J2ME:
The Complete Reference

James Keogh

McGraw-Hill/Osborne

New York Chicago San Francisco
Lisbon London Madrid Mexico City
Milan New Delhi San Juan
Seoul Singapore Sydney Toronto

The **McGraw·Hill** Companies

McGraw-Hill/Osborne
2600 Tenth Street
Berkeley, California 94710
U.S.A.

To arrange bulk purchase discounts for sales promotions, premiums, or fund-raisers,
please contact **McGraw-Hill/**Osborne at the above address. For information on
translations or book distributors outside the U.S.A., please see the International
Contact Information page immediately following the index of this book.

J2ME: The Complete Reference

1234567890 CUS CUS 019876543

ISBN 0-07-222710-9

Publisher
Brandon A. Nordin

Vice President & Associate Publisher
Scott Rogers

Editorial Director
Wendy Rinaldi

Project Editor
Mark Karmendy

Acquisitions Coordinator
Athena Honore

Technical Editor
Amar Mehta

Copy Editor
Judith Brown

Proofreader
Claire Splan

Indexer
Jack Lewis

Computer Designers
Apollo Publishing Services,
Lucie Ericksen, Tara A. Davis

Illustrators
Michael Mueller, Lyssa Wald,
Melinda Moore Lytle

Series Design
Peter F. Hancik

This book was composed with Corel VENTURA™ Publisher.

This book is dedicated to Anne, Sandy,
Joanne, Amber-Leigh Christine, and Graaf,
without whose help and support
this book couldn't be written.

About the Author

Jim Keogh teaches courses on Java Application Development, including J2EE, at Columbia University and is a member of the Java Community Process Program. He developed the first e-commerce track at Columbia and became its first chairperson. Jim spent more than a decade developing advanced systems for major Wall Street firms. Jim introduced PC Programming nationally in his *Popular Electronics Magazine* column in 1982, four years after Apple Computer started in a garage. He was also a team member who built one of the first Windows applications by a Wall Street firm, featured by Bill Gates in 1986. Jim is the author of 55 books, including his most recent book, *J2EE: The Complete Reference*. He is also a faculty member in the Graduate School, Saint Peter's College, New Jersey City, NJ.

Contents

Part I

J2ME Basics

Part II

J2ME User Interface

Part III

J2ME Data Management

Introduction

Java technology has evolved from a programming language designed to create machine-independent embedded systems into a robust, vendor-independent, machine-independent, server-side technology, enabling the corporate community to realize the full potential of web-centric applications.

Java began with the release of the Java Development Kit (JDK). It was obvious from the start that Java was on a fast track to becoming a solution to the problems of many corporate systems. More interface and libraries were extended in the JDK as the corporate world demanded—and received—application programming interfaces (API) that addressed real-world situations.

JDK API extensions fully integrated into the JDK with the release of the Java 2 Standard Edition (J2SE) of the JDK. J2SE contains all the APIs needed to build industrial strength Java applications. However, the corporate world felt J2SE lacked the strength required for developing enterprise-wide applications and for servicing the needs of developers of mobile and embedded systems.

Again the corporate community pushed Sun Microsystems, Inc. to revise Java technology to address needs of an enterprise. Sun Microsystems, Inc. then launched the Java Community Program (JCP) that brought together corporate users, vendors, and technologists to develop a standard for enterprise Java APIs. The result is the

Java 2 Platform Enterprise Edition, commonly referred to as Java 2 Enterprise Edition (J2EE), and the Java 2 Micro Edition (J2ME).

Enterprise systems traditionally are designed using the client/server model, where client-side systems request processing from service-side systems. However, enterprise systems were undergoing their own evolution. A new model called Web services gradually replaced the client/server model in corporations.

Application programmers assembled applications from an assortment of processing components called Web services. Each Web service was independent from other Web services and independent from applications. A client-side application communicates with a middle-tier, server-side application, which in turns interacts with the necessary Web services that are also located on the server side.

With the adoption of the Web services model in corporations, the JCP realized that J2ME must also go through another evolutionary cycle. With the introduction of new specifications, the Java community has merged J2ME technology with Web services technology.

In addition to the acceptance of Web services, corporations are also seeking to merge mobile technology such as Personal Digital Assistants and cellular phones with corporate mainstream applications. J2ME, with the new PIM API, enables developers to create sophisticated, wireless applications that have direct access to native PDA databases. This enables corporate executives to use corporation's PDA systems to interact with data mantained by PDA native applications.

What's Inside

This book covers in detail all aspect of J2ME, Web services, PDA, and cellular phone application development. The book is divided into these five parts:

- Part I: J2ME Basics
- Part II: J2ME User Interface
- Part III: J2ME Data Management
- Part IV: J2ME Personal Information Manager Profile
- Part V: J2ME Networking and Web Services

Part I: J2ME Basics

The new web-centric corporation is changing the way in which it delivers highly efficient, enterprise-wide distributive systems to meet the round-the-clock instantaneous demand expected by thousands of concurrent users—anywhere at any time. The old way of building enterprise systems won't solve today's corporate IT requirements.

Technologists at Sun Microsystems, Inc. and the Java Community Program rewrote the way developers build large-scale, web-centric distributive systems by using Java 2 Enterprise Edition (J2EE), and Java 2 Micro Edition (J2ME). J2EE addresses complex server-side issues faced by programmers who develop these systems while J2ME addresses the need to create mobile and embedded components that makes these systems accessible from other than the desktop.

Part I of this book introduces you to basic concepts used in J2ME technology and in Web services technology. These concepts focus on four areas of interest, beginning with an overview of J2ME that defines J2ME and illustrates J2ME's role in the evolutionary process of computer programming.

The next area of interest examines the J2ME architecture. It is here where you roll up your sleeves and get your hands into the guts of J2ME to investigate how J2ME works within the Web services infrastructure.

At first glance, you might feel overwhelmed by the power of J2ME. However, that feeling is short-lived because the third area of interest in Part I discusses J2ME best practices, showing you commonly used design principles used by J2ME programmers to build advanced J2ME Web centric distributive systems.

Part I concludes with a look at J2ME design patterns used to solve common programming problems that crop up during the development of a J2ME application. After reading Part I you'll have a solid basis for learning how to build your own J2ME applications.

Part II: J2ME User Interface

Nearly every J2ME application that you develop requires a way for a user to interact with it unless the application is an embedded closed system. An embedded closed system such as those that control an automobile's engine doesn't require input from the user but instead receives input from electro-mechanical devices.

A user interface for a J2ME application is similar to yet different from a user interface that you find on a desktop application. They are similar in that both display options available to the user and then receive and process the option selected by the user. However, a J2ME user interface is less sophisticated than those found on a desktop application because of the limited resources (i.e., screen size) that are available on a J2ME device (i.e., cellular phone).

In Part II you'll learn database concepts of the J2ME user interface. You'll also explore the details of building a J2ME user interface for your application.

Part III: J2ME Data Management

At the center of nearly every J2ME application is a repository of information that is accessed and manipulated by both service-side components, such as Web services, and client-side applications. A repository is a database management system that stores, retrieves, and maintains the integrity of information stored in its databases.

A J2ME application uses Java data objects, JDBC, and other technology that is necessary to interact with a database management system to provide information to the J2ME application.

In Part III you'll learn database concepts in relation to Java data objects. You'll also explore the details of JDBC, which is used to connect to and interact with popular— and some not so popular—database management systems. And you'll also learn how to create and send requests for information and integrate the results of a request into your J2ME application.

Part IV: J2ME Personal Information Manager Profile

Many corporations have practically made PDAs the *de facto* standard as a mobile communicator, especially since PDA and cell phone technologies have merged, causing a blur between PDAs and cell phones. That is, a PDA can be used as a cell phone and cell phones have incorporated PDA applications.

Until recently, J2ME applications lacked the capability to interact with native PDA databases such as those used to store calendar, to-do list, and address information.

The Java Community Process released a new Personal Information Manager (PIM) API, which is used to develop sophisticated J2ME applications. This enables J2ME applications to interact with the J2ME device's personal information database, which is used by the device's address book, notepad, and calendar applications.

In Part IV of this book you'll explore this API and learn how to implement it in your J2ME application.

Part V: J2ME Networking and Web Services

The glue that enables J2ME applications to interact with external applications, including server-side components, is networking capabilities. In Part V you'll learn how to implement routines that take advantage of a J2ME device's network features to open communications with other applications using a hard-wire or wireless network connection.

You'll also learn how to utilize Web services to expand the horizon of your J2ME application. Web services is a web of services where services are software building blocks that are available on a network from which programmers can efficiently create large-scale distributive systems.

You won't learn how to create Web services, but you will learn how to utilize them to increase the functionality of your J2ME application beyond the limited resources found on a J2ME device. In Part V, you'll also learn about Service Oriented Architecture Protocol (SOAP), Universal Description, Discovery, and Web Services Description Language (WSDL), and how to implement them in your J2ME application.

A Book for All Programmers

J2ME: The Complete Reference is designed for all Java programmers, regardless of their experience level. It does assume, however, that a reader is able to create at least a runtime Java program. If you are just learning Java, this book will make an excellent companion to any Java tutorial and serve as a source of answers to your specific questions. Experienced Java, J2EE, and J2ME pros will find the coverage of the many new Web services features.

Don't Forget: Code on the Web

Remember, the source code for all of the programs in this book is available free of charge on the Web at http://www.osborne.com. Downloading this code prevents you from having to type in the examples.

The
Complete
Reference

J2ME

Part I

J2ME Basics

The
Complete
Reference

Chapter 1

J2ME Overview

The term "computer" conjures many images, such as desktop and laptop computers and servers stored in some highly protected remote location. And while these images accurately portray a computer, there are many more computers that lack the familiar computer shape but contain the same basic components found in desktop and laptop computers. Cell phones, digital set-top boxes for cable television, car navigation systems, pagers, and personal digital assistants are all computers. And computers are also used to control the operation of automobiles, industrial equipment, and household appliances. This new breed of computers, referred to as *small computing devices*, is distinguishable from more traditional computers by their reduced resource availability. Resources such as memory, permanent storage, and power are plentiful in traditional computers but are precious in small computing devices.

Along with the new breed of computers came a new platform, on which developers can build and implement programs to control small computing devices. The platform is called Java 2 Micro Edition (J2ME). You'll be introduced to J2ME in this chapter.

Java 2 Micro Edition and the World of Java

The computer revolution of the 1970s increased the demand for sophisticated computer software to take advantage of the ever-increasing capacity of computers to process data. The C programming language became the linchpin that enabled programmers to build software that was just as robust as the computer it ran on.

As the 1980s approached, programmers were witnessing another spurt in the evolution of programming language. Computer technology advanced beyond the capabilities of the C programming language. The problem wasn't new. It occurred previously and caused the demise of generations of programming languages. The problem was that programs were becoming too complicated to design, write, and manage to keep up with the capabilities of computers. It was around this time that a design concept based on Simula 67 and Smalltalk (from the late 1960s) moved programming to the next evolutionary step. This was the period when object-oriented programming (OOP), and with it a new programming language called C++, took programmers by storm.

In 1979, Bjarne Stroustrup of Bell Laboratories in New Jersey enhanced the C programming language to include object-oriented features. He called the language C++. (The ++ is the incremental operator in the C programming language.) C++ is truly an enhancement of the C programming language, and it began as a preprocessor language that was translated into C syntax before the program was processed by the compiler.

Stroustrup built on the concept of a *class* (taken from Simula 67 and Smalltalk), from which instances of objects are created. A class contains data members and member functions that define an object's data and functionality. He also introduced the concept of *inheritance*, which enabled a class to inherit some or all data members and member functions from one or more other classes—all of which complements the concepts of object-oriented programming. By 1988, ANSI officials standardized Stroustrup's C++ specification.

Enter Java

Just as C++ was becoming the language of choice for building industrial-strength applications, another growth spurt in the evolution of programming language was budding, fertilized by the latest disruptive technology—the World Wide Web. The Internet had been a well-kept secret for decades before the National Science Foundation (who oversaw the Internet) removed barriers that prevented commercialization. Until 1991 when it was opened to commerce, the Internet was the almost exclusive domain of government agencies and the academic community. Once the barrier to commercialization was lifted, the World Wide Web—one of several services offered on the Internet—became a virtual community center where visitors could get free information about practically anything and browse through thousands of virtual stores.

Browsers power the World Wide Web. A *browser* translates ASCII text files written in HTML into an interactive display that can be interpreted on any machine. As long as the browser is compatible with the correct version of HTML and HTTP implementation, any computer running the browser can use the same HTML document without having to modify it for a particular type of computer, which was something unheard of at the time. Programs written in C or C++ are machine dependent and cannot run on a different machine unless the program is recompiled.

The success of the Internet gave renewed focus to developing a machine-independent programming language. And the same year the Internet was commercialized, five technologists at Sun Microsystems set out to do just that. James Gosling, Patrick Naughton, Chris Warth, Ed Frank, and Mike Sheridan spent 18 months developing the programming language they called Oak, which was renamed Java when this new language made its debut in 1995. Java went through numerous iterations between 1991 and 1995, during which time many other technologists at Sun made substantial contributions to the language. These included Bill Joy, Arthur van Hoff, Jonathan Payne, Frank Yelin, and Tim Lindholm.

Although Java is closely associated with the Internet, it was developed as a language for programming software that could be embedded into electronic devices regardless of the type of CPU used by the device. This is known as the EmbeddedJava platform and is in continuous use today for closed systems.

The Java team from Sun succeeded in creating a portable programming language, something that had eluded programmers since computers were first programmed. Their success, however, was far beyond their wildest dreams. The same concept used to make Java programs portable to electronic devices also could be used to make Java programs run on computers running Microsoft Windows, UNIX, and Macintosh.

Timing was perfect. The Internet/intranet had whetted corporate America's appetite for cost-effective, portable programs that could replace mission-critical applications within the corporation. And Java had proven itself as a programming language used to successfully develop machine-independent applications.

It was in the mid-1990s when the team from Sun realized that Java could be easily adapted to develop software for the Internet/intranet. And toward the turn of the century, many corporations embraced Java and began replacing legacy applications—many of which were written in C and C++—with Java Internet/intranet-enabled applications. In keeping with the genealogical philosophy that only the dominant genes are passed on to the next generation, the Java development team at Sun incorporated the best of Smalltalk (automatic garbage collection) and C++ into Java and left out features of C++ that were inefficient and not programmer friendly. The team also created new features that gave Java the dynamics necessary for Internet-based programming.

Java Virtual Machine

Writing Java programs is similar to writing C++ programs in that the programmer writes source code that contains instructions into an editor, or in an integrated development environment, and then the source code is compiled. However, that's where Java and C++ part ways. The compiling and linking process of a C++ program results in an executable that can be run on an appropriate machine. In contrast, the Java compiler converts Java source code into bytecode that is executed by the Java Virtual Machine (JVM).

Machine-specific instructions are not included in bytecode. Instead, they already reside in the JVM, which is machine specific. This means that the bytecode might contain fewer instructions that need to be translated than a comparable C++ program.

Although the Java compiler generates bytecode that must be interpreted by the JVM at run time, the number of instructions that need translation are usually minimal and have already been optimized by the Java compiler.

J2EE and J2SE

Java itself has undergone an evolution that rivals the evolution of programming languages in general. Originally designed for programs that control electronic devices, Java made waves in the Internet development community by providing a means to give intelligence to passive web pages. The Java development team's design has made Java the programming language of choice for programming enterprise-wide, web-centric applications.

Information technology departments had always sought ways to create cost-effective computer applications. One approach is client/server architecture that uses a two-tier architecture in which client-side software requests services from server-side software. For example, software running on the client captures a request for information from a user and then formats the request into a query that is sent over the network to the database server for processing. The database server then transmits the requested data to the client, where software presents data to the user (Figure 1-1).

Increasingly, back-end systems and infrastructure grew as information technology departments streamlined operations to deliver information and technology services to the desktop. Client/server architecture exploded from a two-tier architecture to a multi-tier web services architecture in which a client's request to server-side software generates requests to special software called a web service (Figure 1-2). This is very similar to asking a travel agent to arrange for your vacation. The travel agent contacts hotels, airlines, the car rental company, restaurants, and other vendors that are necessary to fulfill your request.

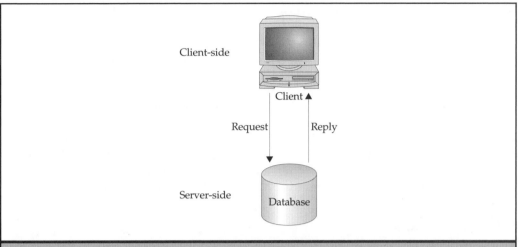

Figure 1-1.   *In client/server architecture, client-side software sends requests to server-side software for processing.*

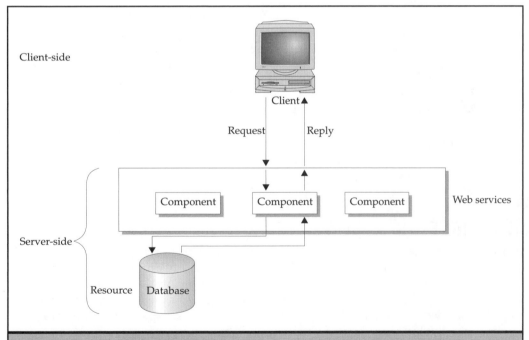

Figure 1-2.   *Multi-tier web services architecture uses server-side software to receive requests from client-side software that is processed by web services.*

Although multi-tier architecture provides services efficiently, it also complicates the design, creation, debugging, distribution, and maintenance of an application because a programmer must be assured that all tiers work together. However, the Java development team enhanced the capabilities of Java to dramatically reduce the complexity of developing a multi-tier application.

The team grouped features of Java into three editions, each having a software development kit (SDK). The original edition of Java, called the Java 2 Standard Edition (J2SE), consists of application programming interfaces (APIs) needed to build a Java application or applet. The Java 2 Micro Edition (J2ME) contains the API used to create applications for small computing devices, including wireless Java applications. And the Java 2 Enterprise Edition (J2EE), an embellished version of the J2SE to accommodate n-tier architecture, has the API to build applications for multi-tier architecture.

The Birth of J2EE

Java is an evolving programming language that began with the release of the Java Development Kit (JDK). During this evolutionary process, the Java development team included more interfaces and libraries as programmers demanded new APIs. These new features were called *extensions*—APIs that were add-ons to the JDK. Sun Microsystems incorporated these extensions into a new Java development kit called J2SE.

Information technology departments of corporations look toward web-centric applications as a way to economize while offering streamlined services to employees and customers. An increased emphasis was placed on server-side programming and on development of vendor-independent APIs to access server-side systems. Sun responded by creating the Java Community Process Program that invited corporate users, vendors, and technologists to develop a standard for enterprise Java APIs. The Java Community Process Program effort resulted in J2EE.

J2EE is a combination of several technologies that offer a cohesiveness to bond together server-side systems and services to produce an industrial-strength scalable environment within which web-centric applications can thrive. A critical ingredient in the development of J2EE is the collaborative environment fostered by Sun, within which vendors and technologists come together in the Java Community Process Program to create and implement Java-based technologies.

Back to the Future: J2ME

Remember that Java began as a programming language to create programs for embedded systems—microcomputers found in consumer and industrial products such as those used to control automobiles and appliances. The development team at Sun worked on Java in the early 1990s to address the programming needs of the fledgling embedded computer market, but that effort was sidetracked by more compelling opportunities presented by the Internet.

As those opportunities were addressed, a new breed of portable communications devices opened other opportunities at the turn of the century. Cell phones expanded from voice communications devices to voice and text communications devices. Pocket electronic telephone directories evolved into personal digital assistants. Chipmakers were releasing new products at this time that were designed to transfer computing power from a desktop computer into mobile small computers that controlled gas pumps, cable television boxes, and an assortment of other appliances.

The time was right for the next evolution of Java. However, instead of beefing up Java with additional APIs, the team at Sun, along with the Java Community Process Program, dismantled both the Java programming language and the Java Virtual Machine. They stripped down Java APIs and the JVM to the minimum coding required to provide intelligence to embedded systems and microcomputer devices. This was necessary because of resource constraints imposed upon the hardware design of these devices. The result of their efforts is J2ME. J2ME is a reduced version of the Java API and Java Virtual Machine that is designed to operate within the sparse resources available in the new breed of embedded computers and microcomputers.

Inside J2ME

J2ME made its debut at the JavaOne Developers Conference in mid-1999 and is targeted to developers of intelligent wireless devices and small computing devices who need to incorporate cross-platform functionality in their products.

Consumers of mobile and small computing devices have high performance expectations for these devices. They demand quick response time, compatibility with companion services, and full-featured applications in a small computing device. Consumers expect the same software and capabilities found on their desktop and laptop computers to be available on their cell phones and personal digital assistants.

To meet these expectations, developers have to rethink the way they build computer systems. Developers need to harness the power of existing front-end and back-end software found on business computers and transfer this power onto small, mobile, and wireless computing devices. J2ME enables this transformation to occur with minimal modifications, assuming that applications are scalable in design so that an application can be custom-fitted to resources available on a small computing device.

Developers seeking to build applications that run on cell phones, personal digital assistants, and various consumer and industrial appliances must strike a balance between a thick client and a thin client. A *thick client* is front-end software that contains the logic to handle a sizable amount of data processing for the system (Figure 1-3). A *thin client* is front-end software that depends on back-end software for much of the system processing (Figure 1-4).

Developers must determine the minimum client processing that will meet the end user's expectations of quick response time that is feasible within the limited resources available on the small computing device. You'll learn how to make this decision in Chapter 4.

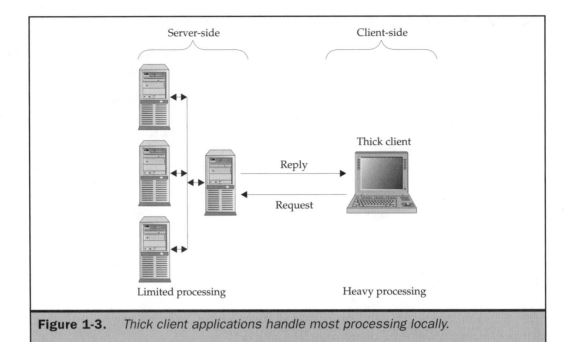

Figure 1-3.   *Thick client applications handle most processing locally.*

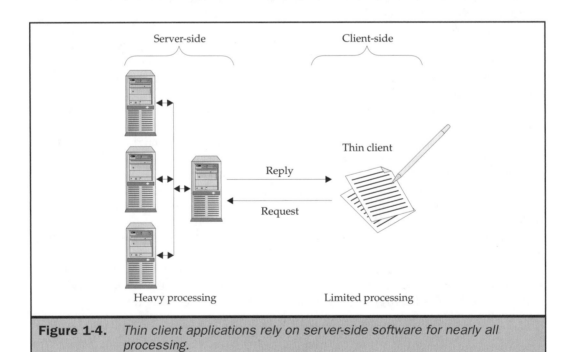

Figure 1-4.   *Thin client applications rely on server-side software for nearly all processing.*

J2ME BASICS

Let's say that a wireless small computing device is used to transact orders on the floor of a stock exchange. The wireless device has software to handle user interactions such as displaying an electronic form on the screen, collecting user input, processing the input, and displaying results of the processing on the screen. The order form is displayed on the screen, and the user enters information into the order form using various input conventions commonly found in small wireless devices. The device collects the order information and then processes the order using a combination of software on the wireless device and software running on a back-end system that receives the order through a wireless connection.

Processing on the wireless device might involve two steps: First the software performs a simple validation process to assure that all fields on the form contain information. Next the order is transmitted to the back-end system. The back-end system handles adjusting account balances and other steps involved in processing the order. A confirmation notice is returned by the back-end system to the wireless device, which displays the confirmation notice on the screen (Figure 1-5).

A key benefit of using J2ME is that J2ME is compatible with all Java-enabled devices. A Java-enabled device is any computer that runs the Java Virtual Machine. Ericsson,

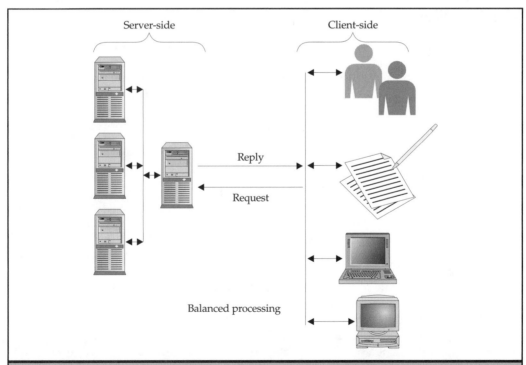

Figure 1-5.   *A J2ME application is a balance between local and server-side processing.*

Motorola, Nextel, Nokia, Panasonic, and RIM all have Java-enabled devices. In addition, J2ME maintains the powerful security features found in the Java language and enables wireless and small computing devices to access resources that are within an organization's firewall.

How J2ME Is Organized

Traditional computing devices use fairly standard hardware configurations such as a display, keyboard, mouse, and large amounts of memory and permanent storage. However, the new breed of computing devices lacks hardware configuration continuity among devices. Some devices don't have a display, permanent storage, keyboard, or mouse. And memory availability is inconsistent among small computing devices.

The lack of uniform hardware configuration among the small computing devices poses a formidable challenge for the Java Community Process Program, which is charged with developing standards for the JVM and the J2ME for small computing devices.

J2ME must service many different kinds of small computing devices, including screen-phones, digital set-top boxes used for cable television, cell phones, and personal digital assistants. The challenge for the Java Community Process Program is to develop a Java standard that can be implemented on small computing devices that have nonstandard hardware configurations.

The Java Community Process Program has used a twofold approach to addressing the needs of small computing devices. First, they defined the Java run-time environment and core classes that operate on each device. This is referred to as the *configuration*. A configuration defines the Java Virtual Machine for a particular small computing device. There are two configurations, one for handheld devices and the other for plug-in devices. Next, the Java Community Process Program defined a profile for categories of small computing devices. A *profile* consists of classes that enable developers to implement features found on a related group of small computing devices.

J2ME Configurations

There are two configurations for J2ME as of this writing. These are Connected Limited Device Configuration (CLDC) and the Connected Device Configuration (CDC). The CLDC is designed for 16-bit or 32-bit small computing devices with limited amounts of memory. CLDC devices usually have between 160KB and 512KB of available memory and are battery powered. They also use an inconsistent, small-bandwidth network wireless connection and may not have a user interface. CLDC devices use the KJava Virtual Machine (KVM) implementation, which is a stripped-down version of the JVM. CLDC devices include pagers, personal digital assistants, cell phones, dedicated terminals, and handheld consumer devices with between 128KB and 512KB of memory.

CDC devices use a 32-bit architecture, have at least two megabytes of memory available, and implement a complete functional JVM. CDC devices include digital set-top boxes, home appliances, navigation systems, point-of-sale terminals, and smart phones.

J2ME Profiles

A profile consists of Java classes that enable implementation of features for either a particular small computing device or for a class of small computing devices. Small computing technology continues to evolve, and with that, there is an ongoing process of defining J2ME profiles. Seven profiles have been defined as of this writing. These are the Foundation Profile, Game Profile, Mobile Information Device Profile, PDA Profile, Personal Profile, Personal Basis Profile, and RMI Profile.

- The Foundation Profile is used with the CDC configuration and is the core for nearly all other profiles used with the CDC configuration because the Foundation Profile contains core Java classes.

- The Game Profile is also used with the CDC configuration and contains the necessary classes for developing game applications for any small computing device that uses the CDC configuration.

- The Mobile Information Device Profile (MIDP) is used with the CLDC configuration and contains classes that provide local storage, a user interface, and networking capabilities to an application that runs on a mobile computing device such as Palm OS devices. MIDP is used with wireless Java applications.

- The PDA Profile (PDAP) is used with the CLDC configuration and contains classes that utilize sophisticated resources found on personal digital assistants. These features include better displays and larger memory than similar resources found on MIDP mobile devices (such as cell phones).

- The Personal Profile is used with the CDC configuration and the Foundation Profile and contains classes to implement a complex user interface. The Foundation Profile provides core classes, and the Personal Profiles provide classes to implement a sophisticated user interface, which is a user interface that is capable of displaying multiple windows at a time.

- The Personal Basis Profile is similar to the Personal Profile in that it is used with the CDC configuration and the Foundation Profile. However, the Personal Basis Profile provides classes to implement a simple user interface, which is a user interface that is capable of displaying one window at a time.

- The RMI Profile is used with the CDC configuration and the Foundation Profile to provide Remote Method Invocation classes to the core classes contained in the Foundation Profile.

There will likely be many profiles as the proliferation of small computing devices continues. Industry groups within the Java Community Process Program (java.sun.com/aboutjava/communityprocess) define profiles. Each group establishes the standard profile used by small computing devices manufactured by that industry.

A CDC profile is defined by expanding upon core Java classes found in the Foundation Profile with classes specifically targeted to a class of small computing device. These device-specific classes are contained in a new profile that enables developers to create industrial-strength applications for those devices. However, if the Foundation Profile is specific to CDC, not all profiles are expanded upon the core classes found in the Foundation Profile.

Keep in mind that applications can access a small computing device's software and hardware features only if the necessary classes to do so are contained in the JVM and in the profile used by the developer.

J2ME and Wireless Devices

With the dramatic increase and sophistication of mobile communications devices such as cell phones came demand for applications that can run on those devices. Consumers and corporations want to expand mobile communications devices from voice communications to applications traditionally found on laptops and PCs. They want to send and receive email, store and retrieve personal information, perform sophisticated calculations, and play games.

Developers, mobile communications device manufacturers, and mobile network providers are anxious to fill this need, but there is a serious hurdle: mobile communications devices utilize a number of different application platforms and operating systems. Without tweaking the code, an application written for one device cannot run on another device. Mobile communications devices lack a standard application platform and operating system, which has made developing applications for mobile communications devices a risky economic venture for developers.

The lack of standards is nothing new to computing or to any developing technology. Traditionally, manufacturers of hardware devices try to corner the market and enforce their own proprietary standard as the de facto standard for the industry. Usually one upstart succeeds, as in the case of Microsoft. Other times, industry leaders form a consortium, such as the Java Community Process Program, to collectively develop a standard.

The Wireless Application Protocol (WAP) forum became the initial industry group that set out to create standards for wireless technology. Ericsson, Motorola, Nokia, and Unwired Planet formed the WAP forum in 1997, and it has since grown to include nearly all mobile device manufacturers, mobile network providers, and developers. The WAP forum created mobile communications device standards referred to as the WAP standard. The WAP standard is an enhancement of HTML, XML, and TCP/IP. One element of this standard is the Wireless Markup Language specification, which consists of a blend of HTML and XML and is used by developers to create documents that can be displayed by a microbrowser. A *microbrowser* is a diminutive web browser that operates on a mobile communications device.

The WAP standard also includes specifications for a Wireless Telephony Application Interface (WTAI) specification and the WMLScript specification. WTAI is used to create an interface for applications that run on a mobile communications device. WMLScript is a stripped-down version of JavaScript.

While the WAP forum provided the framework within which developers can build mobile communications device applications, they still had to overcome a common hurdle found in every rapidly developing technology. The sophistication of mobile communications devices, phenomenal growth of the market, and high demand for industrial-strength mobile communications applications out-paced the ability to define and implement new mobile communications device standards.

Many sophisticated applications designed for mobile communications devices require the device to process information beyond the capabilities of the WAP specification. J2ME provided the standard to fill this gap. For example, a sales representative wants to check available flights and hotel accommodations, purchase an airline ticket, book the hotel and car rental, and then send the itinerary to a client, all while sitting in a taxi in traffic. The sales representative also wants the itinerary stored on the mobile communications device and retrieved during the trip.

J2ME applications referred to as a *MIDlet* can run on practically any mobile communications device that implements a JVM and MIDP. This encourages developers to invest time and money in building applications for mobile communications devices without the risk that the application is device dependent. However, J2ME isn't seen as a replacement for the WAP specification because both are complementary technologies. Developers whose applications are light-client based continue to use WML and WMLScript. Developers turn to J2ME for heavier clients that require sophisticated processing on the mobile communications device.

What J2ME Isn't

The hype about any technology can cause misperceptions about the capabilities of an evolving technology, and J2ME isn't immune to such misunderstandings. Therefore, it is important to understand the limitations of J2ME.

Although J2ME is J2SE without some classes, developers shouldn't assume that existing Java applications would run in the J2ME environment without requiring modification to the code. The write-once-run-anywhere philosophy of Java is a bit overstated when it comes to J2ME because of resource constraints imposed by small computing devices.

Some J2SE applications require classes that are not available in J2ME. Likewise, resources required by the J2SE application may not be available on the small computing device. This means that developers must expect to test existing J2SE applications in the J2ME environment and probably pare down the application to run using limited resources.

Another misconception about J2ME is the Java Virtual Machine implementation on the small computing device. Small computing devices use one of two Java Virtual Machine implementations. Devices that use the CDC configuration use the full Java Virtual Machine implementation, while devices that use the CLDC configuration use the KJava Virtual Machine implementation.

A MIDlet is not invoked the same way as a J2SE application is invoked because many small computing devices don't have a command prompt. MIDlets are controlled by application management software (AMS). The manufacturer of a small computing device provides AMS, although third-party vendors might also create AMS. AMS interacts with native operations of a small computing device and controls the life cycle of a MIDlet. The life cycle consists of installation and upgrades as well as version management and uninstalling the application. Likewise, AMS is responsible for starting, managing execution, and stopping the MIDlet.

Other Java Platforms for Small Computing Devices

J2ME isn't the only Java platform designed for small computing devices. Other Java platforms—EmbeddedJava, JavaCard, and PersonalJava—predate J2ME.

EmbeddedJava is the Java platform used for small computing devices that are dedicated to one purpose and have a 32-bit processor and 512KB of ROM and RAM. EmbeddedJava is based on JDK 1.1 and is being replaced by the CDLC configuration. For more information about EmbeddedJava, visit java.sun.com/products/embeddedjava.

JavaCard is the Java platform used for smart cards, the smallest computing device that supports Java. The JavaCard VM runs on small computing devices that have 16KB of nonvolatile memory and 512 bytes of volatile memory. However, unlike the EmbeddedJava platform, there isn't any movement to replace JavaCard with J2ME because of the resource constraints of the current generation of smart cards. Future smart card generations will probably have great resources available and be compatible with the CDLC configuration. You can find more information about JavaCard in java.sun.com/products/javacard.

PersonalJava is the Java platform used for small computing devices that have a maximum of 2MB of ROM and a minimum of 1MB of RAM, such as large PDAs and mobile communications devices. PersonalJava uses JDK 1.1.8 and the JVM and will be replaced by the CDC configuration and the Personal Basis Profile and Personal Profile. More information about PersonalJava is available at java.sun.com/products/personaljava.

The
Complete
Reference

Chapter 2

Small Computing Technology

"Beam me up Scotty" is a famous line from *Star Trek*. Captain Kirk made this request using a clamshell-shaped communicator. Granted there has yet to be anyone transported on light waves, but clamshell-shaped communicators are used everyday. We call it a cellular telephone.

Today we can speak with anyone, anywhere, anytime. And tomorrow we'll read any book, shop in any store, check up on our kids and our house, pay our bills, and do more by using small computing devices and mobile communications devices. These devices have already changed our lives. A friend of mine is responsible for building alliances among corporate executives and investment bankers. Very few people know where my friend physically works—and no one really cares. Calls are directed to a cellular telephone and roll over to voice mail when there is no answer. Emails are retrieved using a laptop that is sometimes connected to the email server through a traditional telephone line and other times linked using a wireless connection. My friend's office is where my friend is.

This is all made possible by software developers exploiting features of small computing and mobile computing devices. Before you learn to build those applications, you should become familiar with the technology that makes this possible. In this chapter you'll explore the technology used in small computing devices and mobile computing devices.

Wireless Technology

Wireless technology that is used in small computing devices and mobile communications devices is the same radio technology Guglielmo Marconi used to provide an alternative communication means to the telegraph and the telephone.

Radio technology is based on the wave phenomenon. A wave is a characteristic of vibrating molecules, which you see whenever you move a knife up and down in the still water of a dishpan (Figure 2-1). The force of the knife against the surface of the water causes water molecules to vibrate and form a wave along the surface of the water.

The force used to propel the knife determines the wave height. The greater the force, the higher the wave and the greater the distance the wave travels across the surface of the water. The number of times the knife is moved up and down in the water determines the frequency of the wave. Each time the knife is plunged into the water another wave is generated, causing a rippling effect across the water's surface.

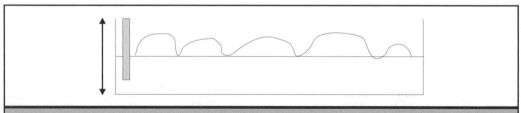

Figure 2-1.   *Moving a knife up and down in water causes the formation of a wave.*

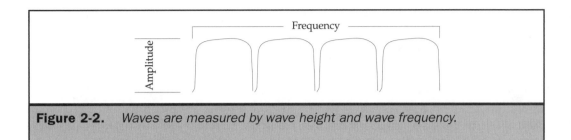

Figure 2-2.   *Waves are measured by wave height and wave frequency.*

Waves are measured in two ways: by the wave height and by the wave frequency. The wave height is referred to as the wave's amplitude, and the frequency of the wave is simply called frequency, which is measured as the number of waves per second (Figure 2-2).

The frequency of a wave causes the wave to take on specific characteristics. For example, a low-frequency wave called a sound wave produces a frequency that can be heard by humans. Sound waves travel a short distance through air. A higher-frequency wave called a radio wave cannot be heard but can travel long distances in all directions and through solid objects. And even higher frequencies called light waves take on other characteristics. Light waves can be seen, travel a long distance in a limited direction, and cannot penetrate solid objects.

Waves are grouped according to frequencies that have similar characteristics in the electromagnetic spectrum (Figure 2-3). For example, there is an audio spectrum, a radio spectrum, and a light spectrum. There are also subgroups within each spectrum, each of which has a variation of the characteristics of the spectrum. The radio spectrum has divisions for television, microwave, and X-ray frequencies. The light spectrum has divisions for infrared light, visible light, and ultraviolet light.

Many small computing devices and mobile communications devices use radio waves and light waves to transmit and receive information. Radio waves are used by cellular telephones, wireless modems, and wireless personal digital assistants (PDAs) for communication. Infrared light waves are used by PDAs to exchange information between PDAs and laptop/desktop computers and among other PDAs.

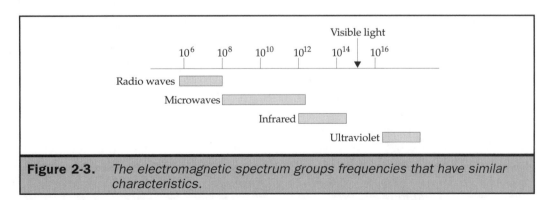

Figure 2-3.   *The electromagnetic spectrum groups frequencies that have similar characteristics.*

Radio signals are transmitted in the frequency range from 10 kilohertz to 300,000 megahertz. A hertz is one wave per second, kilohertz is 1,000 waves per second, and a megahertz is a million waves per second.

Radio Transmission

Radio transmission consists of two components. These are a transmitter and a receiver, both of which must be tuned to the same frequency. A transmitter broadcasts a steady wave called a carrier signal that does not contain any information (Figure 2-4). Conceptually, you can think of a telephone dial tone as a carrier signal.

A carrier signal has two purposes. First, the carrier signal establishes a communications channel with the receiver (Figure 2-5). The receiver knows the channel is open when the carrier signal is detected. The carrier signal also serves as the wave that is encoded with information during transmission.

A radio transmitter encodes patterns of sound waves detected by a microphone by modifying the carrier signal wave (Figure 2-6). The receiver decodes the pattern from the carrier wave and translates the pattern into electrical current that directs a speaker to regenerate the sound waves captured by the microphone attached to the transmitter.

Limitations of Radio Transmissions

The distance a radio signal travels is based on the amount of energy used to transmit the radio wave. This is similar to the energy used to plunge the knife into the dishpan of water. Using a relatively small amount of energy causes the wave to barely reach the side of the dishpan. However, plunging the knife into the dishpan with force causes the wave to overflow the sides of the dishpan.

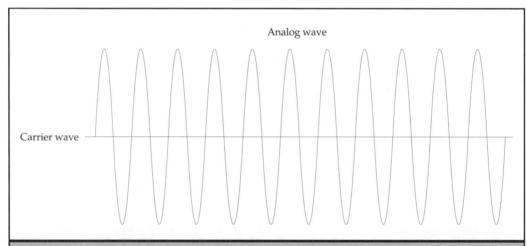

Figure 2-4. *A carrier signal is a broadcast wave that does not contain any information.*

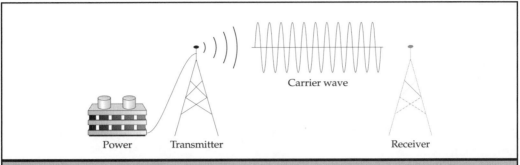

Figure 2-5. *A carrier signal is used to establish a communications channel.*

Radio waves are measured in watts. A radio signal transmitted at 50 megawatts travels twice the distance a 25-megawatt radio signal travels. A radio signal gradually loses power the farther it travels away from the transmitter. Radio engineers extend the range of transmission by using a repeater. A *repeater* (Figure 2-7) is both a radio receiver and radio transmitter, also known as a *transceiver*. A repeater receives a radio signal and then retransmits the signal, thereby increasing the distance the signal travels. Retransmission introduces new energy to power the signal for longer distances.

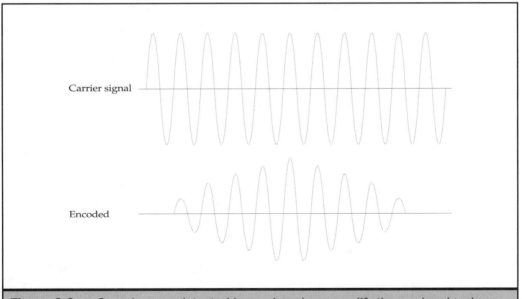

Figure 2-6. *Sound waves detected by a microphone modify the carrier signal.*

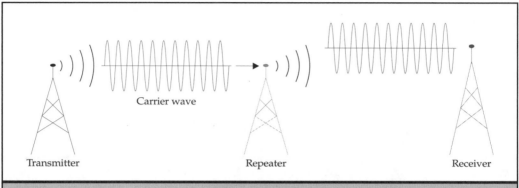

Carrier wave

Transmitter   Repeater   Receiver

Figure 2-7.   *A repeater receives and retransmits a signal.*

Radio Data Networks

Radio transmissions are commonly used to broadcast analog voice information on radio waves that travel 360 degrees over the air and through many physical obstructions. However, radio technology is also used to transmit digital information on those same waves.

Information is traditionally encoded as variations of an aspect of the wave. Encoding is achieved by modifying the amplitude of the wave, known as *amplitude modulation* (AM), or modifying the frequency of the wave, called *frequency modulation* (FM). Encoding uses many values to represent information using AM and FM.

Hundreds of thousands of radio waves are simultaneously and independently transmitted. Sometimes a radio receiver picks up an erroneous radio signal while tuned to its primary frequency. The erroneous radio signal is known as *interference* and can disrupt the accurate decoding of the transmitted information.

Today information is digitally encoded using binary values to represent information transmitted on radio waves. Digitizing information enables receivers to accurately decode transmitted information because the degree of uncertainty in the encoded information is far less than experienced in analog encoded information.

Both an analog signal and a digital signal are waves. They differ by the way information is encoded into the signal. Information is represented in an analog signal as many values. The receiver must determine whether each value is a component of the signal or is interference. The same information is represented in a digital signal as one of two discrete binary values. The receiver ignores a signal whose value is not a binary value. Furthermore, error-checking software in the receiver determines whether an erroneous digital signal is received.

Radio transmitters, repeaters, and receivers are organized to form a radio network that extends transmissions over great distances. Radio networks are scalable because repeaters are placed in the network to increase the distance that the original transmission travels.

There are three types of wireless radio networks: low-power single frequency, high-power single frequency, and spread spectrum. Low-power single frequency covers an area of 30 meters, which is about the area of a small building such as a warehouse or a stock exchange trading floor. A high-power single frequency wireless radio network can cover a metropolitan area.

Both low-power single frequency and high-power single frequency radio networks are exposed to the same security risk. Anyone tuned into the radio frequency receives the transmitted signal. Therefore, all transmissions must be encrypted to hinder eavesdropping on the signal.

A spread-spectrum wireless radio network uses multiple frequencies to transmit a signal using either direct sequence modulation or frequency hopping. *Direct sequence modulation* breaks down information into parts and then simultaneously transmits each part over a different frequency. The receiver must tune to each frequency to receive each part, then reassemble parts into the full message. *Frequency hopping* transmits information rotating among a set of frequencies. The receiver must be tuned to each frequency according to the transmission rotation.

Most radio frequencies are controlled by the Federal Communications Commission and require an FCC license before a wireless radio network can be established.

Data Packets

Radio transmitters send one message at a time over a communications channel. This is similar to sending one telephone call at a time over a telephone line. Each telephone call is placed in a queue while waiting for the current telephone call to end. As you can imagine, telephone calls could easily back up whenever there are more calls than there are empty telephone lines.

Digital radio networks use packet switching technology to transmit multiple messages simultaneously over a communications channel. Each message is divided into small pieces and placed in an electronic envelope called a *packet* (Figure 2-8). A packet contains information that identifies the sender and the receiver, a digitized portion of the message, the sequence number of the packet, and error-checking information. To reassemble

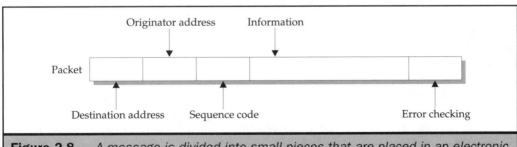

Figure 2-8. *A message is divided into small pieces that are placed in an electronic envelope called a packet.*

packets, the receiver uses the packet sequence number. A transmitter continuously sends packets from multiple messages over a communications channel.

Packet switching technology is more efficient than traditional transmission methods because packet switching utilizes pauses in a transmission to send packets. A transmission pause is caused when a message isn't ready for transmission. This is similar to a pause in a telephone conversation.

Software running on the transmitter manages multiple outgoing messages to assure that each message is divided and placed into packets and the packets are transmitted. Software running on the receiver manages incoming packets, reconstructs packets into original messages, and forwards messages to the appropriate application software for future processing.

Microwave Technology

Microwave is a subspectrum of the radio spectrum and has many characteristics of radio waves discussed previously in this chapter. However, microwaves travel in one unobstructed direction. Any obstruction, such as a mountain or building, disrupts microwave transmission.

There are two kinds of microwave networks: terrestrial and satellites. Terrestrial microwave networks transmit a microwave signal over a terrain, such as buildings in an office complex. Satellite microwave networks transmit a microwave signal between a ground station and orbiting satellites and among orbiting satellites (Figure 2-9).

Earth-to-satellite transmissions are slower than terrestrial microwave transmissions, which causes unnatural pauses to occur in the transmission. This is noticeable during a live international television broadcast when a pause occurs between the time a television news anchor questions a reporter and the reporter's response. Therefore, satellite microwave transmission may not be suitable for real-time two-way communications where nearly instantaneous transmission is expected.

Satellite Networks

A satellite is an orbiting repeater that receives a microwave transmission from an earth station or from other satellites, then retransmits the signal to a microwave receiver located on the ground or in another satellite. The first generation of satellites used for the military were stationed in geosynchronous orbit at a fixed location 22,300 miles above the surface of the earth. However, the geosynchronous orbit hampers real-time transmission because of the signal delay between earth and the satellite, which makes geosynchronous orbiting satellites unacceptable for commercial two-way real-time communication.

A newer breed of satellite technology, called Low Earth Orbiting Satellite (LEOS), overcame the communications delay by positioning satellites lower than geosynchronous orbit—between 435 miles and 1,500 miles above the earth. LEOS eliminated delays in communication, but introduced two new problems. First, LEOS covers a smaller area of the earth, and therefore more satellites are required to cover the same ground area as

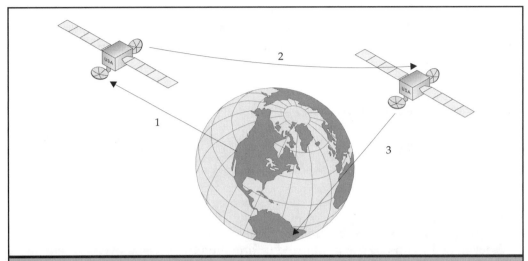

Figure 2-9. *A microwave signal is used to communicate among orbiting satellites and ground stations.*

covered by geosynchronous satellites. The other problem is the orbital speed. LEOS travels faster than the earth's rotation and requires ground stations to locate LEOS before beginning transmission. Geosynchronous satellites always remain in the same position above the ground station.

In an effort to compromise between LEOS and geosynchronous satellites, another breed of satellites called the Middle Earth Orbit (MEO) was developed. MEO orbits between LEOS and geosynchronous satellites—6,000 to 13,000 miles—and thus has less delay than geosynchronous satellites and poses less difficulty than LEOS for ground stations to locate.

Mobile Radio Networks

The infrastructure of cellular telephone technology is the backbone of wireless small computing mobile communications and enables these devices to connect to traditional communications systems. The forerunner of cellular telephone technology is a private radio technology. Service and trucking companies and government agencies use private radio technology to communicate with employees over frequencies isolated from other radio frequencies. For example, package carriers like Federal Express use private radio networks to track packages. Private radio transmitted analog information when first introduced but later expanded into digital communication as the need for paging and messaging services materialized.

Companies can operate their own private radio network by acquiring broadcast rights to a specified radio frequency from the Federal Communications Commission and purchasing the necessary broadcast equipment. Alternatively, companies can lease broadcast time from organizations that offer Specialized Mobile Radio (SMR) network services.

Cellular Telephone Networks

A cellular telephone network comprises mobile transceivers, called cellular telephones, and a network of fixed transceivers, called base stations, that are strategically positioned along the terrain (Figure 2-10). Base stations are used to connect cellular telephones to the ground-based telephone system.

There are two kinds of cellular networks: analog and digital. Cellular telephones began in the 1970s with the expansion of AT&T into the mobile telephone service market. Cellular telephones used analog technology at that time. This changed in mid-1995 when IBM developed technology that digitized information transmitted over the cellular telephone network. Cellular telephone networks then became capable of transmitting both voice and data.

The transmission range of a cellular telephone is determined by the strength of the battery powering the phone and the location of the nearest base station. Transmission range drops as power is drained from the cellular telephone and the telephone is taken farther from a base station.

Engineers can provide reliable cellular telephone transmissions by strategically positioning many base stations around the country so that a cellular telephone is always within the vicinity of a base station. Cellular transceivers are also designed to minimize the power drain that occurs from transmitting and receiving signals.

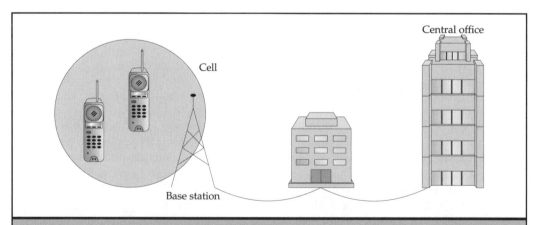

Figure 2-10. *Fixed transceivers called base stations form a communications cell.*

A cellular telephone is in continuous communication with base stations as it moves throughout the cellular network. Transmission from a cellular telephone is broadcast 360 degrees and is received by a base station closest to the cellular telephone. Cellular telephone networks are designed so that the signal is automatically transferred to the next closest base station using a technique called a *hand-off*: the connection between the cellular telephone and the cellular telephone network is dropped for a fraction of a second, the cellular telephone moves between base stations, and the next base station reestablishes the signal.

The area covered by a base station is called a *cell*. The split-second gap during the hand-off goes unnoticed most times, as long as cells are near each other. The hand-off doesn't have a negative effect on voice communications because persons on the call adjust for the slight break in communication. However, the communications drop has a dramatic effect on data communication over a cellular telephone network. Analog cellular telephone networks lose data during transmissions when a hand-off occurs, which is unacceptable for data communications. Digital cellular telephone networks also lose connection during hand-off, but a digital cellular telephone network uses software to recover lost data by requesting that the transceiver resend the data.

Digital cellular telephone networks trap and correct errors. Analog cellular telephone networks lack error-control capability. Analog networks transmit one long burst of information over a communications channel that can either be used for transmitting or receiving information but not both simultaneously, which is called *half-duplex*. In contrast, digital cellular telephone networks transmit information in small packets, called frames or cells, as described previously in this chapter. Pauses between transmissions give the receiver an opportunity to notify the transmitter if an error occurred in receiving a packet.

Cellular Digital Packet Data

IBM pioneered digital cellular telephone networks with the introduction of their Cellular Digital Packet Data (CDPD) protocol, commonly known as IP wireless. IP wireless requires that an Internet protocol (IP) address be assigned to each cellular transceiver in the cellular telephone network. An IP address uniquely identifies each device within the cellular telephone network and is used to reestablish a connection if communication is lost during a hand-off.

Base stations have multiple entry points called ports, each of which is identified by a unique port number. A transceiver is assigned to a base station port in the cellular telephone network. A transceiver continues to transmit to the port number until a hand-off occurs, at which time the transceiver is assigned another port number associated with the next base station.

IBM developed a special modem called a CDPD modem for transmitting digital information over an analog cellular telephone network. The CDPD modem transmits small bursts of encrypted data, which frees the communication channel between bursts to transmit error messages.

Speed is the major stumbling block in using a cellular telephone network to transmit data. The standard analog transmission rate of a cellular telephone network is 9,600 bits per second, which is increased to 14,400 bits per second using CDPD. These speeds are sufficient to transmit delivery information, inquire about the status of an order, or provide remote access to email, but are insufficient for full Internet access.

Digital Wireless Transmissions

A digital cellular telephone network can transmit both voice and data simultaneously using multiplex transmission. There are three multiplex transmission methods used on a digital cellular telephone network: Code Division Multiple Access (CDMA), Time Division Multiple Access (TDMA), and a third-generation wireless standard called 3G.

CDMA uses spread-spectrum transmission to use multiple communications channels for transmission, which dramatically increases data throughput over the network. The cellular telephone temporarily uses on-board memory in transceivers to store data to keep transmissions flowing during a hand-off. This is called a soft hand-off. TDMA uses one communications channel shared among transmissions by using time slots. Transmission time is divided into time slots, and then each packet is assigned to a time slot. The 3G multiplexing technique uses either CDMA or TDMA to increase the throughput to 56 kilobits per second.

Cell Phones and Text Input

Traditional cellular telephones have a keypad that contains numbers and letters. (European traditional cellular telephones have only numbers.) Letters were designed to identify telephone exchanges—local switching stations that serviced a group of customers. Each switching station was referred to by a name that implied the location of the switching station. For example, there was a switching station called Murray Hill that covered the Murray Hill section of New York City.

The first two letters of the name of the switching station were used to replace the first two digits of a seven-digit phone number. Let's say a customer was assigned Murray Hill 5 1000 as a telephone number. A caller dials MU 5 1000. Today the person would call 685-1000 since the switching station naming convention was dropped decades ago.

Today customers expect to be able to enter textual information using the cellular telephone keypad. However, there are two problems with the keypad. First, the keypad doesn't contain the letters Q or Z. And each numeric key, except for the first key, contains three letters. A common solution to this problem is for software in the cellular telephone to count the number of times a key on the keypad is pressed to determine which letter of the alphabet was entered. For example, here's how the name Jim is entered using a cellular telephone keypad: Press the number 5 once, then pause. Press the number 4 three times without pausing. And press the number 6 and pause.

Another solution is to use T9 technology. T9 technology uses special glasses that track eye movement, enabling a person to type by moving her eyes in one of eight directions. Multiple letters are assigned to each direction. An algorithm was developed that predicted which one of the multiple letters a person wanted to type based on the previous letters that she selected. Let's say you entered 546. The number 5 could represent the letters *JKL*.

Bluetooth Wireless Network

Many small computing devices such as those used in consumer appliances communicate with each other by using a low-power radio network that uses Bluetooth technology. Bluetooth technology broadcasts within a 400-foot radius, which is expected to extend to nearly 4,000 feet, and so is perfect for a wireless network in an office.

Transmission consists of short data packets to maximize throughput to one megabit per second. The short size of a packet reduces retransmission time when errors are detected and packets must be resent. Security is provided through frequency hopping that occurs at 1,600 hops per second, practically eliminating the risk that the signal will be intercepted. Data is also encrypted before being broadcast. So even if the signal is intercepted, the receiver still requires the key to decipher the data.

The number 4 could represent the letters *GHI*. And the number 6 could represent the letters *MNO*. Only one English word can be created by combining these letters, which is the word "JIM." However, all legitimate words that can be formed using the selected numbers are displayed on the cell phone screen. The person is then prompted to select the correct word.

Counting keypresses and T9 technology are limited. Other technology such as voice recognition and new mobile communications devices have capitalized on these limitations and provide more efficient means to enter and send textual information over the cellular telephone network.

Messaging

One of the first popular wireless mobile communications devices was a pager. A *pager* displays any series of numbers that were sent by a caller. Technically, the series of numbers represented the caller's telephone number and implied that the call be returned. Practically, the series of numbers could represent anything to which the caller and the receiver agreed on. For example, it was common for systems administrators to have their system send a 911 call to a pager whenever there was a systems problem. Some systems administrators even devised a code that was sent indicating which system transmitted the call and the nature of the problem. Drug dealers were also notorious for using pagers to send encoded messages of drug deliveries. A buyer would call the pager and send a series of numbers that told the dealer the type of drug, quantity, and delivery location for the buy.

Today's wireless mobile communications devices offer text messaging services that enable short textual messages to be sent to the device from any device that has access to the service. Cellular telephone companies offer three types of messaging services: Short Message Service (SMS), Cell Broadcast Service (CBS), and Unstructured Supplementary Services Data (USSD).

SMS type of messaging is capable of sending a maximum of 160 characters on the control channel of a cellular telephone network. A *control channel* is a communications channel used to manage cellular telephone calls. Messages sent using SMS are sent and received during a cellular telephone call because the telephone call and the message use different communications channels for transmission. However, there may be a slight delay between transmission of a message and when the message is received because SMS messaging uses store-forwarding technology, where the message is temporarily stored in a mailbox before being delivered to the receiver.

The CBS type of messaging broadcasts a maximum of 15 pages of 93 characters per page to every device on the network. Everyone on the network receives the same message, which is why CBS messaging has had limited success in the market.

The USSD type of messaging transmits a maximum of 182 characters along the control channel, similar to SMS messaging. However, USSD messaging does not use store-forwarding technology. Instead, USSD messaging sends the message directly to the receiver, which enables the receiver to respond instantaneously.

Personal Digital Assistants

A personal digital assistant (PDA) is probably the most commonly used small mobile computing device next to a cellular telephone. PDAs are lightweight and small enough to fit in a pocket, and they run essential applications. PDA is a generic name that applies to a simple digital telephone directory and to more elaborate mobile computing devices that run a spreadsheet, word processor, email, and a variety of customized programs.

All PDAs are small computing devices that contain an operating system, processor, memory, and a port to connect the PDA to peripherals and external computing devices. There are three commonly used operating systems on a PDA: EPOC, Palm OS, and Windows CE. EPOC is used in the Psion product line, Palm OS in the Palm PDAs, and Windows CE on various pocket PC devices.

There is an assortment of processors designed for the PDA market that include the DragonBall processor built by Motorola and used in the Palm PDA. The DragonBall has a 16 MHz clock speed. The StrongARM processor, manufactured by Intel, is another PDA processor used in the Psion product line and some pocket PCs. The StrongARM has a clock speed of 200 MHz. Another competitor in the PDA processor market is the Crusoe processor manufactured by Transmeta, which is also found in some pocket PC PDAs.

Avoid equating a PDA's processing speed with that of a desktop or laptop computer. Some operating systems, such as Windows CE, require more processing than a Palm OS PDA to perform a similar task, and the extra processing power running under Windows CE does not necessarily perform a task any faster than a Palm.

Memory is precious in a PDA. A PDA does not have permanent storage, therefore all the applications and data running in a PDA must reside in memory. PDAs use ROM and RAM. ROM is used to store bundled applications from the factory. These include a word processor, spreadsheet, diary, telephone directory, and other kinds of programs that you expect to find in a PDA. Applications that are not bundled with the PDA, and data for all applications including those that reside in ROM, are stored in RAM.

PDAs use one of three types of RAM: Dynamic RAM (DRAM), Enhanced Data Output (EDO), and Synchronous Dynamic RAM (SDRAM). DRAM is the least expensive RAM. EDO is found in some PDAs, and SDRAM is very rarely used. Generally the more RAM installed in a computer, the better the computer's performance, but this is not necessarily true with PDAs. The amount of RAM that affects performance depends on the PDA's operating system. Windows CE requires more memory (32MB) to perform basic functions than a Palm (4MB).

Some PDAs have an expansion slot for Compact Flash (CF+) cards that contain components such as a modem, cellular telephone, network card used to connect to a local area network, or additional memory that slips into an expansion slot on the PDA to enhance the PDA's functionality.

PDAs have the same problem as all mobile devices. They need batteries to operate—and they drain batteries quickly. You'll learn more about batteries later in this chapter. PDAs also don't have a user-friendly keyboard to enter data.

Designers attempt to overcome the lack of a keyboard by creating a virtual keyboard on a touch-sensitive screen that requires the user to hunt-and-peck to enter data. Another approach to data entry is to use handwriting recognition software. Software running in the PDA analyzes marks made on a touch-sensitive screen and guesses the character that the user wants to enter. Pocket PCs that run Windows CE can use an autocorrect feature that minimizes errors in handwriting recognition. Palm uses its own brand of shorthand called Graffiti.

Mobile Power

Power is the primary challenge facing the mobile small computing industry. Consumer expectations are high for mobile small computing devices. They want desktop performance anytime and anywhere they power up. Unfortunately, improvements in power storage technology haven't kept pace with mobile computing technology.

Every mobile small computing device is powered by one or more batteries that have a limited life span after which there is no electricity to operate the device. Engineers reduce power consumption by removing power-hungry components and impose power-saving techniques such as deactivating components when a component is not in use.

The length of time a mobile small computing device is operational depends on how well and how long a battery holds its electrical charge. For example, a PDA might operate steadily for 20 hours, while a cellular telephone remains operational for 10 hours. The actual time a battery remains charged depends on a number of factors. These include the type of battery in use, the condition of the battery, and the power consumption of each operation. For example, standby operation for a cellular telephone consumes less power than transmitting a signal.

Power is measured in watt-hours, which means the number of hours the battery can supply one watt of power. A cellular telephone battery is rated at 10 watt-hours, so the battery can supply one watt of power for ten hours. A PDA battery has a rating of 2 watt-hours, supplying one watt of power for two hours.

The amount of watts used by a mobile computing device varies depending on the power-hungry components built into the device. In addition, power consumption depends on the state of the device. Mobile computing devices have three states: active, standby, and off. The active state is when the device is being used. The standby state, also known as the sleep mode, is when all but critical components are powered down, minimizing the drain on the battery. When the device is turned off, the off state still drains power from the battery to maintain information such as a telephone directory in memory.

There are two general classes of batteries: non-rechargeable and rechargeable. Non-rechargeable batteries are further classified as alkaline and zinc-carbon. These are found in PDAs and as an emergency backup power for cellular telephones. Alkaline batteries have a higher capacity to retain an electrical charge than zinc-carbon batteries. Rechargeable batteries fall into four subclasses: lead acid batteries, nickel cadmium (NiCAD) batteries, nickel metal hydride (NiMH) batteries, and lithium ion (LiON) batteries.

Cellular telephone manufacturers originally used lead acid batteries because they can be recharged many times; however, lead acid is a dangerous ingredient, and therefore the manufacturers moved to the safer nickel cadmium battery. NiCAD batteries can be recharged 1,000 times before the battery discharges. However, NiCAD batteries must be fully discharged before being recharged, otherwise the battery may not fully recharge. Consumers complained about this recharging limitation, and therefore manufacturers dropped NiCAD batteries for either the nickel metal hydride battery or the lithium ion battery.

The NiMH battery does not have to be fully discharged before recharging. It also has a quarter more charging capacity than a NiCAD battery. A lithium ion battery has a longer life and more charging capacity than the NiMH battery. Both NiMH and LiON batteries are considered "smart" batteries because each has a power meter that indicates the electrical charge of the battery.

Set-Top Boxes

With the onset of cable television and satellite television came a demand for another type of small computing device called a set-top box. A *set-top box* is the device that connects a television to a cable signal or satellite signal received from a service provider. Set-top box technology has evolved with the increasing demand by consumers for television and related services such as email and video on demand. The first-generation set-top box had a simple function: it received a scrambled analog television transmission from the service provider, unscrambled the signal, and sent the unscrambled signal to the television.

The next generation set-top box enabled two-way digital transmissions between the service provider and the consumer. A digital incoming signal from the service provider contained the television signal, and the outgoing signal from the customer carried requests for service, such as pay-per-view access to programming.

The latest in set-top box technology enables service providers to offer fully interactive services that include video on demand, interactive advertising, TV-centric applications, email, and Internet access. Set-top boxes have progressed from being a simple embedded signal decoder to a dedicated personal computer.

There are three categories of set-top boxes: broadcast TV, enhanced TV, and advanced services. A broadcast TV set-top box provides traditional broadcast television and has no return channel. Signals are received in an MPEG-formatted data stream. An enhanced TV set-top box is similar to a broadcast TV set-top except the enhanced TV set-top box has a return channel from the customer to the service provider. An advanced services set-top box is basically a dedicated personal computer that has sufficient computing power to provide rapid processing for interactive, multimedia services.

Inside Look at a Set-Top Box

All modern set-top boxes perform five common operations. These are to decode a digital signal received from the service provider, authenticate access rights, transmit a signal to a television, transmit audio information to create surround sound, and provide interactive services such as access to the Internet and email.

Multiple signals are received by the set-top box from the service provider, each of which is transmitted over its own communications channel. The tuner circuit within the set-top box filters all communications channels except the channel selected by the consumer. The signal from the selected channel is sent to the demodulator circuit. The *demodulator circuit* is a chip that converts the signal into binary data before sending the binary signal to the demultiplexer chip.

The demultiplexer has a number of functions within the set-top box. First, with the assistance of the built-in security system, it determines whether the consumer has the right to access the service transmitted on the selected channel. The consumer is notified if access to the service is denied, otherwise the demultiplexer separates the binary signal into a video signal and an audio signal and then forwards each to the proper decoder circuit. The decoder circuit transforms each signal into a signal used to display the video and replay audio.

Set-top boxes are controlled by an operating system that is usually proprietary, although some manufacturers use a third-party operating system for their set-top box. The most commonly used operating systems are PowerTV OS, VxWorks (also used in cellular phones and car navigation systems), pSOSystem, DAVID OS-9, Windows CE, ChorusOS, JavaOS (also used for automobile computers and private telephone systems), and Linux.

Smart Cards

A *smart card* is a mobile small computing device that is used to store secured information. Smart cards are replacing magnetic strip cards such as credit cards. Typically, a smart card has an 8-bit CPU and 64KB of EEPROM along with a modest amount of memory. And similar to set-top boxes, there are many operating systems used in smart cards. The more commonly used smart card operating systems include Java Card from Sun, MultOS from MasterCard, Smart Card for Windows from Microsoft, and Visa Open Platform.

Smart cards are used to provide real-time, interactive access to secured data stored in the memory of the smart card. A security plan protects this information from unauthorized access and manipulation of information stored in memory.

Let's say that a smart card is used as an electronic checkbook. A consumer's identification information, checking account number, and balance are stored in the smart card's memory. When the consumer makes a purchase, the smart card is inserted into a smart card reader. A smart card reader is an input/output device that is attached to a bank's merchant network and is used to transfer payment from the consumer's account to the merchant's account.

The bank's merchant network first authenticates the consumer by prompting the consumer to present proper identification, which is commonly a personal identification number that the consumer enters into the smart card reader. Once the customer is properly identified to the bank's merchant network, the network determines the portion of the secured data contained on the smart card filing system that can be accessed by the merchant. If the merchant isn't permitted to access the consumer's checking account information, the transaction terminates.

If access is permitted, the necessary information stored in memory to complete the transaction is deciphered, and the transaction commences. The bank's merchant network deducts the transaction amount from the checking account balance on the smart card and within the bank's own system and credits the merchant's account. The revised checking account balance is then rewritten to the smart card. The process by which the bank's merchant network verifies the transaction is called *nonrepudiation*.

The
Complete
Reference

Chapter 3

J2ME Architecture and Development Environment

U sing J2ME you can develop practically any application that you can imagine for a small computing device. The only limitations are those posed by available resources on the small computing device and your skills as a J2ME programmer. A small computing device is constrained by its resources, as you learned previously in this book. These restrictions are inflexible and require you to design your J2ME application to work within these limitations. Fortunately, J2ME technology provides tools to build an industrial-strength Java application designed to run on a small computing device.

Writing a J2ME application is not unlike writing any Java application. You use the same basic programming constructs as used in a J2SE application. However, some routines commonly used in a J2SE application must be modified or excluded from a J2ME application. In this chapter, you'll learn more about the J2ME architecture and how constraints of the architecture restrict the use of routines that you probably employ in your J2SE applications. Furthermore, you'll be introduced to the J2ME development environment and learn techniques for building your first J2ME application.

J2ME Architecture

The modular design of the J2ME architecture enables an application to be scaled based on constraints of a small computing device. J2ME architecture doesn't replace the operating system of a small computing device. Instead, J2ME architecture consists of layers located above the native operating system, collectively referred to as the Connected Limited Device Configuration (CLDC). The CLDC, which is installed on top of the operating system, forms the run-time environment for small computing devices.

The J2ME architecture comprises three software layers (Figure 3-1). The first layer is the configuration layer that includes the Java Virtual Machine (JVM), which directly interacts with the native operating system. The configuration layer also handles interactions between the profile and the JVM. The second layer is the profile layer, which consists of the minimum set of application programming interfaces (APIs) for the small computing device. The third layer is the Mobile Information Device Profile (MIDP). The MIDP layer contains Java APIs for user network connections, persistence storage, and the user interface. It also has access to CLDC libraries and MIDP libraries.

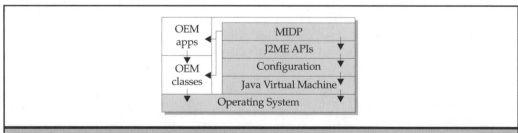

Figure 3-1. *Layers of the J2ME architecture*

A small computing device has two components supplied by the original equipment manufacturer (OEM). These are classes and applications. OEM classes are used by the MIDP to access device-specific features such as sending and receiving messages and accessing device-specific persistent data. OEM applications are programs provided by the OEM, such as an address book. OEM applications can be accessed by the MIDP.

A word of caution: accessing OEM classes and OEM applications from the MIDP restricts the portability of a J2ME application since not all small computing device manufacturers use the same OEM classes or OEM applications.

Small Computing Device Requirements

There are minimum resource requirements for a small computing device to run a J2ME application. First the device must have a minimum of 96 × 54 pixel display that can handle bitmapped graphics and have a way for users to input information, such as a keypad, keyboard, or touch screen. At least 128 kilobytes (KB) of nonvolatile memory is necessary to run Mobile Information Device (MID), and 8KB of nonvolatile memory is needed for storage of persistent application data. To run JVM, 32KB of volatile memory must be available. The device must also provide two-way network connectivity.

Besides minimal hardware requirements, there are also minimal requirements for the native operating system. The native operating system must implement exception handling, process interrupts, be able to run the JVM, and provide schedule capabilities. Furthermore, all user input to the operating system must be forwarded to the JVM, otherwise the device cannot run a J2ME application. Although the native operating system doesn't need to implement a file system to run a J2ME application, it must be able to write and read persistent data (data retained when the device is powered down) to nonvolatile memory.

Run-Time Environment

A MIDlet is a J2ME application designed to operate on an MIDP small computing device. A MIDlet is defined with at least a single class that is derived from the javax.microedition.midlet.MIDlet abstract class. Developers commonly bundle related MIDlets into a MIDlet suite, which is contained within the same package and implemented simultaneously on a small computing device. All MIDlets within a MIDlet suite are considered a group and must be installed and uninstalled as a group (Figure 3-2).

Members of a MIDlet suite share resources of the host environment and share the same instances of Java classes and run within the same JVM. This means if three MIDlets from the same MIDlet suite run the same class, only one instance of the class is created at a time in the Java Virtual Machine. A key benefit of the relationship among MIDlet suite members is that they share the same data, including data in persistent storage such as user preferences.

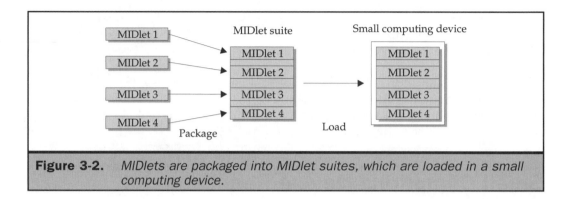

Figure 3-2.   *MIDlets are packaged into MIDlet suites, which are loaded in a small computing device.*

Sharing data among MIDlets exposes each MIDlet to data errors caused by concurrent read/write access to data. This risk is reduced by synchronization primitives on the MIDlet suite level that restrict access to volatile data and persistent data. However, if a MIDlet uses multi-threading, the MIDlet is responsible for coordinated access to the record store.

Data cannot be shared between MIDlets that are not from the same MIDlet suite because the MIDlet suite name is used to identify data associated with the suite. A MIDlet from a different MIDlet suite is considered an unreliable source.

A MIDlet suite is installed, executed, and removed by the application manager running on the device. The manufacturer of the small computing device provides the application manager. Once a MIDlet suite is installed, each member of the MIDlet suite is given access to classes of the JVM and CLDC by the application manager. Likewise, a MIDlet can access classes defined in the MIDP to interact with the user interface, network, and persistent storage.

The application manager also makes the Java archive (JAR) file and the Java application descriptor (JAD) file available to members of the MIDlet suite.

Inside the Java Archive File

All the files necessary to implement a MIDlet suite must be contained within a production package called a Java archive (JAR) file. These files include MIDlet classes, graphic images (if required by a MIDlet), and the manifest file. The manifest file contains a list of attributes and related definitions that are used by the application manager to install the files contained in the JAR file onto the small computing device. Nine attributes are defined in the manifest file; all but six of these attributes are optional.

Table 3-1 lists attributes contained in a manifest file. Of these, the first six attributes are required for every manifest file. Failure to include them in the manifest file causes the application manager to halt the installation of the JAR file.

Listing 3-1 is a manifest file that contains the minimum number of attributes. As you'll see in the section "Hello World J2ME Style" later in this chapter, you use an

Manifest File Attribute	Description
MIDlet-Name	MIDlet suite name.
MIDlet-Version	MIDlet version number.
MIDlet-Vendor	Name of the vendor who supplied the MIDlet.
MIDlet-n	Attribute per MIDlet. Values are MIDlet name, optional icon, and MIDlet class name.
MicroEdition-Profile	Identifies the J2ME profile that is necessary to run the MIDlet.
MicroEdition-Configuration	Identifies the J2ME configuration that is necessary to run the MIDlet.
MIDlet-Icon	Icon associated with MIDlet, must be in PNG image format (optional).
MIDlet-Description	Description of MIDlet (optional).
MIDlet-Info-URL	URL containing more information about the MIDlet.

Table 3-1.   *Attributes of the Manifest File*

editor to create a manifest file as a text file with the .txt file extension. The manifest file's extension is changed to .mf when the MIDlet is prepared for deployment.

Listing 3-1
A manifest file

```
MIDlet-Name: Best MIDlet
MIDlet-Version: 2.0
MIDlet-Vendor: MyCompany
MIDlet-1: BestMIDlet, /images/BestMIDlet.png, Best.BestMIDlet
MicroEdition-Profile: MIDP-1.0
MicroEdition-Configuration: CLDC-1.0
```

Entries in the manifest are name:value pairs and therefore can appear in any order within the manifest file. Each pair must be terminated with a carriage return. Whitespace between the colon and the attribute value is ignored when the application manager reads the manifest file.

Let's step through the manifest file shown in Listing 3-1. The MIDlet-Name attribute specifies the name of the MIDlet suite, which is Best MIDlet in this example. The MIDlet-Version and MIDlet-Vendor attributes identify the version number of the MIDlet suite and the company or person who provided the MIDlet suite.

The MIDlet-*n* attribute contains information about each MIDlet that is in the JAR file. The number of the MIDlet replaces the letter *n*. In this example, the *n* is replaced with the digit 1 because there is only one MIDlet in the MIDlet suite.

The MIDlet-*n* attribute can contain three values that describe the MIDlet. A comma separates each value. The first value is the name of the MIDlet, which is BestMIDlet. Next is an optional value that specifies the icon that will be used with the MIDlet. In this example, BestMIDlet.png is the icon. The icon must be in the PNG image format. And the last value for the MIDlet-*n* attribute is the MIDlet class name, which is Best.BestMIDlet. The application manager uses the class name to load the MIDlet.

The next MIDlet-*n* attribute is the MicroEdition-Profile whose value is the J2ME profile that is required to run the MIDlet. In this example the MIDP-1.0 profile is required. And the last MIDlet-*n* attribute is the MicroEdition-Configuration. The MicroEdition-Configuration attribute identifies the J2ME configuration that is necessary to run the MIDlet.

Inside the Java Application Descriptor File

You may include a Java application descriptor (JAD) file within the JAR file of a MIDlet suite as a way to pass parameters to a MIDlet without modifying the JAR file (see Chapter 4). A JAD file is also used to provide the application manager with additional content information about the JAR file to determine whether the MIDlet suite can be implemented on the device.

A JAD file is similar to a manifest in that both contain attributes that are name:value pairs. Name:value pairs can appear in any order within the JAD file. There are five required system attributes for a JAD file:

MIDlet-Name
MIDlet-Version
MIDlet-Vendor
MIDlet-*n*
MIDlet-Jar-URL

A system attribute is an attribute that is defined in the J2ME specification. Table 3-2 contains a complete list of system attributes. Listing 3-2 illustrates a typical JAD file. All JAD files must have the .jad extension.

The JAD file shown in Listing 3-2 contains a few attributes that are also found in the manifest file in Listing 3-1. The first three attributes in the JAD file are identical to attributes in the manifest file.

Listing 3-2
A JAD file

```
MIDlet-Name: Best MIDlet
MIDlet-Version: 2.0
MIDlet-Vendor: MyCompany
MIDlet-Jar-URL: http://www.mycompany.com/bestmidlet.jar
MIDlet-1: BestMIDlet, /images/BestMIDlet.png, Best.BestMIDlet
```

The MIDlet-Jar-URL attribute contains the URL of the JAR file, which in this example is called bestmidlet.jar. And the last required attribute in the JAD file is the MIDlet-*n* attribute that defines a MIDlet of the MIDlet suite identical to the MIDlet-*n* attribute of the manifest. A MIDlet-*n* attribute is required for each MIDlet in the MIDlet suite.

A word of caution: the values of the MIDlet-Name, MIDlet-Version, and MIDlet-Vendor attributes in the JAD file must match the same attributes in the manifest. If the values are different, the JAR file is not installed. Other attributes that are not the same are overridden by attributes in the descriptor.

JAD File Attribute	Description
MIDlet-Name	MIDlet suite name.
MIDlet-Version	MIDlet version number.
MIDlet-Vendor	Name of the vendor who supplied the MIDlet.
MIDlet-*n*	Attribute per MIDlet. Values are MIDlet name, optional icon, and MIDlet class name.
MIDlet-Jar-URL	Location of the JAR file.
MIDlet-Jar-Size	Size of the JAR file in bytes (optional).
MIDlet-Data-Size	Minimum size (in bytes) for persistent data storage (optional).
MIDlet-Description	Description of MIDlet (optional).
MIDlet-Delete-Confirm	Confirmation required before removing the MIDlet suite (optional).
MIDlet-Install-Notify	Send installation status to given URL (optional).

Table 3-2.   *Attributes for a JAD File*

A developer can include application attributes in a JAD file. An application attribute is a name:value pair that contains a value unique to the application. Any name can be given to an application attribute as long as it does not begin with MIDlet-.

MIDlet Programming

Programming a MIDlet is similar to creating a J2SE application in that you define a class and related methods. However, a MIDlet is less robust than a J2SE application because of the restrictions imposed by the small computing device. The following overview gives you a glimpse of how a MIDlet is created. You'll learn the details of building your own MIDlet in the "Hello World J2ME Style" section later in this chapter.

A MIDlet is a class that extends the MIDlet class and is the interface between application statements and the run-time environment, which is controlled by the application manager. A MIDlet class must contain three abstract methods that are called by the application manager to manage the life cycle of the MIDlet. These abstract methods are startApp(), pauseApp(), and destroyApp().

The startApp() method is called by the application manager when the MIDlet is started and contains statements that are executed each time the application begins execution (Figure 3-3). The pauseApp() method is called before the application manager temporarily stops the MIDlet. The application manager restarts the MIDlet by recalling the startApp() method. The destroyApp() method is called prior to the termination of the MIDlet by the application manager.

Listing 3-3 illustrates the basic shell of a MIDlet. In this example, the MIDlet class called BasicMIDletShell extends the MIDlet class. Any name can be used for a class as long as it conforms to the Java class naming convention.

Listing 3-3
The basic MIDlet shell

```
public class BasicMIDletShell extends MIDlet
{
  public void startApp()
  {
  }
  public void pauseApp()
  {
  }
  public void destroyApp( boolean unconditional)
  {
  }
}
```

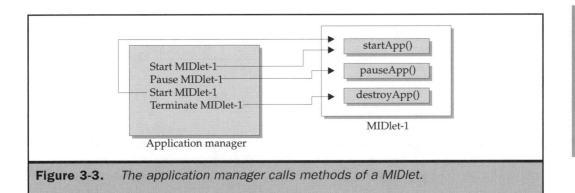

Figure 3-3.   *The application manager calls methods of a MIDlet.*

Both the startApp() and pauseApp() methods are public and have no return value nor parameter list. The destroyApp() method is also a public method without a return value. However, the destroyApp() method has a boolean parameter that is set to true if the termination of the MIDlet is unconditional, and false if the MIDlet can throw a MIDletStateChangeException telling the application manager that the MIDlet does not want to be destroyed just yet.

At the center of every MIDlet are the MIDP API classes used by the MIDlet to interact with the user and handle data management. User interactions are managed by user interface MIDP API classes. These APIs enable a developer to display screens of data and prompt the user to respond with an appropriate command. The command causes the MIDlet to execute one of three routines: perform a computation, make a network request, or display another screen.

The data-handling MIDP API classes enable the developer to perform four kinds of data routines: write and read persistent data, store data in data types, receive data from and send data to a network, and interact with the small computing device's input/output features.

Event Handling

A MIDlet is an event-based application. All routines executed in the MIDlet are invoked in response to an event reported to the MIDlet by the application manager. The initial event that occurs is when the MIDlet is started and the application manager invokes the startApp() method.

The startApp() method in a typical MIDlet contains a statement that displays a screen of data and prompts the user to enter a selection from among one or more options. The nature and number of options is MIDlet and screen dependent.

A Command object is used to present a user with a selection of options to choose from when a screen is displayed. Each screen must have a CommandListener.

A CommandListener monitors user events with a screen and causes the appropriate code to execute based on the current event. You'll learn more about screens, Command objects, and CommandListeners in the "Hello World J2ME Style" section later in this chapter.

User Interfaces

The design of a user interface for a MIDlet depends on the restrictions of a small computing device. Some small computing devices contain resources that provide a rich user interface, while other more resource-constrained devices offer a modest user interface. A rich user interface contains the following elements, and a device with a minimal user interface has some subset of these elements as determined by the profile used for the device.

A Form is the most commonly invoked user interface element found in a MIDlet and is used to contain other user interface elements. Text is placed on a form as a StringItem, a List, a ChoiceGroup, and a Ticker.

A StringItem contains text that appears on a form that cannot be changed by the user. A List is an itemized options list from which the user can choose an option. A ChoiceGroup is a related itemized options list. And a Ticker is text that is scrollable.

A user enters information into a form by using the Choice element, TextBox, TextField, or DateField elements. The Choice element returns an option that the user selected. TextBox and TextField elements collect textual information from a user and enable the user to edit information that appears in these user interface elements. The DateField is similar to a TextBox and TextField except its contents are a date and time.

An Alert is a special Form that is used to alert the user that an error has occurred. An Alert is usually limited to a StringItem user interface element that defines the nature of the error to the user.

You will learn more about the full range of user interface elements and how to deploy them later in this book.

Device Data

Small computing devices don't have the resources necessary to run an onboard database management system (DBMS). In fact some of these devices lack a file system. Therefore, a MIDlet must read and write persistent data without the advantage of a DBMS or file system.

A MIDlet can use an MIDP class—RecordStore—and two MIDP interfaces—RecordComparator and RecordFilter—to write and read persistent data. A RecordStore class contains methods used to write and read persistent data in the form of a record. Persistent data is read from a RecordStore by using either the RecordComparator interface or the RecordFilter interface. You'll learn how to use RecordStore, RecordComparator, and RecordFilter later in this book.

Java Language for J2ME

CDC implements the full J2SE available, but CLDC implements a stripped-down J2SE because of the limited resources in small computing devices. In this section you'll learn about three prominent features of J2SE that you cannot implement in J2ME.

Floating-point math is probably the most notable missing feature of J2ME. Floating-point math requires special processing hardware to perform floating-point calculations. However, most small computing devices lack such hardware and therefore are unable to process floating-point calculations. This means that your MIDlet cannot use any floating-point data types or calculations.

The second most notable difference between the Java language used in J2SE and J2ME is the absence of support for the finalize() method. The finalize() method in J2SE is automatically called before an instance of a class terminates and typically contains statements that free previously allocated resources. However, resources in a small computing device are too scarce to process the finalize() method.

Another dramatic difference is the reduced number of error-handling exceptions that are supported in J2ME. Table 3-3 lists error-handling exceptions available in J2ME. Exception handling drains system resources, which are precious in a small computing device and therefore the primary reason for trimming the number of error-handling exceptions. Typically, run-time errors are automatically responded to by the native operating system by restarting the small computing device.

Changes were also made in the Java Virtual Machine that runs on a small computing device because of resource constraints. One such change occurs with the class loader. JVM for small computing devices requires a custom class loader that is supplied by the device manufacturer and cannot be replaced or modified.

Another feature lacking in the JVM is the ThreadGroup class. You cannot group threads. All threads are handled at the object level, although there is a workaround (see Chapter 4). Also, you cannot call other programming languages' methods and APIs, primarily because of the memory requirements to execute such calls. Two other features of J2SE that are missing from J2ME are weak references and the Reflection classes.

The standard JVM uses class file verification to protect applications from malicious code through the use of a security manager. However, this process is replaced with a two-step process because of the limited resources available on small computing devices. The first step is called preverification and occurs outside the small computing device prior to loading the MIDlet. Preverification requires that additional attributes called stack maps are inserted into a class file by software before the second step runs. *Stack maps* describe the MIDlet's variables and operands located on the interpreter stack.

After preverification is completed, the MIDlet class is loaded into the device, and the verifier within the small computing device validates each instruction in the MIDlet class. The MIDlet class is automatically rejected if the verifier detects an error.

System Classes		
java.lang.Class	java.lang.Runtime	java.lang.System
java.lang.Object	java.lang.String	java.lang.Thread
java.lang.Runnable	java.lang.StringBuffer	java.lang.Throwable
Data Type Classes		
java.lang.Boolean	java.lang.Character	java.lang.Long
java.lang.Byte	java.lang.Integer	java.lang.Short
Collection Classes		
java.util.Enumeration	java.util.Stack	
java.util.Hashtable	java.util.Vector	
Input/Output Classes		
java.io.ByteArrayInputStream	java.io.DataOutputStream	java.io.PrintStream
java.io.ByteArrayOutputStream	java.io.InputStream	java.io.Reader
java.io.DataInput	java.io.InputStreamReader	java.io.Writer
java.io.DataInputStream	java.io.OutputStream	
java.io.DataOutput	java.io.OutputStreamWriter	
Calendar and Time Classes		
java.util.Calendar	java.util.Date	java.util.TimeZone

Table 3-3.   *J2ME Support Classes*

Utility Classes

java.lang.Math	java.util.Random

Exception Classes

java.io.EOFException	java.lang.ClassNotFoundException	java.lang.NegativeArraySizeException
java.io.InterruptedIOException	java.lang.Exception	java.lang.NullPointerException
java.io.IOException	java.lang.IllegalAccessException	java.lang.NumberFormatException
java.io.UnsupportedEncodingException	java.lang.IllegalArgumentException	java.lang.RuntimeException
java.io.UTFDataformatException	java.lang.IllegalMonitorStateException	java.lang.SecurityException
java.lang.ArithmeticException	java.lang.IllegalThreadStateException	java.lang.StringIndexOutOfBoundsException
java.lang.ArrayIndexOutOfBoundsException	java.lang.IndexOutOfBoundsException	java.util.emptyStackException
java.lang.ArrayStoreException	java.lang.InstantiationException	java.util.NoSuchElementException
java.lang.ClassCastException	java.lang.InterruptedException	

Error Classes

java.lang.Error	java.lang.OutOfMemoryError	java.lang.VirtualMachineError

Internationalization

java.io.InputStreamReader	java.io.OutputStreamWriter

Table 3-3.   *J2ME Support Classes (continued)*

J2ME Software Development Kits

A MIDlet is built using free software packages that are downloadable from the java.sun .com web site, although you can purchase third-party development products such as Borland JBuilder Mobile Set, Sun One Studio 4 (formerly Forte for Java), and WebGain VisualCafe Enterprise Suite. Three software packages need to be downloaded from java.sun.com. These are the Java Development Kit (1.3 or greater) (java.sun.com/ j2se/downloads.html), Connected Limited Device Configuration (CLDC) (java.sun. com/products/cldc/), and the Mobile Information Device Profile (MIDP) (java.sun.com/ products/midp/). You'll also need the J2ME Wireless Toolkit to develop MIDlets for handheld devices (java.sun.com/products/j2mewtoolkit/download.html).

Each of these software packages contains installation instructions that you need to follow closely in order to assure proper installation of each package. However, there are a few tips that will help you during the installation. First, install the Java development kit. The Java development kit contains the Java compiler and the jar.exe, which is used to create Java archive files as described previously in this chapter. After downloading the Java development kit package, unzip the package and run the installation program. It is best to accept the default directory, although you are free to choose a different directory for the Java development kit.

Once the Java development kit is installed, place the c:\jdk\bin directory, or whatever directory you selected for the Java development kit, on the PATH environment variable (see "Setting the Path in Windows" sidebar). This enables you to invoke the Java compiler from anywhere on your computer.

Setting the Path in Windows
Windows 2000 and Windows NT

1. Choose System from the Control Panel.

2. Select Environment or Advanced/Environment.

3. Locate the PATH environment variable.

4. Enter the directory at the end of the path. Be sure to separate entries with a semicolon.

Windows 98 and Windows 95

1. Select Start.

2. Select Run.

3. Enter **sysedit**.

4. Select OK.

5. Locate the autoexec.bat dialog box.

6. Add the directory to the PATH environment variable.

J2ME BASICS

Install the CLDC once the Java development kit is installed. Unzip the downloaded CLDC files from the java.sun.com web site onto the d:\j2me directory (J2ME_HOME) on your computer. You'll need to create the j2me directory if one doesn't exist. Unzipping the CLDC package creates the j2me_cldc subdirectory below the j2me directory.

The j2me_cldc has a bin subdirectory that contains the K Virtual Machine and the preverifier executable files for an assortment of platforms such as win32. Each platform is in its own subdirectory under j2me_cldc. Add the j2me\j2me_cldc\bin\win32 subdirectory to the PATH environment variable (see "Setting the Path in Windows" sidebar). You should substitute win32 subdirectory with the appropriate subdirectory for your platform.

Next, download and unzip the MIDP file. Be sure to use \j2me as the directory for the MIDP file. Unzipping the MIDP file creates a midp directory. The name of this directory might vary depending on the version that you download. Some versions create a midp-fcs directory, while the 1.0.3 version creates a %J2ME_HOME%\ midp1.0.3fcs directory. This chapter references the %J2ME_HOME%\midp1.0.3fcs directory. You can replace references to this directory with the directory relevant to your midp version. The midp1.0.3fcs directory also contains a bin subdirectory. And you'll need to include the \j2me\midp1.0.3fcs\bin subdirectory in the PATH environment variable.

Next, create two environment variables. These are CLASSPATH and MIDP_HOME. The CLASSPATH environment variable identifies the path to be searched whenever a class is invoked. The MIDP_HOME environment variable identifies the location of the \lib directory that contains the internal.config file and the system.config file.

Set the CLASSPATH to

```
d:\j2me\midp1.0.3fcs\classes;.
```

Notice that the CLASSPATH terminates with a period. The period implies the current directory and will cause the current directory to be searched if a class is not found in the \j2me\midp1.0.3fcs\classes directory.

Modifying the internal.config File

The internal.config file is used to describe preferences that affect features of MIDP. Preferences are identified by name:value pairs. You can change values of name:value pairs by modifying the file with an editor. For example, MIDP contains an emulator for J2ME devices, such as cellular telephones. An emulator enables you to test the performance of your MIDlet without having to load the MIDlet into the real device.

You can modify the color configuration of the emulated device by changing the value of the system.display.screen_depth attribute to 1, 2, 4, or 8. The value 1 causes the emulator to display black and white colors. The value 2 forces the emulator to display a 4-color grayscale. The value 4 displays a 15-color grayscale, and the value 8 changes the emulator to 256 possible colors.

Set the MIDP_HOME environment variable to

```
d:\j2me\midp1.0.3fcs
```

Hello World J2ME Style

You can create your first MIDlet once the Java development kit, Connected Limited Device Configuration (CLDC), and Mobile Information Device Profile (MIDP) are installed. And keeping tradition alive, let's begin by creating a directory structure within which you can create and run MIDlets. Here are the directories that are used for examples in this chapter:

- j2me
- j2me\src
- j2me\src\greeting
- j2me\tmp_classes
- j2me\midlets

You'll create two MIDlets in this section, which will illustrate the basic concept of making and running a J2ME application. The first MIDlet is called HelloWorld and the other MIDlet is GoodbyeWorld. The HelloWorld MIDlet shows how to create a simple MIDlet that can be invoked directly from the class and from a Java archive file. Later in this section you'll learn how to create a MIDlet suite that contains two MIDlets. These are HelloWorld and GoodbyeWorld.

Let's begin by creating the HelloWorld MIDlet. Enter the code shown in Listing 3-4 into a text editor such as Notepad, and save the file in the j2me\src\greeting directory as HelloWorld.java.

The HelloWorld MIDlet performs three basic functions that are found in nearly all MIDlets. These are to display a text box and a command on the screen, then listen to events that occur while the MIDlet is running.

The HelloWorld MIDlet is created by defining a class called HelloWorld that extends the MIDlet class and implements a CommandListener. The HelloWorld class contains three private data members and four methods. The data members are a Display object, a text box, and a command. The methods are startApp(), pauseApp(), and destroyApp(), which are discussed earlier in this chapter. The fourth method is called commandAction() and is invoked by the application manager whenever an event occurs.

Listing 3-4 illustrates a typical HelloWorld MIDlet. Two packages must be imported at the beginning of the MIDlet to access MIDlet classes and lcdui classes. MIDlet classes are screen oriented and create a Display object and then place components of the screen into the Display object. The Display object is then invoked later in the MIDlet to display the screen on the small computing device.

Listing 3-4
HelloWorld
MIDlet
source code

```
package greeting;
import javax.microedition.midlet.*;
import javax.microedition.lcdui.*;
public class HelloWorld extends MIDlet implements CommandListener
{
  private Display display ;
  private TextBox textBox ;
  private Command quitCommand;
  public void startApp()
  {
    display  = Display.getDisplay(this);
    quitCommand = new Command("Quit", Command.SCREEN, 1);
    textBox  = new TextBox("Hello World", "My first MIDlet", 40, 0);
    textBox .addCommand(quitCommand);
    textBox .setCommandListener(this);
    display .setCurrent(textBox );
  }
  public void pauseApp()
  {
  }
  public void destroyApp(boolean unconditional)
  {
  }
  public void commandAction(Command choice, Displayable displayable)
  {
    if (choice == quitCommand)
    {
      destroyApp(false);
      notifyDestroyed();
    }
  }
}
```

The Display object in this example is called display and will contain a TextBox object called textBox and a Command object called quitCommand. All three objects are private and are defined at the beginning of the HelloWorld class definition.

The startApp() method contains the necessary statements to invoke previously defined objects. The startApp() method begins by creating an instance of the Display object by calling the getDisplay() method. The instance of the Display object is assigned to the display Display object that is previously defined in the class. Calling getDisplay multiple times always returns the same Display reference for the specified MIDlet.

Next, an instance of a command object is created. There are three values required when creating a command object. The first value is the label of the command that will appear on the screen. The label in this example is Quit. The next value is the type of command, which is a screen command. The third parameter determines the priority of the command, which is the first priority—the higher the number, the lower the priority. The application manager uses priority to determine the order in which a command appears in a menu if the MIDlet uses a menu.

The last instance of an object that is created in the startApp() is a TextBox object. Four values are necessary to create an instance of a TextBox object. The first is the caption for the TextBox object followed by the text that will appear in the TextBox object. In this example, Hello World is the caption and My first MIDlet is the text. The other two values are coordinates used by the application manager to position the TextBox object on the screen.

Next, the Command object must be associated with the TextBox message. This is accomplished by calling the addCommand() method of the TextBox object and passing the addCommand() method the Command object. Once the Command object is associated with the TextBox object, the CommandListener must be associated with the TextBox object in order for the CommandListener to respond to events occurring when the TextBox object is displayed on the screen. The setCommandListener() method of the TextBox object is used to associate the TextBox object with the CommandListener.

And the final statement within the startApp() method associates the TextBox object with the Display object by calling the setCurrent() method of the Display object and passing the setCurrent() method the TextBox object.

When the application manager of the small computing device runs the HelloWorld MIDlet, the startApp() method is the first method that is invoked, which causes the display that contains the Hello World message and the Quit command to be shown on the screen.

The HelloWorld MIDlet is required to define a pauseApp() method and a destroyApp() method, but these methods can remain empty because no special action is taken when the HelloWorld MIDLet is paused or destroyed.

The commandAction() method contains statements that evaluate events that occur while the HelloWorld MIDLet is running. The command selected by the user is passed to the commandAction() method as the first parameter. The second parameter is a Displayable object, which is a reference to the TextBox that is associated with the command. A TextBox along with other interface objects are Displayable objects.

An if statement is used to determine whether the user selected the Command object that is associated with the Hello World TextBox object. If so, the destroyApp() method is invoked and is passed a boolean false. The destroyApp() method is called before the MIDlet is destroyed; afterwards the notifyDestroyed() method is called to notify the application manager that the HelloWorld MIDLet has entered into the destroyed state. Prior to invoking the notifyDestroyed() method, a MIDlet should have completed its own garbage collection.

Compiling Hello World

The Hello World source code files should be saved in the new j2me\src\greeting directory as HelloWorld.java. Next, you'll need to compile the HelloWorld MIDlet. Compiling a MIDlet is a two-step process. The first step is to use the Java compiler to transform the source file into a class file. The second step is to preverify the class file, as described previously in this chapter. The preverification generates a modified class file.

Make j2me\src\greeting the current directory, and then enter the following command at the command line. The d: drive is used in this example. You can replace the d: with the drive letter that is appropriate for your file structure.

```
javac -d d:\j2me\tmp_classes -target 1.1 -bootclasspath
d:\j2me\midp1.0.3fcs\classes HelloWorld.java
```

The bootclasspath option must be used when compiling a MIDlet. The bootclasspath option points to the startup class files commonly referred to as the Java bootstrap files. The startup classes are MIDP classes. If you fail to use the bootclasspath option, the compiler uses JDK classes instead of the MIDP classes.

The compiler produces a file called HelloWorld.class in the j2me\tmp_classes\ greeting directory. The greeting directory is created because of the package greeting declaration in the source code. The J2SDK 1.4 compiler outputs class files for JVM 1.2. However, the preverification expects classes for JVM 1.1. Therefore, you need to specify JVM 1.1 in the target option so the compiler generates classes for the JVM 1.1.

Next, you'll need to preverify the HelloWorld.class that was generated by the compiler. Make sure that j2me\src\greeting is the current directory and enter the following command:

```
preverify -d d:\j2me\classes -classpath d:\j2me\midp1.0.3fcs\classes
d:\j2me\tmp_classes
```

You must use two preverify options. The -d option places the class file within the tmp_classes directory. The second option is -classpath, which points to the location of the library classes that come with the MIDP. Preverification files are contained in the midp1.0.3fcs\classes directory. The output of the javac compiler is in the tmp_classes directory.

You can exclude the -classpath option if the CLASSPATH environment variable points to the d:\j2me\midp1.0.3fcs\classes directory. In this case, you simply invoke the preverify using:

```
preverify -d d:\j2me\classes d:\j2me\tmp_classes
```

A word of caution: the preverifier overwrites the HelloWorld.class file generated by the compiler if the directory specified in the -d option is the same directory that contains the HelloWorld.class file. Replacing the HelloWorld.class file isn't a problem because the post-preverified HelloWorld.class is the file used to invoke the class.

Running Hello World

A MIDlet should be tested in an emulator before being downloaded to a small computing device. An *emulator* is software that simulates how a MIDlet will run in a small computing device. Once you're satisfied that a MIDlet is operating properly, you can deploy the MIDlet as part of a MIDlet suite, which you'll learn to do a little later in the chapter.

There are two ways to run a MIDlet. These are either by invoking the MIDlet class or by creating a JAR file, then running the MIDlet from the JAR file. Let's begin by running the MIDlet class without the need of a JAR file. Make sure that j2me\src\ greeting is the current directory, and then enter the following command. Figure 3-4 illustrates how the MIDlet appears in the emulator. Click the right telephone handset icon to close the MIDlet.

```
midp -classpath d:\j2me\classes  greeting.HelloWorld
```

Deploying Hello World

A MIDlet should be placed in a MIDlet suite after testing is completed. The MIDlet suite is then packaged into a JAR file along with other related files for downloading to a small computing device. This process is commonly referred to as *packaging*.

In the HelloWorld example, the MIDlet suite contains one MIDlet, which is the HelloWorld.class. Before packaging the MIDlet into a JAR file, you'll need to use an editor to create the manifest file shown in Listing 3-5. The manifest describes the JAR file. The manifest file should be saved as manifest.txt in the j2me\src\greeting directory. Notice that the MIDlet description within the manifest file contains a graphic call, /greeting/mylogo.png, that is associated with the HelloWorld MIDlet. Any PNG-formatted image file can be used in place of mylogo.png. However, all image files must be in the PNG format. You can also remove references to an image file by replacing the name of the image file with a space, such as:

```
MIDlet-1: HelloWorld, , greeting.HelloWorld
```

Listing 3-5
The manifest file for Hello World

```
MIDlet-Name: Hello World
MIDlet-Version: 1.0
MIDlet-Vendor: Jim
MIDlet-1: HelloWorld, /greeting/myLogo.png, greeting.HelloWorld
MicroEdition-Configuration: CLDC-1.0
MicroEdition-Profile: MIDP-1.0
```

Figure 3-4.   *The HelloWorld MIDlet running in the emulator*

You can create the JAR file once the manifest.txt file is saved in the j2me\src\ greeting directory. Make sure the j2me\src\greeting directory is the current directory, and then create the JAR file by entering the following command:

```
jar -cfvm d:\j2me\midlets\HelloWorld.jar manifest.txt -C d:\j2me\classes greeting
```

The final piece of the Hello World package is a JAD file. Create the JAD file shown in Listing 3-6 using an editor, and save the JAD file in the j2me/src/greeting directory.

Listing 3-6
The JAD
file for
HelloWorld

```
MIDlet-Name: Hello World
MIDlet-Version: 1.0
MIDlet-Vendor: Jim
```

```
MIDlet-Description: My First MIDlet suite
MIDlet-1: HelloWorld, /greeting/myLogo.png, greeting.HelloWorld
MIDlet-Jar-URL: HelloWorld.jar
MIDlet-Jar-Size: 1428
```

Copy the HelloWorld.jad file into the j2me/midlets directory, and then make j2me/midlets the current directory. Invoke the MIDlet by entering the following command. The image of the mobile cellular telephone is displayed on the screen (Figure 3-4). Click the right telephone handset icon to close the MIDlet.

```
midp -classpath HelloWorld.jar -Xdescriptor HelloWorld.jad
```

Once you are satisfied that the MIDlet suite packaged in a JAR file is operating properly in the emulator, you can download the JAR file to a small computing device. The downloading process is device dependent, and therefore you must refer to the device's documentation or the manufacturer's web site for steps for downloading your JAR file.

What to Do When Your MIDlet Doesn't Work Properly

Sometimes a MIDlet won't compile or run properly. Although each MIDlet is unique, there are a few common problems that cause a MIDlet to fail. Here are areas to investigate if you experience a failure.

If the compiler, preverifier, JAR program, or emulator doesn't run from the command line, review the value of the PATH, CLASSPATH, and MIDP_HOME environment variables to be sure you have included the exact path to these programs. Also make sure that the current directory reference (a period) is included in the CLASSPATH environment variable.

Running out of environment space is a common problem on some platforms. This results in not enough room to store the complete value of an environment variable such as the PATH. You can work around this problem by creating an executable file, such as a batch file in Windows, that sets the environment variables for J2ME components. Run this executable file before compiling and testing your MIDlet to temporarily reset environment variables. The environment variables return to their original values the next time you restart your computer or log in.

Many types of errors can occur during the compiling and packaging process. Some are syntax errors, which you'll be able to fix quickly by reviewing the source code. Other errors can be caused by poorly formed command line options and arguments, such as failing to insert a space between an option and a period when referencing the current directory.

Another common occurrence is for a MIDlet suite to run fine in test but fail to run after downloaded to the small computing device. In this case, the application manager on the small computing device might reject the MIDlet suite because the MIDlet suite cannot be run on the device. An oversize MIDlet suite is a likely suspect.

Multiple MIDlets in a MIDlet Suite

In the real world, multiple MIDlets are distributed in a single MIDlet suite. The application manager then displays each MIDlet as a menu option, enabling the user to run one of the MIDlets. Let's create another MIDlet to illustrate how to deploy a multiple MIDlet suite.

The new MIDlet is called GoodbyeWorld and is shown in Listing 3-7. Enter this code into a text editor and save the file as GoodbyeWorld.java in the j2me\src\greeting directory. Make the j2me\src\greeting directory the current directory. Compile both the HelloWorld.java and GoodbyeWorld.java files by entering the following command at the command line:

```
javac -d d:\j2me\tmp_classes -target 1.1 -bootclasspath
d:\j2me\midp1.0.3fcs\classes *.java
```

Preverify these files by entering the following command at the command line:

```
preverify -d d:\j2me\classes -classpath d:\j2me\midp1.0.3fcs\classes
d:\j2me\tmp_classes
```

Listing 3-7
GoodbyeWorld
MIDlet source
code

```java
package greeting;
import javax.microedition.midlet.*;
import javax.microedition.lcdui.*;
public class GoodbyeWorld extends MIDlet implements CommandListener
{
  private Display display ;
  private TextBox textBox ;
  private Command quitCommand;
  public void startApp()
  {
    display   = Display.getDisplay(this);
    quitCommand = new Command("Quit", Command.SCREEN, 1);
    textBox   = new TextBox("Goodbye World", "My second MIDlet", 40, 0);
    textBox .addCommand(quitCommand);
    textBox .setCommandListener(this);
    display .setCurrent(textBox );
  }
  public void pauseApp()
  {
  }
  public void destroyApp(boolean unconditional)
  {
  }
  public void commandAction(Command choice, Displayable displayable )
```

```
    {
      if (choice == quitCommand)
      {
        destroyApp(false);
        notifyDestroyed();
      }
    }
  }
}
```

Next, create a manifest.txt file, as illustrated in Listing 3-8, and save the file in the j2me/src/greeting directory. You can modify the manifest.txt file created in the previous example as an alternative to writing a new manifest file by including a description of the GoodbyeWorld class as shown in Listing 3-8.

Create the HelloWorld.jar file by entering the following command. Make sure that the j2m/src/greeting directory is the current directory.

```
jar -cfvm d:\j2me\midlets\HelloWorld.jar manifest.txt -C d:\j2me\classes greeting
```

You'll also be required to create or modify the existing JAD file to resemble Listing 3-9. Save the HelloWorld.jar file in 2me/src/greeting. Next, copy the HelloWorld.jar file and the HelloWorld.jad file to the j2me/midlets directory.

Make the j2me/midlets directory the current directory, and then enter the following command on the command line to run the J2ME application:

```
midp -classpath HelloWorld.jar -Xdescriptor HelloWorld.jad
```

Listing 3-8
The manifest file for HelloWorld/GoodbyeWorld MIDlet suite

```
MIDlet-Name: Hello World
MIDlet-Version: 1.0
MIDlet-Vendor: Jim
MIDlet-1: HelloWorld, /greeting/myLogo.png, greeting.HelloWorld
MIDlet-2: GoodbyeWorld, /greeting/myLogo.png, greeting.GoodbyeWorld
MicroEdition-Configuration: CLDC-1.0
MicroEdition-Profile: MIDP-1.0
```

Listing 3-9
The JAD file for HelloWorld/GoodbyeWorld

```
MIDlet-Name: Hello World
MIDlet-Version: 1.0
MIDlet-Vendor: Jim
MIDlet-Description: My First MIDlet suite
MIDlet-1: HelloWorld, /greeting/myLogo.png, greeting.HelloWorld
MIDlet-2: GoodbyeWorld, /greeting/myLogo.png, greeting.GoodbyeWorld
```

```
MIDlet-Jar-URL: HelloWorld.jar
MIDlet-Jar-Size: 4048
```

The cellular phone emulator displays the image of a cellular phone on the screen, as shown in Figure 3-5. Notice that the emulator's application manager displays both the HelloWorld and GoodbyeWorld MIDlets as menu options.

Click on the up or down arrow keys on the emulator to move the cursor up and down the menu options. Click on the center button to launch either the HelloWorld MIDlet or the GoodbyeWorld MIDlet. For example, if you move the cursor to the GoodbyeWorld MIDlet and select the center button on the emulator, the emulator's application manager launches the GoodbyeWorld MIDlet, as shown in Figure 3-6. Click the left cellular telephone handset icon to return to the menu.

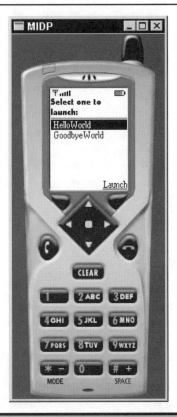

Figure 3-5.   *The HelloWorld MIDlet running in the emulator*

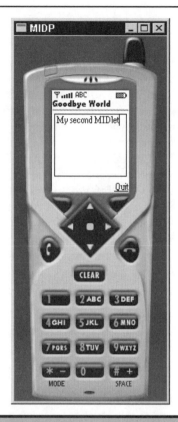

Figure 3-6. *The GoodbyeWorld MIDlet running in the emulator*

J2ME Wireless Toolkit

Building and running a J2ME application at the command line is cumbersome, to
say the least, when you are creating a robust application consisting of several MIDlets.
Creating your application within an integrated development environment is more
productive than developing applications by entering commands at the command line.

There are a number of popular integrated development environments on the market
designed for developing J2ME applications. These include Borland's JBuilder and Sun
Microsystems' Forte. Another integrated development environment is the J2ME Wireless
Toolkit that is downloadable from java.sun.com/products/j2mewtoolkit/download.html.

The J2ME Wireless Toolkit is used to develop and test J2ME applications by selecting a few buttons from a toolbar. However, the J2ME Wireless Toolkit is a stripped-down integrated development environment in that it does not include an editor, a full debugger, and other amenities found in a third-party integrated development environment.

Building and Running a Project

Download the J2ME Wireless Toolkit from the Sun web site. The Toolkit file is a self-extracting executable file. Run this executable after downloading the file, and the installation program creates all the directories required to run the Toolkit. The installed J2ME Wireless Toolkit is placed in the WTK104 directory, although the directory might have a variation of this name depending on the version of the Toolkit that you download.

Ktoolbar is the executable within the directory that launches the Toolkit. The main window is displayed (see Figure 3-7) when you run ktoolbar. You'll notice that the main window is sparse compared with other integrated development environments.

Let's create a new project by selecting the New Project button from the toolbar. You'll be prompted to enter a project name and class name (see Figure 3-8). Enter **Hello World** as the project name and **greeting.HelloWorld** as the class name, which is the name of the first MIDlet that is associated with the project.

After selecting the Create Project button, the J2ME Wireless Toolkit automatically creates a directory structure for the project and also creates the manifest file and JAD file. You can see and modify attributes of these files by selecting the Settings option, which displays a dialog box containing a series of tabs. The first tab displayed, Required (see Figure 3-9), contains a list of attributes that are necessary for the manifest file and JAD

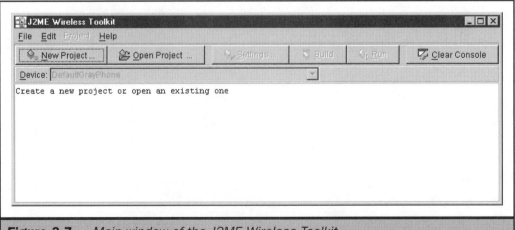

Figure 3-7.   *Main window of the J2ME Wireless Toolkit*

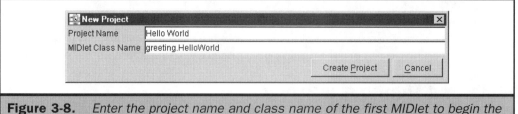

Figure 3-8. *Enter the project name and class name of the first MIDlet to begin the project.*

file, as previously discussed in this chapter. The Optional tab (see Figure 3-10) contains attributes that are common to many projects but not required to build and deploy a J2ME application.

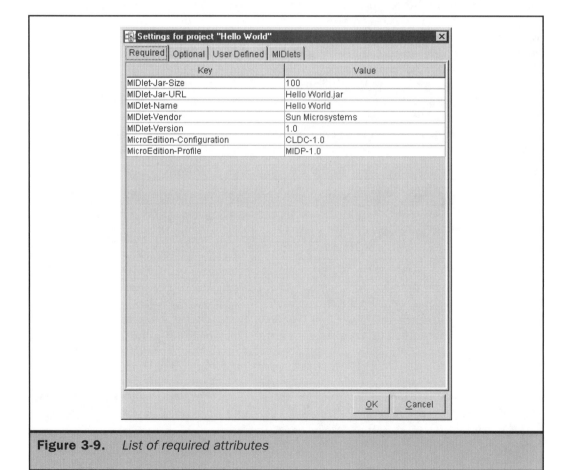

Figure 3-9. *List of required attributes*

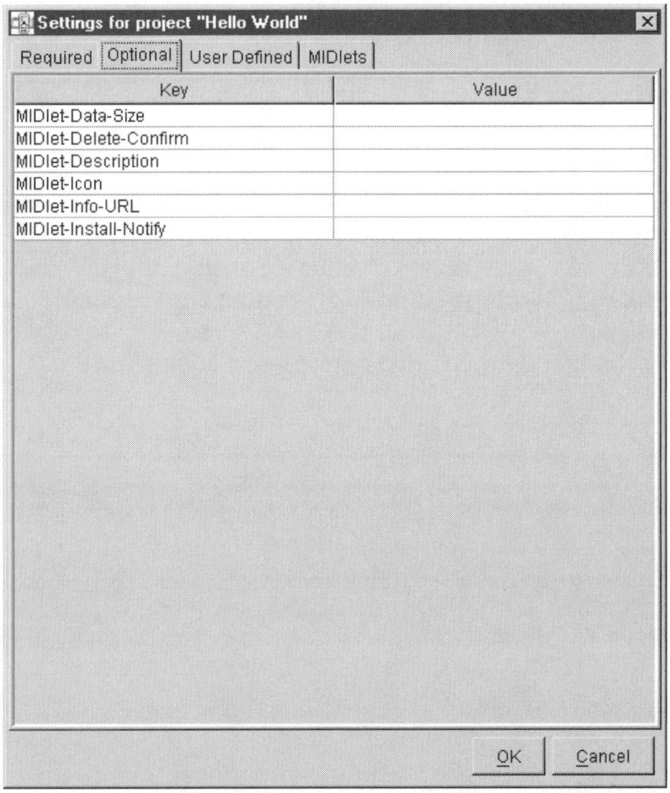

Figure 3-10. *List of optional attributes*

The User Defined tab (Figure 3-11) contains optional attributes specific to your application, as discussed previously in this chapter. This tab will be empty until you select the Add button and insert your own attributes. The MIDlets tab (Figure 3-12) lists MIDlets of your project. Notice that the HelloWorld MIDlet is listed in the tab, which is the MIDlet you entered as the class name when beginning the project.

A well-organized file structure is automatically created for your project as a result of starting a new project. Within the WTK104 directory, you'll see an apps subdirectory in which the projects you create are stored. Browse the apps subdirectory to see a subdirectory called Hello World, which is the name that you gave to your project. A subdirectory of the apps directory is created for every project. And within the project's subdirectory is another set of subdirectories. These are

■ src, containing source code

■ bin, containing the manifest.mf file, JAD file, and JAR file

- classes, containing the compiled classes
- tmpclasses, containing the preverify classes
- res, containing image, data, and other files required by the application

Hello World Project

Let's re-create the Hello World and Goodbye World application that you created previously in this chapter. Create a new project called Hello World following the directions in the "Hello World J2ME Style" section. Next, create a greeting directory beneath the src directory. Copy the HelloWorld.java file and GoodbyeWorld.java file that you created previously, and place those files into the project's src\greeting subdirectory, which is Hello World\src\greeting if you named your project Hello World.

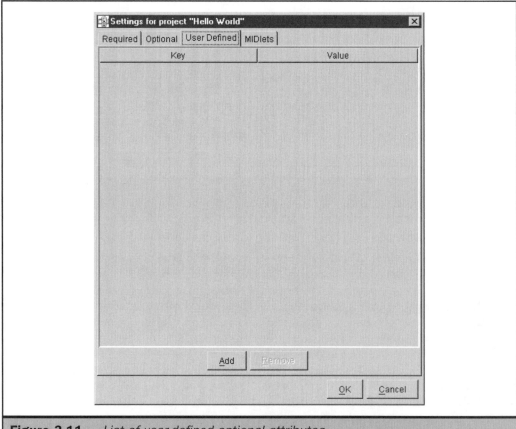

Figure 3-11. *List of user-defined optional attributes*

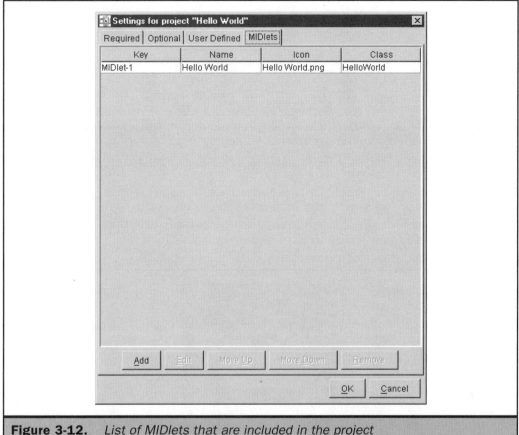

Figure 3-12.   *List of MIDlets that are included in the project*

Select the Settings button and the MIDlets tab. You'll need to insert the
GoodbyeWorld.java MIDlet into the MIDlet list. Select the Add button to display
the Enter MIDlet Details dialog box (Figure 3-13), and enter **Goodbye World** as the
name of the MIDlet, then **greeting.GoodbyeWorld** as the MIDlet class. Leave the Icon
empty until you have a PNG image that you want to use with the MIDlet. Select OK
to return to the main screen.

 *If you choose not to create the greeting subdirectory, you'll need to remove the package
greeting statement from the source code.*

Select the Build button from the toolbar. The J2ME Wireless Toolkit compiles,
preverifies, and packages the application in one step, which previously required three
steps using the command line.

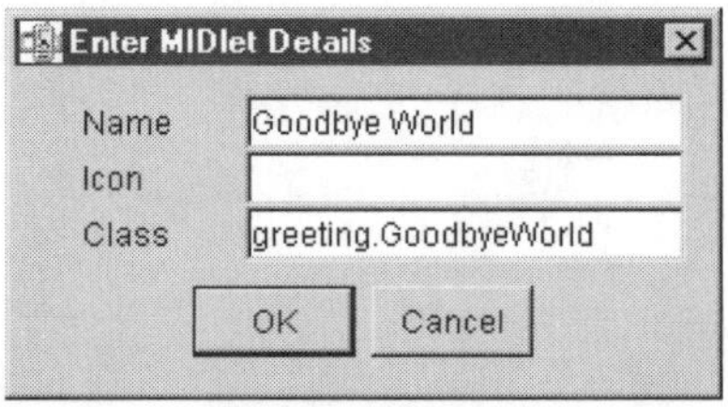

Enter MIDlet Details
Name
Goodbye World
Icon
Class
greeting.GoodbyeWorld
OK
Cancel

Figure 3-13. *Enter the name of the MIDlet and the MIDlet class name.*

The Device drop-down box contains a list of emulators available for testing your application. Select DefaultColorPhone, and then select the Run button. The image of a color cellular telephone is displayed running your application (see Figure 3-14).

DefaultColorPhone
Select one to launch:
Hello World
Goodbye World
Launch
CLEAR
MODE
SPACE

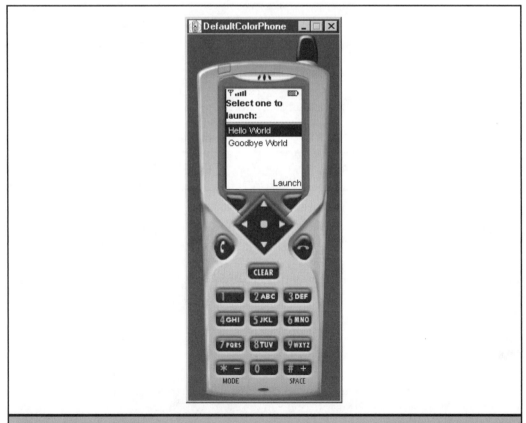

Figure 3-14. *The DefaultColorPhone emulator*

Rerun your application several times, alternating among device emulators. Figure 3-15 simulates your application running a DefaultGrayPhone, and Figure 3-16 emulates the Motorola i85S cellular telephone.

MIDlets on the Internet

The Wireless Toolkit can run MIDlets that access Internet resources by configuring the emulator to interact with a proxy server and let you monitor activities between the MIDlet and the Internet for debugging purposes. You configure the emulator for the Internet by selecting Edit | Preferences. The Network Configuration tab is used to set the port number and server name of the proxy server. The Trace tab is used to set preferences

Figure 3-15. *The DefaultGrayPhone emulator*

Figure 3-16.   *The Motorola cellular telephone emulator*

for monitoring the interactions between the MIDlet and the Internet. There are four options that you can set by selecting the appropriate check boxes (Figure 3-17).

The Trace Garbage Collection option displays the status of objects that include memory allocation of existing objects, the number of objects on the heap, and the size of the largest free object. The status is displayed whenever the garbage collector is invoked.

The Trace Class Loading option will display the name of each class as it is loaded into the emulator. The Trace Class Method Calls option logs object and related methods when they are called. Display Exceptions causes all exceptions to be displayed regardless of whether they are caught or uncaught.

The Performance, Monitor, and Storage tabs are used to fine-tune the Wireless Toolkit for those aspects of an emulator.

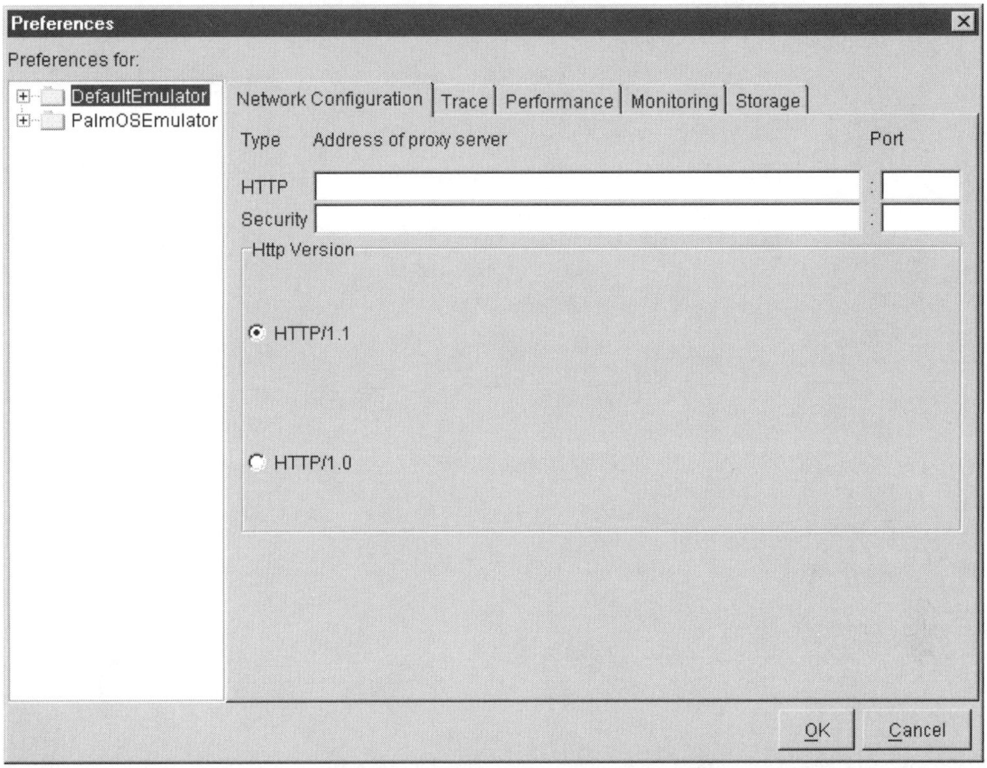

Figure 3-17.   *The Trace tab contains preferences for monitoring MIDlets over the Internet.*

The
Complete
Reference

Chapter 4

J2ME Best Practices and Patterns

Designing applications for small computing devices is a challenge, to say the least, primarily because of the limited resources found in these devices. You must assume that the small computing device contains minimal memory and storage room for persistent data, as discussed in the first two chapters of this book.

Many traditional systems design methods and best practices are simply not appropriate for building applications to run on small computing devices. This means that you must rethink your approach to designing an application earmarked for a small computing device. Fortunately, there are best practices and patterns that you can implement in your design that overcome many limitations inherent in small computing devices. In this chapter you'll learn about best practices and patterns for developing J2ME applications.

The Reality of Working in a J2ME World

A small computing device has a radically different hardware configuration than traditional computing devices such as desktop computers and servers. It is for this reason that you must take into account the device's hardware configuration when designing your J2ME application. Consider the following differences between traditional computing devices and small computing devices.

Traditional computing devices are under continuous power from the power grid, while some small computing devices such as cellular telephones rely on battery power that diminishes during the course of operation. A power grid powers other small computing devices such as set-top boxes and appliances.

Another important difference between traditional computing devices and small computing devices is the network connection. Unlike traditional computing devices, mobile small computing devices connect to a network via a radio or infrared connection whose quality varies depending on the distance of the device from a network receiver and the strength of the signal generated by the device. Some nonmobile small computing devices such as set-top boxes use a hard-wired network connection similar to traditional computing devices. Inconsistency in a network connection and the diminishing longevity of power typically require the user of a small computing device to synchronize data and applications frequently with a desktop computer or server.

As you learned in Chapter 1, programs and data are stored in a small computer device's memory, commonly referred to as *primary storage*. These are lost when the device drops power, although many devices have a secondary battery to retain programs and data as long as possible. Once lost, programs and data must be reloaded into the device. Secondary storage is not usually available on a small computing device. Therefore, a J2ME application should rely on data stored offline in a desktop computer or server rather than data stored in the device's primary storage. Data stored offline can be reloaded into the device using a network connection.

Don't expect a mobile small computing device to transmit and receive data at the same rate as a device on a hard-wired network. Data transmission between a mobile small computing device and a traditional computing device is slow in comparison to a hard-wired network connection because radio and infrared technology offers a narrower transmission bandwidth than that found in hard-wired network connections. A bandwidth is the number of communications channels available to transmit bits of data simultaneously.

Many users of your J2ME application expect the same response from your application as they experience from desktop computer applications. Therefore, you must design your J2ME application to minimize and optimize data transmission with offline data sources. One way to optimize your J2ME application is called ROMizing the application for run-time operations. ROMizing creates a machine code image of an application before the application is deployed on the small computing device. In comparison, using a just-in-time compiler, or other techniques employed by the Java Virtual Machine, optimizes J2SE and J2EE applications.

Best Practices

Over time and through trial and error, J2ME developers have come up with the best way to solve complex J2ME programming problems. And these techniques are called best practices and patterns. *Best practices* are proven design and programming techniques used to build J2ME systems. *Patterns* are routines that solve common programming problems that occur in such systems.

Professional developers use best practices and patterns to avoid making common mistakes when designing and building a J2ME application. You can benefit from the experiences of professional J2ME developers by incorporating appropriate best practices and patterns in the design of your J2ME application. You'll learn about these best practices and patterns in the following sections.

Keep Applications Simple

You must adapt to a new mind-set when creating applications for small computing devices because of limited resources available and the inability to easily expand resources to meet application requirements. Typically, you design an application by dividing it into objects that have associated data and methods. Let's use an order form as an example. An order form is an object that has an order number, customer number, product number, and related data. Likewise, an order form has functionality associated with it, such as inserting a new order, modifying an existing order, and deleting an order. And the order form has one or more menu options that enable a user to navigate the order form.

You design a J2ME application by also dividing the application into pieces. However, the divisions of a J2ME application are much finer divisions than those found in a typical application. For example, a common division of a J2ME application is a menu option rather than a menu object or menu method of an object. Each menu option is its own MIDlet. Menu option MIDlets are packaged in the same MIDlet suite along with other MIDlets related to the application.

The J2ME device's application manager is used to present each MIDlet (menu option) on the device's menu and in this way reduces processing resources normally required to run the application's own menu (Figure 4-1).

The best practice is to keep your application design simple. Limit your design to minimum functionality required to meet user expectations. Place each functional component in its own MIDlet where possible, and package the application's MIDlets in the same MIDlet suite. This enables the device's application manager to manage MIDlets and the resources used by MIDlets.

Keep Applications Small

The size of your J2ME application is critical to deploying the application efficiently. The best practice is to remove unnecessary components of your application in order to reduce the size of the overall application. Fancy bells and whistles that have become the hallmark of many desktop applications also increase the size of an application. While elaborate applications work well on the desktop, they tend to be less adaptive to small computing devices.

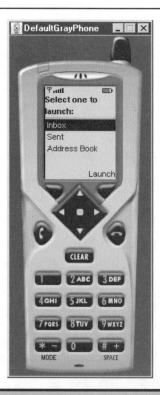

Figure 4-1. *Make each menu option a MIDlet, and let the application menu display each menu option.*

Anyone who uses a J2ME application expects the application to download quickly to the small computing device and run among other applications on the device. A smaller application meets these expectations because fewer bytes need to be downloaded and stored in memory on the device.

Besides stripping away the bells and whistles and other unnecessary features from your J2ME application, you should also deploy your application as a JAR file. A JAR file, as you learned in the previous chapter, is a compressed version of a J2ME application.

On some occasions, you'll discover that even a stripped-down version of your application takes too long to download or simply is too large to run on the small computing device. In these situations, divide your application into several MIDlets, and then combine the MIDlets in a MIDlet suite, as described in the previous chapter.

Limit the Use of Memory

In addition to removing unnecessary features from your application, design your application to manage memory efficiently. There are two types of memory management that should be used in the J2ME application. These are overall memory management and peak time memory management. Overall memory management is designed to reduce the total memory requirements of an application. Peak memory management focuses on minimizing the amount of memory the application uses at times of increased memory usage on the device.

A primary way to reduce total memory requirements of your application is to avoid using object types. Instead, use scalar types, which use less memory than object types. Likewise, always use the minimum data type suited for storing data. For example, some developers use an int as a binary flag where only one of two values is assigned to the variable. A boolean value requires less memory and therefore should be used in place of an int. This and similar data management subtleties usually have little or no noticeable impact on a non-J2ME application. However, this kind of attention to detail will have a dramatic impact on the performance of a J2ME application.

Peak time memory management requires you to manage garbage collection. J2ME does have a garbage collector, but as with J2SE, you don't know when the garbage collector will collect your garbage. Therefore, it is critical that you clean up after the application is finished using memory.

Here are a few ways to manage your own garbage collection: First, allocate an object immediately before the object is used in the application rather than at the beginning of your application. Allocating memory at the beginning of the application reserves memory long before the object will be used within the application. This memory could be utilized by other parts of the application until the application requires the object. Next, set all references to objects to null once the application no longer needs the object. This decreases the memory application of the object to the minimum memory necessary to store an object reference.

Always reuse objects instead of creating new objects. This reduces both memory allocation and the need for processing power. Memory allocation is reduced because multiple references can use the same object at different times in the application's life cycle. Obviously, both objects that use the same memory cannot run simultaneously. The need for processing power is reduced because a portion of the processing required to allocate new memory doesn't need to be invoked since memory has already been allocated when the object is instantiated.

Reducing the likelihood of exceptions is another technique for lowering memory usage of your application. The fewer exceptions that might be thrown, the less memory your application requires. And the last best practice to reduce memory usage is to release all resources immediately following their use within your application. Releasing a resource makes the resource and related memory available to other components of your application and to other applications running on the small computing device along with your application.

Off-Load Computations to the Server

Small computing devices are designed to run applications that do not require intensive processing because processing power common to desktop computers is not available on these devices. This means that you must design your J2ME application to perform minimal processing on the small computing device. However, the reality is that sophisticated, industrial-strength applications require processing that is beyond the capabilities of these devices. At first glance, you might assume that small computing devices are unable to run processing-intensive applications, and you'd be correct in your assumptions. But there is an alternative that lets you combine the convenience of a small computing device with an application that requires intense processing.

The alternative is to build a client-service J2ME application or web services J2ME application. There are two levels of operation in a client-service application. These are the client level and the server level. The small computing device runs the client level that provides user interface and presentation functionality to the application. The server-side level processes client requests and returns the result to the small computing device for presentation to the user. Nearly all processing occurs on the server side of the application.

There are three tiers in web services. The first layer is the client tier, sometimes referred to as the presentation tier. This is where a person interacts with an application. The second layer contains the business logic that is used to fulfill requests from a client by calling appropriate software on the processing tier. Processing software returns results to the business logic layer, and in turn, those results are returned to the client for presentation to the user.

Let's say an overnight delivery person is unsure of the recipient's address and uses client software in his handheld computing device to query the company's database for the recipient's telephone number. The request is captured by client software and sent over a wireless network connection to the business logic software running on the corporate server (Figure 4-2). The business logic software assesses what web services are necessary to fulfill the request and proceeds to invoke those web services, passing the necessary information from the query to respond to the client's request.

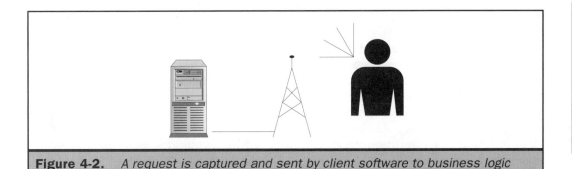

Figure 4-2. *A request is captured and sent by client software to business logic software for processing.*

In this example, the business logic software determines that the database management system (DBMS) software (processing tier) is required to locate the customer's telephone number in the database. The DBMS running on the processing layer handles processing required to locate the telephone number in the database and forwards the telephone number to the business logic layer, which sends the telephone number to the delivery person's handheld computer.

Processing on the client is limited to displaying the user interface, capturing a user request, opening and maintaining a network connection to the back-end systems, sending (request) and receiving information (telephone number), and presenting incoming information to the user of the small computing device.

Manage Your Application's Use of a Network Connection

Besides lightening the processing load on the small computing device, you must also be concerned about the availability of a network connection. Some small computing devices are mobile, wireless devices where a network connection is not always available, and even when available, the connection might be broken during transmission due to the positioning of the transmitter and receiver (for example, when moving from one cell to another in a cellular telephone network).

Cellular telephone networks use technology that attempts to maintain connection as the mobile device moves from one cell to another cell. In reality there are dead zones where the mobile device is outside the range of the cellular telephone transceiver. The connection is broken in these dead zones, and sometimes it cannot be automatically reestablished by the telephone company. The drop in communication can occur without warning, as many cellular telephone users have experienced.

Although you cannot avoid a break in communication, you can take steps to reduce the impact on the user of your application. Begin by keeping transmissions short—transfer the minimum information necessary to accomplish a task. Let's say your application is designed to retrieve email messages from a server. Instead of retrieving all emails in an inbox, you can retrieve the "From," "Subject," and "Data received" fields from the last ten emails that were placed in the inbox. Your J2ME application can present these fields on the screen and then give the user the options to select an email to read, select a preview for an email, delete an email, or retrieve the next ten emails.

Consider using store-forwarding technology and a server-side agent whenever your J2ME application requests a lot of information. A *server-side agent* is software running on the server that receives a request from a mobile device and then retrieves requested information from a data source, which is very similar to the business logic layer of web services technology. The results of the query are then held by the agent until the mobile device asks for the information, at which time the information is forwarded to the mobile device.

The request from the mobile device consists of a small amount of data. The agent can accumulate large amounts of data from database management software to fulfill the request and then forward small amounts of data to the mobile device.

Let's say that a customer stopped an overnight delivery carrier on the street corner and asked for a shipping status. The customer doesn't have any particulars about the shipment except for her company name, address, and destination. The delivery service's mobile tracking system can be designed to efficiently respond to the customer's request by using store-forwarding technology and a server-side agent (Figure 4-3). The mobile device could send a request to the agent for all shipments from the company made from the zip code given to the carrier by the customer.

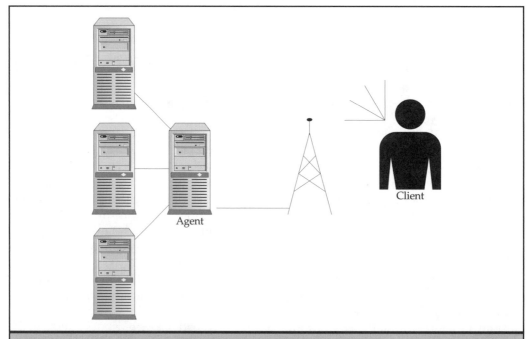

Figure 4-3.   *An agent works on the server side to act on behalf of client software running on the small computing device.*

The agent forwards the request to the tracking system's database management software, which returns complete information for 30 shipments. Software running on the mobile device polls the agent periodically (once per second), asking for the latest, next, or previous shipping number and destination, depending on the option selected by the carrier. The carrier then reviews the destinations of the ten shipments with the customer to narrow the search for the customer's shipment. Once the customer identifies the correct shipment, the mobile device requests status information about the shipment from the agent.

Always build into your mobile application a mechanism for recovering from a transmission drop. For example, retain key information about a request on the mobile device until the request is fulfilled. The mobile application can then use the retained key information to resubmit the request either automatically or as a user option if there is a breakdown in communication.

Simplify the User Interface

Most desktop applications have a standard set of graphical user interface objects such as text boxes, combo boxes, radio buttons, check boxes, and push buttons. These objects are accessible to the user through a mouse, keyboard, and other input devices commonly associated with a desktop computer. However, small computing devices use a variety of user display and input devices. Some devices, such as a cellular telephone, have an inch-square display and a telephone keypad for data input. Other devices, such as personal data assistants, have wide rectangular screens and a hunt-and-peck keyboard.

There is a standard display and input for desktop computers, but you cannot say the same about small computing devices. The variety of shapes and hardware configurations found in devices classified as small computing devices makes it nearly impossible to standardize on a set of user interface objects for these devices. Given this limitation, you still need to provide a user interface for your J2ME application. Here are several practices that you should consider following when designing a user interface for a small computing device.

It is critical that you design a user interface that takes advantage of convenient features found on a small computing device and avoid user interactions that are awkward to perform. For example, entering personal information using a small computer device such as a cellular telephone or PDA is difficult, to say the least, although the information can be entered given the time and patience. A more convenient approach is to design a desktop companion application in which personal information is entered and then downloaded to the device by selecting a menu option on the device's keypad.

Where possible, take advantage of the user interface provided by the device's application manager, rather than designing your own. As you saw in the previous chapter, the application manager lists each MIDlet in the MIDlet suite as a menu option, avoiding the need for the programmer to develop a menu.

If you decide to create a user interface containing a menu, consider the available input mechanisms of the small computer device before beginning your design. Some devices have touch screens that enable you to use icons, rather than words, to represent menu options. Other devices, such as cellular telephones, have limited keypads. Therefore, you should carefully select shortcut keys that activate menu selection to conform to the keyboard. Let's say three options are presented in a list on the screen. Typically, you identify each option with a shortcut key that is a sequence of letters (A, B, C), or numbers (1, 2, 3), or a letter within the name of the option.

Selecting letters A, B, and C is easy on a standard keyboard, but awkward on a cellular telephone keypad because all three letters are assigned to one key. Some keypad algorithms recognize a letter by the number of times the key is pressed—press once for the letter A, twice for B, and three times for C. A better design is to avoid using sequential letters as such and either use the first letter of keys on the keypad or numbers as a shortcut key (Figure 4-4).

Limit the amount of user input into your application to simple menu selections and an occasional few fields of text or numbers, depending on the design of the small computing device. The rule of thumb: a user should be able to interact with your application by using a thumb while holding the device in one hand.

Figure 4-4. *Select letters as shortcut keys that are easily entered into the small computing device.*

Use Local Variables

Limited resource is the theme that echoes through design considerations for applications that run on small computing devices. As a developer, you cannot assume there are sufficient resources on every small computing device to run your application. Failure to seriously recognize this theme will result in your application being unable to run on many small computing devices. Therefore, it is critical to evaluate processing requirements of each routine within your application. Your objective is to exclude routines that increase processing overhead if a less processing-intense routine can accomplish the same task.

You'll find this line of thought radically different from the mind-set used to write applications for desktop devices and server devices, where you can safely assume that sufficient resources exist to run an application. Desktop devices and server devices typically have more than enough resources available to process an application efficiently.

Data storage is a key area within an application for reducing excessive processing. In many applications, developers assign values to data members of a class rather than using a local variable. Assigning data to a class member adheres to object-oriented design philosophy, which is prevalent in application design.

Although encapsulating data within an object tightly controls access to the data, this advantage is realized at the expense of additional processing time whenever the application accesses the data member. Accessing a data member of a class requires more processing steps than accessing the same data if the data is stored as a local variable. Therefore, accessing a local variable is less processing intense than accessing a class member.

You can increase processing of your application if you eliminate the extra steps of accessing a data member of a class by assigning values to local variables. Of course, you'll need to weigh the gains in processing against the benefits of encapsulating data in a class. However, you'll find processing considerations an overriding factor in data-intense applications that run on a small computing device.

Don't Concatenate Strings

Concatenating strings is another processing drain that can be avoided by designing an application to eliminate concatenations or at least reduce the number of concatenations to the minimum necessary to achieve the objective of the application.

Concatenation also increases the application's use of memory in addition to increasing the application's processing requirements, which becomes apparent by comparing processing a string with processing a concatenated string.

A *string* is an array of characters terminated by a NULL and stored sequentially in memory. Let's assume the application wants to compare two strings, both of which are four characters and reside in memory. The application instructs the small computing device to copy the first character of each string into the CPU for comparison. This process continues until either the null character is reached or a letter pair is different. The entire process might require ten reading instructions and five comparison instructions, depending on when a mismatch is discovered (see Figure 4-5).

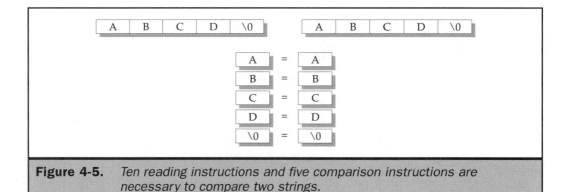

Figure 4-5.   *Ten reading instructions and five comparison instructions are necessary to compare two strings.*

However, additional processing steps are necessary if one of those strings is a concatenated string. Let's divide the first string into two strings, as shown in Figure 4-6. The left string must be concatenated into the first string; afterwards, the first string and the target string are compared.

The concatenation process introduces six additional processing steps: three instructions to read each character of the second string and three more instructions to write those characters to the end of the first string.

Besides the increase in processing steps, concatenation also requires more memory than if the first string and second string did not have to be concatenated. Notice in Figure 4-6 that the second string remains in memory after the strings have been concatenated. Therefore, you can reduce processing time and memory usage by avoiding concatenating strings. An alternative is to concatenate strings before the string is loaded into the small computing device.

If there is a need to concatenate strings, use a StringBuffer object. This makes efficient use of memory when strings are appended to the buffer, although there is additional processing overhead.

Avoid Synchronization

It is very common for developers to invoke one or multiple threads within an operation. Invoking a thread is a way of sharing a routine among other operations. For example, a sort routine can be shared simultaneously by multiple operations that must sort data. Each operation invokes the sort routine independent of other operations, although the same code is being executed for all operations. Deadlocks and other conflicts might arise when multiple operations use the same routine. These problems are avoided by synchronizing the invocations of a thread, as you probably remember when you learned Java programming.

Always use a thread whenever an operation takes longer than a tenth of a second to run because a thread requires less overhead than non-thread invocation methods, and therefore you'll see a performance increase in your application.

J2ME BASICS

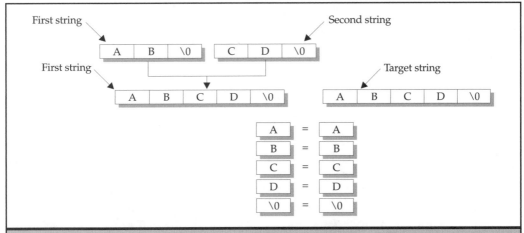

Figure 4-6.   *Concatenating strings requires processing and memory allocation not required if strings are concatenated before being loaded into the small computing device.*

Another way to increase performance is to avoid using synchronization where possible. Synchronization requires additional processing steps that are not necessary when synchronization is deactivated. However, you must consider the performance trade-off with possible conflicts among operations that use the same threaded routine. As a general rule, avoid using synchronization unless there is a high likelihood that conflicts among operations will occur.

Thread Group Class Workaround

A common way of reducing the overhead of starting a new thread is to create a group of thread objects that are assigned threads as needed by operations within an application. Less processing is required to assign a thread to an existing thread object than to create a new thread object.

Grouping thread objects is made possible by the ThreadGroup class, but J2ME does not support this class. You can work around it, however, by creating your own grouping using the Collection class. You can store groups of thread objects in a collection and then use standard collection methods to start and stop threads in the collection and assign threads to particular thread objects within the collection.

Upload Code from the Web Server

Version management is always a concern of application developers, especially when applications are invoked from within a small computing device. It can be a nightmare keeping track of various versions of an application once an application is distributed.

You can reduce and possibly eliminate problems associated with multiple versions of the same application by requiring invocation of the application from a web server. Every device that invokes the application will then use the same copy of the application that is stored on a web server accessible from the Internet, extranet, or intranet.

Here's how a small computing device can invoke a web server–based J2ME application:

```
midp -transient http://www.mycompany.com/welcome.jad
```

Rather than running a local JAD file, the -transient option specifies that the JAD file is located on a web server identified by the URL on the command line. In this way, the developer only needs to update one copy of the application, and distribution is handled by making the latest version of the application available on the web server.

This technique is ideal for set-top boxes that are connected to a web server via a cable television connection or satellite connection. Software can be updated each time the set-top box comes online without the user or a technician having to reinstall the application.

Reading Settings from JAD Files

There will likely be occasions when you need to have your application perform in a certain way, depending on the type of small computing device that runs the application. Although you can create versions of your application for specific small computing devices, there is a more efficient approach to tailoring an application to a device.

First, design your application with switches that activate and/or deactivate routines depending on the value of a setting. A setting is a value assigned to a variable that is either created within the application or passed to the application as a command line parameter.

However, J2ME applications are capable of reading the value of a setting from a JAD file and manifest file. A setting is a user-defined value created in either file, as discussed in Chapter 3. A good practice is to create a user-defined value within the JAD file rather than within the manifest file because the JAD file can be modified without having to repackage your application. A manifest file is a component of a package (see Chapter 3).

Listing 4-1 shows a typical JAD file that includes a user-defined value called Model-Version: M253. The J2ME program in Listing 4-2 illustrates how to read this user-defined value during run time without having to recompile or repackage the application.

A user-defined value is read by invoking the getAppProperty() method and passing the name of the user-defined value to the getAppProperty() method. The getAppProperty() returns the user-defined value from either the manifest file or the JAD file depending on which of these files contains the user-defined value.

Listing 4-2 reads the Model-Version user-defined value defined in the JAD file and displays the value on the screen. Of course, you can create a compound statement that invokes the getAppProperty() method and then assigns the returned value to a variable or uses the return value directly in an expression.

Listing 4-1
A JAD file containing a user-defined value

```
MIDlet-Name: Best MIDlet
MIDlet-Version: 2.0
MIDlet-Vendor: MyCompany
MIDlet-Jar-URL: http://www.mycompany.com/bestmidlet.jar
MIDlet-1: BestMIDlet, /images/BestMIDlet.png, Best.BestMIDlet
Model-Version: M253
```

Listing 4-2
A program that reads a user-defined value from the JAD file

```
public class BasicMIDletShell extends MIDlet
{
  public void startApp()
  {
    System.out.println(getAppProperty("Model-Version"));
  }
  public void pauseApp()
  {
  }
  public void destroyApp( boolean unconditional)
  {
  }
}
```

Populating Drop-down Boxes

A drop-down box is a convenient way for users to choose an item from a list of possible items, such as an abbreviation for a state. Traditionally, content of a drop-down box is loaded from the data source once when the application is invoked and remains in memory until the application terminates.

While caching the contents in memory is a best practice in Java programming, caching is a questionable practice when developing a J2ME application. Loading a list of data for a drop-down box when the J2ME application is invoked is efficient if this is a short list that doesn't require substantial memory resources.

Load the list dynamically from a server whenever the list is long. Release the list once the user has made a selection, and then reload the list the next time the drop-down box is invoked. In this way, memory used to store the list can be reused between calls to the drop-down box.

The question that you're bound to be asking is what constitutes a short or long list of items. You'll need to test your application loading the list once and then loading the list dynamically for each invocation to determine which method delivers the best performance. Be sure to test in real-world conditions when loading a list from a server. Any processing delay by the server responding to a request for the list can severely impact your application's user response time. Likewise, transmission delays will also deliver a negative user experience with your application.

In contrast, caching a long list limits memory availability to other routines within your application and to other applications running on the small computing device. This might result in some features of your application becoming unavailable or worse—a user won't be able to load another application if your application is loaded in memory.

Minimize Network Traffic

Developing a J2ME application is a balancing act between deciding whether processing should be performed by the small computing device or by a server. The choice depends upon many factors, including the amount of transmission that must occur for each process. A good practice is to off-load as much processing as is reasonable to a server and minimize the number of processes that need to be invoked by the J2ME application in order to reduce network transmissions.

Collect all the information from the user that is required by the process at one time, and then forward the information to the server when invoking the process. For example, your application might be used to retrieve a list of customers that the user may later filter to remove unwanted customers or reorder the customer list into a more appropriate sequence. You can reduce the number of processes and network transmission by requiring the user to select the filter and sequence as part of the request for the customer list (Figure 4-7). In this way, the database server can create the customer list in the desired order without having the user make subsequent requests to manipulate the customer information.

Dealing with Time

J2ME applications that rely on current time might incur a problem that is not realized in desktop computer and server applications. Current time is determined by the date/time setting on the device. Desktop computers and servers are stationary, and therefore current time reflects the time zone where these devices are located. However, the same isn't true of a mobile small computing device because the device can be moved to multiple time zones.

The problem of time-sensitive data is further compounded by the fact that the date/time setting is device dependent. For example, a number of cellular telephones have a geographic positioning feature that enables the device's operating system to know the exact location of the device. Some geographic positioning systems use a global position system (GPS) that pinpoints the device by triangulating satellite-transmitted signals. Other

J2ME BASICS

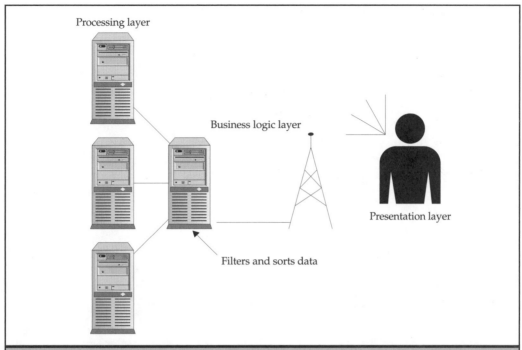

Processing layer

Business logic layer

Presentation layer

Filters and sorts data

Figure 4-7.   *Let the business logic layer filter and sort data rather than filtering and sorting data in the small computing device.*

geographic positioning systems determine a device's time zone based on the cellular telephone network's cell that receives the device's transmission (Figure 4-8).

Those mobile small computing devices that have a built-in geographic positioning system typically adjust the date/time setting on the device automatically as the device moves to a new time zone. However, not all mobile small computing devices have a geographic positioning system on board (for example, PDAs) and therefore rely on the user to adjust the date/time setting when crossing into another time zone.

Unfortunately, there isn't any practice that guarantees a user will adjust the date/ time setting to reflect the current time zone, although you can remind the user of the importance of making such an adjustment. Knowing the time zone used when the time-sensitive data was entered into your J2ME application is critical when analyzing the data. For example, the data might be time stamped 9:30 A.M., but you still need to know the time zone in order to properly evaluate the time the data was entered into your application.

The best practice is to always store time based on Greenwich Mean Time (GMT) by using the getTime() method of the Date class. In this way, the time stamp of all the data is recorded in a uniform time zone, facilitating the data analysis.

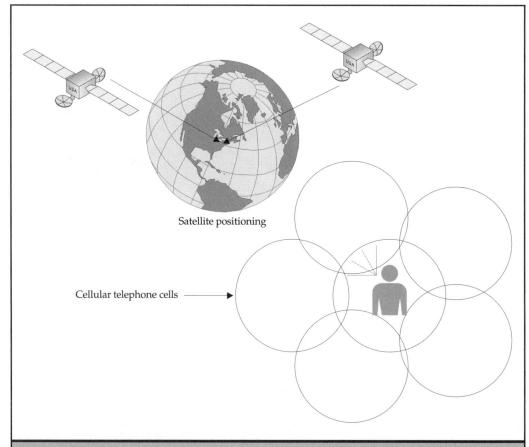

Figure 4-8. *Geographic positioning systems in a mobile small computing device detect the location of the device, enabling the operating system to make time zone adjustments.*

Automatic Data Synchronization

As discussed at the beginning of this chapter, a small computing device is typically used to store and manipulate data that changes over time, such as a list of clients and financial records. Storage of data in a small computing device is temporary because the device usually doesn't have secondary storage. All data is stored in primary storage (memory) and can be lost whenever the device loses power.

Data is permanently stored in secondary storage on a traditional computing device such as a desktop computer or server. Therefore, it is critical to the success of your application that you provide a mechanism to efficiently update data in the small computing device with data stored on the traditional computer's secondary storage.

Failure to do this will cause both devices to become unsynchronized, resulting in erroneous data being displayed and manipulated by the small computing device.

A good practice is to build into your J2ME application a routine that automatically uploads the latest data when the J2ME application is invoked. Likewise, your J2ME application should automatically download data that has changed to the secondary storage device prior to the termination of the application.

The small computing device must be connected to the network for both actions to occur. It is common for the device to automatically log onto the network when the device is activated. However, some devices might require the user to log onto the network. If the user doesn't log onto the network, your application is unable to update data in the small computing device with data stored in the secondary storage device.

A good practice is to prompt the user to open a network connection while your J2ME application begins running or right before the application terminates. The prompt should give the user two choices: open a network connection or skip opening a network connection until the next time the J2ME application is opened. The prompt should also explain that if the user postpones opening a network connection, the data retained in the small computing device might become outdated and might be lost should the device lose power.

Updating Data that Has Changed

Keep in mind that synchronizing data can be a time-consuming process, depending on the speed of the network connection and the amount of data that is being updated. Therefore, you should balance the response time of your application with the need to retain updated data. Data can become outdated in two ways: when data changes on the small computing device and when data changes on the secondary storage device, which is usually the server.

A good practice is to offer the user of your application three options for updating data: incremental updates, batch updates, and full updates. Incremental updates require an exchange of data to occur whenever data changes, either on the small computing device or on the secondary storage device. And only the changed data is exchanged between devices.

Performance decreases as the number of incremental data changes occur because the changed data is transmitted following the modification of the data. The batch update option eliminates the need for incremental updates by updating a batch of data either periodically or on demand, controlled by the user of the application. A batch update only transmits data that is changed by either the small computing device or the secondary storage device.

For example, you might design the application to automatically send a batch when the application begins, terminates, or during an idle period when the application runs. Likewise, you should offer the user an option that enables a manual transfer of modified data as a way for the user to back up changes to the data.

A full update should be available as a user-invoked option because of the time required to update all data. Typically, this option is used in an emergency to restore data when incremental and batch updates are unsynchronized.

Be Careful of the Content of the startApp() Method

As you learned in Chapter 3, a MIDlet consists of required methods, each of which is callable by the small computing device's application manager. One of those methods is startApp(), which is called each time the MIDlet is invoked. Intuitively you might assume that the startApp() method is called once during the life of the MIDlet and therefore is a perfect place within your application to store code that is to execute once each time the MIDlet is invoked.

Tips for Developing J2ME Applications

- Applications are typically single-threaded.
- One application runs at a time.
- Applications are event driven.
- Users change from one application to another rather than terminating an application.
- Mobile small computing devices are used intermittently.
- Applications use multiple subscreens, each displaying only relevant information.
- Mobile small computing devices are typically used in two-minute sessions 30 times a day.
- Applications must accomplish a task within two minutes; otherwise the user is likely to turn off the mobile small computing device.
- Limit user input to a few keystrokes. Develop a PC-based component of your application that is used for data input.
- Users want an instant response from an application.
- Off-load processing to a server or desktop computer.
- Avoid power-consuming tasks such as communications, animation, and sound.
- Reduce data communication to the bare minimum because users pay for transmission by byte, usually in the range of 50,000 to 300,000 bytes per month.
- Preload as many files as possible into a mobile small computing device in order to reduce data transmissions.

However, a MIDlet is started more than once by the device's application manager. For example, the application manager might pause the MIDlet while another MIDlet is processing and then restart the MIDlet by calling the startApp() method. This means that only statements that must be executed following a pause should appear within the startApp() method. Statements that should run once during the lifetime of the MIDlet should not be placed in the startApp() method and instead should appear within the MIDlet constructor.

Let's say your application uses a variable to accumulate the total of several operations within the MIDlet. Typically, you initialize the variable once when the MIDlet is invoked the first time. The initialization must be performed in the MIDlet constructor and not in the startApp() method, otherwise the total will be reset to zero each time the MIDlet is activated after a pause in operations.

The Complete Reference

Part II

J2ME User Interface

The
Complete
Reference

Chapter 5

Commands, Items,
and Event Processing

Nearly every J2ME application has an interface that enables user interactions with the application. The user interface can be as simple as pressing a button on the small computing device, which causes the application to react, or as complex as displaying a form containing check boxes, radio buttons, lists, and other objects common to many applications.

Selections made by a user are considered events that are forwarded to your application by the device's application manager for processing. The application's developer must write code that recognizes an event and then reacts to the event by performing a task based on the nature of the application. In this chapter you'll be introduced to techniques used to create a user interface for a J2ME application and to process events that are generated by the user interacting with your application.

J2ME User Interfaces

A user interface is a set of routines that displays information on the screen, prompts the user to perform a task, and then processes the task. For example, a J2ME email application might display a list of menu options, such as Inbox, Compose, and Exit, and then prompt the user to make a selection by moving the cursor keys and pressing a key on the small computing device. The device's application manager passes the selection to the application, where it is compared with known options. If a match occurs, the application performs the steps necessary to process the option.

A developer can use one of three kinds of user interfaces for an application. These are a command, form, or canvas. A command-based user interface consists of instances of the Command class. An instance of the Command class is a button that the user presses on the device to enact a specific task. For example, Exit is an instance of the Command class associated with an Exit button on the keypad to terminate the application. The Help button is also an instance of the Command class that is linked to the Help key on the device, which is used whenever the user requires assistance.

A form-based user interface consists of an instance of the Form class that contains instances derived from the Item class such as text boxes, radio buttons, check boxes, lists, and other conventions used to display information on the screen and to collect input from the user. A form is similar to an HTML form.

A canvas-based user interface consists of instances of the Canvas class within which the developer creates images such as those used in a game. In this chapter you'll learn about the Command class and be introduced to forms. You'll learn how to incorporate items onto a form in Chapter 6. Chapter 7 introduces you to techniques for developing the canvas user interface.

Display Class

Before learning how to incorporate instances of the Command class and the Item class into your application, let's take a moment to explore how your application interacts with the small computing device's screen. The device's screen is referred to as the display, and you interact with the display by obtaining a reference to an instance of the MIDlet's Display class. Each MIDlet has one and only one instance of the Display class. Every J2ME MIDlet that displays anything on the screen must obtain a reference to its Display instance. This instance is used to show instances of Displayable class on the screen.

The Displayable class has two subclasses. These are the Screen class and the Canvas class. The Screen class contains a subclass called the Item class, which has its own subclasses used to display information or collect information from a user (such as forms, check boxes, radio buttons). The Screen class and its derived classes are referred to as high-level user interface components.

The Canvas class is used to display graphical images such as those used for games. Displays created using the Canvas class are considered a low-level user interface and are used whenever you need to display a customized screen.

Instances of classes derived from the Displayable class are placed on the screen by calling the setCurrent() method of the Display class. The object that is to be displayed is passed to the setCurrent() method as a parameter. It is important to note that instances of derived classes of the Item class are not directly displayable and must be contained within an instance of a Form class. An instance of an Item class appears on the screen when the setCurrent() method is used to show the form. The getCurrent() method of the Display class is used by a MIDlet to retrieve information about the instances of derivatives of the Displayable class.

You obtain an instance of the Display class by declaring a reference to the instance and then assigning the instance to the reference by invoking the getDisplay() method,

Determining the Color Attribute of a Device

Listed here are the steps required to determine the color attribute of a device:

1. Create references.
2. Create a Display object.
3. Create an instance of the Command class to exit the MIDlet.
4. Call isColor() method.
5. Evaluate the return value of isColor() method.
6. Create an instance of the TextBox class that describes results of isColor() method.
7. Associate the instances of the Command class with the instances of the TextBox class.
8. Associate a CommandListener with the instance of the TextBox class.
9. Display the instance of the TextBox class on the screen.
10. Terminate the MIDlet when the Exit command is entered.

as illustrated in the following code segment. Multiple calls to the getDisplay(this) method return the same Display instance.

```
private Display display;
display = Display.getDisplay(this);
```

Once an instance of the Display object is created, you use the Display API (see "Quick Reference Guide" at the end of the chapter) to display instances of classes derived from the Display class on the screen and to retrieve information about the screen and currently displayed objects.

Listing 5-1 contains the JAD file for this MIDlet, and Listing 5-2 illustrates how the Display class is used to determine the color attribute of the small computing device's screen. In this example, the MIDlet invokes the isColor() method of the Display class to determine whether the screen is capable of displaying color. If so, the MIDlet displays an instance of the TextBox class reporting that the device has a color screen; otherwise the instance reports that the device is incapable of displaying color. Of course, in a real-world MIDlet, the response returned by the isColor() method is used within the MIDlet either to activate or deactivate routines that manipulate color on the screen.

Listing 5-1
A JAD file

```
MIDlet-Name: CheckColor
MIDlet-Version: 1.0
MIDlet-Vendor: MyCompany
MIDlet-Jar-URL: CheckColor.jar
MIDlet-1: CheckColor, CheckColor.png, CheckColor
MicroEdition-Configuration: CLDC-1.0
MicroEdition-Profile: MIDP-1.0
MIDlet-JAR-SIZE: 100
```

Listing 5-2
Using the Display class to determine whether the screen is capable of displaying color

```
import javax.microedition.midlet.*;
import javax.microedition.lcdui.*;
public class CheckColor extends MIDlet implements CommandListener
  private Display display;
  private Form form;
  private TextBox textbox;
  private Command exit;
  public CheckColor()
  {
    display = Display.getDisplay(this);
    exit = new Command("Exit", Command.SCREEN, 1);
    String message=null;
    if (display.isColor())
```

```
    {
      message="Color display.";
    }
    else
    {
     message="No color display";
    }
    textbox = new TextBox("Check Colors", message, 17, 0);
    textbox.addCommand(exit);
    textbox.setCommandListener(this);
  }
  public void startApp()
  {
   display.setCurrent(textbox);
  }
  public void pauseApp()
  {
  }
  public void destroyApp(boolean unconditional)
  {
  }
  public void commandAction(Command command,
                            Displayable displayable)
  {
   if (command == exit)
   {
     destroyApp(true);
     notifyDestroyed();
   }
  }
}
```

The MIDlet is called CheckColor and begins by creating references for instances used in the MIDlet. These instances are for the Display class, Form class, TextBox class, and Command class. You'll learn about the Form class, TextBox class, and Command class later in this chapter. For now it is sufficient to understand that the instance of the Display class displays a form that contains a text box and the Exit command. The color status appears in the text box, and the Exit command terminates the MIDlet.

The constructor is defined next. Remember, statements within the constructor are executed once during the life of the MIDlet when the MIDlet is invoked. The first statement in the constructor creates an instance of the Display class by calling the getDisplay() method, which is assigned to the display reference.

Next, an instance of the Command class is created. A later section of this chapter explains the Command class. For now it is sufficient to understand that the label of the instance of the Command class in this example is Exit and the instance is assigned to the exit reference. An instance of the TextBox class is then created. The caption of this instance is "Check Colors" and is assigned to the form reference.

The instance of the Command class is then associated with the instance of the TextBox class by calling the addCommand() method and passing the method reference to the Command class instance, which in this example is called exit.

As you'll learn in the section "Command Class," a MIDlet must associate a CommandListener whenever a Command class is instantiated. A CommandListener listens for command events to occur during the execution of the MIDlet. A command event is the selection of a Command object by the user of the MIDlet. You associate a CommandListener with a MIDlet by specifying the listener as an argument to the setCommandListener() method.

The MIDlet then calls the isColor() method, which returns a boolean value. A true indicates that the device can display color. A false is returned if the device is incapable of displaying colors. The instance of the TextBox class is displayed with a message, depending on the return value of the isColor() method. You'll learn about the TextBox class later in this chapter and in Chapter 6. However, understand that the first parameter is the caption of the text box, and the second parameter is the text that appears in the text box.

The Exit command is also associated with the text box, so the user can terminate the MIDlet when the text box appears on the screen. Likewise, a CommandListener is also specified for the text box Exit command, which in this case is the MIDlet itself because the MIDlet implements the CommandListener.

Once the constructor is defined, you must define the standard methods required by a MIDlet. These are the startApp() method, pauseApp() method, and destroyApp() method. The startApp() is called by the device's application manager whenever the MIDlet is started or restarted following a pause in operation. The startApp() method contains a statement that calls the setCurrent() method and is passed reference the instance of TextBox class that will be shown on the screen. You can include additional statements in the startApp() method as needed by your MIDlet.

The pauseApp() method definition and the destroyApp() method definition are empty in this example because there are no special statements that must be executed when the MIDlet is paused by the device's application manager. The commandAction() method must be defined to receive event reports from the device's application manager. Whenever the user selects a command, the commandAction() method is invoked by the application manager to process the command.

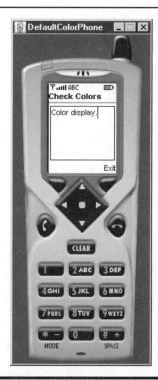

Figure 5-1.   *The text "Color Display" appears when you run the MIDlet in the default color phone emulator in the J2ME Wireless Toolkit.*

The application manager passes the commandAction() method reference to the selected command, which is then compared to known commands that were created for the MIDlet. In this sample the commandAction statement matches the Exit command, which invokes a destroyApp() method to unconditionally terminate the MIDlet. Right after the execution of the destroyApp() method, the notifyDestroyed() method is called to notify the application manager that the MIDlet is terminating. Figure 5-1 and Figure 5-2 show how this program appears on a generic cellular telephone and the Palm PDA.

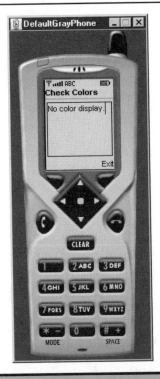

Figure 5-2.   *The text "No color display" appears when you run the MIDlet in the default gray phone emulator in the J2ME Wireless Toolkit.*

The Palm OS Emulator

Before you can run the Palm OS emulator in the J2ME Wireless Toolkit, you'll need to download Palm OS ROM files from the Palm web site (www.palmos.com/dev). The ROM file contains the Palm OS required for the emulator to properly perform like a Palm PDA. You'll also need to join the Palm OS Developer Program (free) and agree to the online license (free) for ROM files before you are permitted to download them. Be prepared to spend a few minutes downloading since ROM files are fairly large, even when compressed into a zip file.

Several ROM files are available for download, each representing a different version of the Palm OS and each suited for a particular Palm product. Always choose the latest version of the Palm OS for downloading unless you are designing a MIDlet to run on

Running MIDlets

It is strongly suggested that you avoid compiling and executing MIDlets at the command line because you'll find yourself being bogged down by entering long command line statements to compile and run a MIDlet. Consider using the J2ME Wireless Toolkit, or another integrated development environment such as JBuilder, to compile and run your J2ME MIDlets, instead of working at the command line. All the examples in this chapter were compiled and executed using the J2ME Wireless Toolkit.

The Toolkit automatically creates a directory structure for your MIDlet development project, sets default values for the JAD file, and creates its own JAR file. You can change settings in the JAD file by using a graphical user interface provided in the Toolkit. Furthermore, you can quickly test your MIDlet in a variety of cellular telephone emulators, Palm emulators, and Black Berry pagers by selecting the appropriate emulator from a drop-down box.

a particular type of Palm device. If your MIDlet is Palm device specific, you'll need to download the ROM file that corresponds to the Palm OS that runs on that Palm device.

Don't fret if you download the wrong ROM, because the Palm OS emulator displays an error when running your MIDlet, indicating the proper version of the Palm OS that is required to run your MIDlet on the Palm device that is being tested in the emulator. You'll be prompted to enter the location of the ROM file on your hard disk into a dialog box the first time that you run the Palm OS emulator. Subsequently, the Palm OS emulator uses that ROM file.

Command Class

You create an instance of the Command class by using the Command class constructor within your J2ME application. The Command class constructor requires three parameters. These are the command label, the command type, and the command priority. The Command class constructor returns an instance of the Command class.

The following example illustrates a cancel command. The first parameter of the command declaration is Cancel. Any text can be placed here and will appear on the screen as the label for the command. The second parameter is the predefined command types. Table 5-1 lists all the predefined command types. The last parameter is the priority, which is set to 1. The command created by this declaration is assigned to cancel.

```
cancel = new Command("Cancel", Command.CANCEL, 1);
```

Command Type	Description
BACK	Move to the previous screen
CANCEL y	Cancel the current operation
EXIT	Terminate the application
HELP	Display help information
ITEM	Map the command to an item on the screen
OK	Positive acknowledgment
SCREEN	No direct key mapping available on device; command will be mapped to object on a form or canvas
STOP	Stop the current operation

Table 5-1. *Command Types*

It is important to understand that although a command type is mapped to a key on the device's keypad, the device does not process the command. When the user selects the command, the application manager detects the event and passes the selected command to your application for processing.

Your selection of command type is a request and not a directive to the small computing device to map the command to a particular keypad key. The device always has the option to ignore your request and map the command in any way it wishes.

Priority indicates your preference as to the importance of each command object created by your application. Priority is established by the value that you assigned to the third parameter of the command declaration. A low value has a higher priority than a higher value. The device's application manager has the option of ignoring the priority or using the priority to resolve conflicts between two commands. For example, an application manager may use the priority to determine the order in which command labels appear on the screen.

A word of caution: you have no control over how the device's application manager uses the priority of command objects created by your application.

CommandListener

Every J2ME application that creates an instance of the Command class must also create an instance that implements the CommandListener interface. The CommandListener is notified whenever the user interacts with a command by way of the commandAction() method. Classes that implement the CommandListener must implement the commandAction() method, which accepts two parameters. The first parameter is a reference to an instance of the Command class, and the other parameter is a reference to the instance of the Displayable class, as illustrated in Listing 5-3.

Listing 5-3
Creating a command-Action() method

```
public void commandAction(Command command, Displayable displayable)
{
  if (command == cancel)
  {
    destroyApp(false);
    notifyDestroyed();
  }
}
```

The device's application manager calls the commandAction() method and passes the command selected by the user. You must evaluate the command to determine the command selected by the user. An if statement is used in this example to evaluate the command.

Compare the command with the reference to the instance of the Command class that was returned when you created the command within your application. The Exit command was created in the previous section of this chapter and is used within the if statement in Listing 5-1 to determine whether the user selected the Exit command.

The commandAction() method must contain all the processing that is to occur when the user selects a command. The destroyApp() method is called to unconditionally terminate the application; and before the application terminates, the notifyDestroyed() method is called to notify the device's application manager that the application is terminating. You learned about these methods in Chapter 3.

Online Help Example

Providing online help is a routine common to nearly every well-written J2ME application. Online help instructs users on interacting with the application. Instructions are displayed in a text box that the application displays when the user selects the Help command (Figure 5-3). You'll learn more about using a text box in the next chapter.

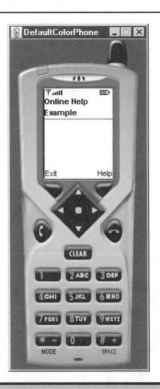

Figure 5-3.   *Select the button below the Help command to display the help screen on the default color phone emulator.*

The user returns to the previous screen by selecting the Back command (Figure 5-4). The Back command removes the Help text box from the screen and returns the user to the original screen. The last command that is found in all J2ME applications is the Exit command. The Exit command terminates the application.

You can also run this MIDlet in the Palm OS emulator by selecting the Palm OS emulator in the Wireless Toolkit before selecting the Run button. Select the OnlineHelp icon when the Palm appears on the screen. This runs the MIDlet. Next, press the Menu icon on the bottom left of the screen. You'll notice that a menu appears at the top of the screen. Select the Options menu item and then the Help menu item to display the help text created by the MIDlet (Figure 5-5).

Listing 5-4 contains the JAD file for Listing 5-5. Listing 5-5 illustrates how to use commands to create an online help routine for your application. You can enhance the online help routine by using instances of the Item class other than a text box, which you'll learn about in the next chapter.

Listing 5-4
A JAD file for
online help

```
MIDlet-Name: OnlineHelp
MIDlet-Version: 1.0
MIDlet-Vendor: MyCompany
MIDlet-Jar-URL: OnlineHelp.jar
MIDlet-1: OnlineHelp, , OnlineHelp
MicroEdition-Configuration: CLDC-1.0
MicroEdition-Profile: MIDP-1.0
MIDlet-JAR-SIZE: 100
```

Listing 5-5
Online help
routine using
Command
objects

```java
import javax.microedition.midlet.*;
import javax.microedition.lcdui.*;
public class OnlineHelp extends MIDlet implements CommandListener
{
  private Display display;
  private Command back;
  private Command exit;
  private Command help;
  private Form form;
  private TextBox helpMesg;
  public OnlineHelp()
  {
    display = Display.getDisplay(this);
    back = new Command("Back", Command.BACK, 2);
    exit = new Command("Exit", Command.EXIT, 1);
    help = new Command("Help", Command.HELP, 3);
    form = new Form("Online Help Example");
    helpMesg = new TextBox("Online Help", "Press Back to return
to the previous screen or press Exit to close this
program.", 81, 0);
    helpMesg.addCommand(back);
    form.addCommand(exit);
    form.addCommand(help);
    form.setCommandListener(this);
    helpMesg.setCommandListener(this);
  }
  public void startApp()
  {
    display.setCurrent(form);
  }
  public void pauseApp()
  {
  }
```

J2ME
USER INTERFACE

```
public void destroyApp(boolean unconditional)
{
}
public void commandAction(Command command,
                          Displayable displayable)
{
  if (command == back)
  {
    display.setCurrent(form);
  }
  else if (command == exit)
  {
   destroyApp(false);
   notifyDestroyed();
  }
  else if (command == help)
  {
   display.setCurrent(helpMesg);
  }
}
}
```

The MIDlet begins by creating an OnlineHelp class that extends the MIDlet class and implements the CommandListener, which is used to trap events that occur while the MIDlet is running. Five variables are declared that will be used to reference instances in this MIDlet. The first variable is used to reference the Display class instance that is used to display other Displayable class instances on the screen. Next are three variables that reference the Back command, Exit command, and Help command. The last variable references the instance of the Form class that contains commands and the instance of the TextBox class, which is referenced with the helpMesg variable.

Next, the MIDlet defines a constructor for the OnlineHelp class. The constructor contains statements that are executed once when the MIDlet is invoked. Remember from Chapter 4 that the constructor is not the same as the startApp() method. The startApp() is called by the device's application manager each time the MIDlet is started, including after the MIDlet is paused. This means that the startApp() might be called several times after the invocation of the MIDlet.

The constructor is where you create instances and associate them with other instances. The constructor begins by obtaining a reference to the instances of the OnlineHelp MIDlet's Display class. The next three instances (Command class, a Form class, and TextBox class) are then created.

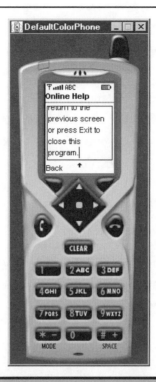

Figure 5-4. *Select the button below the Back command to return to the previous screen in the default color phone emulator.*

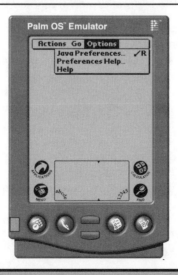

Figure 5-5. *Select Help to run the MIDlet.*

Creating Online Help

Listed here are the steps required to create online help.

1. Declare references.

2. Obtain a reference to the instance of the Display class.

3. Create an instance of the Command class to return from the help page.

4. Create an instance of the Command class to exit the MIDlet.

5. Create an instance of the Form class.

6. Create an instance of the TextBox class that contains the help text.

7. Associate the instance of the Back Command class with the instance of the TextBox class.

8. Associate the instance of the Exit Command class and the instance of the Help Command class with the instance of the Form class.

9. Associate a CommandListener with the instance of the Form class.

10. Associate a CommandListener with the instance of the TextBox class.

11. Display the form.

12. Evaluate the command that the user entered into the small computing device.

13. If the command is the Back command, display the form.

14. If the command is the Exit command, terminate the MIDlet.

15. If the command is the Help command, display the text box.

The instantiation of the Command class sets the label for each command, the reference to the instance type, and the suggested priority for each command. The Form class constructor is used to set the caption to "Online Help Example."

The TextBox class constructor is where you specify the title and text. The TextBox class constructor requires four parameters. First is the title of the text box, which is "Online Help." Next is the text that appears in the text box. You'll notice in Figure 5-4 that there are too many lines of text for all the text to appear simultaneously on the screen. Therefore, you should take into consideration the screen size when preparing any text display in order to reduce the need for the user to scroll through the text. You can use multiple screens and an additional command (such as Forward) to enable the user to page through your screens.

The third parameter is the number of characters in the message, which in this example is 81. The last parameter is a TextField constraint, which is zero in this example and explained in detail in Chapter 6.

Once classes are instantiated, the MIDlet then associates instances with other instances to create a cohesive form. The addCommand() method of the text box is called to associate the Back command with the helpMesg text box. This causes the Back command to be available when the helpMesg text box is displayed. The Exit command and the Help command are then associated with the form by calling the addCommand() method. The last two statements within the constructor associate a CommandListener for the form and the text box.

The startApp() method is the next component of the MIDlet that you need to define. The startApp() method is called whenever the MIDlet is started by the device's application manager. The startApp() contains one statement that calls the setCurrent() method of the Display class. The setCurrent() method requires one parameter, which is the form that is to be placed on the display.

The pauseApp() method and the destroyApp() method are left empty because we don't require any special task to be performed when the MIDlet is paused or destroyed. Both methods must be defined in every MIDlet, as you remember from Chapter 3.

The commandAction() method is where commands are processed. The commandAction() method requires two parameters. The first parameter is a reference to the instance of the Command class selected by the user and passed to the commandAction() method by the device's application manager. The other parameter is the variable that references the Displayable instance of the event.

A series of if and if else statements are used to compare known commands to the command passed to the commandAction() method. First, the method tests if the command is the Back command. If so, the setCurrent() method is called once again to return to the original form.

Next, the commandAction() method tests if the Exit command was selected. If so, the destroyApp() method and notifyDestroyed() method are called, as described previously in this section of the chapter. The commandAction() then determines whether the Help command is selected. If so, the setCurrent() method is invoked and is passed the helpMesg TextBox, which is displayed on the screen.

Item Class

The Item class is derived from the Form class, and that gives an instance of the Form class character and functionality by implementing text fields, images, date fields, radio buttons, check boxes, and other features common to most graphical user interfaces. The Item class has derivative classes that create those features. You'll learn how to implement derivative classes of the Item class in Chapter 6. For now, we'll examine how to insert an instance of the Item class into the form of your J2ME application.

In many ways, the Item class has similarities to the Command class in that instances of both classes must be declared and then added to the form. Likewise, a listener processes instances of both the Item class and the Command class.

The user interacts with your application by changing the status of instances of derived classes of the Item class, except for instances of the ImageItem class and StringItem class. These instances are static and not changeable by the user. An instance of the ImageItem class causes an image to appear on the form, and an instance of the StringItem class causes text to be displayed on the form. For example, your application might present options in the form of an instance of the ChoiceGroup class, which is derived from the Item class. An instance of a ChoiceGroup class is a check box or radio button. The user makes a selection by choosing a check box or radio button.

A change in the status of an instance of the Item class is processed by the itemStateChanged() method (defined in the ItemStateListener interface), which is called automatically by the method for an application that utilizes the Item class. You must create one itemStateChanged() method for an application that implements an instance of the Item class.

The itemStateChanged() method is similar to the actionCommand() method used to respond to the invocation of a command by the user of your application. Although these methods are similar in design, you cannot combine them into one method because the application manager specifically calls the itemStateChanged() method and actionCommand() method independently of each other.

It is important to understand precisely when the itemStateChanged() method is called because subtle differences in when the method is invoked can alter the way your application reacts to change in the state of an instance of the Item class. The state is changed by the user or by your application. For example, based on a user's selection of a radio button or check box, your application may change the text of a text field. The change made by the user to a radio button or check box is detected by the listener and causes the device's application manager to call the itemStateChanged() method. However, the state change of the text field by your program doesn't invoke the itemStateChanged() method, although it too is a change of state of an instance of the Item class.

In contrast, the itemStateChanged() method is invoked if the user changed the content of the text field. The assumption is if the user caused the state to change, then your application needs to consider processing the change in state. However, if your application caused the change, then no additional processing is necessary because the assumption is that any necessary processing would have been completed by your application prior to changing the state.

The itemStateChanged() method is not like a trigger found in many database management systems. A trigger is a method automatically called whenever an event occurs regardless of what caused the event to occur. The itemStateChanged() method is automatically called only when a user event changes the state.

The application manager invokes the itemStateChanged() method when the user changes focus from the current instance of the Item class to another instance, if the current instance state changed because of user interaction with the instance. The itemStateChanged() method processes the change before focus is set on the other instance.

Creating an Item Class

Listed here are the steps required for creating an Item class.

1. Declare references.
2. Declare an instance of the Display class.
3. Create an instance of the ChoiceGroup class.
4. Associate options with the instance of the ChoiceGroup class.
5. Set the default choice.
6. Create an Exit command.
7. Create an instance of the Form class.
8. Associate the instance of the ChoiceGroup class to the instance of the Form class.
9. Associate the Exit command with the form.
10. Associate a CommandListener with the form.
11. Associate an ItemStateListener with the form.
12. Display the form.
13. Evaluate the command entered by the user.
14. If the command is the Exit command, terminate the MIDlet.
15. If an instance of the Item class changes state, read the selection from the instances of the ChoiceGroup class.
16. Display the selection on the screen.

In effect, the itemStateChanged() method processes each instance of the Item class as the state is changed by the user. Let's say a form contains a text field and a set of check boxes. The user enters information into the text field and then selects check boxes. Between the time the focus leaves the text field and arrives at the check boxes, the device's application manager calls the itemStateChanged() method, passing it the text of the text field. Only after the itemStateChanged() is processed will the user be able to select check boxes.

The following statement illustrates how to create a text field. The text field requires four values. These are title, text, maximum number of characters that can be entered into the text field, and the TextField constraint, which is zero to indicate there isn't any constraint. You'll learn about TextField constraints in Chapter 6.

```
textbox = new TextField("Title", "Text", 4, 0);
```

Item Listener

Each MIDlet that utilizes instances of the Item class within a form must have an itemStateChanged() method to handle state changes in these instances. The itemStateChanged() method, as shown in Listing 5-5, contains one parameter, which is an instance of the Item class. The instance passed to the itemStateChanged() method is the instance whose state was changed by the user.

Listing 5-5
The itemState-Changed() method

```
public void itemStateChanged(Item item)
{
  if (item == selection)
  {
    StringItem msg = new StringItem("Your color is ",
        radioButtons.getString(radioButtons.getSelectedIndex()));
    form.append(msg);
  }
}
```

Since there is one itemStateChanged() per MIDlet, you must include logic within the itemStateChanged() method to identify the Item object that is passed by the device's application manager to the itemStateChanged() method. In this example, an if statement is used to compare the incoming instance to one of two instances that the MIDlet created on the form. These instances are a text field and radio buttons.

Logic within the itemStateChanged() method is similar to that used within the actionCommand() method. First the itemStateChanged() method determines whether the incoming instance is a text field. If so, the MIDlet displays a message that indicates the state of the text field has been changed by the user. However, if the incoming instance is not the text field and is a radio button, then a similar statement is displayed at the command line indicating that the user changed the radio button state. The device's application manager must pass the two instances specified in the itemStatechanged() method for a statement to be displayed.

Of course, the itemStateChanged() method would have appropriate logic to process a change in each instance rather than displaying a statement at the command line.

Listing 5-6 contains the JAD for Listing 5-7. Listing 5-7 illustrates how to construct a MIDlet that creates an instance of the ChoiceGroup class and associates the instance with a form. The instance of the ChoiceGroup class in this example is a set of radio buttons. The MIDlet begins with the declaration of references for instances of the Display class, Form class, Exit Command class, the Item class, and ChoiceGroup class, and two integers that reference the index of the instances of the ChoiceGroup class.

Listing 5-6
A JAD file

```
MIDlet-Name: RadioButtons
MIDlet-Version: 1.0
```

```
MIDlet-Vendor: MyCompany
MIDlet-Jar-URL: RadioButtons.jar
MIDlet-1: RadioButtons, , RadioButtons
MicroEdition-Configuration: CLDC-1.0
MicroEdition-Profile: MIDP-1.0
MIDlet-JAR-SIZE: 100
```

Listing 5-7
Selecting an
option from a
ChoiceGroup
object

```java
import javax.microedition.midlet.*;
import javax.microedition.lcdui.*;
public class RadioButtons extends MIDlet
            implements ItemStateListener, CommandListener
{
  private Display display;
  private Form form;
  private Command exit;
  private Item selection;
  private ChoiceGroup radioButtons;
  private int defaultIndex;
  private int radioButtonsIndex;
  public RadioButtons()
  {
    display = Display.getDisplay(this);
    radioButtons = new ChoiceGroup(
                        "Select Your Color",
                        Choice.EXCLUSIVE);
    radioButtons.append("Red", null);
    radioButtons.append("White", null);
    radioButtons.append("Blue", null);
    radioButtons.append("Green", null);
    defaultIndex = radioButtons.append("All", null);
    radioButtons.setSelectedIndex(defaultIndex, true);
    exit = new Command("Exit", Command.EXIT, 1);
    form = new Form("");
    radioButtonsIndex = form.append(radioButtons);
    form.addCommand(exit);
    form.setCommandListener(this);
    form.setItemStateListener(this);
  }
  public void startApp()
  {
     display.setCurrent(form);
  }
```

```
public void pauseApp()
{
}
public void destroyApp(boolean unconditional)
{
}
public void commandAction(Command command,
                          Displayable displayable)
{
  if (command == exit)
  {
     destroyApp(true);
     notifyDestroyed();
  }
}
public void itemStateChanged(Item item)
{
 if (item == radioButtons)
 {
    StringItem msg = new StringItem(Your color is ",
          radioButtons.getString(radioButtons.getSelectedIndex())));
    form.append(msg);
 }
 }
}
```

Next in the MIDlet is the constructor that contains statements executed once during the life cycle of the MIDlet. The constructor begins by obtaining a reference to the instance of the MIDlet's Display class by calling the getDisplay() method. The instance is assigned the display reference.

An instance of the ChoiceGroup class is created next. The instance has a title called "Select Your Color" and a type, which in this example is EXCLUSIVE. As you'll learn in Chapter 6, the type of an instance of the ChoiceGroup class determines its display and functionality. The EXCLUSIVE type causes the instance to appear and function as a set of radio buttons. The MULTIPLE type transforms the instance into check boxes.

The next five statements call the append() method, and each creates an option in the instance of the ChoiceGroup class and assigns the option an appropriate label. The first parameter of the append() method is the label, and the other parameter is the image used to represent the option. The second option is used to associate an image with the option. A null is passed as the second option because no image is used in this example.

The append() method returns the index number of the option that is appended to the instance of the ChoiceGroup class. An index number is an integer within the instance of the ChoiceGroup class that uniquely identifies an option. The index number is used within the MIDlet to reference an option, which is illustrated in the statement that calls the setSelectedIndex() method.

It is always wise to set one radio button as the default choice to assure that the user doesn't overlook selecting a radio button. You set the default by calling the setSelectedIndex() method. The setSelectedIndex() method requires two parameters. The first parameter is the index of the option selected as the default choice. The second parameter indicates whether the selectedIndex should be selected (true) or not selected (false)—see Figure 5-6.

In this example, the index of the All option is assigned to the defaultIndex variable when the append() method appends the All option to the instance of the ChoiceGroup class. The defaultIndex variable is passed as the first parameter to the setSelectedIndex() method, and a true value is passed to select the All option when the MIDlet is invoked.

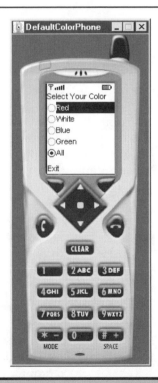

Figure 5-6.   *The All option is the default selection when the MIDlet runs on the default color phone emulator.*

Next, the MIDlet creates an Exit command and an instance of the Form class, both of which are assigned to appropriate references. Notice that the form does not contain a caption, but still requires double quotations in place of the caption.

The instance of the ChoiceGroup class is then associated with the form by calling the append() method and passing the append() method reference to the instance of the ChoiceGroup class. The Exit command is then associated with the form by calling the addCommand() and passing it the reference to the Exit command. The form is also associated with a CommandListener and an ItemStateListener.

The form is displayed on the screen when the setCurrent() method is called each time the device's application manager invokes the startApp() method. The MIDlet is notified of both commandAction() and itemStateChanged() events because the MIDlet implements CommandListener and ItemStateListener for actions taking place on the form.

Command events are forwarded to the commandAction() method where the command is compared to the Exit command to determine whether the user selected the Exit command. If so, the destroyApp() method is called and passed a boolean true, indicating an unconditional termination of the MIDlet. The notifyDestroyed() method is then called to send notification to the application manager that the MIDlet has entered the destroyed state and is ready to be terminated.

The radio button MIDlet, by virtue of implementing ItemStateListener, is notified of Item state changes of the ChoiceGroup object on the form (Figure 5-7). The Item whose state changed is passed to the itemStateChanged() method, where the Item object is evaluated and compared to the radio button ChoiceGroup.

If the radio button is the Item whose state changed, the MIDlet calls the getSelectedIndex() method to determine the index number of the radio button that was selected. The index number is then passed to the getString() method to retrieve the text of that option, which becomes a component of an instance of the StringItem class. This instance is assigned to a reference that is passed to the append() method so the label of the selected option is displayed on the form.

Exception Handling

As you learned in Chapter 3, the small computing device's application manager oversees the operation of a MIDlet. The application manager calls the startApp(), pauseApp(), and destroyApp() methods whenever the user or the device requires a MIDlet to begin, pause, or terminate. However, there are times when the disruption of processing by complying with the application manager's request might cause irreparable harm. For example, a MIDlet might be in the middle of a communication session or saving persistent data when the destroyApp() method is called by the device's application manager. Complying with the request would break off communications or corrupt data.

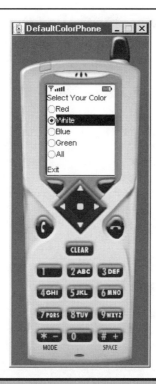

Figure 5-7. *Move the up and down arrow keys to highlight an option, and then press the center button to select the highlighted option on the default color phone emulator.*

You can regain a little control of the MIDlet's operation by causing a MIDletStateChangeException to be thrown. A MIDletStateChangeException is used to temporarily reject a request from the application manager either to start the MIDlet (startApp()) or to destroy the MIDlet (destroyApp()). A MIDletStateChangeException cannot be thrown within the pauseApp() method.

You should incorporate routines that throw a MIDletStateChangeException whenever your MIDlet has processing that should not be interrupted by the application manager. Many developers place routines that throw a MIDletStateChangeException in the destroyApp() method since terminating a MIDlet during critical processing might have a fatal effect on communication or data.

Throwing a MIDletStateChangeException

Listing 5-8 is the JAD file for Listing 5-9. Listing 5-9 illustrates the technique for throwing a MIDletStateChangeException from within the destroyApp() method. Remember that a MIDletStateChangeException can also be thrown from the startApp() method using an approach similar to the one used in Listing 5-9.

Listing 5-8
A JAD file

```
MIDlet-Name: ThrowException
MIDlet-Version: 1.0
MIDlet-Vendor: MyCompany
MIDlet-Jar-URL: ThrowException.jar
MIDlet-1: ThrowException, ThrowException.png, ThrowException
MicroEdition-Configuration: CLDC-1.0
MicroEdition-Profile: MIDP-1.0
MIDlet-JAR-SIZE: 100
```

Listing 5-9
Throwing a
MIDletState-
Change-
Exception in
destroyApp()

```
import javax.microedition.midlet.*;
import javax.microedition.lcdui.*;
public class ThrowException extends MIDlet
                   implements CommandListener
{
  private Display display;
  private Form form;
  private Command exit;
  private boolean isSafeToQuit;
  public ThrowException()
  {
    isSafeToQuit = false;
    display = Display.getDisplay(this);
    exit = new Command("Exit", Command.SCREEN, 1);
    form = new Form("Throw Exception");
    form.addCommand(exit);
    form.setCommandListener(this);
  }
  public void startApp()
  {
   display.setCurrent(form);
  }
  public void pauseApp()
  {
```

```
    }
    public void destroyApp(boolean unconditional)
                    throws MIDletStateChangeException
    {
      if (unconditional == false)
      {
       throw new MIDletStateChangeException();
      }
    }
    public void commandAction(Command command,
                              Displayable displayable)
    {
      if (command == exit)
      {
        try
        {
          if (exitFlag == false)
          {
            StringItem msg = new StringItem (
                              "Busy", "Please try again.");
            form.append(msg);
            destroyApp(false);
          }
          else
          {
           destroyApp(true);
           notifyDestroyed();
          }
        }
        catch (MIDletStateChangeException exception)
        {
          isSafeToQuit = true;
        }
      }
    }
}
```

Listing 5-9 requires the user to select the Exit command twice to terminate the MIDlet (Figure 5-8). When the user selects the Exit command the first time, the device's application manager calls the destroyApp() method where a MIDletStateChangeException is thrown,

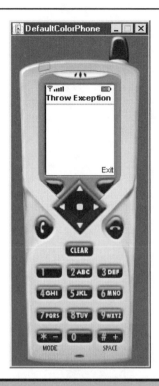

Figure 5-8. *The Exit command must be selected twice to terminate the MIDlet on the default color phone emulator.*

causing the message "Busy Please try again." to be displayed on the screen (Figure 5-9). The MIDlet successfully terminates the second time the user selects the Exit button.

Listing 5-9 begins by declaring references that are later used to point to objects and variables within the MIDlet. These references are for the Display object, Form object, and Exit Command object. Also declared is the boolean isSafeToQuit variable that is used to indicate whether it is safe to terminate the MIDlet.

In the constructor, the isSafeToQuit is assigned a false, implying that the MIDlet should not be terminated. Likewise in the constructor there are statements that obtain instances to the Display class, Command class, and Form class, each of which is assigned to the proper reference. The command is also associated with the form using the addCommand() method, and a CommandListener is associated with the form.

When the MIDlet is loaded into the device, the application manager executes the constructor and calls the startApp() method, where the setCurrent() method is invoked to display the form on the screen. The MIDlet then waits for the user to select the Exit command button. When this happens, the CommandListener "hears" the event and calls

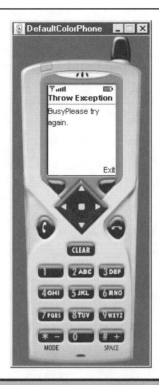

Figure 5-9.   *A message is displayed before the exception is thrown by the MIDlet on the default color phone emulator.*

the commandAction() method, passing the command selected by the user to the method. The selected command is then compared to known commands within the MIDlet, which in this example is the Exit command.

The MIDlet enters the try { } block within the commandAction() method if the Exit command was selected by the user. The value of the exitFlag is then evaluated within the try { } block. If the value is false, an instance of the StringItem class is created and is displayed on the screen by passing the instance to the append() method. The destroyApp() method is then called and passed a false value. A false value means that there is not an unconditional termination of the MIDlet because processing cannot be disrupted. For the sake of this example, we're assuming that processing is ongoing and a fatal error would occur should it not be allowed to complete before the MIDlet is terminated.

However, the destroyApp() method is passed a true value if the value of the exitFlag is true, indicating that the MIDlet can be terminated unconditionally. Notification of the pending destruction of the MIDlet is then sent by invoking the notifyDestroyed() method.

Notice that the destroyApp() method is capable of throwing a MIDletState-ChangeException. A MIDletStateChangeException is thrown if the destroyApp() method is passed a false value indicating there is a condition to termination of the MIDlet. The MIDletStateChangeException is trapped by the catch { } block in the commandAction() method where the value of the exitFlag is set to true. The next time the user selects the Exit command the destroyApp() is called and passed a true value, meaning the MIDlet can terminate unconditionally.

Steps for Throwing a MIDletStateChangeException
Listed here are the steps required for throwing a MIDletStateChangeException.

1. Declare references.

2. Set default value for the exit flag to false.

3. Obtain a reference to an instance of the Display class.

4. Create an instance of the Command class to exit the MIDlet.

5. Create an instance of the Form class.

6. Associate the command to the form.

7. Associate a CommandListener with the form.

8. Display the form on the screen.

9. Evaluate the command selected by the user.

10. If the Exit command is selected, determine whether conditions are safe to terminate the MIDlet.

11. If conditions are not safe to terminate the MIDlet, create an instance of the StringItem class with the message "Busy, please try again."

12. Display the instance of the StringItem class on the screen.

13. Call the destroyApp() method with a conditional termination notice.

14. If conditions are safe to terminate the MIDlet, call the destroyApp() method with an unconditional termination notice, and notify the application manager of pending termination of the MIDlet.

15. When the destroyApp() method is called, evaluate the status of the unconditional parameter.

16. If the unconditional parameter is false, throw a MIDletStateChangeException; otherwise terminate the MIDlet.

17. Trap exceptions thrown within the commandAction() method.

18. If the MIDletStateChangeException is thrown, indicate that conditions are now safe to terminate the MIDlet by assigning a true value to the exit flag.

19. Terminate the MIDlet when the Exit command is entered the second time.

Quick Reference Guide

This quick reference guide provides a brief overview of classes used by J2ME for the Display class, Command class, and Item class. Full details of these classes and all Java classes and interfaces are available at java.sun.com.

javax.microedition.lcdui.Display Class

Method	Description
static Display getDisplay(MIDlet midlet)	Retrieve an instance of the Display class
Displayable getCurrent()	Retrieve the current instance of Displayable class
void setCurrent(Alert alert, Displayable displayable)	Display the specified instance of the alert dialog box and then the specified instance of the Displayable class
void setCurrent (Displayable displayable)	Display the specified instance of the Displayable class
boolean isColor()	Determine whether the device supports color
int numColors()	Retrieve the number of colors or shades of gray that are available on the device
void callSerial(Runnable runnable)	Call an instance of the Runnable class after repainting

javax.microedition.lcdui.Displayable Class

Method	Description
void addCommand(Command command)	Associate a command to an instance of the Displayable class
void removecommand(Command command)	Disassociate a command from an instance of the Displayable class
void setCommandListener(CommandListener commandlistener)	Associate a CommandListener to an instance of the Displayable class
boolean isShown()	Determine whether an instance of the Displayable class is shown on the screen

javax.microedition.lcdui.Command Class

Method	Description
Command(String label, int commandType, int priority)	Create an instance of the Command class that displays the specified label and is of the specified commandType and has the specified priority
int getCommandType()	Retrieve the commandType of a command
String getLabel()	Retrieve the label of a command
int getPriority()	Retrieve the priority of a command

javax.microedition.lcdui.CommandListener Interface

Method	Description
void commandAction (Command command, Displayable displayable)	Process an instance of the Command class

javax.microedition.lcdui.Item Class

Method	Description
String getLabel()	Retrieve the label associated with an instance of the Item class
void setLabel(String label)	Assign a label to an instance of the Item class

javax.microedition.lcdui.ItemStateListener Interface

Method	Description
void itemStateChanged (Item item)	Process changes to an instance of the Item class

javax.microedition.midlet.MIDlet Class

Method	Description
abstract void destroyApp (boolean unconditional)	MIDlet is going to shut down
abstract void pauseApp()	MIDlet is going to pause
abstract void startApp()	MIDlet is in the active state
final void notifyDestroyed()	Requesting to shut down the MIDlet
final void notifyPaused()	Requesting to pause the MIDlet
final void resumeRequest()	Requesting to activate the MIDlet
final String getAppProperty(String key)	Retrieve attributes from a JAD or JAR file

javax.microedition.midlet.MIDletStatechangeException Class

Method	Description
MIDletStateChangeException()	Create a new MIDletStateChangeException object without a test
MIDletStateChangeException(String string)	Create a new MIDletStateChangeException object with a message

J2ME
USER INTERFACE

The Complete Reference

Chapter 6

High-Level Display: Screens

The display is a crucial component of every J2ME application since it contains objects used to present information to the person using the application and in many cases prompts the person to enter information that is processed by the application. You were introduced to the basic concepts of the J2ME display in the previous chapter and shown how to create a simple graphical user interface for your application. To say the least, this user interface is wanting and lacks sophistication that most of us expect from a J2ME application.

The J2ME Display class is the parent of Displayable, which you'll recall from the previous chapter. The Displayable class has two subclasses of its own: Screen and Canvas. The Screen class is used to create high-level J2ME displays in which the methods of its subclasses handle details of drawing objects such as radio buttons and check boxes. In contrast, the Canvas class and its subclasses are used to create low-level J2ME displays. The methods give you pixel-level control of the display, enabling you to draw your own images and text such as those used to create games.

In this chapter we'll continue exploring techniques for building a J2ME high-level display by focusing on the Screen class and its derived classes. You'll learn how to create a low-level display using the Canvas class in the next chapter.

Screen Class

You will probably spend most of your time using the Screen class and its derived classes when developing a user interface for your J2ME application. These classes contain methods that generate radio buttons, check boxes, lists, and other familiar objects that users expect to find on the screen when interacting with your application. The following illustrates the Display class hierarchy, which helps you learn the inheritance structure of the Screen class. Every MIDlet has one Display object but can have many Displayable objects, which you discovered in the previous chapter. A Displayable object is any object that can be displayed on the small computing device's screen.

```
public class Display
      public abstract class Displayable
            public abstract class Screen extends Displayable
                  public class Alert extends Screen
                  public class Form extends Screen
                  public class List extends Screen implements Choice
                  public abstract class Item
                        public class ChoiceGroup extends Item implements Choice
                        public class DateField extends Item
                        public class TextField extends Item
                        public class Gauge extends Item
                        public class ImageItem extends Item
                        public class StringItem extends Item
                  public class TextBox extends Screen
```

```
              public class Command
              public class Ticker
              public class Graphics
              public interface Choice
public abstract class Canvas extends Displayable
              public class Graphics
```

You already know that the Displayable class has two derived classes, Screen and Canvas. The Screen class has its own set of derived classes. These are TextBox, List, Alert, Form, and Item classes. The Canvas class also has its own derived class, the Graphics class, which you'll learn about in the next chapter.

The TextBox class is used to display multi-line text on the screen. The List class is used to display a list of items, as in a menu, and enables the user to choose one of those items. The Alert class displays a dialog box containing a message such as a warning. And the Form class is a container class that can display multiple classes derived from the Item class.

The Item class has six derived classes, any number of which can be displayed within a Form object on the screen:

- ChoiceGroup class used to display radio buttons and check boxes
- DateField class used for inputting a date into an application
- TextField class used for inputting text into an application
- Gauge class used to graphically show progress
- ImageItem class used to display an image stored in a file
- StringItem class used to display text on the screen

The Command class is used to create a Command object that can be associated with practically any class except the Alert class. You created Command objects for MIDlets that you built in the previous chapter. The Ticker is a variable of the Screen class that causes text to scroll on the screen like a stock exchange ticker tape. You'll see how to implement the Ticker in your own application later in this chapter.

The Graphics class is a base class used by derived classes to create and display custom graphical images on the screen. Objects that display options to the person using an application implement the Choice interface. You'll see how the Graphics class is used in the next chapter and how the Choice interface is used later in this chapter when you learn how to create a ChoiceGroup object.

Alert Class

An alert is a dialog box displayed by your program to warn a user of a potential error such as a break in communication with a remote computer. An alert can also be used to display any kind of message on the screen, even if the message is not related to an error. For example, an alert is an ideal way of displaying a reminder on the screen. You implement an alert by creating an instance of the Alert class in your program using the following statement. Once created, the instance is passed to the setCurrent() method of the Display object to display the alert dialog box on the screen.

```
alert = new Alert("Failure", "Lost communication link!", null, null);
display.setCurrent(alert);
```

The Alert constructor requires four parameters. The first parameter is the title of the dialog box, which is "Failure" in this example. The next parameter is the text of the message displayed within the dialog box. "Lost communication link!" is the text that appears when the Failure dialog box is shown on the screen. The third parameter is the image that appears within the dialog box. The previous example doesn't use an image; therefore the third parameter is set to null. The last parameter is the AlertType. The AlertType is a predefined type of alert. None of the predefined AlertTypes is used in the previous example, and therefore a null is used as the fourth parameter. Table 6-1 contains a list of predefined AlertTypes.

A word of caution: An alert dialog box is not designed to retrieve input from a user other than the selection of the OK button to close the dialog box. This means displayable objects such as ChoiceGroup and TextBox cannot be used within an alert dialog box. Likewise, you cannot insert your own Command objects as buttons.

An alert dialog box reacts in one of two ways depending on the value of the default timeout for the Alert object. The alert dialog box can remain visible until the user selects the OK button, or the alert dialog box can be visible for a specified number of milliseconds. An alert dialog box is referred to as a *modal* dialog box if the user must select the OK button to terminate the dialog box. Otherwise, it is considered a *timed* dialog box that terminates when the default timeout value is reached.

Type	Description
ALARM	Your request has been received.
CONFIRMATION	An event or processing is completed.
ERROR	An error is detected.
INFO	A nonerror alert occurred.
WARNING	A potential error could occur.

Table 6-1.   *Predefined AlertTypes for the Alert Object*

The value passed to the setTimeout() method determines whether an alert dialog box is a modal dialog box or a timed dialog box. The setTimeout() method has one parameter, which is the default timeout value. Use Alert.FOREVER as the default timeout value for a modal alert dialog box, or pass a time value in milliseconds indicating time to terminate the alert dialog box. The following example illustrates how to create a modal alert dialog box:

```
alert = new Alert("Failure", "Lost communication link!", null, null);
alert.setTimeout(Alert.FOREVER);
display.setCurrent(alert);
```

You can always retrieve the current default timeout by calling the getDefaultTimeout() method of the instance of the Alert class. The getDefaultTimeout() method returns the integer value of Alert.FOREVER or the default timeout in milliseconds.

The device's application manager determines the screen that appears when the user dismisses the alert dialog box. However, you can control what appears following the dialog box by passing reference to the next object as the second parameter to the setCurrent() method. The second parameter is reference to the displayable object that appears on the screen once the alert dialog box is closed, as illustrated in the next code segment.

Let's assume that an instance of the Form class contains instances of classes necessary to open a communications link with a remote computer. In this example, the instance of the Form class is titled "Communications Link." Notice that instances of both the Alert class and the Form class are passed to the setCurrent() method. Once the user selects OK to dismiss the alert dialog box, the device's application manager displays the instances of the Form object, enabling the user to reestablish communication with the remote computer.

```
form = new Form("Communication Link");
alert = new Alert("Failure", "Lost communication link!", null, null);
alert.setTimeout(Alert.FOREVER);
display.setCurrent(alert, form);
```

An alternative way to control which instance of a class appears on the screen once an alert dialog box is terminated is simply to invoke the setCurrent() method twice. Pass reference to the instance of the Alert class to the first invocation of the setCurrent(), and then pass reference to the next instance the next time that the setCurrent() method is called, as shown below. Calling the setCurrent() method twice using one parameter or once using two parameters achieves the same results without penalties.

```
form = new Form("Communication Link");
alert = new Alert("Failure", "Lost communication link!", null, null);
```

```
alert.setTimeout(Alert.FOREVER);
display.setCurrent(alert);
display.setCurrent(form);
```

Listing 6-1 contains the JAD file for Listing 6-2, which illustrates how to incorporate an alert in your MIDlet. This listing is similar to Listing 5-9 (in the previous chapter), where the person using the MIDlet must select Exit twice before the MIDlet terminates. The purpose of this example is to highlight the technique for preventing termination of a MIDlet before critical processing, such as data transfer to a remote computer, is completed.

A warning message was displayed on the screen in Listing 5-9 informing the user that the MIDlet was busy and asking her to make another attempt to exit the MIDlet. The warning message was displayed as an instance of the StringItem class. Listing 6-2 performs basically the same task, except the instance of the StringItem class is replaced with an alert dialog box (Figure 6-1). The alert dialog box is modal and requires the user to close the box before making a second attempt to terminate the MIDlet.

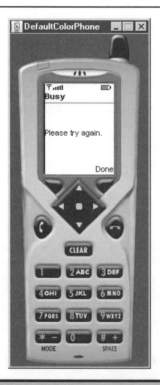

Figure 6-1. *An alert dialog box displays a message on the screen.*

The MIDlet in Listing 6-2 is called DisplayAlert and begins by declaring references to instances of the Display class, Alert object, Form object, and Command object. There is also a boolean variable, which is used to flag whether or not the user made one attempt to terminate the MIDlet.

Next, the constructor is defined, first by assigning a false value to the exitFlag variable. The false value is the default value and indicates that the person hasn't made the first attempt to exit the MIDlet. Three instances are then created and assigned to the appropriate reference. These are instances of the Display class, Command class, and Form class.

The instance of the Command class is associated with the instance of the Form class by calling the addCommand() method and passing it reference to the instances of the Command class. The last statement in the constructor associates a CommandListener to the instance of the Form class by invoking the setCommandListener() method. The registered CommandListener is notified of command events as they occur.

The startApp() method is then defined with one statement that calls the setCurrent() method to display the instance of the Form class on the screen. The startApp() method is invoked by the device's application manager. The pauseApp() is defined as an empty method. Remember that every MIDlet must have a pauseApp() defined, even if no statements are executed when the application manager calls the pauseApp() method.

The destroyApp() method also must be defined in every MIDlet and is the method called before the MIDlet terminates. The destroyApp() method is passed a boolean value that indicates whether termination of the MIDlet is conditional or unconditional. Conditional termination requires that a particular condition be met prior to termination. The condition in this example is that the value of the boolean parameter is false, indicating that the MIDlet hasn't finished processing, although the user requested that the MIDlet terminate. An exception is thrown when this occurs. An unconditional termination indicates that no condition must be met before the MIDlet terminates, which happens in this example when the user selects the Exit command for the second time.

The commandAction() method processes command events trapped by the CommandListener. The commandAction() is called when the person selects any command available on the device. The CommandListener's commandAction() method processes command events as notified by the system/application manager. Only the Exit command is evaluated in this example.

The MIDlet flow enters the try { } block when the Exit command is received by the commandAction() method, and the MIDlet evaluates whether or not the value of the exitFlag variable is false. If false, this means that the user has selected the Exit command only once. This causes the creation of an instance of the Alert class, which is assigned to the appropriate reference.

The title of the alert instance is "Busy," and the message is "Please try again." No image is being used with the alert instance; therefore the third parameter is null. The AlertType of the alert instance is WARNING.

The alert dialog box is modal, so the timeout setting must be set to Alert.FOREVER. This is accomplished by calling the setTimeout() method and passing it the Alert.FOREVER integer.

Creating an Alert Dialog Box

Listed here are the steps required to create an alert dialog box:

1. Declare references.

2. Set default value for the exit flag to false.

3. Obtain a reference to the instance of the Display class.

4. Create an instance of a Command class to exit the MIDlet.

5. Create an instance of the Form class.

6. Associate the instance of the Command class to the instance of the Form class.

7. Associate a CommandListener with the instance of the Form class.

8. Display the instance of the Form class on the screen.

9. Evaluate the command selected by the user.

10. If the Exit command is selected, determine whether conditions are safe to terminate the MIDlet.

11. If conditions are not safe to terminate the MIDlet, create a modal instance of the Alert class with the message "Busy" "Please try again."

12. Display the instance of the Alert class on the screen.

13. Call the destroyApp() method with a conditional termination notice.

14. If conditions are safe to terminate the MIDlet, call the destroyApp() method with an unconditional termination notice, and notify the application manager of pending termination of the MIDlet.

15. When the destroyApp() method is called, evaluate the status of the unconditional parameter.

16. If the unconditional parameter is false, throw a MIDletStateChangeException; otherwise, terminate the MIDlet.

17. Trap exceptions thrown within the commandAction() method.

18. If the MIDletStateChangeException is thrown, indicate that conditions are now safe to terminate the MIDlet by assigning a true value to the exit flag variable.

19. Terminate the MIDlet when the Exit command is entered the second time.

Next, the destroyApp() method is called and is passed a false, indicating there is a condition associated with the termination of the MIDlet. That is, the user must make two attempts to terminate the MIDlet, and only one attempt has been made so far.

However, the destroyApp() method is invoked and passed a boolean true if the value of the exitFlag variable is true, which begins the termination process. The MIDlet then returns from the destroyApp() to call the notifyDestroyed() method, which notifies the application manager of the termination.

The catch { } traps a MIDletStateChangeException thrown by the destroyApp() when a conditional termination notice is received. The exception causes the value of the exitFlag variable to be set to true, meaning the MIDlet terminates unconditionally the next time the user selects the Exit command.

Listing 6-1
The JAD file for Listing 6-2

```
MIDlet-Name: DisplayAlert
MIDlet-Version: 1.0
MIDlet-Vendor: MyCompany
MIDlet-Jar-URL: DisplayAlert.jar
MIDlet-1: DisplayAlert, , DisplayAlert
MicroEdition-Configuration: CLDC-1.0
MicroEdition-Profile: MIDP-1.0
MIDlet-JAR-SIZE: 100
```

Listing 6-2
Displaying a modal alert dialog box when an exception is thrown

```
import javax.microedition.midlet.*;
import javax.microedition.lcdui.*;
public class DisplayAlert extends MIDlet implements CommandListener
{
  private Display display;
  private Alert alert;
  private Form form;
  private Command exit;
  private boolean exitFlag;
  public DisplayAlert()
  {
    exitFlag = false;
    display = Display.getDisplay(this);
    exit = new Command("Exit", Command.SCREEN, 1);
    form = new Form("Throw Exception");
    form.addCommand(exit);
    form.setCommandListener(this);
  }
  public void startApp()
  {
   display.setCurrent(form);
  }
  public void pauseApp()
  {
```

```
    }
    public void destroyApp(boolean unconditional)
          throws MIDletStateChangeException
    {
      if (unconditional == false)
      {
       throw new MIDletStateChangeException();
      }
    }
    public void commandAction(Command command, Displayable displayable)
    {
      if (command == exit)
      {
        try
        {
          if (exitFlag == false)
          {
           alert = new Alert("Busy", "Please try again.",
                             null, AlertType.WARNING);
           alert.setTimeout(Alert.FOREVER);
           display.setCurrent(alert, form);
           destroyApp(false);
          }
          else
          {
           destroyApp(true);
           notifyDestroyed();
          }
        }
        catch (MIDletStateChangeException exception)
        {
          exitFlag = true;
        }
      }
    }
  }
```

Alert Sound

Each AlertType has an associated sound that automatically plays whenever the alert
dialog box appears on the screen. The sound, which is different for each AlertType, is
used as an audio cue to indicate that an event is about to occur. Users of your MIDlet

will learn to identify events by sound cue over time and will become less dependent on the visual cue presented by the alert dialog box.

An audio cue can be sounded without having to display the alert dialog box. You do this by calling the playSound() method and passing it reference to the instance of the Display class, as illustrated in the following code segment. This is a modification of the if statement in Listing 6-1. The sound associated with the AlertType WARNING is heard when the playSound() method is called.

```
if (exitFlag == false)
{
  AlertType.WARNING.playSound(display);
  destroyApp(false);
}
```

Form Class

The Form class is a container for other displayable objects that appear on the screen simultaneously. Any derived class of the Item class can be placed within an instance of the Form class. For example, instances of the StringItem class can be displayed by inserting those instances within the instance of the Form class, then showing the instance of the Form class.

Small computing device screens vary in size, so you can expect that some instances within the instance of the Form class won't fit on the screen. However, devices typically implement scrolling, which allows the user to bring instances out of view onto the screen. An instance is placed with the instance of the Form class by calling one of two methods. These are insert() method and append() method. The insert() method places the instance in a particular position on the form as specified by parameters passed to the insert() method. The append() method places the instance after the last object on the form.

The following code segment illustrates how to create an instance of the Form class and call the append() method to place an instance of the StringItem class onto the form. After declaring referencing for the instance of the Form class and for the instance of the StringItem class, a new Form instance is created and given the title "My Form." Next, a StringItem instance with the message "Welcome, glad you could come." is created. You'll learn the details of creating and using the StringItem object later in this chapter. The append() method is called once when both instances are created. Reference to the StringItem instance is then passed to the form, thereby placing the StringItem instance as the last object on the form.

```
private Form form;
private StringItem message;
form = new Form("My Form");
```

```
message = new StringItem("Welcome, ", "glad you could come.");
form.append(message);
```

Each instance placed on a form has an index number associated with it, beginning with the value zero. You can use the index number to reference the instance within your MIDlet, for example, when you want to insert an instance onto the form.

The following segment of code shows you how to insert another StringItem instance onto a form before the first StringItem instance. This example is nearly identical to the previous example, except there are four changes. First, two StringItem references are declared, called message1 and message2. An int is also declared and is used to store the index number of the first StringItem instance placed on the form.

The same Form instance and StringItem instance as in the previous example are created and assigned to the proper reference. However, a second StringItem instance is also created. Notice that the index number of the first message appended to the Form instance is stored in the index1 variable. The index1 variable is passed as the first parameter to the insert() method to place the second message on the form before the first message. Reference to the second message is passed as the second parameter to the insert() method.

```
private Form form;
private StringItem message1, message2;
private int index1;
form = new Form("My Form");
message1 = new StringItem("Welcome, ", "glad you could come.");
message2 = new StringItem("Hello, ", "Mary.");
index1 = form.append(message1);
form.insert(index1,message2);
```

An alternative to using the insert() and append() methods for associating instances of the Item class with a form is to create an array of instances of the Item class and then pass the array to the constructor when the instance of the Form class is created. This is an excellent technique for initially populating the instance of the Form class. You can then use the insert() method, append() method, set() method, and delete() method to manage instances of the Item object on the form throughout the life of the MIDlet.

Listing 6-3 contains the JAD file for Listing 6-4, which illustrates how to populate an instance of the Form class with an array of instances of the Item class. This example creates an array of StringItem instances. Each element of the array is then assigned a StringItem instance. The array is passed as the second parameter to the constructor when the instance of the Form class is created, and the instance of the Form class

Creating an Instance of the Form Class

Listed here are the steps required to create an instance of the Form class:

1. Declare references.
2. Obtain a reference to the instance of the Display class.
3. Create an instance of a Command class to exit the MIDlet.
4. Create two instances of the StringItem class.
5. Assign each instance of the StringItem class to an array element.
6. Create an instance of the Form class.
7. Associate the instance of the Command class to the instance of the Form class.
8. Associate a CommandListener with the instance of the Form class.
9. Display the instance of the Form class on the screen.
10. Evaluate the command selected by the user.
11. If the Exit command is selected, terminate the MIDlet.

J2ME USER INTERFACE

is displayed within the startApp() method by calling the setCurrent() method, as described in Listing 6-3.

Listing 6-3
The JAD file for Listing 6-4

```
MIDlet-Name: CreatingFormWithItems
MIDlet-Version: 1.0
MIDlet-Vendor: MyCompany
MIDlet-Jar-URL: CreatingFormWithItems.jar
MIDlet-1: CreatingFormWithItems, , CreatingFormWithItems
MicroEdition-Configuration: CLDC-1.0
MicroEdition-Profile: MIDP-1.0
MIDlet-JAR-SIZE: 100
```

Listing 6-4
Creating a form with items

```
import javax.microedition.midlet.*;
import javax.microedition.lcdui.*;
public class CreatingFormWithItems
```

```
                  extends MIDlet implements CommandListener
{
  private Display display;
  private Form form;
  private Command exit;
  public CreatingFormWithItems ()
  {
    display = Display.getDisplay(this);
    exit = new Command("Exit", Command.SCREEN, 1);
    StringItem messages[] = new StringItem[2];
    message[0] = new StringItem("Welcome, ", "glad you could come.");
    message[1] = new StringItem("Hello, ", "Mary.");
    form = new Form("Display Form with Items", messages);
    form.addCommand(exit);
    form.setCommandListener(this);
  }
  public void startApp()
  {
   display.setCurrent(form);
  }
  public void pauseApp()
  {
  }
  public void destroyApp(boolean unconditional)
  {
  }
  public void commandAction(Command command, Displayable displayable)
  {
    if (command == exit)
    {
      destroyApp(true);
      notifyDestroyed();
    }
  }
}
```

An instance of the Item class that appears on the form can be replaced by another instance of the Item class by calling the set() method. The set() method requires two parameters. The first parameter is the index number of the instance of the Item class that is being replaced, and the other parameter is reference to the instance of the Item object that is replacing the existing Item class.

Likewise, you can remove an instance of the Item class from a form by invoking the delete() method. The delete() method requires one parameter, which is the index number of the instance of the Item class that is being removed from the form.

Item Class

An Item class is a base class for a number of derived classes that can be contained within a Form class. These derived classes are ChoiceGroup, DateField, Gauge, ImageItem, StringItem, and TextField, each of which is discussed in detail later in this chapter. Some classes derived from the Item class, such as ChoiceGroup, DateField, and TextField, are used for data entry. The ChoiceGroup class is used to create check boxes or radio buttons on a form, and the DateField class and TextField class are used to capture date and free-form text from the user of the MIDlet.

The state of an instance of a class derived from the Item class changes whenever a user enters data into the instance, such as when a check box is selected. You can capture this change by associating an ItemStateListener with an instance of a class derived from an Item class (ChoiceGroup, for example). An ItemStateListener monitors events during the life of the MIDlet and traps events that represent changes in the state of any Item class contained in a form on the screen.

The class implementing the ItemStateListener interface (the MIDlet in this case) becomes the registered listener (callback) whose itemStateChanged() method is called when an item event occurs. The device's application manager detects the event and calls the itemStateChanged() method of the MIDlet. This similar process occurs with the CommandListener when a command event occurs, except when the commandAction() method is invoked.

Logic within the itemStateChanged() method compares the reference to known items on the form and then initiates processing. The nature of this processing is application dependent, but processing is likely to retrieve the value that the user entered into the item.

The following code segment illustrates how to associate an ItemStateListener with an instance of the Item object and how to define the itemStateChanged() method. This example creates an instance of the ChoiceGroup class, which is derived from the Item class. The instance of the ChoiceGroup class is displayed as a set of radio buttons collectively titled "Pick One." No radio buttons are shown in this code segment, but you'll see how to create them in the next section of this chapter. For now, assume that the instance of the ChoiceGroup class contains several radio buttons.

The instance of the ChoiceGroup class is then placed on the form by calling the append() method, which is passed reference to the instance of the ChoiceGroup class. Next, an ItemStateListener is associated with the form by calling the setItemStateListener() method. As you'll see in the next section, the creation of an instance of the ChoiceGroup class, appending the instance to the form, and associating an ItemStateListener with the form are performed within the constructor of the MIDlet.

The itemStateChanged() method is defined outside the constructor and contains logic to evaluate the item passed to the method. An if statement is used in this example to determine whether the selected item is the instance of the ChoiceGroup class. If so, the item is processed according to the business rules of the application.

```
private Form form;
private ChoiceGroup choiceGroup;
....
choiceGroup = new ChoiceGroup("Pick One", Choice.EXCLUSIVE);
form.append(choiceGroup);
form.setItemStateListener(this);
....
public void itemStateChanged(Item item)
{
  if (item == choiceGroup)
  {
   // do some processing
  }
}
```

ChoiceGroup Class

You are probably familiar with check boxes and radio buttons used in graphical user interfaces for choosing one or multiple choices from a selection of options. Likewise, check boxes and radio buttons are used to display selected options that were previously chosen. Check boxes and radio buttons are often grouped into sets of options, although there are times when one check box, rather than multiple check boxes, is required by an application. Radio buttons are almost always displayed in a set of radio buttons.

The primary difference between a set of check boxes and a set of radio buttons, besides their obvious appearance, is the number of check boxes or radio buttons that users can select. Users can choose multiple check boxes within a set of check boxes, while they can choose only one radio button within a set of radio buttons. For example, radio buttons are used on a form to identify the user's gender. The user can be either male or female, and therefore selection of one precludes the other. In contrast, a set of check boxes is used to identify preferences, such as choice of movies. Each check box within the set is a movie category. The selection of one category does not preclude the selection of other categories.

J2ME classifies check boxes and radio buttons as the ChoiceGroup class. An instance of the ChoiceGroup class can be one of two types: exclusive or multiple. An *exclusive* instance appears as a set of radio buttons, and a *multiple* instance contains one or a set of check boxes. You determine the format of an instance of a ChoiceGroup class by passing the ChoiceGroup class constructor a choice type, as shown in Table 6-2.

Choice Type	Description
EXCLUSIVE	Only one selection available at any time (radio button).
MULTIPLE	Zero or more selections available at any time (check box).
IMPLICIT	Only one selection at any time. The selection generates a command event automatically. No icon is used (menu list).

Table 6-2.   *Choice Types for ChoiceGroup Object and List Object*

When the user selects either a radio button or check box, the device's application manager detects the event and calls the itemStateChanged() method of the MIDlet, as described in the "Item Class" section of this chapter. The itemStateChanged() method determines whether the item selected is an instance of the ChoiceGroup. If so, then either the getSelectedFlags() method or getSelectedIndex() method must be called to retrieve the item selected by the user.

The getSelectedFlags() method returns an array that contains the status of the selected flag for each member of the instance of the ChoiceGroup class (each radio button or each check box). The MIDlet must step through each element of the array to determine whether the selected flag status is true or false. If true, the radio button or check box that corresponds to the index of the array element was selected by the user. If false, the user did not make a selection.

The getSelectedIndex() method returns the index number of the item selected by the user, such as a radio button. The index number is typically passed to the getString() method, which returns the text of the selected radio button or check box. You'll learn this technique in the next section of this chapter.

Instead of using the ItemStateListener and itemStateChanged() methods, you can place a Command on the screen and implement a CommandListener and define an actionCommand() method. As you'll recall from Chapter 5, the device's application manager notifies the CommandListener when a command is selected, and then the actionCommand() method you define in the MIDlet is called. The actionCommand() method then calls either the getSelectedFlags() method or the getSelectedIndex() method to identify the item selected by the user.

The "Quick Reference Guide" section of this chapter contains methods that you can use with instances of the ChoiceGroup class.

Creating and Accessing Check Boxes

Listing 6-5 contains the JAD file for Listing 6-6, which illustrates how to use a MULTIPLE type to create check boxes in a MIDlet. This example displays a list of movie categories in the form of check boxes within an instance of the Form class and then prompts the user to select kinds of movies he would like to see. Those choices are then displayed as a string on the screen (Figure 6-2).

Listing 6-6 begins with the declaration of references for instances of classes that are used within the application. The declarations are for the Display class, Form class, Command class, and ChoiceGroup class as well as two integers that are later used to identify the instance of the ChoiceGroup class.

The constructor is where instances are created and associated with the instance of the Form class. First obtain a Display instance by calling the getDisplay() method. Next, the instance of the ChoiceGroup class, called "movies," is created. Two parameters are passed to the constructor of the ChoiceGroup class. The first parameter is the title of the instance, and the other parameter is the type of ChoiceGroup, which is MULTIPLE because we want the instance to appear as check boxes.

The append() method is called once for each check box. The append() method requires two parameters. The first parameter is the label of the check box, and the other parameter is reference to an image that appears along with the label. No images are used in this example, so the second parameter is set to a null value.

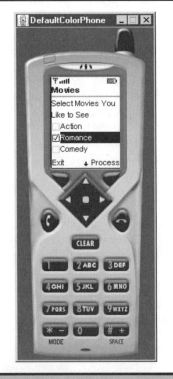

Figure 6-2. *Displaying check boxes on a form*

Two Command instances are created next. These are the Exit command and the Process command. The Exit command terminates the MIDlet, and the Process command causes the MIDlet to evaluate each check box to determine the user's preferences. Once these Command instances are created, the MIDlet creates an instance of the Form class that will become the container that holds other instances. The constructor of the Form class is passed the title of the form, called "Movies."

The next series of statements associates the instance of the ChoiceGroup class and instances of the Command class with the form. Notice that the entire instance referenced by movies is passed as a parameter to the append() method. This automatically appends all the check boxes of the instance to the form. You don't need to append each check box to the form.

The append() method returns the index number of the instance placed on the form. As you learned previously in this chapter, the index number uniquely identifies an instance on the form and is used throughout the MIDlet to reference the instance. The index number of the movies instance is stored in the movieIndex int so we can reference the movies instance later in the MIDlet. You don't need to store the index number of an instance if the instance is not referenced within the MIDlet.

The MIDlet then associates commands and a CommandListener with the form and processes all user selections immediately when the Process command activates. Alternatively, the MIDlet can implement an ItemStateChangeListener, which is notified whenever the state of an item changes. Many developers prefer to use a CommandListener instead of an ItemStateChangeListener.

The instance of the Form object containing check boxes is displayed on the screen by calling the setCurrent() method from within the startApp(). The setCurrent() method is passed reference to the instance of the form as a parameter. The pauseApp() method and the destroyApp() method are defined as required by J2ME specifications but are left empty because the application doesn't require any special statements to be executed when the device's application manager calls both of these methods.

The actionCommand() method is where all the processing occurs. The device's application manager detects when the user selects a command and notifies the MIDlet using the CommandListener to call the commandAction() method, where the command is evaluated. The if statement within the commandAction() method compares the incoming command to the Process command. If they match, the instance of the ChoiceGroup class is processed; otherwise the command is compared to the Exit command and terminates the MIDlet if they match.

The MIDlet performs some interesting processing when the user selects the Process command. First, an array of boolean types is created. Notice that the dimension of the array is set by calling the size() method of the instance of the ChoiceGroup. The size() method returns the number of check boxes in the set. The size() method is also used to create an array of instances of the StringItem object. These instances are used to display the user's selections.

Next, the boolean array is passed to the getSelectedFlags() method. The getSelectedFlags() method populates the boolean array with the state of each check

Creating Check Boxes

Listed here are the steps required to create check boxes:

1. Declare references.
2. Obtain a reference to the instance of the Display class.
3. Create an instance of a ChoiceGroup of MULTIPLE type.
4. Append check boxes to the instance of the ChoiceGroup.
5. Create an instance of a Command class to exit the MIDlet.
6. Create an instance of a Command class to process the check boxes.
7. Create an instance of a ChoiceGroup class.
8. Create an instance of the Form class.
9. Associate the instance of the ChoiceGroup to the instance of the Form class.
10. Associate the instance of the Command class to the instance of the Form class.
11. Associate a CommandListener with the instance of the Form class.
12. Display the instance of the Form class on the screen.
13. Evaluate the command selected by the user.
14. If the Exit command is selected, terminate the MIDlet.
15. If the Process command is selected, process the check boxes.
16. Read the selected status of each check box.
17. Evaluate the selected status of each check box.
18. If the selected status is true, retrieve the string of the check box.
19. Display the string of the check box on the form.
20. Remove the check box from the form.

box. A for loop is then used to step through the boolean array, evaluating the value of each array element. The picks array length variable is used instead of the size() method to set the maximum iterations of the loop.

If the value of the boolean array element is true, the MIDlet calls the getString() method, passing it the index number of the check box. Each check box is assigned an index number relative to other check boxes within the set and is used to uniquely identify the check box.

The getString() method returns the label of the check box, which is then passed to the setText() method of the next instance of the StringItem class and is later displayed on the screen by appending the string to the form. The instance of the ChoiceGroup

class and the Process command are both removed from the form by calling the delete()
method and the removeCommand() method, respectively.

**J2ME
USER INTERFACE**

Listing 6-5
The JAD
file for
Listing 6-6

```
MIDlet-Name: CheckBoxes
MIDlet-Version: 1.0
MIDlet-Vendor: MyCompany
MIDlet-Jar-URL: CheckBoxes.jar
MIDlet-1: CheckBoxes, , CheckBoxes
MicroEdition-Configuration: CLDC-1.0
MicroEdition-Profile: MIDP-1.0
MIDlet-JAR-SIZE: 100
```

Listing 6-6
Creating and
accessing
check boxes

```
import javax.microedition.midlet.*;
import javax.microedition.lcdui.*;
public class CheckBoxes extends MIDlet implements CommandListener
{
  private Display display;
  private Form form;
  private Command exit;
  private Command process;
  private ChoiceGroup movies;
  private int movieIndex;
  public CheckBoxes()
  {
    display = Display.getDisplay(this);
    movies = new ChoiceGroup("Select Movies You Like to See",
                             Choice.MULTIPLE);
    movies.append("Action", null);
    movies.append("Romance", null);
    movies.append("Comedy", null);
    movies.append("Horror", null);
    exit = new Command("Exit", Command.EXIT, 1);
    process = new Command("Process", Command.SCREEN,2);
    form = new Form("Movies");
    movieIndex = form.append(movies);
    form.addCommand(exit);
    form.addCommand(process);
    form.setCommandListener(this);
  }
  public void startApp()
  {
    display.setCurrent(form);
```

```
    }
    public void pauseApp()
    {
    }
    public void destroyApp(boolean unconditional)
    {
    }
    public void commandAction(Command command, Displayable displayable)
    {
      if (command == process)
      {
        boolean picks[] = new boolean[movies.size()];
        StringItem message[] = new StringItem[movies.size()];
        movies.getSelectedFlags(picks);
        for (int x = 0; x < picks.length; x++)
        {
          if (picks[x])
          {
           message[x] = new StringItem("",movies.getString(x)+"\n");
           form.append(message[x]);
          }
        }
        form.delete(movieIndex);
        form.removeCommand(process);
      }
      else if (command == exit)
      {
          destroyApp(false);
          notifyDestroyed();
      }
    }
}
```

Creating and Accessing Radio Buttons

Listing 6-7 contains the JAD file for Listing 6-8, which shows how to create a ChoiceGroup object that displays radio buttons on the screen as part of a form. This MIDlet displays two radio buttons, each representing a gender, and then prompts the user to select one or the other gender (Figure 6-3). After making a selection, the user clicks the Process command, causing the MIDlet to read the selected radio button and display the label of the radio button on the form.

Like Listing 6-6, Listing 6-8 begins by declaring references and integers that are used later in the program. Instances are created within the constructor, one of which

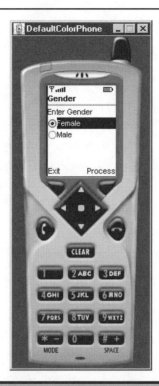

Figure 6-3.   *Displaying radio buttons on a form*

is an instance of the ChoiceGroup class. The ChoiceGroup class constructor is passed
a title in the first parameter and the type in the second parameter. Notice that the type
is EXCLUSIVE, which limits selection to only one set of choices within the group.

The append() method is called twice to add two radio buttons to the group. These
are Female and Male. The Male radio button is the default selection. You set a default
selection by first storing the index number of the Male radio button that is returned
by the append() method. This index number is then passed as the first parameter to
the setSelectedIndex() method. The setSelectedIndex() method's second parameter is
a boolean value indicating whether the radio button is on or off. In this example, a true
value is passed to turn on the radio button.

The remaining statements within the constructor create instances of the Command
class and associate them and other instances with the form. This is nearly identical to
similar statements within the constructor of Listing 6-6. The form is then displayed
by calling the setCurrent() method in the startApp() method. Command events are
detected, and the commandAction() method is called to process those events, as
described previously in the "Item Class" section of this chapter.

Creating Radio Buttons

Listed here are the steps required to create radio buttons:

1. Declare references.
2. Obtain a reference to the instance of the Display class.
3. Create an instance of a ChoiceGroup of EXCLUSIVE type.
4. Append radio buttons to the instance of the ChoiceGroup.
5. Set the Male radio button as the default radio button.
6. Create an instance of a Command class to exit the MIDlet.
7. Create an instance of a Command class to process the radio buttons.
8. Create an instance of the Form class.
9. Associate the instance of the ChoiceGroup to the instance of the Form class.
10. Associate the instance of the Command class to the instance of the Form class.
11. Associate a CommandListener with the instance of the Form class.
12. Display the instance of the Form class on the screen.
13. Evaluate the command selected by the user.
14. If the Exit command is selected, terminate the MIDlet.
15. If the Process command is selected, process the radio button.
16. Read the selected radio button.
17. Retrieve the string of the selected radio button.
18. Display the string of the radio button on the form.
19. Remove the radio button from the form.
20. Remove the Process command from the form.

The MIDlet invokes the getSelectedIndex() method of the gender object if the incoming command is the Process command. The getSelectedIndex() returns an integer representing the index of the gender object selected by the user. The index is passed to the getString() method, which returns the radio button's label and assigns the label to an instance of the StringItem class. This instance is then displayed on the form by calling the append() method; afterward the gender instance and the Process command are removed from the form.

Listing 6-7
The JAD
file for
Listing 6-8

```
MIDlet-Name: RadioButtons
MIDlet-Version: 1.0
MIDlet-Vendor: MyCompany
```

```
MIDlet-Jar-URL: RadioButtons.jar
MIDlet-1: RadioButtons, , RadioButtons
MicroEdition-Configuration: CLDC-1.0
MicroEdition-Profile: MIDP-1.0
MIDlet-JAR-SIZE: 100
```

Listing 6-8
Creating and
accessing
radio buttons

```
import javax.microedition.midlet.*;
import javax.microedition.lcdui.*;
public class RadioButtons extends MIDlet implements CommandListener
{
  private Display display;
  private Form form;
  private Command exit;
  private Command process;
  private ChoiceGroup gender;
  private int currentIndex;
  private int genderIndex;
  public RadioButtons()
  {
    display = Display.getDisplay(this);
    gender = new ChoiceGroup("Enter Gender", Choice.EXCLUSIVE);
    gender.append("Female", null);
    currentIndex = gender.append("Male ", null);
    gender.setSelectedIndex(currentIndex, true);
    exit = new Command("Exit", Command.EXIT, 1);
    process = new Command("Process", Command.SCREEN,2);
    form = new Form("Gender");
    genderIndex = form.append(gender);
    form.addCommand(exit);
    form.addCommand(process);
    form.setCommandListener(this);
  }
  public void startApp()
  {
    display.setCurrent(form);
  }
  public void pauseApp()
  {
  }
  public void destroyApp(boolean unconditional)
  {
  }
```

```
   public void commandAction(Command command, Displayable displayable)
   {
     if (command == exit)
     {
           destroyApp(false);
           notifyDestroyed();
     }
     else if (command == process)
     {
       currentIndex = gender.getSelectedIndex();
       StringItem message = new StringItem("Gender: ",
gender.getString(currentIndex));
       form.append(message);
       form.delete(genderIndex);
       form.removeCommand(process);
     }
   }
}
```

DateField Class

The DateField class is used to display, edit, or input date and/or time into a MIDlet.
A DateField class is instantiated by specifying a label for the field, a field mode, and a
time zone, although time zone is optional. Table 6-3 lists the available DateField modes.
Both methods are illustrated in the following two statements:

```
DateField datefield = new DateField("Today", DateField.DATE);
DateField datefield = new DateField("Time", DateField.TIME, timeZone);
```

Once a DateField class is instantiated, you can use DateField class methods to enter
a date and time into the date field and retrieve the date and time value that has already
been entered into the date field. You place a date or time into the date field by calling the

Mode	Description
DATE	Display, edit, and input a date
TIME	Display, edit, and input a time
DATE_TIME	Display, edit, and input both date and time

Table 6-3. *DateField Modes*

setDate() method. The setDate() method requires one parameter, which is an instance of the Date class containing the date/time value that will appear in the date field.

The getDate() method is called to retrieve the date/time value of the date field. You can use the date/time value in a number of ways within your MIDlet, such as in a calculation. Listing 6-9 contains the JAD file for Listing 6-10, which illustrates how to place a date/time value into a date field and read a date/time value from a date field that is later used in a calculation.

Besides storing and retrieving date/time values using DateField class methods, you can also replace the DateField mode and retrieve the DateField mode of an instance of a DateField class. You'll find these methods handy to use whenever you need to change the mode on the fly. The setInputMode() method replaces the existing DateField mode with the mode passed as a parameter to the setInputMode() method. The getInputMode() method is used to retrieve the mode of an instance of a DateField.

Creating and Manipulating an Instance of a DateField Object

The example in Listing 6-10 creates an instance of the DateField class that is initialized with current date and time of the system's clock, which is displayed on the screen (Figure 6-4).

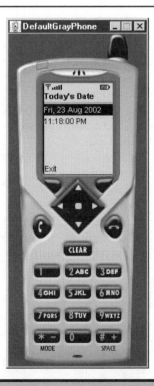

Figure 6-4.   *Displaying the date field on a form*

Creating an Instance of the DateField Class

Listed here are the steps required to create an instance of the DateField class:

1. Declare references.

2. Obtain a reference to the instance of the Display class.

3. Create an instance of the Form class.

4. Create an instance of the DateField class.

5. Set the instance of the DateField class to the system's date.

6. Create an instance of a Command class to exit the MIDlet.

7. Associate the instance of the DateField class to the instance of the Form class.

8. Associate the instance of the Command class to the instance of the Form class.

9. Associate a CommandListener with the instance of the Form class.

10. Display the instance of the Form class containing the system's date on the screen.

11. Evaluate the command selected by the user.

12. If the Exit command is selected, terminate the MIDlet.

You'll notice that, like other listings in this chapter, Listing 6-10 begins by declaring references to instances of classes that are used in the MIDlet. These classes are instantiated in the constructor and assigned to variables.

The instance of the DateField class is placed in the DATE_TIME mode since both date and time are displayed. The date and time is set by passing the Date() construction a date/time value in milliseconds since January 1, 1970. The System.currentTimeMillis() method returns the current time in milliseconds—the number of milliseconds since January 1, 1970.

The instance of the DateField class, along with the Exit commands and the CommandListener, are then associated with the instance of the Form class. The form is then displayed on the screen by calling the setCurrent() method within the startApp() method. After the user selects the Exit command, the device's application manager calls the commandAction() method, where the command is evaluated. The MIDlet terminates when the user selects the Exit command.

Listing 6-9
The JAD
file for
Listing 6-10

```
MIDlet-Name: DateToday
MIDlet-Version: 1.0
MIDlet-Vendor: MyCompany
MIDlet-Jar-URL: DateToday.jar
MIDlet-1: DateToday, , DateToday
MicroEdition-Configuration: CLDC-1.0
```

```
MicroEdition-Profile: MIDP-1.0
MIDlet-JAR-SIZE: 100
```

Listing 6-10
Displaying
the system's
date

```java
import java.util.*;
import javax.microedition.midlet.*;
import javax.microedition.lcdui.*;
 public class DateToday extends MIDlet implements CommandListener
{
  private Display display;
  private Form form;
  private Date today;
  private Command exit;
  private DateField datefield;
  public DateToday()
  {
    display = Display.getDisplay(this);
    form = new Form("Today's Date");
    today = new Date(System.currentTimeMillis());
    datefield = new DateField("", DateField.DATE_TIME);
    datefield.setDate(today);
    exit = new Command("Exit", Command.EXIT, 1);
    form.append(datefield);
    form.addCommand(exit);
    form.setCommandListener(this);
  }
  public void startApp ()
  {
    display.setCurrent(form);
  }
  public void pauseApp()
  {
  }
  public void destroyApp(boolean unconditional)
  {
  }
  public void commandAction(Command command, Displayable displayable)
  {
   if (command == exit)
   {
    destroyApp(false);
    notifyDestroyed();
   }
  }
}
```

Gauge Class

The Gauge class creates an animated progress bar that graphically represents the status of a process. The indicator on the gauge generated by the Gauge class moves from one end to the other proportionally to the completion of the process measured by the gauge. Although movement of the indicator appears to be automatically driven by the underlying process that is being measured, this movement is completed under the control of the MIDlet. There is no direct, automatic link between a Gauge class and the associated process.

The Gauge class provides methods to display the gauge and move the indicator. The developer must build the routine into the MIDlet to move the indicator. This means that the routine must monitor the progress of the underlying process and move the indicator of the Gauge class to a position that corresponds to the status of the process.

Let's say a MIDlet performs 100 calculations, and you want to use a gauge to indicate the number of calculations made. Each time a calculation is completed, you must move the indicator one tick. The user of the MIDlet can also control the indicator if the instance of the Gauge class is set in the interactive mode. In interactive mode the user can move the indicator of the gauge to a desired value, such as increasing the volume of a device. The developer must then include a routine in the MIDlet to read the value of the gauge indicator and incorporate the user's input into the MIDlet's processing.

You create an instance of the Gauge class by using the following code segment:

```
Gauge gauge = new Gauge("Like/Dislike Gauge", true, 100, 0);
```

This statement creates an interactive gauge with the caption "Like/Dislike Gauge" and a scale of zero to 100. The first parameter passed to the constructor of the Gauge class is a string containing the caption that is displayed with the gauge. The second parameter is a boolean value indicating whether or not the gauge is interactive. The third parameter is the maximum value of the gauge, and the last parameter is the gauge's initial value.

Although a gauge is set to the interactive mode, you can still change the current value of the gauge indicator by calling the setValue() method. The setValue() method requires one parameter, which is the integer representing the new value. You must write the logic in your MIDlet to calculate the new value. Many times you will want to increment or decrement the current value of the gauge by a specific amount. Therefore, you'll need to determine the current value of the gauge by calling the getValue() method. The getValue() method returns an integer representing the gauge's current value.

Before setting a new value for the gauge, be sure the new value doesn't exceed the maximum value of the gauge, otherwise the indicator on the gauge won't be able to display the new value. You can determine the maximum value of the gauge by calling the getMaxValue() method, which returns the integer representing the current maximum value. If your new value exceeds the maximum value, you can reset the maximum value before setting the new value by calling the setMaxValue() method and passing the method an integer representing the new maximum value.

Creating and Manipulating an Instance of a Gauge Class

Listing 6-11 contains the JAD file for Listing 6-12, which shows how to create a noninteractive gauge. This example simulates monitoring a process and reporting the status of the process by moving the indicator on the gauge through the range of values from zero to 100 (Figure 6-5). The monitoring begins when the user selects the Start command. The commandAction() method then loops through moving the indicator by retrieving the current value of the indicator, incrementing that value, and then repositioning the indicator on the gauge. It is within this loop that you place statements that evaluate the status of a process, which is then reflected by positioning the indicator.

Like other examples in this chapter, Listing 6-12 begins by declaring variables that are used to reference instances of classes created within the MIDlet, including an instance of the Gauge class. These instances are created with the GaugeNonInteractive constructor. The Gauge class constructor is passed four parameters. The first is the caption for the gauge, "Progress Tracking." The second parameter is a boolean false value indicating that the gauge isn't interactive. The third parameter is the maximum value of the gauge, which is set to 100. And the last parameter is the initial value of the gauge.

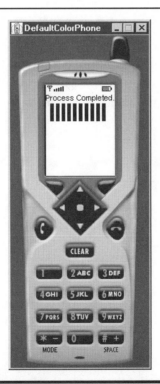

Figure 6-5.   *Displaying a noninteractive gauge on a form*

J2ME USER INTERFACE

Creating an Instance of the Gauge Class

Listed here are the steps required to create an instance of the Gauge class:

1. Declare references.
2. Obtain a reference to the instance of the Display class.
3. Create an instance of the Gauge class.
4. Create an instance of a Command class to exit the MIDlet.
5. Create an instance of a Command class to start processing the selection.
6. Create an instance of the Form class.
7. Associate the instance of the Gauge class to the instance of the Form class.
8. Associate instances of the Command class to the instance of the Form class.
9. Associate a CommandListener with the instance of the Form class.
10. Display the instance of the Form class on the screen.
11. Evaluate the command selected by the user.
12. If the Exit command is selected, terminate the MIDlet.
13. If the Start command is selected, process the gauge.
14. Make sure the current value of the instance of the Gauge class is less than the maximum value of the instance.
15. If the value is less than the maximum, increment the current value of the gauge by one and reposition the indicator.
16. Remove the Start command.
17. Change the label of the gauge to indicate that processing is completed.

Instances of the Command class, the Gauge class, and the CommandListener are then associated with the form. The form is then displayed on the screen when the startApp() method is called by the device's application manager.

The commandAction() method is invoked any time a command event is detected. This method evaluates the incoming command by comparing the command to the Exit and Start commands created by the MIDlet. If the Exit command was selected, the commandAction() method causes the MIDlet to terminate, as described in previous listings in this chapter. If the Start command was selected, the MIDlet enters the while loop.

The loop continues as long as the current value of the gauge, as reported by the getValue() method, is less than the maximum value of the gauge returned by the getMaxValue() method. The MIDlet then retrieves the current value again, increments the value by one, and passes the sum as the parameter to the setValue() method, thereby resetting the gauge indicator to show the new status of processing within the while loop.

Once the current value is equal to the maximum value of the gauge, the loop is terminated. The Start command is removed from the form, and the setLabel() method is called, resetting the label of the gauge to "Process Completed."

Listing 6-11
The JAD
file for
Listing 6-12

```
MIDlet-Name: GaugeNonInteractive
MIDlet-Version: 1.0
MIDlet-Vendor: MyCompany
MIDlet-Jar-URL: GaugeNonInteractive.jar
MIDlet-1: GaugeNonInteractive, , GaugeNonInteractive
MicroEdition-Configuration: CLDC-1.0
MicroEdition-Profile: MIDP-1.0
MIDlet-JAR-SIZE: 100
```

Listing 6-12
Implementing
a noninter-
active gauge

```
import javax.microedition.midlet.*;
import javax.microedition.lcdui.*;
 public class GaugeNonInteractive
                extends MIDlet implements CommandListener
{
  private Display display;
  private Form form;
  private Command exit;
  private Command start;
  private Gauge gauge;
  private boolean isSafeToExit;
  public GaugeNonInteractive()
  {
    display = Display.getDisplay(this);
    gauge = new Gauge("Progress Tracking", false, 100, 0);
    exit = new Command("Exit", Command.EXIT, 1);
    start = new Command("Start", Command.SCREEN, 1);
    form = new Form("");
    form.append(gauge);
    form.addCommand(start);
    form.addCommand(exit);
    form.setCommandListener(this);
    isSafeToExit = true;
  }
  public void startApp()
  {
   display.setCurrent(form);
  }
  public void pauseApp()
  {
  }
```

```
public void destroyApp(boolean unconditional)
               throws MIDletStateChangeException
{
  if (!unconditional)
  {
    throw new MIDletStateChangeException();
  }
}
public void commandAction(Command command, Displayable displayable)
{
  if (command == exit)
  {
    try
    {
      destroyApp(isSafeToExit);
      notifyDestroyed();
    }
    catch (MIDletStateChangeException Error)
    {
      Alert alert = new Alert("Busy", "Please try again.", null, AlertType.WARNING);
      alert.setTimeout(1500);
      display.setCurrent(alert, form);
    }
  }
  else if (command == start)
  {
    form.remove.Command(start);
    new Thread(new GaugeUpdater()).start();
  }
}
class GaugeUpdater implements Runnable
{
  GaugeUpdater()
  {
  }
  public void run()
  {
    isSafeToExit = false;
    try
    {
    while (gauge.getValue() < gauge.getMaxValue())
    {
      Thread.sleep(1000);
      gauge.setValue(gauge.getValue() + 1);
    }
      isSafeToExit = true;
      gauge.setLabel("Process Completed.");
```

```
        }
        catch (InterruptedException Error)
        {
           throw new RuntimeException(Error.getMessage());
        }
    }
  }
}
```

As mentioned earlier, an instance of a Gauge class can become interactive, enabling the user to adjust the indicator of the gauge. Listing 6-13 contains the JAD file for Listing 6-14, which illustrates how to create an interactive gauge (Figure 6-6). Listing 6-14 prompts the user to rate a movie by moving the indicator on a gauge, then selecting the Vote command to register her rating. The rating is then displayed on the screen in an alert dialog box.

You'll notice that this listing is very similar to Listing 6-12 in that references to instances of classes are declared at the beginning of the list and are assigned instances after instances of classes are created in the GaugeInteractive constructor.

Creating an Interactive Gauge

Listed here are the steps required to create an interactive gauge:

1. Declare references.

2. Obtain a reference to the instance of the Display class.

3. Create an instance of the Gauge class.

4. Create an instance of a Command class to exit the MIDlet.

5. Create an instance of a Command class to start processing the selection.

6. Create an instance of the Form class.

7. Associate the instance of the Gauge class to the instance of the Form class.

8. Associate instances of the Command class to the instance of the Form class.

9. Associate a CommandListener with the instance of the Form class.

10. Display the instance of the Form class on the screen.

11. Evaluate the command selected by the user.

12. If the Exit command is selected, terminate the MIDlet.

13. If the Vote command is selected, process the value of the gauge.

14. Read the current value of the gauge.

15. Display the value of the gauge in an alert dialog box.

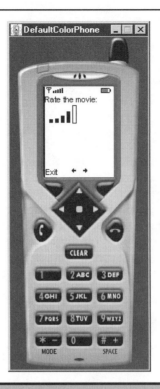

Figure 6-6. *Displaying an interactive gauge on a form*

The instance of the Gauge class has a caption called "Rate the movie:" and has an initial value of one and a maximum value of five. Notice that the second parameter of the Gauge constructor is a boolean true value, which makes the gauge interactive.

Instances are then associated with the form, and the form is displayed when the startApp() method is invoked. The actionCommand() method traps the selection of the Start command and displays an alert dialog box captioned "Ranking," using the return value from the getValue() method as its message. The getValue() method retrieves the current value of the indicator gauge, which reflects the user's ranking of the movie. The MIDlet terminates when the Exit command is selected.

Listing 6-13
The JAD file for Listing 6-14

```
MIDlet-Name: GaugeInteractive
MIDlet-Version: 1.0
MIDlet-Vendor: MyCompany
MIDlet-Jar-URL: GaugeInteractive.jar
```

```
MIDlet-1: GaugeInteractive, , GaugeInteractive
MicroEdition-Configuration: CLDC-1.0
MicroEdition-Profile: MIDP-1.0
MIDlet-JAR-SIZE: 100
```

Listing 6-14
Implementing
an interactive
gauge

```
import javax.microedition.midlet.*;
import javax.microedition.lcdui.*;
public class GaugeInteractive extends MIDlet implements CommandListener
{
  private Display display;
  private Form form;
  private Command exit;
  private Command vote;
  private Gauge gauge;
  public GaugeInteractive ()
  {
    display = Display.getDisplay(this);
    gauge = new Gauge("Rate the movie: ", true, 5, 1);
    exit = new Command("Exit", Command.EXIT, 1);
    vote = new Command ("Vote", Command.SCREEN, 1);
    form = new Form("");
    form.addCommand(exit);
    form.addCommand(vote);
    form.append(gauge);
    form.setCommandListener(this);
  }
  public void startApp()
  {
    display.setCurrent(form);
  }
  public void pauseApp()
  {
  }
  public void destroyApp(boolean unconditional)
  {
  }
  public void commandAction(Command command, Displayable displayable)
  {
    if (command == exit)
    {
      destroyApp(false);
      notifyDestroyed();
```

```
    }
    else if (command == vote)
    {
     String msg = String.valueOf(gauge.getValue());
     Alert alert = new Alert("Ranking", msg, null, null);
     alert.setTimeout(Alert.FOREVER);
     alert.setType(AlertType.INFO);
     display.setCurrent(alert);
    }
  }
}
```

StringItem Class

Previously in this chapter, you used an instance of a StringItem class to display a message on the screen. We'll discuss the details of creating this instance in this section. The purpose of using a StringItem class is to display a text that cannot be modified or deleted by the user of the MIDlet.

A StringItem class is different from other classes derived from the Item class in that a StringItem class does not recognize events. This means that an instance of a StringItem class can never cause an event because the user cannot modify the text of the string item. Other instances of the Item class, such as an instance of the ChoiceGroup class, recognize an event whenever the value of the instance changes, such as selecting a radio button or check box.

Although an instance of the StringItem class cannot cause an event to occur, you can modify the instance from within the MIDlet as a result of an event caused by instances of other classes. For example, the text of an instance of the StringItem class can be changed as a result of the user selecting a radio button.

You create an instance of a StringItem class by passing the StringItem class constructor two parameters. The first parameter is a string representing the label of the instance. The other parameter is a string of text that will appear on the screen.

You can retrieve the text of the instance of a StringItem class once the instance is created by calling the getText() method. The getText() method returns a string containing the text. Likewise, you can replace the text by calling the setText() method. The setText() method requires one parameter, which is the new text that replaces the current text of the instance.

The label of the instance can be changed by calling the setLabel() method. The setLabel() method requires one parameter, which is the replacement label. You can retrieve a label from an instance by invoking the getLabel() method. The getLabel() method returns a string consisting of the label of the instance.

Creating and Manipulating an Instance of a StringItem Object

Listing 6-15 contains the JAD file for Listing 6-16, which demonstrates how to create an instance of a StringItem class and then manipulate the label and text after the instance is displayed on the screen. This example tells the user a joke. A question is posed to the user, and then he has the option either to terminate the MIDlet or give up and have the MIDlet display the punch line in answer to the question (Figure 6-7).

The program starts like other listings in this chapter, so we'll jump to statements pertinent to the StringItem class instead of reviewing each statement. The instance is created within the StringItemExample constructor. Two strings are passed to the StringItem class constructor. The first parameter is the label called "Question:", and the other parameter is the question. The instance of the StringItem class is then associated with the form, along with other instances of other classes created by the MIDlet. The form is then displayed by the startApp() method.

Creating an Instance of a StringItem Class

Listed here are the steps required to create an instance of the StringItem class:

1. Declare references.
2. Obtain a reference to the instance of the Display class.
3. Create an instance of the StringItem class.
4. Create an instance of a Command class for the answer to the joke.
5. Create an instance of a Command class to exit the MIDlet.
6. Create an instance of the Form class.
7. Associate the instance of the StringItem class to the instance of the Form class.
8. Associate instances of the Command class to the instance of the Form class.
9. Associate a CommandListener with the instance of the Form class.
10. Display the instance of the Form class on the screen.
11. Evaluate the command selected by the user.
12. If the Exit command is selected, terminate the MIDlet.
13. If the Giveup command is selected, process the instance of the StringItem class.
14. Change the label of the instance to "Answer:".
15. Change the text of the instance to the answer to the joke.
16. Remove the Giveup command.

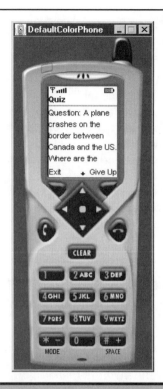

Figure 6-7. *Displaying a string item on a form*

The user selects the Giveup command if unable to answer the question. The if statement within the commandAction() method then enables the setLabel() method and setText() method to be invoked. The setLabel() method replaces the "Question:" label of the StringItem class instance with the "Answer:" label. Likewise, the text of the instance is replaced with the punch line when the setText() method is called. The Giveup command is then removed from the form.

Listing 6-15
The JAD file for Listing 6-16

```
MIDlet-Name: StringItemExample
MIDlet-Version: 1.0
MIDlet-Vendor: MyCompany
MIDlet-Jar-URL: StringItemExample.jar
MIDlet-1: StringItemExample, , StringItemExample
MicroEdition-Configuration: CLDC-1.0
MicroEdition-Profile: MIDP-1.0
MIDlet-JAR-SIZE: 100
```

Listing 6-16
Implementing
the StringItem
class

```java
import javax.microedition.midlet.*;
import javax.microedition.lcdui.*;
public class StringItemExample extends MIDlet
                                  implements CommandListener
{
  private Display display;
  private Form form;
  private StringItem question;
  private Command giveup;
  private Command exit;
  public StringItemExample()
  {
    display = Display.getDisplay(this);
    question = new StringItem("Question: ",
               "A plane crashes on the border between Canada
                and the US. Where are the survivors buried?");
    giveup = new Command("Give Up", Command.SCREEN, 1);
    exit = new Command("Exit", Command.EXIT, 1);
    form = new Form("Quiz");
    form.addCommand(exit);
    form.addCommand(giveup);
    form.append(question);
    form.setCommandListener(this);
  }
  public void startApp()
  {
    display.setCurrent(form);
  }
  public void pauseApp()
  {
  }
  public void destroyApp(boolean unconditional)
  {
  }
  public void commandAction(Command command, Displayable displayable)
  {
    if (command == giveup)
    {
      question.setLabel("Answer: ");
      question.setText("Survivors are not buried.");
      form.removeCommand(giveup);
    }
    else if (command == exit)
```

```
   {
    destroyApp(false);
    notifyDestroyed();
   }
  }
 }
```

TextField Class

The TextField class is used to capture one line or multiple lines of text entered by the user. The number of lines of a text field depends on the maximum size of the text field when you create an instance of the TextField class. You instantiate the TextField class by using the following statement, passing the TextField constructor four parameters:

```
textfield = new TextField("First Name:", "", 30, TextField.ANY);
```

The first parameter is the label that appears when the instance is displayed on the screen. The second parameter is text that you want to appear as the default text for the instance, which the user can edit. The third parameter is the maximum number of characters that can be held by the instance. A word of caution: The character count that you enter is a request to the device's application manager and not a directive. This means the maximum number of characters that can be entered into the text field might be lower than the value passed to the constructor.

You can determine the actual character size of a text box by calling the getMaxSize() method once the text field is instantiated. Always check the maximum size of a text field before populating it if your MIDlet is likely to populate the text field with a lot of text. In this way you can prevent an error from occurring during run time.

You can also change the maximum size by calling the setMaxSize() method. The setMaxSize() method requires one parameter, which is the new value for the maximum size for the text field. Any time that you need to know the length of the text in the text field you can call the size() method, which returns an integer representing the number of characters existing in the text field.

Also keep in mind that not all characters in a text field will appear on the screen. Characters that don't fit on the screen are still available to the user by scrolling. The device handles scrolling for you.

The last parameter passed to the constructor of the TextField class is the constraint (if any) that is used to restrict the type of characters that the user can enter into the text field. Table 6-4 lists the constraints recognized by the TextField class. The instance of the TextField class accepts any character if the ANY constraint is set. You can restrict entry to numeric characters by passing the NUMERIC constraint to the constructor. All non-numeric characters are excluded from the text field.

Constraint	Description
CONSTRAINT_MASK	Used to determine the constraint's current value
ANY	Input any character
EMAILADDR	Input only valid email address characters
NUMERIC	Input positive and negative numbers; cannot exclude either positive or negative numbers
PASSWORD	Hide input
PHONENUMBER	Input characters valid to a phone number sometimes specific to locality and device
URL	Input characters valid to a URL

Table 6-4.   *TextField Object Constraints*

Three special-purpose constraints—EMAILADDR, PHONENUMBER, and URL—act as filters to assure that only valid characters can be entered into the text field for email addresses, phone numbers, and URLs. All other characters are treated as an error and therefore are prevented from being stored in the text field. The PASSWORD constraint can be combined with other constraints to hide characters from being displayed. An asterisk or other character determined by the device is displayed in place of the actual character placed in the text box. The CONSTRAINT_MASK constraint is used to determine the constraint's current value.

There are two methods you can use to retrieve characters entered into a text field by the user of your MIDlet. These are the getString() method and the getChars() method. The getString() method returns the content of the text field as a string, and the getChars() method returns the text field content as a character array. The getChars() method requires that you pass it a character array as a parameter.

You place text into a text field by calling either the setString() method or the setChars() method. The setString() method requires one parameter, which is the string containing text that should appear in the text field. The setChars() method requires three parameters. The first is the character array whose data will populate the text field. The second is the position of the first character within the array that will be placed into the text field. The last parameter is the length of characters of the character array that will be placed into the text field. Characters in the character array will replace the entire content of the text field.

You can insert characters within the text field without overwriting the entire content of the text field by calling the insert() method. The insert() method has two signatures, one for strings and the other for character arrays. The insert() method used to insert a string into the contents of a text field requires two parameters. The first parameter is the string that will be inserted into the text field. The other parameter is the character position of the current string where the new text is inserted. The text that exists there now will be shifted down to make room for the inserted text.

The insert() method used to insert a character array requires four parameters. The first parameter is reference to the array. The second parameter is the position of the first character within the array that will be placed into the text field. The third parameter is the number of characters contained in the array that will be placed into the text field. And the last parameter is the character position of the current text that will be shifted down to make room for the inserted text.

Text can be removed from the text field by calling the delete() method, which requires two parameters. The first is the position of the first character to be deleted. The other parameter is the length of characters that are to be deleted.

The constraint of a text field can be changed after the instance is created by calling the setConstraints() method. The setConstraints() method requires you to pass the new constraint as a parameter to the setConstraints() method. You can also determine the current constraint by calling the getConstraints() method.

Another sometimes handy method is the getCaretPosition() method. A *caret* is the cursor within the text field, and as you probably guessed, the getCaretPosition() method returns the current position of the cursor. For example, you might design an application that requires the user to select a section of text by positioning the cursor at the first character of the section and then selecting a command. In response, your MIDlet calls the getCaretPosition() method and uses the returned position to extract the section of text from the contents of the text field.

Creating and Manipulating an Instance of a TextField Class

We will look at two common ways to use a TextField class in a MIDlet. Listing 6-17 contains the JAD file for Listing 6-18, which shows how to create an instance of a TextField class, capture user input, and then replace the text in the text field with text generated by the MIDlet. Listing 6-19 contains the JAD file for Listing 6-20, which illustrates the technique for using the PASSWORD constraint when prompting the user to enter a password into a text field. This MIDlet also shows you how to change the constraint from within your program and replace the password text with text of your own.

Let's begin with Listing 6-18. This MIDlet begins much the same way as other examples shown in this chapter, by declaring variables, then creating instances of classes within the TextCapture constructor. Those instances are then assigned to variables and associated with the Form object.

Creating an Instance of a TextField Class

Listed here are the steps required to create an instance of a TextField class:

1. Declare references.
2. Obtain a reference to the instance of the Display class.
3. Create an instance of a Command class for the Submit class.
4. Create an instance of a Command class to exit the MIDlet.
5. Create an instance of the TextField class.
6. Create an instance of the Form class.
7. Associate the instance of the TextField class to the instance of the Form class.
8. Associate instances of the Command class to the instance of the Form class.
9. Associate a CommandListener with the instance of the Form class.
10. Display the instance of the Form class on the screen.
11. Evaluate the command selected by the user.
12. If the Exit command is selected, terminate the MIDlet.
13. If the Submit command is selected, process the instance of the TextField class.
14. Retrieve the text of the instance.
15. Concatenate the text to the "Hello," greeting.
16. Replace the text in the instance.
17. Remove the Submit command.

Notice that an instance of a TextField class is created within the TextCapture constructor. This text field is labeled "First Name:" and can receive up to 30 characters of any kind. Initially, the text field is empty. Also notice that instances of two commands are created. One command is called Submit and is selected after the user enters a first name in the text box. The other command is the Exit command and is used to terminate the MIDlet. The form containing the text field is displayed on the screen by calling the setCurrent() method in the startApp() method (Figure 6-8).

The Submit command is detected and processed by the commandAction() method, as described in the "Item Class" section of this chapter. If the command passed to the commandAction() method is the Submit command, the MIDlet calls the getString()

Figure 6-8. *Displaying a text field on a form*

method to retrieve the string from the text field. The content of the text field is then concatenated to the word "Hello," which is then passed to the setString() method, causing the new string to replace the existing string in the text field (Figure 6-9). The Submit command is then removed from the screen, forcing the user to select the Exit command to terminate the MIDlet.

Listing 6-20 is practically the same MIDlet as Listing 6-18 with a few exceptions. The text field in Listing 6-20 is labeled "Password:" and has two constraints. The first constraint is ANY, enabling any character to be entered into the text field. The other constraint is PASSWORD, which displays an asterisk (or another character selected by the device) in place of each character that the user enters in the text field. Notice that the bitwise OR operator (|) is used to join constraints.

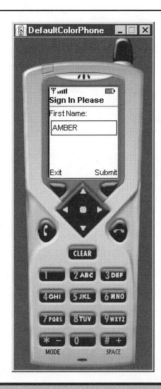

Figure 6-9. *A sign-in screen is displayed after the Submit command is selected.*

If you drop down to the commandAction() method, you'll see that the setConstraints() method is called, changing the constraint from ANY | PASSWORD to ANY, which causes characters placed in the text field to be displayed unchanged. The MIDlet also calls the setString() method to replace the hidden content of the text field with the "Thank you." string.

Listing 6-17
The JAD
file for
Listing 6-18

```
MIDlet-Name: TextFieldCapture
MIDlet-Version: 1.0
MIDlet-Vendor: MyCompany
MIDlet-Jar-URL: TextFieldCapture.jar
MIDlet-1: TextFieldCapture, , TextFieldCapture
MicroEdition-Configuration: CLDC-1.0
MicroEdition-Profile: MIDP-1.0
MIDlet-JAR-SIZE: 100
```

```
import javax.microedition.midlet.*;
import javax.microedition.lcdui.*;
public class TextFieldCapture extends MIDlet
                                    implements CommandListener
{
  private Display display;
  private Form form;
  private Command submit;
  private Command exit;
  private TextField textfield;
  public TextFieldCapture()
  {
   display = Display.getDisplay(this);
   submit = new Command("Submit", Command.SCREEN, 1);
   exit = new Command("Exit", Command.EXIT, 1);
   textfield = new TextField("First Name:", "", 30, TextField.ANY);
   form = new Form("Sign In Please");
   form.addCommand(exit);
   form.addCommand(submit);
   form.append(textfield);
   form.setCommandListener(this);
  }
  public void startApp()
  {
   display.setCurrent(form);
  }
  public void pauseApp()
  {
  }
  public void destroyApp(boolean unconditional)
  {
  }
  public void commandAction(Command command, Displayable displayable)
  {
   if (command == submit)
   {
     textfield.setString("Hello, " + textfield.getString());
     form.removeCommand(submit);
   }
   else if (command == exit)
   {
      destroyApp(false);
      notifyDestroyed();
```

```
      }
    }
  }
```

Listing 6-19
The JAD
file for
Listing 6-20

```
MIDlet-Name: HideText
MIDlet-Version: 1.0
MIDlet-Vendor: MyCompany
MIDlet-Jar-URL: HideText.jar
MIDlet-1: HideText, , HideText
MicroEdition-Configuration: CLDC-1.0
MicroEdition-Profile: MIDP-1.0
MIDlet-JAR-SIZE: 100
```

Listing 6-20
Hiding text in
a text field

```
import javax.microedition.midlet.*;
import javax.microedition.lcdui.*;
public class HideText extends MIDlet implements CommandListener
{
  private Display display;
  private Form form;
  private Command submit;
  private Command exit;
  private TextField textfield;
  public HideText()
  {
   display = Display.getDisplay(this);
   submit = new Command("Submit", Command.SCREEN, 1);
   exit = new Command("Exit", Command.EXIT, 1);
   textfield = new TextField("Password:", "", 30, TextField.ANY | TextField.PASSWORD);
   form = new Form("Enter Password");
   form.addCommand(exit);
   form.addCommand(submit);
   form.append(textfield);
   form.setCommandListener(this);
  }
  public void startApp()
  {
   display.setCurrent(form);
  }
  public void pauseApp()
  {
  }
  public void destroyApp(boolean unconditional)
  {
  }
  public void commandAction(Command command, Displayable displayable)
```

```
        {
         if (command == submit)
         {
           textfield.setConstraints(TextField.ANY);
           textfield.setString("Thank you.");
           form.removeCommand(submit);
         }
         else if (command == exit)
         {
            destroyApp(false);
            notifyDestroyed();
         }
       }
     }
```

ImageItem Class

There are two types of images that can be displayed. These are immutable images and mutable images. An *immutable image* is loaded from a file or other resource and cannot be modified once the image is displayed. Icons associated with MIDlets are immutable images. A *mutable image* is drawn on the screen using methods available in the Graphics class. Once drawn, your MIDlet can redraw any portion of the image.

An immutable image is drawn on a screen, and a mutable object is drawn on a canvas. As you learned at the beginning of the chapter, the Displayable class has two derived classes—the Screen class and the Canvas class. Immutable images are displayed using an instance of the ImageItem class, which inherits from the Item class. Mutable images are displayed using the Graphics class, which is derived from the Canvas class. You'll learn techniques for drawing and displaying mutable images in the next chapter, which discusses the low-level MIDlet interface. This section focuses on displaying immutable images.

The first step in displaying an immutable image is to create an instance of the Image class by calling the createImage() method. The createImage() method requires one parameter that contains the name of the file containing the image. Make sure that you include the full path to the file in the parameter. The next step is to create an instance of the ImageItem class. The constructor of the ImageItem class requires four parameters. The first is a string that becomes the label for the image. The second parameter is reference to the instance of the Image class created in step one. The third parameter is the layout directive. And the last parameter is a string referred to as alternate text that is displayed in place of the image if for some reason the image cannot be displayed by the device. Some applications won't require you to specify a label or alternate text; therefore, use a null as the value of the parameter in place of a string.

The layout directive is a request to the device's application manager to position the image at a particular location on the screen. The device's application manager determines the actual location where the image appears. Table 6-5 lists layout directives. The bitwise OR operator combines layout directives (|), which is illustrated in Listing 6-22.

Value	Description
LAYOUT_DEFAULT	Use the device's default layout
LAYOUT_LEFT	Place image left
LAYOUT_RIGHT	Place image right
LAYOUT_CENTER	Center image
LAYOUT_NEWLINE_BEFORE	Start a new line and then draw the image
LAYOUT_NEWLINE_AFTER	Draw the image and then start a new line

Table 6-5.   *ImageItem Layout Directives*

You can modify the image layout after the image is displayed on the screen by calling the getLayout() method and setLayout() method. The getLayout() method returns the current layout directive of an instance of an ImageItem. The setLayout() method replaces the current layout with a new layout whose directive is passed as a parameter to the setLayout() method.

Likewise, you can modify the label and alternate text associated with an image by calling the getLabel() method, setLabel method, getAltText() method, and setAltText() method. The getLabel() and getAltText() methods retrieve the current label and alternate text, and the setLabel() and setAltText() methods are called to replace them. Both the setLabel() and setAltText() methods require one parameter, which is the replacement text.

The image itself is replaceable by calling the getImage() method and the setImage() method. The getImage() method fetches the current image associated with the instance of the ImageItem, and the setImage() method associates a new image with the instance. The setImage() method requires you to pass it an instance of an Image class. Therefore, you'll need to create a new instance of the Image class for the new image before calling the setImage() method.

Creating an Instance of an ImageItem Class

Listing 6-21 contains the JAD file for Listing 6-22, which illustrates how to create instances of an Image class and an ImageItem class and then display an immutable image on the screen. The necessary variables are declared at the beginning of the program and are assigned relative objects within the ImmutableImage constructor.

The ImmutableImage constructor is slightly different from constructors of other examples in this chapter because it includes a try { } block. The try { } block contains statements that create an instance of the Image class and an instance of the ImageItem class and then associates the image item with the form. These statements are placed within the try { } block to detect an exception that is thrown if the file name passed to the createImage() method isn't found.

Creating an Instance of an ImageItem Class

Listed here are the steps required to create an instance of an ImageItem class:

1. Declare references.

2. Obtain a reference to the instance of the Display class.

3. Create an instance of a Command class to exit the MIDlet.

4. Create an instance of the Form class.

5. Associate the instance of the Command class to the instance of the Form class.

6. Associate a CommandListener with the instance of the Form class.

7. Create an instance of the Image class.

8. Create an instance of the ImageItem class.

9. Place the image on its own line to the left of the screen and display "My Image" whenever the image cannot be displayed.

10. Associate the instance of the ImageItem class to the form.

11. Display an alert dialog box if the image cannot be found.

12. Display the instance of the Form class on the screen.

13. Evaluate the command selected by the user.

14. If the Exit command is selected, terminate the MIDlet.

The first statement within the try { } block calls the createImage() method and passes the name of the file that contains the image we want displayed on the screen. Obviously, you should replace the image "myimage.png" with the file name of your own image.

The next statement creates an instance of an ImageItem class. Notice that a null is passed as the first parameter to the constructor of the ImageItem class because there is no label for the image. The next parameter is reference to the image created by calling the createImage() method in the previous statement. The third parameter contains three layout directives. The first directive states that the image must appear below the previous image or text on the screen. The second layout directive requests that the image appear left on the screen. And the last layout directive states that no other images or text should appear on the same line on the screen as the image. The image item is then appended to the form.

An exception is thrown if for some reason myimage.png cannot be loaded into the instance of the Image class. The catch { } block traps the exception and displays an alert message that a problem exists with the myimage.png file. Barring an exception being thrown, the form and image are displayed on the screen when the startApp() method is called to invoke the setCurrent() method. The rest of Listing 6-22 is nearly identical to previous listings shown in this chapter.

Listing 6-21
The JAD
file for
Listing 6-22

```
MIDlet-Name: ImmutableImage
MIDlet-Version: 1.0
MIDlet-Vendor: MyCompany
MIDlet-Jar-URL: ImmutableImage.jar
MIDlet-1: ImmutableImage, , ImmutableImage
MicroEdition-Configuration: CLDC-1.0
MicroEdition-Profile: MIDP-1.0
MIDlet-JAR-SIZE: 100
```

Listing 6-22
Displaying an
immutable
image

```
import javax.microedition.midlet.*;
import javax.microedition.lcdui.*;
public class ImmutableImage extends MIDlet
                               implements CommandListener
{
  private Display display;
  private Form form;
  private Command exit;
  private Image image;
  private ImageItem imageItem;
  public ImmutableImage()
  {
    display = Display.getDisplay(this);
    exit = new Command("Exit", Command.EXIT, 1);
    form = new Form("Immutable Image Example");
    form.addCommand(exit);
    form.setCommandListener(this);
    try
    {
      image = Image.createImage("myimage.png");
      imageItem = new ImageItem(null, image,
                    ImageItem.LAYOUT_NEWLINE_BEFORE |
                    ImageItem.LAYOUT_LEFT |
                    ImageItem.LAYOUT_NEWLINE_AFTER, "My Image");
     form.append(imageItem);
    }
    catch (java.io.IOException error)
    {
     Alert alert = new Alert("Error", "Cannot load myimage.png.",
                           null, null);
     alert.setTimeout(Alert.FOREVER);
     alert.setType(AlertType.ERROR);
     display.setCurrent(alert);
```

```
      }
    }
    public void startApp()
    {
      display.setCurrent(form);
    }
    public void pauseApp()
    {
    }
    public void destroyApp(boolean unconditional)
    {
    }
    public void commandAction(Command command, Displayable Displayable)
    {
      if (command == exit)
        {
          destroyApp(false);
          notifyDestroyed();
        }
    }
}
```

List Class

The List class is used to display a list of items on the screen from which the user can select one or multiple items. There are three formats for the List class: radio buttons, check boxes, and an implicit list that does not use a radio button or check box icon (see Table 6-2). As you can probably gather from the description of a List class, it is functionally similar to the ChoiceGroup class discussed previously in this chapter. This is because both the List class and the ChoiceGroup class implement the Choice interface. The Choice interface defines methods to retrieve a selection and remove a selection, among other maintenance functionality.

A List class differs from the ChoiceGroup class by the way events of each instance are handled by a MIDlet. As you recall from the discussion about the ChoiceGroup class, an ItemStateListener is used to listen to events generated by an instance of a ChoiceGroup class. Those events are then passed along to the itemStateChanged() method for processing. Likewise, a commandAction() method is used to process command events, as described in the "Item Class" section of this chapter.

In contrast, a list does not generate an item state change event; therefore, a Command needs to be added to initiate processing. For example, no event is generated when a user selects a radio button or check box item with a list. Those selections are received by the MIDlet only after an instance of a Command class is chosen. However, a command event is automatically generated when the user selects an item from an instance of an implicit formatted List class. Typically, an implicit formatted List class is used to create a menu. The commandAction() method is automatically called to process the menu selection without requiring the user to select a command to process the selection.

A List class is derived from the Screen class and does not require a container. In contrast, the ChoiceGroup class is derived from the Item class and requires an instance of a Form class to contain the instance of the ChoiceGroup class.

You can create an instance of the List class with or without list items. An instance is created without list items by passing the constructor of the List class two parameters. The first parameter is a string that contains the titles of the list, and the other parameter is the format of the list (see Table 6-2), commonly referred to as the listType.

You can include list items when creating the instance of a List class by passing two additional parameters to the List class constructor. The first two parameters are title and listType. The third parameter is a string array whose elements contain list items that can be selected by the user of your MIDlet. The fourth parameter is an array of instances of the Image class, each associated with a corresponding list item.

List items can be added to an instance of a List object by calling the append() method or insert() method. The append() method requires two parameters. The first parameter is the string that contains the new list item, and the second parameter is an instance of the Image class of an image that is associated with the new list item. The new list item is appended to the end of the list.

The insert() method is very similar in design to the append() method, except the new list item is inserted within the list. Three parameters are necessary for the insert() method. The first parameter is the index number of the list item above which the new list item is inserted. The other two parameters are the same as the parameters of the append() method.

You can retrieve the list item selected by the user by calling the getSelectedIndex() method. The getSelectedIndex() method returns the index number of the selected list item. You pass the returned index number as the parameter to the getString() method, which returns the string of the selected list item, which is then processed by the commandAction() method.

If the instance of the List class is a check box, then call the getSelectedFlag() method. The getSelectedFlag() method requires one parameter, which is a boolean array. The method then populates the boolean array with the selected flag value of each list item. You can then evaluate each array element to determine which list items the user selected. The size() method returns the number of items on the list and can be used to set the size of the boolean array.

One or more list items can become the default selection by calling the setSelectedIndex() method or the setSelectedFlags() method. The setSelectedFlags() method is used to set the selected flag of one list item and requires two parameters. The first parameter is the index number of the list item being selected, and the other parameter is a boolean value, where true signifies that the list item is selected and false signifies unselected. The setSelectedIndex() method performs an operation similar to the setSelectedFlags(), except the setSelectedIndex() sets the selected status for all list items. The setSelectedIndex()

requires one parameter, which is a boolean array containing the selected status for the entire list.

Any list item can be replaced by calling the set() method. The set() method requires three parameters. The first is the index number of the list item being replaced. The second parameter is the string replacing the string of the specified list item. And the last parameter is an Image object that contains the image associated with the replacement list item.

A list item can be removed from the list by calling the delete() method. The delete() method requires one parameter, which is the index number of the list item being deleted.

Creating an Instance of a List Class

The listings in this section illustrate how to implement the three formats of a List class in your MIDlet. Listing 6-23 contains the JAD file for Listing 6-24, which creates an instance of an implicit List class. Listing 6-25 contains the JAD file for Listing 6-26, which creates a check box instance of a List class, and Listing 6-27 is the JAD file for Listing 6-28, which creates a radio button instance of a List class.

Listing 6-24 creates an implicit list called "Menu:" that contains two options: New and Open (Figure 6-10). This listing is constructed like other listings in this chapter,

Figure 6-10. *Displaying an implicit list on the screen*

by declaring variables at the beginning of the MIDlet and then creating objects and assigning those objects to variables within the ListImplicit constructor.

Passing two parameters to the constructor of the List object creates the instance of the List class. The first parameter is the title of the instance, "Menu:", and the other parameter is the List object format type IMPLICIT.

You can modify this listing and assign list items and related images when creating the instance by also passing an array of list items as the third parameter and the array of images as the fourth parameter to the constructor. However, in this example the append() method is called to append list items to the instance. The first parameter to the append() method is the string that is displayed on the list, and the other parameter is null because no image is associated with the list item. You pass an instance of the Image object referencing the image as the second parameter of the append() method if you want to associate an image with a list item.

Notice that the Exit command is added to the instance of the List object. In previous examples, the Exit command was added to an instance of a Form object. Remember that the List class and the Form class are both directly derived from the Screen class. Therefore, the List class isn't contained within the Form class, requiring that instances of the Command class be directly added to the instance of the List class.

The instance of the List class is then passed to the setCurrent() method within the startApp() method to display the list on the screen. Also remember that a command event is automatically generated when the user selects an item on the list. This command is identified as List.SELECT_COMMAND, which is tested within the commandAction() method. The List.SELECT_COMMAND simply informs the MIDlet that an item on the list was selected. It does not identify the selected item.

Creating an Instance of an Implicit List Class

Listed here are the steps required to create an instance of an implicit List class:

1. Declare references.

2. Obtain a reference to the instance of the Display class.

3. Create an instance of a Command class to exit the MIDlet.

4. Create an instance of the List class using the IMPLICIT type.

5. Append items to the instance of the List class.

6. Associate the instance of the Command class to the instance of the List class.

7. Associate a CommandListener with the instance of the List class.

8. Display the instance of the List class on the screen.

9. Evaluate the command selected by the user.

10. If the Exit command is selected, terminate the MIDlet.

11. If an item from the instance of the List class is selected, display the text of the item in an alert dialog box.

First, the getSelectedIndex() method is called to return the index number of the selected list item. Index numbers are assigned sequentially beginning with zero as each item is appended to the list. This means that the first item is "New" and has the index value zero. The second item has the index number of one as a string value of "Open."

The if statement evaluates the value returned by the getSelectedIndex() method. An alert is displayed when a match occurs. The alert shows the list item selected by the user of the MIDlet. The MIDlet terminates like the other examples in this chapter— when the user selects the Exit command.

Listing 6-23
The JAD
file for
Listing 6-24

```
MIDlet-Name: ListImplicit
MIDlet-Version: 1.0
MIDlet-Vendor: MyCompany
MIDlet-Jar-URL: ListImplicit.jar
MIDlet-1: ListImplicit, , ListImplicit
MicroEdition-Configuration: CLDC-1.0
MicroEdition-Profile: MIDP-1.0
MIDlet-JAR-SIZE: 100
```

Listing 6-24
Displaying
an implicit
List class

```
import javax.microedition.midlet.*;
import javax.microedition.lcdui.*;
public class ListImplicit extends MIDlet implements CommandListener
{
  private Display display;
  private List list;
  private Command exit;
  Alert alert;
  public ListImplicit()
  {
    display = Display.getDisplay(this);
    exit = new Command("Exit", Command.EXIT, 1);
    list = new List("Menu:", List.IMPLICIT);
    list.append("New",null);
    list.append("Open",null);
    list.addCommand(exit);
    list.setCommandListener(this);
  }
  public void startApp()
  {
    display.setCurrent(list);
  }
  public void pauseApp()
  {
```

```
      }
   public void destroyApp(boolean unconditional)
   {
   }
   public void commandAction(Command command, Displayable displayable)
   {
      if (command == List.SELECT_COMMAND)
      {
         String selection = list.getString(list.getSelectedIndex());
         alert = new Alert("Option Selected", selection, null, null);
         alert.setTimeout(Alert.FOREVER);
         alert.setType(AlertType.INFO);
         display.setCurrent(alert);
      }
      else if (command == exit)
      {
         destroyApp(false);
         notifyDestroyed();
      }
   }
}
```

Listing 6-26 displays an instance of a List class in the form of check boxes (Figure 6-11). This instance is created similar to Listing 6-12 except that the format type of the instance is MULTIPLE. Four items are added to the list by calling the append() method. None of the items is associated with an image, so the second parameter of the append() method is null.

Unlike the implicit formatted instance of the List class, the multiple format does not automatically generate a command event. Instead, you must create an instance of the Command object that, when selected, causes the MIDlet to process the list. The Submit command is used in this example for that purpose. The list is displayed the same way as in Listing 6-24.

The if statement within the actionCommand() method traps the submit event and causes statements within the if statement to process the user selections. First, a boolean array is declared having the size of the value returned by calling the size() method, which is the number of items in the instance of the List class. The StringBuffer is also created.

Next, the getSelectedFlags() method is called and is passed the boolean array. The getSelectedFlags() method populates the boolean array with the selected status of each item on the list. The MIDlet then steps through each item using a for loop. The selected flag status of the boolean array element is compared to the boolean value true for each iteration of the for loop. If the value of the boolean array element is true, the getString() method is called and passed the index number of the current boolean array element, which is the same index number of the item on the list. The getString() method returns

Figure 6-11.   *Displaying a list in the form of check boxes*

the text of that item, which is then appended to the instance of the StringBuffer class called message.

An alert is displayed on the screen containing the text of each item selected by the user. The Submit command is then removed from the screen, leaving the user to close the alert dialog box and then terminate the MIDlet by selecting the Exit command.

Listing 6-25
The JAD
file for
Listing 6-26

```
MIDlet-Name: ListCheckBox
MIDlet-Version: 1.0
MIDlet-Vendor: MyCompany
MIDlet-Jar-URL: ListCheckBox.jar
MIDlet-1: ListCheckBox, , ListCheckBox
MicroEdition-Configuration: CLDC-1.0
MicroEdition-Profile: MIDP-1.0
MIDlet-JAR-SIZE: 100
```

Creating an Instance of a Check Box–Formatted List Class

Listed here are the steps required to create an instance of a check box–formatted List class:

1. Declare references.
2. Obtain a reference to the instance of the Display class.
3. Create an instance of the List class using the MULTIPLE type.
4. Append items to the instance of the List class.
5. Create an instance of a Command class to exit the MIDlet.
6. Create an instance of a Command class to submit the instance of the List class for processing.
7. Associate instances of the Command class to the instance of the List class.
8. Associate a CommandListener with the instance of the List class.
9. Display the instance of the List class on the screen.
10. Evaluate the command selected by the user.
11. If the Exit command is selected, terminate the MIDlet.
12. If the Submit command is selected, process the instance of the List class.
13. Retrieve the status of the selected flags of each item on the list.
14. Evaluate each status of the selected flags.
15. If the status is true, append the text to the message.
16. Display the message containing text of the selected check boxes within an alert dialog box.

Listing 6-26
Displaying and manipulating a check box List class

```
import javax.microedition.midlet.*;
import javax.microedition.lcdui.*;
public class ListCheckBox extends MIDlet implements CommandListener
{
    private Display display;
    private Command exit;
    private Command submit;
    private List list;
    public ListCheckBox()
    {
```

```
    display = Display.getDisplay(this);
    list = new List("Select Media", List.MULTIPLE);
    list.append("Books", null);
    list.append("Movies", null);
    list.append("Television", null);
    list.append("Radio", null);
    exit = new Command("Exit", Command.EXIT, 1);
    submit = new Command("Submit", Command.SCREEN,2);
    list.addCommand(exit);
    list.addCommand(submit);
    list.setCommandListener(this);
}
public void startApp()
{
  display.setCurrent(list);
}
public void pauseApp()
{
}
public void destroyApp(boolean unconditional)
{
}
public void commandAction(Command command, Displayable Displayable)
{
  if (command == submit)
  {
    boolean choice[] = new boolean[list.size()];
    StringBuffer message = new StringBuffer();
    list.getSelectedFlags(choice);
    for (int x = 0; x < choice.length; x++)
    {
      if (choice[x])
      {
        message.append(list.getString(x));
        message.append(" ");
      }
    }
    Alert alert = new Alert("Choice", message.toString(),
                            null, null);
    alert.setTimeout(Alert.FOREVER);
    alert.setType(AlertType.INFO);
    display.setCurrent(alert);
```

```
        list.removeCommand(submit);
    }
    else if (command == exit)
    {
      destroyApp(false);
      notifyDestroyed();
    }
  }
}
```

Listing 6-28 displays a list of radio buttons. You'll notice that the construction of Listing 6-28 is nearly identical to the check box listing in Listing 6-26 (Figure 6-12). There are two differences between these listings. First, the instance of the List class uses the EXCLUSIVE format in Listing 6-28. This of course is the radio button format. The other difference is within the commandAction() method.

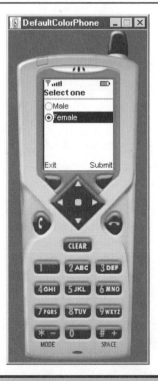

Figure 6-12.   *Displaying a list in the form of radio buttons*

Creating an Instance of a Radio Button–Formatted List Class

Listed here are the steps required to create an instance of a radio button–formatted List class:

1. Declare references.
2. Obtain a reference to the instance of the Display class.
3. Create an instance of the List class using the EXCLUSIVE type.
4. Append items to the instance of the List class.
5. Create an instance of a Command class to exit the MIDlet.
6. Create an instance of a Command class to submit the instance of the List class for processing.
7. Associate instances of the Command class to the instance of the List class.
8. Associate a CommandListener with the instance of the List class.
9. Display the instance of the List class on the screen.
10. Evaluate the command selected by the user.
11. If the Exit command is selected, terminate the MIDlet.
12. If the Submit command is selected, process the instance of the List class.
13. Retrieve the index number of the selected item from the instance of the List class.
14. Retrieve the text of the selected item using the item's index number.
15. Display the text of the selected radio button in an alert dialog box.

The user of this MIDlet still must select an item from the list and activate the Submit command before the selection is processed. Since there is only one possible selection, the MIDlet calls the getSelectedIndex() method to return the index number of the selected list item. This index number is then passed to the getString() method to retrieve the text of the item, which is used as the second parameter to the constructor of the Alert class. As with Listing 6-26, the alert dialog box displays the list item that was selected by the user. The remaining code in Listing 6-28 is the same as in Listing 6-26.

Listing 6-27
The JAD file for Listing 6-28

```
MIDlet-Name: ListRadioButtons
MIDlet-Version: 1.0
MIDlet-Vendor: MyCompany
MIDlet-Jar-URL: ListRadioButtons.jar
MIDlet-1: ListRadioButtons, , ListRadioButtons
```

```
MicroEdition-Configuration: CLDC-1.0
MicroEdition-Profile: MIDP-1.0
MIDlet-JAR-SIZE: 100
```

```java
import javax.microedition.midlet.*;
import javax.microedition.lcdui.*;
public class ListRadioButtons extends MIDlet implements CommandListener
{
  private Display display;
  private Command exit;
  private Command submit;
  private List list;
  public ListRadioButtons()
  {
    display = Display.getDisplay(this);
    list = new List("Select one", List.EXCLUSIVE);
    list.append("Male", null);
    list.append("Female", null);
    exit = new Command("Exit", Command.EXIT, 1);
    submit = new Command("Submit", Command.SCREEN,2);
    list.addCommand(exit);
    list.addCommand(submit);
    list.setCommandListener(this);
  }
  public void startApp()
  {
    display.setCurrent(list);
  }
  public void pauseApp()
  {
  }
  public void destroyApp(boolean unconditional)
  {
  }
  public void commandAction(Command command, Displayable Displayable)
  {
    if (command == submit)
    {
      Alert alert = new Alert("Choice",
                      list.getString(list.getSelectedIndex()),
                      null, null);
      alert.setTimeout(Alert.FOREVER);
```

```
                alert.setType(AlertType.INFO);
                display.setCurrent(alert);
                list.removeCommand(submit);
            }
            else if (command == exit)
            {
                destroyApp(false);
                notifyDestroyed();
            }
        }
    }
```

TextBox Class

The TextBox class is very similar to a TextField class, discussed previously in this chapter. Both are used to receive multiple lines of textual data from a user and constrain text that can be entered using the constraint directives shown in Table 6-4. You can request that a maximum number of characters be allowed in instances of both the TextBox class and the TextField class. However, the device determines the actual size of both of these instances. Characters that exceed the display area of the screen become scrollable in many devices.

The TextBox class and TextField class differ in that the TextBox class is derived from the Screen class, while the TextField class is derived from the Item class. This means that an instance of the Form class cannot contain an instance of the TextBox class, while an instance of a TextField class must be contained within an instance of the Form class.

Another important difference between the TextBox class and the TextField class is that the TextBox class uses a CommandListener and cannot use an ItemStateListener. An ItemStateListener is used with an instance of the TextField class, although many times the content of an instance of the TextField class is retrieved and processed when the user selects a command associated with a form that contains the text field.

An instance of the TextBox class is created by passing four parameters to the TextBox class constructor. The first parameter is the title of the text box. The second parameter is text used to populate the instance. The third parameter is the maximum number of characters that can be entered into the instance. Keep in mind that this parameter is a request and may not be fulfilled by the device. The device determines the maximum number of characters for an instance of the TextBox class. The last parameter is the constraint used to limit the types of characters that can be placed within the instance.

The TextBox class has the same methods as found in the TextField class. Refer to the "TextField Class" section of this chapter for details on how to use these methods. You'll also find TextBox class methods in the "Quick Reference Guide" section at the end of this chapter.

Creating an Instance of a TextBox Class

Listing 6-29 contains the JAD file for Listing 6-30, which illustrates how to create an instance of the TextBox class and manipulate text entered into the text box by the user of this MIDlet. This listing displays a text box and prompts the user to enter a first name, then select the Submit command (Figure 6-13).

> **Tip** *Many of the keys on a telephone keypad are associated with three letters. Select each letter associated with a key by pressing the key multiple times. For example, the letter I is the third letter associated with key 4. You can display the letter I on the screen by pressing the key three times.*

When the Submit command is selected, it is processed by the commandAction() method (see "Item Class," earlier in this chapter). The name is copied from the text box and used to form a greeting, which then replaces the first name on the screen (Figure 6-14).

Figure 6-13. *Displaying a text box on the screen*

Figure 6-14. *Displaying the greeting on the screen*

Listing 6-30 begins very much like the other listings in this chapter, by declaring variables and then creating objects within the TextBoxCapture constructor, which are then assigned to those variables. You'll notice that an instance of a TextBox class is created with the title "First Name:". The instance does not contain any text when first displayed on the screen. The instance can receive any characters based on the ANY constraint, and a request is made to limit the number of characters that can be contained in the instance to 30 characters.

After the user enters a first name and selects the Submit command, the MIDlet calls the getString() method from within the commandAction() method to retrieve the contents of the text box. The first name is then concatenated to the expression "Hello," and the concatenated string is passed as a parameter to the setString() method. The setString() method replaces the contents of the text box with the string passed as the parameter.

Creating an Instance of a TextBox Class

Listed here are the steps required to create an instance of a TextBox class:

1. Declare references.
2. Obtain a reference to the instance of the Display class.
3. Create an instance of a Command class to submit the instance of the List class for processing.
4. Create an instance of a Command class to exit the MIDlet.
5. Create an instance of a TextBox class and accept any characters.
6. Associate instances of the Command class to the instance of the TextBox class.
7. Associate a CommandListener with the instance of the TextBox class.
8. Display the instance of the TextBox class on the screen.
9. Evaluate the command selected by the user.
10. If the Exit command is selected, terminate the MIDlet.
11. If the Submit command is selected, process the instance of the TextBox class.
12. Retrieve the text of the instance of the TextBox class.
13. Concatenate the text to the greeting "Hello,".
14. Replace the text of the instance with the concatenated text.
15. Remove the Submit command from the screen.

The Submit command is then removed from the screen, making the Exit command the only available option for the user to select. The Exit command terminates the MIDlet.

Listing 6-29
The JAD file for Listing 6-30

```
MIDlet-Name: TextBoxCapture
MIDlet-Version: 1.0
MIDlet-Vendor: MyCompany
MIDlet-Jar-URL: TextBoxCapture.jar
MIDlet-1: TextBoxCapture, , TextBoxCapture
MicroEdition-Configuration: CLDC-1.0
MicroEdition-Profile: MIDP-1.0
MIDlet-JAR-SIZE: 100
```

Listing 6-30
Interacting
with an
instance of a
TextBox class

```
import javax.microedition.midlet.*;
import javax.microedition.lcdui.*;
public class TextBoxCapture extends MIDlet implements CommandListener
{
  private Display display;
  private TextBox textbox;
  private Command submit;
  private Command exit;
  public TextBoxCapture()
  {
   display = Display.getDisplay(this);
   submit = new Command("Submit", Command.SCREEN, 1);
   exit = new Command("Exit", Command.EXIT, 1);
   textbox = new TextBox("First Name:", "", 30, TextField.ANY);
   textbox.addCommand(exit);
   textbox.addCommand(submit);
   textbox.setCommandListener(this);
  }
  public void startApp()
  {
   display.setCurrent(textbox);
  }
  public void pauseApp()
  {
  }
  public void destroyApp(boolean unconditional)
  {
  }
  public void commandAction(Command command, Displayable displayable)
  {
   if (command == submit)
   {
     textbox.setString("Hello, " + textbox.getString());
     textbox.removeCommand(submit);
   }
   else if (command == exit)
   {
      destroyApp(false);
      notifyDestroyed();
   }
  }
}
```

Ticker Class

The Ticker class is used to scroll text horizontally on the screen much like a stock ticker scrolls stock prices across the screen. An instance of the Ticker class can be associated with any class derived from the Screen class and be shared among screens. An instance of a Ticker object is created by passing the constructor of the Ticker class a string containing the text that is to be scrolled across the screen. You cannot control the location on the screen where scrolling occurs. Likewise, there is no control over the speed of the scrolling. The device that runs the MIDlet controls both location and speed.

You can retrieve the text associated with an instance of the Ticker class by calling the getString() method. You can replace the text currently scrolling across the screen by calling the setString() method. The setString() method requires one parameter, which is a string containing the replacement text.

Listing 6-31 contains the JAD file for Listing 6-32, which illustrates how to create an instance of the Ticker class and associate the instance with an instance of a List class.

Creating an Instance of a Ticker Class

Listed here are the steps required to create an instance of a Ticker class:

1. Declare references.
2. Obtain a reference to the instance of the Display class.
3. Create an instance of a Command class to exit the MIDlet.
4. Create an instance of a Command class to begin processing.
5. Create an instance of the Ticker class and initialize text of the instance.
6. Create an instance of the List class.
7. Append items to the instance of the List class.
8. Associate instances of the Command class to the instance of the List class.
9. Associate a CommandListener with the instance of the List class.
10. Associate the instance of the Ticker class with the instance of the List class.
11. Display the instance of the List class on the screen.
12. Evaluate the command selected by the user.
13. If the Exit command is selected, terminate the MIDlet.
14. If the Submit command is selected, process the selection.
15. Change the text of the instance of the Ticker class to reflect the selection.

This example creates a set of radio buttons that contain two options (Figure 6-15). The first option is called "Technology" and the other "Entertainment." When the MIDlet runs, fictitious stock symbols and stock prices representing the technology industry scroll across the screen. The user is prompted to select a radio button, then select the Submit command. The Submit command causes the MIDlet to display the desired industry stock symbols and prices scrolling across the ticker.

This listing begins like the other listings in this chapter. You'll notice that an instance of the Ticker class is created within the TickerList constructor. Technology stock symbols and prices are the default text appearing on the ticker. The MIDlet then creates an EXCLUSIVE instance of the List class and assigns the instance two list items called Technology and Entertainment by calling the append() method. The second parameter of the append() method is null since no image is associated with these list items. The ticker is then associated with the list by calling the setTicker() and passing the reference to the ticker instance as a parameter to the setTicker() method.

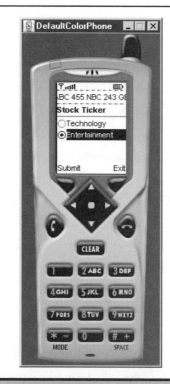

Figure 6-15. *Displaying a ticker on the screen*

The actionCommand() method is the place in the MIDlet where the request is processed. First, the actionCommand() determines whether the Submit command is selected. If so, the getSelectedIndex() method is called to retrieve the index number of the item that the user selected from the list. Remember, index number zero is the first item appended to the list. Index numbers are assigned sequentially as items are appended to the list.

Depending on the user's selection, the MIDlet replaces the current text of the ticker with new text by calling the setString() method. Text continues to flow across the screen until the user selects the Exit command to terminate the MIDlet.

Listing 6-31
The JAD
file for
Listing 6-32

```
MIDlet-Name: TickerList
MIDlet-Version: 1.0
MIDlet-Vendor: MyCompany
MIDlet-Jar-URL: TickerList.jar
MIDlet-1: TickerList, , TickerList
MicroEdition-Configuration: CLDC-1.0
MicroEdition-Profile: MIDP-1.0
MIDlet-JAR-SIZE: 100
```

Listing 6-32
Interacting
with an
instance of a
Ticker class

```
import javax.microedition.midlet.*;
import javax.microedition.lcdui.*;
public class TickerList extends MIDlet implements CommandListener
{
  private Display display;
  private List list;
  private final String tech;
  private final String entertain;
  private Ticker ticker;
  private Command exit;
  private Command submit;
  public TickerList()
  {
    display = Display.getDisplay(this);
    tech = new String ("IBM 55 MSFT 32 SUN 52 CISCO 87");
    entertain = new String ("CBS 75 ABC 455 NBC 243 GE 21");
    exit = new Command("Exit", Command.SCREEN, 1);
    submit = new Command("Submit", Command.SCREEN, 1);
    ticker = new Ticker(tech);
    list = new List("Stock Ticker", Choice.EXCLUSIVE);
    list.append("Technology", null);
```

```
      list.append("Entertainment", null);
      list.addCommand(exit);
      list.addCommand(submit);
      list.setCommandListener(this);
      list.setTicker(ticker);
  }
  public void startApp()
  {
    display.setCurrent(list);
  }
  public void pauseApp()
  {
  }
  public void destroyApp(boolean unconditional)
  {
  }
  public void commandAction(Command command, Displayable display)
  {
    if (command == exit)
    {
      destroyApp(true);
      notifyDestroyed();
    }
    else if (command == submit)
    {
      if (list.getSelectedIndex() == 0)
      {
        ticker.setString (tech);
      }
      else
      {
        ticker.setString(entertain);
      }
    }
  }
}
```

Quick Reference Guide

This guide provides an overview of classes used by J2ME for the Screen object and derived classes, along with the Ticker object. Full details of these classes and all Java classes and interfaces are available at java.sun.com.

javax.microedition.lcdui.Screen Class

Method	Description
String getTitle()	Retrieve the screen's title.
void setTitle(String string)	Set the screen's title.
Ticker getTicker()	Retrieve the screen's Ticker.
void setTicker(Ticker ticker)	Set the screen's Ticker.

javax.microedition.lcdui.Alert Class

Method	Description
Alert(String title)	Create an instance of the Alert class.
Alert(String title, String message, Image image, AlertType, alertType)	Create an instance of the Alert class with an Image and AlertType.
Image getImage()	Retrieve an instance of the Alert class image.
void setImage(Image image)	Associate an image with an instance of the Alert class.
String getString()	Get an instance of the Alert class message.
void setString(String str)	Set an instance of the Alert class message.
int getDefaultTimeout()	Retrieve an instance of the Alert class default time.
int getTimeout()	Retrieve actual time an instance of the Alert class will be displayed.
void setTimeout(int time)	Set the display time of an instance of the Alert class.
AlertType getType()	Retrieve the AlertType of an instance of the Alert class.
void setType(AlertType type)	Set the AlertType of an instance of the Alert class.

Javax.microedition.lcdui.Form Class

Method	Description
Form (String title)	Create an instance of the Form class with a title.
Form (String title, Item[] items)	Create an instance of the Form class and append the specified list of array items onto the instance.
Int append(Image image)	Append an instance of the Image class to an instance of the Form class.
Int append(Item item)	Append an instance of the Item class or subclass to an instance of the Form class.
Int append(String string)	Append an instance of the String class to an instance of the Form class.
Void delete(int index)	Remove an instance of the Item class or subclass specified by the index from an instance of the Form class.
Void insert (int index, Item item)	Insert an instance of the Item class or subclass before the instance of the Item class whose position is specified by the index.
Item get(int index)	Retrieve an instance of the Item class or subclass whose position is specified by the index.
Void set(int index, Item item)	Replace an existing instance of the Item class or subclass whose position is specified by the index with the instance of the Item class or subclass reference in the second parameter.
Void setItemStateListener(ItemStatelistener itemStateListener)	Associate an ItemStateListener with an instance of the Item class or subclass.
Int size()	Retrieve the number of instances of the Item class or subclass in an instance of the Form class.
String getLabel()	Retrieve the label associated with an instance of an Item class.
Void setLabel(String label)	Associate a label with an instance of an Item class.

javax.microedition.lcdui.ChoiceGroup Class

Method	Description
ChoiceGroup (String label, int choiceType)	Create an instance of an empty ChoiceGroup class, where label is the title of the instance and choiceType is the type of instance.
ChoiceGroup(String label, int choiceType, String[] string, Image image)	Create an instance of the ChoiceGroup class, where label is the title of the instance and choiceType is the type of instance, and use the image with the instance. Also populate the instance with options contained in the string.
int append (String string, Image image)	Place an option at the end of other options in an instance of the Choice Group class, and associate the image with the option.
void delete (int index)	Remove the option identified by the index number from an instance of the ChoiceGroup class, and associate the image with the option.
void insert (int index, String string, Image image)	Insert an option into an instance of the ChoiceGroup class before the option identified by the index number.
void set (int index, String string, Image image)	Replace an option identified by the index number with the option specified in the string and image.
String getString (int index)	Retrieve the string associated with the option identified by the index number.
Image getImage(int index)	Retrieve the image associated with the option identified by the index number.
int getSelectedIndex()	Retrieve the index associated with an option.
void setSelectedIndex(int index, boolean selected)	Select the option identified by the index and whether the option is selected (true) or unselected (false).
int getSelectedFlags (boolean[] array)	Retrieve the selection status of options and store them in an array.

javax.microedition.lcdui.ChoiceGroup Class

Method	Description
void setSelectedFlag (boolean[] array)	Set the selection status of options stored in an array.
boolean isSelected (int index)	Determine whether the user selected the option identified by the index number.
int size()	Determine the number of options there are in an instance of the ChoiceGroup.

javax.microedition.lcdui.DateField Class

Method	Description
DateField (String label, int mode)	Create an instance of the DateField class that contains the specified label and uses the specified mode.
DateField (String label, int mode, TimeZone timeZone)	Create an instance of the DateField class that contains the specified label and uses the specified mode and time zone.
Date getDate()	Retrieve the date/time from an instance of the DateField class.
void setDate (Date date)	Set the date for an instance of the DateField class.
int getInputMode()	Retrieve the input mode of an instance of the DateField class.
void setInputMode(int mode)	Replace the existing date field mode with a different mode.

javax.microedition.lcdui.Gauge Class

Method	Description
Gauge(String label, boolean interactive, int maxValue, int initialValue)	Create an instance of the Gauge class, where label is the caption for the instance, interactive is a boolean value indicating whether the instance is interactive, maxValue is the maximum value displayed in the gauge, and the initialValue is the beginning value displayed in the gauge.
int getValue()	Retrieve the current value of the gauge.

javax.microedition.lcdui.Gauge Class

Method	Description
void setValue (int value)	Set a new value for the gauge.
int getMaxValue()	Retrieve the maximum value of the gauge.
void setMaxValue(int maxValue)	Set the maximum value of the gauge.
boolean isInteractive()	Determine whether the gauge is interactive.

javax.microedition.lcdui.StringItem Class

Method	Description
StringItem (String label, String text)	Create an instance of a StringItem class, where the label is text describing the StringItem class, and text is the text displayed on the screen.
String getText()	Retrieve the text portion of an instance of a StringItem class.
Void setText (String text)	Replace the text portion of an instance of a StringItem class.
String getLabel()	Retrieve the label portion of an instance of a StringItem class.
Void setLabel (String text)	Replace the label portion of an instance of a StringItem class.

javax.microedition.lcdui.TextField Class

Method	Description
TextField (String label, String text, int maxSize, int constraint)	Create an instance of a TextField class.
void delete (int offset, int length)	Remove characters from a TextField class at a specified offset.
void insert (String src, int position)	Insert String at a specified offset in a TextField class at a specified offset.
void insert (char[] data, int offset, int length, int position)	Insert characters from an array into a TextField class at a specified offset.
void setChars (char[] data, int offset, int length)	Replace characters of a TextField class with characters from an array.

javax.microedition.lcdui.TextField Class

Method	Description
void setString(String text)	Replace characters of a TextField class with characters in a string.
int getChars (char[] data)	Copy contents of a TextField class into an array.
String getString()	Copy contents of the TextField class into a string.
int getConstraints()	Retrieve the constraint of a TextField class.
void setConstraints (int constraint)	Set the constraint of a TextField class.
int getMaxSize()	Retrieve the maximum number of characters of a TextField class.
int setMaxSize (int maxsize)	Set the maximum number of characters of a TextField class.
int getCaretPosition()	Retrieve the cursor position within a TextField class.
int size()	Retrieve the number of characters in a TextField class.

javax.microedition.lcdui.Image Class

Method	Description
static Image create Image (String name)	Create an immutable image, where name is the name of a resource.
Static Image createImage (Image source)	Create an immutable image, where source is reference to an existing Image.
Static Image createImage(byte[] imageData, int imageOffset, int imageLength)	Create an immutable image, where byte is an array of data representing the image, imageOffset is the starting position of the image, and imageLength is the length of the image.
Static Image createImage(int width, int height)	Create a mutable image that has a specified width and height.
Graphics getGraphics()	Retrieve reference to an instance of the Graphics class.
Int getHeight()	Retrieve the image height.
Int getwidth()	Retrieve the image width.
boolean isMutable()	Determine whether an image is a mutable image.

javax.microedition.lcdui.ImageItem Class

Method	Description
ImageItem(String label, Image im, int layout, String altText)	Create an instance of the ImageItem class, where label is text describing the image, im is reference to the image, layout is the layout directive, and altText is displayed if the image cannot be shown on the device.
Image getImage()	Retrieve an image associated with an ImageItem class.
voaid setImage (image im)	Associate an image with an ImageItem class.
int getLayout()	Retrieve the layout directive of an ImageItem instance.
void setLayout (int layout)	Replace the layout directive of an ImageItem instance.
String getAltText()	Retrieve the alternate text of an ImageItem instance.
void setAltText(String text)	Replace the alternate text of an ImageItem instance.

javax.microedition.lcdui.List Class

Method	Description
List (String title, int listType)	Create an instance of the List class without assigning elements to the list. The title is the title of the list, and the listType is the type of list being created.
List (String title, int listType, String[] stringElements, Image[] imageElements)	Create an instance of the List class and assign elements to the list. The title is the title of the list; the listType is the type of list being created; stringElements is an array of strings containing text for the list; and imageElements is an array of images associated with each list element.
int append (String stringPart, Image imagePart)	Append an element to the end of the list, where stringPart is the text of the element, and imagePart is the image associated with the element.
void delete(int indexNum)	Remove an element from a list, where the element being removed is identified by the indexNum.

javax.microedition.lcdui.List Class

void insert (int indexNum, String stringPart, Image imagePart)	Insert an element into the list at a specific position within the list, where indexNum is the position within the list where the element will be located; stringPart is the text of the element; and imagePart is the image associated with the element.
void set(int indexNum, String stringPart, Image imagePart)	Replace an element in the list at a specific position within the list, where indexNum is the position within the list where the element will be located; stringPart is the text of the element; and imagePart is the image associated with the element.
String getString (int indexNum)	Retrieve the text of an element from a specific position in the list, where indexNum identifies the position of the element.
Image getImage(int indexNum)	Retrieve the image of an element from a specific position in the list, where indexNum identifies the position of the element.
int getSelectedIndex()	Retrieve index of a selected element of a list.
void setSelectedIndex(int indexNum, boolean selected)	Set the default selected flag of an element within the list, where indexNum is the index number of the element, and selected is either true or false.
int getSelectedFlag (boolean[] selectedArray_return)	Retrieve the selection status and store them in the selectedArray.
void setSelectedFlags(boolean[] selectedArray)	Set the selection status based on values stored in the selectedArray.
boolean isSelected(int indexNum)	Determine whether the element identified by indexNum is selected.
int size()	Number of elements in list.

javax.microedition.lcdui.TextBox Class

Method	Description
TextBox(String title, String text, int maxSize, int constraint)	Create a new instance of the TextBox class, where title is the title of the text box; text is the text used to populate the text box; maxSize is the requested maximum number of characters that can be entered into the text box; and constraint identifies character restrictions.

javax.microedition.lcdui.TextBox Class

Method	Description
void delete(int offset, int length)	Remove characters from a text box. Characters to be removed begin with the character specified by offset character position until the specified length is reached.
void insert(String src, int position)	Insert characters from a string into the text box, where src is the string, and position is the position within the text box to insert the characters.
void insert(char[] data, in offset, int length, int position)	Insert characters from an array into the text box, where data is the array; offset is the starting position within the array; length is the number of characters to insert; and position is the place within the text box to insert the characters.
void setChars(char[] data, int offset, int length)	Replace contents of the text box with characters in an array, where data is the array; offset is the starting position within the array; and length is the number of characters to insert.
int getChars(char[] data)	Retrieve the contents of a text box into an array, where data is the array that receives the contents of the text box.
string getString()	Retrieve the contents of a text box into a string.
int getConstraints()	Retrieve the constraints of the text box.
void setConstraints(int constraints)	Replace the constraints of a text box, where constraints contains the new constraints.
int getMaxSize()	Retrieve the maximum number of characters that can be stored in a text box.
int setMaxSize(int maxSize)	Set the maximum number of characters that can be stored in a text box, where maxSize is the requested maximum number of characters.
int getCaretPosition()	Retrieve the current cursor position within the text box.
int size()	Retrieve the current number of characters in a text box.

javax.microedition.lcdui.Ticker Class

Method	Description
Ticker(String str)	Create a new Ticker, where str is the text that appears in the ticker.
String getString()	Retrieve the text displayed by the Ticker.
void setString(String str)	Set the text displayed by the Ticker, where str is the text.

The
Complete
Reference

J2ME

Chapter 7

Low-Level Display:
Canvas

Small computing devices are still in their formative years as they evolve into *Star Trek*–like devices that handle our mundane, and some not so mundane, tasks—at any time and anywhere. However, many of these devices have already grown to a level of sophistication that is necessary for implementing a wide range of applications. Today's small computing devices are capable of running form-based applications, games that challenge the best of us, and applications that interact with remote computers. Practically any application you can imagine can be designed to operate within the confines of a small computing device.

Many applications that you develop will use a high-level user interface, usually thought of as an object that handles its own display and consists of lists, radio buttons, check boxes, images, and text. You learned how to create a high-level user interface in the previous chapter. Classes associated with the high-level interface handle the pixel-level detail necessary to draw radio buttons, check boxes, and other objects on the screen. You basically call methods and let the methods handle display.

Occasionally, you may be called upon to create an application that sizzles and wows the user with fancy graphics and animation. To get the sizzle and wow into your application, you'll need to go beyond the high-level user interface and get down and dirty into the pixel level of your application, where you control the position of every picture element that appears on the screen. This is referred to as the *low-level user interface*. You'll learn how to become the master of the low-level user interface in this chapter.

The Canvas

As you'll recall from Chapter 6, each MIDlet has one instance of the Display class, and the Display class has one derived class called the Displayable class. Everything a MIDlet displays on the screen is created by an instance of a class that is derived from the Displayable class. The Display class hierarchy is shown here:

```
public class Display
        public abstract class Displayable
                public abstract class Screen extends Displayable
                public abstract class Canvas extends Displayable
        public class Graphics
```

The Displayable class has two subclasses: Screen and Canvas. The Screen class and its derivatives are used to create high-level components that you learned about in the previous chapter. The Canvas class and its derivatives are used to gain low-level access to the display, which is necessary for graphic- and animation-based applications. A graphic is used with a canvas.

You can think of an instance of the Canvas class as an artist's canvas on which you draw images that might include text. An instance of the Graphics class is similar to the artist's tools that are used to draw an image. For example, color, lines, and arcs are some of the graphic tools available to create an image on the canvas. The Canvas class and the Graphics class give you pixel control over everything that appears on the canvas. This low-level control is particularly noticeable whenever text is placed on the canvas because you control every aspect of how characters are formed to display the text.

Let's step back to recall how you display text using the high-level user interface. First, you create an instance of a text field, text box, or string item and then associate text with the instance. Next, the setCurrent() is called and passed the instance (or a container such as a form that contains the instance). You don't need to be concerned about describing how the device's application manager is to form each character of the text on the screen.

However, displaying text using the Graphics class requires you to specify the height, width, and other characteristics that describe how each character of the text is to be drawn on the screen. Your application is actually drawing each character as compared to simply specifying the text that you want displayed. You'll learn how to draw characters later in this chapter.

A Canvas is created by instantiating a concrete subclass, which is discussed later in this chapter.

The Layout of a Canvas

The canvas is divided into a virtual grid in which each cell represents one pixel. Coordinates mark the column and row of a cell within the grid (Figure 7-1). The x coordinate represents the column, and the y coordinate represents the cell's row. The first cell located in the upper-left corner of the grid has the coordinate location of 0, 0, where the first zero is the x coordinate and the other zero is the y coordinate.

As you probably imagine, the size of the canvas is device dependent since canvas size and the screen size are the same. The screen size of a mobile telephone might be different from the screen size of a PDA, and yet both devices are capable of running the same MIDlet. Your MIDlet should determine the canvas size of the device that implements your graphic application before drawing on the screen. The canvas size is measured in pixels. Your MIDlet should determine the canvas size of the device by calling the getWidth() and getHeight() methods of the Canvas class.

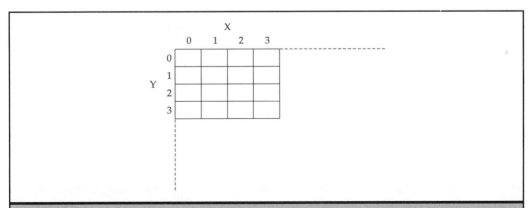

Figure 7-1.   *Coordinates mark the column and row of a cell within a grid.*

Proportional Coordinates

The values (in pixels) returned by the getWidth() and getHeight() methods can be used to draw an image at a given location that is proportional to the size of the canvas by using relative coordinates rather than exact coordinates on the canvas. Let's say that the first element of the image you want drawn on the canvas is located in the center of the canvas. The question you need to answer is what coordinate is the center of the canvas? The answer depends on the canvas size, which depends on the small computing device that runs your MIDlet. You work around this problem by letting your MIDlet calculate the center coordinate based on the return value of the getWidth() and getHeight() methods.

Here's what you need to do. Assume the size of the canvas is 200 pixels wide (columns) and 200 pixels high (rows). The coordinate of the center of the canvas is 99, 99 (remember that coordinates are zero based), calculated as:

```
x = getWidth()/2
y = getHeight()/2
```

Now assume the same MIDlet is running on a small computing device with a canvas size of 400 pixels wide by 400 pixels high. The same calculation determines the center coordinate as 199, 199. Therefore, the MIDlet can use the calculation to determine the center coordinate of any size canvas, which means that the image will appear in the same canvas location when the MIDlet runs on any device.

Calculating a specific coordinate rather than specifying a fixed coordinate solves one problem facing a developer of a J2ME application. Another problem is scaling an image to fit a canvas size that is device dependent. If you knew the size of the canvas, you could plot each pixel that is required to draw an image. The image will be symmetrical within the screen. However, the symmetry is disrupted when the size of the canvas changes and the image size remains the same.

Let's say that you want to draw a line across the top of the canvas, but leave a one-pixel border around the line. If the screen size is 200 pixels wide by 200 pixels high, the starting coordinate of the line is 1, 1 (the cell in the second column and second row beginning at the left corner). The ending coordinate is 1, 198. However, the line takes on a different appearance if the size of the canvas is 400 pixels by 400 pixels. The line stops at the top center of the canvas because row 198 is halfway to the right of the canvas.

Therefore, you should write code that draws images proportional to the size of the canvas if being symmetrical within the canvas is critical to your application. This means that you'll need to use relative coordinates to draw an image rather than specific coordinates by having your MIDlet calculate the specific coordinate of each element of your image. For example, here is how to identify the coordinates for the line so that the length of the line is always proportional to the canvas size. The starting coordinates are set as specific values because the line always begins one pixel from the left and top of the canvas. Likewise, the x coordinate will always be the second row and can be fixed at row coordinate one. However, the column coordinate used to specify the termination of the line must be calculated so that the line always appears one pixel away from the right end of the canvas regardless of the size of the canvas.

```
startX = 1
startY = 1
endX = 1
endY = getWidth() – 1
```

You can use the concepts presented in this section to create your own calculations that determine specific coordinates based on the canvas size of the device running your MIDlet.

The Pen

An image is drawn on a canvas using a virtual pen. Using a virtual pen is very similar to using a real pen to draw an image on paper. That is, the pen is dropped on the canvas at a specified coordinate, filling the cell with the color of ink used in the pen. Cells change from their present color to the color of the ink as the pen is repositioned on the canvas. For example, a horizontal line forms on the canvas when the virtual pen is dragged horizontally across the canvas. Likewise, dragging the virtual pen vertically down the canvas draws a vertical line.

A virtual pen is used by instances of the Graphics class to draw rectangles, arcs, and other graphical image components on the canvas. You don't directly create and use a virtual pen.

Painting

Graphical components used to create an image on a canvas are drawn on the canvas when the paint() method of the Displayable class is called. This is referred to as *painting*. The paint() method is an abstract method that is used both by instances and derivatives of the Screen class and Canvas class.

Java specifications require that a concrete class provide implementation for any abstract methods defined in its parent class. Therefore, an instance of the Screen class and Canvas class must define a paint() method. The contents of the paint() method are statements that draw images on the screen.

Derivatives from the Screen class have two predefined methods used to paint the screen. Images painted by derivatives of the Screen class (Textbox, List, Alert, and Form) are radio buttons, check boxes, list, text, and other constructs that you find in a graphical user interface, which you learned about in the previous chapter. The first predefined method is paint(), which contains instructions that set parameters for drawing an image, such as defining the virtual pen. The other method is paintContent(), which is called at the end of the paint() method and contains statements to actually draw the image.

The developer doesn't become directly involved with the paint() method or the paintContent() method when building an application that uses the high-level user interface because details on how to display images are already defined by the derivative of the

Screen class. The same cannot be said when you develop an application that uses the low-level user interface by creating instances of classes derived from the Canvas class. You are responsible for defining the paint() method for your canvas-based application.

The paint() method requires one parameter, which is reference to the instance of the Graphics class created by your application. You'll learn how to use the Graphics class later in this chapter. Here is a paint() method that draws a rectangle on the canvas. Let's assume that an instance of the Graphics class referenced as graphics was created. The drawRect() is one of the many methods available from the Graphics class that draw predefined images on the canvas. The first two parameters of the drawRect() method specify the cell of the upper-left corner of the rectangle, and the last two parameters specify the width and height of the rectangle, where 40 is the width and 20 is the height.

```
protected void paint(Graphics graphics)
{
  graphics.drawRect(12, 6, 40, 20));
}
```

The paint() and repaint() Methods

You don't call the paint() method directly. Instead, the paint() method is called automatically by the setCurrent() method when the MIDlet is started. You call the repaint() whenever the canvas or a portion of the canvas must be refreshed.

Let's say that you want to draw text on a canvas that is already displayed on the screen. First, you create the text using a graphic, which you'll learn how to do later in this chapter. Next, you call the repaint() method to have the entire canvas redrawn, which includes text and images that currently exist on the screen and the new text, unless you've removed existing text or images.

There are two versions of the repaint() method. One version requires no parameters and repaints the entire canvas. The other version requires four parameters that define the region of the canvas that is to be repainted. The first two parameters are the x and y coordinates for the upper-left corner of the region, and the last two parameters are the width and height of the region.

You specify a region of the canvas to repaint whenever only a portion of the canvas has changed and when you don't want to waste time repainting the entire canvas, such as when an animated image is displayed on the screen. This is known as *clipping*.

Animation is the illusion of movement caused by rapidly changing images on the screen, where each image is slightly different from the previous image. Each image displayed on the screen is referred to as a *frame*. A key to successful animation is speed. You must change frames in such a way that users don't notice the change. Typically, a small portion of a frame changes in an animated image. The repaint() method is capable of repainting only the portion of the frame that changed rather than the entire frame, which dramatically reduces the time that is necessary to change a frame on the screen.

The serviceRepaints() method is another painting method that you'll use when developing a low-level user interface for your application. A paint request is one of many requests a MIDlet can make to the application manager of a small computing device. Other requests can be made to store data or to communicate with a remote computer. Sometimes outstanding requests can be given a higher process priority by the device's application manager than a paint request. However, you'll need to override outstanding requests to have the canvas repainted whenever an image is being animated; otherwise, a delay in repainting the canvas destroys the effect of animation.

The serviceRepaints() method directs the device's application manager to override outstanding requests for service with the repaint request. The repaint request becomes the next request to be processed by the application manager.

showNotify() and hideNotify()

The device's application manager calls the showNotify() method immediately before the application manager displays the canvas. You define the showNotify() method with statements that prepare the canvas for display, such as initializing resources by beginning threads or assigning values to variables as required by your application.

The hideNotify() method is called by the application manager after the canvas is removed from the screen. You define the hideNotify() method with statements that free resources that were allocated when the showNotify() method was called. This includes deactivating threads and resetting values assigned to variables as necessary.

User Interactions

One of two techniques can be used to receive user input into your low-level J2ME application. The first technique is to create one or more instances of the Command class, which you learned about in the previous chapter. Once an instance of a command is created, the instance is associated with the instance of the Canvas class by calling the addCommand() method illustrated in Chapter 6. If you associate a command with a canvas, you'll also need to associate a CommandListener to the canvas in order to monitor command events generated by the user selecting a command. Likewise, you'll need to define a commandAction() method (see Chapter 6) that is called by the device's application manager to process the command event.

The other technique is to use low-level user input components that generate low-level user events. These components are key codes, game actions, and pointers.

- A *key code* is a numerical value sent by the small computing device when the user of your application selects a particular key. Each key on the device's keypad is identified by a unique key code.

- A *game action* is a keystroke that a person uses to play a game on the small computing device. MIDP defines a set of constants that represent keystrokes common to game controllers.

- A *pointer event* is input received from a pointer device attached to the small computing device, such as a touch screen or mouse.

Working with Key Codes

Each key on an ITU-T keypad, which is used on cellular telephones, is mapped to a standard set of key codes that are shown in Table 7-1. J2ME associates key code values with constants; however, use the constant instead of the constant value. You'll find that using constants within your code clarifies the reference to a key because the name of the constant contains the name of the key associated with the key code.

All small computing devices that use the ITU-T keypad adhere to these key codes. Some of these devices also have other keys on the keypad, each of which is also assigned a key code. The manufacturer's specification for the device usually lists key codes used by the device for keys outside of those on the standard ITU-T keypad.

 Your MIDlet can detect and process any key code—including keys other than those found on the standard ITU-T keypad—using techniques described later in this section. However, keys outside of the standard ITU-T keypad may not be available in all small computing devices, resulting in a possible portability problem with your MIDlet. So avoid using keys other than those on the standard ITU-T keypad unless your MIDlet will run exclusively on a specific make and model device that contains those keys.

Constant	Value
KEY_NUM0	48
KEY_NUM1	49
KEY_NUM2	50
KEY_NUM3	51
KEY_NUM4	52
KEY_NUM5	53
KEY_NUM6	54
KEY_NUM7	55
KEY_NUM8	56
KEY_NUM9	57
KEY_STAR	42
KEY_POUND	35

Table 7-1. *Key Code Constants and Key Code Values*

There are three empty methods that are called when a particular key event occurs while your MIDlet is running. You should override these methods if your application needs to call them. These methods are keyPressed(), keyReleased(), and keyRepeated(). The keyPressed() method is called by the application manager whenever a key is pressed by the user. Likewise, the keyReleased() method is called when the key selected by the user is released. And the keyRepeated() method is called by the application manager when the user holds down the key, causing the key to be automatically repeated. A word of caution: not all devices support repeated keys. Your MIDlet can inquire whether or not the repeated key feature is supported by calling the hasRepeatEvents() method. (See "Quick Reference Guide" at the end of this chapter.)

All of these methods have empty implementation. You must override each method if your application needs to process the related key events. However, many of the applications you create that implement a low-level user interface will only need to override the keyPressed() method because you'll need to know which key was selected by the user. The keyRelease() method and the keyRepeated() method are overridden only for applications that have special processing whenever a person releases a key or holds down a key for an extended period.

All three methods require one parameter, which is an integer that represents the value of the key code passed to the method by the device's application manager. An if statement or switch case statement is used to compare the incoming key code with key code constants that are processed by the MIDlet.

Listing 7-1 illustrates the basic way in which you detect and process key codes of keys selected by the person using the MIDlet. This example designates the 2, 8, 4, and 6 keys as directional keys, where the 2 and 8 are up and down and 4 and 6 are left and right. The MIDlet displays text that describes the direction selected by the user. Of course, in a real application you would likely reposition an image, such as a game piece, on the screen whenever a direction key is detected rather than display text. You'll see how this is done later in this chapter.

Detecting and Processing Key Codes

A MIDlet that uses a low-level user interface extends the MIDlet as illustrated in Listing 7-1. Listing 7-2 contains the JAD file for Listing 7-1. This listing displays a menu (Figure 7-2) on the screen prompting the user to press a key displayed on the menu. Each key represents a direction. The name of the direction is drawn on the canvas after the key is selected (Figure 7-3).

The MIDlet begins by declaring two variables. The first variable references an instance of the Display class, much the same as you saw in the previous chapter. The other variable references a developer-defined class called MyCanvas, which is defined later in this listing.

You'll notice that most of the work occurs outside of the constructor, which is different from the high-level user interface (see Chapter 6), where a number of tasks are performed in the constructor. Tasks normally performed in the constructor of a MIDlet that uses the

Figure 7-2.   *A menu is displayed prompting the user to select a menu option.*

high-level user interface are performed in the developer-defined class that extends the Canvas class.

Two instances of classes are created within the KeyCodeExample constructor. These are the Display class and the MyCanvas class. Notice that the remainder of code within the KeyCodeExample class definition is nearly identical to examples shown in the previous chapter. This is because a MIDlet that uses the low-level user interface must contain the same required method definitions as a MIDlet that uses the high-level user interface.

Let's turn to the end of the listing where the MyCanvas class is defined. The first statement declares a reference to an instance of the Command class that is used to terminate the MIDlet. You've seen that command used many times in the high-level user interface MIDlets in the previous chapter. Next, reference to a String called direction is declared, followed by the creation of an instance of the KeyCodeExample class.

The constructor of MyCanvas is passed an instance of the KeyCodeExample class that is referenced internally to the constructor. The direction string is initialized with

Figure 7-3.   *The name of the direction selected by the user is drawn on the canvas.*

text that describes directional keys; the text is displayed on the screen when the device's application manager calls the paint() method.

Next, an instance of the Command class is created and associated with the instance of MyCanvas. Likewise, a CommandListener is associated with the instance of MyCanvas in order to monitor command events occurring while the MIDlet runs. The commandAction() method defined later in the class definition is called by the device's application manager to process a command event—identical to how the same method is used in the high-level user interface.

The paint() method is defined next. It uses an instance of the Graphics class, which is passed as the parameter to the paint() method, to draw an image on the canvas, as discussed previously in this chapter. There are four statements within the paint() method. The first statement sets the color to white. Each of the three integers passed to the setColor() method represents a color value of red, green, and blue. You'll learn about setting colors later in this chapter. For now understand that the higher the number, the lighter the value; so the values 255, 255, 255 whiten the canvas and thereby erase existing images from the canvas.

Next, a filled rectangle is drawn on the screen. The color of the filled rectangle is white, and drawing the rectangle has the effect of erasing images from the canvas. The first two parameters of the fillRect() method are the coordinates of the upper-left corner of the rectangle. The last two parameters are the width and height of the rectangle. You'll learn more about drawing rectangles later in this chapter.

Once the canvas is erased, the color is set to red, and then the drawString() method, which actually paints text on the canvas, is called. There are four parameters to the drawString() method. The first parameter is the string of text that will be painted on

Detecting and Processing Key Codes

Listed here are the steps for detecting and processing key codes:

1. Declare references to classes.

2. Create instances of classes and assign those instances to references.

3. Display the instance of the Canvas class whenever the MIDlet is started.

4. Terminate the MIDlet when the Exit command is selected.

5. Define a class derived from the Canvas class that implements a CommandListener.

6. Within the derived class, declare references.

7. Within the derived class, define a constructor that initializes text to be displayed on the canvas.

8. Within the derived class, create an instance of the Command class.

9. Within the derived class, associate the instance of the Command class with the canvas.

10. Within the derived class, associate the CommandListener with the canvas.

11. Within the derived class, define a paint() method that erases the canvas and draws the string on the canvas.

12. Within the derived class, define a commandAction() method to process the Exit command.

13. Within the derived class, define a keyPressed() method to process keys selected by the user while the MIDlet runs.

14. Compare the incoming key code value with game action constants for KEY_NUM2, KEY_NUM8, KEY_NUM4, and KEY_NUM6.

15. If matched, indicate the direction selected by the player.

16. Erase the canvas and redraw the text on the canvas.

the canvas. The next two parameters specify the location on the canvas to paint the text. The first is the x (column) coordinate, and the other is the y (row coordinate). The fourth parameter of the drawString() method is the anchor point. You'll learn about anchor points later in this chapter when the drawString() method is discussed in detail. For now, consider an anchor point as a construct used to align text with other objects on the canvas.

The last method defined in the MyCanvas class is the keyPressed() method. The keyPressed() method, as described previously in this section, is called by the device application manager whenever the user presses a key on the keypad. The key code of that key is passed to the keyPressed() method for processing.

In this example, a switch case statement is used to compare the incoming key code to the directional keys recognized by the MIDlet. If the incoming key code matches the key code constant, text describing the direction selected by the user is assigned to the direction string, and then the repaint() method is called. The repaint() method causes the paint() method to be invoked, which erases the canvas and displays the value of the direction string on the canvas.

Listing 7-1
Capturing
and
processing
key codes

```
import javax.microedition.midlet.*;
import javax.microedition.lcdui.*;
public class KeyCodeExample extends MIDlet
{
  private Display  display;
  private MyCanvas canvas;
  public KeyCodeExample ()
  {
    display = Display.getDisplay(this);
    canvas  = new MyCanvas(this);
  }
  protected void startApp()
  {
    display.setCurrent(canvas);
  }
  protected void pauseApp()
  {
  }
  protected void destroyApp( boolean unconditional )
  {
  }
  public void exitMIDlet()
  {
    destroyApp(true);
    notifyDestroyed();
  }
}
class MyCanvas extends Canvas implements CommandListener
{
```

```
private Command exit;
private String direction;
private KeyCodeExample keyCodeExample;
public MyCanvas (KeyCodeExample keyCodeExample)
{
  direction = "2=up 8=dn 4=lt 6=rt";
  this.keyCodeExample = keyCodeExample;
  exit = new Command("Exit", Command.EXIT, 1);
  addCommand(exit);
  setCommandListener(this);
}
protected void paint(Graphics graphics)
{
  graphics.setColor(255,255,255);
  graphics.fillRect(0, 0, getWidth(), getHeight());
  graphics.setColor(255, 0, 0);
  graphics.drawString(direction, 0, 0,
                      Graphics.TOP | Graphics.LEFT);
}
public void commandAction(Command command, Displayable displayable)
{
  if (command == exit)
  {
    keyCodeExample.exitMIDlet();
   }
}
protected void keyPressed(int key)
{
  switch ( key ){
   case KEY_NUM2:
     direction = "up";
     break;
   case KEY_NUM8:
     direction = "down";
     break;
   case KEY_NUM4:
     direction = "left";
     break;
   case KEY_NUM6:
     direction = "right";
     break;
  }
  repaint();
}
}
```

Listing 7-2
The JAD
file for
Listing 7-1

```
MIDlet-Name: KeyCodeExample
MIDlet-Version: 1.0
MIDlet-Vendor: MyCompany
MIDlet-Jar-URL: KeyCodeExample.jar
MIDlet-1: KeyCodeExample, , KeyCodeExample
MicroEdition-Configuration: CLDC-1.0
MicroEdition-Profile: MIDP-1.0
MIDlet-JAR-SIZE: 100
```

Working with Game Actions

The theme may differ among computer games, but the way players interact with a game is fairly constant across all computer games. Players can move up, down, left, right, and they can fire. Typically, directional movement causes a game piece to move in a corresponding direction or changes the viewpoint of the player, depending on the nature of the game. Fire causes an event to occur within the game, such as releasing a bullet from a gun.

Directional movement and fire are referred to as game actions, and MIDP game action defines constants that enable you to utilize game actions within your MIDlet without being concerned about the appropriate key code that is assigned to each action. Nearly all small computing devices accommodate game action keys either by associating each game action with a dedicated key, such as a key labeled "fire," or by associating each game action to a generic key, such as numbers on a keypad.

Each game action is associated with one or more keys on the keypad. For example, the down game action might be associated with a down directional key and a number on the keypad. Pressing either key causes the same game action to occur. However, each key can be assigned to only one game action. This means pressing the down game action key doesn't also generate an up game action.

You don't need to be concerned about key mapping of game actions if you use game action constants to refer to game actions within your MIDlet. Table 7-2 contains game action constants that are used when developing a game for a small computing device. You can reference either the name of the constant or the value of the constant within your MIDlet to determine the game action selected by the player. However, it is always best to reference the constant rather than the constant value.

A game action causes the keyPressed() method, keyReleased() method, and keyRepeated() method to be called, depending on the key pressed by the player. You can detect which game action occurred by calling the getGameAction() method. The getGameAction() method requires one parameter—the key code of the key selected by the player—which is passed as a parameter to the keyPressed(), keyReleased(), or keyRepeated() method.

Game Action Constant	Description	Game Action Constant Value
UP	Move up	1
DOWN	Move down	6
LEFT	Move left	2
RIGHT	Move right	5
FIRE	Fire	8
GAME_A	Device defined	9
GAME_B	Device defined	10
GAME_C	Device defined	11
GAME_D	Device defined	12

Table 7-2. *Game Action Constants*

An if statement or a switch case statement can be used to compare the incoming key code to game action constants. Each game action constant is a data member of the Canvas class and is referenced by using the name of the game action constant, such as Canvas.LEFT, Canvas.RIGHT, Canvas.UP, Canvas.DOWN, and Canvas.FIRE.

There are two alternative ways to detect the game action key selected by the player. The first is to compare key code values by calling the getKeyCode() method. The getKeyCode() method requires one parameter, which is the name of the game action constant. The getKeyCode() returns the key code value associated with the game action constant that can then be directly compared to the incoming key code value passed to the keyPressed(), keyReleased(), or keyRepeated() method.

Let's say that you need to determine whether the player selected the FIRE game action key. You call the getKeyCode() method and pass it the name of the FIRE game action constant, which is FIRE. The return value is then compared with the incoming game action key code, as illustrated in the following code segment. The keycode variable is an int representing the value of the key code selected by the player.

```
if (getKeyCode(FIRE) == keycode)
{
  //fire
}
```

The other way to determine the player's selection is to retrieve the name of the key that is associated with the incoming key code by calling the getKeyName() method. The getKeyName() method requires one parameter, which is the key code value. The getKeyName() method returns the name of the key represented by the key code value. A word of caution: the name returned by the getKeyName() method is not necessarily the name of the game action. Instead, it is the name of the key.

Let's say that the player pressed the left game action key, which has a game action constant value of 2 (Table 7-2). The actual name for the key might be KEY_4 if the device uses the key labeled 4 as the left directional key on the keypad. In this example, the name KEY_NUM4 is returned by the getKeyName() method.

In order to use the getKeyName() method to detect the game action key selected by the player, you must first determine the key name for each of the game action keys. You do this by calling the getKeyCode() method, passing it the game action constant name, and then passing the return value from the getKeyCode() method to the getKeyName() method, which returns the name of the key associated with the key code value. This technique is illustrated in the following code segment:

```
if (getKeyName(getKeyCode(FIRE).equals(getKeyName(keycode))))
{
   //fire
}
```

Detecting and Processing Game Actions

Listing 7-3 illustrates how to detect and process game actions selected by a player. Listing 7-4 is the JAD file for Listing 7-3. You'll notice that Listing 7-3 is very similar to Listing 7-1, except this example relocates text on the screen based upon the game action selected by the player.

This listing begins the same as Listing 7-1, by declaring references that are later assigned instances of the Display class and the MyCanvas class in the GameActionExample constructor. And as in Listing 7-1, MyCanvas is declared later in the listing. The instance of MyCanvas class is displayed by passing it to the setCurrent() method within the startApp() method of the MIDlet.

Nearly all the action in Listing 7-3 happens in the definition of the MyCanvas class. The class definition begins by declaring references similar to references declared in Listing 7-1. However, two additional variables are declared in Listing 7-3. These are x and y integers whose values represent canvas coordinates used to position text on the canvas.

The initial coordinate is 5, 5, which identifies the cell in the upper-left region of the canvas. This is the cell where the device draws the line of text assigned to the message variable in the constructor (see Figure 7-4). The other statements within the constructor are the same as statements used in Listing 7-1.

Figure 7-4. *Text assigned to the message variables in the constructor is displayed on the screen.*

The paint() method erases images from the canvas and draws the string called "message" at the x, y coordinate. Initially, the value of the x, y coordinate is 5, 5. However, you'll notice that statements within the keyPressed() method definition modify the initial values, depending on the game action key selected by the player.

The commandAction() method is defined next and has the same definition as the commandAction() command contained in Listing 7-1. The purpose of the commandAction() method is to process the Exit command when the player terminates the MIDlet.

The keyPressed() method is called to detect and process game action keys. As in Listing 7-1, a switch case statement is used to compare the incoming key code value to a constant. This example uses game action constants to detect the game action key selected by the player. The key selected by the user is retrieved by calling the getGameAction(key) method.

Based on the selected key, the appropriate case statement replaces the string assigned to the message variable and then adjusts the value of either the x or y coordinate to

Detecting and Processing Game Action Keys

Listed here are the steps for detecting and processing game action keys:

1. Declare references to classes.

2. Create instances of classes and assign those instances to references.

3. Display the instance of the Canvas class whenever the MIDlet is started.

4. Terminate the MIDlet when the Exit command is selected.

5. Define a class derived from the Canvas class that implements a CommandListener.

6. Within the derived class, declare references.

7. Within the derived class, define a constructor that initializes text to be displayed on the canvas.

8. Within the derived class, create an instance of the Command class.

9. Within the derived class, associate the instance of the Command class with the canvas.

10. Within the derived class, associate the CommandListener with the canvas.

11. Within the derived class, define a paint() method that erases the canvas and draws the string on the canvas.

12. Within the derived class, define a commandAction() method to process the Exit command.

13. Within the derived class, define a keyPressed() method to process keys selected by the user while the MIDlet runs.

14. Compare the incoming key code value with game action constants for UP, DOWN, LEFT, RIGHT, and FIRE.

15. If matched, indicate the direction selected by the player and adjust the coordinate appropriately to position the text on the canvas in the direction selected by the player.

16. Erase the canvas and redraw the text on the canvas.

reposition the text on the canvas. Next the repaint() method is called, which calls the paint() method to erase the canvas and draw the new text on the canvas.

Listing 7-3
Capturing and processing game actions

```
import javax.microedition.midlet.*;
import javax.microedition.lcdui.*;
public class GameActionExample extends MIDlet
{
```

```java
  private Display  display;
  private MyCanvas canvas;
  public GameActionExample()
  {
    display = Display.getDisplay(this);
    canvas  = new MyCanvas (this);
  }
  protected void startApp()
  {
    display.setCurrent(canvas);
  }
  protected void pauseApp()
  {
  }
  protected void destroyApp( boolean unconditional )
  {
  }
  public void exitMIDlet()
  {
    destroyApp(true);
    notifyDestroyed();
  }
}
class MyCanvas extends Canvas implements CommandListener
{
  private Command exit;
  private String message;
  private GameActionExample gameActionExample;
  private int x, y;
  public MyCanvas (GameActionExample gameActionExample)
  {
    x = 5;
    y = 5;
    direction = "Use Game Keys";
    this.gameActionExample = gameActionExample;
    exit = new Command("Exit", Command.EXIT, 1);
    addCommand(exit);
    setCommandListener(this);
  }
  protected void paint(Graphics graphics)
  {
    graphics.setColor(255,255,255);
    graphics.fillRect(0, 0, getWidth(), getHeight());
    graphics.setColor(255, 0, 0);
    graphics.drawString(message, x, y, Graphics.TOP | Graphics.LEFT);
  }
  public void commandAction(Command command, Displayable displayable)
  {
    if (command == exit)
```

```
        {
          gameActionExample.exitMIDlet();
        }
    }
    protected void keyPressed(int key)
    {
      switch ( getGameAction(key) ){
        case Canvas.UP:
          message = "up";
          y--;
          break;
        case Canvas.DOWN:
          message = "down";
          y++;
          break;
        case Canvas.LEFT:
          message = "left";
          x--;
          break;
        case Canvas.RIGHT:
          message = "right";
          x++;
          break;
        case Canvas.FIRE:
          message = "FIRE";
          break;
      }
      repaint();
    }
}
```

Listing 7-4
The JAD
file for
Listing 7-3

```
MIDlet-Name: GameActionExample
MIDlet-Version: 1.0
MIDlet-Vendor: MyCompany
MIDlet-Jar-URL: GameActionExample.jar
MIDlet-1: GameActionExample, , GameActionExample
MicroEdition-Configuration: CLDC-1.0
MicroEdition-Profile: MIDP-1.0
MIDlet-JAR-SIZE: 100
```

Working with Pointer Devices

A pointer device is something other than a keyboard or keypad that is used to interact
with an application. The most commonly used pointer devices are a touch screen and a
mouse, although you can be sure that new pointer devices are bound to find their way
into the marketplace in the future. Fortunately, as a J2ME developer, you don't become
involved in the details of how a pointer device interfaces with a small computer or how

someone uses the pointer device to interact with your MIDlet. The device manufacturer and the implementation of the Java Virtual Machine handle those details. However, you are responsible for developing routines within your MIDlet to process pointer events. A pointer event occurs whenever the person uses a pointer device to interact with your MIDlet. There are three pointer events that your MIDlet must process. These are when the person presses a pointer device, releases a pointer device, and drags a pointer device.

A person presses a pointer device by applying pressure to a portion of a touch screen or by clicking the mouse button. This causes a *press event*. A *release event* occurs once pressure is removed from the touch screen or the mouse button. And your MIDlet is notified of a *drag event* whenever the person moves the pointer device during a press event.

Your MIDlet processes pointer events by defining three methods that are automatically called by the device's application manager when a pointer event occurs. These methods are the pointerPressed() method, the pointerReleased() method, and the pointerDragged() method. All three methods require two parameters. The first parameter is an integer representing the x coordinate of the pointer device, and the other parameter is an integer representing the y coordinate. Typically, your MIDlet will use these parameters to change the image that appears on the screen.

Let's say that your MIDlet prompts the user to draw a line across the screen using a pointer device. A line is drawn by pressing the pointer device at a particular location on the canvas, then while pressed (or while holding down the mouse button), the person drags the pointer device to another position on the canvas before releasing the pointer device.

Here's what happens behind the scenes in the MIDlet. A press event is detected and the pointerPressed() method is called when the pointer device is pressed. The pointerPressed() method receives the coordinate of the pointer on the canvas. Let's call that the starting coordinate.

Dragging the pointer device is a drag event and causes the pointerDragged() method to be invoked continuously until the person stops dragging the pointer device. The pointerDragged() method is called each time the pointer device is dragged and is passed the coordinate of the pointer device when the drag event occurs. Let's call this coordinate the current coordinate.

Finally, the release event occurs when the person removes pressure from the pointer device (removes the finger or implement from the touch screen or releases the mouse button). The pointerReleased() method is then called and passed the pointer device's coordinate on the canvas where the person released the pointer device. We'll call this the end coordinate.

In this example, the color of the pixel at the coordinate must be changed to the color of the line to give the illusion that a line is being drawn on the screen. The pointerPressed() method, pointerDragged() method, and pointerReleased() method all must contain statements that change the color of the pixel at the coordinate passed to each method by the device's application manager.

Detecting and Processing Pointer Events

Listing 7-5 shows how to write a MIDlet that draws a line on the canvas based on pointer events generated by the user of the application. Listing 7-6 is the JAD file for Listing 7-5. Each time a pointer event occurs, the MIDlet redraws the line as determined by the coordinate passed to the appropriate pointer event method.

Listing 7-5 follows the same basic structure as other listings discussed previously in this chapter. The PointerExample class definition is technically the same as the GameActionExample class definition in Listing 7-3, except the class name is different. Therefore, we'll jump down to the definition of the MyCanvas class.

Several variables are declared at the beginning of the MyCanvas class. Two variables are used to reference commands. These are the Exit command used by the user to terminate the MIDlet and the Erase command. The Erase command is used whenever the user wants to remove the line from the screen.

Next, a boolean variable called eraseFlag is declared and is initialized to a false value. The eraseFlag is used throughout the MIDlet to indicate whether the user wants the screen erased. There are also four integers declared. These integers are used to hold the start and current coordinates when the line is being drawn. And the last variable is reference to the instance of the PointerExample class.

The MyCanvas class constructor definition assigns commands to references and associates commands and the CommandListener with the instance of the Canvas class. This is the same technique illustrated in other listings in this chapter.

You'll notice that the paint() method is a bit more complex than paint() methods defined in other listings in this chapter because the paint() method must perform several tasks. First, the paint() method must determine whether the user wants the screen erased by evaluating the value of the eraseFlag. If the eraseFlag is true, images on the canvas are erased, otherwise the paint() method draws the line on the canvas.

The canvas is erased by calling the setColor() method to white. Remember from our previous discussion about the setColor() method that you must pass the setColor() method three parameters. These are color values for red, green, and blue. The higher the color value, the brighter the color. The highest—and therefore brightest—color value is 255, which is white.

The fillRect() method is then called to paint a rectangle on the canvas with the current color, which is white. The fillRect() method requires four parameters. The first two parameters are the coordinates of the upper-left corner and lower-right corner of the rectangle. The upper-left corner of the rectangle is the first cell of the canvas. The lower-right corner is determined by the getWidth() and getHeight() methods, both of which return the maximum width and height of the filled rectangle. You'll be formally introduced to the setColor() method, the fillRect() method, and other graphic methods in the next section of this chapter.

Once the canvas is erased, the eraseFlag, start, and current coordinates are initialized to false and zero, respectively. The paint() method is then abruptly terminated with the return statement because the remaining statements in the paint() method draw a line on the screen, which is not what the user requested. However, if the user didn't select the Erase command, statements that erase the canvas within the paint() method are skipped, and the MIDlet proceeds to draw a line on the screen. This process begins by calling the setColor() method and setting each parameter to zero. Zero is the darkest color value, which is black. This means images drawn on the canvas after the color is set to zero are drawn in black.

The drawLine() method is called once the color is set to black. The drawLine() method requires four parameters. The first two parameters identify the starting coordinates for the line, and the other parameters identify the end coordinates of the line. The values of these parameters are the current values of sX, sY, cX, cY variables.

Detecting and Processing Pointer Events

Listed here are the steps for detecting and processing pointer events:

1. Declare references to classes.
2. Create instances of classes and assign those instances to references.
3. Display the instance of the Canvas class whenever the MIDlet is started.
4. Terminate the MIDlet when the Exit command is selected.
5. Define a class derived from the Canvas class that implements a CommandListener.
6. Within the derived class, declare references.
7. Within the derived class, create instances of the Command class—one command used to terminate the MIDlet and the other to erase the screen.
8. Within the derived class, associate instances of the Command class with the canvas.
9. Within the derived class, associate the CommandListener with the canvas.
10. Within the derived class, define a paint() method either to erase the canvas or draw a line segment on the canvas.
11. Within the derived class, define a commandAction() method to process the Exit command and the Erase command.
12. Within the derived class, define a pointerPressed() method to process the pointer pressed event by resetting the starting coordinates of the line to coordinates that identify the position of the pointer device when the pointer device is pressed.
13. Within the derived class, define a pointerDragged() method to process the pointer drag event by resetting the current coordinates of the line to coordinates that identify the position of the pointer device as the pointer device is dragged across the screen.

The values of the sX, sY, cX, cY variables are modified by the pointer event methods that are defined later in the MyClass class definition. Before the MIDlet leaves the paint() method, the values of the current coordinates (cX and cY) are assigned to the starting coordinates (sX and sY). This means that the next segment of the line is drawn at the end of the current line.

The commandAction() method is similar to the commandAction() method used in other listings with one exception. When the commandAction() method detects that the user selected the Erase command, the eraseFlag is set to true and the repaint() method is called. The repaint() method invokes the paint() method, which erases the canvas.

Two other methods are defined in the MyClass class. These are the pointerPressed() method and the pointerDragged() method. We didn't define the pointerReleased() method because the MIDlet doesn't perform any special processing when the user releases the pointer device.

The pointerPressed() method receives coordinates of where the pointer device was located on the canvas when the user pressed the pointer device. This coordinate is always the starting coordinate of the line. Notice that the repaint() method isn't called within the pointerPressed() method because we expect that the user doesn't want a pixel to appear unless the pointer device is dragged.

The pointerDragged() method receives coordinates of each position of the canvas over which the user drags the pointer device. As each drag event is captured, the pointerDragged() method is called and the current coordinate variables (cX and cY) are assigned the value of the pointer device. The repaint() method is called once the coordinates are assigned to these variables. The repaint() method calls the paint() method, as previously described, and uses the value of the current coordinate variables and the start coordinate variables to draw the next segment of the line.

Listing 7-5
Capturing and processing pointer events

```
import javax.microedition.midlet.*;
import javax.microedition.lcdui.*;
public class PointerExample extends MIDlet
{
  private Display  display;
  private MyClass canvas;
  public PointerExample()
  {
    display = Display.getDisplay(this);
    canvas  = new MyClass (this);
  }
  protected void startApp()
  {
    display.setCurrent( canvas );
  }
  protected void pauseApp()
  {
  }
  protected void destroyApp( boolean unconditional )
  {
```

J2ME
USER INTERFACE

```java
    }
  public void exitMIDlet()
  {
    destroyApp(true);
    notifyDestroyed();
  }
}
class MyClass extends Canvas implements CommandListener
{
  private Command exit;
  private Command erase;
  private boolean eraseFlag = false;
  private boolean isFirstPaint;
  private int sX = 0,sY = 0, cX = 0, cY = 0;
  private PointerExample pointerExample;
  public MyClass (PointerExample pointerExample)
  {
    this.pointerExample = pointerExample;
    exit = new Command("Exit", Command.EXIT, 1);
    erase = new Command("Erase", Command.SCREEN, 1);
    addCommand(exit);
    addCommand(erase);
    setCommandListener(this);
    isFirstPaint = true;
  }
  protected void paint(Graphics graphics)
  {
    if (eraseFlag || isFirstPaint)
    {
      graphics.setColor(255, 255, 255);
      graphics.fillRect(0, 0, getWidth(), getHeight());
      eraseFlag = isFirstPaint = false;
      sX = 0;
      sY = 0;
      cX = 0;
      cY = 0;
      return;
    }
    graphics.setColor(0, 0, 0);
    graphics.drawLine(sX, sY, cX, cY);
    sX = cX;
    sY = cY;
  }
  public void commandAction(Command command, Displayable displayable)
  {
    if (command == exit)
      pointerExample.exitMIDlet();
    else if (command == erase)
    {
```

```
            eraseFlag = true;
            repaint();
        }
    }
    protected void pointerPressed(int x, int y)
    {
        sX = x;
        sY = y;
    }
    protected void pointerDragged(int x, int y)
    {
        cX = x;
        cY = y;
        repaint();
    }
}
```

Listing 7-6
The JAD
file for
Listing 7-5

```
MIDlet-Name: PointerExample
MIDlet-Version: 1.0
MIDlet-Vendor: MyCompany
MIDlet-Jar-URL: PointerExample.jar
MIDlet-1: PointerExample, , PointerExample
MicroEdition-Configuration: CLDC-1.0
MicroEdition-Profile: MIDP-1.0
MIDlet-JAR-SIZE: 100
```

Graphics

As you recall from earlier in this chapter, the screen of the low-level user interface is a canvas, which is an instance of the Canvas class. The canvas is organized into a grid in which each cell of the grid is a pixel. Coordinates, as explained in the previous sections, identify each cell. An image is drawn on the canvas by using a virtual graphical device called a *graphic context*, such as the rectangle and line. A graphic context is an instance of the Graphics class. You'll learn about these virtual graphical devices in this section.

Reference to the graphic context is passed to the paint() method. A mutable image, as you'll remember, is an image that can be altered by your MIDlet. You've seen how to create a graphic context in previous listings that defined the paint() method. Reference to the graphic context passed to a paint() method exists for the duration of the paint() method. Once the MIDlet leaves the paint() method, the graphic context goes out of scope. The graphic context can no longer be used to draw on the canvas, even if reference to the graphic context is retained. In contrast, a graphic context created in association with a mutable image remains available to the MIDlet as long as reference to the image and the image itself remains in scope. You'll learn how to create a graphic context using a mutable image later in this chapter.

Stroke Style and Color

Every graphic context has two characteristics you can control from within the MIDlet. These are stroke style and color. Stroke style defines the appearance of lines used to draw an image on the canvas, and color specifies the background and foreground color of the image.

You can use two kinds of stroke styles when drawing images on the canvas: solid and dotted. As the names imply, the solid stroke style causes the graphic context to use a solid line when drawing the image, and the dotted stroke style results in the image being drawn using a dotted line. The solid stroke style is the default.

Skipping pixels along the lines of the image creates the dotted stroke. The small computing device determines the number of pixels skipped. You cannot modify the appearance of the dotted stroke, and you might discover that skipped pixels may affect the appearance of the image. For example, a pixel at the corner of a rectangle might be missing and therefore ruin the illusion of a square-cornered rectangle.

Calling the setStrokeStyle() method determines the stroke style that will be used by a graphic context. A stroke style setting is particular to each graphic context and does not affect other graphic contexts. For example, one graphic context can be set to a dotted stroke style and another set to a solid stroke style. Both graphic contexts can be used to draw images on the same canvas without affecting each other's stroke style.

The setStrokeStyle() method requires one parameter, which is a constant that represents a stroke style. There are two constants, SOLID and DOTTED, both of which are members of the Graphics class. You can change the stroke style of a graphic context anytime within your MIDlet by calling the setStrokeStyle() and passing the setStrokeStyle() the constant that represents a different stroke style. You determine the current stroke style of a graphic context by calling the getStrokeStyle(). This method returns an integer that can be compared within your MIDlet to the stroke style constants.

Colors

You've already seen how combining degrees of red, green, and blue creates the foreground and background color of a graphic context. The degree of each color is specified as an integer value within the range of 0 to 255. Zero produces the darkest possible value of the color, and 255 produces the lightest possible value. For example, color values 0, 0, 0 (red, green, blue) produce black, and color values 255, 255, 255 produce white. Values between these extremes produce shades of various colors. All integers in Java are 32 bits. Of those 32 bits, 8 bits are used to represent red, blue, and green. All color values are stored in one integer. The 8 highest order bits are not used.

A word of caution: Your choice of colors for a graphic context is a request and not a directive. The actual color of a graphic context is device dependent. Every effort is made to draw an image in the requested colors, but sometimes the device doesn't support the colors you select or doesn't support color at all. In these cases, the device automatically uses colors that closely match your request, or it converts your color selection to shades of gray. You don't have any control over color choices made by a device.

> **Tip**   *The gray scale uses a range from 0 to 255, where zero is black and 255 is white.*

You can determine whether a device supports color and the number of colors or shades of gray that are supported by calling the appropriate Display class method within your MIDlet. The isColor() method returns a boolean value that is true if color is supported; otherwise a false value is returned, indicating that the device supports the gray scale instead of color. The numColors() method returns an integer representing the number of colors or shades of gray supported by the device. You can use both of these return values to reset a color choice for the graphic context that is appropriate for the colors available on the small computing device.

You set the color of a graphic context by calling the setColor() method of the Graphics class. The setColor() method requires either one parameter or three parameters depending on how you represent your choice of color. A color can be represented as one integer or three integers, where each of the three integers represents a color value of red, green, and blue.

Let's take a closer look at how color values are represented in order to understand the technique used to represent a color by a single integer. Remember that the highest order bits are not used to represent color values. The color is represented by the next 24 bits. The 24 bits are divided into three 8-bit groups. The first 8-bit group represents the color value of red. The second 8-bit group represents the color value of green. And the third 8-bit group represents the color value of blue.

Background Colors

Technically there isn't any way to distinguish between foreground and background colors because the concept of background colors is not supported in J2ME. All colors are foreground colors. However, you can work around this limitation by drawing a filled rectangle over the complete canvas before drawing other images on the canvas.

You've seen this technique used in Listing 7-3 to erase the canvas. In this example the following code segment is used to draw a filled rectangle the size of the canvas and fill the rectangle with the color white:

```
graphics.setColor(255, 255, 255);
graphics.fillRect(0, 0, getWidth(), getHeight());
```

Once the filled rectangle is drawn on the canvas, you can use another graphic context to draw an image on the canvas. Of course, that graphic context must have a color setting other than white; otherwise, you won't be able to see the new image on the screen.

Normally, you will determine the color to use with a graphic context by assigning a color value to each color group (red, green, blue), as discussed previously in this section. The bitwise shift operator (<<) and the bitwise OR operator (|) are then used to insert each of the color values into the appropriate place within the 24 bits that represent the color.

Let's use this example to illustrate. Suppose we use the following color values: red = 50, green = 200, and blue = 150. You can set the color of a graphic context by calling setColor(50, 200, 150). You can also pass the combined values of red, green, and blue to the setColor() method. Here's how these values are combined and passed to the setColor() method:

```
setColor((50 << 16) | (200 << 8) | 150);
```

First, the red color value 50 is bit shifted 16 places to the left, so it now occupies the second high order byte of an integer. Next, the green color value is bit shifted 8 places to the left, so it now occupies the third high order byte of an integer. No shifting is done to the blue value since it is already where it is supposed to be, namely, the lowest order byte of an integer. Next, all the values are bitwise ORed together, resulting in a single integer whose highest order byte is 0, second highest order byte is the value 50, third highest is 200, and the lowest order byte is 150.

Looking at the red, green, and blue color values in binary rather than decimal illustrates how these values are combined into one 24-bit value. Here are the decimal values for each color:

Red	50	00110010
Green	200	11001000
Blue	150	10010110

When these values are combined into one 32-bit value they appear as:

00000000001100101100100010010110

There are two techniques available for determining the current color setting of a graphic context. They involve determining the value of each component of the color (red, green, blue) either by calling the appropriate method for each component or by masking the color value. The simplest way to determine the color is to call the getRedComponent() method, getGreenComponent() method, and getBlueComponent() method. Each returns an integer representing the color value of the corresponding component.

An alternative technique is to retrieve the 32-bit color value by calling the getColor() method, then using a bit mask to extract each component of the color. The following code segment illustrates how to use this technique. Assume that red, green, and blue are integer variables and graphics is the instance of the Graphics class. The getColor() method returns the color value setting of the instance of the Graphics class, which is the graphic context. The first statement masks all but the first 8 bits of the color value, which represents the red component of the color. The second statement masks all but the second 8 bits of the color value. This is the green component. And the last statement masks the last 8 bits of the color, which is the blue component.

```
red = graphics.getColor()   & 0x00ff0000;
red = red >> 16;
green = graphics.getColor() & 0x0000ff00;
green = green >> 8;
blue = graphics.getColor()   & 0x000000ff;
```

Lines

Lines are drawn on the canvas by calling the drawLine() method, which is illustrated in Listing 7-6. The drawLine() method creates a line from a starting coordinate to an ending coordinate. Four parameters are required by the drawLine() method. The first two parameters are integers representing the starting x, y coordinate of the line. The other two parameters are integers representing the ending x, y coordinate of the line.

The thickness of the line, referred to as the *weight*, is typically measured in point size, where zero is the thinnest possible line. Unfortunately, you cannot easily change the weight of a line drawn on the canvas because the weight is always one pixel. The only way to create a heavier (thicker) line is to draw multiple, abutting lines, which appear as one thicker line on the screen. You can simulate point size by controlling the number of abutting lines used to draw the line on the canvas. A single line equates practically to zero point. You can approximate an increase in point size each time another line abuts the existing line.

The color of the line is determined by the color setting of the graphic context used to draw the line. You can set the color of the line by calling the setColor() method before invoking the drawLine() method. The setColor() method is discussed in the previous section of this chapter. Remember, the setColor() method determines the foreground color of the line. To paint the background color, you'll need to draw a filled rectangle that has the same dimensions as the canvas (see previous section).

Rectangles

A rectangle is an area of the canvas defined by four corners, just like a rectangle that you can draw using paper and pencil. You define a rectangle's dimensions by identifying coordinates for the upper-left corner and the lower-right corner. Four types of rectangles can be drawn on a canvas. These are an outlined rectangle, filled rectangle, outlined rectangle with rounded corners, and a filled rectangle with rounded corners. An outlined rectangle is one where only line segments connecting the corners are drawn. The inside of the rectangle remains the same color as the outside of the rectangle. The filled rectangle also draws line segments to connect corners, but the inside of the rectangle is filled with the same color as the drawn line segments. And as the names imply, each of these types of rectangles can have squared corners or rounded corners.

You create an outlined rectangle by calling the drawRect() method and the filled rectangle by calling the fillRect() method. Both methods create a square-cornered rectangle and require four parameters. The first two parameters are the coordinates of the upper-left corner of the rectangle (x1, y1), and the last two parameters are the width and height of the rectangle (x2, y2).

The color used to draw a rectangle must be set using the setColor() method (discussed previously in this chapter) before drawing the rectangle. Otherwise the current color of the graphic context is used both to color the outline and fill the inside of the rectangle, depending on the type of rectangle being drawn.

By setting the color of the graphic context that draws a filled rectangle to 255, 255, 255 and using 0, 0, getWidth(), getHeight() as the coordinates of the rectangle, you can erase all images from the canvas.

Creating a round-cornered rectangle is nearly identical to creating a square-cornered rectangle, except you must specify the horizontal and vertical diameter of the arc used to create the round corners. The horizontal diameter is referred to as the *arc width,* and the vertical diameter is referred to as the *arc height.*

The diameter represents the sharpness of the corner, where the smaller the diameter, the sharper the corner appears. Both the horizontal and vertical diameters are defined as integers. You should experiment using different diameter values before deciding on the diameters that are best to use with your application.

You create a round-cornered rectangle by calling the drawRoundRect() method and fillRoundRect() method, respectively. Both methods require six parameters. The first four parameters identify the upper-left corner and lower-right corner of the rectangle. The fifth and sixth parameters are integers representing the horizontal diameter and vertical diameter of the corners.

Drawing a Rectangle

We are going to look at two ways to draw a rectangle on the canvas. Listing 7-7 draws two outlined rectangles, one with square corners and the other with rounded corners. Listing 7-8 contains the JAD file for Listing 7-7. Listing 7-9 draws the same two rectangles, except these are filled rectangles. Its JAD file appears in Listing 7-10. The listings begin like the other listings discussed in this chapter, by declaring references for instances of the Display class and the MyCanvas class, which is defined within these listings. These instances are created and assigned within the constructor. The required methods for a MIDlet are then defined.

The structure of the MyCanvas class definition also resembles those of other listings that you've explored previously in this chapter. First, references are declared for the Exit command and the instances of the MIDlet class. The actual instances are created in the constructor of the MyCanvas definition where they are also assigned to these references. The Exit command and the CommandListener are both then associated with the canvas.

You'll notice that the definition of the paint() methods of Listing 7-7 and Listing 7-9 are different from each other. The paint() method in Listing 7-7 draws an outlined rectangle with square corners using the default color of the graphic context. This rectangle appears in the upper-left portion of the canvas, where the upper-left corner is located at coordinate 2, 2 and the width and height of the rectangle is 20, 20.

Next, a rounded corner outlined rectangle is drawn on the same canvas at a location lower than the first rectangle. The upper-left corner of this rectangle is at coordinate 20, 20, and the width and height are 60, 60. Since this is a round-cornered rectangle, we also need

J2ME USER INTERFACE

Drawing a Rectangle

Listed here are the steps for drawing a rectangle:

1. Declare references to classes.

2. Create instances of classes and assign those instances to references.

3. Display the instance of the Canvas class whenever the MIDlet is started.

4. Terminate the MIDlet when the Exit command is selected.

5. Define a class derived from the Canvas class that implements a CommandListener.

6. Within the derived class, declare references.

7. Within the derived class, create an instance of the Command class.

8. Within the derived class, associate the instance of the Command class with the canvas.

9. Within the derived class, associate the CommandListener with the canvas.

10. Within the derived class, define a paint() method to define the rectangular area of the canvas where the rectangle is to be drawn. Specify the horizontal and vertical diameters of the arc if rounded corners are used in the rectangle. Specify the color to be used to draw and fill the rectangle unless the default color is being used.

11. Within the derived class, define a commandAction() method to process the Exit command.

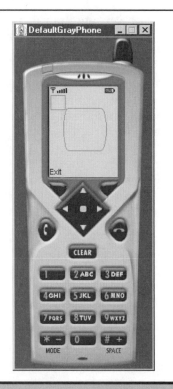

Figure 7-5. *An outlined rectangle with rounded corner*

to specify the horizontal and vertical diameter of the arc that forms the corner of the rectangle. In this example, the horizontal diameter is 15, and the vertical diameter is 45.

The definition of the paint() method in Listing 7-9 begins by erasing the canvas of images by setting the color to white and then drawing a filled rectangle. Next, the color is set to red. Remember, parameters to the setColor() method represent the integer color value of red, green, and blue. Green and blue are set to the darkest color value, while the color value for red is set to the brightest color value.

The same rectangles drawn in Listing 7-7 are also drawn in Listing 7-9. However, these rectangles are filled with the color blue rather than outlined in the default color as they are in Listing 7-7 (Figure 7-5 and Figure 7-6). Both Listing 7-7 and Listing 7-9

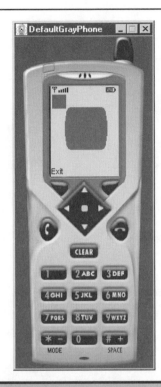

Figure 7-6. *A filled rectangle with rounded corner*

define the commandAction() method that is used to detect and process the selection
of the Exit command to terminate the MIDlet.

Listing 7-7
Drawing a
rectangle and
a rounded
rectangle

```
import javax.microedition.midlet.*;
import javax.microedition.lcdui.*;
public class RectangleExample extends MIDlet
{
  private Display  display;
  private MyCanvas canvas;
  public RectangleExample ()
  {
```

J2ME USER INTERFACE

```
    display = Display.getDisplay(this);
    canvas  = new MyCanvas (this);
  }
  protected void startApp()
  {
    display.setCurrent( canvas );
  }
  protected void pauseApp()
  {
  }
  protected void destroyApp( boolean unconditional )
  {
  }
  public void exitMIDlet()
  {
    destroyApp(true);
    notifyDestroyed();
  }
}
class MyCanvas extends Canvas implements CommandListener
{
  private Command exit;
  private RectangleExample rectangleExample;
  public MyCanvas (RectangleExample rectangleExample)
  {
    this.rectangleExample = rectangleExample;
    exit = new Command("Exit", Command.EXIT, 1);
    addCommand(exit);
    setCommandListener(this);
  }
  protected void paint(Graphics graphics)
  {
      graphics.setColor(255,255,255);
      graphics.fillRect(0, 0, getWidth(), getHeight());
      graphics.setColor(255,0,0);
      graphics.drawRect(2, 2, 20, 20);
      graphics.drawRoundRect(20, 20, 60, 60, 15, 45);
  }
  public void commandAction(Command command, Displayable displayable)
  {
    if (command == exit)
    {
     rectangleExample.exitMIDlet();
    }
  }
}
```

Listing 7-8
The JAD
file for
Listing 7-7

```
MIDlet-Name: RectangleExample
MIDlet-Version: 1.0
MIDlet-Vendor: MyCompany
MIDlet-Jar-URL: RectangleExample.jar
MIDlet-1: RectangleExample, , RectangleExample
MicroEdition-Configuration: CLDC-1.0
MicroEdition-Profile: MIDP-1.0
MIDlet-JAR-SIZE: 100
```

Listing 7-9
Drawing
a filled
rectangle
and a filled
rounded
rectangle

```
import javax.microedition.midlet.*;
import javax.microedition.lcdui.*;
public class FilledRectangleExample extends MIDlet
{
  private Display  display;
  private MyCanvas canvas;
  public FilledRectangleExample ()
 {
    display = Display.getDisplay(this);
    canvas  = new myCanvas(this);
  }
  protected void startApp()
  {
    display.setCurrent( canvas );
  }
  protected void pauseApp()
  {
  }
  protected void destroyApp( boolean unconditional )
  {
  }
  public void exitMIDlet()
  {
    destroyApp(true);
    notifyDestroyed();
  }
}
class MyCanvas extends Canvas implements CommandListener
{
  private Command exit;
  private FilledRectangleExample filledRectangleExample;
  public MyCanvas (FilledRectangleExample filledRectangleExample)
  {
    this. filledRectangleExample = filledRectangleExample;
    exit = new Command("Exit", Command.EXIT, 1);
    addCommand(exit);
```

```
    setCommandListener(this);
  }
  protected void paint(Graphics graphics)
  {
    graphics.setColor(255,255,255);
    graphics.fillRect(0, 0, getWidth(), getHeight());
    graphics.setColor(0, 0, 255);
    graphics.fillRect(2, 2, 20, 20);
    graphics.fillRoundRect(20, 20, 60, 60, 15, 45);
  }
  public void commandAction(Command command, Displayable displayable)
  {
    if (command == exit)
    {
      filledRectangleExample.exitMIDlet();
    }
  }
}
```

Listing 7-10
The JAD
file for
Listing 7-9

```
MIDlet-Name: FilledRectangleExample
MIDlet-Version: 1.0
MIDlet-Vendor: MyCompany
MIDlet-Jar-URL: FilledRectangleExample.jar
MIDlet-1: FilledRectangleExample, , FilledRectangleExample
MicroEdition-Configuration: CLDC-1.0
MicroEdition-Profile: MIDP-1.0
MIDlet-JAR-SIZE: 100
```

Arcs

An arc is a curved line segment that is used to draw circles, ovals, and other curved images. As you'll soon discover, drawing an arc is a bit tricky because you must define the area of the canvas that will be covered by the arc and the angle used to draw the arc. The first step in drawing an arc is to decide the area of the canvas that will be covered by the arc. The area is defined as a rectangle rather than the circumference of the arc. Think of this as defining a box within which the angle is drawn. A rectangle is defined by specifying two sets of coordinates. The first set of coordinates (x1, y1) set the upper-left corner of the rectangle. The other set of coordinates (x2, y2) set the lower-right corner of the rectangle.

Once the rectangle is defined, you must define two angles used to draw the arc. An angle is defined in degrees from 0 to 360 degrees. The first angle is the starting point of the arc, and the other angle is the end point of the arc. Picture a clock. The 3 o'clock position is 0 degree. Degrees are incremented as you move counterclockwise. The 12 o'clock position is 90 degrees, 9 o'clock is 180 degrees, and 6 o'clock is 270 degrees. Degrees decrement as you move clockwise. Based on the picture of the clock, you must select the angle where the arc begins to be drawn. Likewise, you select the angle where the arc terminates.

Let's say that you want to draw a smile on the canvas. A smile is an arc. The starting point of the smile is at angle 180 (9 o'clock) and the end point at angle 360 (3 o'clock). It might take some trial and error, but you'll quickly learn to determine the proper angles to use when defining an arc to be drawn on the canvas.

Now with the theory under your belt, let's see how an arc is drawn from within a MIDlet. You can draw two kinds of arcs—an outlined arc and a filled arc. In an outlined arc, only the circumference of the arc is drawn (like a smile). In a filled arc, the circumference of the arc is drawn, and the area within the center and the circumference is filled with the color of the graphic context used to draw the arc (a colored circle, for example).

An outlined arc is drawn by calling the drawArc() method, and the filled arc is drawn by calling the fillArc() method. Both methods require six parameters, all of which are integers. The first two parameters set the coordinates for the upper-left corner of the rectangle that contains the arc (x1, y1). The next two parameters are the width and height of that rectangle (x2, y2). The fifth parameter is the start angle, and the last parameter is the end angle of the arc.

| Tip | *The rectangle is used as a reference when drawing the arc. The rectangle is not drawn on the canvas.* |

Drawing an Arc

Two listings are presented here, showing how to draw an arc within a MIDlet. Both programs perform basically the same task, except Listing 7-11 draws an outlined arc (see Figure 7-7), with the JAD file in Listing 7-12; while Listing 7-13 draws a filled arc (see Figure 7-8). Listing 7-14 contains the JAD file for Listing 7-13. The outlined arc is a smile using the default color. The filled arc is a half circle colored red.

Let's begin with Listing 7-11. This listing begins like other listings in this chapter, by declaring references to instances of the Display class and MyCanvas class, which is defined within the MIDlet. Instances are assigned to these variables in the constructor. The rest of the ArcExample class definition follows the structure used in other classes that we've discussed previously in this chapter.

Most of the action in Listing 7-11 and Listing 7-13 occurs in the MyCanvas class definition. The class definition begins by declaring references to the Exit command and an instance of the ArcExample class. The Exit command and the CommandListener are then associated with MyCanvas in the constructor of the MyCanvas class.

The paint() method definition is where the MIDlet draws the arc by calling the drawArc() method. First the rectangular area of the canvas that will contain the arc is

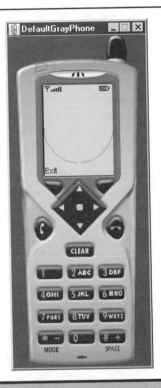

Figure 7-7. *An outlined half-circle arc*

defined by the first four parameters to the drawArc() method. The upper-left corner is at x, y coordinate 0, 0. The lower-right corner is calculated based on the size of the canvas. The getWidth() method and the getHeight() method return integers that represent the width and height of the canvas, which you learned about previously in this chapter.

The last two parameters of the drawArc() method specify the angle where the device begins drawing the arc on the canvas and the angle representing the end point of the arc. Drawing begins at the 180-degree angle position, which is 9 o'clock on the face of a clock. Drawing continues counterclockwise until another 180-degree angle position is reached. This is the 3 o'clock position.

The definition of the paint() method in Listing 7-13 is nearly the same as Listing 7-7's paint() method except that the paint() method in Listing 7-13 calls the fillArc() method instead of the drawArc() method. Both methods use the same parameters.

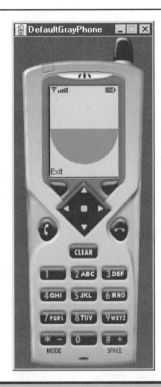

Figure 7-8. *A filled half-circle arc*

The last method defined in the MyCanvas class is the commandAction() method that is used to detect and process the Exit command whenever the user decides to terminate the MIDlet.

Listing 7-11
Drawing an
outlined arc

```
import javax.microedition.midlet.*;
import javax.microedition.lcdui.*;
public class ArcExample extends MIDlet
{
  private Display  display;
  private MyCanvas canvas;
  public ArcExample()
  {
```

```
      display = Display.getDisplay(this);
      canvas  = new MyCanvas (this);
   }
   protected void startApp()
   {
      display.setCurrent( canvas );
   }
   protected void pauseApp()
   {
   }
   protected void destroyApp( boolean unconditional )
   {
   }
   public void exitMIDlet()
   {
      destroyApp(true);
      notifyDestroyed();
   }
}
class MyCanvas extends Canvas implements CommandListener
{
   private Command exit;
   private ArcExample arcExample;
   public myCanvas (ArcExample arcExample)
   {
      this.arcExample = arcExample;
      exit = new Command("Exit", Command.EXIT, 1);
      addCommand(exit);
      setCommandListener(this);
   }
   protected void paint(Graphics graphics)
   {
      graphics.setColor(255,255,255);
      graphics.fillRect(0, 0, getWidth(), getHeight());
      graphics.setColor(255,0,0);
      graphics.drawArc(0, 0, getWidth(), getHeight(), 180, 180);
   }
   public void commandAction(Command command, Displayable displayable)
   {
```

```
            if (command == exit)
            {
               arcExample.exitMIDlet();
            }
         }
      }
```

Listing 7-12
e JAD file for
Listing 7-11

```
MIDlet-Name: ArcExample
MIDlet-Version: 1.0
MIDlet-Vendor: MyCompany
MIDlet-Jar-URL: ArcExample.jar
MIDlet-1: ArcExample, , ArcExample
MicroEdition-Configuration: CLDC-1.0
MicroEdition-Profile: MIDP-1.0
MIDlet-JAR-SIZE: 100
```

Listing 7-13
Drawing a
filled arc

```
import javax.microedition.midlet.*;
import javax.microedition.lcdui.*;
public class ArcFilledExample extends MIDlet
{
   private Display  display;
   private MyCanvas canvas;
   public ArcFilledExample()
   {
      display = Display.getDisplay(this);
      canvas  = new MyCanvas (this);
   }
   protected void startApp()
   {
      display.setCurrent( canvas );
   }
   protected void pauseApp()
   {
   }
   protected void destroyApp( boolean unconditional )
   {
   }
   public void exitMIDlet()
   {
```

```
      destroyApp(true);
      notifyDestroyed();
   }
}
class MyCanvas extends Canvas implements CommandListener
{
  private Command exit;
  private ArcFilledExample arcFilledExample;
  public MyCanvas (ArcFilledExample arcFilledExample)
  {
    this.arcFilledExample = arcFilledExample;
    exit = new Command("Exit", Command.EXIT, 1);
    addCommand(exit);
    setCommandListener(this);
  }
  protected void paint(Graphics graphics)
  {
    graphics.setColor(255,255,255);
    graphics.fillRect(0, 0, getWidth(), getHeight());
    graphics.setColor(255,0,0);
    graphics.fillArc(0, 0, getWidth(), getHeight(), 180, 180);
  }
  public void commandAction(Command command, Displayable displayable)
  {
    if (command == exit)
    {
      arcFilledExample.exitMIDlet();
    }
  }
}
```

Listing 7-14
The JAD file for
Listing 7-13

```
MIDlet-Name: ArcFilledExample
MIDlet-Version: 1.0
MIDlet-Vendor: MyCompany
MIDlet-Jar-URL: ArcFilledExample.jar
MIDlet-1: ArcFilledExample, , ArcFilledExample
MicroEdition-Configuration: CLDC-1.0
MicroEdition-Profile: MIDP-1.0
MIDlet-JAR-SIZE: 100
```

Drawing an Arc

Listed here are the steps for drawing an arc:

1. Declare references to classes.

2. Create instances of classes and assign those instances to references.

3. Display the instance of the Canvas class whenever the MIDlet is started.

4. Terminate the MIDlet when the Exit command is selected.

5. Define a class derived from the Canvas class that implements a CommandListener.

6. Within the derived class, declare references.

7. Within the derived class, create an instance of the Command class.

8. Within the derived class, associate the instance of the Command class with the canvas.

9. Within the derived class, associate the CommandListener with the canvas.

10. Within the derived class, define a paint() method to define the rectangular area of the canvas within which to draw the arc, and define angles where the arc begins and where the arc ends. Also set the color used to outline the arc or the fill area of the arc, unless the default color value is going to be used by the MIDlet.

11. Within the derived class, define a commandAction() method to process the Exit command.

Text

Displaying text using the low-level user interface differs from displaying text with the high-level user interface discussed in the previous chapter. The difference is based on who controls the details used to display the text. Using the high-level user interface, text is displayed by calling one of several methods and passing the text as a parameter to those methods. Each method determines how to display the text without requiring any direction from you. This is not the situation when displaying text using the low-level user interface because you control the details of how text is displayed.

Many developers pay little attention to how text appears on the screen (other than color and position), although displaying text is a complex operation. For example, someone must determine the appearance of each letter of the text, the height and width of every character, and the size of the space between characters, among other such details.

The font used to display text determines the appearance of text on the screen. There are thousands of fonts, as you have probably seen when you write a document using a word processor. We identify fonts by name, such as Times Roman and Arial. A font name actually represents a set of font metrics that determine the pixels necessary to generate alphanumeric characters and symbols on the screen and on a printed page.

The J2SE specification defines the FontMetrics class that is used to specify every detail of the font; but the J2ME specification does not support the FontMetrics class, and therefore you are limited to the font metrics that you can control from within your MIDlet. There are three font metrics that are controllable by a MIDlet. These are the font face, the font style, and the font size.

Selecting the *font face* is similar to selecting the font name in a word processing document, although your selections are limited to the default system font face, monospace font face, and proportional font face. The default system is the font face that the device chooses. Monospace is a font face in which all characters are the same width. Proportional is a font face in which the width of a character is determined by the nature of the character. For example, the letter *W* is wider than the letter *A*, and the letter *I* has a smaller width than *A*.

There are four *font styles* to choose from, which are identical to styles available in a word processor. These are plain, bold, italic, and underlined. You can apply multiple font styles to text by using the OR (|) operator. *Font sizes* are small, medium, and large. The small computing device determines the actual size of the font. Unlike a word processor, in which you can set font sizes to 10 points or 12 points, you cannot select specific type sizes. Instead, you must limit your choices to small, medium, or large.

Font faces, font styles, and font sizes are associated with font constants (Table 7-3) that are used to identify your font request. It is important to understand that your selection of a font is a request and not a directive to the device. The device will match your request to available fonts, but there is no guarantee that your request will be fulfilled. For example, you might request a monospace font face and an italic font style, but the text might be displayed using a monospace, plain font if the device doesn't have a monospace font in the italic font style.

You set a font by calling the setFont() method, which is a member of the Graphics class. The setFont() method requires one parameter, which is an instance of the Font class. You obtain the instance of the Font class by calling the getFont() method. The getFont() method requires three parameters. The first parameter is the font face, the second parameter is the font style, and the last parameter is the font size.

The following code segment illustrates how to set a font to the proportional font face that has bold and underline styles, and uses small size characters. Notice that the getFont() method is a member of the Font class, as are the font constants. Also notice that the OR (|) operator is used to combine font styles. Text displayed by that graphic context appears in the font once the font is set.

```
graphics.setFont(Font.getFont(Font.PROPORTIONAL,
              Font.BOLD | Font.ITALIC, Font.SMALL);
```

Font Constant	Description	Font Constant Value
FACE_SYSTEM	System font face	0
FACE_MONOSPACE	Monospace font face	32
FACE_PROPORTIONAL	Proportional font face	64
STYLE_PLAIN	Plain font style	0
STYLE_BOLD	Bold font style	1
STYLE_ITALIC	Italicized font style	2
STYLE_UNDERLINED	Underlined font style	4
SIZE_SMALL	Small font size	8
SIZE_MEDIUM	Medium font size	0
SIZE_LARGE	Large font size	16

Table 7-3. *Font Constants*

You can determine the font face, font style, and font size of an instance of the Font class by calling the getFace() method, getStyle() method, and the getSize() method, respectively. These methods return an integer that represents the value of the font constant listed in Table 7-3.

The integer returned by the getStyle() method represents the combined style of the instance of the Font class, such as Font.BOLD | Font.ITALIC. You can use a series of other methods to query the individual font styles associated with a font. These methods are isPlain(), isBold(), isItalic(), and isUnderlined(). Each of these methods returns a boolean value that is true if the corresponding style is used in the font, otherwise a false value is returned.

Aligning Text

Aligning text is probably the trickiest routine that you'll encounter when drawing text on the canvas because you'll need to know measurements of text that is already on the canvas as well as measurements of text being drawn. Text is drawn within a virtual bounding box, which is an invisible box that defines the boundaries of the text. First you specify a position on the screen by setting coordinates. Let's call them x, y. Next, you specify an anchor point that identifies the relationship of the coordinate to the bounding box.

Anchor Point Constant	Description
LEFT	Coordinates represent the left edge of the boundary box.
HCENTER	Coordinates represent the horizontal center of the boundary box.
RIGHT	Coordinates represent the right edge of the boundary box.
TOP	Coordinates represent the top edge of the boundary box.
BASELINE	Coordinates represent the baseline for the text.
BOTTOM	Coordinates represent the bottom edge of the boundary box.

Table 7-4. *Anchor Point Constants*

Suppose you want the coordinates to be the upper-left corner of the boundary box. You then specify the anchor point TOP | LEFT. Let's say that you want the coordinates to represent the lower-right corner of the boundary box. You then use the BOTTOM | RIGHT anchor point. The width and height of the text determine the coordinate of the opposite corner of the boundary box. Anchor points are represented by anchor point constants, as shown in Table 7-4.

There are three horizontal values, LEFT, HCENTER, and RIGHT, and three vertical values, TOP, BASELINE, and BOTTOM. Horizontal and vertical values define the location within the bounding box of the specified coordinate. The values are combined to define an anchor point. Here's how this is done. You pick a location on the screen, and if you want that position to be the upper-right of the bounding box, you set the anchor point to GRAPHICS.TOP | GRAPHICS.RIGHT.

The question that remains to be answered is how do you know which anchor point to use to draw your text? However, there isn't a clear-cut answer. Other text that abuts the boundary box usually determines text alignment within the boundary box. Text is measured by ascent, descent, leading, font height, and advance.

Ascent is the measurement from the baseline of the text to the top of the highest character in the text. *Descent* is from the baseline to the lowest character in the text. Let's examine the following text to identify the ascent and descent: "We work together." The ascent is the distance between the bottom and the top of the *W* because the *W* is the highest character in the text. The bottom of the *W* is the baseline. The descent is the distance between the bottom of the *g* and the bottom of the *W*, or the bottom of any of the other characters of the text, because the *g* is the lowest character within the text.

Leading is the distance between the descent and ascent of abutting lines of text. The *font height* is the sum of the ascent, leading, and descent. And the *advance* is the text length, including spaces between characters.

You can use methods of the Font class to determine these measurements. You can determine the advance by calling the charWidth() method, the charsWidth() method, or the substringWidth() method. The charWidth() method measures the width of one character and requires one parameter, which is a character. This method returns an integer representing the width of the character in pixels.

The charsWidth() method measures a series of characters in a character array. This method requires three parameters. The first parameter is the character array. The second parameter is an integer representing the first character of the series being measured. The last parameter is an integer representing the length of the series.

The substringWidth() method measures a substring of characters within a string and also requires three parameters. The first parameter is the string. The second parameter is an integer representing the first character of the substring, and the last parameter is an integer representing the length of the substring.

The ascent is measured by calling the getBaselinePosition() method. No parameters are required by this method because the method analyzes text already associated with the graphic context used to draw text on the canvas. The getBaselinePosition() method returns an integer that represents the pixels between the baseline and the top character within the text.

The font height is measured by calling the getHeight() method. The getHeight() method does not require any parameters and returns an integer representing the pixel measurement of the font height.

You use these measurements to determine the alignment adjustments that must be made to the anchor point of the text. Let's say you draw two lines of text, and you want to align both lines. The first line is already drawn, and you're about to draw the second line. First, set the boundary box of the second line of text two pixels below the boundary box of the first line of text. Next, determine the font height of both lines. Let's assume that the font height for the first line of text is higher than the second line because the first line has descending characters and the second line does not have either ascending or descending characters.

You may want to anchor the second line of text toward either the horizontal center or bottom of the boundary box in order to avoid the appearance of cramping the descending character of the first line of text.

Be forewarned that aligning text using text metrics and anchor points is tedious and requires patience, but your efforts will show in the results on the screen.

Drawing Methods

There are four methods that you can use to draw text on the canvas. Your choice depends on whether the text is a character, array of characters, a string, or a substring. Call the drawChar() method if you are drawing one character on the canvas. The drawChar() method requires four parameters. The first parameter is the character. The next two parameters are the x, y coordinates of the upper-left corner of the boundary box. And the last parameter is the anchor point.

The drawChars() method is used to draw an array of characters or a subset of a character array. The drawChars() method requires six parameters. The first parameter is the character array. The second parameter is an integer representing the offset in the array where the first character to be drawn is located. The third parameter indicates how many characters are to be drawn starting at the offset specified by the second parameter. The fourth and fifth parameters are the x, y coordinates of the boundary box's anchor point.

There are two methods you can use when drawing a string on the canvas. These are the drawString() method and the drawSubstring() method. The drawString() method requires four parameters. The first parameter is the string. The second and third parameters are the x, y coordinates that specify the anchor point coordinate. And the last parameter specifies the part of the boundary box to locate the anchor point.

The drawSubstring() method is very similar in structure to the drawChars() method in that the same six parameters are required, except the first parameter is the string that contains the substring that is being drawn on the canvas.

Drawing Text

Listing 7-15 illustrates how to draw a line of text on the canvas. Listing 7-16 is the JAD file for Listing 7-15. The text is short but sufficient to demonstrate this technique. This example uses the proportional font face, bold style, and small font size to draw the text in the center of the boundary box, which is located near the upper-left corner of the canvas.

The TextExample class definition is structured identically to other listings in this chapter. Likewise, the definition of the myCanvas class is very similar to the myCanvas class definitions used in other examples. However, the definition of the paint() method is where all the action takes place to draw the text.

The first two statements within the paint() method are used to erase the canvas, as discussed in previous sections of this chapter. The third statement sets the font for the graphic context used to draw the text. The setFont() method requires reference to an instance of the Font class, which is returned by the getFont() method. Notice that we pass the font face, font style, and font size that we want to the getFont() method. This assures that the instance of the Font class returned to the MIDlet has those properties.

The last statement draws the string by calling the drawString() method (see Figure 7-9). The text is "Profound statement.", which is passed as the first parameter to the drawString() method. The next two parameters are coordinates of the anchor point. The last parameter defines the position of the string using the HCENTER | BASELINE constants. It tells drawString() that the center of the bounding box and where the baseline occurs is at pixel coordinate (50, 10).

Figure 7-9. *This draws a string on the canvas by calling the drawString() method.*

The commandAction() method is the last method defined in the myCanvas class. This class definition is the same as used in other examples in this chapter.

Listing 7-15
Drawing text on the canvas

```
import javax.microedition.midlet.*;
import javax.microedition.lcdui.*;
public class TextExample extends MIDlet
{
  private Display  display;
  private MyCanvas canvas;
  public TextExample ()
  {
    display = Display.getDisplay(this);
    canvas  = new MyCanvas (this);
  }
```

```java
  protected void startApp()
  {
    display.setCurrent(canvas);
  }
  protected void pauseApp()
  {
  }
  protected void destroyApp( boolean unconditional )
  {
  }
  public void exitMIDlet()
  {
    destroyApp(true);
    notifyDestroyed();
  }
}
class MyCanvas extends Canvas implements CommandListener
{
  private Command exit;
  private TextExample textExample;
  public MyCanvas (TextExample textExample)
  {
    this. textExample = textExample;
    exit = new Command("Exit", Command.EXIT, 1);
    addCommand(exit);
    setCommandListener(this);
  }
  protected void paint(Graphics graphics)
  {
    graphics.setColor(255,255,255);
    graphics.fillRect(0, 0, getWidth(), getHeight());
    graphics.setColor(255,0,0);
    graphics.setFont(Font.getFont(Font.FACE_PROPORTIONAL,
                        Font.STYLE_BOLD, Font.SIZE_SMALL));
    graphics.drawString("Profound statement.", 50, 10,
Graphics.HCENTER|Graphics.BASELINE);
  }
  public void commandAction(Command command, Displayable displayable)
  {
    if (command == exit)
    {
      textExample.exitMIDlet();
```

```
      }
    }
  }
```

Listing 7-16
The JAD
file for
Listing 7-15

```
MIDlet-Name: TextExample
MIDlet-Version: 1.0
MIDlet-Vendor: MyCompany
MIDlet-Jar-URL: TextExample.jar
MIDlet-1: TextExample, , TextExample
MicroEdition-Configuration: CLDC-1.0
MicroEdition-Profile: MIDP-1.0
MIDlet-JAR-SIZE: 100
```

Drawing Text

Listed here are the steps for drawing text:

1. Declare references to classes.
2. Create instances of classes and assign those instances to references.
3. Display the instance of the Canvas class whenever the MIDlet is started.
4. Terminate the MIDlet when the Exit command is selected.
5. Define a class derived from the Canvas class that implements a CommandListener.
6. Within the derived class, declare references.
7. Within the derived class, create an instance of the Command class.
8. Within the derived class, associate the instance of the Command class with the canvas.
9. Within the derived class, associate the CommandListener with the canvas.
10. Within the derived class, define a paint() method to create a font that has a proportional font face, bold font style, and small font size. The paint() method must also draw the text "Profound statement."
11. Within the derived class, define a commandAction() method to process the Exit command.

Images

An image is an instance of an Image object that has been previously created either by your MIDlet using a graphic context (discussed earlier in this chapter), or by graphics software. Recall from the previous chapter, there are two kinds of images: a mutable image can be modified by your MIDlet, and an immutable image cannot be modified by your MIDlet.

You create an instance of an Image by calling the createImage() method. The createImage() method requires one parameter or two parameters depending on whether you are drawing a mutable or immutable image. One parameter is required for the createImage() method if the instance is used to draw an immutable image. The parameter is the file name of the image, including the full directory path. The following code segment illustrates this technique:

```
Image image = Image.createImage("/myImage.png");
```

Two parameters are required for the createImage() method if the instance is used to draw a mutable image. These parameters define the height and width in pixels of the memory block used to store the mutable image as it is being drawn. The following code segment creates a block of memory 20 pixels high and 10 pixels wide for a total image size of 200 pixels.

```
Image tmpImg = Image.createImage(20, 10);
```

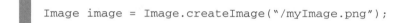

Tip *Some developers sketch a mutable image on graph paper to get a rough layout of the image and an estimate of the memory block size required to draw the image.*

You'll use the instance as a parameter to the drawImage() method, which draws the image on the canvas. You'll see how this is done later in this section. The instance of the image is also used to create a mutable image.

You create a mutable image by calling the getGraphics() method of the Image class to return an instance of the Graphics class, which is the graphic context used to draw the mutable image. Methods discussed in the "Graphics" section earlier in this chapter are used to draw elements of the mutable image.

Let's say that you want to create a mutable image of a line. The following code segment shows you how this is done. First, you must create an instance of the Image class by calling the createImage() method. Next, you'll need an instance of the Graphics class that is created by calling the getGraphics() method. And then you call the drawLine() method, as described previously in this chapter.

```
Image image = Image.createImage(20, 10);
Graphics graphic = image.getGraphics();
graphic.drawLine(5, 5, 20, 20);
```

Of course, your mutable graphic would be more complex than a simple line because you'll probably use other methods of the Graphics class to build an attractive image. Each of these methods, however, must be called from the same instance of the Graphics class that is derived from the instance of the image you created in your MIDlet.

The drawImage() method is used to draw a mutable or immutable image on the canvas. The drawImage() requires four parameters. The first parameter is the instance of the Image class that references the image. The next two parameters are integers that represent the coordinate used to position the image on the canvas. The image is drawn within a virtual boundary box similar to the boundary box used to draw text on the canvas (see "Text"). The coordinate represents the upper-left corner of the boundary box.

The last parameter is an integer that represents the portion of the image bounding box that is anchored at the specified coordinate. The image anchor point is used to finely adjust the location of the image within the boundary box. Table 7-5 lists constants used to represent image anchor points. Two anchor points must be specified in the drawImage() method—one for the horizontal position and the other for the vertical position. This is nearly identical to the way anchor points are specified in the text drawing methods.

Here is a code segment that shows how to draw an image on the canvas. This method is used to draw both mutable and immutable images. The code segment centers the image

Anchor Point Constant	Description
LEFT	Coordinates represent the left edge of the boundary box.
HCENTER	Coordinates represent the horizontal center of the boundary box.
RIGHT	Coordinates represent the right edge of the boundary box.
TOP	Coordinates represent the top edge of the boundary box.
VCENTER	Coordinates represent the baseline for the text.
BOTTOM	Coordinates represent the bottom edge of the boundary box.

Table 7-5.   *Image Anchor Point Constants*

horizontally and vertically at 5, 20, which is the center of the image bounding box specified by the coordinate.

```
graphics.drawImage(image, 5, 20, Graphics.HCENTER | Graphics.VCENTER);
```

Drawing an Image

Listing 7-17 creates a mutable image of a filled arc (see Figure 7-10) and then draws the image. The JAD file is in Listing 7-18. Listing 7-19 draws an immutable image; Listing 7-20 contains the JAD file.

Let's begin with Listing 7-17. The structure of this listing is very similar to other listings discussed in this chapter, so we'll move to the definition of the MyCanvas class that contains statements not used in previous listings. The MyCanvas definition begins by declaring references that include a reference to an instance of the Image class, which is set to null. The constructor of the MyCanvas class creates an Exit command and assigns the Exit command and a CommandListener to the canvas.

Figure 7-10. *A drawing of a mutable image of a filled arc*

Next, the memory block is requested for the image by calling the createImage() method. The memory block is 70 pixels high and 70 pixels wide. The createImage() method returns an instance of the Image class, which is then assigned to the image variable.

The instance of the Image class is then used to create a graphic context by calling the getGraphics() method. The getGraphics() method returns an instance of the Graphics class. The setColor() method is then called to set the color of the image to red. This is followed by a call to the fillArc() method that draws a filled arc (see "Arcs") in the memory block that was requested for the image.

You can't assume that the device will be able to reserve the block of memory for the image or be able to create the image. Therefore, you should place these statements within a try {} block and create a catch {} block to respond to any errors that might occur during this process. The catch {} block in this example displays an alert dialog box should an error happen (see Chapter 6).

Drawing an Image

Listed here are the steps for drawing an image:

1. Declare references to classes.

2. Create instances of classes and assign those instances to references.

3. Display the instance of the Canvas class whenever the MIDlet is started.

4. Terminate the MIDlet when the Exit command is selected.

5. Define a class derived from the Canvas class that implements a CommandListener.

6. Within the derived class, declare references.

7. Within the derived class, create an instance of the Command class.

8. Within the derived class, associate the instance of the Command class with the canvas.

9. Within the derived class, associate the CommandListener with the canvas.

10. Request a block of memory sufficient to hold the image, and then create the image, if you are using a mutable image. Otherwise, identify the file name that contains the immutable image. Display an error message if there is a problem creating the image or opening the file that contains the image.

11. Within the derived class, define a paint() method that determines whether the image was successfully created or the image file was successfully opened. If so, then draw the image on the canvas.

12. Within the derived class, define a commandAction() method to process the Exit command.

The definition of the paint() method is also different from paint() methods used in previous listings in this chapter. The paint() method uses an if statement to determine whether the image variable is referencing an image memory block. You'll recall that the image variable was initialized to null at the beginning of the MyCanvas class definition. If the allocation of the memory block failed in the constructor, the image variable is still null, otherwise the null value is replaced with a reference to the image memory block.

The drawImage() method is called once the paint() method verifies that the image variable isn't null. The drawImage() is passed the image variable and the coordinate of the image boundary box. The image is then positioned in the vertical and horizontal center of the image boundary box as indicated by the image anchor point parameter. The commandAction() method definition is the same as in other listings discussed in this chapter.

Listing 7-19 is similar to Listing 7-17 except for statements within the try {} block and catch {} block in the definition of the MyCanvas class constructor. You'll notice that the try {} block contains one statement that calls the createImage() method. The createImage() is passed the name of the immutable image that will be associated with the instance of the Image class returned by the createImage() method. No other statements are necessary because the image is already created and the createImage() method automatically requests a block of memory to store the image.

However, there is a possibility that the device is unable to load the image into memory; for example, it may not be able to locate the image file that is passed to the createImage() method. Therefore, you still need to place the call to the createImage() method within a try {} block. The catch{} block is practically the same as in Listing 7-17, except the message that appears in the alert dialog box reports that the image file cannot be opened.

Listing 7-17
Drawing a mutable image on the canvas

```
import javax.microedition.midlet.*;
import javax.microedition.lcdui.*;
public class MutableImageExample extends MIDlet
{
  private Display  display;
  private MyCanvas canvas;
  public MutableImageExample ()
  {
    display = Display.getDisplay(this);
    canvas  = new MyCanvas (this);
  }
  protected void startApp()
  {
    display.setCurrent( canvas );
  }
  protected void pauseApp()
  {
```

```
}
protected void destroyApp( boolean unconditional )
{
}
public void exitMIDlet()
{
  destroyApp(true);
  notifyDestroyed();
}
class MyCanvas extends Canvas implements CommandListener
{
  private Command exit;
  private MutableImageExample mutableImageExample;
  private Image image = null;
  public myCanvas(MutableImageExample mutableImageExample)
  {
    this. mutableImageExample = mutableImageExample;
    exit = new Command("Exit", Command.EXIT, 1);
    addCommand(exit);
    setCommandListener(this);
    try
    {
      image = Image.createImage(70, 70);
      Graphics graphics = image.getGraphics();
      graphics.setColor(255, 0, 0);
      graphics.fillArc(10, 10, 60, 50, 180, 180);
    }
    catch (Exception error)
    {
      Alert alert = new Alert("Failure",
                   "Creating Image", null, null);
      alert.setTimeout(Alert.FOREVER);
      display.setCurrent(alert);
    }
  }
  protected void paint(Graphics graphics)
  {
    if (image != null)
    {
     graphics.setColor(255,255,255);
     graphics.fillRect(0, 0, getWidth(), getHeight());
     graphics.drawImage(image, 30, 30,
```

```
                              Graphics.VCENTER | Graphics.HCENTER);
        }
      }
      public void commandAction(Command command, Displayable display)
      {
        if (command == exit)
        {
          mutableImageExample.exitMIDlet();
        }
      }
    }
}
```

Listing 7-18
The JAD
file for
Listing 7-17

```
MIDlet-Name: MutableImageExample
MIDlet-Version: 1.0
MIDlet-Vendor: MyCompany
MIDlet-Jar-URL: MutableImageExample.jar
MIDlet-1: MutableImageExample, , MutableImageExample
MicroEdition-Configuration: CLDC-1.0
MicroEdition-Profile: MIDP-1.0
MIDlet-JAR-SIZE: 100
```

Listing 7-19
Drawing an
immutable
image on
the canvas

```
import javax.microedition.midlet.*;
import javax.microedition.lcdui.*;
public class ImmutableImageExample extends MIDlet
{
  private Display  display;
  private MyCanvas canvas;
  public ImmutableImageExample ()
  {
    display = Display.getDisplay(this);
    canvas  = new MyCanvas (this);
  }
  protected void startApp()
  {
    display.setCurrent( canvas );
  }
  protected void pauseApp()
  {
  }
  protected void destroyApp( boolean unconditional )
```

```
  {
  }
public void exitMIDlet()
{
  destroyApp(true);
  notifyDestroyed();
}
class MyCanvas extends Canvas implements CommandListener
{
  private Command exit;
  private ImmutableImageExample immutableImageExample;
  private Image image = null;
  public MyCanvas (ImmutableImageExample immutableImageExample)
  {
    this. immutableImageExample = immutableImageExample;
    exit = new Command("Exit", Command.EXIT, 1);
    addCommand(exit);
    setCommandListener(this);
    try
    {
      image = Image.createImage("/myImage.png");
    }
    catch (Exception error)
    {
      Alert alert = new Alert("Failure",
                   "Can't open image file.", null, null);
      alert.setTimeout(Alert.FOREVER);
      display.setCurrent(alert);
    }
  }
  protected void paint(Graphics graphics)
  {
    if (image != null)
    {
      graphics.drawImage(image, 0, 0,
                    Graphics.VCENTER | Graphics.HCENTER);
    }
  }
  public void commandAction(Command command, Displayable display)
  {
    if (command == exit)
    {
```

```
                immutableImageExample.exitMIDlet();
        }
    }
}
}
```

```
MIDlet-Name: ImmutableImageExample
MIDlet-Version: 1.0
MIDlet-Vendor: MyCompany
MIDlet-Jar-URL: ImmutableImageExample.jar
MIDlet-1: ImmutableImageExample, , ImmutableImageExample
MicroEdition-Configuration: CLDC-1.0
MicroEdition-Profile: MIDP-1.0
MIDlet-JAR-SIZE: 100
```

Repositioning Text and Images

Each position on a canvas is organized by a row and column grid, where each coordinate identifies a pixel. The upper-left corner of the canvas is always coordinate 0, 0, as previously discussed in this chapter. Coordinates are used with methods of a graphic context to identify locations on the canvas for drawing and positioning an image, as illustrated through listings in this chapter.

Coordinates are passed explicitly to these methods by providing exact coordinates, such as 5, 10, or implicitly by referencing an offset of an explicit coordinate, such as 5 + 3, 10 + 3. In either case, coordinates are based on the 0, 0 coordinate being the upper-left corner of the canvas.

You might need to proportionally shift all text and images to a new location on the canvas. There are two techniques you can use to make this move. First, you can change all coordinates of an image to reflect its new position, or you can move the entire grid and let the device adjust all the coordinates based on the new position of the upper-left corner of the grid on the canvas. This technique, called *translating coordinates,* is a more efficient way of moving text and images than modifying coordinates within your MIDlet.

You translate coordinates by calling the translate() method of the Graphics class. The translate() method requires two parameters that are integers representing the x, y coordinate of the new position of the upper-left corner of the grid.

Let's say you draw an arc where the upper-left corner of the image boundary box is at coordinate 0, 0 on the canvas. You then want to modify your MIDlet to move the arc and any other text and images on the canvas down and across 15 pixels. You can achieve this by calling the translate() and passing the coordinates of the new location of the first cell of the grid before the image is drawn on the screen. This is illustrated in Listing 7-21.

You'll notice that the coordinate for the drawImage() method is 0, 0. However, the coordinate passed to the translate() method is 15, 15. Reference to coordinate 0, 0 is automatically adjusted to the coordinate of the new upper-left corner of the grid, which is 15, 15.

At any point in your MIDlet you can reset the first pixel on the canvas to the original position by calling the translate() method and passing it 0, 0 as the coordinate for the upper-left corner of the canvas. Remember that the translate() method only affects the position of text and images called after the translate() method is invoked. Text and images previously drawn on the canvas are unaffected.

You can determine the coordinate of the upper-left corner of the canvas by calling the getTranslateX() method and getTranslateY() method to return the x, y coordinate.

Translating Coordinates in a MIDlet

Listing 7-21 is a modification of Listing 7-17, which creates a mutable image of a filled arc drawn on the canvas using the drawImage() method. Listing 7-22 is the JAD file for Listing 7-21. Refer to the "Drawing an Image" section of this chapter for a detailed explanation of Listing 7-17, which also applies to Listing 7-21.

Translating Coordinates

Listed here are the steps for translating coordinates:

1. Declare references to classes.

2. Create instances of classes and assign those instances to references.

3. Display the instance of the Canvas class whenever the MIDlet is started.

4. Terminate the MIDlet when the Exit command is selected.

5. Define a class derived from the Canvas class that implements a CommandListener.

6. Within the derived class, declare references.

7. Within the derived class, create an instance of the Command class.

8. Within the derived class, associate the instance of the Command class with the canvas.

9. Within the derived class, associate the CommandListener with the canvas.

10. Request a block of memory sufficient to hold the image, and then create the image, if you are using a mutable image. Otherwise, identify the file name that contains the immutable image. Display an error message if there is a problem creating the image or opening the file that contains the image.

11. Within the derived class, define a paint() method that determines whether the image was successfully created or the image file was successfully opened. If so, translate the coordinates of the first pixel on the grid, and then draw the image on the canvas.

12. Within the derived class, define a commandAction() method to process the Exit command.

You'll notice that the instance of the Image class is created in the constructor of the definition of the myCanvas class. Creation of the instance also reserves a block of memory that is used to draw the filled arc. The instance is also used to create an instance of the Graphics class that provides the graphic contexts needed to draw the filled arc. The color is set to red, and the fillArc() method is called to draw the filled arc with the reserved block of memory.

Let's jump down to the definition of the paint() method in Listing 7-21 to see how the image of the filled arc is drawn on the screen using the translate() method. Once the MIDlet determines that an image has been created by using the if statement, the translate() method is called and passed the coordinate 45, 45, which is the new coordinate for the upper-left corner of the grid.

Notice that the drawImage() method is passed 0, 0 as the coordinate used to draw the image on the canvas. Coordinate 0, 0 refers to the first pixel on the canvas. However, the translate() method redefined the coordinate of the first pixel as being 45, 45. Therefore, the image is drawn at cell 45, 45 on the original grid rather than 0, 0 (see Figure 7-11). This happens without your having to modify the coordinates passed to the drawImage() method.

Figure 7-11.   *An image is drawn at cell 45, 45 on the original grid rather than at cell 0, 0.*

```
import javax.microedition.midlet.*;
import javax.microedition.lcdui.*;
public class TranslateCoordinates extends MIDlet
{
  private Display  display;
  private MyCanvas canvas;
  public TranslateCoordinates ()
  {
    display = Display.getDisplay(this);
    canvas  = new MyCanvas (this);
  }
  protected void startApp()
  {
    display.setCurrent( canvas );
  }
  protected void pauseApp()
  {
  }
  protected void destroyApp( boolean unconditional )
  {
  }
  public void exitMIDlet()
  {
    destroyApp(true);
    notifyDestroyed();
  }
  class MyCanvas extends Canvas implements CommandListener
  {
    private Command exit;
    private TranslateCoordinates translateCoordinates;
    private Image image = null;
    public myCanvas(TranslateCoordinates translateCoordinates)
    {
      this. translateCoordinates = translateCoordinates;
      exit = new Command("Exit", Command.EXIT, 1);
      addCommand(exit);
      setCommandListener(this);
      try
      {
        image = Image.createImage(70, 70);
        Graphics graphics = image.getGraphics();
        graphics.setColor(255,0,0);
```

```
          graphics.fillArc(10, 10, 60, 50, 180, 180);
        }
        catch (Exception error)
        {
          Alert alert = new Alert("Failure",
                          "Creating Image", null, null);
          alert.setTimeout(Alert.FOREVER);
          display.setCurrent(alert);
        }
      }
      protected void paint(Graphics graphics)
      {
        if (image != null)
        {
         graphics.setColor(255,255,255);
         graphics.fillRect(0, 0, getWidth(), getHeight());
         graphics.translate(45, 45);
         graphics.drawImage(image, 0, 0,
                      Graphics.VCENTER | Graphics.HCENTER);      }
        }
      public void commandAction(Command command, Displayable display)
      {
        if (command == exit)
        {
          translateCoordinates.exitMIDlet();
        }
      }
    }
  }
}
```

```
MIDlet-Name: TranslateCoordinates
MIDlet-Version: 1.0
MIDlet-Vendor: MyCompany
MIDlet-Jar-URL: TranslateCoordinates.jar
MIDlet-1: TranslateCoordinates, , TranslateCoordinates
```

```
MicroEdition-Configuration: CLDC-1.0
MicroEdition-Profile: MIDP-1.0
MIDlet-JAR-SIZE: 100
```

Clipping Regions

The drawImage() method used in previous listings in this chapter draws an image on the canvas based on a clipping region. A *clipping region* is a rectangular piece of an image defined by two sets of coordinates. The first set identifies the upper-left corner of the clipping region, and the second set is the width and height of the clipping region. Only the portion of the image that appears within the clipping region is drawn on the canvas. Other portions of the image still exist within the image but are not drawn. The entire canvas is the default clipping region and is used to draw the complete image whenever the drawImage() method is called.

Let's return to the filled arc created and drawn in Listing 7-17 to see how adjusting the clipping region changes the way an image is drawn on the canvas. The image boundary box of the filled arc in Listing 7-17 has the coordinates 10, 10, 60, 60. This means the upper-left corner of the box appears at cell 10, 10 and has a width of 60 and height of 60. The clipping region is the entire canvas. We can show a piece of the filled arc by setting the clipping region to 35, 35, 40, 40, which is what happens in Listing 7-23. Only a portion of the filled arc is drawn when the drawImage() method is called.

You set the clipping region by calling the setClip() method of the Graphics class. The setClip() method requires four parameters. The first two parameters are integers representing the upper-left corner coordinates of the clipping region, and the third and fourth parameters are integers representing the width and height of the clipping region.

You can also reduce the size of a clipping region by calling the clipRect() method. The clipRect() method also requires the same four parameters as the setClip(), except coordinates passed to the clipRect() method refer to the new clipping region.

There are four other methods that you might find handy when working with a clipping region. These are the getClipX() method, getClipY() method, getClipHeight() method, and getClipWidth() method. The getClipX() method and getClipY() method return upper-left coordinates of the existing clipping region. Similarly, the getClipHeight() method returns the height and getClipWidth() method returns the width of the existing clipping region.

Creating a Clipping Region

Listed here are the steps for creating a clipping region:

1. Declare references to classes.
2. Create instances of classes and assign those instances to references.
3. Display the instance of the Canvas class whenever the MIDlet is started.
4. Terminate the MIDlet when the Exit command is selected.
5. Define a class derived from the Canvas class that implements a CommandListener.
6. Within the derived class, declare references.
7. Within the derived class, create an instance of the Command class.
8. Within the derived class, associate the instance of the Command class with the canvas.
9. Within the derived class, associate the CommandListener with the canvas.
10. Request a block of memory sufficient to hold the image, and then create the image, if you are using a mutable image. Otherwise, identify the file name that contains the immutable image. Display an error message if there is a problem creating the image or opening the file that contains the image.
11. Within the derived class, define a paint() method that determines whether the image was successfully created or the image file was successfully opened. If so, create a new clipping region and draw the image on the canvas.
12. Within the derived class, define a commandAction() method to process the Exit command.

Creating a Clipping Region

Listing 7-23 illustrates how to set a clipping region in a MIDlet. Listing 7-24 contains the JAD file for Listing 7-23. This example draws a filled arc, which you have seen in Listing 7-17 (see Figure 7-12). However, only a portion of the filled arc is actually drawn on the canvas because a clipping region is defined as being smaller than the filled arc (see Figure 7-13).

Figure 7-12. *A filled arc is drawn without using a clipping region.*

Listing 7-23 is basically the same as Listing 7-17, so refer back to the "Drawing an Image" section if you are unsure of how each statement in the MIDlet works. For now, we'll turn our attention to the definition of the paint() method since this is where the clipping region is created.

The filled arc is created and drawn in the myCanvas class constructor and drawn on the screen by calling the drawImage() method in the definition of the paint() method. However, the clipping region is created prior to calling the drawImage() method since the drawImage() method draws the image on the current clipping region, which is the full canvas if we didn't precede the drawImage() method with the setClip() method.

Figure 7-13. *A filled arc is drawn using a clipping region.*

The setClip() method is passed two coordinates. The first coordinate identifies the upper-left cell of the clipping region, which is 35, 35. The second coordinate identifies the width and height of the region, which is 40, 40.

Listing 7-23
Creating
a clipping
region

```
import javax.microedition.midlet.*;
import javax.microedition.lcdui.*;
public class  ClippingRegion extends MIDlet
{
  private Display  display;
  private MyCanvas canvas;
  public ClippingRegion()
  {
    display = Display.getDisplay(this);
    canvas  = new MyCanvas(this);
```

```
}
protected void startApp()
{
  display.setCurrent( canvas );
}
protected void pauseApp()
{
}
protected void destroyApp( boolean unconditional )
{
}
public void exitMIDlet()
{
  destroyApp(true);
  notifyDestroyed();
}
class MyCanvas extends Canvas implements CommandListener
{
  private Command exit;
  private ClippingRegion clippingRegion;
  private Image image = null;
  public MyCanvas (ClippingRegion clippingRegion)
  {
    this. clippingRegion = clippingRegion;
    exit = new Command("Exit", Command.EXIT, 1);
    addCommand(exit);
    setCommandListener(this);
    try
    {
      image = Image.createImage(70, 70);
      Graphics graphics = image.getGraphics();
      graphics.setColor(255,0,0);
      graphics.fillArc(10, 10, 60, 50, 180, 180);
    }
    catch (Exception error)
    {
      Alert alert = new Alert("Failure", "Creating Image",
                        null, null);
      alert.setTimeout(Alert.FOREVER);
      display.setCurrent(alert);
    }
  }
```

```
      protected void paint(Graphics graphics)
      {
        if (image != null)
        {
         graphics.setColor(255,255,255);
         graphics.fillRect(0, 0, getWidth(), getHeight());
         graphics.setClip(35, 35, 40, 40);
         graphics.drawImage(image, 30, 30,
                       Graphics.VCENTER | Graphics.HCENTER);
        }
      }
      public void commandAction(Command command, Displayable display)
      {
        if (command == exit)
        {
          clippingRegion.exitMIDlet();
        }
      }
    }
  }
```

Listing 7-24
The JAD file for
Listing 7-23

```
MIDlet-Name: ClippingRegion
MIDlet-Version: 1.0
MIDlet-Vendor: MyCompany
MIDlet-Jar-URL: ClippingRegion.jar
MIDlet-1: ClippingRegion, , ClippingRegion
MicroEdition-Configuration: CLDC-1.0
MicroEdition-Profile: MIDP-1.0
MIDlet-JAR-SIZE: 100
```

Animation

Animation is the simulation of motion on the screen caused by the timed drawing of a series of related images. Each image is referred to as a *cell* in animation terminology; however, we'll use the term *image* instead because a cell also refers to an intersection of the grid used for positioning objects on the canvas.

Each image in the animation must relate to the image currently displayed and the next image to be displayed. Let's say the animation shows a ball bouncing up and down. At least two images are necessary to create this illusion of motion. One image is the ball in the air, and the other is the ball on the ground. The animation begins by showing the image of the ball in the air followed by the image of the ball on the ground and then back to displaying the ball in the air.

You can enhance the quality of the animation by inserting other images in this sequence. For example, one image might be the ball striking the ground followed by another image that shows the ball being flattened by the ground, and then the image of the rounded ball on the ground is displayed before the ball is shown in the air.

Our brain is able to retain the current image for the fraction of a second until the next image is displayed. We don't notice that the image has changed. That is, we don't notice unless the time between displaying images is longer than the length of time our brain retains the image, or if the next image isn't logically associated with the current image.

For example, suppose there is an animation of a ball being dropped from a rooftop to the ground. The ball bounces after striking the ground. The animation begins with the image of the ball on the rooftop followed by the ball in the air, giving the illusion of the ball falling. The next image we'd expect to see is the ball hitting the ground. Let's say that the next image isn't the ball hitting the ground but is the image of the ball on the rooftop again. The sequence of images isn't logical and therefore disrupts the illusion of the bouncing ball.

Simulated movement becomes realistic if 30 images (sometimes called frames) are displayed per second. This is the display rate used in films and television. However, you can probably use a slower rate for animation on the small computing device. The slower the rate (fewer images per second), the more jerky the movement appears.

Animation appears to move smoothly if each image in the series represents a small progression toward the final image. Let's return to the bouncing ball. The ball appears to move roughly if there are three images: one image at the top of the roof; another midway to the ground; and the last image of the ball hitting the ground. However, by showing other images of the ball at different stages of falling in a logical sequence, the ball appears to fall smoothly from the roof.

The first step in animation is to carefully lay out the progression of images that you'll need to display in order to create the illusion of movement. Next, create each image so that each is slightly different from the previous image. You can create these images as either mutable or immutable. A mutable image is created using methods described in this chapter. An immutable image is created using graphics software or digital photography.

Once images are drawn or loaded from a file, you display each image by first calling the createImage() method to create an instance of the Image class and then calling the drawImage() method. Timing the display of each image is controlled by a timing loop (sometimes within a while loop) so that the animation recycles to the first image after the last image is displayed.

Another way to incorporate animation in your MIDlet is to create one large image that is a composite of each image in the animation. You then change the clipping region each time an image is to be displayed. The coordinate of the clipping region changes to the coordinate of the image that is to be displayed. This technique draws the image once and then displays portions of the image as required to create the illusion of movement.

Quick Reference Guide

This quick reference guide provides an overview of classes used by J2ME for the low-level user interface. Full details of these classes and all Java classes and interfaces are available at java.sun.com.

javax.microedition.lcdui.Canvas Class

Method	Description
int getWidth()	Return the width of the canvas in pixels.
int getHeight()	Return the height of the canvas in pixels.

Paint

Method	Description
abstract void paint(Graphic g)	Draw an image on the canvas using the instance of the Graphics class passed as a parameter.
final void repaint()	Repaint the full canvas.
final void repaint(int x, int y, int width, int height)	Repaint the specified region of the canvas.
final void servicePaints()	A pending paint request must be processed before other outstanding requests.
boolean isDoubleBuffered()	Determine whether the device supports double buffering.

Notify

Method	Description
void showNotify()	Called before the application manager displays the canvas.
void hideNotify()	Called after the application manager removes the canvas from the screen.

Key and Game Actions

Method	Description
void keyPressed(int keycode)	Called whenever a key is pressed and used to process the key code of that key.
void keyReleased(int keycode)	Called whenever a key is released and used to process the key code of that key.
void keyRepeated(int keycode)	Called whenever a key is held down and used to process the key code of that key (not supported by all devices).
boolean hasRepeatEvents()	Determine whether the device supports repeated keys.
String getKeyName(int keycode)	Return the text associated with the key.

javax.microedition.lcdui.Canvas Class

Key and Game Actions

Method	Description
int getKeyCode(int gameActionConstant)	Return the key code value for the game action constant.
int getGameAction(int keycode)	Return the game action for a key code value.
String getKeyname(int keycode)	Return the name of the key for a key code. The name returned is not the name of the game action, but is the name of the actual key.

Pointer Events

Method	Description
boolean hasPointerEvents()	Determine whether the device supports a pointer device.
boolean hasPointerMotionEvents()	Determines whether the device detects the press, drag, and release motion of a pointer device.
void pointerDragged(int x, int y)	Called in response to a pointer drag event.
void pointerPressed(int x, int y)	Called in response to a pointer press event.
void pointerReleased(int x, int y)	Called in response to a pointer release event.

javax.microedition.lcdui.Graphics Class

Method	Description
void setColor(int RGB)	Change the current color to the integer represented by RGB. Red, green, and blue color values are consolidated into one integer value and passed to the setColor() method.
void setColor(int red, int green, int blue)	Change the current color to integers represented by red, green, and blue color values.
int getColor()	Retrieve the integer value that represents the current color.
int getBlueComponent()	Retrieve the blue color value.
int getGreenComponent()	Retrieve the green color value.
int getRedComponent()	Retrieve the red color value.
void setGrayScale(int value)	Change the value of the current gray scale.
int getGrayScale()	Retrieve the value of the current gray scale.

javax.microedition.lcdui.Graphics Class

Method	Description
Stroke Style	
int getStrokeStyle()	Retrieve the stroke style of a graphic context.
void setStrokeStyle(int style)	Set the stroke style of a graphic context, where style is either SOLID or DOTTED.
Line	
void drawLine(int x1, int y1, int x2, int y2)	Draw a line beginning at coordinate x1, y1 and ending at coordinate x2, y2.
Arc	
Void drawArc(int x1, int y1, int x2, int y2, startAngle, endAngle)	Draw an outline arc within the rectangle defined as the first four parameters beginning with the startAngle and terminating with the endAngle.
Void fillArc(int x1, int y1, int x2, int y2, startAngle, endAngle)	Draw a filled arc within the rectangle defined as the first four parameters beginning with the startAngle and terminating with the endAngle.
Rectangle	
void drawRect(int x1, int y1, int x2, int y2)	Draw a rectangle, where x1, y1 represents the coordinate of the upper-left corner of the rectangle, and x2, y2 represents the width and height of the rectangle.
void drawroundRect(int x1, int y1, int x2, int y2, int arcW, int arcH)	Draw a rounded rectangle, where x1, y1 represents the coordinate of the upper-left corner of the rectangle, and x2, y2 represents the width and height of the rectangle. arcW is the angle for the width of the arc, and arcH is the angle for the height of the arc.
void fillRect(int x1, int y1, int x2, int y2)	Draw a filled rectangle, where x1, y1 represents the coordinate of the upper-left corner of the rectangle, and x2, y2 represents the width and height of the rectangle.
void fillRoundedRect (int x1, int y1, int x2, int y2, int arcW, int arcH)	Draw a rounded filled rectangle, where x1, y1 represents the coordinate of the upper-left corner of the rectangle, and x2, y2 represents the width and height of the rectangle. arcW is the angle for the width of the arc, and arcH is the angle for the height of the arc.

javax.microedition.lcdui.Graphics Class

Method	Description
Text	
void drawChar(char character, int x, int y, int anchor)	Draw a character at the x, y coordinate on the canvas using the specified anchor point.
void drawChars(char[] data, int offset, int len, int x, int y, int anchor)	Draw a subset of a character array the length specified by len and beginning with the character indicated by the offset. Draw the subset at the x, y coordinate on the canvas using the specified anchor point.
void drawString (String str, int x, int y, int anchor)	Draw a string at the x, y coordinate on the canvas using the specified anchor point.
void drawSubstring(String str, int offset, int len, int x, int y, int anchor)	Draw a substring the length specified by len and beginning with the character indicated by the offset. Draw the substring at the x, y coordinate on the canvas using the specified anchor point.
Font getFont()	Return the font of the graphic context.
void setFont(Font font)	Set the font of the graphic context, where font is the new font.
Image	
void drawImage(Image img, int x, int y, int anchor)	Draw the image specified in img, where the upper-left corner of the image is positioned at coordinate x, y using anchor point referenced by anchor.
Translate	
void translate (int x, int y)	Translate the specified by x, y coordinate.
int getTranslateX()	Retrieve the translated x coordinate.
int getTranslateY()	Retrieve the translated y coordinate.
Clip Region	
void setClip (int x1, int y1, int x2, int y2)	Set the coordinates for the clipping region, where x1, y1 represents the coordinate of the upper-left corner of the region, and x2, y2 represents the coordinate of the lower-right corner of the clipping region.

J2ME
USER INTERFACE

javax.microedition.lcdui.Graphics Class

Clip Region

Method	Description
void clipRect(int x1, int y1, int x2, int y2)	Create a rectangle defined by x1, y1 and x2, y2 coordinates that establish a new clipping region by intersecting the existing clipping region. The coordinate x1, y1 represents the upper-left corner of the region, and x2, y2 represents the coordinate of the lower-right corner of the new clipping region.
int getClipX()	Retrieve the x1 coordinate of the upper-left corner of the clipping region.
int getClipY()	Retrieve the y1 coordinate of the upper-left corner of the clipping region.
int getClipHeight()	Retrieve the x2 coordinate of the lower-right corner of the clipping region.
int getclipWidth()	Retrieve the y2 coordinate of the lower-right corner of the clipping region.

javax.microedition.lcdui.Font Class

Method	Description
static Font getFont(int face, int style, int size)	Create an instance of the Font class that has the specified font face, font style, and font size.
static Font getDefaultfont()	Create an instance of the Font class that uses the default font face, font style, and font size.

Face, Style, Size

int getFace()	Retrieve the font face.
int getStyle()	Retrieve the combination of font styles.
int getSize()	Retrieve the font size.
boolean isPlain()	Determine whether the font uses the plain style.
boolean isBold()	Determine whether the font uses the bold style.
boolean isItalic()	Determine whether the font uses the italic style.
boolean isUnderlined()	Determine whether the font uses the underlined style.

javax.microedition.lcdui.Font Class

Method	Description
	Height/Width
int getHeight()	Return the font height.
int getBaselinePosition()	Return the ascent of the text.
int charWidth(char ch)	Return the advance of a character.
int charsWidth(char[] ch, int offset, int length)	Return the advance of a series of characters in a character array that begins with character represented by the offset and has a length represented by the integer length.
int substringWidth(String str, int offset, int length)	Return the advance of a substring that begins with character represented by the offset and has a length represented by the integer length.

The Complete Reference

Part III

J2ME Data Management

The
Complete
Reference

Chapter 8

Record Management System

Practically every J2ME application that you develop requires persistence. *Persistence* is the retention of information during operation of the MIDlet and when it is not running. The nature of the information is application dependent, but typically stretches the breadth of data storage from application settings to information common to a database. Persistence is common to every Java application written in J2SE, J2EE, or J2ME. However, the manner in which persistence is maintained in a J2ME application differs from persistence in J2SE or J2EE applications because of the limited resources available in small computing devices that run J2ME applications.

Many small computing devices lack disk drives and access to a network database server or file server, which are the typical resources used for persistence in J2SE and J2EE applications. Therefore, J2ME applications must store information in nonvolatile memory using the Record Management System (RMS). The RMS is an application programming interface that is used to store and manipulate data in a small computing device using a J2ME application. In this chapter you'll learn how to use the Record Management System for your application's persistence.

Record Storage

Many operating environments contain a file system that is used to store information in nonvolatile resources such as a CD-ROM and disk drive. Groups of related information are stored under the same file name. Not all small computing devices have a file system and therefore are unable to store information in the manner that you are accustomed to when working with a PC, server, and other traditional computing devices.

The Record Management System provides a file system–like environment that is used to store and maintain persistence in a small computing device. RMS is a combination file system and database management system that enables you to store data in columns and rows similar to the organization of data in a table of a database. And you can use RMS to perform the functionality of database management software (DBMS). That is, you can insert records, read records, search for particular records, and sort records stored by the RMS.

Although RMS provides database functionality, RMS is not a relational database, and therefore you cannot use SQL to interact with the data. Instead, you'll use the RMS application programming interface and the enumeration application programming interface to sort, search, and otherwise manipulate information stored in persistence.

The Record Store

RMS stores information in a record store. A *record store* compares to a flat file used for data storage in a traditional file system and to a table of a database. A record store contains information referenced by a single name, similar to a flat file and like a table. A record store is a collection of records organized as rows (records) and columns (fields).

Columns contain like data such as first name. Rows contain related data such as a first name, middle name, last name, street, city, state, and postal code. RMS automatically assigns to each row a unique integer that identifies the row in the record store, which is called the record ID. The record ID is in its own column within the record store. The record ID is considered the primary key of the record store. A primary key of the record store serves the same purpose as a primary key in a table of a database, which is to uniquely identify each record in a table.

Although conceptually you can envision a record store as rows and columns, technically there are two columns. The first column is the record ID, and the other column is an array of bytes that contains the persistent data, which you'll learn more about later in this chapter.

Record Store Scope

You can create multiple record stores as required by your MIDlet as long as the name of each record store is unique. The name of a record store must be a minimum of one character and not more than 32 characters. Characters are Unicode, and the name is case sensitive. Record stores can be shared among MIDlets that are within the same MIDlet suite (see Chapter 3) (Figure 8-1). Record stores must be uniquely named within a MIDlet suite, although duplicate names can be used for record stores in other MIDlet suites.

Let's say that MIDlet A collects information about customers from a sales representative. MIDlet B displays customer information collected by MIDlet A. MIDlet B can access customer information if both MIDlet A and MIDlet B are in the same MIDlet suite. However, MIDlet B is unable to access customer information if MIDlet A and MIDlet B are in different MIDlet suites.

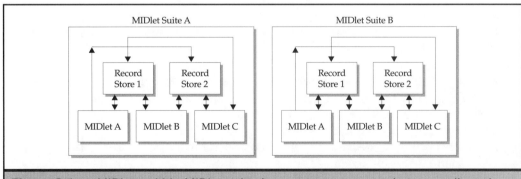

Figure 8-1.   *MIDlets within MIDlet suite A cannot access record stores collected in MIDlet suite B.*

Setting Up a Record Store

The openRecordStore() method is called to create a new record store and to open an existing record store. This method creates or opens a record store depending on whether the record store already exists within the MIDlet suite. The openRecordStore() method requires two parameters. The first parameter is a string containing the name of the record store. The second parameter is a boolean value indicating whether the record store should be created if the record store doesn't exist. A true value causes the record store to be created if the record store isn't in the MIDlet suite and also opens the record store. A false value does not create the record store if the record store isn't located.

You'll find the second version of the openRecordStore() method useful whenever your MIDlet tries to open an existing record store. Let's say that your MIDlet accesses address information stored in a record store created and maintained by another MIDlet in the same MIDlet suite. You don't want your MIDlet to create a new record store if for some reason the record store is unavailable when you tried to open it because another MIDlet creates and maintains the record store.

Internal resources are utilized to make an open record store available to MIDlets within a MIDlet suite. As you know, resources are limited in small computing devices. Therefore, you should make a conscious effort not to tie up resources that can be otherwise used for processing by your MIDlet or other MIDlets running on the small computing device. To that end, always close any record store that is not in use so that resources utilized by the record store can be reused by other processes. You close a record store by calling the closeRecordStore() method. The closeRecordStore() method does not require any parameters.

A record store remains in nonvolatile memory even after the small computing device is powered down. Nonvolatile memory is a scarce resource that needs to be properly managed to ensure that sufficient memory is available when required to store information collected by a MIDlet. You can help manage nonvolatile memory by removing all record stores that are no longer being used by MIDlets running on the device. A record store can be deleted by calling the deleteRecordStore() method. This method requires one parameter, which is a string containing the name of the record store that is to be removed from the device.

Creating, Opening, Closing, and Removing a Record Store

Listing 8-1 illustrates how to create a new record store, close it, and then remove it from the small computing device. All information contained in the record store is lost when the record store is removed. Listing 8-2 is the JAD file for Listing 8-1.

Listing 8-1 begins by declaring three references for instances of the Display class, Alert class, and RecordStore class. The instance of the Display class is required because an alert dialog box (see Chapter 6) is shown should an error be detected by this MIDlet; otherwise, an instance of the Display class is not necessary unless the MIDlet has a user interface. A user interface is not required to interact with a record store, although many MIDlets that interact with a record store have a user interface.

All the actions in this listing occur in the commandAction() method. Typically, routines to create, open, close, and remove a record store are located in appropriate methods throughout the MIDlet, which you'll see in examples shown later in this chapter.

Once the instance of the Display class is created, the listing enters the first of three try {} blocks. In the first try {} block, the listing attempts to create the record store by calling the openRecordStore() method and passing it the name of the record store and a boolean value. The boolean value indicates that the record store should be created if there isn't an existing record store of the same name. Errors occurring when creating the record store are trapped by the catch {} block, where an alert dialog box is displayed describing the error.

Typically, the MIDlet will read from and/or write to the record store at this point in the listing. We'll move on to showing how to close the record store since the purpose of this listing is to provide a framework for working with a record store rather than illustrating how to interact with the record store. You'll see how to read and write in the next section of this chapter.

The closeRecordStore() method is called within the second try {} block to close the record store and release resources used to maintain an open record store. Remember, you can always reopen the record store by calling the openRecordStore() method and passing it the name of the record store that you want to open.

The catch {} responds to errors that happen if a problem arises when closing the record store. The second catch {} block, similar to other catch {} blocks in this listing, displays an alert dialog box that contains the error and informs the user that an error occurred.

Creating, Closing, and Removing a Record Store

Here are the steps required to create, close, and remove a record store:

1. Declare references to classes.
2. Create instances of classes and assign those instances to references.
3. Open a record store and create a new record store if the record store doesn't exist.
4. Display any errors that occur when opening/creating a record store.
5. Close the record store.
6. Display any errors that occur when closing the record store.
7. Remove the record store.
8. Display any errors that occur when removing the record store.

Next, the listing determines whether the small computing device contains record stores in nonvolatile memory by calling the listRecordStores() method. The listRecordStores() returns a null value if no record stores exist on the device.

The listing proceeds if at least one record store exists, by entering the third try {} block, where the deleteRecordStore() method is called. The deleteRecordStore() method requires one parameter, which is a string containing the name of the record store that is to be removed from the device. Any errors occurring during this process are trapped by the catch {} block and displayed in an alert dialog box. The remainder of the listing contains the same structure that you learned about in previous chapters.

Listing 8-1
Create, close, and remove a record store

```
import javax.microedition.rms.*;
import javax.microedition.midlet.*;
import javax.microedition.lcdui.*;
import java.io.*;
public class RecordStoreExample
            extends MIDlet implements CommandListener
{
  private Display display;
  private Alert alert;
  private Form form;
  private Command exit;
  private Command start;
  private RecordStore recordstore = null;
  private RecordEnumeration recordenumeration = null;
  public RecordStoreExample ()
  {
    display = Display.getDisplay(this);
    exit = new Command("Exit", Command.SCREEN, 1);
    start = new Command("Start", Command.SCREEN, 1);
    form = new Form("Record Store");
    form.addCommand(exit);
    form.addCommand(start);
    form.setCommandListener(this);
  }
  public void startApp()
  {
    display.setCurrent(form);
  }
  public void pauseApp()
  {
  }
  public void destroyApp( boolean unconditional )
  {
```

```
}
public void commandAction(Command command, Displayable displayable)
{
  if (command == exit)
  {
    destroyApp(true);
    notifyDestroyed();
  }
  else if (command == start)
  {
    try
    {
      recordstore = RecordStore.openRecordStore("myRecordStore",
                                                true );
    }
    catch (Exception error)
    {
      alert = new Alert("Error Creating", error.toString(),
                        null, AlertType.WARNING);
      alert.setTimeout(Alert.FOREVER);
      display.setCurrent(alert);
    }
    try
    {
      recordstore.closeRecordStore();
    }
    catch (Exception error)
    {
      alert = new Alert("Error Closing", error.toString(),
                        null, AlertType.WARNING);
      alert.setTimeout(Alert.FOREVER);
      display.setCurrent(alert);
    }
    if (RecordStore.listRecordStores() != null)
    {
      try
      {
        RecordStore.deleteRecordStore("myRecordStore");
      }
      catch (Exception error)
      {
        alert = new Alert("Error Removing", error.toString(),
```

```
                                        null, AlertType.WARNING);
                    alert.setTimeout(Alert.FOREVER);
                    display.setCurrent(alert);
                }
            }
        }
    }
}
```

```
MIDlet-Name: RecordStoreExample
MIDlet-Version: 1.0
MIDlet-Vendor: MyCompany
MIDlet-Jar-URL: RecordStoreExample.jar
MIDlet-1: RecordStoreExample, , RecordStoreExample
MicroEdition-Configuration: CLDC-1.0
MicroEdition-Profile: MIDP-1.0
MIDlet-JAR-SIZE: 100
```

Writing and Reading Records

Once your MIDlet opens a record store, the MIDlet can write records to the record store and read information already stored there using one of two techniques for writing and reading records. The first technique is used to write and read a string of data and is used primarily whenever you have one data column in the record store such as a list of abbreviations of states. The other technique is used to write and read multiple columns of data of different types such as string, integer, and boolean.

Let's begin by exploring the technique for writing a string to a record store. The addRecord() method is used to write a record to the record store. The addRecord() method requires three parameters. The first is a byte array containing the byte value of the string being written to the record store. The second is an integer representing the index of the first byte of the byte array that is to be written to the record store. The third is the total number of bytes that is to be written to the record store.

The first step in writing a string to a record store is to create an instance of a String and assign text to the instance. Next, the string must be converted to a byte array by calling the getBytes() method, as shown here. The getBytes() method returns a byte array.

```
string.getBytes()
```

The second parameter of the addRecord() method is usually zero, and the third parameter is the length of the byte array, indicating that the entire byte array should be written to the record store.

Typically, information is read from a record store a record at a time and stored in a byte array. The byte array is then converted to a string, which is then displayed on the screen or processed further based on the needs of the application.

Your MIDlet needs to know the number of records in a record store in order to read all the records from the record store. The getNumRecords() method of the RecordStore class returns an integer that represents the total number of records in the record store. You should use this value as the maximum value for a for loop used to step through each record in the record store, as you'll see in Listing 8-3.

Call the getRecord() method of the RecordStore class for each iteration of the for loop. The getRecord() method returns bytes from the RecordStore, which are stored in a byte array that you create. The getRecord() method requires three parameters. The first parameter is the record ID, as described earlier in this chapter. The second parameter is the byte array that you create for storing the record. The third parameter is an integer representing the position in the record from which to begin copying into the byte array.

For example, the following code segment reads the second record from the record store and copies that record, beginning with the first byte of the record, from the record store into the byte array. Typically, the first parameter of the getRecord() method is the integer of the for loop, and the third parameter is zero, indicating the entire record is to be copied into the byte array.

```
recordstore.getRecord(2, myByteArray, 0)
```

Creating a New Record and Reading an Existing Record

Listing 8-3 illustrates the technique for writing a record to a record store and reading records from the record store. Figure 8-2 shows the output of running this MIDlet. Listing 8-4 is the JAD file for this listing. You'll notice that Listing 8-3 is similar in design to Listing 8-1 in that nearly all the action occurs within the commandAction() method.

Many programmers separate routines to write and read records into their own methods. These routines are shown in the commandAction() method rather than in separate methods in order to simplify the design and make it easier to understand the technique of writing and reading records. You can rewrite the program to separate these functionalities once you feel comfortable working with a record store.

Listing 8-3 performs five routines. First a record store is created, and then one record is written to the record store. Next, the record is read from the record store and displayed within an alert dialog box. Once the user dismisses the alert dialog box, the MIDlet closes the record store, then removes the record store from the small computing device.

The record store is created by calling the openRecordStore() method, as described in Listing 8-1. An exception is thrown if the MIDlet is unable to create the record store, at which time the exception is displayed in an alert dialog box. The MIDlet then enters the routine that writes a record to the record store. This routine begins with the creation of

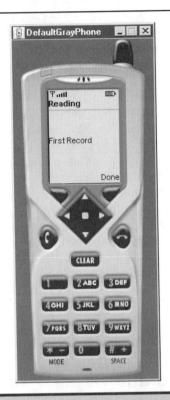

Figure 8-2. *Reading a record from a record store and displaying the record on the screen*

a string called "First Record." The string must be stored as a byte array. Therefore, the bytes that make up the string are retrieved by calling the getBytes() method.

Finally, the addRecord() method is called to write the string to the record store. The addRecord() method is passed three parameters. The first parameter is the byte array that contains the string. The second parameter is the index of the first byte, and the third parameter is the total number of bytes that are to be written to the record store. The first byte is the first element of the byte array (zero), and the total number of bytes is the number stored in byteOutputData.length. Exceptions thrown when writing the record are displayed in an alert dialog box called within the related catch {} block.

The next routine reads the record that was written to the record store. The routine begins by declaring a byte array that is used to store the bytes read from the record store. An integer is also declared and is used when converting the byte array to a string. The routine is written to read all records from the record store, not simply the one record that the MIDlet wrote to the record store in the previous routine, although that is the only record in the record store.

A for loop is used to step through records in the record store. The maximum iteration of the for loop is set as the return value from the getNumRecords() method, which returns the number of records in the record store. The value of the for loop integer (x) represents the record ID. Record IDs begin with one—not zero—therefore the value of the for loop is initialized to one.

There is always the possibility that the record size exceeds the byte array allocation. You can avoid this potential problem by evaluating this condition with an if statement, as shown in this routine. If the current record size is greater than the length of the allocated byte array, the MIDlet creates a new byte array the size of the value returned by the getRecordSize() method.

The getRecord() method is called to retrieve a record from the record store. The getRecord() method requires three parameters. The first is the record ID that is being

Writing and Reading String-Based Records

Here are the steps required to write and read string-based records:

1. Declare references to classes.
2. Create instances of classes and assign those instances to references.
3. Open a record store and create a new record store if the record store doesn't exist.
4. Display any errors that occur when opening/creating a record store.
5. Create data in the form of a string.
6. Convert data to a byte array.
7. Write the byte array to the record store.
8. Create a byte array before reading data from the record store.
9. Determine the number of records in the record store.
10. Loop through each record in the record store.
11. Determine whether the size of the current record exceeds the length of the byte array. If so, then create a new byte array large enough to hold the record.
12. Copy the current record from the record store to the byte array.
13. Convert the byte array to a string and display the string on the screen.
14. Close the record store and display any errors that occur as the record store is closed.
15. Remove the record store and display any errors that occur as the record store is being removed.

read, which is the current value of the for loop variable. The second is the name of the byte array into which the record is copied. The third is the index position of the first byte that is to be copied into the byte array.

The getRecord() method copies the record from the record store and into the byteInputData byte array and returns an integer representing the length of the record. Remember that the record is still in a byte array and must be converted to a string before the record is displayed within the alert dialog box.

Notice that the message parameter of the Alert method creates a new string using the byte array that contains the record read from the record store. Three parameters are necessary to create the string from the context of the byte array. The first parameter is reference to the byte array. The next two parameters define the first index of the byte array and the last index, which is the number of bytes read by the getRecord() method (length). The second parameter is almost always zero, and the third parameter is the length of the record read from the record store, which is the value assigned to the length integer variable.

The record read from the record store is displayed in the alert dialog box. Once the alert dialog box is dismissed, the MIDlet closes the record store by calling the closeRecordStore() method and then removes the record store by calling the deleteRecordStore() method, as described previously in this chapter. The remainder of Listing 8-3 contains the structure that is standard to all MIDlets as discussed previously in this book.

Listing 8-3
Write and read records

```
import javax.microedition.rms.*;
import javax.microedition.midlet.*;
import javax.microedition.lcdui.*;
import java.io.*;
public class WriteReadExample extends MIDlet implements CommandListener
{
  private Display display;
  private Alert alert;
  private Form form;
  private Command exit;
  private Command start;
  private RecordStore recordstore = null;
  public WriteReadExample()
  {
    display = Display.getDisplay(this);
    exit = new Command("Exit", Command.SCREEN, 1);
    start = new Command("Start", Command.SCREEN, 1);
    form = new Form("Record");
    form.addCommand(exit);
    form.addCommand(start);
    form.setCommandListener(this);
```

```
}
public void startApp()
{
  display.setCurrent(form);
}
public void pauseApp()
{
}
public void destroyApp( boolean unconditional )
{
}
public void commandAction(Command command, Displayable displayable)
{
  if (command == exit)
  {
    destroyApp(true);
    notifyDestroyed();
  }
  else if (command == start)
  {
    try
    {
     recordstore = RecordStore.openRecordStore(
                              "myRecordStore", true );
    }
    catch (Exception error)
    {
      alert = new Alert("Error Creating",
                    error.toString(), null, AlertType.WARNING);
      alert.setTimeout(Alert.FOREVER);
      display.setCurrent(alert);
    }
    try
    {
      String outputData = "First Record";
      byte[] byteOutputData = outputData.getBytes();
      recordstore.addRecord(byteOutputData, 0,
                byteOutputData.length);
    }
    catch ( Exception error)
    {
      alert = new Alert("Error Writing",
```

```
                 error.toString(), null, AlertType.WARNING);
    alert.setTimeout(Alert.FOREVER);
    display.setCurrent(alert);
  }
  try
  {
    byte[] byteInputData = new byte[1];
    int length = 0;
    for (int x = 1; x <= recordstore.getNumRecords(); x++)
    {
      if (recordstore.getRecordSize(x) > byteInputData.length)
      {
        byteInputData = new byte[recordstore.getRecordSize(x)];
      }
      length = recordstore.getRecord(x, byteInputData, 0);
    }
      alert = new Alert("Reading", new String(byteInputData, 0,
                     length), null, AlertType.WARNING);
      alert.setTimeout(Alert.FOREVER);
      display.setCurrent(alert);


  }
  catch (Exception error)
  {
    alert = new Alert("Error Reading", error.toString(),
                      null, AlertType.WARNING);
    alert.setTimeout(Alert.FOREVER);
    display.setCurrent(alert);
  }
  try
  {
    recordstore.closeRecordStore();
  }
  catch (Exception error)
  {
    alert = new Alert("Error Closing", error.toString(),
                   null, AlertType.WARNING);
    alert.setTimeout(Alert.FOREVER);
    display.setCurrent(alert);
  }
  if (RecordStore.listRecordStores() != null)
```

```
        {
          try
          {
            RecordStore.deleteRecordStore("myRecordStore");
          }
          catch (Exception error)
          {
           alert = new Alert("Error Removing", error.toString(),
                        null, AlertType.WARNING);
           alert.setTimeout(Alert.FOREVER);
           display.setCurrent(alert);
          }
        }
      }
    }
}
```

Listing 8-4
The JAD
file for
Listing 8-3

```
MIDlet-Name: WriteReadExample
MIDlet-Version: 1.0
MIDlet-Vendor: MyCompany
MIDlet-Jar-URL: WriteReadExample.jar
MIDlet-1: WriteReadExample, , WriteReadExample
MicroEdition-Configuration: CLDC-1.0
MicroEdition-Profile: MIDP-1.0
MIDlet-JAR-SIZE: 100
```

Writing and Reading Mixed Data Types

It is common for records to consist of mixed data types such as string, boolean, and integer (see Figure 8-3). Let's say that you are saving information. You might store the customer name, customer number, and gender. A string is used to store a customer name, an integer to store the customer number, and a boolean to indicate gender.

ID	Column 1	Column 2	Column 3
1	First Record	15	true
2	Second Record	10	false
3	Third Record	5	true

Figure 8-3. *A record store typically stores data of multiple data types such as a string, integer, and boolean.*

The routine that you'll need to write to save a record of mixed data types is slightly different from the routine in Listing 8-3 that saves string information to the record store. Listing 8-5 shows how to write and read mixed data types. Listing 8-6 contains the JAD file for this listing. Figure 8-4 shows the output of Listing 8-5.

You'll notice that Listing 8-5 has basically the same structure as Listing 8-3. This MIDlet writes a string, an integer, and a boolean value to a record store that is created by the MIDlet. Once the record is written, the MIDlet reads the context of the record, which is displayed in an alert dialog box.

The MIDlet begins by declaring references to objects that are used within the MIDlet. Instances of these objects are created within the class constructor. The MIDlet creates a record store called myRecordStore after retrieving reference to the display. Any errors occurring while the record store is being created are caught by the catch {} block and displayed in an alert dialog box.

Next, the MIDlet creates an array of bytes called outputRecord followed by the creation of the string, integer, and boolean values of the first record. Two streams are used to write the record to the record store. The first stream is a byte array output

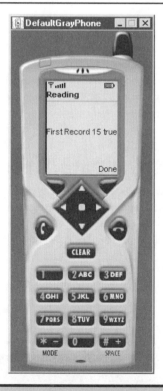

Figure 8-4. *Displaying mixed data types read from a record store*

stream created by calling the ByteArrayOutputStream() constructor. The other stream—a data output stream used to output the byte array output stream—is created by calling the DataOutputStream() constructor and passing it reference to the byte array output stream.

The objective is to write data to a buffer, then write the buffered data to the stream. The data stream is then converted to a byte array. The byte array is then written to the record store.

The DataOutputStream class has methods that write specific data types to a buffer. Three of these methods are used in this example. These are writeUTF() method, writeBoolean() method, and writeInt() method. Each is passed the appropriate data.

The buffered data is placed in the data stream by calling the flush() method. The stream is converted to a byte array by calling the toByteArray() method, which returns a reference to the byte array of the stream. This reference is passed to the addRecord() method, as described in the previous section, which saves the byte array as a new record in the record store. The ByteArrayOutputStream object's internal store is cleared by calling the reset() method.

Next, the output stream and the data output stream are both closed. Any errors occurring while the data is being written to the record store are trapped by the catch {} block and displayed in an alert dialog box. The MIDlet then focuses on retrieving the record from the record store. This process begins by declaring appropriate references and an array. The array size is set to 100 bytes. You must be sure that the size of the array is sufficient to hold all the bytes of the record.

Reading a mixed data type record from a record store is similar to the routine that writes mixed data types. First, you create an instance of the ByteArrayInputStream class. The constructor of this class is passed the byte array that was just created. You also create an instance of the DataInputStream class and pass reference to the ByteArrayInputStream class to the DataInputStream class constructor.

The routine used to read records from a record store must assume that more than one record exists, and therefore you need to include a for loop so the MIDlet continues to read records from a record store until the last record is read.

You'll notice that the construction of the for loop is very similar to the for loop in Listing 8-3 to read string data from a record store. The getRecord() method is called for each iteration. Remember that the value of x is the record ID number of the record you want to retrieve. The contents of the record are copied from the record store and into the byte array that is passed to the getRecord() method. This places bytes of the record into the input data stream.

The appropriate method is called to extract the string, integer, and boolean values from the copy of the record in the input data stream and to store those values in the appropriate variable. A word of caution: you must read data from the data stream in the order in which the data appears in the record.

The reset() method is called to enable reuse of the ByteArrayInputStream's buffer. The MIDlet then returns to the top of the for loop and evaluates whether or not to read another record from the record store. If so, the process begins again. If not, the input

Writing and Reading Mixed Data Type Records

Here are the steps required to write and read mixed data type records:

1. Declare references to classes.
2. Create instances of classes and assign those instances to references.
3. Open a record store and create a new record store if the record store doesn't exist.
4. Display any errors that occur when opening/creating a record store.
5. Create data in the appropriate data type.
6. Convert data to a byte array output stream.
7. Create a data output stream using the byte array output stream.
8. Write each column of the record to the data output stream.
9. Convert the data output stream to a byte array.
10. Write the record to the record store.
11. Close the output byte array output stream and the data output stream.
12. Display any errors that might occur while writing to the record store.
13. Create a buffer of bytes sufficient to hold a record.
14. Create a byte array input stream and a data input stream.
15. Loop through the record store, copying each column from the record store to a variable.
16. Display the data in a dialog box.
17. Display any errors that occur when reading records from the record store.
18. Close and remove the record store.

stream and input data stream are closed, and the contents of the variables are displayed within an alert dialog box. Errors that occur while records are read from the record store are displayed in an alert dialog box. The record store is then closed and deleted from the device.

Listing 8-5
Write and read records of mixed data types

```
import javax.microedition.rms.*;
import javax.microedition.midlet.*;
import javax.microedition.lcdui.*;
import java.io.*;
public class WriteReadMixedDataTypesExample
        extends MIDlet implements CommandListener
```

```
{
  private Display display;
  private Alert alert;
  private Form form;
  private Command exit;
  private Command start;
  private RecordStore recordstore = null;
  public WriteReadMixedDataTypesExample ()
  {
    display = Display.getDisplay(this);
    exit = new Command("Exit", Command.SCREEN, 1);
    start = new Command("Start", Command.SCREEN, 1);
    form = new Form("Mixed Record");
    form.addCommand(exit);
    form.addCommand(start);
    form.setCommandListener(this);
  }
  public void startApp()
  {
    display.setCurrent(form);
  }
  public void pauseApp()
  {
  }
  public void destroyApp( boolean unconditional )
  {
  }
  public void commandAction(Command command, Displayable displayable)
  {
    if (command == exit)
    {
      destroyApp(true);
      notifyDestroyed();
    }
    else if (command == start)
    {
      try
      {
       recordstore = RecordStore.openRecordStore(
                      "myRecordStore", true );
      }
      catch (Exception error)
      {
        alert = new Alert("Error Creating",
                  error.toString(), null, AlertType.WARNING);
        alert.setTimeout(Alert.FOREVER);
        display.setCurrent(alert);
```

```
      }
      try
      {
        byte[] outputRecord;
        String outputString = "First Record";
        int outputInteger = 15;
        boolean outputBoolean = true;
        ByteArrayOutputStream outputStream = new ByteArrayOutputStream();
        DataOutputStream outputDataStream =
                    new DataOutputStream(outputStream);
        outputDataStream.writeUTF(outputString);
        outputDataStream.writeBoolean(outputBoolean);
        outputDataStream.writeInt(outputInteger);
        outputDataStream.flush();
        outputRecord = outputStream.toByteArray();
        recordstore.addRecord(outputRecord, 0, outputRecord.length);
        outputStream.reset();
        outputStream.close();
        outputDataStream.close();
      }
      catch ( Exception error)
      {
        alert = new Alert("Error Writing",
                error.toString(), null, AlertType.WARNING);
        alert.setTimeout(Alert.FOREVER);
        display.setCurrent(alert);
      }
      try
      {
        String inputString = null;
        int inputInteger = 0;
        boolean inputBoolean = false;
        byte[] byteInputData = new byte[100];
        ByteArrayInputStream inputStream = new ByteArrayInputStream(byteInputData);
        DataInputStream inputDataStream =
                new DataInputStream(inputStream);
        for (int x = 1; x <= recordstore.getNumRecords(); x++)
        {
         recordstore.getRecord(x, byteInputData, 0);
         inputString = inputDataStream.readUTF();
         inputBoolean = inputDataStream.readBoolean();
         inputInteger = inputDataStream.readInt();
         inputStream.reset();
        }
        inputStream.close();
        inputDataStream.close();
        alert = new Alert("Reading", inputString + " " +
```

```
                              inputInteger + " " +
                              inputBoolean, null, AlertType.WARNING);
        alert.setTimeout(Alert.FOREVER);
        display.setCurrent(alert);
      }
      catch (Exception error)
      {
        alert = new Alert("Error Reading",
                error.toString(), null, AlertType.WARNING);
        alert.setTimeout(Alert.FOREVER);
        display.setCurrent(alert);
      }
      try
      {
        recordstore.closeRecordStore();
      }
      catch (Exception error)
      {
        alert = new Alert("Error Closing",
                error.toString(), null, AlertType.WARNING);
        alert.setTimeout(Alert.FOREVER);
        display.setCurrent(alert);
      }
      if (RecordStore.listRecordStores() != null)
      {
        try
        {
          RecordStore.deleteRecordStore("myRecordStore");
        }
        catch (Exception error)
        {
          alert = new Alert("Error Removing",
                  error.toString(), null, AlertType.WARNING);
          alert.setTimeout(Alert.FOREVER);
          display.setCurrent(alert);
        }
      }
    }
  }
}
```

Listing 8-6
The JAD
file for
Listing 8-5

```
MIDlet-Name: WriteReadMixedDataTypesExample
MIDlet-Version: 1.0
MIDlet-Vendor: MyCompany
MIDlet-Jar-URL: WriteReadMixedDataTypesExample.jar
MIDlet-1: WriteReadMixedDataTypesExample, ,
```

```
                    WriteReadMixedDataTypesExample
MicroEdition-Configuration: CLDC-1.0
MicroEdition-Profile: MIDP-1.0
MIDlet-JAR-SIZE: 100
```

Record Enumeration

A record store is more like a flat file than a database management system and therefore lacks many sophisticated features that you find in a database management system. For example, you cannot send an SQL query to a record store, nor can you ask a record store to search for keywords or sort records, which is commonly performed by a database management system. However, you can still perform searches and sorts of records in a record store by using the RecordEnumeration interface. An Enumeration provides a way to traverse data elements. The Enumeration object manages how data is retrieved from the record store. Changes to the record store are reflected when the record store's content is iterated.

You obtain a record enumeration by calling the enumerateRecords() method. The enumerateRecords() method requires three parameters. The first is the record filter used to exclude records returned from the record store. The second is reference to the record comparator, which is a method used to compare records returned from the record store. The last parameter is a boolean value indicating whether or not the enumeration is automatically updated when changes are made to the underlying record store.

The enumerateRecords() method returns a RecordEnumeration, as illustrated in the following code segment. There isn't any filter or comparator method, and the record enumeration is not automatically updated when a change is made to the record store. You'll see how to create a record enumeration that uses a filter and comparator method later in this chapter.

```
RecordEnumeration recordEnumeration = recordstore.enumerateRecords(null, null,
false);
```

You then use methods of the RecordEnumeration (see "Quick Reference Guide" at the end of this chapter) to interact with records in the RecordEnumeration.

One of the most common interactions that you'll have with a RecordEnumeration is to step through each record of the RecordEnumeration. The following code segment illustrates how this is done. The hasNextElement() method is called to evaluate whether or not there is another record in the RecordEnumeration. A boolean true is returned if another record exists; otherwise, a boolean false is returned.

```
while ( recordEnumeration.hasNextElement())
{
    //do something
}
```

You can retrieve a record from the RecordEnumeration using one of two techniques. The first technique is designed to read a record that has a single data type such as a string from the RecordEnumeration. The other technique reads a record that has a compound data type. The next code segment shows how to read a record that has a single data type, which in this case is a string. You'll learn about reading records having compound data types later in this chapter.

This code segment calls the nextRecord() method, which returns a copy of the next record in the RecordEnumeration. The record is passed to the constructor of the String class and is assigned to the string variable. You would place this code segment within a conditional loop, such as the while loop shown previously in this section, to be assured that a record exists in the RecordEnumeration before attempting to copy the record to the string. Of course, you probably would use an array of strings if a while loop is used; otherwise the MIDlet would be overwriting the previous record assigned to the string, unless you plan to process the record within the while loop.

```
String string = new String(recordEnumeration.nextRecord());
```

You can move forward or back within the RecordEnumeration by calling either the nextRecord() method, which moves to the next record, or the previousRecord() method, which moves back one record. Both the nextRecord() method and the previousRecord() method return a byte array containing a copy of the record.

You are positioned at the top of the RecordEnumeration when the RecordEnumeration is created. The top is not the first record; you must call the nextRecord() method to move to the first record. You can move to the last record by calling the previousRecord() method while at the top of the RecordEnumeration. You can return to the top of the RecordEnumeration by calling the reset() method.

Before moving in either direction through the RecordEnumeration, you should always determine whether there are records in the RecordEnumeration, and if so, whether there is a next record or previous record.

Call the numRecords() method to determine the number of records there are in the RecordEnumeration. The numRecords() method returns an integer representing the total number of records. If the return value is greater than zero, then evaluate whether there is a next record or previous record depending on the desired direction. The hasNextElement() method is called to determine whether there is a next record, which is illustrated in a previous code segment. Call the hasPreviousElement() method to determine whether there is a previous record. Both methods return a boolean value indicating whether or not there is another record.

You can track your progress through the RecordEnumeration by retrieving the record IDs of records in the RecordEnumeration. Let's say that you determine there are ten records in the RecordEnumeration by calling the numRecords() method. The ID of the first record in the RecordEnumeration is zero, and the ID of the last record is nine. You can determine the record ID of the next record by calling the nextRecordId() method. The nextRecordId() method returns an integer representing the ID of the next record. Likewise, you call the previousRecordId() method to retrieve the ID of the previous record.

Sometimes record IDs can be misleading when the RecordEnumeration is automatically updated whenever a change is made to the underlying record store. There are two ways in which automatic updating is activated or deactivated. The first way is when the RecordEnumeration is created. As you'll recall, the last parameter in the enumerateRecords() method is a boolean value that if set to true, causes the RecordEnumeration to update automatically. The RecordEnumeration is not changed when the underlying record store changes if the boolean value is false.

The other way to set automatic updating of the RecordEnumeration is by calling the keepUpdated() method. The keepUpdated() method has one parameter, which is a boolean value indicating whether or not the RecordEnumeration is automatically updated.

You can check the status of the automatic updating feature by calling the isKeptUpdated() method. This method returns a boolean value indicating whether or not the RecordEnumeration is automatically updated. This is important to know if you are relying on record IDs to plot your way through the RecordEnumeration, because each time a record is inserted or removed from the RecordEnumeration, record IDs are reindexed.

You can manually cause the RecordEnumeration to be rebuilt by calling the rebuild() method. The rebuild() method should be called whenever records in the underlying record store change and the automatic update feature is deactivated.

Obviously, you'll know when your MIDlet changes the underlying record store and therefore needs to call the rebuild() method. However, many times other MIDlets within the same MIDlet suite can also change the record store without notifying your MIDlet. In this case, you should create a RecordListener, which notifies your MIDlet that the associated record store has changed and that the MIDlet needs to call the rebuild() method. You'll learn more about the RecordListener later in this chapter.

You can call the destroy method to empty the contents of a RecordEnumeration and release resources used by the RecordEnumeration. This should be done as soon as the MIDlet no longer requires the RecordEnumeration in order to free those resources for other purposes. Remember, a small computing device has limited resources, unlike a PC or server.

Reading a Record of a Simple Data Type into a RecordEnumeration

We'll look at two listings to show how to read records from a record store into a RecordEnumeration. Listing 8-7 reads three records, each a string type from a record store, and displays them in an alert dialog box (Figure 8-5). The JAD file is in Listing 8-8. Listing 8-9 reads three mixed data type records from a record store and also displays them in an alert dialog box. Listing 8-10 contains the JAD file for this listing.

Let's begin with a look at Listing 8-7. The structure is very similar to Listing 8-3, which inserted a record into a record store and then read the record from the record store, displaying the record in an alert dialog box. You'll notice the first difference from Listing 8-3 occurs in the second try {} block. Three strings are created and assigned to a String array. One string was used in Listing 8-3. Each element of the String array is then written to the record store using the same technique as illustrated in Listing 8-3.

Reading a Record of a String Data Type into a RecordEnumeration

Here are the steps required to read a record of a string data type into a RecordEnumeration:

1. Declare references to classes.
2. Create instances of classes and assign those instances to references.
3. Open a record store and create a new record store if the record store doesn't exist.
4. Display any errors that occur when opening/creating a record store.
5. Create data in the appropriate data type.
6. Convert data to a byte array.
7. Write the record to the record store.
8. Display any errors that might occur while writing to the record store.
9. Create a RecordEnumeration.
10. Loop through the RecordEnumeration, copying each record to a variable.
11. Display the data in a dialog box.
12. Display any errors that occur when reading records from the RecordEnumeration.
13. Close and remove the RecordEnumeration and the record store.

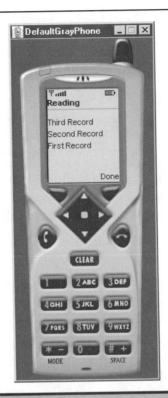

Figure 8-5.   *Displaying a simple data type from a RecordEnumeration*

Another change is in the third try {} block, where records from the record store are copied into the RecordEnumeration and then displayed on the screen. The first statement in this try {} block creates a RecordEnumeration by calling the enumerateRecords() method. The RecordEnumeration doesn't use a filter or comparator and is not automatically updated when changes are made to the underlying record store.

Before entering the while loop, the MIDlet calls the hasNextElement() method to determine whether there is a next record in the RecordEnumeration. Remember that the RecordEnumeration is not at the first record, so the hasNextElement() method determines whether there is a record in the record store. A boolean true is returned if a record exists, otherwise a false is returned.

If a true is returned by the hasNextElement(), the MIDlet copies the first record of the RecordEnumeration into a string, which is then displayed in an alert dialog box. Of course, you can further process the record instead of displaying the record, depending on the nature of your application. This process continues until the hasNextElement() method returns a false, indicating no more records exist in the RecordEnumeration.

The last modification of Listing 8-3 occurs in the fifth try {} block of Listing 8-7. This is where the record store is deleted. The destroy() method is called in this example to release resources used by the RecordEnumeration and thereby having the effect of deleting records in the RecordEnumeration.

```java
import javax.microedition.rms.*;
import javax.microedition.midlet.*;
import javax.microedition.lcdui.*;
import java.io.*;
public class RecordEnumerationExample
            extends MIDlet implements CommandListener
{
  private Display display;
  private Alert alert;
  private Form form;
  private Command exit;
  private Command start;
  private RecordStore recordstore = null;
  private RecordEnumeration recordEnumeration = null;
  public RecordEnumerationExample ()
  {
    display = Display.getDisplay(this);
    exit = new Command("Exit", Command.SCREEN, 1);
    start = new Command("Start", Command.SCREEN, 1);
    form = new Form("RecordEnumeration");
    form.addCommand(exit);
    form.addCommand(start);
    form.setCommandListener(this);
  }
  public void startApp()
  {
    display.setCurrent(form);
  }
  public void pauseApp()
  {
  }
  public void destroyApp( boolean unconditional )
  {
  }
  public void commandAction(Command command,
            Displayable displayable)
  {
```

```
if (command == exit)
{
  destroyApp(true);
  notifyDestroyed();
}
else if (command == start)
{
  try
  {
    recordstore = RecordStore.openRecordStore(
                "myRecordStore", true );
  }
  catch (Exception error)
  {
    alert = new Alert("Error Creating",
            error.toString(), null, AlertType.WARNING);
    alert.setTimeout(Alert.FOREVER);
    display.setCurrent(alert);
  }
  try
  {
    String outputData[] = {"First Record",
            "Second Record", "Third Record"};
    for (int x = 0; x < 3; x++)
    {
      byte[] byteOutputData = outputData[x].getBytes();
      recordstore.addRecord(byteOutputData,
                0, byteOutputData.length);
    }
  }
  catch ( Exception error)
  {
    alert = new Alert("Error Writing",
            error.toString(), null, AlertType.WARNING);
    alert.setTimeout(Alert.FOREVER);
    display.setCurrent(alert);
  }
  try
  {
    StringBuffer buffer = new StringBuffer();
```

```
    recordEnumeration =
          recordstore.enumerateRecords(null, null, false);
    while (recordEnumeration.hasNextElement())
    {
      buffer.append(new String(recordEnumeration.nextRecord()));
      buffer.append("\n");
    }
    alert = new Alert("Reading",
          buffer.toString(), null, AlertType.WARNING);
    alert.setTimeout(Alert.FOREVER);
    display.setCurrent(alert);
}
catch (Exception error)
{
  alert = new Alert("Error Reading",
            error.toString(), null, AlertType.WARNING);
  alert.setTimeout(Alert.FOREVER);
  display.setCurrent(alert);
}
try
{
  recordstore.closeRecordStore();
}
catch (Exception error)
{
  alert = new Alert("Error Closing",
          error.toString(), null, AlertType.WARNING);
  alert.setTimeout(Alert.FOREVER);
  display.setCurrent(alert);
}
if (RecordStore.listRecordStores() != null)
{
  try
  {
    RecordStore.deleteRecordStore("myRecordStore");
    recordEnumeration.destroy();
  }
  catch (Exception error)
  {
   alert = new Alert("Error Removing",
          error.toString(), null, AlertType.WARNING);
```

```
                    alert.setTimeout(Alert.FOREVER);
                    display.setCurrent(alert);
                }
            }
        }
    }
}
```

Listing 8-8
The JAD
file for
Listing 8-7

```
MIDlet-Name: RecordEnumerationExample
MIDlet-Version: 1.0
MIDlet-Vendor: MyCompany
MIDlet-Jar-URL: RecordEnumerationExample.jar
MIDlet-1: RecordEnumerationExample, , RecordEnumerationExample
MicroEdition-Configuration: CLDC-1.0
MicroEdition-Profile: MIDP-1.0
MIDlet-JAR-SIZE: 100
```

Reading a Mixed Data Type Record into a RecordEnumeration

Listing 8-9 is very similar to Listing 8-5. Both write and read mixed data type records. Listing 8-9 creates an array of strings, integers, and boolean and assigns values to each element of these arrays. Each of these is a record. Listing 8-5 created one record. The process of writing mixed data type records to the record store is the same as the process used in Listing 8-5 with one small difference. Listing 8-9 uses a loop to write all three records to the record store.

The next records from the record store are copied into the RecordEnumeration. This process is very similar to the same process in Listing 8-5 that is used to read records from the record store, but there are a few subtle differences that you need to notice. First, the enumerateRecords() method is called to build a RecordEnumeration. The enumerateRecords() method doesn't use a filter or comparator and is not updated automatically as changes occur to the record store. Next, the hasNextElement() is called to determine whether there is a record in the RecordEnumeration. Statements within the while block are skipped if a false is returned; otherwise, the MIDlet proceeds to the current record by calling the getRecord() method. The getRecord() method requires one parameter, which is the record ID of the record that is being copied into the RecordEnumeration. The record ID is returned by the nextRecordId() method.

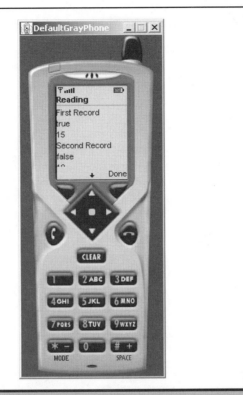

Figure 8-6. *Records of mixed data types in the RecordEnumeration are displayed.*

The readUTF() method, readBoolean() method, and readInt() method are then called to return their respective data from the current record of the RecordEnumeration. These return values are then concatenated and assigned to a string. The string is then displayed in an alert dialog box (Figure 8-6). The same process occurs for each record in the RecordEnumeration.

And as with Listing 8-7, Listing 8-9 releases resources used by the RecordEnumeration by calling the destroy() method in the fifth try {} block.

Listing 8-9
Reading
a record of a
mixed data
type into
a Record-
Enumeration

```
import javax.microedition.rms.*;
import javax.microedition.midlet.*;
import javax.microedition.lcdui.*;
import java.io.*;
public class MixedRecordEnumerationExample
```

```
          extends MIDlet implements CommandListener
{
  private Display display;
  private Alert alert;
  private Form form;
  private Command exit;
  private Command start;
  private RecordStore recordstore = null;
  private RecordEnumeration recordEnumeration = null;
  public MixedRecordEnumerationExample ()
  {
    display = Display.getDisplay(this);
    exit = new Command("Exit", Command.SCREEN, 1);
    start = new Command("Start", Command.SCREEN, 1);
    form = new Form("Mixed RecordEnumeration");
    form.addCommand(exit);
    form.addCommand(start);
    form.setCommandListener(this);
  }
  public void startApp()
  {
    display.setCurrent(form);
  }
  public void pauseApp()
  {
  }
  public void destroyApp( boolean unconditional )
  {
  }
  public void commandAction(Command command, Displayable displayable)
  {
    if (command == exit)
    {
      destroyApp(true);
      notifyDestroyed();
    }
    else if (command == start)
    {
      try
      {
```

```
        recordstore = RecordStore.openRecordStore(
                "myRecordStore", true );
    }
    catch (Exception error)
    {
      alert = new Alert("Error Creating",
                error.toString(), null, AlertType.WARNING);
      alert.setTimeout(Alert.FOREVER);
      display.setCurrent(alert);
    }
    try
    {
      byte[] outputRecord;
      String outputString[] = {"First Record",
                "Second Record", "Third Record"};
      int outputInteger[] = {15, 10, 5};
      boolean outputBoolean[] = {true, false, true};
      ByteArrayOutputStream outputStream =
                new ByteArrayOutputStream();
      DataOutputStream outputDataStream =
                new DataOutputStream(outputStream);
      for (int x = 0; x < 3; x++)
      {
        outputDataStream.writeUTF(outputString[x]);
        outputDataStream.writeBoolean(outputBoolean[x]);
        outputDataStream.writeInt(outputInteger[x]);
        outputDataStream.flush();
        outputRecord = outputStream.toByteArray();
        recordstore.addRecord(outputRecord, 0,
                    outputRecord.length);
      }
      outputStream.reset();
      outputStream.close();
      outputDataStream.close();
    }
    catch ( Exception error)
    {
      alert = new Alert("Error Writing",
                error.toString(), null, AlertType.WARNING);
      alert.setTimeout(Alert.FOREVER);
```

J2ME
DATA MANAGEMENT

```
                display.setCurrent(alert);
            }
            try
            {
                StringBuffer buffer = new StringBuffer();
                byte[] byteInputData = new byte[300];
                ByteArrayInputStream inputStream = new ByteArrayInputStream(byteInputData);
                DataInputStream inputDataStream =
                        new DataInputStream(inputStream);
                recordEnumeration = recordstore.enumerateRecords(
                            null, null, false);
                while (recordEnumeration.hasNextElement())
                {
                    recordstore.getRecord(recordEnumeration.nextRecordId(),
                            byteInputData, 0);
                    buffer.append(inputDataStream.readUTF());
                    buffer.append("\n");
                    buffer.append(inputDataStream.readBoolean());
                    buffer.append("\n");
                    buffer.append(inputDataStream.readInt());
                    buffer.append("\n");
                    alert = new Alert("Reading", buffer.toString(),
                            null, AlertType.WARNING);
                    alert.setTimeout(Alert.FOREVER);
                    display.setCurrent(alert);
                }
                inputStream.close();
            }
            catch (Exception error)
            {
                alert = new Alert("Error Reading",
                        error.toString(), null, AlertType.WARNING);
                alert.setTimeout(Alert.FOREVER);
                display.setCurrent(alert);
            }
            try
            {
                recordstore.closeRecordStore();
```

```
      }
      catch (Exception error)
      {
        alert = new Alert("Error Closing",
              error.toString(), null, AlertType.WARNING);
        alert.setTimeout(Alert.FOREVER);
        display.setCurrent(alert);
      }
      if (RecordStore.listRecordStores() != null)
      {
       try
       {
         RecordStore.deleteRecordStore("myRecordStore");
         recordEnumeration.destroy();
       }
       catch (Exception error)
       {
        alert = new Alert("Error Removing",
              error.toString(), null, AlertType.WARNING);
        alert.setTimeout(Alert.FOREVER);
        display.setCurrent(alert);
       }
      }
    }
  }
}
```

Listing 8-10
The JAD
file for
Listing 8-9

```
MIDlet-Name: MixedRecordEnumerationExample
MIDlet-Version: 1.0
MIDlet-Vendor: MyCompany
MIDlet-Jar-URL: MixedRecordEnumerationExample.jar
MIDlet-1: MixedRecordEnumerationExample, ,
            MixedRecordEnumerationExample
MicroEdition-Configuration: CLDC-1.0
MicroEdition-Profile: MIDP-1.0
MIDlet-JAR-SIZE: 100
```

J2ME
DATA MANAGEMENT

Reading a Mixed Data Type Record into a RecordEnumeration

Here are the steps required to read a mixed data type record into a RecordEnumeration:

1. Declare references to classes.
2. Create instances of classes and assign those instances to references.
3. Open a record store and create a new record store if the record store doesn't exist.
4. Display any errors that occur when opening/creating a record store.
5. Create data in the appropriate data type.
6. Convert data to a byte array output stream.
7. Create a data output stream using the byte array output stream.
8. Write each column of the record to the data output stream.
9. Convert the data output stream to a byte array.
10. Write the record to the record store.
11. Close the output byte array output stream and the data output stream.
12. Display any errors that might occur while writing to the record store.
13. Create a buffer of bytes sufficient to hold a record.
14. Create a byte array input stream and a data input stream.
15. Create a RecordEnumeration.
16. Loop through the RecordEnumeration, copying each column from the record store to a variable.
17. Display the data in a dialog box.
18. Display any errors that occur when reading records from the record store.
19. Close and remove the RecordEnumeration and the record store.

Sorting Records

Records within a RecordEnumeration are sorted by defining a comparator class that is an implementation of the RecordComparator interface. Within the comparator class you define a method that has the logic to compare each record to determine whether the record is equal to the current record or should precede or follow the current record within the RecordEnumeration. This method, called compare(), requires two parameters, which are two byte arrays that contain the current record and the next record. These byte arrays are then converted to two strings that are compared by using the compareTo() method of the String class.

The compareTo() method returns an integer that is equal to zero, less than zero, or greater than zero. A zero indicates that both strings are the same. An integer less than zero indicates that the next record precedes the current record in the RecordEnumeration. An integer greater than zero indicates that the next record follows the current record in the RecordEnumeration.

Based on the return value of the compareTo() method, the compare() method returns a predefined comparison value. These are RecordComparator.EQUIVALENT, RecordComparator.PRECEDES, and RecordComparator.FOLLOW (see Table 8-1).

You pass reference to the instance of the RecordComparator() as the second parameter of the enumerateRecords() method. The enumerateRecords() then calls the compare() method whenever there is a need to sort records within the RecordEnumerator. The direction of the sort is controlled by the logic that you create within the compare() method. If you want the sort to appear in ascending order, then return the RecordComparator .PRECEDES when the return value of the compareTo() string is less than the current record and RecordComparator.FOLLOW when the return value is greater than the current record.

You create a descending sort by reversing these operations: return the RecordComparator.FOLLOW when the return value of the compareTo() string is less than the current record and RecordComparator.PRECEDES when the return value is greater than the current record.

Value	Description
EQUIVALENT	Records passed to the compare() method are the same.
FOLLOW	The record passed as the first parameter follows the record passed as the second parameter.
PRECEDES	The record passed as the first parameter precedes the record passed as the second parameter.

Table 8-1. *Comparison Values for the compare() Method*

Sorting Single Data Type Records in a RecordEnumeration

Listing 8-11 illustrates how to sort a RecordEnumeration that contains a single data type record, which is a string (Figure 8-7). Listing 8-12 contains the JAD file for Listing 8-11. You'll notice that Listing 8-11 is very similar to Listing 8-7 in that both create a record store that contains three strings. Each record in the RecordEnumeration is then displayed in an alert dialog box.

The difference between Listing 8-7 and Listing 8-11 is that Listing 8-11 presents records contained in the RecordEnumeration in sort order. Notice in the second try {} block that three strings are created. These are different from the strings created in Listing 8-7. The strings First Record, Second Record, and Third Record are replaced with the names Mary, Bob, and Adam in order to illustrate sorting.

Figure 8-7. *Sorting a single data type record in a RecordEnumeration*

The next change occurs in the third try {} block where an instance of the RecordComparator() interface is created and passed as the second argument to the enumerateRecords() method. A null was passed as the second parameter to the enumerateRecords() method in Listing 8-7 because the RecordEnumeration was not sorted.

The final change occurs at the end of the listing where the compare() method is defined. The compare() method receives two parameters called record1 and record2; both are byte arrays supplied by the enumerateRecords() method. Those byte arrays are transformed into strings, which are evaluated by the compareTo() method. The compareTo() method requires one argument that is the value of the second parameter passed to the compare() method. In this example, record2 is referenced to the second parameter.

Sorting a Single Data Type of a Record in a RecordEnumeration

Here are the steps required to sort using a data type of a record in a RecordEnumeration:

1. Declare references to classes.

2. Create instances of classes and assign those instances to references.

3. Open a record store and create a new record store if the record store doesn't exist.

4. Display any errors that occur when opening/creating a record store.

5. Create data in the appropriate data type.

6. Convert data to a byte array.

7. Write the record to the record store.

8. Display any errors that might occur while writing to the record store.

9. Create a Comparator class with a method that compares two records and returns a value indicating whether the next record should follow, precede, or is equivalent to the current record.

10. Create an instance of the Comparator class and use the instance when creating the RecordEnumeration.

11. Loop through the RecordEnumeration, copying each record to a variable.

12. Display the data in a dialog box.

13. Display any errors that occur when reading records from the RecordEnumeration.

14. Close and remove the RecordEnumeration and the record store.

An if...if else...else statement evaluates the return value of the compareTo() method, and then the appropriate comparison value is returned to the compareTo() method.

```java
import javax.microedition.rms.*;
import javax.microedition.midlet.*;
import javax.microedition.lcdui.*;
import java.io.*;
public class SortExample extends MIDlet implements CommandListener
{
  private Display display;
  private Alert alert;
  private Form form;
  private Command exit;
  private Command start;
  private RecordStore recordstore = null;
  private RecordEnumeration recordEnumeration = null;
  private Comparator comparator = null;
  public SortExample ()
  {
    display = Display.getDisplay(this);
    exit = new Command("Exit", Command.SCREEN, 1);
    start = new Command("Start", Command.SCREEN, 1);
    form = new Form("Mixed RecordEnumeration", null);
    form.addCommand(exit);
    form.addCommand(start);
    form.setCommandListener(this);
  }
  public void startApp()
  {
    display.setCurrent(form);
  }
  public void pauseApp()
  {
  }
  public void destroyApp( boolean unconditional )
  {
  }
  public void commandAction(Command command, Displayable displayable)
  {
    if (command == exit)
    {
      destroyApp(true);
```

```
      notifyDestroyed();
  }
  else if (command == start)
  {
    try
    {
      recordstore = RecordStore.openRecordStore(
                    "myRecordStore", true );
    }
    catch (Exception error)
    {
      alert = new Alert("Error Creating",
            error.toString(), null, AlertType.WARNING);
      alert.setTimeout(Alert.FOREVER);
      display.setCurrent(alert);
    }
    try
    {
      String outputData[] = {"Mary", "Bob", "Adam"};
      for (int x = 0; x < 3; x++)
      {
        byte[] byteOutputData = outputData[x].getBytes();
        recordstore.addRecord(byteOutputData, 0,
                  byteOutputData.length);
      }
    }
    catch ( Exception error)
    {
     alert = new Alert("Error Writing",
              error.toString(), null, AlertType.WARNING);
     alert.setTimeout(Alert.FOREVER);
     display.setCurrent(alert);
    }
    try
    {
      StringBuffer buffer = new StringBuffer();
      Comparator comparator = new Comparator();
      recordEnumeration = recordstore.enumerateRecords(
                      null, comparator, false);
      while (recordEnumeration.hasNextElement())
      {
        buffer.append(new String(recordEnumeration.nextRecord()));
```

```
        buffer.append("\n");
      }
      alert = new Alert("Reading", buffer.toString() ,
             null, AlertType.WARNING);
      alert.setTimeout(Alert.FOREVER);
      display.setCurrent(alert);
    }
    catch (Exception error)
    {
      alert = new Alert("Error Reading",
              error.toString(), null, AlertType.WARNING);
      alert.setTimeout(Alert.FOREVER);
      display.setCurrent(alert);
    }
    try
    {
     recordstore.closeRecordStore();
    }
    catch (Exception error)
    {
      alert = new Alert("Error Closing",
                error.toString(), null, AlertType.WARNING);
      alert.setTimeout(Alert.FOREVER);
      display.setCurrent(alert);
    }
    if (RecordStore.listRecordStores() != null)
    {
      try
      {
        RecordStore.deleteRecordStore("myRecordStore");
        recordEnumeration.destroy();
      }
      catch (Exception error)
      {
       alert = new Alert("Error Removing",
              error.toString(), null, AlertType.WARNING);
       alert.setTimeout(Alert.FOREVER);
       display.setCurrent(alert);
      }
    }
  }
}
```

```
    }
class Comparator implements RecordComparator
{
  public int compare(byte[] record1, byte[] record2)
  {
    String string1 = new String(record1),
              string2= new String(record2);
    int comparison = string1.compareTo(string2);
    if (comparison == 0)
      return RecordComparator.EQUIVALENT;
    else if (comparison < 0)
      return RecordComparator.PRECEDES;
    else
      return RecordComparator.FOLLOWS;
  }
}
```

Listing 8-12
The JAD
file for
Listing 8-11

```
MIDlet-Name: SortExample
MIDlet-Version: 1.0
MIDlet-Vendor: MyCompany
MIDlet-Jar-URL: SortExample.jar
MIDlet-1: SortExample, , SortExample
MicroEdition-Configuration: CLDC-1.0
MicroEdition-Profile: MIDP-1.0
MIDlet-JAR-SIZE: 100
```

Sorting Mixed Data Type Records in a RecordEnumeration

Listing 8-13 shows how to sort a RecordEnumeration that contains records of mixed data types (Figure 8-8). Listing 8-14 is the JAD file for Listing 8-13. Listing 8-13 is a modification of Listing 8-9 that wrote and read mixed data types to and from a record store.

Both Listing 8-9 and Listing 8-13 are structured similarly, so we'll concentrate on exploring the modifications made to Listing 8-9 to sort records in the RecordEnumeration. Listing 8-13 writes three records containing two columns of data. The first column consists of strings and the second column integers. This is different from Listing 8-9 where a boolean column is also written to the record store. The boolean column was excluded from this example to simplify the code.

The next modification occurs in the third try {} block of Listing 8-13 where an instance of the RecordComparator interface is referenced and passed as the second parameter to the enumerateRecords() method. The RecordComparator implementation is defined at the end of Listing 8-13.

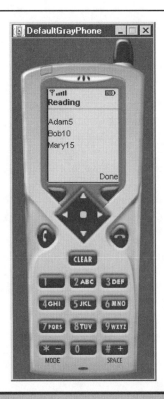

Figure 8-8.   *Sorting mixed data type records in a RecordEnumeration*

Another modification is made in the fifth try {} block where a call is made to the compareClose() method of the RecordComparator interface. The compareClose() method closes streams opened by the RecordComparator interface to facilitate comparing records.

At the end of Listing 8-13 you'll find the definition of the Comparator implementation of the RecordInterface. The Comparator defines two methods: compare() and compareClose(). The compare() method is called by the enumerateRecords() method to compare the next record with the current record within the RecordEnumeration. Both records are passed as byte arrays to the compare() method.

Records passed as parameters to the compare() method contain both columns—first a string and then an int. In real projects you can expect to have multiple columns of different data types. However, the technique used in this example can easily be expanded to handle records of any number of columns and data types.

The compare() method begins by creating a byte array input stream from the first record and then using the byte array input stream to create a data input stream. This is the same process used in Listing 8-9 to read mixed data type records from the RecordEnumeration.

Sorting a Mixed Data Type Record in a RecordEnumeration

Here are the steps required to sort a mixed data type record in a RecordEnumeration:

1. Declare references to classes.

2. Create instances of classes and assign those instances to references.

3. Open a record store and create a new record store if the record store doesn't exist.

4. Display any errors that occur when opening/creating a record store.

5. Create data in the appropriate data type.

6. Convert data to a byte array output stream.

7. Create a data output stream using the byte array output stream.

8. Write each column of the record to the data output stream.

9. Convert the data output stream to a byte array.

10. Write the record to the record store.

11. Close the output byte array output stream and the data output stream.

12. Display any errors that might occur while writing to the record store.

13. Create a buffer of bytes sufficient to hold a record.

14. Create a byte array input stream and a data input stream.

15. Create a Comparator class with a method that compares two records and returns a value indicating whether the next record should follow, precede, or is equivalent to the current record.

16. Create an instance of the Comparator class and use the instance when creating the RecordEnumeration.

17. Loop through the RecordEnumeration, copying each column from the record store to a variable.

18. Display the data in a dialog box.

19. Display any errors that occur when reading records from the record store.

20. Close and remove the RecordEnumeration and the record store.

J2ME
DATA MANAGEMENT

Each column in the record is read using the appropriate read*XXX*() method, as described previously in this chapter. It is important to remember to read each column in the order in which the column appears in the record. In this example, the first column is a string, and the second column is an integer. Therefore, the readUTF() method must be called before calling the readInt() method. This is also true if the record has other columns.

Only the return value of the readInt() method is assigned to a variable in this example because the value of the second column is being used to sort the record. The return value of the readUTF() method is not retained because the value of this column is not being sorted. You don't need to read columns of a record beyond the column that is the key to the sort because only the column with the sort key is processed.

The same process is used to extract the column used as the sort key for the second record passed to the compare() method. The integer columns from both records are then compared, and the appropriate comparison value is returned by the compare() method.

```
import javax.microedition.rms.*;
import javax.microedition.midlet.*;
import javax.microedition.lcdui.*;
import java.io.*;
public class SortMixedRecordDataTypeExample
        extends MIDlet implements CommandListener
{
  private Display display;
  private Alert alert;
  private Form form;
  private Command exit;
  private Command start;
  private RecordStore recordstore = null;
  private RecordEnumeration recordEnumeration = null;
  private Comparator comparator = null;
  public SortMixedRecordDataTypeExample ()
  {
    display = Display.getDisplay(this);
    exit = new Command("Exit", Command.SCREEN, 1);
    start = new Command("Start", Command.SCREEN, 1);
    form = new Form("Mixed RecordEnumeration");
    form.addCommand(exit);
    form.addCommand(start);
    form.setCommandListener(this);
  }
  public void startApp()
  {
    display.setCurrent(form);
  }
  public void pauseApp()
```

```
{
}
public void destroyApp( boolean unconditional )
{
}
public void commandAction(Command command, Displayable displayable)
{
  if (command == exit)
  {
    destroyApp(true);
    notifyDestroyed();
  }
  else if (command == start)
  {
    try
    {
      recordstore = RecordStore.openRecordStore(
               "myRecordStore", true );
    }
    catch (Exception error)
    {
      alert = new Alert("Error Creating",
               error.toString(), null, AlertType.WARNING);
      alert.setTimeout(Alert.FOREVER);
      display.setCurrent(alert);
    }
    try
    {
      byte[] outputRecord;
      String outputString[] = {"Mary", "Bob", "Adam"};
      int outputInteger[] = {15, 10, 5};
      ByteArrayOutputStream outputStream =
               new ByteArrayOutputStream();
      DataOutputStream outputDataStream =
               new DataOutputStream(outputStream);
      for (int x = 0; x < 3; x++)
      {
        outputDataStream.writeUTF(outputString[x]);
        outputDataStream.writeInt(outputInteger[x]);
        outputDataStream.flush();
        outputRecord = outputStream.toByteArray();
        recordstore.addRecord(outputRecord, 0,
               outputRecord.length);
        outputStream.reset();
      }
      outputStream.close();
      outputDataStream.close();
```

```
      }
      catch ( Exception error)
      {
        alert = new Alert("Error Writing",
              error.toString(), null, AlertType.WARNING);
        alert.setTimeout(Alert.FOREVER);
        display.setCurrent(alert);
      }
      try
      {
          String[] inputString = new String[3];
          int z = 0;
          byte[] byteInputData = new byte[300];
          ByteArrayInputStream inputStream =
                    new ByteArrayInputStream(byteInputData);
          DataInputStream inputDataStream =
                    new DataInputStream(inputStream);
          StringBuffer buffer = new StringBuffer();
          comparator = new Comparator();
          recordEnumeration = recordstore.enumerateRecords(
                          null, comparator, false);
          while (recordEnumeration.hasNextElement())
          {
           recordstore.getRecord( recordEnumeration.nextRecordId(),
                              byteInputData, 0);
           buffer.append(inputDataStream.readUTF());
           buffer.append(inputDataStream.readInt());
           buffer.append("\n");
           inputDataStream.reset();
          }
          alert = new Alert("Reading", buffer.toString(), null,
                          AlertType.WARNING);
          alert.setTimeout(Alert.FOREVER);
          display.setCurrent(alert);
          inputDataStream.close();
          inputStream.close();
      }
      catch (Exception error)
      {
        alert = new Alert("Error Reading",
                          error.toString(), null, AlertType.WARNING);
        alert.setTimeout(Alert.FOREVER);
        display.setCurrent(alert);
      }
      try
      {
        recordstore.closeRecordStore();
```

```
      }
      catch (Exception error)
      {
        alert = new Alert("Error Closing",
                    error.toString(), null, AlertType.WARNING);
        alert.setTimeout(Alert.FOREVER);
        display.setCurrent(alert);
      }
      if (RecordStore.listRecordStores() != null)
      {
        try
        {
          RecordStore.deleteRecordStore("myRecordStore");
          comparator.compareClose();
          recordEnumeration.destroy();
        }
        catch (Exception error)
        {
         alert = new Alert("Error Removing",
                    error.toString(), null, AlertType.WARNING);
         alert.setTimeout(Alert.FOREVER);
         display.setCurrent(alert);
        }
      }
    }
  }
}
class Comparator implements RecordComparator
{
  private byte[] comparatorInputData = new byte[300];
  private ByteArrayInputStream comparatorInputStream = null;
  private DataInputStream comparatorInputDataType = null;
  public int compare(byte[] record1, byte[] record2)
  {
    int record1int, record2int;
    try
    {
      int maxlen = Math.max(record1.length, record2.length);
      if (maxlen > comparatorInputData.length)
      {
        comparatorInputData = new byte[maxlen];
      }
      comparatorInputStream = new ByteArrayInputStream(record1);
      comparatorInputDataType =
              new DataInputStream(comparatorInputStream);
      comparatorInputDataType.readUTF();
      record1int = comparatorInputDataType.readInt();
```

```
      comparatorInputStream = new ByteArrayInputStream(record2);
      comparatorInputDataType =
              new DataInputStream(comparatorInputStream);
      comparatorInputDataType.readUTF();
      record2int = comparatorInputDataType.readInt();
      if (record1int == record2int)
      {
        return RecordComparator.EQUIVALENT;
      }
      else if (record1int < record2int)
      {
        return RecordComparator.PRECEDES;
      }
      else
      {
        return RecordComparator.FOLLOWS;
      }
    }
    catch (Exception error)
    {
      return RecordComparator.EQUIVALENT;
    }
  }
  public void compareClose()
  {
    try
    {
      if (comparatorInputStream!= null)
      {
        comparatorInputStream.close();
      }
      if (comparatorInputDataType!= null)
      {
        comparatorInputDataType.close();
      }
    }
    catch (Exception error)
    {
    }
  }
}
```

```
MIDlet-Name: SortMixedRecordDataTypeExample
MIDlet-Version: 1.0
MIDlet-Vendor: MyCompany
```

```
MIDlet-Jar-URL: SortMixedRecordDataTypeExample.jar
MIDlet-1: SortMixedRecordDataTypeExample, ,
          SortMixedRecordDataTypeExample
MicroEdition-Configuration: CLDC-1.0
MicroEdition-Profile: MIDP-1.0
MIDlet-JAR-SIZE: 100
```

Searching Records

Searching is referred to as *filtering*, where the filter is defined by the search criteria. Records that match the search criteria are copied into the RecordEnumeration. Those not matching the search criteria are filtered from the RecordEnumeration. Searching for a record in a record store is very similar to sorting records in that you define an implementation of an interface. In this case the implementation you define filters records contained in a record store rather than sorting records in a RecordEnumeration.

The RecordFilter interface is used when searching for a record. You must define two methods when defining an implementation of the RecordFilter interface. These are the matches() method and the filterClose() method.

The constructor accepts the search criteria as a parameter when your MIDlet creates an instance of the implementation class. The matches() method contains the logic necessary to determine whether a column fits the search criteria and returns a boolean value indicating whether or not there is a match. The filterClose() method frees resources used by the implementation of the RecordFilter interface once the search is completed.

Logic contained in the matches() method reads one or multiple columns from the current record and then applies logical operators to determine whether the record meets the search criteria. You determine the logic used to decide whether or not a record should or should not be included in the RecordEnumeration. Furthermore, you can sort the filtered records by first searching for a subset of records in the record store, then sorting those records.

The next two sections illustrate how to search a record store that contains records of a single data type and records containing multiple data types.

Searching Single Data Type Records

Listing 8-15 shows how to search records that contain a single data type (Figure 8-9). Listing 8-16 is the JAD file for Listing 8-15. You'll notice that Listing 8-15 is a modified version of Listing 8-13. Both listings write three records to a record store. Each record has one column that is a String data type. Listing 8-15 searches for one of those records and displays the results of the search in an alert dialog box.

You'll notice in the third try {} block that a statement creating an instance of the Filter replaces the statement that creates an instance of the Comparator. The Filter is the implementation of the RecordFilter that is defined at the end of the listing. The constructor of the Filter is passed the word "Bob," which is the search criteria.

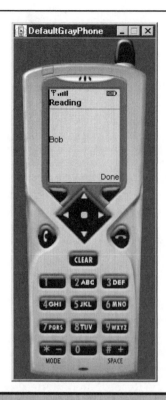

Figure 8-9. *Searching a single data type record in a RecordEnumeration*

The statement beneath the statement that created the instance of the Filter creates the RecordEnumeration. The enumerateRecords() method is passed three parameters. The first is reference to the filter. The second is reference to the Comparator. This is set to null because a Comparator isn't used in this example. The last parameter is a boolean value indicating that the RecordEnumeration should not be automatically updated when changes are made to the underlying record store.

The next modification occurs at the end of the listing where the implementation of the RecordFilter is defined. This implementation is called Filter, and its constructor is passed the search criteria, which is assigned the String search. The search criteria is immediately converted to all lowercase characters. As you'll notice, the record is also changed to lowercase characters before comparing the record to the search criteria.

The matches() method is automatically called to filter records that don't meet the search criteria. The matches() method requires one parameter, which is the record that is being matched to the search criteria. The record is an array of bytes passed by the enumerateRecords() method. The record is then converted to lowercase characters and assigned to a String variable.

The if statement expression is used to determine whether the record should be included in or excluded from the RecordEnumeration. Two conditions must be met for the record to be included in the RecordEnumeration. The record must not be null, and the comparison of the record and the search criteria must not be –1. The matches() method returns a boolean true or false to the enumerateRecords() method indicating whether or not the record should be included in the RecordEnumeration. A true value implies that the record should be included.

Searching with a Data Type of a Record

Here are the steps required to search using a data type of a record:

1. Declare references to classes.
2. Create instances of classes and assign those instances to references.
3. Open a record store and create a new record store if the record store doesn't exist.
4. Display any errors that occur when opening/creating a record store.
5. Create data in the appropriate data type.
6. Convert data to a byte array.
7. Write the record to the record store.
8. Display any errors that might occur while writing to the record store.
9. Create a Filter class with a method that compares the search criteria to a record and returns a value indicating whether the record matches the search criteria. If so, include the record in the RecordEnumeration.
10. Create an instance of the Filter class and use the instance when creating the RecordEnumeration.
11. Loop through the RecordEnumeration, copying each record to a variable.
12. Display the data in a dialog box.
13. Display any errors that occur when reading records from the RecordEnumeration.
14. Close and remove the RecordEnumeration and the record store.

The last method defined in the RecordFilter implementation, filterClose(), is used to free the ByteArrayInputStream and the DataInputStream used by the implementation. This method is called in the fifth try {} block.

```
import javax.microedition.rms.*;
import javax.microedition.midlet.*;
import javax.microedition.lcdui.*;
import java.io.*;
public class SearchExample extends MIDlet implements CommandListener
{
  private Display display;
  private Alert alert;
  private Form form;
  private Command exit;
  private Command start;
  private RecordStore recordstore = null;
  private RecordEnumeration recordEnumeration = null;
  private Filter filter = null;
  public SearchExample ()
  {
    display = Display.getDisplay(this);
    exit = new Command("Exit", Command.SCREEN, 1);
    start = new Command("Start", Command.SCREEN, 1);
    form = new Form("Mixed RecordEnumeration", null);
    form.addCommand(exit);
    form.addCommand(start);
    form.setCommandListener(this);
  }
  public void startApp()
  {
    display.setCurrent(form);
  }
  public void pauseApp()
  {
  }
  public void destroyApp( boolean unconditional )
  {
  }
  public void commandAction(Command command, Displayable displayable)
  {
    if (command == exit)
    {
```

```
    destroyApp(true);
    notifyDestroyed();
}
else if (command == start)
{
  try
  {
    recordstore = RecordStore.openRecordStore(
                      "myRecordStore", true );
  }
  catch (Exception error)
  {
    alert = new Alert("Error Creating",
              error.toString(), null, AlertType.WARNING);
    alert.setTimeout(Alert.FOREVER);
    display.setCurrent(alert);
  }
  try
  {
    String outputData[] = {"Mary", "Bob", "Adam"};
    for (int x = 0 ; x < 3; x++)
    {
      byte[] byteOutputData = outputData[x].getBytes();
      recordstore.addRecord(byteOutputData, 0,
                    byteOutputData.length);
    }
  }
  catch ( Exception error)
  {
    alert = new Alert("Error Writing",
            error.toString(), null, AlertType.WARNING);
    alert.setTimeout(Alert.FOREVER);
    display.setCurrent(alert);
  }
  try
  {
    filter = new Filter("Bob");
    recordEnumeration = recordstore.enumerateRecords(
                  filter, null, false);
    if (recordEnumeration.numRecords() > 0)
    {
      String string = new String(recordEnumeration.nextRecord());
```

```
        alert = new Alert("Reading", string,
                    null, AlertType.WARNING);
        alert.setTimeout(Alert.FOREVER);
        display.setCurrent(alert);
    }
}
catch (Exception error)
{
 alert = new Alert("Error Reading",
            error.toString(), null, AlertType.WARNING);
 alert.setTimeout(Alert.FOREVER);
 display.setCurrent(alert);
}
try
{
 recordstore.closeRecordStore();
}
catch (Exception error)
{
  alert = new Alert("Error Closing",
            error.toString(), null, AlertType.WARNING);
  alert.setTimeout(Alert.FOREVER);
  display.setCurrent(alert);
}
if (RecordStore.listRecordStores() != null)
{
  try
  {
   RecordStore.deleteRecordStore("myRecordStore");
   recordEnumeration.destroy();
   filter.filterClose();
  }
  catch (Exception error)
  {
   alert = new Alert("Error Removing",
            error.toString(), null, AlertType.WARNING);
   alert.setTimeout(Alert.FOREVER);
   display.setCurrent(alert);
  }
}
```

```
        }
    }
}
class Filter implements RecordFilter
{
  private String search = null;
  private ByteArrayInputStream inputstream = null;
  private DataInputStream datainputstream = null;
  public Filter(String search)
  {
    this.search = search.toLowerCase();
  }
  public boolean matches(byte[] suspect)
  {
    String string = new String(suspect).toLowerCase();
    if (string!= null && string.indexOf(search) != -1)
      return true;
    else
      return false;
  }
  public void filterClose()
  {
    try
    {
      if (inputstream != null)
      {
        inputstream.close();
      }
      if (datainputstream != null)
      {
        datainputstream.close();
      }
    }
    catch ( Exception error)
    {
    }
  }
}
```

Listing 8-16
The JAD
file for
Listing 8-15

```
MIDlet-Name: SearchExample
MIDlet-Version: 1.0
MIDlet-Vendor: MyCompany
MIDlet-Jar-URL: SearchExample.jar
MIDlet-1: SearchExample, , SearchExample
MicroEdition-Configuration: CLDC-1.0
MicroEdition-Profile: MIDP-1.0
MIDlet-JAR-SIZE: 100
```

Searching Mixed Data Type Records

Listing 8-17 illustrates how to search records that contain multiple columns, each possibly having different data types (Figure 8-10). Listing 8-18 is the JAD file for Listing 8-17. Listing 8-17 is similar in structure to Listing 8-15, which is used to sort single data type records. Therefore, we'll focus on sections of the example that are

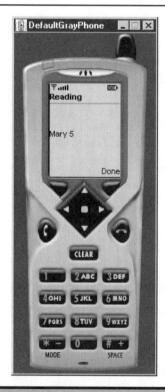

Figure 8-10. *Searching mixed data type records in a RecordEnumeration*

modifications to Listing 8-15. Refer to Listing 8-15 for a complete discussion of each line of code that isn't modified in this example.

The first modification is found in the third try { } block where an instance of the Filter class is created. The Filter class is an implementation of the RecordFilter interface. The constructor of the Filter class is passed the search criteria, which is the integer 10.

Reference to the instance of the Filter class is passed as the first parameter to the enumerateRecords() method, which returns a RecordEnumeration. The enumerateRecords() method calls methods defined in the Filter class. Notice that a null is passed as the second parameter to the enumerateRecords() since a RecordComparator is not being used to sort the RecordEnumeration.

Let's move toward the end of the example and review the definition of the Filter class where three methods are defined. The first method is the constructor, which receives the search criteria as a parameter. The search criteria is assigned to locate an integer variable, which has previously been initialized to zero. The matches() method is the next method defined in the Filter class. This is the method called by the enumerateRecords() method to determine whether the current record should or should not be included in the RecordEnumeration.

The enumerateRecords() method passes the matches() method a byte array containing the current record. This byte array is then converted to a byte array input stream, which is further converted to a data input stream.

The read*XXX*() method is then called to read each column from the data input stream. Columns must be read in the order they are written using the appropriate read*XXX*() method that reflects the data type of the column, as discussed previously in this chapter. You don't need to assign the results of the read*XXX*() method to a variable unless the value of the column is being compared to the search criteria. Furthermore, you can stop reading columns from the data input stream once the column used for the comparison has been read.

In this example, the first column is a string containing a person's name, and the second column is an integer. The first column is read, but the value of the first column is not assigned to a variable because this column is not matched to the search criteria. We still must read this column because columns are read sequentially within a record. Once a column is read, the next column is pointed to within the data input stream.

Next, the second column is read. However, the value of the column is assigned to an integer variable because this is the value within the record that is being compared to the search criteria.

Any errors that occur while reading the data input stream are trapped by the catch {} block where instead of displaying an error message, a boolean false is returned to the enumerateRecords() method indicating that the current record should not be included in the RecordEnumeration.

The if statement is used to compare the string value of the data input stream to the search criteria. If there is a match, a boolean true is returned to the enumerationRecords() method; otherwise, a boolean false is returned.

Searching a Mixed Data Type Record

Here are the steps required to search a mixed data type record:

1. Declare references to classes.
2. Create instances of classes and assign those instances to references.
3. Open a record store and create a new record store if the record store doesn't exist.
4. Display any errors that occur when opening/creating a record store.
5. Create data in the appropriate data type.
6. Convert data to a byte array output stream.
7. Create a data output stream using the byte array output stream.
8. Write each column of the record to the data output stream.
9. Convert the data output stream to a byte array.
10. Write the record to the record store.
11. Close the output byte array output stream and the data output stream.
12. Display any errors that might occur while writing to the record store.
13. Create a buffer of bytes sufficient to hold a record.
14. Create a byte array input stream and a data input stream.
15. Create a Filter class with a method that compares the search criteria to a record and returns a boolean value true or false. If true, then include the record in the RecordEnumeration.
16. Create an instance of the Filter class and use the instance when creating the RecordEnumeration.
17. Loop through the RecordEnumeration, copying each column from the record store to a variable.
18. Display the data in a dialog box.
19. Display any errors that occur when reading records from the record store.
20. Close and remove the RecordEnumeration and the record store.

The last method defined in the Filter class implementation of the RecordFilter is the filterClose() method. This method, called in the fifth try {} block, closes the input stream and data input stream used by the Filter class.

```
import javax.microedition.rms.*;
import javax.microedition.midlet.*;
import javax.microedition.lcdui.*;
```

```java
import java.io.*;
public class SearchMixedRecordDataTypeExample
      extends MIDlet implements CommandListener
{
  private Display display;
  private Alert alert;
  private Form form;
  private Command exit;
  private Command start;
  private RecordStore recordstore = null;
  private RecordEnumeration recordEnumeration = null;
  private Filter filter = null;
  public SearchMixedRecordDataTypeExample ()
  {
    display = Display.getDisplay(this);
    exit = new Command("Exit", Command.SCREEN, 1);
    start = new Command("Start", Command.SCREEN, 1);
    form = new Form("Mixed RecordEnumeration");
    form.addCommand(exit);
    form.addCommand(start);
    form.setCommandListener(this);
  }
  public void startApp()
  {
    display.setCurrent(form);
  }
  public void pauseApp()
  {
  }
  public void destroyApp( boolean unconditional )
  {
  }
  public void commandAction(Command command, Displayable displayable)
  {
    if (command == exit)
    {
      destroyApp(true);
      notifyDestroyed();
    }
    else if (command == start)
    {
      try
      {
        recordstore = RecordStore.openRecordStore(
                "myRecordStore", true );
      }
      catch (Exception error)
      {
        alert = new Alert("Error Creating",
```

```
                    error.toString(), null, AlertType.WARNING);
    alert.setTimeout(Alert.FOREVER);
    display.setCurrent(alert);
}
try
{
  byte[] outputRecord;
  String outputString[] = {"Adam", "Bob", "Mary"};
  int outputInteger[] = {15, 10, 5};
  ByteArrayOutputStream outputStream = new ByteArrayOutputStream();
  DataOutputStream outputDataStream =
          new DataOutputStream(outputStream);
  for (int x = 0; x < 3; x++)
  {
    outputDataStream.writeUTF(outputString[x]);
    outputDataStream.writeInt(outputInteger[x]);
    outputDataStream.flush();
    outputRecord = outputStream.toByteArray();
    recordstore.addRecord(outputRecord, 0, outputRecord.length);
    outputStream.reset();
  }
  outputStream.close();
  outputDataStream.close();
}
catch ( Exception error)
{
 alert = new Alert("Error Writing",
         error.toString(), null, AlertType.WARNING);
 alert.setTimeout(Alert.FOREVER);
 display.setCurrent(alert);
}
try
{
 String inputString;
 byte[] byteInputData = new byte[300];
 ByteArrayInputStream inputStream =
             new ByteArrayInputStream(byteInputData);
 DataInputStream inputDataStream =
             new DataInputStream(inputStream);
 if (recordstore.getNumRecords() > 0)
 {
   filter = new Filter("Mary");
    recordEnumeration = recordstore.enumerateRecords(
              filter, null, false);
    while (recordEnumeration.hasNextElement())
    {
      recordstore.getRecord(recordEnumeration.nextRecordId(),
```

```
                            byteInputData, 0);
           inputString = inputDataStream.readUTF() +
                            " " + inputDataStream.readInt();
           alert = new Alert("Reading", inputString,
                        null, AlertType.WARNING);
           alert.setTimeout(Alert.FOREVER);
           display.setCurrent(alert);
        }
    }
    inputStream.close();
  }
  catch (Exception error)
  {
    alert = new Alert("Error Reading",
              error.toString(), null, AlertType.WARNING);
    alert.setTimeout(Alert.FOREVER);
    display.setCurrent(alert);
  }
  try
  {
    recordstore.closeRecordStore();
  }
  catch (Exception error)
  {
    alert = new Alert("Error Closing",
              error.toString(), null, AlertType.WARNING);
    alert.setTimeout(Alert.FOREVER);
    display.setCurrent(alert);
  }
  if (RecordStore.listRecordStores() != null)
  {
    try
    {
      RecordStore.deleteRecordStore("myRecordStore");
      filter.filterClose();
      recordEnumeration.destroy();
    }
    catch (Exception error)
    {
     alert = new Alert("Error Removing",
              error.toString(), null, AlertType.WARNING);
     alert.setTimeout(Alert.FOREVER);
     display.setCurrent(alert);
    }
  }
 }
}
```

```
}
class Filter implements RecordFilter
{
  private String search = null;
  private ByteArrayInputStream inputstream = null;
  private DataInputStream datainputstream = null;
  public Filter(String searchcriteria)
  {
    search = searchcriteria;
  }
  public boolean matches(byte[] suspect)
  {
    String string = null;
    try
    {
      inputstream = new ByteArrayInputStream(suspect);
      datainputstream = new DataInputStream(inputstream);
      string = datainputstream.readUTF();
    }
    catch (Exception error)
    {
      return false;
    }
    if (string!= null && string.indexOf(search) != -1)
      return true;
    else
      return false;
  }
  public void filterClose()
  {
   try
   {
     if (inputstream != null)
     {
       inputstream.close();
     }
     if (datainputstream != null)
     {
       datainputstream.close();
     }
   }
   catch (Exception error)
   {
   }
  }
}
```

Listing 8-18
The JAD
file for
Listing 8-17

```
MIDlet-Name: SearchMixedRecordDataTypeExample
MIDlet-Version: 1.0
MIDlet-Vendor: MyCompany
MIDlet-Jar-URL: SearchMixedRecordDataTypeExample.jar
MIDlet-1: SearchMixedRecordDataTypeExample, ,
                SearchMixedRecordDataTypeExample
MicroEdition-Configuration: CLDC-1.0
MicroEdition-Profile: MIDP-1.0
MIDlet-JAR-SIZE: 100
```

RecordListener

Records in a RecordEnumeration might be a subset of records if filtering has been applied, as you learned in previous sections of this chapter. It is possible that the RecordEnumeration becomes out of sync with the record store if the record store is accessible to other MIDlets. You can synchronize the RecordEnumeration and the record store by setting the third parameter of the enumerateRecords() method to true, which has already been illustrated in this chapter. However, besides synchronizing the RecordEnumeration and the record store, there are occasions when you'll want other events to occur whenever a record changes in the record store. For example, you may want to change information on a form to reflect the latest data in the record store.

You can be notified of changes made to a record store by implementing an instance of the RecordListener interface. The instance of the RecordListener interface is notified whenever one of three changes is made to the record store. These are when a record is added, modified, or deleted from the record store.

Your definition of the RecordListener interface must define three methods: recordAdded(), recordChanged(), and recordDeleted(). All three methods require two parameters. The first parameter is reference to the record store that has changed, and the second is an integer indicating the record ID that was added, modified, or removed from the record store. Listing 8-19 contains the structure of a RecordListener.

Once you've defined the implementation of the RecordListener, you'll need to associate the implementation with the record store. You do this by placing the following statement below the statement that creates a record store in the constructor of your MIDlet class.

```
recordstore.addRecordListener( new MyRecordListener());
```

Listing 8-19
Definition
of an imple-
mentation of
a Record-
Listener

```
class MyRecordListener implements RecordListener
{
  public void recordAdded(RecordStore recordstore, int recordid)
  {
```

```
   try
   {
      //do something
   }
   catch (Exception error)
   {
      //do something
   }
}
public void recordDeleted(RecordStore recordstore, int recordid)
{
   try
   {
      //do something
   }
   catch (Exception error)
   {
      //do something
   }
}
public void recordChanged(RecordStore recordstore, int recordid)
{
   try
   {
      //do something
   }
   catch (Exception error)
   {
      //do something
   }
}
}
```

Quick Reference Guide

This quick reference guide provides an overview of classes used by J2ME for the
Record Management System. Full details of these classes and all Java classes and
interfaces are available at java.sun.com.

javax.microedition.rms.RecordStore Class

Method	Description
static RecordStore openRecordStore(String recordStoreName)	Open the record store specified in recordStoreName.
static RecordStore openRecordStore(String recordStoreName, boolean createIfNecessary)	Open the record store specified in recordStoreName. If createIfNecessary is true, create a new record store if the recordStoreName doesn't exist. If createIfNecessary is false, don't create a new record store.
void closeRecordStore()	Close the currently opened record store.
static void deleteRecordStore(String recordStoreName)	Remove the record store specified in recordStoreName.
static String[] listRecordStores()	Return an array of strings containing the names of record stores in the MIDlet suite.
int addRecord(byte[] data, int offset, int numBytes)	Insert a record into a record store, where data is the record, offset is the index within the data of the first byte of the data, and the numBytes is the total number of bytes of the data.
void setRecord (int recordID, byte[] newData, int offset, int numBytes)	Replace data in the specified record, where recordID is the record ID, newData is the data that will overwrite the existing data in the record, the offset is the index of the first byte in the byte array, and numBytes is the total number of bytes to be written to the record store.
void deleteRecord(int recordID)	Remove a record specified by recordID from the record store.
byte[] getRecord(int recordID)	Retrieve a record specified by recordID from the record store.
int getRecord(int recordID, byte[] buffer, int offset)	Retrieve a record specified by recordID from the record store, where buffer is the destination, and offset is the byte within the record where copying begins.
int getRecordSize(int recordID)	Retrieve the size of the record specified in recordID. Size is returned as bytes.
int getNextRecordID()	Retrieve the next record ID.
int getNumRecords()	Retrieve the number of records that are in a record store.

javax.microedition.rms.RecordStore Class

Method	Description
long getLastModified()	Retrieve the date of the last modification made to the record store.
int getVersion()	Retrieve the version number of the record store.
String getName()	Retrieve the name of the record store.
int getSize()	Retrieve the size of the record.
int getSizeAvailable()	Retrieve the space available within a record store to store records.
RecordEnumeration enumerateRecords(Recordfilter filter, RecordComparator comparator, boolean keepUpdate)	Create an enumeration of records, where filter specifies the argument for placing records within the enumeration, comparator specifies the argument for comparing records, and keepUpdate is a boolean value that determines whether the enumeration should be updated when changes occur to the underlying record store.
void addRecordListener(RecordListener listener)	Associate a RecordListener to the record store.
void removeRecordListener(recordListener listener)	Remove the RecordListener that is associated with a record store.

javax.microedition.rms.RecordEnumeration Interface

Method	Description
int numRecords()	Return the number of records in the RecordEnumeration.
byte[] nextRecord()	Return the next record in the RecordEnumeration.
int nextRecordId()	Return the next record ID in the RecordEnumeration.
byte[] previousRecord()	Return the previous record in the RecordEnumeration.
int previousRecordId()	Return the previous record ID in the RecordEnumeration.

javax.microedition.rms.RecordEnumeration Interface

Method	Description
boolean hasNextElement()	Determine whether the enumeration has more records going forward.
boolean hasPreviousElement()	Determine whether there is a previous record in the RecordEnumeration.
void keepUpdated(boolean keepUpdated)	Set the automatic update feature of the RecordEnumeration, where keepUpdated is a boolean value indicating whether or not the feature is activated.
boolean isKeptUpdated()	Determine whether the RecordEnumeration is automatically updated.
void rebuild()	Rebuild the index of the RecordEnumeration.
void reset()	Return to the beginning of the RecordEnumeration.
void destroy()	Release resources reserved for the RecordEnumeration.

javax.microedition.rms.RecordComparator Interface

Method	Description
int compare(byte[], rec1, byte[] rec2)	Compare two records represented as byte array rec1 and byte array rec2 to determine the sort sequence of a RecordEnumeration.

javax.microedition.rms.RecordFilter interface

Method	Description
boolean matches(byte[] candidate)	Search a record for a specific value.

javax.microedition.rms.RecordListener Interface

Method	Description
void recordAdded(RecordStore recordStore, int recordId)	This method is called whenever a record is added to the record store, where recordStore is the record store, and recordID is the record that was added.

J2ME
DATA MANAGEMENT

javax.microedition.rms.RecordListener Interface

Method	Description
void recordChanged(RecordStore recordStore, int recordId)	This method is called whenever a record is changed in the record store, where recordStore is the record store, and recordID is the record that was changed.
void recordDeleted(RecordStore recordStore, int recordId)	This method is called whenever a record is deleted from the record store, where recordStore is the record store, and recordID is the record that was deleted.

Record Management System Exceptions

Exception	Description
public InvalidRecordIDException()	An invalid record number was used.
public InvalidRecordIDException(String message)	An invalid record number was used, where message contains the text of the exception.
public RecordStoreException()	General exception with the record store.
public RecordStoreException(String message)	General exception with the record store, where message contains the text of the exception.
public RecordStoreFullException()	Record store is full.
public RecordStoreFullException(String message)	Record store is full, where message contains the text of the exception.
public RecordStoreNotFoundException()	Record store does not exist.
public RecordStoreNotFoundException(String message)	Record store does not exist, where message contains the text of the exception.
public RecordStoreNotOpenException()	Record store is not open.
public RecordStoreNotOpenException(String message)	Record store is not open, where message contains the text of the exception.

The
Complete
Reference

Chapter 9

J2ME Database
Concepts

A J2ME application saves and retrieves data using the Record Management System (RMS), which is discussed in the previous chapter. Applications running on both Connected Limited Device Configuration (CLDC) and Connected Device Configuration (CDC) devices use RMS for local data management. J2ME applications that run on CDC devices are also capable of utilizing a relational database management system (DBMS), which provides industrial-strength database management service to the application. The DBMS is typically located on a server connected to the device over a network, although some CDC devices might have the DBMS stored locally on a hard drive.

As you'll recall from Chapter 1, CLDC devices usually have between 160KB and 512KB of available memory and are battery powered. They also use an inconsistent, small-bandwidth network wireless connection and may not have a user interface. CLDC devices use the KJava Virtual Machine (KVM) implementation, which is a stripped-down version of the JVM. CLDC devices include pagers, personal digital assistants, cell phones, dedicated terminals, and handheld consumer devices with between 128KB and 512KB of memory.

CDC devices use a 32-bit architecture, have at least 2MB of memory available, and implement a complete functional JVM. CDC devices include digital set-top boxes, home appliances, navigation systems, point-of-sale terminals, and smart phones.

A database is a collection of data managed by a DBMS. Many corporations use one of several commercially available DBMSs, such as Oracle, DB2, Sybase, and Microsoft Access (used for small data collections).

A CDC-based J2ME application interacts with commercial DBMSs by using a combination of Java data objects that are defined in the Java Database Connection (JDBC) specification and by using the Structured Query Language (SQL). The JDBC interface forms a communications link with a DBMS, while SQL is the language used to construct the message (called a *query*) that is sent to the DBMS to request, update, delete, and otherwise manipulate data in the DBMS.

This is the first of three chapters that show how to incorporate database interactions into a J2ME application. In this chapter you learn how to transform data elements of a business system into a relational database, which is a common task in development of J2ME applications. You can skip this chapter if you are familiar with this technique. The next chapter focuses on Java data objects—what they are, how they work, and how to use them to communicate with a DBMS. Chapter 11 shows how to write and execute queries, and then interact with the results returned by the DBMS.

Data

You are probably familiar with the term *data* because you use data in everyday life, such as when you dial a telephone number or log into a computer network using a user ID and password. The telephone number, user ID, and password are types of data. Yet the term data is commonly confused with the term *information*. Although these terms have a similar meaning in the vernacular, they are different when related to a DBMS. Information consists of one or more words that collectively infer a meaning, such as a person's address. Data refers to an atomic unit that is stored in a DBMS and is sometimes reassembled into information.

Examples of data are a person's street address, city, state, and zip code. Each of these is an atomic unit that is commonly found in a DBMS. A J2ME application can access one or multiple atomic units as required by the application. Data is organized in a database so that a J2ME application can quickly find, retrieve, update, or delete one or more data elements.

Databases

As mentioned previously in this chapter, a database in the purest sense is a collection of data. While you can use Java and Java's IO classes to create your own database, you'll probably interact with a commercially available DBMS. DBMSs use proprietary and public domain algorithms to assure fast and secure interaction with data stored in the database. Most DBMSs adhere to a widely accepted relational database model. A *database model* is a description of how data is organized in a database. In a *relational database model*, data is grouped into tables using a technique called normalization, which you'll learn about later in this chapter.

Once a database and at least one table are created, a J2ME application can send SQL statements to the DBMS to perform the following:

- Save data
- Retrieve data
- Update data
- Manipulate data
- Delete data

Tables

A table is the component of a database that contains data in the form of rows and columns, very similar to a spreadsheet. A row contains related data such as clients' names and addresses. A column contains like data such as clients' first names. Each column is identified by a unique name, called a column name, that describes the data contained in the column. For example, "client first name" is a likely choice as the name of a column that contains clients' first names. In addition, columns are defined by attributes. An *attribute* describes the characteristic of data that can be stored in the column. Attributes include size, data type, and format. You'll learn about these and other attributes later in this chapter.

Database name, table name, column name, column attributes, and other information that describe database components are known as *metadata*. Metadata is data about data. For example, the size of the client first name column describes the data contained within the column and therefore is referred to as metadata. Metadata is used by J2ME applications to identify database components without needing to know details of a column, table, or the database. For example, a J2ME application can request from the DBMS the data type of a specific column. The column type is used by a J2ME application to copy data retrieved from the DBMS into a Java collection.

Database Schema

A *database schema* (see Figure 9-1) is a document that defines all components of a database, such as tables, columns, and indexes. A database schema also shows relationships between tables; the relationships are used to join rows of two tables. You'll learn about indexes and relating tables later in this chapter.

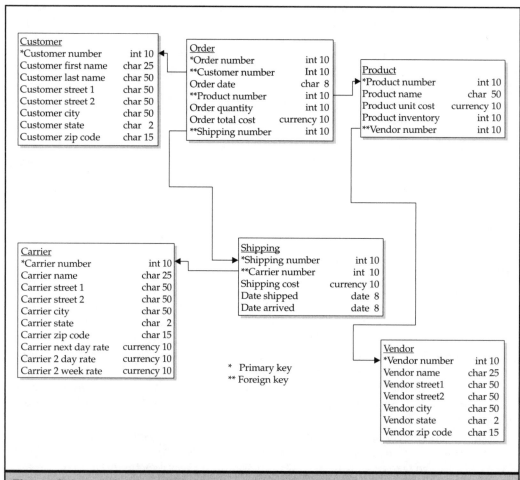

Figure 9-1. *A database schema diagrams the relationships among all components of a database.*

To create a database schema, you must perform six steps:

1. Identify information used in the existing system or legacy system that is being replaced by the J2ME application.
2. Decompose this information into data.
3. Define data.
4. Normalize data into logical groups.
5. Create primary and foreign keys.
6. Group data together into logical groups.

Identifying Information

The initial step in defining a database schema is to identify all information used by the system that is being converted to J2ME technology. Information is associated with objects—also known as *entities*—of the system. An entity is an order form, a product, a customer, a sales representative, for example. Figure 9-2 illustrates the entities for an order system. Each entity is defined by attributes. An attribute is information that describes an entity, such as a customer name for a customer entity.

Don't confuse an entity attribute with data attributes because an entity attribute can be different from data attributes. An entity attribute provides general information about an entity, while a data attribute provides information about data that is used by the entity. Data, as you'll recall, is the atomic level of information. An attribute of an entity is at a more general level than the atomic level. For example, a customer name is an entity attribute, and a customer first name and customer last name are data attributes.

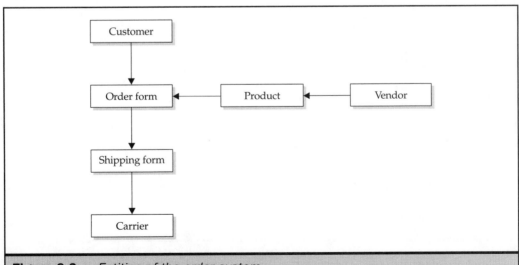

Figure 9-2. *Entities of the order system*

Identifying attributes is intuitive most times because an attribute is information commonly used to describe an entity. For example, a customer name and address are information normally used to describe a customer. Therefore, customer name and address are easily recognizable as attributes of a customer entity. Figure 9-3 contains attributes for entities in the order system. Notice how attributes of an entity uniquely identify the entity.

The best way to identify attributes of an entity is by analyzing instances of the entity. An entity is like an empty order form and an instance is an order form that contains order information. Looking at instances of an entity helps to identify attributes because

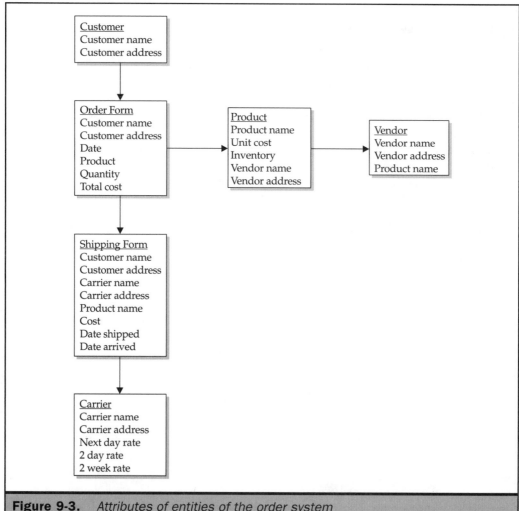

Figure 9-3.   *Attributes of entities of the order system*

you are viewing a real entity. That is, instead of looking at a blank order form, you are looking at an order form that represents a real order. You'll find instances of an entity in the existing system.

Once attributes are identified, you must describe the characteristics of each attribute (see Figure 9-4). Here are common characteristics found in many attributes:

- **Attribute name** The name of the attribute uniquely distinguishes the attribute from other attributes of the same entity. "First name" is an attribute name. Duplicate attribute names within the same entity are prohibited. However, two entities can use the same attribute name. That is, the customer entity and the sales representative entity can both have an attribute called first name.

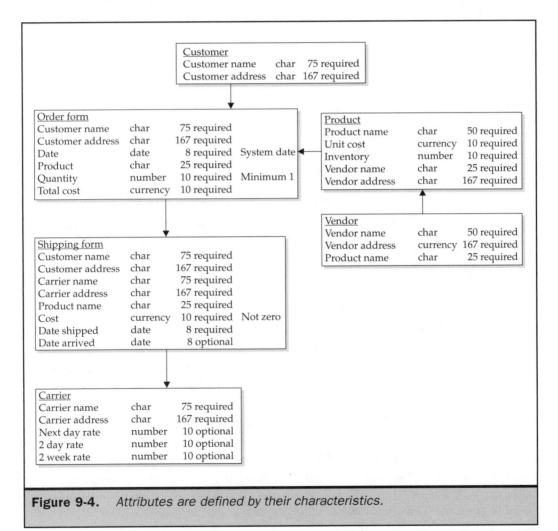

Figure 9-4. *Attributes are defined by their characteristics.*

- **Attribute type**   An attribute type is nearly identical to the data type of a column in a table. Common attribute types include numeric, character, alphanumeric, date, time, Boolean, integer, float, and double, among other attribute types. However, unlike a data type for a column, you do not have to use precise terminology to describe an attribute type. That is, you might call an attribute type "sales in dollars," which is not a valid Java data type but is sufficient to convey the type of information assigned to the entity. It is also advisable to include sample values that are assigned to the entity. This enables you to match the attribute with the most advantageous data type for the DBMS you are using when you create a table for the system.

- **Attribute size**   The attribute size describes the number of characters used to store values of the attribute. This is similar to the size of a column in a table.

- **Attribute range**   An attribute range contains minimum and maximum values that can be assigned to an attribute. For example, the value of the "total amount" attribute of an order entity is likely to be greater than zero and less than 10,000, assuming that no order has ever been received that had a total amount of more than 9,999. This range is then used to throw an error should an order be received with a total amount outside this range.

- **Attribute default value**   An attribute default value is the value that is automatically assigned to the attribute if the attribute isn't assigned a value by the J2ME application. For example, the J2ME application uses the default system date for the date of an order if a sales representative fails to date the order. The system date is the attribute default value.

- **Acceptable values**   An acceptable value for an attribute is one of a set of values established by the business unit and includes zip codes, country codes, methods of delivery, and simply "yes" or "no."

- **Required value**   An attribute may require a value before the attribute is saved to a table. For example, an order entity has an order number attribute that must be assigned an order number.

- **Attribute format**   The attribute format consists of the way an attribute appears in the existing system, such as the format of data.

- **Attribute source**   The attribute source identifies the origin of the attribute value. Common sources are from data entry and J2ME applications (such as using the system date as the value of the attribute).

- **Comments**   A comment is free-form text used to describe an attribute.

Decomposing Attributes to Data

Once attributes of entities are identified, they must be reduced to data elements. This process is called *decomposing*. For the most part, decomposing is an intuitive process because you can easily recognize whether an attribute is already at an atomic level, as illustrated by the customer name and customer address attributes. Both attributes are not atomic, but the atomic level is obvious—first name, last name, city, state, and zip code.

However, decomposing other attributes might be less intuitive. For example, should a customer number attribute be decomposed? At first glance, the response is no because typically, a customer number is already atomic. Consider the following customer number that consists of three numbered segments: 12-24-1001. The first segment (12) represents the sales region where the customer is located. The second segment (24) is the branch in the sales region that handles the relationship with the customer. And the final segment (1001) is the number that identifies the customer within the branch and region.

Since the customer number is in three segments, should the customer number attribute be decomposed into each segment? This isn't an easy question to answer since in some systems it makes sense to further decompose the customer number attribute, and in other systems no further decomposition of the customer number is necessary. The nature of the system will determine whether or not additional decomposition is required for an attribute. For example, in this scenario the customer number probably should be further decomposed if the system references each segment of the customer number, such as using the first segment to select customers of a particular region. Otherwise, the customer number should be treated as atomic.

How to Decompose Attributes

The process of decomposing attributes begins by analyzing the list of entities and their attributes. The list of attributes represents all the information used by the existing system. The objective is to reduce each attribute to a list of data that represents the atomic level of the attribute. Here's how to do this:

1. Look at each attribute and ask yourself if the attribute is atomic.
2. If the attribute isn't atomic, it must be further decomposed. Create a list of data derived from the attribute, as illustrated in Figure 9-5.
3. If the attribute is atomic, no further decomposition is necessary for that attribute.
4. Place the name of the attribute on the data list.
5. Review the data list developed in step 2 and repeat the decomposition process until all attributes are atomic.

Tools for Analysis

Computer-aided software engineering (CASE) tools are designed to automate the process of analyzing a system. Oracle Designer/2000, Rational Rose, and Together J are three of the better CASE tools on the market.

A CASE tool transforms basic information that is entered into the tool into entities, attributes, data, and relationships among entities. CASE tools are beyond the scope of this book. Visit the manufacturers' web sites for more information about CASE tools.

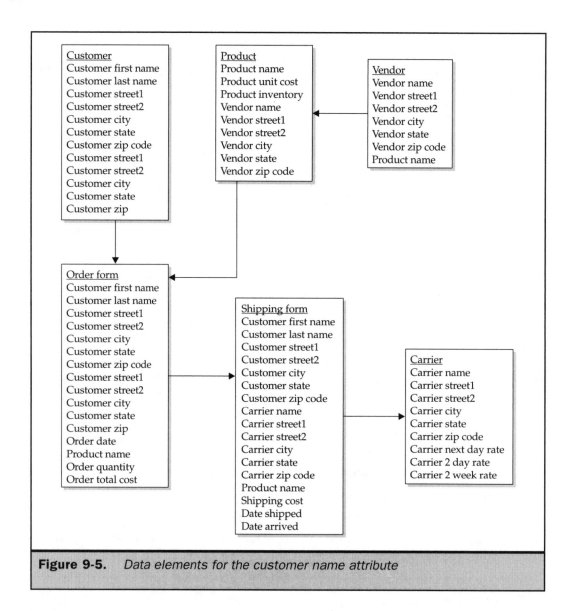

Figure 9-5. *Data elements for the customer name attribute*

Decomposing by Example

Let's work through an example of decomposing attributes using the customer address attribute of a customer entity. The following are attributes for the customer entity:

■ Customer number
■ Customer name

- Customer address
- Customer telephone number

Once the list of attributes is assembled, each attribute on the list must be decomposed. The customer address attribute is decomposed in this example. The same process can be applied to the other attributes.

Review the customer address attribute to determine whether the attribute is atomic, which it isn't. Therefore, the customer address attribute must be decomposed into the following data elements:

- Street address 1
- Street address 2
- City
- State
- Country
- Country code
- Postal code
- Address type (home or business)

Defining Data

Decomposing attributes results in the identification of data elements used by the existing system. Each data element must be defined using techniques similar to those used to describe an attribute. Here are common ways to define a data element:

- **Data name**   The unique name given to the data element, which should reflect the kind of data (see "The Art of Choosing a Name").

- **Data type**   A data type describes the kind of values associated with the data (see the next section, "Data Types").

- **Data size**   The size of text data is the maximum number of characters required to represent values of the data. The size of numeric data is usually either the number of digits or the number of bytes for binary representation (for example, smallint in DB2 is 2 bytes).

Data Types

As previously mentioned in this chapter, a data type describes the characteristics of data associated with a data element. For example, a street address is likely to be an alphanumeric data type because a street address has a mixture of characters and numbers. It is important to use care when selecting the data type of a data element at this stage in the analysis because the data type that you choose typically becomes the data type of the column in the table that contains the data.

The Art of Choosing a Name

Picking a name for a data element might seem intuitive, but can easily become tricky when you realize the name must describe the data, it must be unique, and it may have size and character limitations, depending on the DBMS. The nature of the data provides a hint to the data name, such as "first name" being used as the name for data associated with a person's first name. However, sometimes the obvious choice isn't the best choice. For example, intuitively you might select "telephone number" as the name of data associated with a telephone number. But an entity such as a customer might have more than one telephone number, a home number and business number. This means the name of the data element that contains the telephone number must reflect the kind of telephone number too.

Another twist to selecting a name comes when more than one entity contains similar data. In this example, there could be a customer entity and a sales representative entity, both of which have home and business telephone numbers. The solution is to use the name of the entity as part of the data element name, such as "customer home telephone number" and "customer business telephone number," since this clearly identifies the data.

Keep the length of the name reasonable. The name of a data element typically becomes a column name in a table. Some DBMSs restrict the length of column names and the types of characters that can be used as a column name.

Names of data should have as few characters as possible to identify the data. There are two reasons for this. First, the data name will probably conform to any restrictions imposed by the DBMS. Second, a programmer won't need to type long column names when interacting with the database.

A data name can be abbreviated using components of the name. For example, "customer home telephone number" can be shortened to "cust home phone." When abbreviating data names, make sure the same style of abbreviation is used for naming data. This means that cust is the abbreviation for customer and should be used in other data of the customer entity (for example, cust bus phone).

Be aware that some DBMSs prohibit spaces in column names. You can avoid this problem by removing spaces in the data name. Doing so might make the name unreadable. Readability can be enhanced by capitalizing the first letter of each word in the name, or separating these words with hyphens or underlines as shown here:

- CustHomePhone
- cust-home-Phone
- cust_home_phone

Where possible, limit the choice of data types to those that are common to commercial DBMSs. Not all DBMSs use the same data types; some enhance the standard data type offering. However, if you are unsure of the data type to describe a data element, describe the type of data in your own words and include an example of data values that are associated with the data element. You can refine your choice to available data types in the DBMS when you create the table used to store the data element.

Many commercially available DBMSs have adopted a common set of data types based on the SQL set of data types, which you'll learn about in detail in the next chapter. Some of these are listed here:

- **Character, also referred to as text**   Stores alphabetical characters and punctuation
- **Alpha**   Stores only alphabetical characters
- **Alphanumeric**   Stores alphabetical characters, punctuation, and numbers
- **Numeric**   Stores numbers only
- **Date/Time**   Stores dates and time values
- **Logical (Boolean)**   Stores one of two values: true or false, 0 or 1, or yes or no
- **LOB (large object)**   Stores large text fields, images, and other binary data

Normalizing Data

Normalization is the process of organizing data elements into related groups to minimize redundant data and to assure data integrity. Redundant data elements occur naturally since multiple entities have the same data elements. For example, an order form and invoice are both entities that contain a customer name and address. Therefore, customer name and address are redundant.

For transactional databases, redundant data makes a database complex, inefficient, and exposes the database to problems referred to as *anomalies* when the DBMS maintains the database. Anomalies occur whenever new data is inserted into the database and when existing data is either modified or deleted, and can lead to a breach in referential integrity of the database (see "Referential Integrity" later in this chapter). However, for reporting data, the redundancy rules are bent a little because redundant data is more efficient. It minimizes the number of joins and allows data to be summarized into logical groups.

Errors caused by redundant data are greatly reduced and possibly eliminated by applying the normalization process to the list of data elements that describe all the entities in a system. This is called normalizing the logical data model of a system. The normalization process consists of applying a series of rules called *normal forms* to the list of data elements to:

- Remove redundant data elements.
- Reorganize data elements into groups.
- Define one data element of the group (called a *primary key*) to uniquely identify the group. Often, two or more data elements make up the primary key, which is referred to as a *composite key*.

■ Make other data elements of the group (called *non-key* data elements) functionally dependent on the primary key.

■ Relate one group to another using the primary key.

For example, a customer number is the primary key of a group that contains customer information. Other data contained in the group such as the customer first name and last name are referred to as non-key data elements. Non-key data elements are functionally dependent on the primary key. That is, a customer name, address, and related information cannot exist in the customer group without being assigned a customer number.

The Normalization Process

There are five normal forms. However, many industry leaders have concluded that the fourth and fifth normal forms are difficult to implement and unnecessary. Therefore, we'll confine ourselves to the first three normal forms.

■ First normal form (1NF) requires that information is atomic, as discussed previously in this chapter.

■ Second normal form (2NF) requires data to be in the first normal form. In addition, data elements are organized into groups eliminating redundant data. Each group contains a primary key and non-key data, and non-key data must be functionally dependent on a primary key.

■ Third normal form (3NF) requires that data elements be in the second normal form, and non-key data must not contain transitive dependencies.

Grouping Data

A common way to organize data elements into groups is to first assemble a list of all data elements, as discussed previously in this chapter. When this is done, you'll notice that some data elements are duplicated because they are used by more than one entity. Duplicate data elements must be removed from the list. Although this is an intuitive process, you must be careful because not all data elements with similar sounding names are duplicates.

Let's say there are two data elements, zip code and postal code. At first glance these appear to have the same meaning. A zip code is another term for postal code— or is it? A zip code is a specific kind of postal code used in the United States. Postal code is a general term that also applies to postal codes used by countries other than the United States.

The difference is subtle, but could have an impact if you assume zip code and postal code are the same. For example, many relational databases contain a table of zip codes, where only valid zip codes are stored. The table also contains the city and state that corresponds to a zip code. Postal code data may or may not be contained in a relational database table since it could be difficult to identify all the postal codes from every country and maintain this list as postal codes are modified.

Figure 9-6 contains a list of all data elements before redundant data elements are removed. Figure 9-7 shows the same list after redundant data is removed. Notice that the number of data elements on the list has been dramatically reduced. Figure 9-8 organizes related data into groups.

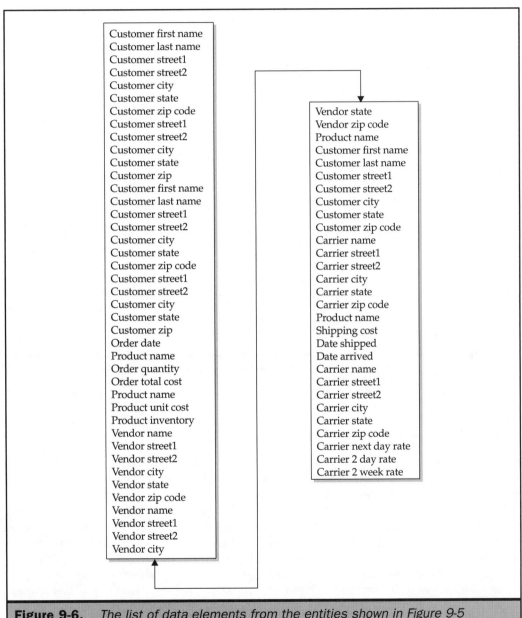

Figure 9-6. *The list of data elements from the entities shown in Figure 9-5*

```
Customer first name
Customer last name
Customer street1
Customer street2
Customer city
Customer state
Customer zip code
Order date
Product name
Order quantity
Order total cost
Product unit cost
Product inventory
Vendor name
Vendor street1
Vendor street2
Vendor city
Vendor state
Vendor zip code
Carrier name
Carrier street1
Carrier street2
Carrier city
Carrier state
Carrier zip code
Shipping cost
Date shipped
Date arrived
Carrier next day rate
Carrier 2 day rate
Carrier 2 week rate
```

Figure 9-7. *The list of data elements shown in Figure 9-6 after redundant data is removed*

Creating Primary Keys

As discussed previously in this chapter, a primary key is a data element that uniquely identifies a row of data elements within a group. The data selected to become the primary key may or may not exist in the data list generated as the result of analyzing entities. Sometimes a data element, such as an order number, is used as the primary key. Other times, the DBMS can be requested to automatically generate a primary key whenever a column in the group isn't suitable to be designated the primary key. Figure 9-8 indicates the primary key of each group with an asterisk.

Let's use a customer entity as an illustration. In the purest sense, a customer has a name and address as attributes. These attributes decompose to first name, last name,

Customer	
*Customer number	int 10
Customer first name	char 25
Customer last name	char 50
Customer street 1	char 50
Customer street 2	char 50
Customer city	char 50
Customer state	char 2
Customer zip code	char 15

Order	
*Order number	int 10
**Customer number	int 10
Order date	char 8
**Product number	int 10
Order quantity	int 10
Order total cost	currency 10
**Shipping number	int 10

Product	
*Product number	int 10
Product name	char 50
Product unit cost	currency 10
Product inventory	int 10
**Vendor number	int 10

Carrier	
*Carrier number	int 10
Carrier name	char 25
Carrier street 1	char 50
Carrier street 2	char 50
Carrier city	char 50
Carrier state	char 2
Carrier zip code	char 15
Carrier next day rate	currency 10
Carrier 2 day rate	currency 10
Carrier 2 week rate	currency 10

Shipping	
*Shipping number	int 10
**Carrier number	int 10
Shipping cost	currency 10
Date shipped	date 8
Date arrived	date 8

*   Primary key
** Foreign key

Vendor	
*Vendor number	int 10
Vendor name	char 25
Vendor street1	char 50
Vendor street2	char 50
Vendor city	char 50
Vendor state	char 2
Vendor zip code	char 15

Figure 9-8.   *Related data is organized into groups.*

street, city, state, and zip code. However, none of these data elements are suited to become a primary key because individually and collectively none uniquely identify a customer.

Intuitively, the customer first name and last name seem to uniquely identify a customer, but upon closer analysis you'll see that more than one customer might have the same first name and last name. Likewise, two people at the same address might have the same name, although it's somewhat unlikely. If neither a single data element nor a combination of data elements uniquely identify a row, then you must create another data element to serve as the primary key of the table, which is what is required in the previous example. Alternatively, you can request the DBMS to generate a primary key automatically.

Nearly all commercial DBMSs can generate primary keys to make the database thread safe and reliable. In contrast, a J2ME application that generates a key must contain the logic to be sure that none of the components running on different servers accidentally generate the same key.

Functional Dependency

A functional dependency occurs when data depends on other data, such as when non-key data is dependent on a primary key. This means that all non-key data has a functional dependency on the primary key within its group.

For example, order product quantity in the orders group cannot exist unless there is an order number. The order number is the primary key of the group, and the order product quantity is non-key data. You can say that order product quantity is functionally dependent on order number. This is noted by the expression

```
order product quantity -> order number
```

Transitive Dependencies

A transitive dependency is a functional dependency between two or more non-key data elements. This is an elusive concept at first, but an example will clearly illustrate transitive dependency. The first grouping in Figure 9-9 shows the Order entity with the two data elements Sales Rep Number and Sales Region, which is the region to which the sales representative is assigned. Salesperson and region have a transitive dependency. The region is functionally dependent on the salesperson, and the salesperson is functionally dependent on the order number. Both salesperson and region are non-key data and are therefore functionally mutually dependent.

The problem lies with the fact that a salesperson cannot be relocated to a different region without having to modify the region data element in the order information group. Therefore, data elements must be regrouped to conform to the third normal form and eliminate transitive dependency.

The second grouping in Figure 9-9 illustrates the regrouping of the Order entity to address the transitive dependency problem. Notice that a new group is formed that contains the Sales Rep Number and the Sales Region. The Sales Rep Number and the Sales Region can be used as a composite key. A composite key, as you recall from an earlier discussion in this chapter, is a primary key that consists of two data elements. In this example, the Sales Rep Number and the Sales Region can be joined to form a composite key. If a sales representative is permitted to make sales in multiple regions, the composite key is used to associate the sales representative with one of many regions and a region to one of many sales representatives.

Identifying transitive dependencies is tricky. You have to carefully analyze the data elements once the list of data elements is in the second normal form to spot transitive dependencies.

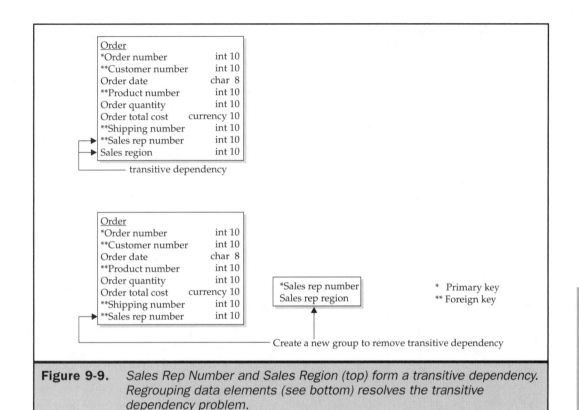

Figure 9-9. *Sales Rep Number and Sales Region (top) form a transitive dependency. Regrouping data elements (see bottom) resolves the transitive dependency problem.*

J2ME
DATA MANAGEMENT

Foreign Keys

As you recall, a foreign key is a primary key of another group used to draw a relationship between two groups of data elements (see ** in Figure 9-8). Relationships between two groups are made using the value of a foreign key and not necessarily the name of a foreign key.

Let's say there are two groups, one contains customer information, and the other contains order information. The primary key in the customer information group is the customer number, and the primary key in the order information group is the order number. Each row in the order group contains the customer number of the customer who placed the order. The customer number in the order group is a foreign key. That is, the customer number in the order group is the primary key of the customer information group.

The DBMS is able to join information about a customer along with information about orders placed by that customer by joining together the customer number in both the customer information group and the order group.

Referential Integrity

The success of a relational database is based on the existence of primary keys and foreign keys of data groups to create relationships among groups. The existence of this relationship is called referential integrity and is illustrated in Figure 9-10.

Referential integrity is enforced by imposing database constraints. This means the DBMS assures referential integrity by preventing primary and foreign keys from being modified or deleted. Likewise, database constraints prevent new rows from being inserted without maintaining referential integrity.

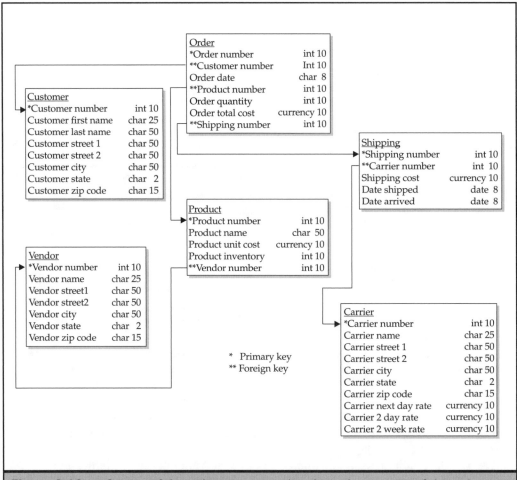

Figure 9-10. *Groups of data elements are related to other groups of data elements by using a combination of foreign keys and primary keys.*

The Art of Indexing

An index is used to quickly locate information in a table, similar to the way information is located in a book. However, instead of page numbers, an index references the row number in the table that contains the search criteria. Conceptually, an index is a table that has two columns. One column is the key to the index, and the other column is the number of the row in the corresponding table that contains the value of the key.

Let's say that you create a table of customer information and use customer number as the primary key to the table. Figure 9-11 contains such a table. An index is created using the primary key as the index key. Notice that each row in the index corresponds to a row in the customer table. However, an index always has two columns regardless of the number of columns in the associated table. The number of columns plays a critical role in finding information quickly in a table because an index has less information for a DBMS to search than a table that contains all the data.

Indexed keys are sorted in alphabetical or numerical order depending on the value of the key. The DBMS begins at the center row of the index when searching for a particular key value. The search criteria is either an exact match to the key value of the center row of the index, is greater than the key value, or less than the key value.

If there is a match, the row that corresponds to the key is retrieved. If the value is greater than the key, the DBMS begins the next search at the center row of the lower

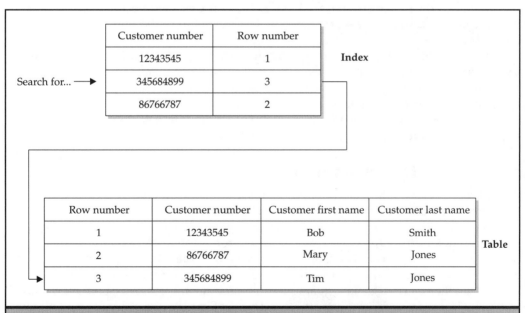

Figure 9-11. *The index key is associated with the row number of the row in the table that contains other information related to the index key.*

half of the index. Likewise, if the value is less than the key, the search continues at the center row of the upper half of the index. The process is repeated until either a match is found or the search criteria cannot be found.

An Index in Motion

Unlike an index of a book, a table can be associated with multiple indexes, each of which contains a different key. For example, a customer information table might have an index based on zip code and another on customer number. The designer of the database determines the number of indexes that are associated with a table, although some DBMSs create their own indexes to speed searches if an appropriate index doesn't exist.

A J2ME application sends the DBMS a query that contains search criteria for information required by the component. Instead of searching the table that contains the search criteria, the DBMS compares the search criteria to keys of indexes, looking for an index to use in the search.

Let's say that a J2ME application needs to retrieve information about a customer. The request for information (called a query) is sent to the DBMS along with the customer number. The DBMS recognizes that the request contains a customer number, then searches a catalog of indexes for an index that uses customer number as its key.

The DBMS always uses an index, if one exists, to locate search criteria. If an index doesn't match the search criteria, the DBMS either creates a temporary index as part of the search or sequentially searches the table. The method used with your DBMS depends on how the manufacturer designed the DBMS.

Once an index is located or a temporary index is created, the DBMS compares the search criteria contained in the request to the index key. When a match is found, the DBMS notes the row number in the second column of the index, then opens the associated table and moves directly to the row that corresponds to the row number. The DBMS then selects columns from the row that contains customer information requested by the J2ME application.

Drawbacks of Using an Index

An index offers an unparalleled advantage for finding information in a table quickly. However, there is a drawback when too many indexes are used with one table. An unacceptable delay can occur whenever a row is inserted into or deleted from the table. Once an index is built, the DBMS is responsible for automatically maintaining the index whenever a row is inserted or deleted from the table. This means that each index associated with a table must be modified whenever a row is inserted or deleted from the table, which can cause performance degradation if a table is associated with many indexes. The trade-off for using multiple indexes is the time necessary for the DBMS to maintain each index.

Performance degradation can be minimized by using a publisher-consumer database design for applications where rows are frequently inserted, deleted, or modified, as in an order processing system. The publisher-consumer database design consists of two or more databases that contain the same information. One database, called the *publisher*, receives requests from the J2ME application to insert a new row, modify, or delete an existing row. J2ME applications don't use the publisher to retrieve information, therefore the publisher database isn't indexed. A *consumer database* receives instructions to insert a new row, modify, or delete an existing row from the publisher. However, the consumer receives requests for information from a J2ME application. Therefore, the consumer database is indexed.

Once the publisher passes data to the consumer, the publisher is free to process the next incoming data, during which time the DBMS is updating the consumer's indexes. There are two major benefits to this design. First, a bottleneck is avoided when many requests are received by the DBMS to insert new information or update existing information. This is because the publisher has two tasks to perform: insert or modify the database, then pass along those changes to the consumer.

The other benefit is that the database becomes scalable. This means that the database can be adjusted to handle an increased volume of requests. Let's say a company begins with a publisher and one consumer. Over time there is an increase in the number of requests for information, which can overwhelm the DBMS and cause performance degradation. This can be remedied by creating a second consumer and routing requests to one or the other consumer, reducing response time by half.

Clustered Keys

A *clustered key* is an index key whose value represents data contained in multiple columns of the corresponding table. Although there is only one column in the index to store the index key, that value can be a combination of data from multiple columns of the table.

Let's say a customer name is used as the index key. Customer name is composed of two data elements: the customer first name and the customer last name. Since there is only one column for the index key, the customer first name and the customer last name are concatenated into one value. That is, the DBMS takes one data element and places it behind the other data element to create a new data element that becomes the index key.

Let's say that the customer first name is Tom and last name is Jones. Here's what they look like when they are concatenated: TomJones. Notice there isn't a space between the first and last name. This is because concatenating places the character of the second value immediately following the last character of the first value.

Clustered keys add overhead to a DBMS because columns are delimited, and the delimiter must be escaped if it appears in the data. This extra step might impede performance of the DBMS. The DBMS treats the index key of a clustered index as it does any index key and uses a combination of trees and hashing algorithms to locate search criteria in the index.

Use concatenation of data elements to:

- Create an index key that uses two or more columns to uniquely identify rows in a table
- Facilitate searching for values of multiple columns, such as a customer name, using one index

Derived Keys

A *derived key* consists of a value that represents part of the value of a column rather than the entire value of the column. Let's say that an order number comprises three components: the first component represents the sales region where the order was placed, the second is the sales representative's number, and the third is a unique number that identifies the order. Although the order number appears in one column of the order table, a component of the order number can be used as an index key. For example, the DBMS can be instructed to derive an index key from the order number by using the first component. This means the index can be used to search for all orders placed within a region that is specified in the search criteria.

Selective Rows

Typically, all the rows in a table are represented in an index associated with that table. However, an index can be created that references a subset of rows in a table. The subset is determined when the index is created.

Let's return to the order number example used in the previous section to illustrate this feature. There might be tens of thousands of orders, each having a row in the order table and in indexes associated with the order table. Suppose a J2ME application is used only to search for orders within a specified region. There will never be an occasion for the component to search other than in the region. Indexes used for searches by the component can be limited to only rows of the table that contain orders placed within the region as identified by the first component of the order number. This means that the index does not contain any references to rows in the order table that are outside the specified region.

A performance benefit is realized by using an index that contains a subset of all the rows of the associated table. This is because rows that will never be searched are excluded from the index, thereby reducing the number of rows of the index that must be searched by the DBMS. The boost in performance, however, is only realized in databases that contain huge amounts of rows. Little if any increase in performance is realized by creating a subset of rows in a typical database because many DBMSs have been optimized to search volumes of data without having to use a subset of rows in an index.

Using a conditional statement when creating an index, which you'll learn to do in the next two chapters, creates a subset. In the order number example, the conditional statement directs the DBMS to include rows in the index where the first component of the order number matches the conditional statement. All other rows are excluded from the index.

Exact Matches and Partial Matches

A DBMS can be instructed to use an index to find an exact or partial match to the search criteria. By default, the DBMS searches for exact matches whenever a query is received from a J2ME application. However, the programmer can construct the query to direct the DBMS to find partial matches.

An exact match requires that all the characters of the search criteria match the index key. If a single character is mismatched, the DBMS does not return data in the corresponding row of the table. A partial match requires that some—not all— of the characters of the index key match the search criteria. That is, if the first character of the search criteria and the index key are the same and the remaining characters are different, the DBMS still considers it a match and returns data in the corresponding row of the table. Exact matches are used whenever a particular value, and only that value, is required, such as a specific customer number. Partial matches are used whenever someone is unsure of the exact value.

Let's say that a sales representative is looking for information about a customer, but she isn't sure if the customer's last name is Johnson or Johnston. She can search using an index of customer names that looks for any customers with the first five letters of "Johns" and any other characters as their last name.

In this example, the customer name index is a concatenated index. The order in which values are concatenated plays a critical role when a DBMS searches for a partial match. This is because the DBMS begins matches left to right. Therefore, the most significant value must be placed first in the concatenated key. The most significant value in the customer name is the customer last name because there are more people with the same first name than the same last name. Therefore, the index key is last name, then first, such as JohnstonMike.

Searching for Phonetic Matches

Some DBMSs feature phonetic searches in which the DBMS returns rows containing index keys that "sound" like the search value. This means that the DBMS stores both exact spelling and phonic spelling of the index key. Phonetic searches are a valuable feature to look for in a DBMS, especially for use with customer service databases. Customer service typically must take bits and pieces of information provided by a customer, and then assemble those pieces into meaningful search criteria.

Many interactions with customers take place over the telephone, and customer service representatives may not have printed materials (such as invoices) that the customer has at hand. This situation typically leads to miscommunication, which aggravates a customer relationship. Although a phonetic search won't guarantee better communication between the customer service representative and the customer, it does give the customer service representative a tool for locating information necessary to respond properly to a customer.

Phonetic searches are made possible by an algorithm built into the DBMS. The phonetic algorithm used by the DBMS defines each index key phonetically. Likewise, the DBMS converts the search criteria into its phonetic spelling before comparing the phonetic spelling of the search criteria to the phonetic spelling of the index key.

The Complete Reference

Chapter 10

JDBC Objects

Many Connected Device Configuration (CDC) device–based J2ME applications save, retrieve, and manipulate information stored in a database using web services provided by a J2ME application. A J2ME application supplies database access using the Java Database Connection (JDBC) interface contained in the JDBC application programming interface (API). The JDBC interface has methods that open a connection to a database management system (DBMS), then transmit messages (queries) to insert, retrieve, modify, or delete data stored in a database.

The DBMS uses the same connection to send messages back to the J2ME application. These messages contain rows of data requested by the J2ME application or information indicating the status of the query being processed by the DBMS. Additional JDBC interfaces are used to interact with data that is returned to the J2ME application by the DBMS.

This is the second of three chapters that focus on how to write a J2ME application to interact with a database. The previous chapter showed how to develop a database schema, which is the database design. This chapter shows how to use the JDBC interface to connect to the DBMS, send queries to the DBMS, and manipulate data returned by the DBMS. The next chapter shows how to use SQL to write queries that interact with the DBMS.

The Concept of JDBC

There are many industrial-strength DBMSs on the market, including Oracle, DB2, Sybase, and many other popular brands. The challenge faced by Sun Microsystems in the late 1990s was to develop a way for Java developers to write high-level code that accesses all popular DBMSs. One major obstacle to overcome was a language barrier. Each DBMS defined its own low-level way to interact with programs to access data stored in its databases. This meant that low-level code written to communicate with an Oracle database might need to be rewritten to access a DB2 database.

Sun met the challenge in 1996 with the creation of the JDBC driver and the JDBC API. Both were created out of necessity because until then Java couldn't access DBMSs and therefore wasn't considered an industrial-strength programming language. The JDBC driver developed by Sun wasn't a driver at all. It was a specification that described the detailed functionality of a JDBC driver. DBMS manufacturers and third-party vendors were encouraged to build JDBC drivers that conformed to Sun's specifications. Those firms who built JDBC drivers for their products could tap into the growing Java applications market.

The specifications required a JDBC driver to be a translator that converts low-level proprietary DBMS messages to low-level messages that are understood by the JDBC API and vice versa. This meant Java programmers could use high-level JDBC interfaces that are defined in the JDBC API to write a routine that interacts with the DBMS. The JDBC interface converts the routine into low-level messages that conform to the JDBC driver specification and sends them to the JDBC driver. The JDBC driver translates the routine into low-level messages that are understood and processed by the DBMS.

JDBC drivers created by DBMS manufacturers have to:

- Open a connection between the DBMS and the J2ME application
- Translate low-level equivalents of SQL statements sent by the J2ME application into messages that can be processed by the DBMS
- Return data that conforms to the JDBC specification to the JDBC driver
- Return information, such as error messages, that conforms to the JDBC specification to the JDBC driver
- Provide transaction management routines that conform to the JDBC specification
- Close the connection between the DBMS and the J2ME application

The JDBC driver makes J2ME applications database independent, which complements Java's philosophy of platform independence. Today, JDBC drivers for nearly every commercial DBMS are available from the Sun web site (www.sun.com) or the DBMS manufacturers' web sites. Java code independence is also extended to implementation of SQL queries. SQL queries are passed from the JDBC API through the JDBC driver to the DBMS without validation. This means it is the responsibility of the DBMS to implement SQL statements contained in the query.

JDBC Driver Types

The JDBC driver specification classifies JDBC drivers into four groups. Each group is referred to as a JDBC driver type and addresses a specific need for communicating with various DBMSs. The JDBC driver types are described in the following sections.

Type 1 JDBC to ODBC Driver

Microsoft was the first company to devise a way to create DBMS-independent database programs when they created Open Database Connectivity (ODBC). ODBC is the basis from which Sun created JDBC. Both ODBC and JDBC have similar driver specifications and an API. The JDBC to ODBC driver, also called the JDBC/ODBC Bridge, is used to translate DBMS calls between the JDBC specification and the ODBC specification. The JDBC to ODBC driver receives messages from a J2ME application that conforms to the JDBC specification, as discussed previously in this chapter. Those messages are translated by the JDBC to ODBC driver into the ODBC message format, which is then translated into the message format understood by the DBMS. However, avoid using the JDBC/ODBC Bridge in a mission-critical application because the extra translation might negatively impact performance.

Type 2 Java/Native Code Driver

The Java/Native Code driver uses Java classes to generate platform-specific code—that is, code only understood by a specific DBMS. The manufacturer of the DBMS provides both the Java/Native Code driver and API classes so the J2ME application can generate the platform-specific code. The obvious disadvantage of using a Java/Native Code driver is the loss of some portability of code. The API classes for the Java/Native Code driver probably won't work with another manufacturer's DBMS.

Type 3 JDBC Driver

The Type 3 JDBC driver, also referred to as the Java Protocol, is the most commonly used JDBC driver. The Type 3 JDBC driver converts SQL queries into JDBC-formatted statements. The JDBC-formatted statements are translated into the format required by the DBMS.

Type 4 JDBC Driver

The Type 4 JDBC driver is also known as the Type 4 Database Protocol. This driver is similar to the Type 3 JDBC driver, except SQL queries are translated into the format required by the DBMS. SQL queries do not need to be converted to JDBC-formatted systems. This is the fastest way to communicate SQL queries to the DBMS.

JDBC Packages

The JDBC API is contained in two packages. The first package is called java.sql and contains core JDBC interfaces of the JDBC API. These include the JDBC interfaces that provide the basics for connecting to the DBMS and interacting with data stored in the DBMS. java.sql is part of the J2SE.

The other package that contains the JDBC API is javax.sql, which extends java.sql and is in the J2ME. Included in the javax.sql package is the JDBC interface that interacts with Java Naming and Directory Interface (JNDI) and the JDBC interface that manages connection pooling, among other advanced JDBC features.

Overview of the JDBC Process

Although each J2ME application is different, J2ME applications use a similar process for interacting with a DBMS. This process is divided into five routines: loading the JDBC driver, connecting to the DBMS, creating and executing a statement, processing data returned by the DBMS, and terminating the connection with the DBMS.

It is sometimes better to get a general understanding of how the process works before delving into the details of each routine of the process. Therefore, the next few sections provide an overview of the process and each routine. A more detailed discussion of each routine is provided later in this chapter.

Load the JDBC Driver

The JDBC driver must be loaded before the J2ME application can connect to the DBMS. The Class.forName() method is used to load the JDBC driver. Suppose a developer wants to work offline and write a J2ME application that interacts with Microsoft Access on the developer's PC. The developer must write a routine that loads the JDBC/ODBC Bridge driver called sun.jdbc.odbc.JdbcOdbcDriver. The driver is loaded by calling the Class.forName() method and passing it the name of the driver, as shown in the following code segment:

```
Class.forName( "sun.jdbc.odbc.JdbcOdbcDriver");
```

Connect to the DBMS

Once the driver is loaded, the J2ME application must connect to the DBMS using the DriverManager.getConnection() method. The java.sql.DriverManager class is the highest class in the java.sql hierarchy and is responsible for managing driver information. The DriverManager.getConnection() method is passed the URL of the database, along with the user ID and password if required by the DBMS. The URL is a String object that contains the driver name and the name of the database that is being accessed by the J2ME application.

The DriverManager.getConnection() returns a Connection interface that is used throughout the process to reference the database. The java.sql.Connection interface is another member of the java.sql package that manages communications between the driver and the J2ME application. It is the java.sql.Connection interface that sends statements to the DBMS for processing. Listing 10-1 illustrates the use of the DriverManager.getConnection() method to load the JDBC/ODBC Bridge and connect to the CustomerInformation database.

Listing 10-1
Open a connection with a database

```
String url = "jdbc:odbc:CustomerInformation";
String userID = "jim";
String password = "keogh";
Statement DataRequest;
private Connection Db;
try {
   Class.forName( "sun.jdbc.odbc.JdbcOdbcDriver");
   Db = DriverManager.getConnection(url,userID,password);
 }
```

Create and Execute an SQL Statement

The next step after the JDBC driver is loaded and a connection is successfully made with a particular database managed by the DBMS is to send an SQL query to the DBMS for processing. An SQL query consists of a series of SQL commands that direct the DBMS to do something, such as return rows of data to the J2ME application. You'll learn how to write queries in the next chapter.

The Connect.createStatement() is used to create a Statement object. The Statement object is then used to execute a query and return a ResultSet object that contains the response from the DBMS, which is usually one or more rows of information requested by the J2ME application. Typically, the query is assigned to a String object, which is passed to the Statement object's executeQuery() method, as illustrated in the next code segment. Once the ResultSet is received from the DBMS, the close() method is called to terminate the statement. Listing 10-2 retrieves all the rows and columns from the Customers table.

Listing 10-2
Retrieve all the rows from the Customers table

```
Statement DataRequest;
ResultSet Results;
try {
      String query = "SELECT * FROM Customers";
      DataRequest = Database.createStatement();
      DataRequest = Db.createStatement();
      Results = DataRequest.executeQuery (query);
      DataRequest.close();
 }
```

Process Data Returned by the DBMS

The java.sql.ResultSet object is assigned the results received from the DBMS after the query is processed. The java.sql.ResultSet object consists of methods used to interact with data that is returned by the DBMS to the J2ME application. Later in this chapter you'll learn the details of using the java.sql.ResultSet object. However, the following code is an abbreviated example that gives you a preview of a commonly used routine for extracting data returned by the DBMS. Error-catching code is purposely removed from this example in order to minimize code clutter. You'll find the completed version of this routine later in this chapter and throughout Chapter 11.

Assume for Listing 10-3 that a J2ME application requested a customer's first name and last name from a table. The result returned by the DBMS is already assigned to the ResultSet object called Results. The first time that the next() method of the ResultSet is called, the ResultSet pointer is positioned at the first row in the ResultSet and returns a boolean value. If false, this indicates that no rows are present in the ResultSet. The if statement in Listing 10-3 traps this condition and displays the "End of data" message on the screen.

A true value returned by the next() method means at least one row of data is present in the ResultSet, which causes the code to enter the do...while loop. The getString() method of the ResultSet object is used to copy the value of a specified column in the current row of the ResultSet to a String object. The getString() method is passed the name of the column in the ResultSet whose content needs to be copied, and the getString() method returns the value from the specified column.

You could also pass the number of the column to the getString() method instead of the name. However, do so only if the columns are specifically named in the SELECT statement. Otherwise you cannot be sure of the order in which the columns appear in the ResultSet, especially since the table might have been reorganized since it was created, and therefore the columns might be rearranged.

In Listing 10-3, the first column of the ResultSet contains the customer's first name, and the second column contains the customer's last name. Both of these are concatenated in this example and assigned to the printrow String object, which is displayed on the screen. This process continues until the next() method, called as the conditional argument to the while statement, returns a false, which means the pointer is at the end of the ResultSet.

Listing 10-3
Retrieving
data from the
ResultSet

```
ResultSet Results;
String FirstName;
String LastName;
String printrow;
boolean Records = Results.next();
if (!Records ) {
   System.out.println( "No data returned");
   return;
}
else
{
 do {
   FirstName = Results.getString (FirstName) ;
   LastName = Results.getString (LastName) ;
   printrow = FirstName + " " + LastName;
   System.out.println(printrow);
 } while ( Results.next() );
}
```

Terminate the Connection to the DBMS

The connection to the DBMS is terminated by using the close() method of the Connection object once the J2ME application is finished accessing the DBMS. The close() method throws an exception if a problem is encountered when disengaging the DBMS. You'll learn how to handle this exception later in this chapter. The following is an example of calling the close() method. Although closing the database connection automatically closes the ResultSet, it is better to close the ResultSet explicitly before closing the connection.

```
Db.close();
```

Database Connection

A J2ME application does not directly connect to a DBMS. Instead, the J2ME application connects with the JDBC driver that is associated with the DBMS. However, before this connection is made, the JDBC driver must be loaded and registered with the DriverManager as mentioned previously in this chapter. The purpose of loading and registering the JDBC driver is to bring the JDBC driver into the Java Virtual Machine (JVM). The JDBC driver is automatically registered with the DriverManager once it is loaded and is therefore available to the JVM and can be used by J2ME applications.

The Class.forName(), as illustrated in Listing 10-4, is used to load the JDBC driver. In this example, the JDBC/ODBC Bridge is the driver that is being loaded. You can replace the JDBC/ODBC Bridge with the appropriate JDBC driver for the DBMS being used in your J2EE application. The Class.forName() throws a ClassNotFoundException if an error occurs when loading the JDBC driver. Errors are trapped using the catch {} block whenever the JDBC driver is being loaded.

Listing 10-4
Load the driver and catch any exceptions that might be thrown during the process

```
try {
    Class.forName( "sun.jdbc.odbc.JdbcOdbcDriver");
}
catch (ClassNotFoundException error) {
    System.err.println("Unable to load the JDBC/ODBC bridge." +
error.getMessage());
    System.exit(1);
}
```

The Connection

After the JDBC driver is successfully loaded and registered, the J2ME application must connect to the database. The database must be associated with the JDBC driver, which is usually performed by either the database administrator or the system administrator. Some students who are learning JDBC programming prefer to use Microsoft Access as the DBMS because the DBMS is usually available on the student's local computer. The "Associating the JDBC/ODBC Bridge with the Database" sidebar shows how to associate the JDBC/ODBC Bridge with a Microsoft Access database.

The data source that the JDBC component will connect to is defined using the URL format. The URL consists of three parts:

- jdbc, which indicates that the JDBC protocol is to be used to read the URL
- <subprotocol>, which is the JDBC driver name
- <subname>, which is the name of the database

Associating the JDBC/ODBC Bridge with the Database

You use the ODBC Data Source Administrator to create the association between the database and the JDBC/ODBC Bridge. Here's what you need to do:

1. Select Start | Settings | Control Panel.
2. Select ODBC 32 to display the ODBC Data Source Administrator.
3. Add a new user by selecting the Add button.
4. Select the driver, and then select Finish. Use the Microsoft Access Driver if you are using Microsoft Access, otherwise select the driver for the DBMS that you are using. If you don't find the driver for your DBMS on the list, you'll need to install the driver. Contact the manufacturer of the DBMS for more information on how to obtain the driver.
5. Enter the name of the database as the Data Source name in the ODBC Microsoft Access Setup dialog box. This is the name that will be used within your Java database program to connect to the DBMS.
6. Enter a description for the data source. This is optional, but will be a reminder of the kind of data stored in the database.
7. Click the Select button. You'll be prompted to browse the directory of each hard drive connected to your computer in order to define the direct path to the database. Click OK once you locate the database, and the directory path and name of the database will be displayed in the ODBC Microsoft Access Setup dialog box.
8. Since this is your database, you can determine whether a login name and password are required to access the database.

   If so, click the Advanced button to display the Set Advanced Options dialog box. This dialog box is used to assign a login name (also referred to as a user ID) and a password to the database. Select OK. If not, skip this step.
9. When the ODBC Microsoft Access Setup dialog box appears, select OK.
10. Select OK to close the ODBC Data Source Administrator dialog box.

The connection to the database is established by using one of three getConnection() methods of the DriverManager object. The getConnection() method requests access to the database from the DBMS. It is up to the DBMS to grant or reject access. A Connection object is returned by the getConnection() method if access is granted, otherwise the getConnection() method throws an SQLException.

Sometimes the DBMS grants access to a database to anyone. In this case, the J2ME application uses the getConnection(String url) method. One parameter is passed to the method because the DBMS only needs the database identified. This is shown in Listing 10-5.

Listing 10-5
Connecting to a database using only the URL

```
String url = "jdbc:odbc:CustomerInformation";
Statement DataRequest;
Connection Db;
try {
    Class.forName( "sun.jdbc.odbc.JdbcOdbcDriver");
    Db = DriverManager.getConnection(url);
}
catch (ClassNotFoundException error) {
    System.err.println("Unable to load the JDBC/ODBC bridge." +
            error);
    System.exit(1);
}
catch (SQLException error) {
    System.err.println("Cannot connect to the database." + error);
    System.exit(2);
}
```

Other databases limit access to authorized users and require the J2EE to supply a user ID and password with the request to access the database. In this case, the J2ME application uses the getConnection(String url, String user, String password) method, as illustrated in Listing 10-6.

Listing 10-6
Connecting to a database using a user ID and password

```
String url = "jdbc:odbc:CustomerInformation";
String userID = "jim";
String password = "keogh";
Statement DataRequest;
Connection Db;
try {
    Class.forName( "sun.jdbc.odbc.JdbcOdbcDriver");
    Db = DriverManager.getConnection(url,userID,password);
}
catch (ClassNotFoundException error) {
    System.err.println("Unable to load the JDBC/ODBC bridge." +
            error);
    System.exit(1);
}
catch (SQLException error) {
    System.err.println("Cannot connect to the database." + error);
    System.exit(2);
}
```

There might be occasions when a DBMS requires information besides a user ID and password before the DBMS grants access to the database. This additional information is referred to as "properties" and must be associated with a Properties object, which is passed to the DBMS as a getConnection() parameter. Typically, properties used to access a database are stored in a text file, the contents of which are defined by the DBMS manufacturer. The J2ME application uses a FileInputStream object to open the file and then uses the Properties object load() method to copy the properties into a Properties object. This is illustrated in Listing 10-7. Notice that the third version of the getConnection() method passes the Properties object and the URL as parameters to the getConnection() method.

Listing 10-7
Using properties to connect to the database

```
Connection Db;
Properties props = new Properties ();
try {
   FileInputStream propFileStream =
                   new fileInputStream("DBProps.txt");
   props.load(propFileStream);
}
catch(IOException err) {
   System.err.print("Error loading propFile: ");
   System.err.println (err.getMessage());
   System.exit(1);
}
try {
   Class.forName( "sun.jdbc.odbc.JdbcOdbcDriver");
   Db = DriverManager.getConnection(url, props);
}
catch (ClassNotFoundException error) {
    System.err.println("Unable to load the JDBC/ODBC bridge." +
           error);
    System.exit(2);
}
catch (SQLException error) {
    System.err.println("Cannot connect to the database." + error);
    System.exit(3);
}
```

Timeout

Competition to use the same database is a common occurrence and can lead to performance degradation. For example, multiple applications might attempt to access a database simultaneously. The DBMS may not respond quickly for a number of reasons, one of which might be that database connections are not available. Rather than wait for a delayed response from the DBMS, the J2ME application can set a timeout period after which the DriverManager will cease trying to connect to the database.

The public static void DriverManager.setLoginTimeout(int seconds) method can be used by the J2ME application to establish the maximum time the DriverManager waits for a response from a DBMS before timing out. Likewise, the public static int DriverManager.getLoginTimeout() method is used to retrieve from the DriverManager the maximum time the DriverManager is set to wait until it times out. The Driver-Manager.getLoginTimeout() returns an int that represents seconds.

Connection Pool

Connecting to a database is performed on a per-client basis. That is, each client must open its own connection to a database, and the connection cannot be shared with unrelated clients. For example, a client that needs to interact frequently with a database must either open a connection and leave the connection open during processing, or open or close and reconnect each time the client needs to access the database. Leaving a connection open might prevent another client from accessing the database should the DBMS have a limited number of connections available. Connecting and reconnecting is simply time consuming and causes performance degradation.

The release of the JDBC 2.1 Standard Extension API introduced connection pooling to address the problem. A *connection pool* is a collection of database connections that are opened once and loaded into memory so these connections can be reused without having to reconnect to the DBMS. Clients use the DataSource interface to interact with the connection pool. The connection pool itself is implemented by the application server and other J2EE-specific technologies, which hide details on how the connection pool is maintained from the client.

There are two types of connections made to the database. The first is the physical connection, which is made by the application server using PooledConnection objects. PooledConnection objects are cached and reused. The other type of connection is the logical connection. A logical connection is made by a client calling the DataSource.getConnection() method, which connects to a PooledConnection object that has already made a physical connection to the database.

Listing 10-8 illustrates how to access a connection from a connection pool. A connection pool is accessible by using the Java Naming and Directory Interface (JNDI). JNDI provides a uniform way to find and access naming and directory services independent of any specific naming or directory service.

First, a J2ME application must obtain a handle to the JNDI context, which is illustrated in the first statement in this code segment. Next, the JNDI lookup() method is called and is passed the name of the connection pool, which returns the DataSource object, called pool in this example. The getConnection() method of the DataSource object is then called, as illustrated earlier in this chapter. The getConnection() returns the logical connection to the database, which is used by the J2ME application to access the database.

The close() method of the DataSource object is called once when the J2ME application is finished accessing the database. The close() method closes the logical connection to the database and not the physical database connection. This means that the same physical connection can be used by the next J2ME application that needs access to the database.

Listing 10-8
Connecting to
a database
using a
connection
pool

```
Context ctext = new InitialContext();
DataSource pool = (DataSource) ctext.lookup("java:comp/env/jdbc/pool");
Connection db = pool.getConnection();
// Place code to interact with the database here
db.close();
```

Statement Objects

Once a connection to the database is opened, the J2ME application creates and sends a query to access data contained in the database. The query is written using SQL, which you'll learn about in the next chapter. One of three types of Statement objects is used to execute the query. These objects are Statement, which executes a query immediately; PreparedStatement, which is used to execute a compiled query; and CallableStatement, which is used to execute store procedures.

The Statement Object

The Statement object is used whenever a J2ME application needs to execute a query immediately without first having the query compiled. The Statement object contains the executeQuery() method, which is passed the query as an argument. The query is then transmitted to the DBMS for processing. The executeQuery() method returns one ResultSet object that contains rows, columns, and metadata that represent data requested by the query. The ResultSet object also contains methods that are used to manipulate data in the ResultSet, which you'll learn about later in this chapter.

The execute() method of the Statement object is used when multiple results may be returned. A third commonly used method of the Statement object is the executeUpdate() method. The executeUpdate() method is used to execute queries that contain UPDATE and DELETE SQL statements, which change values in a row and remove a row, respectively. The executeUpdate() method returns an integer indicating the number of rows that were updated by the query. ExecuteUpdate() is used to INSERT, UPDATE, DELETE, and DDL statements.

Listing 10-9 is an enhanced version of Listing 10-2, used earlier in this chapter to illustrate how to open a database connection. The enhancements are to create a query, execute the query, and return a ResultSet. Two new objects are declared in Listing 10-9: a Statement object called DataRequest and a ResultSet object called Results. In the second try {} block, the query is assigned to the String object query. The query requests that the DBMS return all the rows from the Customers table of the CustomerInformation database.

Next, the createStatement() method of the Connection object is called to return a Statement object. The executeQuery() method of the Statement object is passed the query

J2ME
DATA MANAGEMENT

and returns a ResultSet object that contains data returned by the DBMS. Finally, the close() method of the Statement object is called to close the statement.

The close() method closes all instances of the ResultSet object returned by the Statement. Failure to call the close() method might cause resources used by the Statement object to remain unavailable to other J2ME applications until the garbage routine is automatically run. Java statements used to manipulate the ResultSet are placed between the call to the executeQuery() method and the close() method.

The executeQuery() method throws an SQLException should an error occur during the processing of the query. For example, the query may contain syntax not understood by the DBMS. In this case, the DBMS returns an SQL error message that is passed along to the J2ME application by the executeQuery() method.

Listing 10-9
Using the Statement object to execute a query

```
String url = "jdbc:odbc:CustomerInformation";
String userID = "jim";
String password = "keogh";
Statement DataRequest;
ResultSet Results;
Connection Db;
try {
    Class.forName( "sun.jdbc.odbc.JdbcOdbcDriver");
    Db = DriverManager.getConnection(url,userID,password);
}
catch (ClassNotFoundException error) {
    System.err.println("Unable to load the JDBC/ODBC bridge." +
            error);
    System.exit(1);
}
catch (SQLException error) {
    System.err.println("Cannot connect to the database." + error);
    System.exit(2);
}
try {
    String query = "SELECT * FROM Customers";
    DataRequest = Db.createStatement();
    Results = DataRequest.executeQuery (query);
    //Place code here to interact with the ResultSet
    DataRequest.close();
}
catch ( SQLException error ){
    System.err.println("SQL error." + error);
    System.exit(3);
}
Db.close();
```

Listing 10-10 illustrates how to use the executeUpdate() method of the Statement object. You'll notice that Listing 10-10 is nearly identical to Listing 10-9. However, the query updates a value in the database rather than requesting that data be returned to the J2ME application. You'll learn more about how to write queries to update values in a database in the next chapter.

Three changes are made to Listing 10-9 to illustrate the executeUpdate() method of the Statement object. First, the declaration of the ResultSet object is replaced with the declaration of an int called rowsUpdated. Next, the query is changed. The SQL UPDATE command directs the DBMS to update the Customers table of the CustomerInformation database. The value of the PAID column of the Customers table is changed to 'Y' if the value of the BALANCE column is zero.

Finally, the executeUpdate() method replaces the executeQuery() method and is passed the query. The number of rows that are updated by the query is returned to the executeUpdate() method by the DBMS and is then assigned to the rowsUpdated int. rowsUpdated can be used for many purposes within the J2ME application, such as sending a confirmation notice to the J2ME application that requested database access.

Listing 10-10
Using the execute-Update() method

```
String url = "jdbc:odbc:CustomerInformation";
String userID = "jim";
String password = "keogh";
Statement DataRequest;
Connection Db;
int rowsUpdated;
try {
   Class.forName( "sun.jdbc.odbc.JdbcOdbcDriver");
   Db = DriverManager.getConnection(url,userID,password);
 }
catch (ClassNotFoundException error) {
      System.err.println("Unable to load the JDBC/ODBC bridge." +
             error);
      System.exit(1);
}
catch (SQLException error) {
      System.err.println("Cannot connect to the database." + error);
      System.exit(2);
}
try {
      String query = "UPDATE Customers
                        SET PAID='Y' WHERE BALANCE = '0';
      DataRequest = Db.createStatement();
      rowsUpdated = DataRequest.executeUpdate (query);
      DataRequest.close();
 }
catch ( SQLException error ){
      System.err.println("SQL error." + error);
      System.exit(3);
}
Db.close();
```

PreparedStatement Object

An SQL query must be compiled before the DBMS processes the query. Compiling occurs after one of the Statement object's execution methods is called. Compiling a query is an overhead that is acceptable if the query is called once. However, the compiling process can become an expensive overhead if the query is executed several times by the same instance of the J2ME application during the same session.

An SQL query can be precompiled and executed by using the PreparedStatement object. In this case, the query is constructed similar to queries that were illustrated previously in the chapter. However, a question mark is used as a placeholder for a value that is inserted into the query after the query is compiled. It is this value that changes each time the query is executed.

Listing 10-11 illustrates how to use the PreparedStatement object. Listing 10-11 is very similar to Listing 10-9, in which the Statement object returned information from the Customers table. However, the query directs the DBMS to return all customer information where the customer number equals the customer number specified in the query. Notice that the query has a question mark, which is a placeholder for the value of the customer number that will be inserted into the precompiled query later in the code.

The preparedStatement() method of the Connection object is called to return the PreparedStatement object. The preparedStatement() method is passed the query that is then precompiled. The setXXX() method of the PreparedStatement object is used to replace the question mark with the value passed to the setXXX() method. There are a number of setXXX() methods available in the PreparedStatement object, each of which specifies the data type of the value that is being passed to the setXXX() method (see the section "Data Types" later in the chapter). In Listing 10-11, the setString() is used because the customer number is being passed as a string.

The setXXX() requires two parameters. The first parameter is an integer that identifies the position of the question mark placeholder, and the second parameter is the value that replaces the question mark placeholder. In Listing 10-11, the first question mark placeholder is replaced with the value of the second parameter.

Next, the executeQuery() method of the PreparedStatement object is called. The executeQuery() statement doesn't require a parameter because the query that is to be executed is already associated with the PreparedStatement object.

The advantage of using the PreparedStatement object is that the query is precompiled once and the setXXX() method called as needed to change the specified values of the query without having to recompile the query. The PreparedStatement object also has an execute() method and an executeUpdate() method, as described in the previous section.

The precompiling is performed by the DBMS and is referred to as late binding. When the DBMS receives the request, the DBMS attempts to match the query to a previously compiled query. If found, then parameters passed to the query using the setXXX() methods are bound and the query is executed. If not found, then the query is compiled and retained by the DBMS for later use.

The JDBC driver passes two parameters to the DBMS. One parameter is the query, and the other is an array of late binding variables. Both binding and compiling are performed by the DBMS. The late binding is not associated with the specific object or code block where the preparedStatement() is declared.

Listing 10-11
Using the
Prepared-
Statement
object

```
String url = "jdbc:odbc:CustomerInformation";
String userID = "jim";
String password = "keogh";
ResultSet Results;
Connection Db;
try {
   Class.forName( "sun.jdbc.odbc.JdbcOdbcDriver");
   Db = DriverManager.getConnection(url,userID,password);
 }
catch (ClassNotFoundException error) {
     System.err.println(
             "Unable to load the JDBC/ODBC bridge." + error);
     System.exit(1);
}
catch (SQLException error) {
     System.err.println("Cannot connect to the database." + error);
     System.exit(2);
}
try {
     String query = "SELECT * FROM Customers WHERE CustNumber = ?";
     PreparedStatement pstatement = Db.preparedStatement(query);
     pstatement.setString(1, "123");
     Results = pstatement.executeQuery ();
     //Place code here to interact with the ResultSet
     pstatement.close();
 }
catch ( SQLException error ){
     System.err.println("SQL error." + error);
     System.exit(3);
}
Db.close();
```

CallableStatement

The CallableStatement is used to call a stored procedure from within a J2ME object. A stored procedure is a block of code and is identified by a unique name. The type and style of code depend on the DBMS vendor and can be written in PL/SQL, TransactSQL, C, or another programming language. The stored procedure is executed by invoking the name of the stored procedure.

The CallableStatement object uses three types of parameters when calling a stored procedure. These parameters are IN, OUT, and INOUT. The IN parameter contains any data that needs to be passed to the stored procedure and whose value is assigned using the set*XXX*() method, as described in the previous section. The OUT parameter contains the value returned by the stored procedures, if any. The OUT parameter must be registered using the registerOutParameter() method and then is later retrieved by the J2ME application using the get*XXX*() method. The INOUT parameter is a single parameter used for both passing information to the stored procedure and retrieving information from a stored procedure using the techniques described in the previous two paragraphs.

Listing 10-12 illustrates how to call a stored procedure and retrieve a value returned by the stored procedure. Listing 10-12 is similar to other listings used in this chapter, but has been modified slightly to call a stored procedure.

The first statement in the second try {} block creates a query that calls the stored procedure LastOrderNumber, which retrieves the most recently used order number. The stored procedure requires one parameter that is represented by a question mark placeholder. This parameter is an OUT parameter that will contain the last order number following the execution of the stored procedure.

Next, the preparedCall() method of the Connection object is called and is passed the query. This method returns a CallableStatement object, which is called cstatement. Since an OUT parameter is used by the stored procedure, the parameter must be registered using the registerOutParameter() of the CallableStatement object.

The registerOutParameter() method requires two parameters. The first parameter is an integer that represents the number of the parameter, which is 1, meaning the first parameter of the stored procedure. The second parameter to the registerOutParameter() is the data type of the value returned by the stored procedure, which is Types.VARCHAR.

The execute() method of the CallableStatement object is called next to execute the query. The execute() method doesn't require the name of the query because the query is already identified when the CallableStatement object is returned by the prepareCall() query method.

After the stored procedure is executed, the getString() method is called to return the value of the specified parameter of the stored procedure, which in this example is the last order number.

Listing 10-12
Calling a stored procedure

```
String url = "jdbc:odbc:CustomerInformation";
String userID = "jim";
String password = "keogh";
String lastOrderNumber;
Connection Db;
try {
   Class.forName( "sun.jdbc.odbc.JdbcOdbcDriver");
   Db = DriverManager.getConnection(url,userID,password);
}
catch (ClassNotFoundException error) {
      System.err.println("Unable to load the JDBC/ODBC bridge." +
            error);
      System.exit(1);
}
catch (SQLException error) {
```

```
        System.err.println("Cannot connect to the database." + error);
        System.exit(2);
}
try {
        String query = "{ CALL LastOrderNumber (?)}";
        CallableStatement cstatement = Db.prepareCall(query);
        cstatement.registerOutParameter(1, Types. VARCHAR);
        cstatement.execute();
                        lastOrderNumber = cstatement.getString(1);
        cstatement.close();
 }
catch ( SQLException error ){
     System.err.println("SQL error." + error);
     System.exit(3);
}
Db.close();
```

ResultSet

As you'll remember from previous sections in this chapter, a query is used to update, delete, and retrieve information stored in a database. The executeQuery() method is used to send the query to the DBMS for processing and returns a ResultSet object that contains data requested by the query.

The ResultSet object contains methods that are used to copy data from the ResultSet into a Java collection of objects or variable(s) for further processing. Data in a ResultSet object is logically organized into a virtual table consisting of rows and columns. In addition to data, the ResultSet object also contains metadata, such as column names, column size, and column data type.

The ResultSet uses a virtual cursor to point to a row of the virtual table. A J2ME application must move the virtual cursor to each row, then use other methods of the ResultSet object to interact with the data stored in columns of that row. The virtual cursor is positioned above the first row of data when the ResultSet is returned by the executeQuery() method. This means that the virtual cursor must be moved to the first row using the next() method. The next() method returns a boolean true if the row contains data, otherwise a boolean false is returned, indicating that no more rows exist in the ResultSet.

Once the virtual cursor points to a row, the get*XXX*() method is used to copy data from the row to a collection, object, or variable. As illustrated previously in this chapter, the get*XXX*() method is data type specific. For example, the getString() method is used to copy String data from a column of the ResultSet. The data type of the get*XXX*() method must be the same data type of the column in the ResultSet.

The get*XXX*() method requires one parameter, which is an integer that represents the number of the column that contains the data. For example, getString(1) copies the data from the first column of the ResultSet.

Columns appear in the ResultSet in the order in which column names appeared in the SELECT statement in the query. Let's say a query contained the following SELECT statement:

SELECT CustomerFirstName, CustomerLastName FROM Customer

This query directs the DBMS to return two columns. The first column contains customer first names, and the second column contains customer last names. Therefore, getString(1) returns data in the customer first name column of the current row in the ResultSet.

Reading the ResultSet

Listing 10-13 illustrates a commonly used routine to read values from a ResultSet into variables that can later be further processed by the J2ME application. Listing 10-13 is based on previous code segments in this chapter.

Once a successful connection is made to the database, a query is defined in the second try {} block to retrieve the first name and last name of customers from the Customers table of the CustomerInformation database. The next() method of the ResultSet is called to move the virtual pointer to the first row in the ResultSet. If there is data in that row, the next() returns a true, which is assigned the boolean variable Records. If there isn't any data in that row, Records is assigned a false value. A false value is trapped by the if statement, where the "End of data." message is displayed and the program terminates.

A true value causes the program to enter the do…while in the third try {} block, where the getString() method is called to retrieve values in the first and second columns of the ResultSet. The values correspond to the first name and last name. These values are assigned to their corresponding String object, which is then concatenated and assigned the printrow String object and printed on the screen.

The next() method is called in the while statement to move the virtual cursor to the next row in the ResultSet and determine whether there is data in that row. If so, statements within the do…while loop are executed again. If not, the program breaks out of the loop and executes the close() statement to close the Statement object, as discussed previously in this chapter.

Listing 10-13
Reading data from the ResultSet

```
String url = "jdbc:odbc:CustomerInformation";
String userID = "jim";
String password = "keogh";
String printrow;
String FirstName;
String LastName;
Statement DataRequest;
ResultSet Results;
Connection Db;
try {
   Class.forName( "sun.jdbc.odbc.JdbcOdbcDriver");
```

```
    Db = DriverManager.getConnection(url,userID,password);
 }
catch (ClassNotFoundException error) {
     System.err.println("Unable to load the JDBC/ODBC bridge." +
             error);
     System.exit(1);
}
catch (SQLException error) {
     System.err.println("Cannot connect to the database." + error);
     System.exit(2);
}
try {
     String query = "SELECT FirstName,LastName FROM Customers";
     DataRequest = Db.createStatement();
     Results = DataRequest.executeQuery (query);
}
catch ( SQLException error ){
    System.err.println("SQL error." + error);
    System.exit(3);
}
boolean Records = Results.next();
if (!Records ) {
   System.out.println("No data returned");
   System.exit(4);
}
try {
  do {
     FirstName = Results.getString ( 1 ) ;
     LastName = Results.getString ( 2 ) ;
     printrow = FirstName + " " + LastName;
     System.out.println(printrow);
  } while (Results.next() );
  DataRequest.close();
}
catch (SQLException error ) {
   System.err.println("Data display error." + error);
   System.exit(5);
}
```

Scrollable ResultSet

Until the release of JDBC 2.1 API, the virtual cursor could only be moved down the ResultSet object. But today the virtual cursor can be moved backwards or even positioned at a specific row. The JDBC 2.1 API also enables a J2ME application to specify the number of rows to return from the DBMS. Six methods of the ResultSet object are used to position the virtual cursor, in addition to the next() method discussed in the previous section. These are first(), last(), previous(), absolute(), relative(), and getRow().

The first() method moves the virtual cursor to the first row in the ResultSet. Likewise, the last() method positions the virtual cursor at the last row in the ResultSet. The previous() method moves the virtual cursor to the previous row. The absolute() method positions the virtual cursor at the row number specified by the integer passed as a parameter to the absolute() method.

The relative() method moves the virtual cursor the specified number of rows contained in the parameter. The parameter is a positive or negative integer, where the sign represents the direction the virtual cursor is moved. For example, a –4 moves the virtual cursor back four rows from the current row. Likewise, a 5 moves the virtual cursor forward five rows from the current row. And the getRow() method returns an integer that represents the number of the current row in the ResultSet.

The Statement object that is created using the createStatement() of the Connection object must be set up to handle a scrollable ResultSet by passing the createStatement() method one of three constants. These constants are TYPE_FORWARD_ONLY, TYPE_SCROLL_INSENSITIVE, and TYPE_SCROLL_SENSITIVE.

The TYPE_FORWARD_ONLY constant restricts the virtual cursor to downward movement, which is the default setting. TYPE_SCROLL_INSENSITIVE and TYPE_ SCROLL_SENSITIVE constants permit the virtual cursor to move in both directions. TYPE_SCROLL_INSENSITIVE makes the ResultSet insensitive to data changes made by another J2ME application in the table whose rows are reflected in the ResultSet. The TYPE_SCROLL_SENSITIVE constant makes the ResultSet sensitive to those changes.

Listing 10-14 illustrates how to reposition the virtual cursor in the ResultSet. This listing, which is a modification of the previous code segments used as examples in this chapter, retrieves customers' first names and last names from the Customers table of the CustomerInformation database. Since Listing 10-14 moves the virtual cursor in multiple directions, the TYPE_SCROLL_INSENSITIVE constant is passed to the createStatement(). This enables the use of virtual cursor control methods in the third try {} block. Initially, the virtual cursor moves to the first row of the ResultSet and then to the last row before being positioned at the second to last row of the ResultSet.

Next, the virtual cursor is positioned in the tenth row of the ResultSet using the absolute() method. Finally, the relative() method is called twice. The first time the relative() method is called, the virtual cursor is moved back two rows from the current row, which places the virtual cursor at row eight. The relative( ) method is again called to return the virtual cursor back to its original row by moving the virtual cursor two rows forward.

If you use any of these methods and end up positioning the cursor before the first record or beyond the last record, there won't be any errors thrown.

Listing 10-14
Using a scrollable virtual cursor

```
String url = "jdbc:odbc:CustomerInformation";
String userID = "jim";
String password = "keogh";
String printrow;
String FirstName;
String LastName;
Statement DataRequest;
```

```
ResultSet Results;
Connection Db;
try {
   Class.forName( "sun.jdbc.odbc.JdbcOdbcDriver");
   Db = DriverManager.getConnection(url,userID,password);
 }
catch (ClassNotFoundException error) {
      System.err.println("Unable to load the JDBC/ODBC bridge." +
              error);
      System.exit(1);
}
catch (SQLException error) {
      System.err.println("Cannot connect to the database." + error);
      System.exit(2);
}
try {
      String query = "SELECT FirstName,LastName FROM Customers";
      DataRequest = Db.createStatement(TYPE_SCROLL_INSENSITIVE);
      Results = DataRequest.executeQuery (query);
}
catch ( SQLException error ){
     System.err.println("SQL error." + error);
      System.exit(3);
}
boolean Records = Results.next();
if (!Records ) {
   System.out.println("No data returned");
   System.exit(4);
}
try {
  do {
      Results.first();
      Results.last();
      Results.previous();
      Results.absolute(10);
      Results.relative(-2);
      Results.relative(2);
      FirstName = Results.getString ( 1 ) ;
      LastName = Results.getString ( 2 ) ;
      printrow = FirstName + " " + LastName;
      System.out.println(printrow);
  } while (Results.next() );
  DataRequest.close();
}
catch (SQLException error ) {
   System.err.println("Data display error." + error);
   System.exit(5);
}
```

Not All JDBC Drivers Are Scrollable

Although the JDBC API contains methods to scroll a ResultSet, some JDBC drivers may not support some or all of these features, and therefore they will not be able to return a scrollable ResultSet. Listing 10-15 can be used to test whether or not the JDBC driver in use supports a scrollable ResultSet.

Listing 10-15
Testing whether a driver supports a scrollable ResultSet

```
boolean forward, insensitive, sensitive;
DataBaseMetaData meta = Db.getMetaData();
forward = meta.supportsResultsSetType(ResultSet.TYPE_FORWARD_ONLY);
insensitive = meta.supportsResultsSetType(
                    ResultSet. TYPE_SCROLL_INSENSITIVE);
sensitive = meta.supportsResultsSetType(
                    ResultSet. TYPE_SCROLL_SENSITIVE);
System.out.println("forward: " + answer);
System.out.println("insensitive: " + insensitive);
System.out.println("sensitive: " + sensitive);
```

Specify Number of Rows to Return

When the J2ME application requests rows from the ResultSet, some rows are fetched into the driver and returned at one time. Other times, all rows requested may not be retrieved at the same time. In this case, the driver returns to the DBMS and requests another set of rows that are defined by the fetch size and then discards the current set of rows. This process continues until the J2EE retrieves all rows.

Although the Statement class has a method for setting maximum rows, the method may not be effective since the driver does not implement them. In addition, the maximum row setting is for rows in the ResultSet and not for the number of rows returned by the DBMS. For example, the maximum rows can be set to 100. The DBMS might return 500 rows, but the ResultSet object silently drops 400 of them. This means all 500 rows are still pumped over the network.

The fetch size is set by using the setFetchSize() method, which is illustrated in Listing 10-16. However, all DBMS vendors may not implement the fetch size. Consult the driver documentation to determine whether fetch size is supported. If fetch size isn't supported, the methods will compile and execute, but have no effect. Don't become overly concerned about setting the fetch size because fetch size is in the area of performance tuning, which is handled by the database administrator or the network engineer.

Listing 10-16 illustrates how to set the maximum number of rows returned by the DBMS. The second try {} block in Listing 10-16 calls the createStatement() method of the Connection object and then sets the maximum number of rows to 500 using the setFetchSize() method of the Statement object.

Listing 10-16
Setting the
maximum
number
of rows
returned in
a ResultSet

```
String url = "jdbc:odbc:CustomerInformation";
String userID = "jim";
String password = "keogh";
String printrow;
String FirstName;
String LastName;
Statement DataRequest;
ResultSet Results;
Connection Db;
try {
    Class.forName( "sun.jdbc.odbc.JdbcOdbcDriver");
    Db = DriverManager.getConnection(url,userID,password);
 }
catch (ClassNotFoundException error) {
      System.err.println("Unable to load the JDBC/ODBC bridge." +
            error);
      System.exit(1);
}
catch (SQLException error) {
      System.err.println("Cannot connect to the database." + error);
      System.exit(2);
}
try {
      String query = "SELECT FirstName,LastName FROM Customers";
      DataRequest = Db.createStatement(TYPE_SCROLL_INSENSITIVE);
      DataRequest.setFetchSize(500);
      Results = DataRequest.executeQuery (query);
}
catch ( SQLException error ){
    System.err.println("SQL error." + error);
      System.exit(3);
}
```

Updatable ResultSet

Rows contained in the ResultSet can be updated similar to how rows in a table can be updated. This is made possible by passing the createStatement() method of the Connection object the CONCUR_UPDATABLE. Alternatively, the CONCUR_READ_ONLY constant can be passed to the createStatement() method to prevent the ResultSet from being updated.

There are three ways to update a ResultSet. These are updating values in a row, deleting a row, and inserting a new row. All of these changes are accomplished by using methods of the Statement object.

Update a Value in ResultSet

Once the executeQuery() method of the Statement object returns a ResultSet, the update*XXX*() method is used to change the value of a column in the current row of the ResultSet. The *XXX* is replaced with the data type of the column that is to be updated. The update*XXX*() method requires two parameters. The first is either the number or name of the column of the ResultSet that is being updated, and the second is the value that will replace the value in the column of the ResultSet.

A value in a column of the ResultSet can be replaced with a NULL value by using the updateNull() method. The updateNull() method requires one parameter, which is the number of the column in the current row of the ResultSet. The updateNull() doesn't accept the name of the column as a parameter.

The updateRow() method is called after all the update*XXX*() methods are called. The updateRow() method changes values in columns of the current row of the ResultSet based on the values of the update*XXX*() methods.

Listing 10-17 illustrates how to update a row in a ResultSet. In this example, customer Mary Jones was recently married and changed her last name to Smith before processing the ResultSet. The updateString() method is used to change the value of the last name column of the ResultSet to 'Smith'. The change takes effect once the updateRow() method is called, but this change only occurs in the ResultSet. The corresponding row in the table remains unchanged until an update query is run, which is discussed in the next chapter.

Listing 10-17
Updating the
ResultSet

```
String url = "jdbc:odbc:CustomerInformation";
String userID = "jim";
String password = "keogh";
Statement DataRequest;
ResultSet Results;
Connection Db;
try {
   Class.forName( "sun.jdbc.odbc.JdbcOdbcDriver");
   Db = DriverManager.getConnection(url,userID,password);
 }
catch (ClassNotFoundException error) {
      System.err.println("Unable to load the JDBC/ODBC bridge." +
            error);
      System.exit(1);
}
catch (SQLException error) {
      System.err.println("Cannot connect to the database." + error);
      System.exit(2);
}
try {
      String query = "SELECT FirstName,LastName
                      FROM Customers
                      WHERE FirstName = 'Mary' and
                          LastName = 'Jones'";
```

```
        DataRequest = Db.createStatement(ResultSet.CONCUR_UPDATABLE);
        Results = DataRequest.executeQuery (query);
}
catch ( SQLException error ){
     System.err.println("SQL error." + error);
        System.exit(3);
}
boolean Records = Results.next();
if (!Records ) {
   System.out.println("No data returned");
   System.exit(4);
}
try {
     Results.updateString ("LastName", "Smith");
        Results.updateRow();
        DataRequest.close();
}
catch (SQLException error ) {
   System.err.println("Data display error." + error);
   System.exit(5);
}
```

Delete a Row in the ResultSet

The deleteRow() method is used to remove a row from a ResultSet. Sometimes this is advantageous when processing the ResultSet because this is a way to eliminate rows from future processing. For example, each row of a ResultSet may have to pass three tests. Those that fail to pass the first test could be deleted from the ResultSet, thereby reducing the number of rows that have to be evaluated for the second test. This also deletes the row from the underlying database.

The deleteRow() method is passed an integer that contains the number of the row to be deleted. A good practice is to use the absolute() method, described previously in the chapter, to move the virtual cursor to the row in the ResultSet that should be deleted. However, the value of that row should be examined by the program to assure it is the proper row before the deleteRow() method is called. The deleteRow() method is then passed a zero integer indicating that the current row must be deleted, as shown in the following statement:

```
Results.deleteRow(0);
```

Insert a Row in the ResultSet

Inserting a row into the ResultSet is accomplished using basically the same technique used to update the ResultSet. That is, the updateXXX() method is used to specify the column and value that will be placed into the column of the ResultSet. You can insert one or multiple columns into the new row using the same technique.

The update*XXX*() method requires two parameters. The first parameter is either the name of the column or the number of the column of the ResultSet. The second parameter is the new value that will be placed in the column of the ResultSet. Remember that the data type of the column replaces the *XXX* in the method name.

The insertRow() method is called after the update*XXX*() methods, which causes a new row to be inserted into the ResultSet having values that reflect the parameters in the update*XXX*() methods. This also updates the underlying database.

Listing 10-18 illustrates how to insert a new row in a ResultSet. In this example, the query returns the first name and last name of all customers. The name Tom Smith is inserted into the ResultSet in the third try {} block using the updateString() method. Remember that columns are numbered based on the order that the column names appear in the SELECT statement of the query. The new row is added to the ResultSet after the insertRow() method is called.

Listing 10-18
Inserting a new row into the ResultSet

```
String url = "jdbc:odbc:CustomerInformation";
String userID = "jim";
String password = "keogh";
Statement DataRequest;
ResultSet Results;
Connection Db;
try {
   Class.forName( "sun.jdbc.odbc.JdbcOdbcDriver");
   Db = DriverManager.getConnection(url,userID,password);
 }
catch (ClassNotFoundException error) {
    System.err.println("Unable to load the JDBC/ODBC bridge." +
            error);
    System.exit(1);
}
catch (SQLException error) {
    System.err.println("Cannot connect to the database." + error);
    System.exit(2);
}
try {
    String query = "SELECT FirstName,LastName FROM Customers";
    DataRequest = Db.createStatement(CONCUR_UPDATABLE);
    Results = DataRequest.executeQuery (query);
}
catch ( SQLException error ){
    System.err.println("SQL error." + error);
    System.exit(3);
}
boolean Records = Results.next();
if (!Records ) {
   System.out.println("No data returned");
```

```
       System.exit(4);
   }
   try {
         Results.updateString (1, "Tom");
         Results.updateString (2, "Smith");
         Results.insertRow();
         DataRequest.close();
   }
   catch (SQLException error ) {
      System.err.println("Data display error." + error);
      System.exit(5);
   }
```

Transaction Processing

A transaction may involve several tasks similar to the tasks required to complete a transaction at a supermarket. In a supermarket transaction, each item purchased must be registered, the transaction must be totaled, and the customer must tender the amount of the purchase. The transaction is successfully completed only if each task is completed successfully. If one task fails, the entire transaction fails. Previously completed tasks must be reversed if the transaction fails. For example, goods that were registered must be removed from the register and returned to the shelf.

A database transaction consists of a set of SQL statements, each of which must be successfully completed for the transaction to be completed. If one fails, SQL statements that executed successfully up to that point in the transaction must be rolled back. A database transaction isn't completed until the J2ME application calls the commit() method of the Connection object. All SQL statements executed before the call to the commit() method can be rolled back. However, once the commit() method is called, none of the SQL statements can be rolled back.

The commit() method must be called regardless of whether the SQL statement is part of a transaction or not. This means that the commit() method must be issued in the previous examples in this chapter. However, the commit() method was automatically called in these examples because the DBMS has an AutoCommit feature that is by default set to true.

If a J2ME application is processing a transaction, the AutoCommit feature must be deactivated by calling the setAutoCommit() method and passing it a false parameter. Once the transaction is completed, the setAutoCommit() method is called again, this time passing it a true parameter, which reactivates the AutoCommit feature.

Listing 10-19 illustrates how to process a transaction. The transaction in this example consists of two SQL statements, both of which update the street address of rows in the Customers table. Each SQL statement is executed separately, and then the commit() method is called. However, should either SQL statement throw an SQL exception, the catch {} block reacts by rolling back the transaction before displaying the exception on the screen.

Listing 10-19
Executing
a database
transaction

```
String url = "jdbc:odbc:CustomerInformation";
String userID = "jim";
String password = "keogh";
Statement DataRequest1, DataRequest2 ;
Connection Database;
try {
       Class.forName( "sun.jdbc.odbc.JdbcOdbcDriver");
       Database = DriverManager.getConnection(url,userID,password);
}
catch (ClassNotFoundException error) {
    System.err.println("Unable to load the JDBC/ODBC bridge." +
            error);
    System.exit(1);
}
catch (SQLException error) {
    System.err.println("Cannot connect to the database." + error);
    System.exit(2);
 }
try {
  Database .setAutoCommit(false)
  String query1 = "UPDATE Customers SET Street = '5 Main Street' "
      "WHERE FirstName = 'Bob'";
  String query2 = "UPDATE Customers SET Street = '10 Main Street' " +
      "WHERE FirstName = 'Tim'";
  DataRequest1= Database.createStatement();
  DataRequest2= Database.createStatement();
  DataRequest.executeUpdate (query1 );
  DataRequest.executeUpdate (query2 );
  Database.commit();
  DataRequest1.close();
  DataRequest2.close();
  Database.close();
  }
  catch(SQLException ex) {
   System.err.println("SQLException: " + ex.getMessage());
   if (con != null) {
     try {
       System.err.println("Transaction is being rolled back ");
       con.rollback();
     }
    catch(SQLException excep) {
        System.err.print("SQLException: ");
        System.err.println(excep.getMessage());
    }
   }
  }
```

Savepoints

A transaction may consist of many tasks, some of which don't need to be rolled back should the entire transaction fail. Let's say there are several tasks that occur when a new order is processed. These include updating the customer account table, inserting the order into the pending order table, and sending a customer a confirmation email. Technically all three tasks must be completed before the transaction is considered completed. Suppose the email server is down when the transaction is ready to send the customer a confirmation email. Should the entire transaction be rolled back? Probably not since it is more important that the order continue to be processed (that is, delivered). The confirmation notice can be sent once the email server is back online.

The J2ME application can control the number of tasks that are rolled back by using savepoints. A *savepoint*, introduced in JDBC 3.0, is a virtual marker that defines the task at which the rollback stops. In the previous example, the task before the email confirmation notice is sent can be designated as a savepoint. Listing 10-20 illustrates how to create a savepoint. This is the same code segment as Listing 10-19, but a savepoint is created after the execution of the first UPDATE SQL statement.

There can be many savepoints in a transaction; each is identified by a unique name. The savepoint name is then passed to the rollback() method to specify the point within the transaction where the rollback is to stop. In this example, there is one savepoint called sp1. The name "sp1" is the parameter to the rollback() method in the catch {} block. The purpose of this example is to illustrate how to set and release a savepoint and how to use the savepoint name in the rollback() method. Of course, for commercial applications, you will want more rigorous code that identifies the executeUpdate() method that threw the exception, among other error-checking routines.

The releaseSavepoint() method is called to remove the savepoint from the transaction. The name of the savepoint that is to be removed is passed to the releaseSavepoint() method.

Listing 10-20
Using
savepoints in
a transaction

```
String url = "jdbc:odbc:CustomerInformation";
String userID = "jim";
String password = "keogh";
Statement DataRequest1, DataRequest2 ;
Connection Database;
try {
      Class.forName( "sun.jdbc.odbc.JdbcOdbcDriver");
      Database = DriverManager.getConnection(url,userID,password);
}
catch (ClassNotFoundException error) {
    System.err.println("Unable to load the JDBC/ODBC bridge." +
            error);
    System.exit(1);
}
catch (SQLException error) {
    System.err.println("Cannot connect to the database." + error);
    System.exit(2);
```

```
  }
try {
  Database .setAutoCommit(false)
  String query1 = "UPDATE Customers SET Street = '5 Main Street' " +
      "WHERE FirstName = 'Bob'";
  String query2 = "UPDATE Customers SET Street = '10 Main Street' " +
      "WHERE FirstName = 'Tim'";
  DataRequest1= Database.createStatement();
  Savepoint s1 = Database.setSavepoint ("sp1");
  DataRequest2= Database.createStatement();
  DataRequest.executeUpdate (query1);
  DataRequest.executeUpdate (query2);
  Database.commit();
  DataRequest1.close();
  DataRequest2.close();
  Database.releaseSavepoint ("sp1");
  Database.close();
}
catch ( SQLException error ){
    try {
      Database.rollback(sp1);
    }
    catch ( SQLException error ){
      System.err.println("rollback error." + error.getMessage());
      System.exit(3);
    }
     System.err.println("SQL error." + error. getMessage());;);
    System.exit(4);
}
```

Batch Statements

Another way to combine SQL statements into a transaction is to batch statements together into a single transaction and then execute the entire transaction. You can do this by using the addBatch() method of the Statement object. The addBatch() method receives an SQL statement as a parameter and places the SQL statement in the batch. Once all the SQL statements that make up the transaction are included in the batch, the executeBatch() method is called to execute the entire batch at the same time. The executeBatch() method returns an int array that contains the number of SQL statements executed successfully.

The int array is displayed if a BatchUpdateException error is thrown during the execution of the batch. The batch can be cleared of SQL statements by using the clearBatch() method. The transaction must be committed using the commit() method. Make sure that setAutoCommit() is set to false before executing the batch, as discussed in the previous section.

Listing 10-21 illustrates how to batch SQL statements. In this example, two SQL statements are created, as discussed previously in this chapter. Each SQL statement is added to the batch using the addBatch() method. Once both SQL statements are added to the batch, the executeBatch() method is called to execute each of the SQL statements. The commit() method is then called to commit the changes created by the SQL statement. Until the commit() method is called, the transaction can be rolled back, as described in the previous section.

Listing 10-21
Batching SQL statements into a transaction

```
String url = "jdbc:odbc:CustomerInformation";
String userID = "jim";
String password = "keogh";
Statement DataRequest;
Connection Database;
try {
      Class.forName( "sun.jdbc.odbc.JdbcOdbcDriver");
      Database = DriverManager.getConnection(url,userID,password);
}
catch (ClassNotFoundException error) {
    System.err.println("Unable to load the JDBC/ODBC bridge." +
            error);
    System.exit(1);
}
catch (SQLException error) {
    System.err.println("Cannot connect to the database." + error);
    System.exit(2);
 }
try {
  Database .setAutoCommit(false)
  String query1 = "UPDATE Customers SET Street = '5 Main Street' " +
      "WHERE FirstName = 'Bob'";
  String query2 = "UPDATE Customers SET Street = '10 Main Street' " +
      "WHERE FirstName = 'Tim'";
  DataRequest= Database.createStatement();
  DataRequest.addBatch(query1);
  DataRequest.addBatch(query2);
  int [ ] updated = DataRequest.executeBatch ();
  Database.commit();
  DataRequest1.close();
  DataRequest2.close();
  Database.close();
}
catch(BatchUpdateException error) {
    System.out.println("Batch error.");
    System.out.println("SQL State: " + error.getSQLState());
    System.out.println("Message: " + error.getMessage());
    System.out.println(Vendor: " + error.getErrorCode());
    int [ ] updated  = error.getUpdatecount();
```

```
    int count = updated.length();
    for int - i = 0; i < count; i++) {
        System.out.print (updated[i]);
    }
SQLException sql = error;
While (sql != null)
    {
        System.out.println("SQL error " + sql);
        sql = sql.getnextException();
    }
try{
    DataRequest.clearBatch();
}
catch(BatchUpdateException error) {
    System.out.println("Unable to clear the batch: " +
            error.getMessage());
}
}
```

Keeping ResultSet Objects Open

Whenever the commit() method is called, all ResultSet objects that were created for the transaction are closed. Sometimes a J2ME application needs to keep the ResultSet open even after the commit() method is called. You can control whether or not ResultSet objects are closed following the call to the commit() method (called "holdability") by passing one of two constants to the createStatement() method. These constants are HOLD_CURSORS_OVER_COMMIT and CLOSE_CURSORS_AT_COMMIT.

The HOLD_CURSORS_OVER_COMMIT keeps ResultSet objects open following a call to the commit() method, and CLOSE_CURSORS_AT_COMMIT closes ResultSet objects when the commit() method is called.

RowSet

The JDBC RowSet object is used to encapsulate a ResultSet for use with Enterprise JavaBeans (EJB). A RowSet object contains rows of data from a table or tables that can be used in a disconnected operation. That is, an EJB can interact with a RowSet object without having to be connected to a DBMS, which is ideal for J2ME applications that have PDA clients. You can learn about EJB by picking up a copy of *J2EE: The Complete Reference*, by Jim Keogh (McGraw-Hill/Osborne, 2002).

A row set event is generated every time the cursor is moved in a RowSet and when one or multiple columns of the RowSet change. These events are described in the RowSetEvent.

When an event occurs, the RowSet object creates an instance of a RowSetEvent object and sends the instance to all RowSetListeners that are registered with the RowSet.

A RowSetListener is a class you define that implements the RowSetListener interface. The RowSetListener class must contain three methods, each of which responds to a particular event occurring in a RowSet. These methods are as follows:

```
public void cursorMoved(RowSetEvent event)
public void rowChanged(RowSetEvent event)
public void rowSetChanged(RowSetEvent event)
```

The cursorMoved() method must contain logic that reacts to movement of the cursor within the RowSet. Typically, this method calls ResultSet.getRow() to return the current row of the ResultSet. The rowChanged() method contains logic to respond when a portion of a RowSet is modified, and the rowSetChanged() has logic to respond when the entire RowSet is modified.

Listing 10-22 illustrates how to implement a RowSetListener. First you'll need to create a class that implements the RowSetListener, which is called MyRowSetListener in this example. Next, define the three required methods. Each method is passed an instance of a RowSetEvent created by the RowSet when the event occurs.

After defining the RowSetListener class, you'll need to create an instance of that class, which is called rowsetlistner. The instance of the RowSetListener is then registered with the RowSet by calling the addRowSetListener. This example assumes that the RowSet has already been created. You can deregister a RowSetListener from a RowSet by calling the rowset.removeRowSetListener(rowsetlistner) method.

Listing 10-22
Creating a
RowSet
Listener,
assuming
the instance
rowset has
already been
created

```
MyRowSetListener rowsetlistener = new MyRowSetListener ();
rowset.addRowSetListener (rowsetlistener);
public class MyRowSetListener implements RowSetListener
{
  public void cursorMoved(RowSetEvent event)
  {
   // do something
  }
  public void rowChanged(RowSetEvent event)
  {
    // do something
  }
  public void rowSetChanged(RowSetEvent event)
  {
    // do something
  }
}
```

J2ME
DATA MANAGEMENT

Autogenerated Keys

It is common for a DBMS to automatically generate unique keys for a table as rows are inserted into the table. The getGeneratedKeys() method of the Statement object is called to return keys generated by the DBMS.

The getGeneratedKeys() returns a ResultSet object. You can use the ResultSet.getMetaData() method to retrieve metadata relating to the automatically generated key, such as the type and properties. You can learn more about retrieving metadata in the next section of this chapter.

Metadata

Metadata is data about data, as discussed in Chapter 9. A J2ME application can access metadata by using the DatabaseMetaData interface. The DatabaseMetaData interface is used to retrieve information about databases, tables, columns, and indexes, among other information about the DBMS. A J2ME application retrieves metadata about the database by calling the getMetaData() method of the Connection object. The getMetaData() method returns a DatabaseMetaData object that contains information about the database and its components.

Once the DatabaseMetaData object is obtained, an assortment of methods contained in the DatabaseMetaData object are called to retrieve specific metadata. Here are some of the more commonly used DatabaseMetaData object methods:

- **getDatabaseProductName()**   Returns the product name of the database
- **getUserName()**   Returns the user name
- **getURL()**   Returns the URL of the database
- **getSchemas()**   Returns all the schema names available in this database
- **getPrimaryKeys()**   Returns primary keys
- **getProcedures()**   Returns stored procedure names
- **getTables()**   Returns names of tables in the database

ResultSet Metadata

Two types of metadata can be retrieved from the DBMS: metadata that describes the database (as mentioned in the previous section) and metadata that describes the ResultSet. Metadata that describes the ResultSet is retrieved by calling the getMetaData() method of the ResultSet object. This returns a ResultSetMetaData object, as illustrated in the following code statement:

```
ResultSetMetaData rm = Result.getMetaData()
```

Once the ResultSet metadata is retrieved, the J2ME application can call methods of the ResultSetMetaData object to retrieve specific kinds of metadata. The more commonly called methods are

- **getColumnCount()**   Returns the number of columns contained in the ResultSet
- **getColumnName(int number)**   Returns the name of the column specified by the column number
- **getColumnType(int number)**   Returns the data type of the column specified by the column number

There are many other methods used to retrieve practically any information you need to know about a database and the ResultSet—many more methods than can fit in this chapter. You can obtain detailed information about each of these methods by visiting Sun's web site, java.sun.com.

Data Types

The set*XXX*() and get*XXX*() methods are used throughout this chapter to set a value of a specific data type and to retrieve a value of a specific data type. The *XXX* in the name of these methods is replaced with the name of the data type. Table 10-1 contains a list of data types and their Java equivalents. You can use this list to determine the proper data name to replace the *XXX* in the two methods.

SQL Type	Java Type
CHAR	String
VARCHAR	String
LONGVARCHAR	String
NUMERIC	java.math.BigDecimal
DECIMAL	java.math.BigDecimal
BIT	Boolean
TINYINT	Byte
SMALLINT	Short
INTEGER	Integer
BIGINT	Long
REAL	float

Table 10-1.   *Data Types for Use with the setXXX() and getXXX() Methods*

SQL Type	Java Type
FLOAT	float
DOUBLE	double
BINARY	Byte[]
VARBINARY	Byte[]
LONGVARBINARY	byte[]
BLOB	java.sql.Blob
CLOB	java.sql.Clob
ARRAY	java.sql.Array
STRUCT	java.sql.Struct
REF	java.sql.Ref
DATALINK	java.sql.Types
DATE	java.sql.date
TIME	java.sql.Time
TIMESTAMP	java.sql.Timestamp

Table 10-1. *Data Types for Use with the* setXXX() *and* getXXX() *Methods* (continued)

Exceptions

Three kinds of exceptions are thrown by JDBC methods. These are SQLException, SQLWarning, and DataTruncation. SQLException commonly reflects an SQL syntax error in the query and is thrown by many of the methods contained in the java.sql package. Hopefully the syntax errors in your code get resolved quickly. In production, this exception is most commonly caused by connectivity issues with the database. It can also be caused by subtle coding errors like trying to access an object that's been closed. For example, you try to roll back a transaction in a catch {} clause and don't check first to see if the database connection is still valid. The getNextException() method of the SQLException object is used to return details about the SQL error or a null if the last exception was retrieved. The getErrorCode() method of the SQLException object is used to retrieve vendor-specific error codes.

The SQLWarning throws warnings received by the Connection from the DBMS. The getWarnings() method of the Connection object retrieves the warning, and the getNextWarning() method of the Connection object retrieves subsequent warnings.

Whenever data is lost due to truncation of the data value, a DataTruncation exception is thrown.

Quick Reference Guide

JDBC classes and interfaces contain many methods. This quick reference guide provides an overview of the more commonly used methods. Full details of these methods and all the JDBC classes and interfaces are available at java.sun.com.

java.sql Package public interface CallableStatement

Method	Description
public void registerOutParameter (int parameterIndex, int sqlType) throws SQLException	Register the OUT parameter.
public void registerOutParameter(int parameterIndex, int sqlType,int scale) throws SQLException	Register the OUT parameter.
public boolean wasNull() throws SQLException	Determine an OUT parameter value is null.

set by name

Method	Description
public void setURL(String parameterName, URL val) throws SQLException	Set a parameter to a java.net.URL object.
public void setNull(String parameterName, int sqlType) throws SQLException	Set a parameter to a null value.
public void setBoolean(String parameterName,boolean x) throws SQLException	Set a parameter to a Java boolean value.
public void setByte(String parameterName, byte x)throws SQLException	Set a parameter to a Java byte value.
public void setShort(String parameterName, short x) throws SQLException	Set a parameter to a Java short value.
public void setInt(String parameterName, int x) throws SQLException	Set a parameter to a Java int value.
public void setLong(String parameterName, long x)throws SQLException	Set a parameter to a Java long value.
public void setFloat(String parameterName, float x)throws SQLException	Set a parameter to a Java float value.
public void setDouble(String parameterName, double x) throws SQLException	Set a parameter to a Java double value.
public void setBigDecimal(String parameterName,BigDecimal x) throws SQLException	Set a parameter to a java.math.BigDecimal value.

set by name

Method	Description
public void setString(String parameterName,String x)throws SQLException	Set a parameter to a Java String value.
public void setBytes(String parameterName, byte[] x)throws SQLException	Set a parameter to a Java array of bytes.
public void setDate(String parameterName, Date x)throws SQLException	Set a parameter to a java.sql.Date value.
public void setTime(String parameterName, Time x) throws SQLException	Set a parameter to a java.sql.Time value.
public void setTimestamp(String parameterName,Timestamp x) throws SQLException	Set a parameter to a java.sql.Timestamp value.
public void setBinaryStream(String parameterName, InputStream x, int length) throws SQLException	Set the designated parameter to the given input stream, which will have the specified number of bytes.
public void setObject(String parameterName, Object x,int targetSqlType,int scale)throws SQLException	Set a parameter with the given object.
public void setObject(String parameterName, Object x, int targetSqlType) throws SQLException	Set a parameter with the given object.
public void setObject(String parameterName, Object x)throws SQLException	Set a parameter with the given object.
public void setDate(String parameterName, Date x,Calendar cal) throws SQLException	Set a parameter to a java.sql.Date value.
public void setTime(String parameterName, Time x, Calendar cal)throws SQLException	Set a parameter to a java.sql.Time value.
public void setTimestamp(String parameterName, Timestamp x, Calendar cal) throws SQLException	Set a parameter to a java.sql.Timestamp value.
public void setNull(String parameterName, int sqlType, String typeName)throws SQLException	Set a parameter to a null value.

get by index

Method	Description
public String getString(int parameterIndex) throws SQLException	Determine the value of the designated JDBC CHAR, VARCHAR, or LONGVARCHAR parameter.

get by index

Method	Description
public boolean getBoolean(int parameterIndex) throws SQLException	Determine the value of the designated JDBC BIT parameter.
public byte getByte(int parameterIndex) throws SQLException	Determine the value of the designated JDBC TINYINT parameter.
public short getShort(int parameterIndex) throws SQLException	Determine the value of the designated JDBC SMALLINT parameter.
public int getInt(int parameterIndex) throws SQLException	Determine the value of the designated JDBC INTEGER parameter.
public long getLong(int parameterIndex) throws SQLException	Determine the value of the designated JDBC BIGINT parameter.
public float getFloat(int parameterIndex) throws SQLException	Determine the value of the designated JDBC FLOAT parameter.
public double getDouble(int parameterIndex) throws SQLException	Determine the value of the designated JDBC DOUBLE parameter.
public BigDecimal getBigDecimal(int parameterIndex,int scale) throws SQLException	Determine the value of the designated JDBC NUMERIC parameter.
public byte[] getBytes(int parameterIndex) throws SQLException	Determine the value of the designated JDBC BINARY or VARBINARY parameter.
public Date getDate(int parameterIndex) throws SQLException	Determine the value of the designated JDBC DATE parameter.
public Time getTime(int parameterIndex) throws SQLException	Determine the value of the designated JDBC TIME parameter.
public Timestamp getTimestamp(int parameterIndex) throws SQLException	Determine the value of the designated JDBC TIMESTAMP parameter.
public Object getObject(int parameterIndex)throws SQLException	Determine the value of the designated parameter.
public BigDecimal getBigDecimal(int parameterIndex) throws SQLException	Determine the value of the designated JDBC NUMERIC parameter.
public Object getObject(int i, Map map) throws SQLException	Return an object representing the value of OUT parameter.
public Ref getRef(int i) throws SQLException	Determine the value of the designated JDBC REF parameter.
public Blob getBlob(int i) throws SQLException	Determine the value of the designated JDBC BLOB parameter.
public Clob getClob(int i) throws SQLException	Determine the value of the designated JDBC CLOB parameter.

get by index

Method	Description
public Array getArray(int i) throws SQLException	Determine the value of the designated JDBC ARRAY parameter.
public Date getDate(int parameterIndex, Calendar cal) throws SQLException	Determine the value of the designated JDBC DATE parameter.
public Time getTime(int parameterIndex, Calendar cal) throws SQLException	Determine the value of the designated JDBC TIME parameter.
public Timestamp getTimestamp(int parameterIndex, Calendar cal) throws SQLException	Determine the value of the designated JDBC TIMESTAMP parameter.
public void registerOutParameter (int paramIndex, int sqlType,String typeName)throws SQLException	Register the designated output parameter.
public void registerOutParameter(String parameterName, int sqlType) throws SQLException	Register the OUT parameter named parameterName.
public void registerOutParameter(String parameterName, int sqlType,int scale) throws SQLException	Determine the parameter named parameterName.
public void registerOutParameter(String parameterName, int sqlType, String typeName)throws SQLException	Determine the designated output parameter.
public URL getURL(int parameterIndex) throws SQLException	Determine the value of the designated JDBC DATALINK parameter.

get by name

Method	Description
public String getString(String parameterName) throws SQLException	Determine the value of a JDBC CHAR, VARCHAR, or LONGVARCHAR parameter.
public boolean getBoolean(String parameterName) throws SQLException	Determine the value of a JDBC BIT parameter.
public byte getByte(String parameterName) throws SQLException	Determine the value of a JDBC TINYINT parameter.
public short getShort(String parameterName) throws SQLException	Determine the value of a JDBC SMALLINT parameter.

get by name

Method	Description
public int getInt(String parameterName) throws SQLException	Determine the value of a JDBC INTEGER parameter.
public long getLong(String parameterName) throws SQLException	Determine the value of a JDBC BIGINT parameter.
public float getFloat(String parameterName) throws SQLException	Determine the value of a JDBC FLOAT parameter.
public double getDouble(String parameterName) throws SQLException	Determine the value of a JDBC DOUBLE parameter.
public byte[] getBytes(String parameterName) throws SQLException	Determine the value of a JDBC BINARY or VARBINARY parameter.
public Date getDate(String parameterName) throws SQLException	Determine the value of a JDBC DATE parameter.
public Time getTime(String parameterName) throws SQLException	Determine the value of a JDBC TIME parameter.
public Timestamp getTimestamp(String parameterName) throws SQLException	Determine the value of a JDBC TIMESTAMP parameter.
public Object getObject(String parameterName) throws SQLException	Determine the value of a parameter as an Object.
public BigDecimal getBigDecimal(String parameterName)throws SQLException	Determine the value of a JDBC NUMERIC parameter.
public Object getObject(String parameterName, Map map)throws SQLException	Return an object representing the value of OUT parameter.
public Ref getRef(String parameterName) throws SQLException	Determine the value of a JDBC REF parameter.
public Blob getBlob(String parameterName) throws SQLException	Determine the value of a JDBC BLOB parameter.
public Clob getClob(String parameterName)throws SQLException	Determine the value of a JDBC CLOB parameter.
public Array getArray(String parameterName)throws SQLException	Determine the value of a JDBC ARRAY.
public Date getDate(String parameterName, Calendar cal)throws SQLException	Determine the value of a JDBC DATE parameter.
public Time getTime(String parameterName, Calendar cal)throws SQLException	Determine the value of a JDBC TIME parameter.
public Timestamp getTimestamp(String parameterName, Calendar cal)throws SQLException	Determine the value of a JDBC TIMESTAMP parameter.

J2ME DATA MANAGEMENT

get by name

Method	Description
public URL getURL(String parameterName) throws SQLException	Determine a URL.

java.sql Package public interface Connection Interface

Method	Description
public void close()throws SQLException	Close a Connection.
public boolean isClosed()throws SQLException	Determine whether a Connection object is closed.
public DatabaseMetaData getMetaData()throws SQLException	Retrieve a DatabaseMetaData.
public void setReadOnly(boolean readOnly) throws SQLException	Place a connection in read-only.
public boolean isReadOnly()throws SQLException	Determine whether a Connection object is in read-only.
public String getCatalog()throws SQLException	Determine a Connection's catalog name.

Warnings

Method	Description
public SQLWarning getWarnings()throws SQLException	Retrieve the first warning reported.
public void clearWarnings()throws SQLException	Clear all warnings reported.

Holdability

Method	Description
public void setHoldability(int holdability) throws SQLException	Change the holdability of ResultSet objects.
public int getHoldability() throws SQLException	Determine the holdability of a ResultSet.

Transactions

Method	Description
public Savepoint setSavepoint() throws SQLException	Create an unnamed savepoint.
public Savepoint setSavepoint(String name)throws SQLException	Create a named savepoint.
public void rollback(Savepoint savepoint) throws SQLException	Reverse all changes made after a savepoint was set.
public void releaseSavepoint(Savepoint savepoint)throws SQLException	Remove a Savepoint object.
public void commit()throws SQLException	Make all changes permanent.
public void rollback()throws SQLException	Reverse changes made to a transaction and release any database locks.
public void setAutoCommit(boolean autoCommit)throws SQLException	Set the autocommit mode.
public boolean getAutoCommit()throws SQLException	Determine whether the autocommit mode is set.

CallableStatement

Method	Description
public CallableStatement prepareCall(String sql,int resultSetType, int resultSetConcurrency, int resultSetHoldability)throws SQLException	Create a CallableStatement object that generates a ResultSet.
public CallableStatement prepareCall(String sql,int resultSetType,int resultSetConcurrency)throws SQLException	Create a CallableStatement object that generates a ResultSet.
public CallableStatement prepareCall(String sql)throws SQLException	Create a CallableStatement object.

Statement

Method	Description
public Statement createStatement(int resultSetType,int resultSetConcurrency,int resultSetHoldability) throws SQLException	Create a Statement object that will generate ResultSet.

Statement

Method	Description
public Statement createStatement(int resultSetType,int resultSetConcurrency) throws SQLException	Create a Statement object that generates ResultSet.
public Statement createStatement() throws SQLException	Create a Statement object.

PrepareStatement

Method	Description
public PreparedStatement prepareStatement(String sql) throws SQLException	Create a PreparedStatement object.
public PreparedStatement prepareStatement(String sql,int resultSetType,int resultSetConcurrency,int resultSetHoldability)throws SQLException	Create a PreparedStatement object that will generate ResultSet.
public PreparedStatement prepareStatement(String sql, int[] columnIndexes)throws SQLException	Create a PreparedStatement object that returns autogenerated keys.
public PreparedStatement prepareStatement(String sql,int resultSetType, int resultSetConcurrency)throws SQLException	Create a PreparedStatement object that generates ResultSet.
public PreparedStatement prepareStatement(String sql,String[] columnNames) throws SQLException	Create a PreparedStatement object that returns autogenerated keys.

java.sql Package public interface DatabaseMetaData

Method	Description
public Connection getConnection() throws SQLException	Retrieve the connection that produced metadata.
public boolean supportsSavepoints() throws SQLException	Determine whether a database supports savepoints.
public boolean supportsNamedParameters() throws SQLException	Determine whether a database supports named parameters to callable statements.
public boolean supportsMultipleOpenResults() throws SQLException	Determine whether it is possible to have multiple ResultSet objects returned from a CallableStatement simultaneously.

java.sql Package public interface DatabaseMetaData

public int getMaxUserNameLength() throws SQLException	Determine the maximum number of characters in a user name.
public boolean supportsTransactions() throws SQLException	Determine whether a database supports transactions.
public int getJDBCMajorVersion() throws SQLException	Determine the major JDBC version number of a driver.
public int getJDBCMinorVersion() throws SQLException	Determine the minor JDBC version number of a driver.

Database

Method	Description
public String getURL() throws SQLException	Retrieve the URL for a DBMS.
public String getDatabaseProductName() throws SQLException	Determine the name of a DBMS.
public String getDatabaseProductVersion() throws SQLException	Determine the version number of a DBMS.
public ResultSet getSchemas() throws SQLException	Determine the schema names.
public ResultSet getCatalogs() throws SQLException	Determine the catalog names.
public ResultSet getTypeInfo() throws SQLException	Retrieve a description of standard SQL types supported by a database.
public int getDatabaseMajorVersion() throws SQLException	Determine the major version number of a database.
public int getDatabaseMinorVersion() throws SQLException	Determine the minor version number of a database.

Columns and Rows

Method	Description
public int getMaxColumnNameLength() throws SQLException	Determine the maximum number of characters allowed in a column name.
public int getMaxColumnsInGroupBy() throws SQLException	Determine the maximum number of columns allowed in a GROUP BY clause.
public int getMaxColumnsInIndex() throws SQLException	Determine the maximum number of columns allowed in an index.

Columns and Rows

Method	Description
public int getMaxColumnsInOrderBy() throws SQLException	Determine the maximum number of columns allowed in an ORDER BY clause.
public int getMaxColumnsInSelect() throws SQLException	Determine the maximum number of columns allowed in a SELECT list.
public int getMaxColumnsInTable() throws SQLException	Determine the maximum number of columns allowed in a table.
public int getMaxConnections() throws SQLException	Determine the maximum number of concurrent connections that are possible to a database.
public int getMaxIndexLength() throws SQLException	Determine the maximum number of bytes allowed for an index.
public int getMaxRowSize() throws SQLException	Determine the maximum number of bytes allowed in a row.
public ResultSet getColumns(String catalog, String schemaPattern, String tableNamePattern, String columnNamePattern) throws SQLException	Retrieve a description of table columns.
public ResultSet getColumnPrivileges(String catalog,String schema,String table,String columnNamePattern)throws SQLException	Determine access rights for columns.

Statement

Method	Description
public int getMaxStatementLength() throws SQLException	Determine the maximum number of characters permitted in an SQL statement.
public int getMaxStatements() throws SQLException	Determine the maximum number of active statements that can be open at the same time.
public boolean supportsBatchUpdates() throws SQLException	Determine whether a database supports batch updates.

Table

Method	Description
public int getMaxTableNameLength() throws SQLException	Determine the maximum number of characters in a table name.
public int getMaxTablesInSelect() throws SQLException	Determine the maximum number of tables allowed in a SELECT statement.
public ResultSet getTables(String catalog, String schemaPattern, String tableNamePattern, String[] types) throws SQLException	Determine tables available in a catalog.
public ResultSet getTablePrivileges (String catalog,String schemaPattern,String tableNamePattern)throws SQLException	Determine access rights for each table.

Keys

Method	Description
public ResultSet getPrimaryKeys(String catalog,String schema,String table)throws SQLException	Retrieve a description of a table's primary key.
public ResultSet getIndexInfo(String catalog, String schema,String table,boolean unique, boolean approximate)throws SQLException	Retrieve a description of table's indices and statistics.
public boolean supportsGetGeneratedKeys() throws SQLException	Determine whether autogenerated keys can be retrieved.

Procedure

Method	Description
public ResultSet getProcedureColumns(String catalog,String schemaPattern,String procedureNamePattern,String columnNamePattern)throws SQLException	Determine a catalog's stored procedure parameter and result columns.
public ResultSet getProcedures(String catalog,String schemaPattern,String procedureNamePattern)throws SQLException	Determine the stored procedures available in a catalog.

Holdability

Method	Description
public boolean supportsResultSetHoldability (int holdability) throws SQLException	Determine whether a database supports holdability.

Holdability

Method	Description
public int getResultSetHoldability() throws SQLException	Determine the default holdability of a ResultSet.

java.sql Package public class DriverManager

Method	Description
public static Connection getConnection(String url, Properties info)throws SQLException	Open a connection to a database.
public static Connection getConnection(String url, String user,String password)throws SQLException	Open a connection to a database.
public static Connection getConnection(String url) throws SQLException	Open a connection to a database.

Timeout

Method	Description
public static void setLoginTimeout (int seconds)	Set the maximum time in seconds before the login to the database times out.
public static int getLoginTimeout()	Determine the maximum time in seconds before the login to the database times out.

java.sql Package public interface PreparedStatement

Method	Description
public ResultSetMetaData getMetaData() throws SQLException	Retrieve a ResultSetMetaData object.
public ParameterMetaData getParameterMetaData() throws SQLException	Determine the metadata for a PreparedStatement's parameters.
public void addBatch() throws SQLException	Add a parameter to PreparedStatement batch of commands.

Execute

Method	Description
public ResultSet executeQuery() throws SQLException	Execute a query in a PreparedStatement and return a ResultSet.

Execute

Method	Description
public int executeUpdate() throws SQLException	Execute the SQL statement that contains an INSERT, UPDATE, or DELETE statement in a PreparedStatement.
public boolean execute() throws SQLException	Execute an SQL statement in a PreparedStatement.

Parameters

Method	Description
public void setNull(int parameterIndex,int sqlType)throws SQLException	Set the parameter to a null value.
public void setString(int parameterIndex, String x) throws SQLException	Set the String value.
public void setDate(int parameterIndex, Date x) throws SQLException	Set the java.sql.Date value.
public void setTime(int parameterIndex, Time x) throws SQLException	Set the java.sql.Time value.
public void setTimestamp(int parameterIndex, Timestamp x) throws SQLException	Set the java.sql.Timestamp value.
public void clearParameters() throws SQLException	Clear the current parameter values.
public void setNull(int paramIndex, int sqlType, String typeName)throws SQLException	Set a parameter to a null value.

java.sql Package public interface ResultSet

Method	Description
public void close() throws SQLException	Close a ResultSet.
public ResultSetMetaData getMetaData() throws SQLException	Retrieve metadata.
public Statement getStatement()throws SQLException	Retrieve the Statement object.

Warnings

Method	Description
public SQLWarning getWarnings() throws SQLException	Retrieve the first warning reported on a ResultSet.
public void clearWarnings() throws SQLException	Clear all warnings reported on a ResultSet.

Virtual Cursor Movement

Method	Description
public boolean next() throws SQLException	Move the virtual cursor down one row.
public boolean isFirst()throws SQLException	Determine whether the virtual cursor is on the first row.
public boolean isLast()throws SQLException	Determine whether the virtual cursor is on the last row.
public boolean first()throws SQLException	Move the virtual cursor to the first row.
public boolean last()throws SQLException	Move the virtual cursor to the last row.
public int getRow()throws SQLException	Determine the current row number.
public boolean absolute(int row)throws SQLException	Move the virtual cursor to the row specified by the row parameter.
public boolean relative(int rows)throws SQLException	Move the virtual cursor a relative number of rows.
public boolean previous()throws SQLException	Move the virtual cursor to the previous row.

Fetch Size

Method	Description
public void setFetchSize(int rows) throws SQLException	Give the database driver a hint as to how many rows should be fetched when more rows are needed for this ResultSet.
public int getFetchSize()throws SQLException	Determine the fetch size for this ResultSet.

Rows

Method	Description
public boolean rowUpdated()throws SQLException	Determine whether a row has been updated.
public boolean rowInserted()throws SQLException	Determine whether a row has had an insertion.
public boolean rowDeleted()throws SQLException	Determine whether a row is deleted.
public void updateNull(int columnIndex) throws SQLException	Insert a null into a column.

Rows

Method	Description
public void insertRow()throws SQLException	Insert a row into a ResultSet and into the database.
public void updateRow()throws SQLException	Update the underlying database with the row of this ResultSet.
public void deleteRow()throws SQLException	Delete a row from a ResultSet and from the database.
public void refreshRow()throws SQLException	Refresh the current row with the current value in the database.
public void cancelRowUpdates()throws SQLException	Cancel updates.

java.sql Package public interface ResultSetMetaData

Method	Description
public int getColumnCount()throws SQLException	Retrieve the number of columns in a ResultSet object.
public boolean isCaseSensitive(int column) throws SQLException	Determine whether a column is case sensitive.
public boolean isSearchable(int column) throws SQLException	Determine whether a column can be used in a where clause.
public boolean isCurrency(int column) throws SQLException	Determine whether a column is a cash value.
public int isNullable(int column) throws SQLException	Determine whether a null value can be placed in the column.
public boolean isSigned(int column) throws SQLException	Determine whether values are signed numbers.

Columns

Method	Description
public int getColumnDisplaySize(int column)throws SQLException	Retrieve the column's maximum width in characters.
public String getColumnLabel(int column) throws SQLException	Retrieve the column's label.
public String getColumnName(int column) throws SQLException	Retrieve the column's name.

Columns

Method	Description
public int getPrecision(int column) throws SQLException	Retrieve the column's precision.
public int getColumnType(int column) throws SQLException	Retrieve the data type of the column.
public String getColumnTypeName(int column)throws SQLException	Retrieve the name of the column data type.
public boolean isReadOnly(int column) throws SQLException	Indicate whether a column is read-only.
public boolean isWritable(int column) throws SQLException	Indicate whether a column is writable.

java.sql Package public interface Savepoint

Method	Description
public int getSavepointId()throws SQLException	Retrieve a savepoint ID.
public String getSavepointName() throws SQLException	Retrieve a savepoint name.

java.sql Package public interface Statement

Method	Description
public void close() throws SQLException	Release a Statement object.
public ResultSet getResultSet() throws SQLException	Retrieve the current ResultSet object.
public int getUpdateCount()throws SQLException	Determine the number of rows that were updated.
public Connection getConnection() throws SQLException	Retrieve a Connection object.
public ResultSet getGeneratedKeys() throws SQLException	Retrieve autogenerated keys.

Timeout

Method	Description
public int getQueryTimeout()throws SQLException	Determine the maximum number of seconds for a Statement object to execute.
public void setQueryTimeout(int seconds) throws SQLException	Set the maximum number of seconds for a Statement object to execute.

Rows

Method	Description
public int getMaxRows() throws SQLException	Retrieve the maximum number of rows for a ResultSet object.
public void setMaxRows(int max) throws SQLException	Set the maximum number of rows for a ResultSet object.
public void setFetchSize(int rows) throws SQLException	Give database a hint for how many rows to retrieve when more rows are needed for the ResultSet.
public int getFetchSize()throws SQLException	Determine the number of rows for the fetch size.

Warnings

Method	Description
public SQLWarning getWarnings() throws SQLException	Retrieve the first warning on a Statement object.
public void clearWarnings() throws SQLException	Clear all the warnings reported on a Statement object.

Execute

Method	Description
public boolean execute(String sql) throws SQLException	Execute an SQL statement.
public ResultSet executeQuery(String sql) throws SQLException	Execute an SQL statement and return a ResultSet object.
public int executeUpdate(String sql) throws SQLException	Execute an SQL statement that contains INSERT, UPDATE, or DELETE statements or DDL statements.

Batch

Method	Description
public void addBatch(String sql)throws SQLException	Add an SQL statement to a batch.
public void clearBatch() throws SQLException	Empty a batch of SQL statements.
public int[] executeBatch()throws SQLException	Execute a batch of SQL statements.

javax.sql package public interface DataSource

Method	Description
public Connection getConnection() throws SQLException	Open a connection to a data source.
public Connection getConnection(String username, String password) throws SQLException	Open a connection to a data source.

javax.sql package public interface RowSet

Method	Description
public void setUrl(String url) throws SQLException	Set the URL of a RowSet.
public boolean isReadOnly()	Determine whether a RowSet object is read-only.
public void setReadOnly(boolean value) throws SQLException	Set a RowSet object to read-only.
public int getMaxFieldSize() throws SQLException	Determine the maximum number of bytes that can be placed in a column.
public int getMaxRows() throws SQLException	Determine the maximum number of rows that can be in a RowSet.

DataSource

Method	Description
public String getDataSourceName()	Determine the logical name of the data source for a RowSet.
public void setDataSourceName(String name) throws SQLException	Set the data source name for a RowSet.

User Name and Password

Method	Description
public String getUsername()	Determine the user name used to create a database connection for a RowSet.
public void setUsername(String name) throws SQLException	Set the user name for a RowSet.
public String getPassword()	Determine the password used to create a database connection.
public void setPassword(String password) throws SQLException	Set the database password for a RowSet.

Timeout

Method	Description
public int getQueryTimeout() throws SQLException	Determine the maximum time the driver will wait for a statement to execute.
public void setQueryTimeout(int seconds) throws SQLException	Set the maximum time the driver will wait for a statement to execute.

javax.sql public class RowSetEvent extends java.util.EventObject

Method	Description
public RowSetEvent(RowSet source)	Create an instance of a RowSetEvent that is associated with the RowSet specified by the source parameter.

javax.sql public interface RowSetInternal

Method	Description
public Object[] getParams() throws SQLException	Return an array of Objects containing parameter values for a RowSet.
public Connection getConnection() throws SQLException	Return the Connection object associated with a RowSet. A null is returned if there is no Connection object associated with a RowSet.
public void setMetaData(RowSetMetaData md) throws SQLException	Set the metadata for a RowSet, where md is the RowSetMetaData.
public ResultSet getOriginal() throws SQLException	Return a ResutSet containing the original value of the RowSet.
public ResultSet getOriginalRow() throws SQLException	Return a ResutSet containing the original value of the current row of the RowSet. An exception is thrown if there is no current row.

javax.sql public interface RowSetListener extends java.util.EventListener

Method	Description
public void rowSetChanged(RowSetEvent event)	Send a RowSetListener notification that the entire content of a RowSet has changed. RowSetEvent is the object that contains the RowSet associated with the change.

javax.sql public interface RowSetListener extends java.util.EventListener

Method	Description
public void rowChanged(RowSetEvent event)	Send a RowSetListener notification that the one row of a RowSet has changed. RowSetEvent is the object that contains the RowSet associated with the change.
public void cursorMoved(RowSetEvent event)	Send a RowSetListener notification that the cursor of a RowSet has moved. RowSetEvent is the object that contains the RowSet associated with the cursor.

javax.sql public interface RowSetMetaData extends ResultSetMetaData

Method	Description
public void setColumnCount(int columnCount) throws SQLException	Determine the number of columns in a RowSet, where columnCount specifies the number of columns.
public void setAutoIncrement(int columnIndex, boolean property) throws SQLException	Determine whether the specified column is numbered automatically, where columnIndex is the index of the column, and property is a boolean value indicating whether or not the column is automatically numbered. The property value is false by default.
public void setCaseSensitive(int columnIndex, boolean property) throws SQLException	Determine whether the specified column is case sensitive, where columnIndex is the index of the column, and property is a boolean value indicating whether or not the column is case sensitive. The property value is false by default.
public void setSearchable(int columnIndex, boolean property) throws SQLException	Determine whether the specified column can be used in a where clause, where columnIndex is the index of the column, and property is a boolean value indicating whether or not the column can be used in a where clause. The property value is false by default.
public void setCurrency(int columnIndex, boolean property) throws SQLException	Determine whether the specified column is a cash value, where columnIndex is the index of the column, and property is a boolean value indicating whether or not the column is a cash value. The property value is false by default.

javax.sql public interface RowSetMetaData extends ResultSetMetaData

Method	Description
public void setNullable(int columnIndex, int property) throws SQLException	Determine whether the specified column can be set to null, where columnIndex is the index of the column, and property is an int indicating whether or not the column can be set to null. The property value is one of the following constants: ResultSetMetaData.columnNoNulls, ResultSetMetaData.columnNullable, or ResultSetMetaData.columnNullableUnknown
public void setSigned(int columnIndex, boolean property) throws SQLException	Determine whether the specified column is a signed number, where columnIndex is the index of the column, and property is a boolean value indicating whether or not the column is a signed number. The property value is false by default.
public void setColumnDisplaySize(int columnIndex, int size) throws SQLException	Determine the maximum width in chars when displaying the column, where columnIndex is the index of the column, and property is an int indicating the maximum number of characters that will be displayed.
public void setColumnLabel(int columnIndex, String label) throws SQLException	Determine the suggested label for the column, where columnIndex is the index of the column, and label is the String containing the text of the suggested label.
public void setColumnName(int columnIndex, String columnName) throws SQLException	Determine the name for the column, where columnIndex is the index of the column, and columnName is the String containing the text of the column name.
public void setSchemaName(int columnIndex, String schemaName) throws SQLException	Determine the name of the table's schema that contains the column, where columnIndex is the index of the column, and schemaName is the String containing the text of the schema name.
public void setPrecision(int columnIndex, int precision) throws SQLException	Determine the number of decimal digits, where columnIndex is the index of the column, and precision is an int indicating the maximum number of decimal digits contained in the column.

J2ME
DATA MANAGEMENT

javax.sql public interface RowSetMetaData extends ResultSetMetaData

Method	Description
public void setScale(int columnIndex, int scale) throws SQLException	Determine the number of digits to the right of the decimal point, where columnIndex is the index of the column, and scale is an int indicating the number of digits to the right of the decimal point in the value within the column.
public void setTableName(int columnIndex, String tableName) throws SQLException	Determine the name of the table that contains the column, where columnIndex is the index of the column, and tableName is a String containing the text of the table name.
public void setCatalogName(int columnIndex, String catalogName) throws SQLException	Determine the name of the table catalog that contains the column, where columnIndex is the index of the column, and catalogName is a String containing the text of the catalog.
public void setColumnType(int columnIndex, int SQLType) throws SQLException	Determine SQL type of the column, where columnIndex is the index of the column, and SQLType is an int containing the SQL type.
public void setColumnTypeName(int columnIndex, String typeName) throws SQLException	Determine the name of the column type in the data source of the column, where columnIndex is the index of the column, and typeName is the String containing the text of the column type.

javax.sql public interface RowSetReader

Method	Description
public void readData(RowSetInternal caller) throws SQLException	Read the content of a RowSet, where the caller is the RowSetInternal that is implemented by a RowSet object and is registered with the RowSetReader.

javax.sql public interface RowSetWriter

Method	Description
public boolean writeData(RowSetInternal caller) throws SQLException	Write changes to the RowSet associated with the RowSetWriter to the data source, where caller is the RowSetInternal associated with the RowSetWriter. A true is returned if the data was successfully written to the data source, otherwise a false is returned.

The Complete Reference

Chapter 11

JDBC and Embedded SQL

453

A Connected Device Configuration (CDC) device–based J2ME application interacts with a database management system (DBMS) using Java data objects and SQL statements that are embedded in the J2ME application and executed by the Java data objects. Java data objects are discussed in the previous chapter. This chapter continues with a detailed look at how to create an SQL statement, execute the statement, and interact with rows of data returned to the J2ME application by the DBMS in response to the request for data.

SQL is presented in this chapter using a practical approach. Each section of the chapter focuses on common tasks used in a J2ME application rather than on SQL keywords. This means you can quickly locate a routine in the chapter, then incorporate the routine directly into your J2ME component.

Model Programs

Many programming styles can be used to write the data-access portion of a J2ME component. Two programming styles—referred to as Model A and Model B—are used in this chapter to illustrate how a J2ME application can interact with a DBMS. The Model A program style is used to execute SQL requests that use the execute() or executeUpdate() methods (see Chapter 9) and don't return a ResultSet. The Model B program style is used to execute SQL requests that use the executeQuery() method, which returns a ResultSet. Each of these is described in detail in the next two sections of this chapter.

Both program styles are designed to minimize the code clutter in this chapter. Code clutter occurs whenever many lines of code are used in code examples, but only a few lines of code change between examples. In an effort to reduce code clutter, each complete program model is presented at the beginning of the chapter. One or two comments indicate where within the program model to place code segments that are used to illustrate SQL routines throughout the rest of the chapter. These code segments are contained either within a try {} block or within the DownRow() method. The try {} block is where the SQL statement is created and executed. The DownRow() method is where the J2ME application interacts with the ResultSet.

Let's say that you want to update a row in a database. As you'll remember from the previous chapter, the executeUpdate() method is used to execute the query, and no ResultSet is returned. Therefore, you can replace the second try {} block in the Model A program with the code segment contained in the section of this chapter that shows how to update a row in the database. As you'll see in the next section, the Model A program does not contain a DownRow() method because no ResultSet is returned.

Suppose you want to retrieve data from the database. The executeQuery() method is used in this scenario. The Model B program is used for this purpose because a ResultSet is returned. In this case, the section of this chapter that shows how to retrieve data from a database contains two code segments. The first code segment contains the query, and it replaces the second try {} block in the Model B program. The other code segment replaces the DownRow() method of the Model B program and interacts with the ResultSet.

The next two sections explain how each model program works. Other sections of this chapter discuss commonly used tasks and show how to incorporate those tasks into a J2ME component. Each of these sections also indicates which program model to use with the task.

Model A Program

The Model A program, shown in Listing 11-1, is designed to execute queries that do not return a ResultSet. It is organized into the ModelA() constructor and the main(). The main() creates an instance of the ModelA object called sql1, which causes the execution of the constructor.

The constructor begins by creating three String objects. These are url, userId, and password. The url is assigned the URL of the database. In this example, the JDBC/ODBC bridge is used to connect to the CustomerInformation database. Of course, the URL used in your J2ME application replaces the URL in Model A and will represent the JDBC driver and database that are specific to your J2ME component. Likewise, the database used with your J2ME application may or may not require a user ID and password. If these are required, they will undoubtedly be different from the user ID and password used in Model A.

The first try {} block in Model A uses the Class.forName() method to load the JDBC driver into the Java Virtual Machine (JVM). You will probably need to replace the driver used in Model A with the appropriate JDBC driver for your J2ME component. Once the JDBC driver is loaded, the getConnection() method is called to open a connection to the database using the url, userID, and password String objects. The getConnection() method returns a Connection object called database, which is declared above the definition of the constructor.

Two catch {} blocks follow the first try {} block and are used to trap exceptions that occur while the driver is loaded and a connection is established with the database. You can change the text of messages shown in Model A that are displayed when an exception is caught to a message that is more conducive to your programming style and J2ME requirements.

The second try {} block in Model A contains a comment. You should replace this try {} block with the try {} that appears in the section of this chapter that describes the task you want performed by the J2ME component. You'll notice as you read through this chapter that the try {} block within each section references a Statement object called DataRequest, which is declared as a private member of the ModelA class.

The second try {} block is followed by a catch {} block that traps SQL exceptions that occur during the execution of the query in the second try {} block.

Anytime a database connection is closed, you should first check for a null value on the Connection object. If the connection is no longer valid, the close() method will throw a NullPointerException.

Listing 11-1
A model
J2ME
application
that doesn't
retrieve
information
from a
database
(Model A)

```
import java.sql.*;
public class ModelA
{
  private Connection Database;
  private Statement DataRequest;
  public ModelA ()
  {
    String url = "jdbc:odbc:CustomerInformation";
    String userID = "jim";
    String password = "keogh";
    try {
      Class.forName( "sun.jdbc.odbc.JdbcOdbcDriver");
      Database = DriverManager.getConnection(url,userID,password);
    }
    catch (ClassNotFoundException error) {
      System.err.println("Unable to load the JDBC/ODBC bridge." + error);
      System.exit(1);
    }
    catch (SQLException error) {
      System.err.println("Cannot connect to the database. "+ error);
      if(Database != null) {
        try {
          Database.close();
        }
        catch(SQLException er){}
        }
      System.exit(2);
    }
    try {
      // insert example code here
    }
    catch ( SQLException error ) {
      System.err.println("SQL error." + error);
      if(Database != null) {
        try {
          Database.close();
        }
        catch(SQLException er){}
        }
      System.exit(3);
      }
```

```
      if(Database != null) {
        try {
          Database.close();
        }
        catch(SQLException er){}
        }
      }
  public static void main ( String args [] )
  {
    final ModelA sql1 = new ModelA ();
    System.exit ( 0 ) ;
  }
}
```

Model B Program

The Model B program, shown in Listing 11-2, is designed for use by J2ME components that retrieve information from a database. Notice that the Model B program is similar to the Model A program in that the constructor definition (except for the name of the constructor) and the main() are identical. Therefore, refer to the previous section for a description of the constructor and main().

The second try {} block in Model B is where you place the try {} block contained in sections of this chapter that discuss how to retrieve information from a database. This try {} executes a query and returns a ResultSet object called Results, which is declared as a private member of the ModelB class.

Model B also contains DisplayResults() and DownRow(). DisplayResults() is passed the ResultSet returned in the second try {} block, which is used to move the virtual cursor to the first row of the ResultSet using the next() method (see Chapter 6). The next() returns a boolean value that is assigned to the Records variable. The if statement evaluates the value of Records and displays a "No data returned" message if Records contains a false value indicating that there isn't any data in the row.

However, a true value causes the do…while loop to execute, which is where a call to DownRow() is made, passing it the ResultSet. DownRow() retrieves data stored in columns of the ResultSet and assigns those values to variables. Each section of this chapter that discusses a task that retrieves data from a database has its own DownRow(). Therefore, you need to replace the DownRow() in Model B with the DownRow() that is associated with the task that you want performed by the J2ME component.

After DownRow() extracts data from the current row of the ResultSet, control returns to DisplayResults(), where the next() method is called and the results are evaluated by the while. If the next() method returns a true value, then DownRow() is recalled, otherwise the do…while loop is exited and control returns to the constructor.

DisplayResults() also contains a catch {} block that traps errors thrown by statements within the try {} block.

```java
import java.sql.*;
public class ModelB
{
  private Connection Database;
  private Statement DataRequest;
  private ResultSet Results;
  public ModelB ()
  {
    String url = "jdbc:odbc:CustomerInformation";
    String userID = "jim";
    String password = "keogh";
    try {
      Class.forName( "sun.jdbc.odbc.JdbcOdbcDriver");
      Database = DriverManager.getConnection(url,userID,password);
    }
    catch (ClassNotFoundException error) {
      System.err.println("Unable to load the JDBC/ODBC bridge." + error);
      System.exit(1);
    }
    catch (SQLException error) {
      System.err.println("Cannot connect to the database." + error);
      System.exit(2);
    }
    try {
      // Enter example code here
    }
    catch ( SQLException error ){
      System.err.println("SQL error." + error);
      if(Database != null) {
        try {
          Database.close();
        }
        catch(SQLException er){}
        }
      System.exit(3);
    }
    if(Database != null) {
```

```
      try {
        Database.close();
      }
      catch(SQLException er){}
      }
  }
  private void DisplayResults (ResultSet DisplayResults)
              throws SQLException
  {
    boolean Records = DisplayResults.next();
    if (!Records ) {
      System.out.println( "No data returned");
      return;
    }
    try {
      do {
        DownRow( DisplayResults) ;
      } while ( DisplayResults.next() );
    }
    catch (SQLException error ) {
      System.err.println("Data display error." + error);
      if(Database != null) {
        try {
          Database.close();
        }
        catch(SQLException er){}
        }
      System.exit(4);
    }
  }
  private  void DownRow ( ResultSet DisplayResults )
              throws SQLException
  {
    //Enter new DownRow() code here
  }
  public static void main ( String args [] )
  {
    final ModelB sql1 = new ModelB ();
    System.exit ( 0 ) ;
  }
}
```

Tables

Chapter 5 showed how to design a database. A database design is used as the basis for building tables and indexes that make up a database. Tables and indexes are created using a query written using SQL. Typically, the database administrator writes and executes the query that creates tables and indexes, although it is possible to have a J2ME application or a Java application execute the same query to create tables and indexes.

The following sections demonstrate various techniques used in a query to create a table. Techniques to create indexes are presented later in this chapter. These queries can be executed from within the Model A program, as discussed previously in this chapter, or outside of a Java program using an interface, such as ISQL, that is supplied with a DBMS.

The user ID for logging onto the DBMS and executing the query must have rights to create and drop tables. Dropping a table removes the table from the database, which is discussed later in this chapter. Depending on the policies of your IT department, developers are commonly given rights to create and drop tables in the development environment. Only the database administrator has these rights to do the same in the production environment.

Create a Table

You create a table by formatting an SQL query. The query contains the CREATE TABLE SQL statement that contains the name of the table. In Listing 11-3 the table is called CustomerAddress because the table will contain address information about customers. Following the table name are the column definitions, which are enclosed in parentheses. The first column is called CustomerNumber. The data type of the column and the column size follow the column name. A comma separates each column.

The CustomerAddress table contains four columns. These are

- CustomerNumber, a string of a maximum of 30 characters
- CustomerStreet, a string of a maximum of 30 characters
- CustomerCity, a string of a maximum of 30 characters
- CustomerZip, a string of a maximum of 30 characters

All the SQL commands are enclosed in double quotation marks and assigned to a String object called query. Next, the program creates an SQL statement using the createStatement() method of the Connection object (see Chapter 9). This method returns the handle to the DBMS to the DataRequest object, which is an object of the Statement class.

The query is sent to the DBMS using the executeQuery() method. If successful, the DBMS creates the table. If unsuccessful, the table isn't created and the DBMS returns an error message. The SQL statement is then closed using DataRequest.close().

Listing 11-3
Creating
a table

```
try {
   String query = "CREATE TABLE CustomerAddress (" +
      " CustomerNumber CHAR(30), " +
      " CustomerStreet CHAR(30), " +
      " CustomerCity CHAR(30), " +
      " CustomerZip CHAR(30))";
   DataRequest = Database.createStatement();
   DataRequest.execute(query);
   DataRequest.close();
}
```

Requiring Data in a Column

There are business rules that require a value in specific columns of a row, such as the columns that contain a customer's name. You can require the DBMS to reject rows that are missing a value in specific columns by using the NOT NULL clause in the query when the table is created. Listing 11-4 illustrates how the NOT NULL clause is used in a query.

In this example, a CustomerAddress table is created that contains the same four columns used in Listing 11-3, except all of these columns require a value. In other words, a row that is missing a value in any of these columns is rejected by the DBMS and will not be inserted into a table.

Listing 11-4
Requiring a
value to be
placed in
a column
of a table

```
try {
   String query = "CREATE TABLE CustomerAddress ( " +
      "CustomerNumber CHAR(30) NOT NULL," +
      "CustomerStreet CHAR(30) NOT NULL," +
      "CustomerCity CHAR(30) NOT NULL," +
      "CustomerZip CHAR(30) NOT NULL)";
   DataRequest = Database.createStatement();
   DataRequest.execute (query );
   DataRequest.close();
}
```

Setting a Default Value for a Column

The DBMS can enter a default value into a column automatically if the column is left empty whenever a new row is inserted into the table. You determine the value entered by the DBMS by creating a default value when you create the table. Any value can be used as the default value as long as the value conforms to the data type and size of the column.

Let's say most of your customers reside in the 07660 zip code. Some customers fail to give their sales representative their zip code when placing their first order. They assume that since the zip code is the same as your business, you already know the zip code.

A default value is assigned to a column when you create the table by using the DEFAULT clause. The DEFAULT clause is followed in the query by the value that the DBMS will place in the column if the column is empty in the incoming row. Listing 11-5 illustrates how to set a default value for a column when you create a table.

Listing 11-5
Creating a
default value
for a column

```
try {
    String query = "CREATE TABLE CustomerAddress ( " +
        "CustomerNumber CHAR(30) NOT NULL," +
        "CustomerStreet CHAR(30) NOT NULL," +
        "CustomerCity CHAR(30) NOT NULL," +
        "CustomerZip CHAR(30) NOT NULL DEFAULT '07660')";
    DataRequest = Database.createStatement();
    DataRequest.executeUpdate (query );
    DataRequest.close();
}
```

Drop a Table

A developer may have the right to remove a table, but this is usually reserved for the development environment only. The decision to drop a table shouldn't be made lightly because once a table is dropped you cannot recover it. Instead, the table must be re-created and the data reinserted into the table. In addition to losing data elements stored in the table, dropping a table may affect the integrity of the database and tables that relate to values in the dropped table.

Using the Drop Table statement in the query drops a table. As illustrated in Listing 11-6, the Drop Table statement contains the name of the table that is to be dropped.

Listing 11-6
Dropping
a table

```
try {
    String query = new String ("DROP TABLE CustomerAddress");
    DataRequest = Database.createStatement();
    DataRequest. execute(query);
    DataRequest.close();
}
```

Indexing

The database schema describes indexes along with tables that are used in the database. Writing a query, as illustrated in the next section, creates an index. Likewise, a query is used to remove an existing index, which is referred to as dropping an index. Developers are typically permitted to create or drop indexes within the development environment, and only the database administrator has rights to do the same in the production environment, although these rights may vary according to IT department policy.

Executing the query to create or drop an index follows procedures similar to those for creating and dropping a table. That is, the query can be executed within or outside a J2ME application or Java application. Listings in the following sections should be used with the Model A program since no ResultSet is returned when the query is executed.

Create an Index

An index is created by using the CREATE INDEX statement in a query, as illustrated in Listing 11-7. The CREATE INDEX statement contains the name of the index and any modifier that describes to the DBMS the type of index to be created. In addition, the CREATE INDEX statement uses the ON clauses to identify the name of the table and the name of the column whose value is used for the index.

Listing 11-7 creates an index called CustNum that contains values in the CustomerNumber column of the CustomerAddress table. The CustNum index doesn't have duplicate key values, and therefore the UNIQUE modifier is used in the CREATE INDEX statement to prohibit duplicate key values from being included in the index.

Listing 11-7
Creating a
unique index

```
try {
   String query = "CREATE UNIQUE INDEX CustNum " +
     "ON CustomerAddress (CustomerNumber)";
   DataRequest = Database.createStatement();
   DataRequest.execute (query);
   DataRequest.close();
}
```

Designating a Primary Key

A primary key (see Chapter 9) can be designated when a table is created by using the Primary Key modifier, as illustrated in Listing 11-8. This example contains a query that creates a table, as described previously in this chapter, and one column within the table is designated the primary key. You'll remember that the primary key uniquely identifies each row in a table. Therefore, the column or columns chosen as the primary key must have unique values. That is, the column cannot contain duplicate values.

As shown in Listing 11-8, the OrderNumber column is used as the primary key and is identified in the PRIMARY KEY modifier. Once a column is designated as the primary key, the DBMS prevents duplicate and null values from being placed in the column.

Listing 11-8
Designating a
primary key
for a table

```
try {
    String query = "Create Table Orders ( " +
        "OrderNumber CHAR(30) NOT NULL, " +
        "CustomerNumber CHAR(30),   " +
        "ProductNumber CHAR(30), " +
        "CONSTRAINT ORDERS_PK PRIMARY KEY (OrderNumber))";
    DataRequest = Database.createStatement();
    DataRequest. execute(query);
    DataRequest.close();
}
```

Creating a Secondary Index

A secondary index is created by using the CREATE INDEX statement in a query without the use of the UNIQUE modifier. This means that a secondary index can have duplicate values. Listing 11-9 illustrates how to create a secondary index. In this example, the index is called CustZip, and its key is the CustomerZip column of the CustomerAddress table.

Listing 11-9
Creating a
secondary
index

```
try {
    String query = new String ("CREATE INDEX CustZip " +
        "ON CustomerAddress (CustomerZip) ");
    DataRequest = Database.createStatement();
    DataRequest. execute(query);
    DataRequest.close();
}
```

Creating a Clustered Index

A clustered index is an index whose key is created from two or more columns of a table, as you learned in Chapter 5. For example, combining a customer's last name with a customer's first name is a typical key for a clustered index. Listing 11-10 shows how to create a clustered index. This example creates an index called CustName and uses the LastName and FirstName columns of the Customers table as the key for the index.

The order in which column names appear in the ON clause plays a critical role in the index. As you remember from Chapter 5, the value of the second column is concatenated to the value of the first column that appears in the query. This means that the key in this case would be KeoghJim, assuming Jim Keogh is a value in the FirstName and LastName columns of the table. Therefore, the DBMS may not be able to find the search criteria JimKeogh. Of course, this assumes that the DBMS uses the clustered index for the search.

Listing 11-10
Creating a
clustered
index

```
try {
    String query = "CREATE INDEX CustName " +
        " ON Customers (LastName, FirstName)";
    DataRequest = Database.createStatement();
    DataRequest.execute (query);
    DataRequest.close();
}
```

Drop an Index

An existing index can be removed from the database by using the DROP INDEX
statement, which is similar in construction to the DROP TABLE statement discussed
previously in this chapter. Listing 11-11 shows how to create a query that removes
an index. In this example, the CustName index that is associated with the Customers
table is dropped.

Listing 11-11
Dropping
an index

```
try {
    String query = new String("DROP INDEX CustName ON Customers ");
    DataRequest = Database.createStatement();
    DataRequest. execute(query);
    DataRequest.close();
}
```

Inserting Data into Tables

Once a database, tables, and indexes are created, a J2ME application can insert a new
row into a table. In the next several sections of this chapter, you'll learn the technique
for writing a query that inserts data into all or some of the columns of a new row.

As you learned in Chapter 6, the executeUpdate() method is used to execute a query
that inserts a row, among other tasks. The executeUpdate() method does not return a
ResultSet, therefore you should use the Model A program with code segments shown in
sections that insert a row. These code segments insert a row into the Customers table that
is defined below. Make sure you create this table in the CustomerInformation database
using techniques described previously in this chapter before attempting to insert a new row.

- CustomerNumber, number
- FirstName, VARCHAR, 50
- LastName, VARCHAR, 50
- DateOfFirstOrder, date

Insert a Row

The INSERT INTO statement is used to insert a new row into a table. This is illustrated in Listing 11-12. The INSERT INTO statement contains the name of the table into which the row is to be inserted and the name of the columns in which values are inserted. The VALUES clause is used to define the values to be placed into the row.

Although the column names are optional, you should always use column names because it is a bad practice to assume that columns appear in a particular order in the table. The table might be restructured by the database administrator without your knowledge.

Each value is placed in the VALUES clause in the same order as the corresponding column's name. In Listing 11-12, a new row is being inserted into the Customers table. The first value in the VALUES clause is the customer number, followed by the customer's first name, last name, and date of the first order placed by the customer. This is the same order of the columns' names.

You can exclude a value from appearing in a column by excluding the column from the query. For example, you could have removed the LastName column and corresponding value, and the LastName column will be empty for that row. Be careful that you don't exclude a value that is required by the table, otherwise the DBMS rejects the row, causing an exception to be thrown.

Listing 11-12
Inserting a
row into
a table

```
try {
    String query = "INSERT INTO Customers  " +
        " (CustomerNumber, FirstName, LastName, DateOfFirstOrder) " +
        " VALUES (1,'Mary','Smith','10/10/2001') ";
    DataRequest = Database.createStatement();
    DataRequest.executeUpdate (query);
    DataRequest.close();
}
```

Insert the System Date into a Column

Sometimes business rules require that the current date be placed into a column of a new row. For example, the system date is usually used as the date of a new order. You can place the system date into a column by calling the CURRENT_DATE function. This is not implemented in all versions of DBMSs. If you're using Microsoft Access for your DBMS, for example, you use NOW. Oracle uses SYSDATE, and DB2 uses CURRENT DATE (no underscore).

The CURRENT_DATE function directs the DBMS to use the system date of the server as the value for the column. This is illustrated in Listing 11-13. In this example, the CURRENT_DATE function is called to provide the value for the DateOfFirstOrder column in the new row of the Customers table.

Listing 11-13
Inserting the
system date
into a column

```
try {
   String query = new String (
      "INSERT INTO Customers (CustomerNumber ,FirstName, "+
      " LastName, DateOfFirstOrder )" +
      " VALUES ( 4,'Mary','Jones', CURRENT_DATE)");
   DataRequest = Database.createStatement();
   DataRequest.executeUpdate (query );
   DataRequest.close();
}
```

Insert the System Time into a Column

Call the CURRENT_TIME() function whenever a column requires the current time.
The CURRENT_TIME() function is called by the DBMS when the query is processed,
and it returns the current time of the server. Listing 11-14 illustrates how to call the
CURRENT_TIME() function within a query.

A word of caution: Implementation of dates and time functions has not been
standardized among vendors. This means that some or all date and time functions
discussed in this section may not work with all DBMSs. You should consult your database
administrator or DBMS vendor to determine the proper date and time functions to use
with your DBMS.

Listing 11-14
Inserting the
current time
into a column

```
try {
   String query = new String (
      "INSERT INTO Customers (CustomerNumber ,FirstName, "+
      " LastName, TimeOfFirstOrder ) " +
      " VALUES ( 2,'Bob','Jones', CURRENT_TIME() )") ;
   DataRequest = Database.createStatement();
   DataRequest.executeUpdate(query );
   DataRequest.close();
}
```

Insert a Timestamp into a Column

A timestamp consists of both the current date and time and is used in applications where
both date and time are critical to the operation of the business. For example, Wall Street
firms timestamp orders as they arrive because they must correlate with the market price
of stocks at precisely the date and time the order is processed.

A word of caution: Not all DBMSs support timestamps. Therefore, consult your
database administrator or DBMS vendor for comparable functionality if examples in
this section do not work with your DBMS.

You can place the timestamp into a column by calling the TIMESTAMP() function, as illustrated in Listing 11-15. The server's system date and time is returned by the function and placed into the column.

Listing 11-15
Inserting a
timestamp
into a column

```
try {
  String query = new String (
    "INSERT INTO Customers (CustomerNumber ,FirstName, "+
    " LastName, FirstOrder ) " +
    " VALUES ( 2,'Bob','Jones', CURRENT_TIMESTAMP()) )";
  DataRequest = Database.createStatement();
  DataRequest.executeUpdate (query );
  DataRequest.close();
}
```

Selecting Data from a Table

Retrieving information from a database is the most frequently used routine of J2ME components that interact with a database. Some developers feel that retrieving information is one of the most complex routines to write because there are various ways information can be retrieved. The following sections illustrate the various techniques to retrieve data using the executeQuery() method. As you learned in Chapter 6, the executeQuery() method returns a ResultSet. Therefore, you'll need to use the Model B program with these code segments.

Each section contains a try {} block and a DownRow() method, which replace the second try {} block and the DownRow() method in the Model B program, as described previously in this chapter. Code segments illustrated in these sections retrieve data from the Customers table. Here are the columns in the Customers table, which you should create before executing the code segments:

- FirstName, VARCHAR, 50
- LastName, VARCHAR, 50
- Street, VARCHAR, 50
- City, VARCHAR, 50
- State, VARCHAR, 2
- ZipCode, VARCHAR, 12

Make sure that you insert rows into the Customers table before trying to execute code segments that appear in the following sections. Table 11-1 contains rows of data that you can use in the Customers table.

FirstName	LastName	Street	City	State	ZipCode
Bob	Jones	5 First Street	New York City	NY	07555
Mary	Smith	8 Third Street	Dallas	TX	75553
Bob	Jones	5 First Street	New York City	NY	07555
Mark	Russell	3 Sixth Street	Los Angeles	CA	82272
Susan	Allen	18 Fifth Street	Chicago	IL	45003
Mark	Russell	3 Sixth Street	Los Angeles	CA	82272

Table 11-1.   *Sample Entries in a Customers Table for Practice Selecting Data*

Select All Data from a Table

The SELECT statement is used to retrieve data from a table, as illustrated in Listing 11-16. In this example, all the columns of all the rows of the Customers table are returned in the ResultSet by the DBMS after the query is processed.

As you'll see in the next few sections, names of columns that you want retrieved from the table are included in the SELECT statement. The executeQuery() method, which is used to execute the query, returns a ResultSet object. The ResultSet object is passed to the DisplayResults() method, which is defined in the Model B program at the beginning of this chapter. The DisplayResults() method is responsible for moving through the ResultSet and displaying the contents of the ResultSet on the screen.

As you'll recall from the beginning of this chapter, the DisplayResults() method calls the DownRow() method, which extracts data from the current row of the ResultSet and displays the row on the screen. Listing 11-17 contains the DownRow() method for Listing 11-16. In this example, the DownRow() method is passed the ResultSet object from the DisplayResults() method, as described at the beginning of this chapter.

The DownRow() method then declares String objects that are assigned the value of each column in the ResultSet. There is also a String object called printrow, which is assigned all the other String objects and is used to display the values on the screen.

The getString() method is called to gather the value of a specific column in the ResultSet. Using the number of the column (as described in Chapter 6) specifies the column in the getString() method. The getString() method returns the value of the column, which is assigned to a String object. Remember, the getString() method is really the getXXX() method discussed in Chapter 6. The data type of the column replaces the XXX.

Listing 11-16
Selecting all
data from
a table

```
try {
    String query = new String ("SELECT "  +
      " FirstName, LastName, Street, City, State, ZipCode " +
      " FROM Customers");
    DataRequest = Database.createStatement();
    Results = DataRequest.executeQuery (query);
    DisplayResults (Results);
    DataRequest.close();
}
```

Listing 11-17
Copying
values from
the ResultSet

```
private  void DownRow ( ResultSet DisplayResults ) throws SQLException
{
    String FirstName= new String();
    String LastName= new String();
    String Street= new String();
    String City = new String();
    String State = new String();
    String ZipCode= new String();
    String printrow;
    FirstName = DisplayResults.getString ( 1 ) ;
    LastName = DisplayResults.getString ( 2 ) ;
    Street = DisplayResults.getString ( 3 ) ;
    City = DisplayResults.getString ( 4 ) ;
    State = DisplayResults.getString ( 5 ) ;
    ZipCode = DisplayResults.getString ( 6 ) ;
    printrow = FirstName + " " + LastName + " " +
      City + " " + State +  " " + ZipCode;
    System.out.println(printrow);
}
```

Request One Column

You can specify a column that you want returned from the table by using the column name in the SELECT statement, as illustrated in Listing 11-18. In this example, the LastName column of all the rows in the Customers table is returned in the ResultSet. Listing 11-19 contains the DownRow() method that is used to retrieve data from the ResultSet returned by Listing 11-18.

Listing 11-18
Selecting one
column to be
retrieved
from a table

```
try {
    String query = new String ("SELECT LastName FROM Customers");
    DataRequest = Database.createStatement();
    Results = DataRequest.executeQuery (query);
```

```
      DisplayResults (Results);
      DataRequest.close();
   }
```

Listing 11-19
Copying
values from
the ResultSet

```
   private  void DownRow ( ResultSet DisplayResults )throws SQLException
   {
      String LastName= new String();
      LastName = DisplayResults.getString ( 1 ) ;
      System.out.println(LastName);
   }
```

Request Multiple Columns

Multiple columns can be retrieved by specifying the names of the columns in the SELECT statement similar to the way you select one column in Listing 11-18. This is illustrated in Listing 11-20, where the FirstName and LastName columns for all the rows in the Customers table are returned in the ResultSet. Listing 11-21 shows the DownRow() method that is used to copy and display values from the ResultSet.

Listing 11-20
Requesting
multiple
columns to
be retrieved
from a table

```
   try {
      String query = new String (
              "SELECT FirstName, LastName FROM Customers");
      DataRequest = Database.createStatement();
      Results = DataRequest.executeQuery (query);
      DisplayResults (Results);
      DataRequest.close();
   }
```

Listing 11-21
Copying
values from
the ResultSet

```
   private  void DownRow ( ResultSet DisplayResults )throws SQLException
   {
      String FirstName= new String();
      String LastName= new String();
      String printrow;
      FirstName = DisplayResults.getString ( 1 ) ;
      LastName = DisplayResults.getString ( 2 ) ;
      printrow = FirstName + " " + LastName;
      System.out.println(printrow);
   }
```

Request Rows

Specific rows can be retrieved from a column by using the WHERE clause in conjunction with the SELECT statement. The WHERE clause contains an expression that is used by the DBMS to identify rows that should be returned in the ResultSet. Any logical expression can be used to include or exclude rows based on values in columns of a row, which is discussed later in this chapter.

Listing 11-22 illustrates how to use the WHERE clause to retrieve specific rows. In this example, the SELECT statement retrieves all the columns of rows in the Customers table where the LastName column has the value 'Jones'. You can use the DownRow() method in Listing 11-17 to copy and display values in the ResultSet that is returned by Listing 11-22.

Listing 11-22
Selecting particular rows from a table

```
try {
    String query = new String ("SELECT "  +
        " FirstName, LastName, Street, City, State, ZipCode " +
        " FROM Customers " +
        " WHERE LastName = 'Jones' ");
    DataRequest = Database.createStatement();
    Results = DataRequest.executeQuery (query);
    DisplayResults (Results);
    DataRequest.close();
}
```

Request Rows and Columns

A query can select fewer than all the columns and all the rows of a table by using a combination of techniques shown previously in this chapter, as illustrated in Listing 11-23. In this example, the FirstName and LastName of rows in the Customers table are returned in the ResultSet as long as the value of the LastName column is 'Jones'. You can use the DownRow() method shown in Listing 11-21 to copy and display values of the ResultSet returned by Listing 11-23.

Listing 11-23
Retrieving specific columns and rows

```
try {
    String query = new String("SELECT FirstName, LastName " +
        " FROM Customers " +
        " WHERE LastName = 'Jones' ");
    DataRequest = Database.createStatement();
    Results = DataRequest.executeQuery (query);
    DisplayResults (Results);
    DataRequest.close();
}
```

AND, OR, and NOT Clauses

The WHERE clause in a SELECT statement can evaluate values in more than one column of a row by using the AND, OR, and NOT clauses to combine expressions. As you'll learn in the next three sections, compound expressions in the WHERE clause are individually evaluated, and then the results of these evaluations are further evaluated based on the AND, OR, and NOT clauses in the WHERE clause.

For example, the AND clause requires that both expressions in the compound expression evaluate to true before the WHERE clause expression evaluates true and includes a specified row in the ResultSet. The OR clause requires that at least one of the expressions in the compound expression evaluate to true before the WHERE clause expression evaluates true. And the NOT clause is used to reverse the logic, changing an expression that evaluates true to a false. Each of these clauses is illustrated in the next three sections.

AND Clause

The purpose of the AND clause is to join two subexpressions together to form one compound expression. The AND clause tells the DBMS that the boolean value of both subexpressions must be true for the compound expression to be true. If the compound expression is true, the current row being evaluated by the DBMS is returned to your program.

Listing 11-24 illustrates the use of the AND clause in the WHERE clause. In this example, the FirstName and LastName columns of rows from the Customers table are returned in the ResultSet only if the value of the LastName column is 'Jones' and the value of the FirstName column is 'Bob'. You can use the DownRow() method shown in Listing 11-21 to copy and display values of the ResultSet returned by Listing 11-24.

Listing 11-24
Using the AND clause to form a compound expression in the WHERE clause

```
try {
   String query = new String ("SELECT FirstName, LastName " +
      " FROM Customers " +
      " WHERE LastName = 'Jones' " +
      " AND FirstName = 'Bob'");
   DataRequest = Database.createStatement();
   Results = DataRequest.executeQuery (query);
   DisplayResults (Results);
   DataRequest.close();
}
```

OR Clause

The OR clause is used to create a compound expression using two subexpressions in the same way as the AND clause. However, the OR clause tells the DBMS that the compound expression evaluates to a boolean true if either of the two subexpressions evaluates to a boolean true. Listing 11-25 illustrates the use of the OR clause in the WHERE clause. In this example, the FirstName and LastName columns of rows from the Customers table are returned in the ResultSet only if the value of the FirstName column is 'Mary' or 'Bob'. Listing 11-21 contains the DownRow() method that you can use with Listing 11-25.

Listing 11-25
Using the OR clause to form a compound expression in the WHERE clause

```
try {
   String query = new String ("SELECT FirstName, LastName " +
      " FROM Customers " +
      " WHERE FirstName = 'Mary' " +
      " OR FirstName = 'Bob'");
   DataRequest = Database.createStatement();
   Results = DataRequest.executeQuery (query);
   DisplayResults (Results);
   DataRequest.close();
}
```

NOT Clause

The NOT clause reverses the logic of the subexpression contained in the WHERE NOT clause. If the subexpression evaluates to a boolean true, the NOT clause reverses the logic to return a boolean false. In contrast, if the subexpression evaluates to a boolean false, the compound expression evaluates to a boolean true.

Listing 11-26 illustrates the use of the NOT clause. In this example, only rows that don't contain the value 'Mary' in the FirstName column are returned. Listing 11-21 contains the DownRow() method that can be used with Listing 11-26.

Listing 11-26
Using the NOT clause to form a compound expression in the WHERE clause

```
try {
   String query = new String( "SELECT FirstName, LastName " +
      "FROM Customers " +
      "WHERE NOT FirstName = 'Mary' " );
   DataRequest = Database.createStatement();
   Results = DataRequest.executeQuery (query);
   DisplayResults (Results);
   DataRequest.close();
}
```

Join Multiple Compound Expressions

As just discussed, the AND and OR clauses are used to link together two or more subexpressions, which results in a compound expression. There can be multiple compound expressions within a WHERE clause expression.

Let's say that you want information about Bob Smith, but you are unsure whether he is in Department 42 or 45. You can format a query that uses both the AND clause and the OR clause to retrieve this information. Here's how the WHERE clause might be formatted in this scenario. A word of caution: the AND clause has a higher precedence than the OR clause, so the OR clause must be placed within parentheses in this example.

```
WHERE FirstName = 'Bob' AND
      LastName = 'Smith AND (
      Dept = '42' OR Dept = '45')
```

Although the WHERE clause may appear confusing, you can simplify the expression by identifying subexpressions and compound expressions. From reading the previous section, you probably identified the first compound expression and its subexpressions, shown here:

```
FirstName = 'Bob' AND LastName = 'Smith'
```

The second compound expression is

```
Dept = '42' OR Dept = '45'
```

The second AND clause in the WHERE clause links these two compound expressions. You can use the AND, OR, and NOT clauses to create complex selection expressions. The number of compound expressions that you can use in the WHERE clause is practically endless, although some DBMSs establish a limit. This is because of processing time that is necessary to evaluate a complex WHERE clause expression. Contact your database administrator or the manufacturer of your DBMS to determine the limitations of the DBMS that you are using for your system.

Equal and Not Equal Operators

The equal and not equal operators are used to determine whether the value in the WHERE clause expression is or isn't in the specified column. You've been using the equal operator throughout examples in this chapter. The next section illustrates the use of the not equal operator.

Before running the query in the next section, modify the Customers table by inserting a Sales column. The Sales column is a long data type. After making the modification, place values in the Sales column of the Customers table as shown in Table 11-2.

Not Equal Operator

The not equal operator is used in a WHERE clause expression or subexpression to identify rows that should not be returned by the DBMS. Listing 11-27 illustrates the use of the

FirstName	LastName	Street	City	State	ZipCode	Sales
Bob	Jones	5 First Street	New York City	null	07555	50000
Mary	Smith	8 Third Street	Dallas	TX	75553	20000
Bob	Jones	5 First Street	New York City	null	07555	50000
Mark	Russell	3 Sixth Street	Los Angeles	null	82272	30000
Susan	Allen	18 Fifth Street	Chicago	IL	45003	40000
Mark	Russell	3 Sixth Street	Los Angeles	CA	82272	30000

Table 11-2.   *Sales Column Added to the Customers Table in Table 11-1*

not equal operator. In this example, all columns of rows in the Customers table are returned where the values in the Sales column are not equal to 50000. Listing 11-28 contains the DownRow() method that is used to copy and display values in the ResultSet.

Listing 11-27
Excluding rows from the ResultSet using the not equal operator

```
try {
   String query = new String ("SELECT   " +
      "FirstName, LastName, Street, City, State, ZipCode, Sales " +
      "FROM Customers " +
      "WHERE NOT Sales = 50000 " );
   DataRequest = Database.createStatement();
   Results = DataRequest.executeQuery (query);
   DisplayResults (Results);
   DataRequest.close();
   Database.close();
}
```

Listing 11-28
Copying values from the ResultSet

```
private  void DownRow ( ResultSet DisplayResults )throws SQLException
{
   String FirstName= new String();
   String LastName= new String();
   String Street= new String();
   String City = new String();
   String State = new String();
   String ZipCode= new String();
   long Sales;
   String printrow;
   FirstName = DisplayResults.getString ( 1 ) ;
```

```
    LastName = DisplayResults.getString ( 2 ) ;
    Street = DisplayResults.getString ( 3 ) ;
    City = DisplayResults.getString ( 4 ) ;
    State = DisplayResults.getString ( 5 ) ;
    ZipCode = DisplayResults.getString ( 6 ) ;
    Sales = DisplayResults.getLong ( 7 ) ;
    printrow = FirstName + " " + LastName + " " +
      City + " " + State +  " " + ZipCode + " " + Sales;
    System.out.println(printrow);
}
```

Less Than and Greater Than Operators

The less than and greater than operators direct the DBMS to assess whether or not the value in the specified column of the current row is less than or greater than the value in the WHERE clause expression. Keep in mind that a value in a column that equals the value in the WHERE clause expression is evaluated as a boolean false. Therefore the row containing that value isn't returned in the ResultSet. The value in the column must be less than or greater than but not equal to the value in the WHERE clause expression.

Less Than Operator

Listing 11-29 illustrates the less than operator in the WHERE clause. In this example, all the columns of rows from the Customers table are returned as long as the value of the Sales column is less than 50000. Listing 11-28 contains the DownRow() method that should be used to copy and display the ResultSet returned by Listing 11-29.

Listing 11-29
Using the less than operator in the WHERE clause expression

```
try {
   String query = new String ("SELECT   " +
     "FirstName, LastName, Street, City, State, ZipCode, Sales " +
     " FROM Customers " +
     " WHERE Sales < 50000 " );
   DataRequest = Database.createStatement();
   Results = DataRequest.executeQuery (query);
   DisplayResults (Results);
   DataRequest.close();
}
```

Greater Than Operator

The greater than operator is similar to the less than operator, except the value in the column must be greater than the value in the WHERE clause expression for the row to be returned in the ResultSet. Listing 11-30 illustrates the use of the greater than operator.

In this example, all the columns of rows in the Customers table are returned in the ResultSet if the value of the Sales column is greater than 40000. Listing 11-28 contains the DownRow() method that should be used to copy and display the ResultSet returned by Listing 11-30.

Listing 11-30
Using the greater than operator in the WHERE clause expression

```
try {
   String query = new String ("SELECT   " +
      "FirstName, LastName, Street, City, State, ZipCode, Sales " +
      "FROM Customers " +
      "WHERE Sales > 40000 " );
   DataRequest = Database.createStatement();
   Results = DataRequest.executeQuery (query);
   DisplayResults (Results);
   DataRequest.close();
}
```

Less Than or Equal to and Greater Than or Equal To

A drawback of using the less than and greater than operators is that rows containing the value of the WHERE clause expression are not returned in the ResultSet. Alternatively, the less than or equal to and the greater than or equal to operators can be used to include rows that contain the WHERE clause expression. This is illustrated in the next two sections.

Less Than or Equal To

Listing 11-31 illustrates how to use the less than or equal to operator in the WHERE clause. In this example, all columns of rows in the Customers table are returned if the value of the Sales column of the row is less than or equal to 50000. Listing 11-28 contains the DownRow() method that should be used to copy and display the ResultSet returned by Listing 11-31.

Listing 11-31
Using the less than or equal to operator in the WHERE clause expression

```
try {
   String query = new String ("SELECT   " +
      "FirstName, LastName, Street, City, State, ZipCode, Sales " +
      "FROM Customers " +
      "WHERE Sales <= 50000 " );
   DataRequest = Database.createStatement();
   Results = DataRequest.executeQuery (query);
   DisplayResults (Results);
   DataRequest.close();
}
```

Greater Than or Equal To

As illustrated in Listing 11-32, the greater than or equal to operator is similar to the less than or equal to operator. In this example, all the columns in rows of the Customers table are returned in the ResultSet if the value of the Sales column in the row is greater than or equal to 50000. Listing 11-28 contains the DownRow() method that should be used to copy and display the ResultSet returned by Listing 11-32.

Listing 11-32
Using the greater than or equal to operator in the WHERE clause expression

```
try {
   String query = new String ("SELECT   " +
     "FirstName, LastName, Street, City, State, ZipCode, Sales " +
     "FROM Customers " +
     "WHERE Sales >= 50000 ");
   DataRequest = Database.createStatement();
   Results = DataRequest.executeQuery (query);
   DisplayResults (Results);
   DataRequest.close();
}
```

Between Operator

The BETWEEN operator is used to define a range of values to be used as the value of the selection expression. The range must consist of a sequential series of values, such as 100 to 200. The BETWEEN operator must follow the name of the column in the WHERE clause. The AND operator is used to join the lower and upper values of the range. All values in the range, including the first and last values, are considered when the DBMS evaluates the value of the column specified in the selection expression.

Listing 11-33 illustrates the use of the BETWEEN operator. In this example, all the columns in rows of the Customers table are returned in the ResultSet if the value of the Sales column in the row is between 20000 and 39999.

Listing 11-28 contains the DownRow() method that should be used to copy and display the ResultSet returned by Listing 11-33.

Listing 11-33
Using the BETWEEN operator in the WHERE clause expression

```
try {
   String query = new String("SELECT   " +
     "FirstName, LastName, Street, City, State, ZipCode, Sales " +
     "FROM Customers " +
     "WHERE Sales BETWEEN 20000 AND 39999 " );
   DataRequest = Database.createStatement();
   Results = DataRequest.executeQuery (query);
   DisplayResults (Results);
   DataRequest.close();
}
```

J2ME DATA MANAGEMENT

LIKE Operator

The LIKE operator directs the DBMS to return a row in the ResultSet if a value in a specified column partially matches the value of the WHERE clause expression. The WHERE clause expression must include a character that is an exact match and a wildcard character that is used to match any other character.

A word of caution: the LIKE operator is convenient and powerful, but it also uses a lot of database overhead and therefore should be used with discretion.

Here are the wildcards that are used with the LIKE operator:

■ **Underscore (_)** A single-character wildcard character. For example, if you are unsure whether the customer's last name is Anderson or Andersen, use the underscore in place of the character that is in question, as in Anders_n.

■ **Percent (%)** A multicharacter wildcard character used to match any number of characters. For example, Smi% is used to match a value of a column where the first three characters are Smi followed by any other character(s).

Listing 11-34 illustrates the use of the LIKE operator. In this example, all the columns in rows of the Customers table are returned in the ResultSet if the value of the LastName column in the row has the first three characters Smi and any other characters. Listing 11-28 contains the DownRow() method that should be used to copy and display the ResultSet returned by Listing 11-34.

Listing 11-34
Using the LIKE operator in the WHERE clause expression

```
try {
    String query = new String ("SELECT    " +
        "FirstName, LastName, Street, City, State, ZipCode, Sales " +
        "FROM Customers " +
        "WHERE LastName LIKE 'Smi%' ");
    DataRequest = Database.createStatement();
    Results = DataRequest.executeQuery (query);
    DisplayResults (Results);
    DataRequest.close();
}
```

IS NULL Operator

The IS NULL operator is used to determine whether a specified column does not contain any value. You'll find this useful whenever you need to identify rows in a column that are missing information.

Note that the number zero or a space are not NULL values. For example, a zero value in the Sales column of a table is a real value. Likewise, a column that contains a space isn't NULL because a space is a valid ASCII character. NULL is void of any value and occurs when a row is inserted into a table without having a value, or the value is explicitly set to NULL.

Listing 11-35 illustrates the use of the IS NULL operator. In this example, all the columns in rows of the Customers table are returned in the ResultSet if the value of the State column in the row is NULL. Listing 11-28 contains the DownRow() method that should be used to copy and display the ResultSet returned by Listing 11-35.

Listing 11-35
Using the
IS NULL
operator in
the WHERE
clause
expression

```
try {
    String query = new String ("SELECT  " +
        "FirstName, LastName, Street, City, State, ZipCode, Sales " +
        "FROM Customers " +
        "WHERE State IS NULL ");
    DataRequest = Database.createStatement();
    Results = DataRequest.executeQuery (query);
    DisplayResults (Results);
    DataRequest.close();
}
```

DISTINCT Modifier

The SELECT statement returns all rows in a table unless a WHERE clause is used to exclude specific rows. However, the ResultSet includes duplicate rows unless a primary index is created for the table or only unique rows are required in the table, as you learned previously in this chapter.

There will be occasions when you want to exclude all but one copy of a row from the ResultSet. You can do this by using the DISTINCT modifier in the SELECT statement, as illustrated in Listing 11-36. The DISTINCT modifier tells the DBMS not to include duplicate rows in the ResultSet. You'll find this useful whenever data from multiple sources is combined into one table, as in a mailing list. The DISTINCT modifier filters duplicate rows that contain the same name and address.

A word of caution: This technique requires a lot of system overhead and therefore should be used with discretion. An alternative approach is to write a WHERE clause expression that returns the same results as using the DISTINCT modifier.

In this example, all the columns in rows of the Customers table are returned in the ResultSet exclusive of duplicate rows. Listing 11-28 contains the DownRow() method that should be used to copy and display the ResultSet returned by Listing 11-36.

Listing 11-36
Using the
DISTINCT
modifier

```
try {
    String query = new String ("SELECT DISTINCT  " +
        "FirstName, LastName, Street, City, State, ZipCode, Sales " +
        "FROM Customers ");
    DataRequest = Database.createStatement();
    Results = DataRequest.executeQuery (query);
    DisplayResults (Results);
    DataRequest.close();
}
```

J2ME
DATA MANAGEMENT

IN Modifier

The IN modifier is used to define a set of values used by the DBMS to match values in a specified column. The set can include any number of values and appear in any order. Let's say that you want a list of customers who purchase three products. You place the three product identification numbers in a set; then tell the DBMS to search the order table for orders containing the product numbers in the set. If the product numbers match, customer information associated with the row is returned to your program.

The IN modifier is used in the WHERE clause to define the list of values in the set. This is demonstrated in Listing 11-37, where the DBMS is told to compare values in the Sales column with the three values in the group clause. If any of these three values are found in the Sales column of the current row, the row is returned to the program. Listing 11-28 contains the DownRow() method that should be used to copy and display the ResultSet returned by Listing 11-37.

Listing 11-37
Using the IN modifier in the WHERE clause

```
try {
    String query = new String ("SELECT  " +
      "FirstName, LastName, Street, City, State, ZipCode, Sales " +
      " FROM Customers " +
      " WHERE Sales IN (20000, 30000, 40000) " );
    DataRequest = Database.createStatement();
    Results = DataRequest.executeQuery (query);
    DisplayResults (Results);
    DataRequest.close();
}
```

NOT IN Modifier

The NOT IN modifier is similar to the IN modifier, except the NOT IN modifier reverses the logic. That is, it identifies a set of values that shouldn't match rows returned to the program. Listing 11-38 shows how the NOT IN modifier is used in a program. In this example, all columns of rows in the Customers table where the value of the Sales column isn't 20000, 30000, or 40000 are returned in the ResultSet. Rows with sales of 20000, 30000, or 40000 are not returned. Listing 11-28 contains the DownRow() method that should be used to copy and display the ResultSet returned by Listing 11-38.

Listing 11-38
Using the IN modifier in the WHERE clause

```
try {
    String query = new String ("SELECT " +
      "FirstName, LastName, Street, City, State, ZipCode, Sales " +
      " FROM Customers " +
      " WHERE Sales NOT IN (20000, 30000, 40000) " );
    DataRequest = Database.createStatement();
    Results = DataRequest.executeQuery (query);
```

```
    DisplayResults (Results);
    DataRequest.close();
}
```

Metadata

Metadata is data that describes data, which you learned about in Chapter 6. Metadata is returned with the ResultSet object and can be extracted from the ResultSet object by creating a ResultSetMetaData. Techniques for doing this are described in the next several sections of this chapter. Metadata can be used in a J2ME application for various purposes, such as to display the column name of a column and determine the data type of a column. The most commonly used metadata are

- Column name
- Column number
- Column data type
- Column width

Number of Columns in ResultSet

Listing 11-39 contains the DownRow() method that illustrates how to determine the number of columns in the ResultSet. The getMetaData() method is called to extract metadata from the ResultSet. The getMetaData() method returns a ResultSetMetaData object, which is called metadata in this example.

The ResultSetMetaData object contains several methods that are used to copy specific metadata from the ResultSet. In this example, the getColumnCount() method is called to retrieve the number of columns contained in the result set, which is then assigned to the NumberOfColumns variable and printed on the screen using the println() method. (This doesn't work with all drivers.)

The DownRow() method in Listing 11-39 can replace the DownRow() method in the Model B program and be used in any version of the Model B program presented in this chapter. Of course, the DownRow() method must be modified to copy and display data contained in the ResultSet, as shown previously in this chapter.

Listing 11-39
Determining
the number
of columns in
a ResultSet

```
private  void DownRow ( ResultSet DisplayResults )throws SQLException
{
    ResultSetMetaData metadata = DisplayResults.getMetaData ();
    int NumberOfColumns;
    String printrow;
    NumberOfColumns = metadata.getColumnCount ();
    System.out.println("Number Of Columns: " + NumberOfColumns);
}
```

Data Type of Column

Listing 11-40 illustrates how to determine the data type of a column. You'll notice that this technique is very similar to the technique for retrieving the number of columns in the ResultSet described in the previous section. In this example the getColumnTypeName() method is called to copy the data type from column nine of the result set to the ColumnType object. Any valid column number in the ResultSet can be passed to the getColumnTypeName() method. You can use the data type returned by the getColumnTypeName() method to determine the proper getXXX() method to use to copy data from the ResultSet. The type is returned as the native type, not the SQL type.

Listing 11-40
Determining
the data type
of columns in
a ResultSet

```
private  void DownRow ( ResultSet DisplayResults ) throws SQLException
{
  ResultSetMetaData metadata = DisplayResults.getMetaData ();
  String ColumnType = new String();
  String printrow;
  ColumnType = metadata.getColumnTypeName ( 9 );
  System.out.println("Column Type: " + ColumnType );
}
```

Name of Column

Retrieving the column name from the metadata uses a process similar to copying the data type of a column from the metadata. In the example in Listing 11-41, the getColumnLabel() method is used to copy the column name from a specific column and assign the column name to the String object ColumnName. The number of the column in the ResultSet is passed to the getColumnLabel() method.

Listing 11-41
Determining
the names of
columns in a
ResultSet

```
private  void DownRow ( ResultSet DisplayResults ) throws SQLException
{
  ResultSetMetaData metadata = DisplayResults.getMetaData ();
  String ColumnName = new String();
  String printrow;
  ColumnName = metadata.getColumnLabel (9) ;
  System.out.println("Column Name: " + ColumnName);
}
```

Column Size

The column size, also referred to as the column width, is called the display size and represents the number of characters needed to display the maximum value that might be stored in the column.

You retrieve the display size by using the getColumnDisplaySize( ) method, as illustrated in Listing 11-42. This listing is similar to the others in the metadata sections. The getColumnDisplaySize( ) is called and passed the number of the column whose display size is to be retrieved from the ResultSet. The display size is then shown on the screen.

Listing 11-42
Determining the width of columns in a ResultSet

```
private  void DownRow ( ResultSet DisplayResults ) throws SQLException
{
  ResultSetMetaData metadata = DisplayResults.getMetaData ();
  int ColumnWidth;
  String printrow;
  ColumnWidth = metadata.getColumnDisplaySize ( 9 ) ;
  System.out.println("Column Width:" + ColumnWidth);
}
```

Updating Tables

Modifying data in a database is one of the most common functionalities in every J2ME application that provides database interactions. Generally, any information that is retrievable is also changeable depending on access rights and data integrity issues, which are discussed in Chapter 5. The next several sections illustrate techniques for updating rows in a table of a database. Code segments described in these sections use the executeUpdate() method to process queries. As you recall from Chapter 6, the executeUpdate() method does not return a ResultSet. Therefore, the Model A program described earlier in this chapter should be used with code segments in these sections.

Before executing code segments presented in these sections, you'll need to create a Customers table, as defined here, and then insert the rows of data shown in Table 11-3.

- FirstName, VARCHAR, 50
- LastName, VARCHAR, 50
- Street, VARCHAR, 50
- City, VARCHAR, 50
- State, VARCHAR, 2
- ZipCode, VARCHAR, 12
- Discount, long

Update Row and Column

The UPDATE statement is used to change the value of one or more columns in one or multiple rows of a table. The UPDATE statement must contain the name of the table that is to be updated and a SET clause. The SET clause identifies the name of the column and the new value that will be placed into the column, overriding the current value. The UPDATE statement may have a WHERE clause if a specific number of rows are to be updated. If the WHERE clause is omitted, all rows are updated based on the value of the SET clause.

FirstName	LastName	Street	City	State	Zip	Discount
Bob	Jones	5 First Street	New York City	NY	07555	10
Mary	Smith	8 Third Street	Dallas	TX	75553	20
Tom	Jones	5 First Street	New York City	NY	07555	11
Mark	Russell	23 Eighth Street	Los Angeles	CA	82272	16
Susan	Allen	18 Fifth Street	Chicago	IL	45003	15
Kelly	Russell	32 Fourth Street	Los Angeles	CA	82272	15

Table 11-3. *Discount Column Added to the Customers Table in Table 11-1*

Listing 11-43 illustrates how to update one column. In this example, the value of the Street column of the Customers table is changed to '5 Main Street'. However, the change occurs only where the value of the FirstName column is 'Bob'.

Listing 11-43
Updating
a row and
column

```
try {
    String query = new String("UPDATE Customers " +
        "SET Street = '5 Main Street' " +
        " WHERE FirstName = 'Bob'");
    DataRequest = Database.createStatement();
    DataRequest.executeUpdate (query);
    DataRequest.close();
}
```

Update Multiple Rows

Multiple rows of a table can be updated by formatting the WHERE clause expressions to include criteria that qualify multiple rows for the update. Four common WHERE clause expressions are used to update multiple rows of a table:

- **The IN test** The WHERE clause expression contains multiple values in the IN clause that must match the value in the specified column for the update to occur in the row.

- **The IS NULL test** Rows that don't have a value in the specified column are updated when the IS NULL operator is used in the WHERE clause expression.

- **The comparison test** The WHERE clause expression contains a comparison operator, as described previously in this chapter, that compares the value in the specified column with a value in the WHERE clause expression.

■ **All rows**   A query can direct the DBMS to update the specified column in all
rows of a table by excluding the WHERE clause in the query.

Always be cautious whenever you execute a query that updates multiple rows because
the query has the potential to affect all the information contained in a table. An error in
a query is multiplied by the number of rows in a table whenever the query updates more
than one row.

IN Test

The IN clause provides two or more values that are compared to the value of the
designated column in the IN clause. Rows whose columns contain one of these values
are updated by the UPDATE statement. Listing 11-44 illustrates how the IN test is used
to update rows of the Customers table. In this example, the value of the Discount column
is changed to 25 if the current value of the Discount column is either 12 or 15.

Listing 11-44
Updating
a row using
the IN test

```
try {
   String query = new String ("UPDATE Customers " +
      "SET Discount = 25 " +
      "WHERE Discount IN (12,15)");
   DataRequest = Database.createStatement();
   DataRequest.executeUpdate (query);
   DataRequest.close();
}
```

IS NULL Test

The IS NULL test evaluates the value of a column designated in the test to determine
whether the column is NULL—that is, the column is empty of any value. If so, the IS
NULL test returns a true, and the UPDATE statement updates the column specified in
the SET clause. Listing 11-45 illustrates how to use the IS NULL test in the UPDATE
statement. In this example, the IS NULL test determines whether the LastName column
is NULL. If so, a zero is placed in the Discount column. If not, the value of the Discount
column remains unchanged.

Listing 11-45
Updating a
row using the
IS NULL test

```
try {
   String query = new String ("UPDATE Customers " +
      "SET Discount = 0 " +
      "WHERE LastName IS NULL  ");
   DataRequest = Database.createStatement();
   DataRequest.executeUpdate (query);
   DataRequest.close();
}
```

Update Based on Values in Column

An expression in the WHERE clause can be used to identify rows that are to be updated by the UPDATE statement. All of the WHERE clause expressions discussed previously in the SELECT statement also apply to the UPDATE statement. Review the section "Selecting Data from a Table" for details on how to properly formulate the WHERE clause expression.

Listing 11-46 illustrates how to identify a row to update. In this example, rows in the Customers table that have a Discount greater than 20 will have the value of the Discount changed to 20.

Listing 11-46
Updating a
row based on
a value in a
designated
column

```
try {
   String query = new String ("UPDATE Customers " +
     "SET Discount = 20 " +
     "WHERE Discount > 20 ");
   DataRequest = Database.createStatement();
   DataRequest.executeUpdate (query);
   DataRequest.close();
}
```

Update Every Row

All rows in a table can be updated by excluding the WHERE clause in the UPDATE statement. This technique is illustrated in Listing 11-47. In this example, the value of the Discount column in all rows in the Customers table is changed to zero.

Listing 11-47
Updating
every row in
the table

```
try {
   String query = new String ("UPDATE Customers " +
     "SET Discount = 0 ");
   DataRequest = Database.createStatement();
   DataRequest.executeUpdate (query);
   DataRequest.close();
}
```

Update Multiple Columns

Multiple columns of rows can be updated simultaneously by specifying the column names and appropriate values in the SET clause of the query. Listing 11-48 illustrates this technique. In this example, rows in the Customers table where the LastName column has the value 'Jones' are updated. The SET clause contains the column names and the new values that override the current values of those columns. In this case, the value of the Discount column is changed to 12, and the value of the Street column is changed to 'Jones Street'.

Listing 11-48
Updating
multiple
columns of a
table

```
try {
   String query = new String ("UPDATE Customers " +
      "SET Discount = 12, Street = 'Jones Street'" +
      "WHERE LastName = 'Jones'");
   DataRequest = Database.createStatement();
   DataRequest.executeUpdate (query);
   DataRequest.close();
}
```

Update Using Calculations

The value that replaces the current value in a column does not have to be explicitly defined in the SET clause if the value can be derived from a value in another column of the same row. Let's say that a row contains the retail price of an item purchased by a customer. The customer is granted a percentage discount based on how well the customer is valued by the business. The UPDATE statement can calculate the discounted price and place it in the DiscountPrice column of the row. The value of the discount price doesn't need to be included in the SET clause. Instead, the discount price can be calculated.

Listing 11-49 illustrates how to use the results of a calculation to update a value of a column in a table. In this example, the value placed in the DiscountPrice column is calculated by using values in the Price column and in the Discount column. The results of this calculation override the current value in the DiscountPrice column.

Before running this query, you'll need to create a new Customers table or modify the existing Customers table to reflect the following columns. You'll also need to insert data shown in Table 11-4 into the Customers table.

- FirstName, VARCHAR, 50
- LastName, VARCHAR, 50
- Street, VARCHAR, 50

FirstName	LastName	Street	City	State	Zip	Discount	Price
Bob	Jones	5 First Street	New York City	NY	07555	10	100
Mary	Smith	8 Third Street	Dallas	TX	75553	20	200
Tom	Jones	5 First Street	New York City	NY	07555	20	300
Mark	Russell	23 Eighth Street	Los Angeles	CA	82272	10	400
Susan	Allen	18 Fifth Street	Chicago	IL	45003	15	500
Kelly	Russell	32 Fourth Street	Los Angeles	CA	82272	15	600

Table 11-4. *Price Column Added to the Customers Table in Table 11-2*

J2ME
DATA MANAGEMENT

- City, VARCHAR, 50
- State, VARCHAR, 2
- ZipCode, VARCHAR, 12
- Discount, long
- Price, long
- DiscountPrice, long

Listing 11-49
Updating a
column using
a calculation

```
try {
  String query = new String ("UPDATE Customers " +
    "SET DiscountPrice = Price * ((100 - Discount) / 100) ");
  DataRequest = Database.createStatement();
  DataRequest.executeUpdate (query);
  DataRequest.close();
}
```

Deleting Data from a Table

Deleting rows is necessary to purge erroneous information from the database and to remove information that is no longer needed. However, you must build in safeguards to assure that critical information isn't inadvertently deleted from the database. Before you delete a row from a table, you must be certain that other tables are not negatively affected. The next section illustrates the technique for removing a row from a table by using the DELETE FROM statement. Multiple rows can be deleted by including a WHERE clause in the DELETE FROM statement, as described in detail in the "Updating Tables" section of this chapter.

The query that contains the DELETE FROM statement is executed using the executeQuery() method. As you learned in Chapter 10, the executeQuery() method doesn't return a ResultSet. Therefore, use the Model A program with the code segment described in the next section.

Delete a Row from a Table

The DELETE FROM statement includes the name of the table and a WHERE clause containing an expression that identifies the row or rows to remove from the table. Listing 11-50 illustrates how to use the DELETE FROM statement. In this example, rows in which the value of the LastName column is 'Jones' and the value of the FirstName column is 'Tom' will be deleted from the Customers table. Make sure you have a row that contains these values in the Customers table before running this code segment.

Listing 11-50
Deleting
a row

```
try {
    String query = new String ("DELETE FROM Customers " +
```

```
    "WHERE LastName = 'Jones' and FirstName = 'Tom'");
  DataRequest = Database.createStatement();
  DataRequest.executeUpdate (query);
  DataRequest.close();
}
```

Joining Tables

In Chapter 9 you learned about normalization and how rows of data elements that are placed in tables are related to each other by linking rows using a common value in each row of two tables. Linking rows is called joining tables. Tables are joined in a query using a two-step process. First, both tables that are being joined must be identified in the FROM clause, where tables are listed one after the other and are separated by a comma.

Next, an expression is created in the WHERE clause that identifies the columns used to create the join. Let's say that an Orders table is joined to the Customers table using the customer number. The customer number in the Orders table is in the CustomerNumber column, and the customer number in the Customers table is the CustNum column. The following line contains a WHERE clause expression that joins these tables:

```
WHERE CustomerNumber = CustNum
```

The joined tables create a logical table that has all the columns of both tables. All the tasks performed on a single table (as covered previously in this chapter) can also be applied to joined tables.

Joining too many tables can cause performance degradation and bring response time to a crawl. Typically, five is the maximum number of tables joined. However, the actual number may vary depending on the DBMS, so consult with your database administrator or DBMS manufacturer for the maximum number of tables permitted to be joined using your DBMS.

Before you try examples in this section, you'll need to create a Customers table, ZipCode table, Store table, Products table, and Orders table. These tables are defined below. Insert the rows described in Table 11-5 through Table 11-9 into the appropriate tables before running code segments described in the following sections.

Define the Customers table as follows:

- CustNumber, number, primary key
- FirstName, VARCHAR, 50
- LastName, VARCHAR, 50
- Street, VARCHAR, 50
- Zip, VARCHAR, 12

CustNumber	FirstName	LastName	Street	Zip
591	Anne	Smith	65 Cutter Street	04735
721	Bart	Adams	15 W. Spruce	05213
845	Tom	Jones	35 Pine Street	07660
901	Mary	Smith	5 Maple Street	08513

Table 11-5. *Sample Customers Table for Practice Joining Tables*

ZipCode	City	State
04735	Woodridge	TX
05213	River Ville	CA
07660	West Town	NJ
08513	SunnySide	NY

Table 11-6. *Sample ZipCode Table for Practice Joining Tables*

StoreNumber	ZipCode
278	08513
345	07660
547	05213
825	04735

Table 11-7. *Sample Store Table for Practice Joining Tables*

ProductNumber	ProductName	Unit Price
1052	CD Player	100
3255	VCR	250
5237	DVD Player	325
7466	50-inch TV	532

Table 11-8.   *Sample Products Table for Practice Joining Tables*

Define the ZipCode table as follows:

- ZipCode, VARCHAR, 12, primary key
- City, VARCHAR, 50
- State, VARCHAR, 2

Define the Store table as follows:

- StoreNumber, number, primary key
- ZipCode, VARCHAR, 12

OrderNumber	ProdNumber	CustomerNumber	StoreNumber	Quantity	SubTotal
122	5237	591	345	1	325
334	3255	901	278	1	250
365	3255	901	278	4	1000
534	7466	591	825	3	1596
587	5237	845	345	1	325
717	1052	721	825	2	200
874	7466	721	825	1	532

Table 11-9.   *Sample Orders Table for Practice Joining Tables*

J2ME DATA MANAGEMENT

Define the Products table as follows:

- ProductNumber, number, primary key
- ProductName, VARCHAR, 50
- UnitPrice, long

Define the Orders table as follows:

- OrderNumber, number, primary key
- ProdNumber, number
- CustomerNumber, number
- StoreNumber, number
- Quantity, number
- SubTotal, long

Join Two Tables

Listing 11-51 illustrates the technique used to join two tables. In this example, the Customers table and the ZipCode table are identified in the FROM clause. These are the tables that are being joined.

The WHERE clause expression identifies the Zip column from the Customers table and the ZipCode column from the ZipCode table. The equal operator directs the DBMS to join rows in both the Customers table and the ZipCode table where values of the Zip column and the ZipCode column match. Rows whose columns don't match are excluded from the join (see "Inner and Outer Joins" later in this chapter). If both columns used for the join have the same name, then a column name qualifier is used to associate the column with each table, which is discussed later in this chapter. It's usually considered good practice always to use a table name or alias.

Once the Customers and ZipCode tables are joined, the SELECT statement references column names of both tables to be returned in the ResultSet. In this example, City, State, and ZipCode columns are in the ZipCode table, and the FirstName and LastName columns are in the Customers table.

Listing 11-51 uses the executeQuery() method to execute the query. Therefore, you'll need to use the Model B program to run this example. Listing 11-52 contains the DownRow() method that extracts and displays data from the ResultSet.

Listing 11-51
Joining two tables

```
try {
  String query = new String (
    "SELECT FirstName, LastName, City, State, ZipCode " +
    "FROM Customers, ZipCode " +
    "WHERE Zip = ZipCode");
```

```
    DataRequest = Database.createStatement();
    Results = DataRequest.executeQuery (query);
    DisplayResults (Results);
    DataRequest.close();
}
```

Listing 11-52
The
DownRow()
method used
when joining
two tables

```
private  void DownRow ( ResultSet DisplayResults )
     throws SQLException
{
  String FirstName= new String();
  String LastName= new String();
  String Street= new String();
  String City = new String();
  String State = new String();
  String ZipCode= new String();
  String printrow;
  FirstName = DisplayResults.getString ( 1 ) ;
  LastName = DisplayResults.getString ( 2 ) ;
  Street = DisplayResults.getString ( 3 ) ;
  City = DisplayResults.getString ( 4 ) ;
  State = DisplayResults.getString ( 5 ) ;
  ZipCode = DisplayResults.getString ( 6 ) ;
  printrow = FirstName + " " + LastName + " " +
    City + " " + State +  " " + ZipCode + " " + Sales + " " + Profit;
  System.out.println(printrow);
}
```

Parent-Child Join

A parent-child join is used to join tables that have a parent-child relationship. This means rows in the parent table must exist for rows in the child table to exist, which is illustrated in Listing 11-53. In this example, the Products table and Orders table are joined using the product number value. Only rows that have a matching product number in both tables are placed in the virtual table that consists of rows from both tables. The Products table is the parent table in this relationship because an order cannot be placed without a product appearing in the Products table. Basically, a customer cannot order a product that doesn't exist in the Products table.

Listing 11-53 is executed using the executeQuery() method and therefore returns a ResultSet. This means that you must use the Model B program to run this code segment. Listing 11-54 contains the DownRow() method that retrieves and displays values from the ResultSet.

Listing 11-53
The parent-
child join

```
try {
    String query = new String (" SELECT OrderNumber, ProductName " +
```

```
             " FROM Orders, Products " +
             " WHERE ProdNumber = ProductNumber");
          DataRequest = Database.createStatement();
          Results = DataRequest.executeQuery (query);
          DisplayResults (Results);
          DataRequest.close();
       }
```

```
private  void DownRow ( ResultSet DisplayResults )
       throws SQLException
  {
     int OrderNum, ProdNum;
     String printrow = new String();
     OrderNum = DisplayResults.getInt ( 1 ) ;
     ProdNum = DisplayResults. getInt ( 2 ) ;
     printrow = OrderNum + " " + ProdNum;
     System.out.println(printrow);
  }
```

Multiple Comparison Join

The WHERE clause expression used to join tables can be a compound expression consisting of two or more subexpressions. Each is evaluated separately, as described previously in this chapter. A compound expression is used to specify more than one selection criteria used to join two tables, which is illustrated in Listing 11-55. In this example, the DBMS is directed to join rows of the Products table and rows of the Orders table. There are two components of the subexpression in this example. The first requires the DBMS to match product numbers in both tables. The other subexpression requires that the value in the Quantity column is greater than 2.

The AND operator is used to join both subexpressions. This means that both subexpressions must evaluate true for the DBMS to join rows of both tables. That is, only when the product number matches in both tables and the quantity of the order is greater than 2 will a row be included in the temporary table. If either subexpression evaluates false, the row is not included in the virtual table.

Listing 11-55 is executed using the executeQuery() method and therefore returns a ResultSet. This means that you must use the Model B program to run this code segment. Listing 11-56 contains the DownRow() method that retrieves and displays values from the ResultSet.

```
try {
   String query = " SELECT OrderNumber, ProductName, Quantity " +
      " FROM Orders, Products " +
```

```
   " WHERE ProdNumber = ProductNumber " +
   " AND Quantity > 2";
DataRequest = Database.createStatement();
Results = DataRequest.executeQuery (query);
DisplayResults (Results);
DataRequest.close();
}
```

Listing 11-56
The
DownRow()
method used
with a
multiple
comparison
join

```
private  void DownRow ( ResultSet DisplayResults )
    throws SQLException
{
  int OrderNum, ProdNum, Quantity;
  String printrow = new String();
  OrderNum = DisplayResults.getInt ( 1 ) ;
  ProdNum = DisplayResults. getInt ( 2 ) ;
  Quantity = DisplayResults. getInt ( 3 ) ;
  printrow = OrderNum + " " + ProdNum + " " + Quantity;
  System.out.println(printrow);
}
```

Multitable Join

More than two tables can be joined together by using the name of each table in the join in the FROM clause and by defining the join with the appropriate column names in the WHERE clause expression. Listing 11-57 shows you how to create a multitable join. There are three tables joined in this example—Customers, Orders, and Products, as shown in the WHERE clause.

Notice that all three tables don't need to have a common value used to join them. Each pair of tables has a value common to both of them. Customer numbers that are common between the tables join the Customers table and the Orders table. The Orders table and the Products table are joined by the product number.

You'll need to use the Model B program with this code segment because a ResultSet is returned. Listing 11-58 contains the DownRow() method to use to retrieve and display values in the ResultSet.

Listing 11-57
The multiple
table join

```
try {
   String query = new String (
     "SELECT FirstName, LastName,OrderNumber, ProductName, Quantity " +
     " FROM Customers, Orders, Products " +
```

```
                    " WHERE ProdNumber = ProductNumber " +
                    " AND CustNumber = CustomerNumber");
                DataRequest = Database.createStatement();
                Results = DataRequest.executeQuery (query);
                DisplayResults (Results);
                DataRequest.close();
            }
```

Listing 11-58
The
DownRow()
method
used with
a multiple
table join

```
private  void DownRow ( ResultSet DisplayResults )
        throws SQLException
    {
      int OrderNum, Quantity;
      String FirstName = new String();
      String LastName = new String();
      String ProductName = new String();
      String printrow = new String();
      FirstName = DisplayResults.getString ( 1 ) ;
      LastName = DisplayResults.getString ( 2 ) ;
      OrderNum = DisplayResults.getInt ( 3 ) ;
      ProductName = DisplayResults.getString ( 4 ) ;
      Quantity = DisplayResults. getInt ( 5 ) ;
      printrow = FirstName + " " +
                 LastName + " " +
                 OrderNum + " " +
                 ProductName + " " +
                 Quantity ;
      System.out.println(printrow);
    }
```

Create a Column Name Qualifier

Column names should reflect the kind of data element stored in the column, as you learned in Chapter 5. However, there is likely to be a conflict when two or more tables use the same column name to store the data element. This is the case when both the Products table and the Orders table contain product numbers.

Conflict of column names can be resolved in a join by using a column name qualifier, which identifies the table that contains the column name. Listing 11-59 illustrates how to use a column name qualifier. In this example assume that the Customers table and the Orders table both have a column called CustomerName. Therefore, the name of the CustomerName column must be prefaced with the name of the table.

Listing 11-59 returns a ResultSet. The DownRow() method shown in Listing 11-60 is used along with the Model B program to copy and display values from the ResultSet.

Listing 11-59
Creating a
column name
qualifier

```
try {
   String query = new String ("SELECT Customers.CustNumber, " +
      " FirstName, LastName, OrderNumber, " +
      " ProductName, Quantity " +
      " FROM Customers, Orders, Products " +
      " WHERE ProdNumber = ProductNumber " +
      " AND Customers.CustomerNumber = Orders.CustomerNumber");
   DataRequest = Database.createStatement();
   Results = DataRequest.executeQuery (query);
   DisplayResults (Results);
   DataRequest.close();
}
```

Listing 11-60
The
DownRow()
method
used with a
column name
qualifier

```
private  void DownRow ( ResultSet DisplayResults )
    throws SQLException
{
   int CustomerNumber, OrderNum, Quantity;
   String FirstName = new String();
   String LastName = new String();
   String ProductName = new String();
   String printrow = new String();
   CustomerNumber = DisplayResults. getInt ( 1 ) ;
   FirstName = DisplayResults.getString ( 2 ) ;
   LastName = DisplayResults.getString ( 3 ) ;
   OrderNum = DisplayResults.getInt ( 4 ) ;
   ProductName = DisplayResults.getString ( 5 ) ;
   Quantity = DisplayResults. getInt ( 6 ) ;
   printrow = CustomerNumber + " " +
              FirstName + " " +
              LastName + " " +
              OrderNum + " " +
              ProductName + " " +
              Quantity ;
   System.out.println(printrow);
}
```

Create a Table Alias

A query can be made readable by using table aliases. A table alias is an abbreviation for
the name of the table that is used in place of the table name in the join and in the SELECT
statement. Listing 11-61 shows you how to create and use a table alias in a query. Following

each table name in the FROM clause is a letter used as the table alias. The table alias is used in place of the table name in the column name qualifier.

Any letter or combination of letters can be used as a table alias, but you should make the table alias:

- With as few letters as possible to save space in the query string

- Representative of the table name, such as the first letter(s) of the name

- Unique and not a duplicate of another table name, table alias, or column name

The DownRow() method shown previously in Listing 11-60 is used with Listing 11-61 to extract and display values of the ResultSet.

Listing 11-61
Creating a
table alias

```
try {
   String query = new String ("SELECT c.CustNumber , " +
      " c.FirstName, c.LastName, o.OrderNumber, " +
      " p.ProductName, o.Quantity " +
      " FROM Customers c, Orders o, Products  p" +
      " WHERE o.ProdNumber = p.ProductNumber " +
      " AND c.CustomerNumber = o.CustomerNumber");
   DataRequest = Database.createStatement();
   Results = DataRequest.executeQuery (query);
   DisplayResults (Results);
   DataRequest.close();
}
```

Inner and Outer Joins

The joins shown in previous sections of this chapter link rows that have matching values in the column specified in the join. A row in a table that doesn't match is excluded from the join. There are two kinds of joins, each of which either excludes or includes rows in both tables of the join that don't match. These are

- An *inner join* excludes rows of either table that don't have a matching value.

- An *outer join* includes rows of either table that don't have a matching value.

The following sections discuss each type of join in detail. However, some DBMSs may use their own syntax rather than the SQL syntax for some or all joins. Therefore, consult with your database administrator or DBMS manufacturer for the proper syntax for joins if examples in this book don't work with your DBMS. Code segments used in these sections are executed using the executeQuery() method. Therefore, you'll need to use the Model B program. Remember that joins can also be used with the UPDATE and DELETE statements, in which case the Model A program is used.

Inner Join

Joins discussed previously in this chapter use an inner join to include only rows of both tables that have matching values. Unmatched rows are excluded, and therefore those rows are not returned in the ResultSet.

Listing 11-62 demonstrates the use of an inner join by joining the Orders table and the Products table using product number and joining the Orders table and the Customers table using the customer number. Listing 11-63 contains the DownRow() method used with Listing 11-62 to copy and display the contents of the ResultSet.

```
try {
    String query = new String (" SELECT FirstName, LastName, OrderNumber,
ProductName, Quantity " +
        " FROM Customers,Orders, Products " +
        " WHERE ProdNumber = ProductNumber " +
        " AND Customers.CustNumber = Orders.CustomerNumber");
    DataRequest = Database.createStatement();
    Results = DataRequest.executeQuery (query);
    DisplayResults (Results);
    DataRequest.close();
}
```

```
private  void DownRow ( ResultSet DisplayResults )
    throws SQLException
{
    int OrderNum, Quantity;
    String FirstName = new String();
    String LastName = new String();
    String ProductName = new String();
    String printrow = new String();
    FirstName = DisplayResults.getString ( 1 ) ;
    LastName = DisplayResults.getString ( 2 ) ;
    OrderNum = DisplayResults.getInt ( 3 ) ;
    ProductName = DisplayResults.getString ( 4 ) ;
    Quantity = DisplayResults. getInt ( 5 ) ;
    printrow = FirstName + " " +
            LastName + " " +
            OrderNum + " " +
            ProductName + " " +
            Quantity ;
    System.out.println(printrow);
}
```

Outer Join—Left, Right, Full

An outer join occurs when matching and nonmatching rows of either or both tables are contained in the join. There are three kinds of outer joins:

Left outer join	All matched and unmatched rows of the first table and matched rows of the second table are included in the join.
Right outer join	Matched rows of the first table and matched and unmatched rows of the second table are included in the join.
Full outer join	Matched and unmatched rows of both tables are included in the join.

Left Outer Join   Listing 11-64 shows how to create a left outer join. This example creates a join between the Customers table and the Orders table using the customer number. The *= operator is used in the WHERE clause to create a left outer join. Think of the asterisk as a wildcard that tells the DBMS to use any row in the first table.

Before running Listing 11-64, insert the row shown in Table 11-10 into the Orders table; otherwise there will not be unmatched rows, because all the rows in both tables currently have matching values. Listing 11-65 contains the DownRow() method used with Listing 11-64.

```
try {
   String query = new String (
     " SELECT FirstName, LastName,OrderNumber " +
     "  FROM Customers LEFT JOIN Orders " +
     "  ON Customers.CustNumber = Orders.CustomerNumber");
   DataRequest = Database.createStatement();
   Results = DataRequest.executeQuery (query);
   DisplayResults (Results);
   DataRequest.close();
}
```

```
private  void DownRow ( ResultSet DisplayResults )
     throws SQLException
{
   int, OrderNum;
   String FirstName = new String();
   String LastName = new String();
   String printrow = new String();
   FirstName = DisplayResults.getString ( 1 ) ;
   LastName = DisplayResults.getString ( 2 ) ;
```

```
    OrderNum = DisplayResults.getInt ( 3 ) ;
    printrow = FirstName + " " + LastName + " " + OrderNum;
    System.out.println(printrow);
}
```

Right Outer Join   Listing 11-66 illustrates how to create a right outer join. In this example the Customers table and the Orders table are joined using the customer number. All rows in the Orders table are used in the join regardless of whether the customer number in the Orders table has a corresponding customer number in the Customers table. The WHERE clause contains the right outer join operator (=*), which, as you can see, has the asterisk positioned to the right instead of the left of the equivalent operator.

Before running Listing 11-66, insert the row shown in Table 11-11 into the Orders table; otherwise there will not be unmatched rows, because all the rows in both tables currently have matching values. Listing 11-65 contains the DownRow() method used with Listing 11-66.

Listing 11-66
Creating
a right
outer join

```
try {
   String query = new String (
      " SELECT FirstName, LastName,OrderNumber" +
      " FROM Customers c, Orders o" +
      " WHERE c.CustNumber =* o.CustomerNumber");
   DataRequest = Database.createStatement();
   Results = DataRequest.executeQuery (query);
   DisplayResults (Results);
   DataRequest.close();
}
```

Full Outer Join   A full outer join uses all the rows of both tables regardless of whether they match. Listing 11-67 shows how to create a full outer join. The full outer join operator (*=*) is a combination of the left and right outer join operators, although some DBMSs uses FULL JOIN or other syntax to create a full join. Consult with your database

OrderNumber	ProdNumber	CustomerNumber	StoreNumber	Quantity	SubTotal
733	7466	999	825	1	532

Table 11-10.   *Add These Values to the Orders Table in Table 11-9 to Perform a Left Outer Join.*

OrderNumber	ProdNumber	CustomerNumber	StoreNumber	Quantity	SubTotal
555	1052	999	278	14	1400

Table 11-11.   *Add These Values to the Orders Table in Table 11-9 to Perform a Right Outer Join.*

administrator or the DBMS manufacturer for the syntax used by your DBMS. Listing 11-65 contains the DownRow() method that is used with Listing 11-67.

Listing 11-67
Creating a
full outer join

```
try {
  String query = new String(
    " SELECT FirstName, LastName,OrderNumber " +
    " FROM Customers c, Orders o" +
    " WHERE c.CustNumber *=* o.CustomerNumber");
  DataRequest = Database.createStatement();
  Results = DataRequest.executeQuery (query);
  DisplayResults (Results);
  DataRequest.close();
}
```

Calculating Data

The DBMS can calculate values in a table and return the result of the calculation in the ResultSet by using one of the five built-in calculation functions:

- SUM() tallies values in a column passed to the built-in function.
- AVG() averages values in a column passed to the built-in function.
- MIN() determines the minimum value in a column passed to the built-in function.
- MAX() determines the maximum value in a column passed to the built-in function.
- COUNT() determines the number of rows in a column passed to the built-in function.

The following sections discuss each built-in function and give examples. Before you try the examples, you'll need to create an Orders table, Sales table, and Customers table. These tables are defined next. Insert the rows described in Table 11-12, Table 11-13, and Table 11-14 into the appropriate tables before running code segments described in the following sections of this chapter.

OrderNumber	ProdNumber	CustomerNumber	StoreNumber	Quantity	SubTotal
122	5237	591	345	1	325
334	3255	901	278	1	250
365	3255	901	278	4	1000
534	7466	591	825	3	1596
587	5237	845	345	1	325
717	1052	721	825	2	200
874	7466	721	825	1	532

Table 11-12.   *Sample Entries in an Orders Table for Practice Calculating Data*

StoreNumber	Sales	Estimate
6245	500	450
8644	650	700

Table 11-13.   *Sample Entries in a Sales Table for Practice Calculating Data*

CustNumber	FirstName	LastName	Street	Zip
591	Anne	Smith	65 Cutter Street	04735
721	Bart	Adams	15 W. Spruce	05213
845	Tom	Jones	35 Pine Street	07660
901	Mary	Smith	5 Maple Street	08513

Table 11-14.   *Sample Entries in a Customers Table for Practice Calculating Data*

J2ME
DATA MANAGEMENT

Define the Orders table as follows:

- OrderNumber, number, primary key
- ProdNumber, number
- CustomerNumber, number
- StoreNumber, number
- Quantity, number
- SubTotal, long

Define the Sales table as follows:

- StoreNumber, number, primary key
- Sales, number
- Estimate, number

Define the Customers table as follows:

- CustNumber, number, primary key
- FirstName, VARCHAR
- LastName, VARCHAR
- Street, VARCHAR
- Zip, VARCHAR

SUM()

The SUM() built-in function calculates the sum of the values in the column that is passed to the function. Listing 11-68 illustrates how to use the SUM() built-in function. In this example, values in the Quantity column in the Orders table are passed to the SUM() built-in function.

Listing 11-68 uses the executeQuery() method to execute the query. Therefore, the Model B program should be used with this listing. Listing 11-69 contains the DownRow() method that is used with Listing 11-68.

Listing 11-68
Determining the sum of values in a column

```
try {
    String query = new String ("SELECT SUM(Quantity) " +
        "FROM Orders ");
    DataRequest = Database.createStatement();
    Results = DataRequest.executeQuery (query);
    DisplayResults (Results);
```

```
      DataRequest.close();
}
```

```
private  void DownRow ( ResultSet DisplayResults )
     throws SQLException
{
  long ReturnValue;
  ReturnValue = DisplayResults.getLong ( 1 ) ;
  System.out.println(ReturnValue);
}
```

AVG()

The AVG() built-in function calculates the average value in the column passed to the function. The average is returned in the ResultSet. Listing 11-70 illustrates how to use the AVG() built-in function to calculate the average of the values in the Quantity column of the Orders table. This code segment is used with the Model B program, and Listing 11-69 contains the DownRow() method to retrieve and display the average from the ResultSet.

```
try {
   String query = new String ("SELECT AVG(Quantity) " +
     "FROM Orders ");
   DataRequest = Database.createStatement();
   Results = DataRequest.executeQuery (query);
   DisplayResults (Results);
   DataRequest.close();
}
```

MIN()

The MIN() built-in function returns the lowest value contained in the column passed to the function. Listing 11-71 shows how to use the MIN() built-in function to determine the minimum value in the Quantity column of the Orders table. This code segment is used with the Model B program, and Listing 11-69 contains the DownRow() method to retrieve and display the minimum value from the ResultSet.

```
try {
   String query = new String ("SELECT MIN(Quantity) " +
     "FROM Orders ");
   DataRequest = Database.createStatement();
   Results = DataRequest.executeQuery (query);
```

J2ME
DATA MANAGEMENT

```
      DisplayResults (Results);
      DataRequest.close();
   }
```

MAX()

The MAX() built-in function returns the highest value contained in the column passed to the built-in function. Listing 11-72 shows how to use the MAX() built-in function to determine the maximum value in the Quantity column of the Orders table. This code segment is used with the Model B program, and Listing 11-69 contains the DownRow() method to retrieve and display the value from the ResultSet.

Listing 11-72
Determining the maximum value in a column

```
try {
   String query = new String ("SELECT MAX(Quantity) " +
      "FROM Orders ");
   DataRequest = Database.createStatement();
   Results = DataRequest.executeQuery (query);
   DisplayResults (Results);
   DataRequest.close();
}
```

COUNT()

Counting the number of rows or values in a table is a common calculation. The COUNT() built-in function returns the number of rows in a column. Listing 11-73 uses the COUNT() built-in function to determine the number of values that appear in the Quantity column of the Orders table. The result is returned in the ResultSet. Rows without values in the column are excluded from the count. This means the value returned does not necessarily represent the total number of rows in the table.

This code segment is used with the Model B program, and Listing 11-69 contains the DownRow() method to retrieve and display the value from the ResultSet.

Listing 11-73
Counting the number of values in a column

```
try {
   String query = new String ("SELECT COUNT(Quantity) " +
      "FROM Orders ");
   DataRequest = Database.createStatement();
   Results = DataRequest.executeQuery (query);
   DisplayResults (Results);
   DataRequest.close();
}
```

Count All Rows in a Table

The COUNT() built-in function is also used to return the number of rows in a table. This is accomplished by passing the COUNT() built-in function an asterisk rather than the name of a column. Listing 11-74 illustrates this technique. This code segment is used with the Model B program, and Listing 11-69 contains the DownRow() method to retrieve and display the value from the ResultSet.

Listing 11-74
Counting the number of rows

```
try {
    String query = new String ("SELECT COUNT(*) " +
        "FROM Orders ");
    DataRequest = Database.createStatement();
    Results = DataRequest.executeQuery (query);
    DisplayResults (Results);
    DataRequest.close();
}
```

Retrieve Multiple Counts

Multiple counts can be returned in the ResultSet by using more than one COUNT() built-in function in the SELECT statement. This is illustrated in Listing 11-75, where the ResultSet contains the total number of rows in the Orders table and the number of rows from the Orders table that contain values in the Quantity column.

This code segment is used with the Model B program, and Listing 11-76 contains the DownRow() method to retrieve and display values from the ResultSet.

Listing 11-75
Retrieving multiple counts

```
try {
    String query = new String ("SELECT COUNT(*), COUNT(Quantity) " +
        "FROM Orders ");
    DataRequest = Database.createStatement();
    Results = DataRequest.executeQuery (query);
    DisplayResults (Results);
    DataRequest.close();
}
```

Listing 11-76
The DownRow() method used with multiple calls to the COUNT() built-in function

```
private  void DownRow ( ResultSet DisplayResults )
    throws SQLException
{
    long TotalRows, TotalValues;
    TotalRows = DisplayResults.getLong ( 1 ) ;
    TotalValues = DisplayResults.getLong ( 2 ) ;
    System.out.println(
        "Rows: " + TotalRows + "\nValues: " +
```

```
                    TotalValues);
    }
```

Calculate a Subset of Rows

You can restrict the scope of a built-in calculation function by using a WHERE clause expression to specify the criteria for a row to be included in a calculation. Any valid WHERE clause expression can be used to filter rows to be excluded from the calculation. Likewise, the WHERE clause expression is used to include rows in the calculation. WHERE clause expressions are discussed earlier in this chapter.

Listing 11-77 illustrates how to restrict the scope of a built-in calculation function by using a WHERE clause expression. In this example, the DBMS is told to count the number of values in the OrderNumber column of the Orders table and to average and total the value of the Quantity column of the Orders table. The WHERE clause contains an expression that joins the Customers table and the Orders table using the customer number as the common value between these tables. This means the calculations are performed only on rows that are in the join. Rows whose customer numbers don't appear in both the Customers table and Orders table are excluded from the calculations.

This code segment is used with the Model B program, and Listing 11-78 contains the DownRow() method to retrieve and display values from the ResultSet.

Listing 11-77
Calculating a subset of rows

```
try {
   String query = new String (
      " SELECT COUNT(OrderNumber), AVG(Quantity),   SUM(Quantity) " +
      " FROM Orders o, customers c " +
      " WHERE o.CustomerNumber = c.CustNumber");
   DataRequest = Database.createStatement();
   Results = DataRequest.executeQuery (query);
   DisplayResults (Results);
   DataRequest.close();
   }
```

Listing 11-78
The DownRow() method used when calculating a subset of rows

```
private  void DownRow ( ResultSet DisplayResults )
    throws SQLException
{
  long Orders;
  long Average;
  long Sum;
  Orders = DisplayResults.getLong ( 1 ) ;
  Average = DisplayResults.getLong ( 2 ) ;
  Sum = DisplayResults.getLong ( 3 ) ;
  System.out.println("Total Orders = " + Orders);
  System.out.println("Average Qty  = " + Average);
```

```
      System.out.println("Total Qty  = " + Sum);
   }
```

NULLs and Duplicates

Two common problems that occur when using built-in functions are columns that don't contain a value and rows that contain duplicate values in the same column. Many times you don't want empty columns and duplicate rows included in the calculation.

You can use the DISTINCT modifier to exclude duplicate rows from the calculation. Likewise, problems posed by NULL columns can be avoided by using the IS NULL operator along with the NOT operator in a selection expression. Both of these are discussed earlier in this chapter.

Calculate Without Using Built-in Functions

Although built-in calculation functions are very useful, the DBMS can perform calculations that are defined in the SELECT statement. Listing 11-79 illustrates how to do this. In this example, the DBMS is directed to return to the program the value of the StoreNumber column and the difference between the value in the Sales column and the value in the Estimate column. Neither the Sales column nor the Estimate column data is returned. Instead, only the difference between these two columns is returned. Any arithmetic expression can be used in the SELECT statement along with the appropriate names of columns that contain data elements used in the calculation.

This code segment is used with the Model B program, and Listing 11-80 contains the DownRow() method to retrieve and display values from the ResultSet.

Listing 11-79
Calculating without built-in functions

```
try {
   String query = new String (
     " SELECT StoreNumber, Sales - Estimate " +
     " FROM Sales ");
   DataRequest = Database.createStatement();
   Results = DataRequest.executeQuery (query);
   DisplayResults (Results);
   DataRequest.close();
}
```

Listing 11-80
The DownRow() method used when calculating without built-in functions

```
private  void DownRow ( ResultSet DisplayResults )
     throws SQLException
{
   String Store;
   long Difference;
   Store = DisplayResults.getString ( 1 ) ;
   Difference = DisplayResults.getLong ( 2 ) ;
```

```
    System.out.println("Store = " + Store);
    System.out.println("Difference = " + Difference);
}
```

Grouping and Ordering Data

Columns are returned in the ResultSet in the order that the column names appear in the SELECT statement of the query. The order in which rows appear in the ResultSet can be grouped into similar values or sorted in ascending or descending order by using the GROUP BY clause or the ORDER BY clause, which are discussed in the next few sections of this chapter.

Grouping is the task of organizing rows of data according to similar values within the same column. Let's say that you want to see sales for each store. The ResultSet can be grouped by store number.

Sorting is the task of organizing rows of data in either alphabetical or numerical order according to the value of a column in the result set. A DBMS is capable of creating simple and complex sorting. A simple sort is when the values in a single column are used for the sort. A complex sort is when multiple columns are used for the sort, such as sorting rows by last name and within last names, by first names.

Code segments in the following sections return a ResultSet, therefore the Model B program should be used to execute these code segments. Before executing them, create a Sales table as defined below; then insert rows of data contained in Table 11-15 into the Sales table.

StoreNumber	Sales	Estimate	SalesRepNumber
123	300	200	4
223	450	500	3
123	322	200	4
345	56	30	8
345	125	100	5
223	76	50	2
345	200	156	5

Table 11-15. *Sample Entries in a Sales Table for Practice with Grouping and Sorting Data*

Define the Sales table as follows:

- StoreNumber, number, primary key
- Sales, number
- Estimate, number
- SalesRepNumber, number

GROUP BY

The GROUP BY clause specifies the name of the column whose values are used to group rows in the ResultSet. Listing 11-81 illustrates this technique. In this example, the StoreNumber column and the sum of the values in the Sales column from the Sales table are returned.

The GROUP BY clause organizes the ResultSet by the value in the StoreNumber column. This means that the ResultSet contains the sum of the Sales column for each StoreNumber. Listing 11-82 contains the DownRow() method that is used to retrieve and display values from the ResultSet.

Listing 11-81
Grouping the
ResultSet

```
try {
    String query = new String (" SELECT StoreNumber, SUM(Sales) " +
        " FROM Sales " +
        " Group By StoreNumber");
    DataRequest = Database.createStatement();
    Results = DataRequest.executeQuery (query);
    System.out.println("Store     Sales");
    System.out.println("-----     -----");
    DisplayResults (Results);
    DataRequest.close();
}
```

Listing 11-82
The
DownRow()
method
used when
grouping the
ResultSet

```
private  void DownRow ( ResultSet DisplayResults )
    throws SQLException
{
    long Store;
    long Sum;
    Store = DisplayResults.getLong ( 1 ) ;
    Sum = DisplayResults.getLong ( 2 ) ;
    System.out.println(Store + "          " + Sum);
}
```

Group Multiple Columns

The DBMS can create a subgroup within a group in the ResultSet. For example, the business unit may want to see orders organized by store, and within each store, orders are organized by product. A subgroup is created by placing the name of the column used for the subgroup as the second column name in the GROUP BY clause of the query. Any number of subgroups can be created, depending on the limitations established by the manufacturer of the DBMS used by your program. Column names in the GROUP BY clause must be separated with a comma.

Listing 11-83 illustrates how to create a subgroup. In this example, the ResultSet is grouped by store number, and within each store number group, a subgroup is created using the sales representative number. Listing 11-84 contains the DownRow() method that is used to retrieve and display values from the ResultSet.

Listing 11-83
Creating groupings and subgroupings in the ResultSet

```
try {
   String query = new String (
      " SELECT StoreNumber,SalesRepNumber, SUM(Sales) " +
      " FROM Sales " +
      " Group By StoreNumber, SalesRepNumber");
   DataRequest = Database.createStatement();
   Results = DataRequest.executeQuery (query);
   System.out.println("Store   SalesRep    Sales");
   System.out.println("-----   --------    -----");
   DisplayResults (Results);
   DataRequest.close();
}
```

Listing 11-84
The DownRow() method used when grouping and subgrouping the ResultSet

```
private  void DownRow ( ResultSet DisplayResults )
      throws SQLException
{
   long StoreNumber;
   long SalesRepNumber;
   long Sum;
   StoreNumber = DisplayResults.getLong ( 1 ) ;
   SalesRepNumber = DisplayResults.getLong ( 2 ) ;
   Sum = DisplayResults.getLong ( 3 ) ;
   System.out.println(
             StoreNumber + "          " +
             SalesRepNumber + "          " +
             Sum);
}
```

Conditional Grouping

The number of rows that are included in a group can be limited by a conditional expression in the query. A conditional expression is similar to the WHERE clause expression discussed previously in this chapter. The DBMS uses the conditional expression to qualify whether or not the current row should be included in any group of the ResultSet. Only rows that meet the condition are returned. A row that doesn't meet the condition is excluded. The conditional expression is placed in the HAVING clause of the query. The HAVING clause sets the criteria for a row to be included in a group.

Listing 11-85 demonstrates the use of the HAVING clause in a query. In this example, the value of the StoreNumber column and the total sales for each store from the Sales table are grouped by store number. The HAVING clause excludes from the group, stores that have total sales of less than $401. Listing 11-86 contains the DownRow() method used to retrieve and display values in the ResultSet.

Here are the requirements for using a conditional expression in the HAVING clause:

- The expression must result in a single value.
- The result must appear in every column named in the expression.
- The expression can include a built-in calculation function.

Listing 11-85
Conditional grouping in the ResultSet

```
try {
   String query = new String ("SELECT StoreNumber, SUM(Sales) " +
      " FROM Sales " +
      " Group By StoreNumber" +
      " HAVING SUM(Sales) > 400");
   DataRequest = Database.createStatement();
   Results = DataRequest.executeQuery (query);
   System.out.println("Store  Sales");
   System.out.println("-----   -----");
   DisplayResults (Results);
   DataRequest.close();
}
```

Listing 11-86
The DownRow() method used with conditional grouping in the ResultSet

```
private  void DownRow ( ResultSet DisplayResults )
    throws SQLException
{
  long StoreNumber;
  long Sum;
  StoreNumber = DisplayResults.getLong ( 1 ) ;
  Sum = DisplayResults.getLong ( 2 ) ;
  System.out.println(StoreNumber + "           " + Sum);
}
```

Working with NULL Columns

Empty columns can create unexpected results when you execute a query. This is because, depending on the nature of the query, the empty column may be included or excluded from the operation. As you learned previously in this chapter, the DBMS includes empty columns when calculating average values and counting rows, but excludes empty columns when calculating the minimum or maximum value within a column.

The DBMS may include or exclude a row in a group depending on the conditional expression. Here's how this works:

■ A row is included in a group if the empty column isn't used to group rows or used in the conditional expression in the HAVING clause.

■ A row is excluded from the group if the empty column is used in the conditional expression and the conditional expression normally excludes empty columns from the calculation (as with MIN(), MAX()).

■ A row is included in the group if the empty column is used in the conditional expression and the conditional expression normally includes empty columns from the calculation (as with AVG(), COUNT()).

■ A row is included in the group if the empty column is used to group rows. Rows containing the empty column are placed in their own group.

Sorting Data

The ResultSet can be placed in alphabetical or numerical order by using the ORDER BY clause in the query. Listing 11-87 shows how to use the ORDER BY clause. In this example, values in the StoreNumber column and values in the Sales column from the Sales table are returned in the ResultSet. The ORDER BY clause specifies the StoreNumber column, which sorts the value of the StoreNumber column in ascending numerical order. Listing 11-88 contains the DownRow() method that is used to retrieve and display values from the ResultSet.

Listing 11-87
Sorting the
ResultSet

```
try {
    String query = new String ("SELECT StoreNumber, Sales " +
      " FROM Sales " +
      " ORDER BY StoreNumber");
    DataRequest = Database.createStatement ();
    Results = DataRequest.executeQuery (query);
    System.out.println("Store   Sales");
    System.out.println("-----   -----");
    DisplayResults (Results);
    DataRequest.close ();
}
```

Listing 11-88
The
DownRow()
method used
when sorting
the ResultSet

```
private  void DownRow ( ResultSet DisplayResults )
    throws SQLException
{
  long StoreNumber;
  long Sales;
  StoreNumber = DisplayResults.getLong ( 1 ) ;
  Sales = DisplayResults.getLong ( 2 ) ;
  System.out.println(StoreNumber + "          " + Sales);
}
```

Major and Minor Sort Keys

You can create a sort within a sort by specifying more than one column to be sorted, such as sorting rows by customer last name, and then within last name, sorting by customer first name. The first column specified in the ORDER BY clause is called the *major sort key* and is the initial value used to sort rows. The second and subsequent columns in the ORDER BY clause are called *minor sort keys*. A comma must separate each column name.

Listing 11-89 illustrates how to sort the ResultSet using major and minor sort keys. In this example, the StoreNumber column and Sales column from the Sales table are returned in the ResultSet. The ORDER BY clause sorts the ResultSet by values in the StoreNumber column. Within each StoreNumber value, the value in the Sales column is sorted. Both sorts are ascending numerical sorts. Listing 11-88 contains the DownRow() method that is used to retrieve and display the ResultSet returned by Listing 11-89.

Listing 11-89
Sorting the
ResultSet
using major
and minor
sort keys

```
try {
  String query = new String ("SELECT  StoreNumber, Sales " +
    " FROM Sales " +
    " ORDER BY StoreNumber, Sales");
  DataRequest = Database.createStatement();
  Results = DataRequest.executeQuery (query);
  System.out.println("Store  Sales");
  System.out.println("-----   -----");
  DisplayResults (Results);
  DataRequest.close();
}
```

Descending Sort

In addition to choosing the column to sort, you can also select the direction of the sort by using the ASC or DESC modifier. Listing 11-90 shows how to use the DESC modifier in the ORDER BY clause to specify a descending sort. By default the sort is ascending, although you can use the ASC modifier to explicitly direct that the sort be in ascending order.

The ASC or DESC modifier must appear after the column name in the ORDER BY clause, as illustrated in this example. The ASC or DESC modifier can be used for major and minor sort keys. Listing 11-88 contains the DownRow() method that is used to retrieve and display the ResultSet returned by Listing 11-90.

```
try {
    String query = new String ("SELECT StoreNumber, Sales "
      " FROM Sales " +
      " ORDER BY StoreNumber DESC ");
    DataRequest = Database.createStatement();
    Results = DataRequest.executeQuery (query);
    System.out.println("Store   Sales");
    System.out.println("-----   -----");
    DisplayResults (Results);
    DataRequest.close();
}
```

Sorting on Derived Data

Data that doesn't exist in a table, but comes from the data in a table, such as a calculation (as discussed previously), is derived data. As illustrated in Listing 11-91, placing a calculation in the SELECT statement creates derived data. Listing 11-91 returns the store number and the difference between the value in the Sales column and the value in the Estimate column from the Sales table. The difference is derived data.

Derived data doesn't have a column name. This means that you cannot include a column name in the ORDER BY clause to designate the derived data as the major or minor sort key for the sort. However, you can use the column number of derived data in place of a column name to sort the derived data. The column number of derived data corresponds to the position of the derived data in the SELECT statement.

In this example, the calculation expression that produces the derived data is the second data referenced in the SELECT statement. Therefore, the derived data appears in the second column of the ResultSet. Use 2 in place of the column name in the ORDER BY clause. Listing 11-88 contains the DownRow() method that is used to retrieve and display the ResultSet returned by Listing 11-91.

```
try {
    String query = new String (
      " SELECT StoreNumber, (Sales-Estimate) " +
      " FROM Sales " +
      " ORDER BY 2 ");
    DataRequest = Database.createStatement();
    Results = DataRequest.executeQuery (query);
    System.out.println("Store   Sales");
```

```
     System.out.println("-----   -----");
     DisplayResults (Results);
     DataRequest.close();
}
```

Subqueries

In the real world, you'll find that you need to create complex queries that do more than simply request columns from the database. Instead, you might request columns based on the result of another query. You can direct the DBMS to query the result of a query by creating a subquery. A subquery joins two queries to form one complex query, which efficiently identifies data to be included in the ResultSet.

The format of a subquery is similar to a query, but rows that are selected as a result of the subquery are not returned to your program. Instead, selected rows are queried by another query. Rows chosen by the second query are returned in the ResultSet.

Both queries and subqueries have a SELECT statement and a FROM clause and can also include a WHERE clause and HAVING clause to qualify rows to return. The WHERE clause and HAVING clause are used to express a condition that must be met for a row to be included in the result set.

There are also differences between a query and a subquery. The most noticeable difference is with the ResultSet. The ResultSet of a query is returned to the J2ME component. In contrast, the result set of a subquery is returned to a temporary table, which is then used by a query or another subquery to further extract rows. This means the J2ME application never sees the result of a subquery. Instead, the subquery result is an intermediate step working toward the final selection of data from the database.

You must follow two rules when using a subquery in your program:

- *Return one column from the subquery.* The purpose of a subquery is to derive a list of information from which a query can choose appropriate rows. Only a single column needs to be included in the list.

- *Don't sort or group the result from a subquery.* Since the ResultSet of the subquery isn't going to be returned in the ResultSet of the query, there is no need to sort or group data in the ResultSet of a subquery.

The next several sections illustrate how to create a subquery. These sections can be run using the Model B program, as described previously in this chapter. Before attempting to run these code segments, create the following tables and insert rows shown in Table 11-16 and Table 11-17.

Define the Sales table as follows:

- StoreNumber, number, primary key
- Estimate, number
- SalesRepNumber, number

StoreNumber	Estimate	SalesRepNumber
345	200	4
278	500	3
825	200	2

Table 11-16. *Sample Entries in a Sales Table for Practice with Subqueries*

Define the Orders table as follows:

- OrderNumber, number, primary key
- ProdNumber, number
- CustomerNumber, number
- StoreNum, number
- Amount, number

Create a Subquery

A subquery is a query whose results are evaluated by an expression in the WHERE clause of another query, as illustrated in Listing 11-92. In this example, the subquery is defined below the first WHERE clause. The subquery joins rows of the Sales table and the Order table by store number value, as shown in the second WHERE clause. Once joined, the

OrderNumber	ProdNumber	CustomerNumber	StoreNum	Amount
122	5237	591	345	200
334	3255	901	278	321
365	3255	901	278	433
534	7466	591	825	523
555	1052	999	278	23
717	1052	721	825	75
874	7466	721	825	354

Table 11-17. *Sample Entries in an Orders Table for Practice with Subqueries*

subquery totals the value of the Amount column for each store number and returns the results to a temporary table.

The query then returns a ResultSet that contains store numbers where the value of the Estimate column in the Sales table is equal to the total number of the Amount column returned by the subquery. Listing 11-93 contains the DownRow() method that retrieves and displays the ResultSet from Listing 11-92.

Listing 11-92
Creating a subquery

```
try {
    String query = new String (" SELECT StoreNumber " +
      " FROM Sales "+
      " WHERE Estimate = (SELECT SUM(Amount) " +
      " FROM Orders, Sales " +
      " WHERE StoreNum = StoreNumber) ");
    DataRequest = Database.createStatement();
    Results = DataRequest.executeQuery (query);
    System.out.println("Store");
    System.out.println("-----");
    DisplayResults (Results);
    DataRequest.close();
}
```

Listing 11-93
The DownRow() method used with a subquery

```
private  void DownRow ( ResultSet DisplayResults )
       throws SQLException
{
  long Store;
  Store = DisplayResults.getLong ( 1 ) ;
  System.out.println(Store);
}
```

Conditional Testing

Any conditional expression (as discussed previously in this chapter) can be used to evaluate a relationship between a query and the results of the subquery. You can use four types of conditional tests with a subquery:

- **Comparison test** This test uses comparison operators to compare values in the temporary table with values in the table used by the query.

- **Existence test** This test determines whether a value in the current row of the table used by the query also exists in the temporary table.

- **Set membership test** This test is similar to the existence test in that the DBMS is directed to determine whether a value in the current row of the table used by the query also exists in the temporary table.

■ **Qualified test** This test consists of either the ANY test or the ALL test and determines whether a value in the current row of the table used by the query is in one row of the temporary table or all rows of the temporary table.

The comparison test is illustrated in the previous "Create a Subquery" section. The next several sections show how to perform the other tests. Before executing code segments in these sections, insert rows shown in Table 11-18 in the Sales table.

Existence Test

The existence test is used whenever you need to return rows in the ResultSet where a value in a column is present in the results of the subquery. The existence test requires that you place the EXISTS modifier between the query and the subquery.

Listing 11-94 gives an example of how to use an existence test. The DBMS is told to return a single instance of store numbers from the Sales table only if the store number is in the Orders table. The store number isn't returned if the store hasn't placed an order. Listing 11-93 contains the DownRow() method that can be used with Listing 11-94.

Listing 11-94
Performing the existence test

```
try {
   String query = new String (" SELECT DISTINCT StoreNumber " +
     " FROM Sales   "+
     " WHERE EXISTS " +
     " (SELECT StoreNum " +
     " FROM Orders " +
     " WHERE StoreNum = StoreNumber) ");
   DataRequest = Database.createStatement();
   Results = DataRequest.executeQuery (query);
   System.out.println("Store");
   System.out.println("-----");
   DisplayResults (Results);
   DataRequest.close();
}
```

StoreNumber	Estimate	SalesRepNumber
345	150	5
278	300	6
825	230	7

Table 11-18. *Add These Values to the Sales Table in Table 11-16.*

Membership Test

The IN modifier is used to determine whether a value in the table that is being queried is a member of the results produced by the subquery. If the value appears in both the table and the results of the subquery, the conditional test is evaluated as true and the row that contains the value is returned in the ResultSet; otherwise the row is skipped.

The IN modifier is used in Listing 11-95. In this example, the subquery returns store numbers from the Orders table where the value in the Estimate column of the corresponding row in the Sales table is less than the value in the Amount column of the Orders table.

The IN modifier is used to determine whether the store number in the Sales table is returned in the results of the subquery. If so, then the sales representative's number from the Sales table is returned in the ResultSet; if not, the sales representative's number in the current row of the Sales table is skipped. Listing 11-93 contains the DownRow() method that can be used with Listing 11-95.

Listing 11-95
Performing the membership test

```
try {
   String query = new String (" SELECT SalesRepNumber " +
      " FROM Sales   "+
      " WHERE StoreNumber IN " +
      " (SELECT StoreNum " +
      " FROM Orders " +
      " WHERE Estimate < Amount) ");
   DataRequest = Database.createStatement();
   Results = DataRequest.executeQuery (query);
   System.out.println("Store");
   System.out.println("-----");
   DisplayResults (Results);
   DataRequest.close();
}
```

ANY Test

The ANY test determines whether the value specified in the query is in any of the rows returned by the subquery. If there is at least one match, the row is returned in the ResultSet, otherwise the row is ignored. Listing 11-96 shows how to construct an ANY test. The objective of this program is to return the store number from the Sales table for any store where the estimate is greater than the amount of any of the store's orders in the Orders table.

The ANY test tells the DBMS to include the store number in the ResultSet if the value of the Estimate column for the store in the Sales table is greater than any value in the Amount column for that store in the temporary table. Listing 11-93 contains the DownRow() method that can be used with Listing 11-96.

Rules for the ANY Test

You must conform to a set of rules that govern the use of the ANY test; otherwise, you might experience unexpected results. Here are the rules that you must follow when using the ANY text:

- The ANY test fails if the subquery produces an empty result. Therefore, the query doesn't return any rows in the ResultSet.

- A NULL value returned by the subquery causes the query to return a NULL value. This is because the query is unsure whether the value of the table in the query is in the results of the subquery.

- No value is returned in the ResultSet if the value in the table being queried is not in the results of the subquery.

Listing 11-96
Performing
the ANY test

```
try {
    String query = new String (" SELECT DISTINCT StoreNumber " +
        " FROM Sales  "+
        " WHERE Estimate  > ANY  " +
        " (SELECT Amount" +
        " FROM Orders " +
        " WHERE StoreNumber = StoreNum) ");
    DataRequest = Database.createStatement();
    Results = DataRequest.executeQuery (query);
    System.out.println("Store");
    System.out.println("-----");
    DisplayResults (Results);
    DataRequest.close();
}
```

ALL Test

The ALL test is similar to the ANY test in that the value of the table specified in the query is compared to values returned by the subquery. However, these tests differ in that the ANY test requires at least one match for the row to be included in the ResultSet. The ALL test requires that the value in the table specified in the query matches all the values returned by the subquery.

Listing 11-97 illustrates how to implement the ALL test. In this example, the store number joins the Sales table and the Orders table. Once the tables are joined, the subquery is processed, which returns the value in the Amount column for each store in the Orders table. Next, the value in the Estimate column of the Sales table is compared with each Amount value returned by the subquery. If the Amount value for each row returned by the subquery is less than the value in the Estimate column, then the row in the Sales table is placed in the ResultSet. Otherwise, the row in the Sales table is skipped. The ALL test follows the same rules that apply to the ANY test (see previous section). Listing 11-93 contains the DownRow() method that can be used with Listing 11-97.

Listing 11-97
Performing
the ALL test

```
try {
  String query = new String (" SELECT DISTINCT Store " +
    " FROM Sales  "+
    " WHERE Estimate  > ALL  " +
    " (SELECT Amount" +
    " FROM Orders " +
    " WHERE StoreNumber = StoreNum) ");
  DataRequest = Database.createStatement();
  Results = DataRequest.executeQuery (query);
  System.out.println("Store");
  System.out.println("-----");
  DisplayResults (Results);
  DataRequest.close();
}
```

VIEWs

You can reduce the complexity of your J2ME application by creating one or more views of the database for each user ID that is passed to the J2ME application for data access. A VIEW is similar to creating a table that contains only data the user ID is permitted to access. A VIEW limits columns and rows that can be queried to specific information pertaining to a user ID. A VIEW is like a filter that hides information from a user ID.

Each VIEW is uniquely identified with a name and contains selection criteria for columns and rows that appear in the VIEW when the VIEW is used by a J2ME component. Once a VIEW is created, the J2ME application references a VIEW the same way that a table is referenced in a query.

Rules for Using VIEWs

In many situations, using VIEWs increases the efficiency of interacting with tables in a database. However, there are times when VIEWs are not appropriate for an application. The following is a set of rules that govern how you should use VIEWs in your application:

- Create as many VIEWs as necessary to simplify access to a database.
- Restrict access to a table on need-to-know basis.
- Work with the owner of the data to establish reasonable restrictions.
- Classify users into groups that have similar access requirements to information.
- Create a VIEW for each classification of user rather than for each user.

J2ME
DATA MANAGEMENT

- More than one column can be used in a VIEW.

- More than one table can be used in a VIEW.

- A VIEW is treated as a table in a query regardless of the number of columns and tables that are used to create the VIEW.

- Use a VIEW whenever your program accesses some columns in many tables. The view simplifies the number of tables that a J2ME application needs to access directly.

- Beware of data security restrictions that affect the underlying columns and tables used to create the VIEW. A VIEW inherits data security restrictions from tables used to create the VIEW. Therefore, if the user ID doesn't have rights to information in a table, the VIEW also has the same restrictions.

- Create as many VIEWs as necessary to simplify access to a database. However, querying a VIEW is not necessarily an efficient way to query a database.

The following sections illustrate how to create and use a VIEW. You can execute code segments within each section using the Model A program. Before doing so, create the following tables and insert the rows shown in Table 11-19 and Table 11-20.

Define the Orders table as follows:

- OrderNumber, number, primary key

- ProdNumber, number

- CustomerNumber, number

- StoreNum, number

- Amount, long

OrderNumber	ProdNumber	CustomerNumber	StoreNum	Amount
122	5237	591	345	200
334	3255	901	278	321
365	3255	901	278	433
534	7466	591	825	523
555	1052	999	278	23
717	1052	721	825	75
874	7466	721	825	354

Table 11-19. *Sample Entries in an Orders Table for Practice Using VIEWs*

ProductNumber	ProductName	UnitPrice
1052	CD Player	100
3255	VCR	250
5237	DVD Player	325
7466	50-inch TV	532

Table 11-20. *Sample Entries in a Products Table for Practice Using VIEWs*

Define the Products table as follows:

- ProductNumber, number, primary key
- ProductName, VARCHAR
- UnitPrice, long

Create a VIEW

A VIEW is created by using the CREATE VIEW statement, as illustrated in Listing 11-98. In this example, the CREATE VIEW statement contains the name of the VIEW, which is Store278. Any unique name can be used as the name of a VIEW.

The AS modifier contains the query whose results form the rows and columns that are contained in the VIEW. In this example, all the columns and rows of the Orders table where the value of the StoreNum column is 278 are placed in the VIEW. Only rows that pertain to store 278 are contained in the VIEW. Data from all other stores is excluded.

Listing 11-98
Creating a
VIEW

```
try {
   String query = new String (" CREATE VIEW Store278 AS " +
     " SELECT   *  " +
     " FROM Orders   " +
     " WHERE StoreNum  = 278");
   DataRequest = Database.createStatement();
   DataRequest.execute(query);
   DataRequest.close();
}
```

Select Columns to Appear in the VIEW

You can include or exclude any column in a VIEW. Columns excluded from a VIEW remain in underlying tables used to create the VIEW. However, those columns are hidden from the J2ME component. Listing 11-99 illustrates how to include columns in a VIEW. This example creates a VIEW called StoreProd. The SELECT statement contains column names from the Orders table that are included in the view. All other columns of the Orders table are excluded from the view.

Listing 11-99
Selecting columns to appear in a VIEW

```
try {
    String query = new String (" CREATE VIEW StoreProd AS " +
        " SELECT StoreNum, ProdNumber " +
        " FROM Orders  ");
    DataRequest = Database.createStatement();
    DataRequest.executeQuery (query);
    DataRequest.close();
}
```

Create a Horizontal VIEW

There are two kinds of VIEWs: vertical and horizontal. A vertical VIEW includes all rows of the underlying table and includes some, but not all, columns of the table. This is illustrated in Listing 11-99. A horizontal VIEW contains all columns in the underlying table, but only some rows of the table. This means some rows are excluded from the VIEW and cannot be accessed.

Listing 11-100 shows how to create a horizontal VIEW. In this example, a VIEW called cust901 is created that contains all rows in the Orders table where the value of the CustomerNumber column is 901. Horizontal VIEWs are ideal for situations where access to all columns of a table(s) is required, but not access to all rows.

Listing 11-100
Creating a horizontal VIEW

```
try {
    String query = new String (" CREATE VIEW cust901 AS " +
        " SELECT  *  " +
        " FROM Orders" +
        " WHERE CustomerNumber = 901");
    DataRequest = Database.createStatement();
    Results = DataRequest.execute(query);
    DataRequest.close();
}
```

Create a Multitable VIEW

A multitable VIEW is created like a single table VIEW, but tables used in the view must be joined. Listing 11-101 shows how this is done. Notice that a vertical VIEW is created and contains three columns from the Orders table and the Products table. The Orders table and the Products table are joined together in the WHERE clause using the product number. Although columns in the view come from two tables, columns are treated as if they are from the same table in a query that uses the view.

Listing 11-101
Creating a multitable VIEW

```
try {
    String query = new String (" CREATE VIEW ProdDesc AS " +
        " SELECT  StoreNum, ProdNumber, ProductName " +
        " FROM Orders, Products  " +
        " WHERE ProdNumber = ProductNumber");
    DataRequest = Database.createStatement();
    Results = DataRequest.execute(query);
    DataRequest.close();
}
```

Group and Sort VIEWs

Rows in a VIEW can be grouped and sorted when the VIEW is created rather than grouping or sorting rows in a query that uses the VIEW. A VIEW can be grouped or sorted by using the GROUP BY clause and/or the ORDER BY clause, as discussed previously in this chapter.

Listing 11-102 shows how to sort rows in the VIEW. In this example, a VIEW called GroupProdDesc is created based on the underlying Orders table and Products table, which are joined together by product number. The GroupProdDesc view consists of the store number, product number, and product name that are sorted by the value in the ProdNumber column.

Listing 11-102
Grouping and sorting VIEWs

```
try {
    String query = new String (" CREATE VIEW GroupProdDesc AS " +
        " SELECT  StoreNum, ProdNumber, ProductName " +
        " FROM Orders, Products  " +
        " WHERE ProdNumber = ProductNumber" +
        " ORDER BY ProdNumber  ");
    DataRequest = Database.createStatement();
    Results = DataRequest.execute(query);
    DataRequest.close();
}
```

Modify a VIEW

A VIEW can be modified, and those modifications affect the underlying tables that are used to create the VIEW. There are three ways to modify a VIEW:

- **Update**   Values in one or more columns of a VIEW are changed to values supplied by the query.
- **Insert**   A new row is added to the VIEW and indirectly to the underlying table(s) used to create the VIEW.
- **Delete**   A row is removed from the VIEW and from the underlying table(s) used to create the VIEW.

Rules for Updating a View

A View can be used to update columns and rows in the underlying tables that comprise the View. However, updating a View is possible only if you adhere to a set of rules that govern the use of updating a View.

- Calculation, expressions, and built-in column functions cannot be used in the SELECT statement of the VIEW. Instead, only names of columns can be used.
- Exclude the GROUP BY clause and HAVING clause from the VIEW.
- Duplicate rows must be included in the modification. You cannot use the DISTINCT modifier in the VIEW if values of the view are going to be modified.
- The user ID used in your program must have rights to modify the underlying tables that make up the VIEW.
- Subqueries cannot be used in a VIEW if rows of the VIEW are to be modified.

Updating a View

You can replace values in a view by using the UPDATE statement, as discussed earlier in the section "Update Row and Column." Listing 11-103 illustrates how this is done. In this example, the Store278 VIEW is referenced in the UPDATE statement. The SET clause specifies the Amount column, which is to be updated, and the value that will override the current value in the Amount column. This means the number 700 replaces whatever value is in the column.

The WHERE clause is used to identify rows in the view that are to be updated. Rows that have 334 as the value in the OrderNumber column will have 700 inserted into their Amount column.

Listing 11-103 Updating a VIEW

```
try {
  String query = new String (" UPDATE Store278 " +
    " SET Amount = 700 " +
```

```
                " WHERE OrderNumber  = 334 ");
           DataRequest = Database.createStatement();
           Results = DataRequest.execute(query);
           DataRequest.close();
       }
```

Inserting a Row into a VIEW

A new row can be inserted into the underlying tables that make up a VIEW by using the INSERT INTO statement and referencing the name of the VIEW, as shown in Listing 11-104. In this example, a new row is inserted in the Store278 VIEW using the same technique described in the section "Inserting a Row" earlier in the chapter.

**Listing
11-104**
Inserting
a row into
a VIEW

```
try {
    String query = new String (" INSERT INTO Store278 " +
        " (OrderNumber, ProdNum, CustomerNumber, StoreNum, Amount) " +
        " VALUES (325, 9545 ,301 ,278 ,400) ");
    DataRequest = Database.createStatement();
    Results = DataRequest.execute(query);
    DataRequest.close();
}
```

Deleting a Row from a VIEW

You can remove a row from a VIEW by using the DELETE FROM statement. The DELETE FROM statement requires the name of the VIEW from which the row or rows is to be deleted.

Listing 11-105 illustrates how to delete a row from a VIEW. In this example, one or more rows from the Store278 are deleted. Rows designated to be deleted are identified in the WHERE clause. In this case, rows that have the value 555 in the OrderNumber column are removed from the Orders table, which is the underlying table of the Store278 VIEW.

**Listing
11-105**
Deleting
a row from
a VIEW

```
try {
    String query = new String (" DELETE FROM Store278 " +
        " WHERE OrderNumber = 555   ");
    DataRequest = Database.createStatement();
    Results = DataRequest.execute(query);
    DataRequest.close();
}
```

Dropping a VIEW

A VIEW can be removed by using the DROP VIEW statement. The DROP VIEW statement requires the name of the VIEW that is to be dropped. Two modifiers are used with the DROP VIEW statement:

- **CASCADE**   Remove all VIEWs that depend on the VIEW specified in the DROP VIEW statement as well as the specified VIEW.

- **RESTRICT**   Remove only the VIEW specified in the DROP VIEW statement. All dependent VIEWs remain intact.

A dependent VIEW is a VIEW that has another VIEW, rather than a table, as one of its underlying components. Listing 11-106 shows you how to drop a VIEW. In this example, the Store278 VIEW and all of its dependent VIEWs are dropped (although there aren't any dependent VIEWs). Some DBMSs use DROP TABLE instead of DROP VIEW.

Listing 11-106
Dropping a VIEW

```
try {
    String query = new String (" DROP VIEW  Store278 CASCADE");
    DataRequest = Database.createStatement();
    Results = DataRequest.DataRequest.execute(query);
    DataRequest.close();
}
```

The
Complete
Reference

Part IV

J2ME Personal Information
Manager Profile

The Complete Reference

Chapter 12

Personal Information Manager

The major reason for using a personal digital assistant (PDA) is to store, retrieve, and manage personal information such as addresses, telephone numbers, a calendar, and a to do list. Nearly all PDAs have factory-installed applications to manage this type of information. Although personal information is maintained by PDA applications, any J2ME application running within a CLDC base implementation can access that data through the use of the personal information management (PIM) API. The PIM API contains interfaces and classes that give your MIDP application access to the PDA's database so you can read and modify data stored by other applications and insert your own information into the database, which can then be accessed by other PDA applications.

In this chapter you'll learn how to interact with data stored on the PDA's database by the PDA's to do list, calendar, and address book application. You'll also find a model PIM application that can be modified to meet the needs of your own PIM application.

PIM Databases

The PIM uses three types of databases to store and manage the user's personal information, although a platform may have more than one of each type. These are a contact database, event database, and to do database. The contact database contains names, addresses, phone numbers, and other similar information about personal contacts and follows the IETF vCard 2.1 specification, although optional package PIMs can include 3.0. The vCard 2.1 standard is adhered to for importing and exporting contact data. Databases can contain non-vCard fields. Those fields are mapped to extensions in vCard terminology. You cannot assume that databases comply with the vCard 2.1 format.

The event database and the to do database contain calendar-based information stores that contain the day, month, year, time, and a brief description of activities occurring on a specified date. Both databases adhere to the vCalendar 1.0 standard from the Internet Mail Consortium. The vCalendar 1.0 standard is adhered to for importing and exporting event data. Databases can contain non-vCalendar fields. Those fields are mapped to extensions in vCalendar terminology. You cannot assume that databases comply with the vCalendar 1.0 format.

Two types of interfaces are used with each database. One interface focuses on data elements and gathering data, and the other focuses on persistence for some or all data elements. The data-oriented interface for each database is called Contact, Event, and ToDo. The persistence interface for each database is called ContactList, EventList, and ToDoList. These interfaces determine what data is stored in the database.

Depending on the implementation of the PIM list class, data elements can be placed in a named group called a category. The name of the group is arbitrary, and the list determines whether categories can be assigned and the number of categories that can be assigned for each element. Categories are used to logically group like items together, usually reflected in the UI. For example, a contact database might have personal and work categories, enabling users to classify their contacts.

Three conventions provide general functionality to Contact, Event, ToDo, ContactList, EventList, and ToDoList. These are the PIM class, used to access PIM databases; the PIMItem interface, which provides common element functionality; and the PIMList interface, which provides common list functionality.

The PIM class contains methods that return a list of all ContactList, EventList, and ToDoList names and methods that are used to open each of these lists in either read-only, write-only, or read/write mode. You'll find details of these methods in the "Quick Reference Guide" at the end of this chapter. Each mode is predefined by a field in the PIM class.

The PIMItem interface is a common interface for items of the PIM database. A PIM item is a container created from a particular PIM list that references the item's data through fields. The association between the PIM item and a PIM list lasts for the life of the item. This is similar to a field label within a database, but differs in that field labels are meant for user interfaces and can be localized, while a field is a programmatic reference. A *field* is a logical value identifying a particular group of data in an item. Each field is assigned a name within the PIM API by the implementing class; an example is TEL, which represents a field containing telephone number data. The field is referenced in the PIM API to store data in a PIM item. That is, the field is used to set the value of data and retrieve data.

The PIM API includes definitions for all of the most common fields in PIM databases. However, not every PIM database in the world must support all fields in order to qualify for use by this API. All databases support a subset of these fields, and the subset of fields supported by a particular database is reflected in the API by the PIMList class. This class determines which fields are contained in each PIM item.

Each field has a field data type and a field label in addition to a field. Standard fields— fields that are explicitly defined in the PIM API—already have predefined data types that cannot be changed by an implementation. For example, a TEL field used to store a telephone number always contains String data types. An *extended field* is a nonstandard field defined by a vendor. Vendors may include extended fields whose data types can be retrieved by calling the getFieldDataType(int) method. This method requires one parameter, which is an integer whose value represents the field.

The field label is retrieved by calling the getFieldLabel(int), which also requires that the field be passed as a parameter. The field label is returned as a string. Data can be imported into a PIM item or exported from a PIM item using standard byte-based formats (such as vCard or vCal) defined by the implementing class.

An item contains three types of data: named fields, extended fields, and categories. A *named field* is an item that is referenced by using an explicit field name defined in the class. All fields have attributes, which are qualifiers used to describe the data for a field. For example, ATTR_WORK identifies the field as containing data associated with the work. Attributes appear with all fields unless PIMItem.ATTR_NONE is used, indicating there are no qualifiers for a field. However, attributes are hints to the underlying VM. This means that the VM can ignore attributes if it does not support them.

As mentioned earlier, an extended field is a field that is not explicitly predefined, but has a field ID assigned to it by a vendor's specific PIM list. Extended fields are not included in the standard named fields in the API. For example, a vendor-specific contact database may have a field called MOTHER_IN_LAW. You can determine whether a field is a vendor-specific extended field by comparing the field's value against MIN_EXTENDED_FIELD_VALUE; a field greater than that constant is a field specific to a particular vendor's database. Methods used to interact with a named field are also used to interact with an extended field.

A category is a string item that may correspond to category values already existing in the PIMItem's associated PIMList.

The "Quick Reference Guide" at the end of the chapter contains methods used with this interface. We'll discuss a few of the commonly used methods here.

Your application can place values into a field by calling one of several addXXX() methods. A field is similar to a Vector in that it can store more than one value, and those values are stored in a logical array. These fields are setBinary(int fieldID, byte[] data), setDate(int fieldID, long value), setInt(int fieldID, int value), and setString(int fieldID, String value). Each method requires two parameters. The first parameter is the field ID of the field receiving the value. The other parameter is reference to the data being placed into the field. Once data is placed into fields of a PIM item, you must call the commit() method to persist the data.

You call one of the getXXX() methods to retrieve the value of a field. These are getBinary(int field, int index), getDate(int fielded, int index), getInt(int field, int index), and getString(int field, int index). The getBinary() method returns a byte array. The getDate() method returns a long whose value represents a date. Each method requires an integer parameter, whose value is the field ID of the field, and an index into the field. Indexes are used to access values in a field. The first value assigned to a field using addXXX() resides at index 0, and the value is retrieved using getXXX().

The getFieldDataType(int fieldID) method is used to return the data type of the specified field. The data type is returned as an integer field defined in the PIMItem interface. These are BINARY, DATE, INT, STRING, and STRING_ARRAY.

The getFieldLabel(int fieldID) method is used to retrieve the label of the field specified in the parameter passed to this method. The label is returned as a string.

The "Quick Reference Guide" at the end of this chapter lists methods that can be used to interact with a PIMList.

The Contact Database

The contact database contains personal contact information in the form of a contact entry. A contact entry consists of fields defined in the Contact interface, which is a subset of fields defined by the IETF vCard 2.1 and 3.0 specification [RFC 2426]. There are many predefined fields in a contact entry, as you'll note from reviewing the "Quick Reference Guide" at the end of this chapter. However, the ContactList interface restricts the fields that are retained. That is, some native contact databases do not support all fields defined in a contact entry. The PIMList.isSupportedField(int) method can be called to determine whether a field is supported because the API supports more fields than are associated with any single PIM database. The API supports many different types of PIM databases. The PIMList.isSupportedField(int) method requires an integer parameter whose value is the field ID of the field and returns a boolean value.

For example, a contact entry has a named field used to store a telephone number. However, a contact probably has multiple telephone numbers. Two instances of the named telephone number field can be created, and both can be added via the addString() method. Both telephone numbers can have the same field (Contact.TEL) and can be further distinguished with attributes such as ATTR_HOME and ATTR_MOBILE. The "Quick Reference Guide" at the end of this chapter contains a list of all predefined fields for the Contact interface. Data values of these fields are set and retrieved using the set*XXX*() and get*XXX*() methods that correspond to the data type of the field.

A contact entry is associated with a contact list. The contact list determines what fields from a contact entry are retained when the contract entry is saved to the contact database. This is because all entries in the same list (that is, database tuple) have common fields.

The ContactList interface is used to interact with a contact list. The createContact() method is used to create a contact for a contact list. A contact can be imported into a contact list by calling the importContact(Contact element) method. You use this method when transferring a contact from one contact database to another or when a Contact is created from a vCard data stream. This method requires one parameter, which is reference to the contact being added to the contact list. A contact can be removed from the contact list by calling the removeContact(Contact element) method, passing it reference to the contact that is being removed.

The Event Database

An event is a single entry into the PIM event database, such as noting your significant other's birthday or any calendar event. Fields used in the event database are a subset of the fields defined by the vCalendar 1.0 specification from the Internet Mail Consortium (http://www.imc.org). The subset provides relevant information about an event without compromising the portability of the platform.

The Event interface defines field IDs for use with an event entry. Field IDs include START, END, LOCATION, SUMMARY, NOTE, REVISION, and ALARM. The START and END field IDs designate that the date and time value of the field is the start date and end date for the event entry, respectively. The LOCATION field ID signifies that the field contains the venue for the event entry. SUMMARY and NOTE field IDs state that the field contains free-form text whose value is a synopsis (SUMMARY) or a more complete description (NOTE) of the event. The REVISION field ID indicates that the date and time contained in the field is the last time the event entry was modified. The ALARM field ID implies that an alarm should sound on the date and time specified in the field, indicating that the event is about to occur.

The event list determines which fields from an event entry are retained when the event is saved to the event database. An implementation is not required to support all fields of an event entry. You can query whether or not a field is supported by calling the PIMList.isSupportedField(int), where the value of the integer parameter is the field ID.

You can interact with an event list by using the EventList interface. The EventList interface defines the createEvent() method used to create a new event for the event list. This method returns an Event. You can call the importEvent(Event element) method to import an event into the event list. This method requires one parameter, which is reference to the Event being imported to the event list. The importEvent(Event element) method returns an Event. The removeEvent(Event element) method is called to remove an event from the list. This method requires one parameter, which is reference to the Event that is being removed.

You'll find a complete listing of methods defined by the EventList interface in the "Quick Reference Guide" at the end of this chapter.

Some events happen on a regular schedule, such as a weekly sales meeting. These are considered repeating events, and you use the RepeatRule class to interact with them. The RepeatRule class contains fields used to set the regularity of an event. Regularity is defined in a number of ways, such as happening in a specific month, a specific week within a month, every week, every year, a specific day of the week, at a specific frequency or interval. Examine the "Quick Reference Guide" at the end of this chapter for a complete listing of these fields.

In addition to fields, the RepeatRule class defines methods that can be used to interact with repeated events. The setInt(int fieldID, int value) method is used to set an event to be repeated. Two parameters are required for this method: the first is the ID for the field, and the second is an integer whose value specifies the repeating pattern of the event (RepeatRule class field). See the "Quick Reference Guide" at the end of this chapter for a complete listing of these methods.

The To Do Database

The to do database contains entries for tasks that must be performed and the date and time when they are to be performed. A ToDo entry has fields that are a subset of the fields in the VTODO defined by the vCalendar 1.0 specification from the Internet Mail Consortium.

The ToDo interface defines fields that are used as field IDs for ToDo entries. These field IDs are DUE, SUMMARY, NOTE, REVISON, PRIORITY, COMPLETED, and COMPLETION_DATE. The DUE field ID indicates that the field contains the date when the ToDo entry is due. The SUMMARY and NOTE field IDs contain a synopsis

(SUMMARY) or a more complete description (NOTE) of the task. The REVISION field ID indicates that the date contained in the field is the date the ToDo entry was last modified. The PRIORITY field ID signifies that the ToDo is the priority of the ToDo list. And the COMPLETED field ID states that the ToDo task is completed.

The ToDo list determines the fields from a ToDo entry that are retained in the to do database. Methods defined in the ToDoList interface are used to interact with a ToDo list. The createToDo() method is called to create a new ToDo entry for the ToDo list and returns a ToDo reference to the new entry. The importToDo(ToDo element) method is used to import a ToDo entry into the ToDo list. Reference to the ToDo entry is passed to the method. And the removeToDo(ToDo element) method is called to remove a ToDo entry from the ToDo list. Reference to the ToDo element that is being removed from the ToDo list is passed as a parameter to this method.

Error Handling

Error handling is not consistent across API packages, so you'll need to refer to the implementation's documentation to learn how errors are treated. For example, some implementations, such as AWT, silently ignore optional features that they do not support. Others, such as PIM API, use the "test before use, throw RuntimeException" model, which expects the application to check for features and fields that may or may not be supported before implementing a feature. You don't need to have your application check for features, but failing to do so risks the possibility of RuntimeExceptions being thrown.

A Model PIM Application

The PIMTest application, shown in Listing 12-1, is a model PIM application that you can modify to meet the needs of your own application. It is divided into three areas, each showing how to interact with the address book, calendar, and to do list databases found on most PDAs. The VM implementation defines databases that are accessible to your application. However, your application is not permitted to create new databases.

Your application can interact with the address book by calling one of four methods defined in the model application. These methods are createAContact(), retrieveContacts(), modifyAContact(), and deleteContacts(). As the name of the method implies, the createAContact() method is used to insert information about a new contact into the local address book. Information about contacts can be retrieved by calling the retrieveContacts() method. The retrieveContacts() method returns both information inserted by the createAContact() method and information inserted by other applications into the address book.

Changing contact information in the address book is accomplished by calling the modifyAContact() method. This method enables your application to modify information entered by other applications into the address book in addition to information entered by your own application. The deleteContacts() method is called whenever your application needs to remove contacts from the local address book.

The PDA calendar database is used to store events that occur on a specified date and time. You can insert events into the calendar database by calling the createAnEvent() method, which places an entry into the database. Entries in the calendar database are retrieved by calling the retrieveEvents() method. Your application can process the entry using your own business logic once the entry is retrieved from the database. The retrieveEvents() method retrieves entries inserted by your application as well as entries inserted by other applications.

Any event contained in the calendar database can be modified by calling the modifyEvent() method. This method enables your application to change values of entries that appear in the database. Entries can be removed from the calendar database by calling the deleteEvents() method.

A to do list is used to track activities. Each entry in a to do list is stored in the to do database. Your application can create an entry in the to do list by calling the createAToDo() method. Those entries and entries made by other applications can be retrieved by calling the retrieveToDos() method. Information on a to do list entry can be changed by using the modifyToDos() method. This method is also used to change to do list entries inserted by other applications. The deleteToDos() method removes entries of a to do list.

Listing 12-1
The PIM model application

```
import javax.microedition.pim.*;
import java.util.Enumeration;
import java.util.Calendar;
import java.util.Date;
public class PIMTest   {
    public PIMTest() {
    }
    /*********************************************
    * Contact/ContactList sample code
    *********************************************/
    public void createAContact() {
        // Create a support contact entry in the device's
        //local address bookso that users have the contact
        //information for anything that they
        // need help with about your application
        PIM pim = PIM.getInstance();
        ContactList cl = null;
        Contact new_contact = null;
        try {
            // Open write only since you're just going to
            // add your support contact
            // info to the device's database
            cl = (ContactList)
              pim.openPIMList(PIM.CONTACT_LIST, PIM.WRITE_ONLY);
```

```
} catch (PIMException e) {
    // failed opening the default contact list!
    // Error case - abort this attempt
    System.err.println(
      "Error accessing database - aborting action");
    return;
} catch (SecurityException e) {
    // user rejected application's request for
    //write access to contact list
    // This is not an error condition and can be normal
    System.out.println(
        "Okay, this application won't add the contact");
    return;
}
// Create an "empty" contact to work with
new_contact = cl.createContact();
// Add your company's info: company name,
//two support phone numbers, a support
// email, and a note about what product the user has.  Add whatever
// information the native contact list
//supports and don't add it if
// the field is not supported.
if (cl.isSupportedField(Contact.ORG))
    new_contact.addString(Contact.ORG, PIMItem.ATTR_NONE,
        "Acme, Inc.");
if (cl.isSupportedField(Contact.TEL)) {
    new_contact.addString(Contact.TEL, PIMItem.ATTR_NONE,
        "800-888-8888");
    new_contact.addString(Contact.TEL, PIMItem.ATTR_NONE,
        "800-888-8889");
}
if (cl.isSupportedField(Contact.EMAIL))
    new_contact.addString(Contact.EMAIL,
        PIMItem.ATTR_NONE, "support@acme.com");
if (cl.isSupportedField(Contact.NOTE))
    new_contact.addString(Contact.NOTE, PIMItem.ATTR_NONE,
        "You've purchased application with registration number NNN.");
try {
    // commits it to the list and the native database
    new_contact.commit();
}
catch (PIMException e) {
    // failed committing the contact
     System.err.println(
        "This application cannot add the contact info");
}
 try {
```

```
            cl.close();
        } catch (PIMException e) {
            // failed to close the list
        }
    }
    public void retrieveContacts() {
        // Get all contacts with last name starting with "S" (e.g.
        // Smith, Sanders, Stargell, etc.) for a listing screen
        PIM pim = PIM.getInstance();
        ContactList cl = null;
        Contact search_template = null;
        Enumeration s_contacts = null;
        try {
            cl = (ContactList) pim.openPIMList(PIM.CONTACT_LIST,
                    PIM.READ_ONLY);
        } catch (PIMException e) {
            // failed opening the default contact list!
            System.err.println(
                    "Error accessing database - aborting action");
            return;
        } catch (SecurityException e) {
            // user rejected application's request for
            // read access to contact list
            // This is not an error condition and can be normal
            System.out.println(
                "Okay, this application won't get contacts");
            return;
        }
        // first create a "template" contact which we'll use for matching
        search_template = cl.createContact();
        if (cl.isSupportedArrayElement(Contact.NAME,
                Contact.NAME_FAMILY)) {
            // this particular contact list does contain last names, so we
            // can now do the search
            // now fill in the search parameters of last name
            // starting with 'S'
            String[] name_struct = new String[Contact.NAMESIZE];
            name_struct[Contact.NAME_FAMILY] = "S";
            search_template.addStringArray(Contact.NAME,
                    PIMItem.ATTR_NONE, name_struct);
        }
        else if (cl.isSupportedField(Contact.FORMATTED_NAME)) {
            // the contact implementation doesn't have individual  name
            // fields, so try the single name field FORMATTED_NAME
            search_template.addString(Contact.FORMATTED_NAME,
                PIMItem.ATTR_NONE, "S");
        }
```

```
        try {
            // Get the enumeration of matching elements
            s_contacts = cl.items(search_template);
        } catch (PIMException e) {
            // failed to retrieve elements due to error!
            System.err.println(
                "This application cannot retrieve the contacts");
         }
        try {
            cl.close();
        } catch (PIMException e) {
            // failed to close the list
        }
    }
public void modifyAContact() {
        // Code sample:
        // Update John Smith's home phone number
        // from "555-0000" to "555-1212"
        // since he moved...
        PIM pim = PIM.getInstance();
        ContactList cl = null;
        Enumeration contacts = null;
        try {
            cl = (ContactList) pim.openPIMList(
                PIM.CONTACT_LIST, PIM.READ_WRITE);
        } catch (PIMException e) {
            // failed opening the default contact list!
            System.err.println(
                "This application failed to open the contact list");
        } catch (SecurityException e) {
            // user rejected application's request
            // for read/write access to contact list
            // This is not an error condition and can be normal
            System.out.println(
               "Okay, this application won't get contacts");
            return;
        }
        // first create a "template" contact which we'll use for matching
        // to find John Smith's contact entry
        Contact template = cl.createContact();
        String tel_number = "";
        if (cl.isSupportedField(Contact.NAME)) {
            String[] name_struct = new String[Contact.NAMESIZE];
            name_struct[Contact.NAME_FAMILY] = "Smith";
            name_struct[Contact.NAME_FAMILY] = "John";
            template.addStringArray(
                Contact.NAME, PIMItem.ATTR_NONE, name_struct);
```

```
            }
            if (cl.isSupportedField(Contact.TEL)) {
                template.addString(Contact.TEL, Contact.ATTR_HOME, "555-0000");
            }
            try {
                // Get the enumeration of matching elements
                contacts = cl.items(template);
            } catch (PIMException e) {
                // failed retrieving the items enumeration due to an error
                System.err.println(
                    "This application cannot retrieve the contact");
            }
            // update all John Smith entries with old home numbers of 555-0000
            while (contacts!= null && contacts.hasMoreElements()) {
                Contact c = (Contact) contacts.nextElement();
                for (int index = c.countValues(Contact.TEL); index != 0; index--)
                {
                    if (c.getString(Contact.TEL, index).equals("555-0000")) {
                        c.setString(Contact.TEL, index, Contact.ATTR_HOME,
                          "555-1212");
                        try {
                            // save change to the database
                            c.commit();
                        } catch (PIMException e) {
                            // Oops couldn't save the data...
                            System.err.println(
                              "This application cannot commit the contact info");
                        }
                        break; // go to next matching element
                    }
                }
            }
            try {
                cl.close();
            } catch (PIMException e) {
                // failed to close the list
            }
        }
        public void deleteContacts() {
            // Delete all contacts at company WorldCom
            // since they won't be answering
            // phone calls anymore...
            PIM pim = PIM.getInstance();
            ContactList cl = null;
            Enumeration contacts = null;
            try {
                cl = (ContactList) pim.openPIMList(
```

```
            PIM.CONTACT_LIST, PIM.READ_WRITE);
    } catch (PIMException e) {
        // failed opening the default contact list!
        System.err.println(
            "This application failed to open the contact list");
        return;
    } catch (SecurityException e) {
        // user rejected application's request for
        // read/write access to contact list
        // This is not an error condition and can be normal
        System.out.println(
          "Okay, this application won't get contacts");
        return;
    }
    // first create a "template" contact which we'll use for matching
    // to find WorldCom contact entries
    Contact template = cl.createContact();
    if (cl.isSupportedField(Contact.ORG)) {
        template.addString(Contact.ORG,
            PIMItem.ATTR_NONE, "WorldCom");
        try {
            // Get the enumeration of matching elements
            contacts = cl.items(template);
        } catch (PIMException e) {
            // failed retrieving the items enumeration due to an error
            System.err.println(
                "This application cannot commit the contact info");
        }
    }
    // delete all WorldCom entries
    while (contacts != null && contacts.hasMoreElements()) {
        Contact c = (Contact) contacts.nextElement();
        try {
            cl.removeContact(c);
        } catch (PIMException e) {
            // couldn't delete the entry for some
            // reason (probably shredded)
            System.err.println(
              "This application cannot remove the contact info");
        }
    }
    try {
        cl.close();
    } catch (PIMException e) {
        // failed to close the list
    }
}
```

```
/*********************************************
* Event/EventList sample code
*********************************************/
public void createAnEvent() {
    // Create an event entry in the device's local calendar
    // reminding the user to register your application
    PIM pim = PIM.getInstance();
    EventList el = null;
    Event new_event = null;
    try {
        // Open write only since you're just going to
        //add your registration
        // event info to the device's database
        el = (EventList) pim.openPIMList(
            PIM.EVENT_LIST, PIM.WRITE_ONLY);
    } catch (PIMException e) {
        // failed opening the default event list!
        // Error case - abort this attempt
        System.err.println(
            "Error accessing database - aborting action");
        return;
    } catch (SecurityException e) {
        // user rejected application's request
        // for write access to event list
        // This is not an error condition and can be normal
        System.out.println(
            "Okay, this application won't add the event");
        return;
    }
    // Create an "empty" event to work with
    new_event = el.createEvent();
    // Add a registration reminder event:
    // make it two weeks from now with an
    // alarm 10 minutes before the occurrence, and
    // add a note with the phone or email to call.
    if (el.isSupportedField(Event.START)) {
        Date d = new Date();
        long l = d.getTime() + (long)1209600000;
        new_event.addDate(Event.START, PIMItem.ATTR_NONE, l);
    }
    if (el.isSupportedField(Event.ALARM))
        new_event.addInt(Event.ALARM, PIMItem.ATTR_NONE, 600);
    if (el.isSupportedField(Event.SUMMARY))
        new_event.addString(Event.SUMMARY, PIMItem.ATTR_NONE,
            "Register Your Product!");
    if (el.isSupportedField(Event.NOTE))
        new_event.addString(Event.NOTE, PIMItem.ATTR_NONE,
```

```
                    "You've purchased application XXX with registration number NNN.
                       Please register it now.  Look in the Contact List
                       for information on how to contact us.");
        try {
             // commits it to the list and the native database
            new_event.commit();
        }
        catch (PIMException e) {
            // failed committing the event
            System.err.println("This application cannot add the event")
        }
        try {
            el.close();
        } catch (PIMException e) {
            // failed to close the list
        }
    }
}
public void retrieveEvents() {
    // Get all events occurring for the coming week,
    // for a listing screen
    PIM pim = PIM.getInstance();
    EventList el = null;
    Event search_template = null;
    Enumeration this_weeks_events = null;
    try {
        el = (EventList) pim.openPIMList(
          PIM.EVENT_LIST, PIM.READ_ONLY);
    } catch (PIMException e) {
        // failed opening the default event list!
        System.err.println(
              "Error accessing database - aborting action");
        return;
    } catch (SecurityException e) {
        // user rejected application's request for
        // read access to event list
        // This is not an error condition and can be normal
        System.out.println("Okay, this application won't get events");
        return;
    }
    // calculate today's date and next week's date
    long current_time = (new Date()).getTime();
    long next_week = current_time + 604800000;
    try {
        // Get the enumeration of matching elements
        this_weeks_events = el.items(
          EventList.OCCURRING, current_time, next_week, true);
    } catch (PIMException e) {
```

```
                // failed to retrieve elements due to error!
                // Error case - abort this attempt
                System.err.println(
                   "This application cannot retrieve the events");
            }
            try {
                el.close();
            } catch (PIMException e) {
                // failed to close the list
            }
        }
    public void modifyEvents() {
            // Code sample:
            // Postpone all events from today until
            // tomorrow (sick day today...)
            PIM pim = PIM.getInstance();
            EventList el = null;
            Enumeration todays_events = null;
            try {
                el = (EventList) pim.openPIMList(
                    PIM.EVENT_LIST, PIM.READ_WRITE);
            } catch (PIMException e) {
                // failed opening the default event list!
                System.err.println(
                    "Error accessing database - aborting action");
                return;
            } catch (SecurityException e) {
                // user rejected application's request
                    for read/write access to contact list
                // This is not an error condition and can be normal
                System.out.println(
                     "Okay, this application won't modify any event");
                return;
            }
            // calculate today's start and end times
            Calendar start_of_day = Calendar.getInstance();
            // start of work day is 7am
            start_of_day.set(Calendar.HOUR_OF_DAY, 7);
            Calendar end_of_day = Calendar.getInstance();
            // end of work day is 8pm
            end_of_day.set(Calendar.HOUR_OF_DAY, 20);
            try {
                // Get the enumeration of matching elements
                todays_events = el.items(Event.OCCURRING,
    start_of_day.getTime().getTime(), end_of_day.getTime().getTime(), true);
            } catch (PIMException e) {
                // failed to retrieve elements due to error!
```

```
            System.err.println(
                "This application cannot retrieve the events");
        }
        // update all events by one day
        while (todays_events != null && todays_events.hasMoreElements()) {
            Event e = (Event) todays_events.nextElement();
            e.setDate(Event.START, 0, PIMItem.ATTR_NONE,
                e.getDate(Event.START, 0) + 86400000);
            try {
                // save change to the database
                e.commit();
            } catch (PIMException exe) {
                // Oops couldn't save the data...
                System.err.println(
                    "This application cannot commit the event");
            }
        }
        try {
            el.close();
        } catch (PIMException e) {
            // failed to close the list
        }
    }
    public void deleteEvents() {
        // Delete all events having to do with Christmas (bah humbug!)
        PIM pim = PIM.getInstance();
        EventList el = null;
        Enumeration xmas_events = null;
        try {
            el = (EventList) pim.openPIMList(
                PIM.EVENT_LIST, PIM.READ_WRITE);
        } catch (PIMException e) {
            // failed opening the default event list!
            System.err.println(
                "Error accessing database - aborting action");
            return;
        } catch (SecurityException e) {
            // user rejected application's request
            // for read/write access to event list
            // This is not an error condition and can be normal
            System.out.println(
                "Okay, this application won't modify any event");
            return;
        }
        try {
            // Get the enumeration of matching elements
            xmas_events = el.items("Christmas");
```

```
        } catch (PIMException e) {
            // failed retrieving the items enumeration due to an error
            System.err.println(
                "This application cannot retrieve the events");
            return;
        }
        // delete all event entries containing Christmas
        while (xmas_events != null && xmas_events.hasMoreElements()) {
            Event e = (Event) xmas_events.nextElement();
            try {
                el.removeEvent(e);
            } catch (PIMException exe) {
                // couldn't delete the entry for some reason
                System.err.println(
                 "This application cannot remove the event info");
            }
        }
        try {
            el.close();
        } catch (PIMException e) {
            // failed to close the list
        }
    }
    /*****************************************************
    * ToDo/ToDoList sample code
    *****************************************************/
    public void createAToDo() {
        // Create a todo entry in the device's local todo list
        // reminding the user to register your application
        PIM pim = PIM.getInstance();
        ToDoList tl = null;
        ToDo new_todo = null;
        try {
            // Open write only since you're just going to
            // add your registration
            // todo info to the device's todo database
            tl = (ToDoList) pim.openPIMList(PIM.TODO_LIST, PIM.WRITE_ONLY);
        } catch (PIMException e) {
            // failed opening the default todo list!
            System.err.println(
                "Error accessing database - aborting action");
            return;
        } catch (SecurityException e) {
            // user rejected application's request
            // for write access to todo list
            // This is not an error condition and can be normal
            System.out.println(
```

```
                    "Okay, this application won't add the todo");
            return;
    }
    // Create an "empty" todo to work with
    new_todo = tl.createToDo();
    // Add a registration todo: make it have a
    // due date of two weeks from now
    // with a low priority, and
    // add a note with the phone or email to call.
    if (tl.isSupportedField(ToDo.DUE)) {
        Date d = new Date();
        long l = d.getTime() + (long)1209600000;
        new_todo.addDate(ToDo.DUE, PIMItem.ATTR_NONE, l);
    }
    if (tl.isSupportedField(ToDo.PRIORITY))
        new_todo.addInt(ToDo.PRIORITY, PIMItem.ATTR_NONE, 5);
    if (tl.isSupportedField(ToDo.SUMMARY))
        new_todo.addString(ToDo.SUMMARY, PIMItem.ATTR_NONE,
            "Register Your Product!");
    if (tl.isSupportedField(ToDo.NOTE))
        new_todo.addString(ToDo.NOTE, PIMItem.ATTR_NONE,
                "You've purchased application XXX with
                 registration number NNN. Please register it now.
                 Look in the Contact List for information on
                 how to contact us.");
    try {
            // commits it to the list and the native database
        new_todo.commit();
    }
    catch (PIMException e) {
        // failed committing the todo
        System.err.println("This application cannot add the todo");
    }
    try {
        tl.close();
    } catch (PIMException e) {
        // failed to close the list
    }
}
public void retrieveToDos() {
    // Get all todos due today, for a listing screen
    PIM pim = PIM.getInstance();
    ToDoList tl = null;
    ToDo search_template = null;
    Enumeration todos = null;
    try {
        tl = (ToDoList) pim.openPIMList(PIM.TODO_LIST, PIM.READ_ONLY);
```

```
            } catch (PIMException e) {
                // failed opening the default todo list!
                System.err.println(
                    "Error accessing database - aborting action");
                return;
            } catch (SecurityException e) {
                // user rejected application's request for
                // read access to todo list
                // This is not an error condition and can be normal
                System.out.println(
                    "Okay, this application won't get todo items");
                return;
            }
            // calculate today's start and end times
            Calendar start_of_day = Calendar.getInstance();
            start_of_day.set(Calendar.HOUR_OF_DAY, 0);
            Calendar end_of_day = Calendar.getInstance();
            end_of_day.set(Calendar.HOUR_OF_DAY, 24);
            try {
                // Get the enumeration of matching elements
                todos = tl.items(
                    ToDo.DUE, start_of_day.getTime().getTime(),
                        end_of_day.getTime().getTime());
            } catch (PIMException e) {
                // failed to retrieve elements due to error!
                // Error case - abort this attempt
                System.err.println(
                        "This application cannot retrieve the todos");
            }
            try {
                tl.close();
            } catch (PIMException e) {
                // failed to close the list
            }
        }
    public void modifyToDos() {
        // Mark all stuff from yesterday as completed
        PIM pim = PIM.getInstance();
        ToDoList tl = null;
        ToDo search_template = null;
        Enumeration todos = null;
        try {
            tl = (ToDoList) pim.openPIMList(PIM.TODO_LIST, PIM.READ_ONLY);
        } catch (PIMException e) {
            // failed opening the default todo list!
            System.err.println(
                    "Error accessing database - aborting action");
```

```
            return;
        } catch (SecurityException e) {
            // user rejected application's request for
            // read access to todo list
            // This is not an error condition and can be normal
            System.out.println(
              "Okay, this application won't get todo items");
            return;
        }
        // calculate today's start and end times
        Calendar start_of_day = Calendar.getInstance();
        start_of_day.set(Calendar.HOUR_OF_DAY, 0);
        Calendar end_of_day = Calendar.getInstance();
        end_of_day.set(Calendar.HOUR_OF_DAY, 24);
        try {
            // Get the enumeration of matching elements
            todos = tl.items(
                ToDo.DUE, start_of_day.getTime().getTime() - 86400000,
                end_of_day.getTime().getTime() - 86400000);
        } catch (PIMException e) {
            // failed to retrieve elements due to error!
            // Error case - abort this attempt
            System.err.println("This application cannot retrieve the todos");
        }
        // set all todos due yesterday to completed
        //with updated completion date
        while (todos != null && todos.hasMoreElements()) {
            ToDo t = (ToDo) todos.nextElement();
            if (tl.isSupportedField(ToDo.COMPLETED))
                t.setBoolean(ToDo.COMPLETED, 0, PIMItem.ATTR_NONE, true);
            if (tl.isSupportedField(ToDo.COMPLETION_DATE))
                t.setDate(ToDo.COMPLETION_DATE, 0,
                  PIMItem.ATTR_NONE, (new Date()).getTime());
            try {
                // save change to the database
                t.commit();
            } catch (PIMException exe) {
                // Oops couldn't save the data...
                System.err.println(
                    "This application cannot commit the todo");
            }
        }
        try {
            tl.close();
        } catch (PIMException e) {
            // failed to close the list
        }
    }
```

```java
public void deleteToDos() {
    // Delete all ToDos having to do with
    //    cleaning (hired a maid instead)
    PIM pim = PIM.getInstance();
    ToDoList tl = null;
    Enumeration todos = null;
    try {
        tl = (ToDoList) pim.openPIMList(PIM.TODO_LIST, PIM.READ_WRITE);
    } catch (PIMException e) {
        // failed opening the default todo list!
        System.err.println(
            "Error accessing database - aborting action");
        return;
    } catch (SecurityException e) {
        // user rejected application's request
        // for read/write access to todo list
        // This is not an error condition and can be normal
        System.out.println(
            "Okay, this application won't modify any todo");
        return;
    }
    try {
        // Get the enumeration of matching elements
        todos = tl.items("clean");
    } catch (PIMException e) {
        // failed retrieving the items enumeration due to an error
        System.err.println(
            "This application cannot retrieve the todos");
        return;
    }
    // delete all event entries containing 'clean'
    while (todos != null && todos.hasMoreElements()) {
        ToDo t = (ToDo) todos.nextElement();
        try {
            tl.removeToDo(t);
        } catch (PIMException exe) {
            // couldn't delete the entry for some reason
            System.err.println(
                    "This application cannot remove the todo info");
        }
    }
    try {
        tl.close();
    } catch (PIMException e) {
        // failed to close the list
    }
}
```

Quick Reference Guide

This quick reference guide provides an overview of classes used by J2ME for the PIM API. Full details of these classes and all Java classes and interfaces are available at www.jcp.org.

public interface Contact extends PIMItem

Field	Description
static int ADDR	Specify an address for a Contact.
static int ADDR_COUNTRY	Index into the string array for an address field representing the country of an address.
static int ADDR_EXTRA	Index into the string array for an address field representing any extra info of an address.
static int ADDR_LOCALITY	Index into the string array for an address field representing the locality (for example, a city) of an address.
static int ADDR_POBOX	Index into the string array for an address field representing the post office box of an address.
static int ADDR_POSTALCODE	Index into the string array for an address field representing the postal code (for example, a zip code) of an address.
static int ADDR_REGION	Index into the string array for an address field representing the region (for example, a province, state, or territory) of an address.
static int ADDR_STREET	Index into the string array for an address field, where the data at this index represents the street information of a particular address.
static int ADDRSIZE	The size of an address string array.
static int ATTR_ASST	Attribute classifying data as related to an ASSISTANT.
static int ATTR_AUTO	Attribute classifying a data as related to AUTO.
static int ATTR_FAX	Attribute classifying a data as related to FAX.
static int ATTR_HOME	Attribute classifying a data as related to HOME.

public interface Contact extends PIMItem

Field	Description
static int ATTR_MOBILE	Attribute classifying a data as related to MOBILE.
static int ATTR_OTHER	Attribute classifying a data as "OTHER."
static int ATTR_PAGER	Attribute classifying a data as related to PAGER.
static int ATTR_PREFERRED	Attribute classifying a data with preferred status for retrieval or display purposes (platform specific).
static int ATTR_SMS	Attribute classifying a data as related to SMS.
static int ATTR_WORK	Attribute classifying a data as related to WORK.
static int BIRTHDAY	Field for birthday.
static int CLASS	Field specifying access class for a contact.
static int CLASS_CONFIDENTIAL	Constant indicating contact's class is confidential.
static int CLASS_PRIVATE	Constant indicating contact's class is private.
static int CLASS_PUBLIC	Constant indicating contact's class is public.
static int EMAIL	Field for email address.
static int FORMATTED_ADDR	Field for a formatted version of a contact address.
static int FORMATTED_NAME	Field for a formatted version of a contact name.
static int NAME	Field for a contact name.
static int NAME_FAMILY	Index into the string array for an address field, where the data at this index represents a family name.
static int NAME_GIVEN	Index into the string array for an address field, where the data at this index represents a given name.

public interface Contact extends PIMItem

Field	Description
static int NAME_OTHER	Index into the string array for an address field, where the data at this index represents other alternate name or names.
static int NAME_PREFIX	Index into the string array for an address field, where the data at this index represents a prefix to a name.
static int NAME_SUFFIX	Index into the string array for an address field, where the data at this index represents a suffix to a name.
static int NAMESIZE	Indicate the size of a name string array.
static int NICKNAME	Field where the data is a nickname.
static int NOTE	Field for supplemental information or a comment associated with a Contact.
static int ORG	Field for the organization name or units associated with a Contact.
static int PHOTO	Field for a photo of a Contact.
static int PHOTO_URL	Field for a URL for a photo of a Contact.
static int PUBLIC_KEY	Field for the public encryption key for a Contact.
static int PUBLIC_KEY_STRING	Field for the public encryption key for a Contact.
static int REVISION	Field for the last modification date and time of a Contact item.
static int TEL	Field for a voice telephone number.
static int TITLE	Field for the job title for a Contact.
static int UID	Field for a unique ID for a Contact.
static int URL	Field for the uniform resource locator for a Contact.

Method	Description
int getPreferredIndex(int field)	Return the index of the value marked with the attribute ATTR_PREFERRED for a field.

public interface ContactList extends PIMItem

Method	Description
Contact createContact()	Create a Contact for this contact list.
Contact importContact(Contact contact)	Import the given Contact into this contact list.
void removeContact(Contact contact)	Remove a Contact from the list.

public interface Event extends PIMItem

Field	Description
static int ALARM	Field for the relative time for an Alarm for this Event.
static int CLASS	Field for the desired access class for this contact.
static int CLASS_CONFIDENTIAL	Indicate this event's class is confidential.
static int CLASS_PRIVATE	Indicate this event's class is private.
static int CLASS_PUBLIC	Indicate this event's class is public.
static int END	Field for the noninclusive date and time a single Event ends.
static int LOCATION	Field for the venue for this Event.
static int NOTE	A String for a complete description of an Event.
static int REVISION	Field for the last modification date and time of an Event item.
static int START	Field for the inclusive date and time a single Event starts.
static int SUMMARY	Field for the summary or subject for this Event.
static int UID	Field for a unique ID for an Event.

Method	Description
RepeatRule getRepeat()	Retrieve a RepeatRule object that specifies how often and when this event occurs.
void setRepeat(RepeatRule value)	Set the RepeatRule that specifies how often and when this event occurs.

public interface EventList extends PIMItem

Field	Description
static int ENDING	Represents a search type for Events based on the event end date/time.
static int OCCURRING	Represents a search type for Events based on the event during a time period.
static int STARTING	Represents a search type for Events based on the event start date/time.

Method	Description
Event createEvent()	Create an Event for this event list.
Event importEvent(Event item)	Import the given Event into this list by making a new Event for the list.
java.util.Enumeration items(int searchType, long startDate, long endDate, boolean initialEventOnly)	Return an enumeration of all the Events where at least one of the Event's occurrences falls in the specified startDate to endDate inclusive.
void removeEvent(Event item)	Remove a specific Event from the list.

public class FieldEmptyException extends java.lang.RuntimeException

Method	Description
FieldEmptyException()	Construct an instance of this class with its stack trace filled.
FieldEmptyException(java.lang.String detailMessage)	Construct an instance of this class with its stack trace and message filled.
FieldEmptyException(java.lang.String detailMessage, int field)	Construct an instance of this class with its stack trace, message, and offending field filled.
int getField()	Access the field that caused the exception to be thrown.

public class FieldFullException extends java.lang.RuntimeException

Method	Description
FieldFullException()	Construct an instance of this class with its stack trace filled.

public class FieldFullException extends java.lang.RuntimeException

Method	Description
FieldFullException(java.lang.String detailMessage)	Construct an instance of this class with its stack trace and message filled.
FieldFullException(java.lang.String detailMessage, int field)	Construct an instance of this class with its stack trace, message, and offending field filled.
int getField()	Access the field that caused the exception to be thrown.

public class PIMException extends java.lang.Exception

Field	Description
static int FEATURE_NOT_SUPPORTED	Functionality is not supported in this implementation.
static int GENERAL_ERROR	General PIM exception error.
static int LIST_CLOSED	List is closed and access is attempted.
static int LIST_NOT_ACCESSIBLE	List is no longer accessible by the application, such as if the underlying PIM database is deleted.
static int MAX_CATEGORIES_EXCEEDED	Maximum number of categories is exceeded.
static int UNSUPPORTED_VERSION	Data is in an unsupported PIM version.
static int UPDATE_ERROR	The update could not continue.

Method	Description
PIMException()	Construct an instance of this class with its stack trace filled.
PIMException(java.lang.String detailMessage)	Construct an instance of this class with its stack trace and message filled.
PIMException(java.lang.String detailMessage, int reason)	Construct an instance of this class with its stack trace, message, and reason filled.
int getReason()	Return the reason for the PIM Exception.

public interface PIMItem

Field	Description
static int ATTR_NONE	No additional attributes are applicable to a data value for a field.
static int BINARY	Data is binary in a byte array.
static int BOOLEAN	Data is of boolean primitive data type.
static int DATE	Data is a Date in long primitive data type format expressed in the same long value format as java.util.Date, which is milliseconds since the epoch (00:00:00 GMT, January 1, 1970).
static int EXTENDED_ATTRIBUTE_MIN_VALUE	The minimum possible value for an extended attribute constant.
static int EXTENDED_FIELD_MIN_VALUE	The minimum possible value for an extended field constant.
static int INT	Data is of int primitive data type.
static int STRING	Data is a String object.
static int STRING_ARRAY	Data is an array of related fields returned in a string array.

Method	Description
void addBinary(int field, int attributes, byte[] value, int offset, int length)	Add a binary data value to a field.
void addBoolean(int field, int attributes, boolean value)	Add a boolean value to a field.
void addDate(int field, int attributes, long value)	Add a date value to a field.
void addInt(int field, int attributes, int value)	Add an integer value to a field.
void addString(int field, int attributes, java.lang.String value)	Add a String value to a field.
void addStringArray(int field, int attributes, java.lang.String[] value)	Add an array of related string values as a single entity to a field.

public interface PIMItem

Method	Description
void addToCategory(java.lang.String category)	Add a category to this item.
void commit()	Persist the data in the item to its PIM list.
int countValues(int field)	Return the number of values assigned to a field.
int getAttributes(int field, int index)	Return the attributes associated with the data value at the given index for the indicated field.
byte[] getBinary(int field, int index)	Return a binary data value for a field from the item.
boolean getBoolean(int field, int index)	Return a boolean value from a field in the item.
java.lang.String[] getCategories()	Return all categories for the item.
long getDate(int field, int index)	Return a date value from a field in the item.
int[] getFields()	Return all fields in the item that have data stored for them.
int getInt(int field, int index)	Return an integer value from a field in the item.
PIMList getPIMList()	Return the PIMList associated with this item.
java.lang.String getString(int field, int index)	Return a String value from a field in the item.
java.lang.String[] getStringArray(int field, int index)	Return an array of related values from a field in the item.
boolean isModified()	Return a boolean indicating whether any of this item's fields have been modified since the item was retrieved or last committed.
int maxCategories()	Return the maximum number of categories that this item can be assigned to.
void removeFromCategory (java.lang.String category)	Remove a category from this item.

public interface PIMItem

Method	Description
void removeValue(int field, int index)	Remove the value at the given index for the indicated field in an item.
void setBinary(int field, int index, int attributes, byte[] value, int offset, int length)	Set an existing binary data value in a field to a new value.
void setBoolean(int field, int index, int attributes, boolean value)	Set an existing boolean data value in a field to a new value.
void setDate(int field, int index, int attributes, long value)	Set an existing date data value in a field to a new value.
void setInt(int field, int index, int attributes, int value)	Set an existing int data value in a field to a new value.
void setString(int field, int index, int attributes, java.lang.String value)	Set an existing String data value in a field to a new value.
void setStringArray(int field, int index, int attributes, java.lang.String[] value)	Set an existing String array data value in a field to a new value.

public interface PIMList

Field	Description
static java.lang.String UNCATEGORIZED	Constant for the itemsByCategory (java.lang.String) method to indicate to search for uncategorized items.

Method	Description
void addCategory(java.lang.String category)	Add a category to the PIM list.
void close()	Close the list, releasing any resources.
void deleteCategory(java.lang.String category)	Delete a category from the PIM list.
java.lang.String getAttributeLabel(int attribute)	Return a String label associated with an attribute.
java.lang.String[] getCategories()	Return the categories defined for the PIM list.
int getFieldDataType(int field)	Return an int representing the data type of the data associated with a field.

public interface PIMList

Method	Description
java.lang.String getFieldLabel(int field)	Return a String label associated with a field.
java.lang.String getName()	Return the name of the list.
int[] getSupportedArrayElements (int stringArrayField)	Return an integer array containing all of the supported elements of a string array for a field.
int[] getSupportedAttributes(int field)	Return an integer array containing all of the supported attributes for a field.
int[] getSupportedFields()	Return all fields that are supported in this list.
boolean isCategory(java.lang.String category)	Return whether a category is a valid, existing category for this list.
boolean isSupportedArrayElement(int stringArrayField, int arrayElement)	Return whether or not the element in an array is supported for a field in this PIM list.
boolean isSupportedAttribute(int field, int attribute)	Return whether or not the given attribute is supported in this PIM list for a field.
boolean isSupportedField(int field)	Return whether or not the given field is supported in this PIM list.
java.util.Enumeration items()	Return an Enumeration of all items in the list.
java.util.Enumeration items(PIMItem matchingItem)	Return an Enumeration of all items in the list that contain fields that match all fields specified in the matching item.
java.util.Enumeration items(java.lang.String matchingValue)	Return an Enumeration of all items in the list that contain at least one String field data value that matches the specified string value.
java.util.Enumeration itemsByCategory(java.lang.String category)	Return an enumeration of all items in the PIM list that match the category.
int maxCategories()	Return the maximum number of categories that this list can have.

public interface PIMList

Method	Description
void renameCategory(java.lang.String currentCategory, java.lang.String newCategory)	Rename a category to a new name.
int supportsMultipleValues(int field)	Determine whether a field supports adding more than one value to the field.

public class RepeatRule extends java.lang.Object

Field	Description
static int APRIL	Constant for the month of April.
static int AUGUST	Constant for the month of August.
static int COUNT	Specify the number of times this event repeats, including the first time, starting from the first time the event starts (derived from Event.START) and continuing to the last date of the repeat (defined by RepeatRule.END).
static int DAILY	Indicate frequency when the Event happens every day.
static int DAY_IN_MONTH	Specify the day of the month an Event occurs; for example, 15.
static int DAY_IN_WEEK	Specify the days of the week an Event occurs.
static int DAY_IN_YEAR	Specify the day of the year an Event occurs; for example, 134.
static int DECEMBER	Constant for the month of December.
static int END	Specify the ending date of the repeating event.
static int FEBRUARY	Constant for the month of February.
static int FIFTH	Constant for the fifth week of the month.
static int FIFTHLAST	Constant for the fifth to last week of the month.
static int FIRST	Constant for the first week of the month.

public class RepeatRule extends java.lang.Object

Field	Description
static int FOURTH	Constant for the fourth week of the month.
static int FOURTHLAST	Constant for the fourth to last week of the month.
static int FREQUENCY	Specify the frequency of the Repeat.
static int FRIDAY	Constant for the day of week Friday.
static int INTERVAL	Specify the number of iterations of the frequency between occurring dates, or how often the frequency repeats.
static int JANUARY	Constant for the month of January.
static int JULY	Constant for the month of July.
static int JUNE	Constant for the month of June.
static int LAST	Constant for the last week of the month.
static int MARCH	Constant for the month of March.
static int MAY	Constant for the month of May.
static int MONDAY	Constant for the day of week Monday.
static int MONTH_IN_YEAR	Specify the month in which an event occurs.
static int MONTHLY	Specify the frequency when the Event happens every month.
static int NOVEMBER	Constant for the month of November.
static int OCTOBER	Constant for the month of October.
static int SATURDAY	Constant for the day of week Saturday.
static int SECOND	Constant for the second week of the month.
static int SECONDLAST	Constant for the second to last week of the month.
static int SEPTEMBER	Constant for the month of September.
static int SUNDAY	Constant for the day of week Sunday.
static int THIRD	Constant for the third week of the month.
static int THIRDLAST	Constant for the third to last week of the month.

public class RepeatRule extends java.lang.Object

Field	Description
static int THURSDAY	Constant for the day of week Thursday.
static int TUESDAY	Constant for the day of week Tuesday.
static int WEDNESDAY	Constant for the day of week Wednesday.
static int WEEK_IN_MONTH	Specify which week in a month a particular event occurs.
static int WEEKLY	Specify frequency when the Event happens every week.
static int YEARLY	Specify frequency when the Event happens every year.

Method	Description
RepeatRule()	Default constructor.
void addExceptDate(long date)	Add a Date for which the RepeatRule should not occur.
java.util.Enumeration dates(long startDate, long subsetBeginning, long subsetEnding)	Return an Enumeration of dates on which an Event will occur.
long getDate(int field)	Return a Date field.
java.util.Enumeration getExceptDates()	Return the Dates for which the RepeatRule should not occur.
int[] getFields()	Return a list of fields that currently have values assigned to them.
int getInt(int field)	Return an integer field.
void removeExceptDate(long date)	Delete a Date for which the RepeatRule should not occur.
void setDate(int field, long value)	Set a Date field.
void setInt(int field, int value)	Set an integer field.

public interface ToDo extends PIMItem

Field	Description
static int CLASS	Specify the desired access class for this contact.
static int CLASS_CONFIDENTIAL	Constant indicating the to do's class is confidential.
static int CLASS_PRIVATE	Constant indicating the to do's class is private.
static int CLASS_PUBLIC	Constant indicating the to do's class is public.
static int COMPLETED	Field ID indicating a ToDo has been completed.
static int COMPLETION_DATE	Field ID indicating a ToDo has been completed on the date specified by this field.
static int DUE	The date a ToDo is due expressed in the same long value format as java.util.Date, which is milliseconds since the epoch (00:00:00 GMT, January 1, 1970).
static int NOTE	Specify a more complete description than the SUMMARY for this ToDo.
static int PRIORITY	Specify the priority of this ToDo.
static int REVISION	Specify the last modification date and time of a ToDo item.
static int SUMMARY	Specify the summary or subject for this ToDo.
static int UID	Specify a unique ID for a ToDo.

public interface ToDoList extends PIMList

Method	Description
ToDo createToDo()	Create a ToDo entry for this ToDo list.

public interface ToDoList extends PIMList

Method	Description
ToDo importToDo(ToDo item)	Import the ToDo into this list by making a new ToDo for the list and filling its information with as much information as it can from the provided ToDo.
java.util.Enumeration items(int field, long startDate, long endDate)	Return an enumeration of all the ToDos in the list, where the value of the specified date field falls in the range from startDate to endDate inclusive.
void removeToDo(ToDo item)	Delete a specific ToDo from the list.

public class UnsupportedFieldException extends java.lang.RuntimeException

Method	Description
UnsupportedFieldException()	Construct an instance of this class with its stack trace filled.
UnsupportedFieldException(java.lang .String detailMessage)	Construct an instance of this class with its stack trace and message filled.
UnsupportedFieldException(java.lang .String detailMessage, int field)	Construct an instance of this class with its stack trace, message, and offending field filled.

The Complete Reference

Part V

J2ME Networking and Web Services

Chapter 13

Generic Connection
Framework

The partnership between J2ME and small computing devices opens the possibility of developing a large distributive system that combines the convenience of portable computing with the horsepower of a back-end processing system. A small computing device is compact and has sufficient resources to collect and display information such as an order form, but lacks the capability to fully process and store this information. In contrast, a back-end processing system has the power and storage to handle any data processing requirement, but lacks the convenient size and flexibility to work under any conditions, which are the hallmarks of a small computing device.

J2ME enables you to build an application that overcomes the disadvantages of both by exchanging data between a small computing device and a back-end processing system. You can design an application to utilize a small computing device's capability of data capture and data display and a back-end system's capability for processing and storing the data. The exchange occurs in real time over a connection created by a J2ME application between the small computing device and the remote computer. This connection is created using the Generic Connection Framework (GCF), which you'll learn about in this chapter.

The Connection

A connection is a path between two computing devices that utilizes a hard-wired (cable) technology or wireless technology to transmit and receive data over a network. These devices can be a small computing device and a back-end processing system or two small computing devices. Three pieces of information are required to establish a connection between two computing devices. These are a network address, communications protocol, and communication parameters. (Parameters are not necessarily required depending on the requirements of the remote computing device.)

The *network address* uniquely identifies each computing device on a network. An Internet protocol (IP) address is used on many networks, although other addressing schemes exist. A *communications protocol* is a set of rules that describe how data is transmitted between two computing devices. Both computing devices must agree on a communications protocol before transmitting data. There are three widely used communications protocols: Hypertext Transfer Protocol (HTTP), File Transfer Protocol (FTP), and socket. *Communication parameters* consist of information required to open a connection between two computing devices. Login information such as a user ID and password are commonly used as communication parameters if the remote computer requires authentication before opening the connection with the other computing device.

A connection is opened by calling the Connector.open() method. The Connector.open() method requires one parameter, which is a String containing the communications protocol, network address, and any communication parameters. These components are separated within the String by a colon. You can disregard the last colon if no parameters are used to open the connection. The following code segment illustrates how to open a connection that uses HTTP as the communications protocol and //www.myweb.com as the network address. No communications are necessarily in this example.

```
Connection connection=Connector.Open("http://www.myweb.com");
```

The Class.forName() method is automatically called at run time to determine the class that implements the protocol being used for the connection. The Connector.open() method returns an instance of the Connection Interface, which is used within your J2ME application to transfer information between two computing devices. Figure 13-1 contains the Connection Interface class hierarchy that will be explored throughout this chapter.

Connection and Streams

The Connector class described in the GCF is used to establish network connections. The Connector class is used to access one of seven GCF connection interfaces. GCF connection interfaces provide a basic architecture for network operations and network protocol independence for writing network code. GCF connection interfaces are used the same way regardless of the underlying network protocol. These interfaces are Connection, ContentConnection, DatagramConnection, InputConnection, OutputConnection, StreamConnection, and StreamConnectionNotifier. All of these are located in the javax.microedition.io package.

The Connection interface is the basic connection that can either open or close a connection. The ContentConnection interface is used in a streaming connection that accesses information located on a web server. The DatagramConnection interface is used for packet transmission through the use of a datagram connection. The

```
            Connection Interface
                 InputConnection interface
                      StreamConnection Interface
                           ContentConnection Interface
                                HttpConnection
                 OutputConnection Interface
                      StreamConnection Interface
                           ContentConnection Interface
                                HttpConnection
                 DatagramConnection interface
                 StreamConnectionNotifier Interface
```

Figure 13-1.   *The Connection Interface class hierarchy*

InputConnection interface and OutputConnection interface are used to receive and send data from and to a communications device. The StreamConnection interface is used for two-way transmissions using a communications device. The StreamConnectionNotifier interface is used when a stream connection is established.

The Connector class and related connection interfaces only open (and close) a connection. They do not manage transmission. Think of the Connector class as the code that opens the telephone line for transmission to and from an Internet service provider.

Input/output classes defined in the java.io.package are used to manage transmission over an open connection. It is the input/output classes that write data to an open connection and read data from an open connection.

The InputStream class and the OutputStream class are base classes for all input and output classes. Derived from these classes are input and output classes that stream specific kinds of data. Derived classes are ByteArrayInputStream, ByteArrayOutputStream, DataInputStream, DataOutputStream, and PrintStream. The ByteArrayInputStream class and the ByteArrayOutputStream class buffer internal byte arrays for input and output. The DataInputStream class and the DataOutputStream class are used to input and output data as primitive Java data types. The PrintStream class outputs primitive data individually.

Characters are written and read by using the InputStreamReader class and the OutputStreamWriter class, which are derived from both the InputStream class and Reader class and the OutputStream class and Writer class, respectively.

InputStream Class

The InputStream class defines the basic interface for reading data from an open connection. First, you'll need to open a connection, which you'll learn later in this chapter, and then create an instance of the appropriate class derived from the InputStream class, as discussed in the previous section. Next you call a method of the InputStream class to read data from the connection. There are nine methods in the InputStream class, including three versions of the read() method. These are read(), read(byte b[]), read(byte b[], int off, int len), skip(long n), available(), mark(int readlimit), reset(), markSupported(), and close().

The first read() method returns a byte of data as an integer from the open connection. If the end of the stream is reached, a –1 is returned. You'll need to cast the returned integer as a char when reading characters from the open connection, which you'll see later in this chapter.

The second read() method is used to read multiple bytes from the open connection, which are stored in an array passed as a parameter to the read() method. The return value of this version of the read() method is either the number of bytes read from the open connection or a –1 indicating that the last byte has been read.

The third version of the read() method also reads multiple bytes from an open connection to a byte array. However, you can specify where in the byte array to place bytes read from the connection. This version requires three parameters. The first parameter is the array used to store incoming bytes. The second parameter is an int that specifies the first element of the array used to store the first incoming byte. The third parameter is an int that specifies the total number of bytes to read from the connection. This version of the read() method also returns either the total number of bytes read or a –1.

You can skip bytes in an input stream by calling the skip() method. The skip() method requires one parameter, which is a long that specifies the number of bytes to skip. The skip() method returns either the total number of bytes skipped or a –1 indicating the end of the stream.

The InputStream class uses a blocking technique whenever data is unavailable from the open connection. The blocking technique requires the InputStream class to wait until data becomes available before the application continues. Blocking also occurs with the OutputStream class where the application pauses until data is sent.

You can avoid blocking by calling the available() method before calling the read() method. The available() method returns the number of bytes available to be read from the open connection. If bytes are available, call the read() method; otherwise avoid calling the read() method because it will create a block until bytes are available to be read by your program.

Although your application reads bytes sequentially from a stream, you can read bytes downstream (ahead) and then return upstream to read additional bytes by using the technique called *marking*. Before reading downstream, call the mark() method to mark your current position in the stream. The mark() method requires an int parameter that specifies how many bytes you can read ahead. You return to the marked position in the stream by calling the reset() method. A word of caution: marking may not be available in all implementations; therefore you should call the markSupported() method, which returns a boolean value indicating whether or not marking is supported.

The close() method terminates the input stream, not the connection. Rarely will you need to call the close() method because the input stream is automatically closed when the instance of the InputStream is out of scope. However, it is always a good practice to call the close() method to free up resources.

OutputStream Class

The OutputStream class defines the basic interface for writing data to an open connection. First, you'll need to open a connection and then create an instance of the appropriate class derived from the OutputStream class, as discussed previously in this chapter. Next you call a method of the OutputStream class to write data from the connection. There are five methods in the OutputStream class, including three versions of the write() method. These are write(int b), write(byte b[]), write(byte b[], int off, int len), flush(), and close().

The first version of the write() method writes one byte to the output stream. This byte is passed as an int parameter to the write() method. The second version of the write() method writes multiple bytes to the output stream. Those bytes are contained in the byte array that is passed to the write() method.

The third version of the write() method writes specified elements of a byte array to the output stream. This version requires three parameters. The first parameter is the byte array. The second parameter is an int representing the offset of the first element that will be written to the output stream. The last parameter is an int representing the total number of bytes that are to be written.

The OutputStream class, like the InputStream class, uses blocking. In the case of the OutputStream class, blocking causes the application to wait until all pending bytes are written to the output stream. The flush() method causes any pending bytes to be output to the output stream.

The close() method terminates the output stream, not the connection. Rarely will you need to call the close() method because the output stream is automatically closed when the instance of the OutputStream is out of scope. However, it is always a good practice to call the close() method to free up resources.

Hypertext Transfer Protocol

The communications protocol HTTP is supported by MIDP 1.0 as required by specification. Support for other protocols is implementation dependent. Therefore, you can safely use HTTP in your application with confidence that the device running your application supports it. HTTP requires that a client initiate a request for information from a remote computer. The remote computer is typically a server, although any computing device can respond to a client's request if the computing device supports HTTP.

Communicating using HTTP is very similar in concept to sending and receiving an email. The client creates an email with a request for information. The email contains the address of the person who will supply the information and the return address of the client, which is used to respond to the email. The Uniform Resource Locators (URLs) of the client and remote computer are the addresses used in HTTP.

The network operating system routes the request to the remote computer, where the request is reviewed and a response is returned to the client. Typically, the content of the response is the requested information or a notification message indicating that the information is unavailable or the client is unauthorized to receive the information, depending on the nature of the application.

Creating an HTTP Connection

GCF optimizes mobile devices by providing a level of abstraction for network services enabling the device profile to select network protocols and network services to support. This means devices support only network protocols that they require. However, not all implementations support every network protocol. MIDP implementations are required to support HTTP; therefore, you can count on that support. HTTP is used to connect to web pages.

An HTTP connection is made by calling one of the three versions of the open() method of the Connector class. All three versions require at least a connection string parameter that identifies the connection and throws an IOException error. They also return a Connection. Here's the syntax for the first version of the open() method:

```
static Connection open (String connectString) throws IOException
```

The second version of the open() method requires a second parameter, which is an int that identifies the mode in which the connection is opened. Table 13-1 contains three connector modes: READ, WRITE, and READ_WRITE. The READ mode causes the connection to be used only for data input. The WRITE mode permits data to be sent but not received over the connection. And the READ_WRITE mode enables the connection to be used to send and receive data. Here's the syntax for the second version of the open() method:

```
static Connection open (String connectString, int mode)
                throws IOException
```

The third version of the open() method requires a third parameter consisting of a boolean value that indicates whether or not the application can handle a timeout exception. A timeout exception is thrown whenever an attempt to create the connection fails. The timeout period and other aspects of the timeout exception are implementation dependent. Here's the method definition for the third version of the open() method:

```
static Connection open (String connectString, int mode, boolean timeouts)
                throws IOException
```

The connection string of each version of the open() method contains a unique identifier of the connection that conforms to the Uniform Resource Indicator (URI). The identifier consists of three components: the scheme, the target, and parameters. (Parameters are optional.)

The *scheme* is the name of the network protocol used for the connection. Although you are guaranteed that an implementation supports the HTTP network protocol, some implementations also support socket, datagram, file, and port. Each has its own scheme, as illustrated in Table 13-2.

Mode	Description
READ	Open connection for read only
WRITE	Open connection for write only
READ_WRITE	Open connection for read and write

Table 13-1. *CLDC Connector Modes*

Network Protocol	Scheme	Target	Parameter
HTTP	http://	www.myweb.com	
Socket	socket://	www.mysocket:	1800
Datagram	datagram://	9000	
File	file://	myfile.txt	
Port	comm:	0;	baudrate=9600

Table 13-2. *Values for the Connection String Parameter of the open() Method*

The open() method returns a Connection object that consists of the base interface for the connection. However, you'll probably want to use a specific kind of connection interface, as described previously in this chapter. Therefore, you'll need to cast the returned Connection interface to the interface required for your application. It is common to use the StreamConnection interface for an HTTP connection. Here's how you cast the Connection object returned by the open() method as a StreamConnection interface:

```
StreamConnection connection = (StreamConnection)
        Connector.open("http://www.myweb.com");
```

Reading Data from an HTTP Connection

Once you've opened an HTTP connection and obtained a stream using a connection interface, you are ready to read or write data using an input/output stream class. A common routine is for a J2ME application to request and then receive information from a web server, similar to the technique used by a browser to request and receive web pages. A web page is a text file that contains text and HTML tags that describe how the text should be displayed on the screen. The browser interprets HTML tags and displays the corresponding text accordingly.

Your J2ME program must also interpret the contents of the file that it requests using the HTTP connection. Interpretation of the contents is application dependent. For example, your application might request from a web server a text file that contains customer contact information. Your application must contain the logic necessary to translate raw customer contact information into a meaningful presentation to the user of the application.

The initial step in communicating with a remote computer is to open a connection and a connection interface. The following code segment illustrates how this is done. The first line of code opens an HTTP connection to the web server www.jimkeogh.com and requests access to the index.htm file. The index.htm file is the home page of the web site. You can replace the name of the web server and file with any web server and file that is available to you. Next, the openInputStream() method is called to create an instance of the InputStream.

```
StreamConnect connection = (StreamConnection)
      Connector.open("http://www.jimkeogh.com/index.htm");
InputStream in = connection.openInputStream();
```

The connection and input stream are like a highway between two computers. Once the highway is built, you'll need to send cars along the highway. You do this by calling the read() method, assuming of course that you are reading data from the stream.

The read() method returns an int. The value of the int corresponds to a character if your program is reading a text file. As you recall from learning J2SE, there are a number of ways in which a program can assemble incoming characters into data that can be further manipulated by the program. Probably one of the most common of these techniques is to assemble characters in a line of text, as illustrated in the next code segment.

This code segment begins by creating a string buffer and an int. The read() method is called from within the conditional expression in the while loop. The return value of the read() method is an int, which is assigned to the ch int variable. The value of the ch variable is then compared to a –1 (negative one). A –1 is the value returned by the read() method when there isn't any data left to read from the stream.

Next, the conditional expression in the if statement determines whether the value of the ch variable is the end-of-line character. If not, the append() method is called to append the character to the buffer. The buffer requires one parameter, which is a char. Since the read() method returns an int, you'll need to convert the int to a char and pass the char to the append() method.

If the value of the ch variable is the end-of-line character, the buffer contains the first line of the file and can be processed further within the program. In this code segment, the contents of the buffer are converted to a string by calling the toString() method, and the string is passed as a parameter to the println() method, which displays the line of text on the console—not on the screen of the mobile device. You can process the line of text any way you wish as necessary to fulfill the requirements of the application. After the line of text is processed, you should prepare the string buffer for the next series of characters by resetting the string buffer as shown in the last statement in this code example.

```
StringBuffer buffer = new StringBuffer();
int ch;
while (( ch = in.read()) != -1)
{
   if (ch !=  '\n')
   {
    buffer.append((char) ch);
```

```
   }
   else
   {
    System.out.println(buffer.toString());
    buffer.delete(0, buffer.length());
   }
}
```

Reading and Parsing a Web Page

HTTP is the only protocol guaranteed to be supported by all implementations and is used to retrieve information from a web server. Listing 13-1 illustrates the technique for retrieving such information. Listing 13-2 contains the JAD file for Listing 13-1. A web server can serve information in various kinds of formats, the most common being HTML. As you learned in the previous section, an HTML document contains information and descriptions on how the information is to be displayed.

The purpose of Listing 13-1 is to retrieve the average star rating for my *J2EE: The Complete Reference* book from amazon.com and display it in an alert dialog box. The average star rating indicates how much or how little, on the average, customers enjoyed my book. The rating is recalculated each time a customer reviews the book for amazon.com. To achieve this objective, the MIDlet must connect to the specific HTML document that contains the average star rating, retrieve the document, find the rating within the document, and display it on the screen. You can use this same technique to retrieve any file from a web server.

The listing begins by creating Exit and Start commands that are associated with a form. A CommandListener is also associated with the form. The form is then displayed when the startApp() method is called. Logic within the commandAction() method reacts to the Start command when it is selected by the user of the MIDlet, which causes the MIDlet to actively retrieve and process the information from amazon.com.

Processing begins by creating references to the connection, input stream, and a string buffer before connection is made to amazon.com. The open() method is passed the URL of the specific page on amazon.com that contains information about my book. The URL was determined by manually visiting this book page on amazon.com and then copying the URL from the browser into the listing.

An input stream is then opened once connection is made to amazon.com. The conditional expression in the while loop calls the read() method to return the next integer from the input stream, which is the first character of the HTML document containing information about my book.

Processing continues as long as the value of the integer isn't a –1, which indicates there aren't any characters remaining to be read from the input stream. The MIDlet determines whether the character read from the input stream is a new line character (\n). If not, the character value of the int is appended to the buffer. If so, a line from the HTML document is contained in the buffer.

The content of the buffer is then assigned to a String called line, which is compared to the "out of 5 stars" text. This text is on the same line of the HTML document as the average star rating. I determined this by manually examining the HTML document, looking for a landmark that identifies this line within the document.

The next step is to identify the average star rating within this line of the document. The actual average star rating can be one of a series of values. Therefore, we cannot simply look for a specific value. Instead, the average star rating value is identified by position within the line (see Figure 13-2).

Many commercial web sites position the same kind of information in the same spot of every web page. For example, the average star rating appears five characters from the position of the letter *a* in the HTML tag "alt=". I know this by manually analyzing the line of the HTML tag that contains the average star rating.

Once we know the position of the *a* in the alt= HTML tag in the line that contains the average star rating, we can calculate the position of the rating itself. The indexOf() method is called and passed the alt= HTML tag. The indexOf() method returns an int that represents the character position within the line of the *a* in the alt= tag. This value is assigned to the int position in this MIDlet.

Next the substring() method is called. The substring() method returns a subset of characters contained within the line. The subset is identified by the two parameters passed to the substring() method. The first parameter is an int representing the character position of the first character of the subset. The second parameter is an int representing the character position of the last character of the subset.

In this example, the specific starting and ending positions are unknown because we don't know exactly where within the line the average star rating appears. However, we do know the relative positions of the starting and ending positions of the subset. The starting position is five characters after the *a* in alt=, and the ending position is eight characters after the *a* in alt=. These offset positions were determined by manually analyzing the position of the average star rating in relation to alt=. Regardless of the position of alt= in the line, the subset always began and ended at the same proportional position within the line relative to the character *a*.

```
<li> <b>Publisher:</b> McGraw-Hill Osborne Media; ISBN:
007222472X;
1st edition (September 6, 2002)
<li><b>Average Customer Review:</b>
<img src="http://g-images.amazon.com/images/G/01/detail/stars-5-
0.gif" width=64 height=12 border=0 alt="5.0 out of 5 stars">
Based on 12 reviews.
```

Figure 13-2. *A segment of the HTML document from amazon.com that is read by the MIDlet*

The substring is then displayed in an alert dialog box. Notice that the content of the buffer is erased after each line is read from the input stream by assigning a reference to a new StringBuffer to the buffer variable. This assures there are no residual characters remaining in the buffer from the previous line.

An IOException is thrown whenever the MIDlet is unable to connect to the web server. This error is displayed in an alert dialog box in this example.

Retrieving Information from a Web Server

Here are the steps required to retrieve information from a web server:

1. Declare references.
2. Obtain a reference to the instance of the Display class.
3. Create an instance of a Command class to exit the MIDlet.
4. Create an instance of a Command class to start the MIDlet.
5. Create an instance of the Form class.
6. Associate the instance of the Command class to the instance of the Form class.
7. Associate a CommandListener with the instance of the Form class.
8. Display the instance of the Form class on the screen.
9. If the Start command is selected, create references to a StreamConnection and InputStream.
10. Create a StringBuffer to store characters read from the input stream.
11. Open a connection to the server.
12. Open an input stream.
13. Read each byte from the input stream and append the byte to the StringBuffer.
14. Assign the contents of the StringBuffer to a String after the last character is read from the input stream.
15. Parse the string if necessary, and display the string in an alert dialog box.
16. If the Exit command is selected, terminate the MIDlet.
17. Trap exceptions thrown within the commandAction() method.
18. If the MIDletStateChangeException is thrown, indicate that conditions are now safe to terminate the MIDlet by assigning a true value to the exit flag variable.
19. Terminate the MIDlet when the Exit command is entered the second time.

The same technique illustrated in Listing 13-1 can be used to retrieve and parse any text delivered by a web server. Let's say that account information is stored in a delimited text file called accounts.txt on a web server. You could modify Listing 13-1 to connect to www.myweb.com/accounts.txt and then read each character from the input stream. Logic that you write within the while loop reads each line from the input stream.

Let's assume that each line is a record, and fields within the record are delimited. You can replace the logic in Listing 13-1 that locates the average star ranking with logic that uses the delimiter to parse each field of the current record to extract account information from the input stream.

Listing 13-1
Retrieving
information
from a
web server

```
import javax.microedition.midlet.*;
import javax.microedition.lcdui.*;
import java.io.*;
import javax.microedition.io.*;
import java.util.*;
public class HttpExample extends MIDlet implements CommandListener
{
  private Command exit, start;
  private Display display;
  private Form form;
  private StringItem stars;
  public HttpExample ()
  {
    display = Display.getDisplay(this);
    exit = new Command("Exit", Command.EXIT, 1);
    start = new Command("Start", Command.EXIT, 1);
    form = new Form("Customer Ranking");
    form.addCommand(exit);
    form.addCommand(start);
    form.setCommandListener(this);
  }
  public void startApp() throws MIDletStateChangeException
  {
    display.setCurrent(form);
  }
  public void pauseApp()
  {
  }
  public void destroyApp(boolean unconditional)
  {
  }
  public void commandAction(Command command, Displayable displayable)
  {
    if (command == exit)
    {
      destroyApp(false);
```

```
      notifyDestroyed();
    }
    else if (command == start)
    {
      StreamConnection connection = null;
      InputStream in = null;
      StringBuffer buffer = new StringBuffer();
       try
         {
         connection = (StreamConnection)
Connector.open(
            "http://www.amazon.com/exec/obidos/tg/detail/-/007222472X");
         in = connection.openInputStream();
         int ch;
         while ((ch = in.read()) != -1)
         {
           if (ch != '\n')
           {
             buffer.append((char)ch);
           }
           else
           {
             String line = new String (buffer.toString());
             if(line.equals("out of 5 stars"))
             {
                int position = line.indexOf("alt=");
                Alert alert = new Alert(
                  "Rating", line.substring(position + 5, position + 8), null, null);
                alert.setTimeout(Alert.FOREVER);
                alert.setType(AlertType.ERROR);
                display.setCurrent(alert);
              }
             buffer = new StringBuffer();
           }
        }
      }
      catch (IOException error)
      {
       Alert alert = new Alert("Error", "Cannot connect", null, null);
       alert.setTimeout(Alert.FOREVER);
       alert.setType(AlertType.ERROR);
       display.setCurrent(alert);
      }
    }
  }
}
```

Listing 13-2
The JAD
file for
Listing 13-1

```
MIDlet-Name: httpexample
MIDlet-Version: 1.0
MIDlet-Vendor: MyCompany
MIDlet-Jar-URL: httpexample.jar
MIDlet-1: httpexample, , httpexample
MicroEdition-Configuration: CLDC-1.0
MicroEdition-Profile: MIDP-1.0
MIDlet-JAR-SIZE: 100
```

The File Protocol

The file protocol is used to write information to a file from a MIDlet if the implementation supports the file protocol and if the device supports a file system. Listing 13-3 illustrates the technique used to write information to a file. Listing 13-4 contains the JAD file for this listing. Listing 13-3 is structured similar to Listing 13-1 in that both listings contain a form that has Start and Exit commands associated with it, along with the required CommandListener, which is created within the constructor.

The text is written to the file when a user selects the Start command. Logic to write to the file is contained within the start section of the commandAction() method. First an OutputConnection is created by calling the open() method of the Connector. Two parameters are passed to the open() method. The first parameter is the schema for the file. The schema begins with the protocol identifier called file, which is followed by the full path to the file, including the file name.

The append parameter is at the end of the schema. The append parameter is a boolean value indicating whether or not the text should be written to the end of the file or to the beginning of the file. If true, new text is appended to the end of the file. If false, or if the append parameter is omitted, new text is written at the beginning of the file, overwriting the content of the existing file. The file is automatically created if the file doesn't exist, even if the append parameter is set to true.

The second parameter is the file mode. In this example the file is opened for output. The file could also be opened for input by replacing the Connector.WRITE with Connector.READ. The Connector.WRITE_READ is used to open the file for both input and output.

Once the connection is opened the program creates an OutputStream by calling the openOutputStream() method. The OutputStream is then used to create a PrintStream, which is necessary to write text to a file. You write text to the file by calling the println() method and passing this method the text that is to be written to the file. The stream and connection are both closed once the text is written to the file, and a message is then displayed in an alert dialog box notifying the user that the operation was successful. Any errors that are thrown are caught and displayed in another alert dialog box.

J2ME NETWORKING
AND WEB SERVICES

Writing to a File

Here are the steps required to write to a file:

1. Declare references.

2. Obtain a reference to the instance of the Display class.

3. Create an instance of a Command class to exit the MIDlet.

4. Create an instance of a Command class to start the MIDlet.

5. Create an instance of the Form class.

6. Associate the instance of the Command class to the instance of the Form class.

7. Associate a CommandListener with the instance of the Form class.

8. Display the instance of the Form class on the screen.

9. If the Start command is selected, open an output connection to the server where append is set to true.

10. Open an output stream.

11. Open a PrintStream.

12. Print text to the output stream.

13. Close the output stream.

14. Close the connection.

15. Display message indicating that data has been written.

16. Trap errors thrown during this process.

17. Assign the contents of the StringBuffer to a String after the last character is read from the input stream.

18. Parse the string if necessary, and display the string in an alert dialog box.

19. If the Exit command is selected, terminate the MIDlet.

20. Trap exceptions thrown within the commandAction() method.

21. If the MIDletStateChangeException is thrown, indicate that conditions are now safe to terminate the MIDlet by assigning a true value to the exit flag variable.

22. Terminate the MIDlet when the Exit command is entered the second time.

Listing 13-3
Writing
to a file

```java
import javax.microedition.midlet.*;
import javax.microedition.lcdui.*;
import java.io.*;
import javax.microedition.io.*;
public class FileConnection extends MIDlet implements CommandListener {
  private Command exit, start;
  private Display display;
  private Form form;
  public FileConnection ()
  {
    display = Display.getDisplay(this);
    exit = new Command("Exit", Command.EXIT, 1);
    start = new Command("Start", Command.EXIT, 1);
    form = new Form("Write To File");
    form.addCommand(exit);
    form.addCommand(start);
    form.setCommandListener(this);
  }
  public void startApp() throws MIDletStateChangeException
  {
    display.setCurrent(form);
  }
  public void pauseApp()
  {
  }
  public void destroyApp(boolean unconditional)
  {
  }
  public void commandAction(Command command, Displayable displayable)
  {
    if (command == exit)
    {
      destroyApp(false);
      notifyDestroyed();
    }
    else if (command == start)
    {
      try
      {
        OutputConnection connection = (OutputConnection)
          Connector.open("file://c:/myfile.txt;append=true", Connector.WRITE );
        OutputStream out = connection.openOutputStream();
        PrintStream output = new PrintStream( out );
        output.println( "This is a test." );
        out.close();
```

J2ME NETWORKING
AND WEB SERVICES

```
                      connection.close();
                      Alert alert = new Alert("Completed", "Data Written", null, null);
                      alert.setTimeout(Alert.FOREVER);
                      alert.setType(AlertType.ERROR);
                      display.setCurrent(alert);
                  }
                catch( ConnectionNotFoundException error )
                  {
                    Alert alert = new Alert(
                        "Error", "Cannot access file.", null, null);
                    alert.setTimeout(Alert.FOREVER);
                    alert.setType(AlertType.ERROR);
                    display.setCurrent(alert);
                  }
                catch( IOException error )
                  {
                    Alert alert = new Alert("Error", error.toString(), null, null);
                    alert.setTimeout(Alert.FOREVER);
                    alert.setType(AlertType.ERROR);
                    display.setCurrent(alert);
                  }
              }
          }
      }
```

Listing 13-4
The JAD
file for
Listing 13-3

```
MIDlet-Name: fileconnection
MIDlet-Version: 1.0
MIDlet-Vendor: MyCompany
MIDlet-Jar-URL: fileconnection.jar
MIDlet-1: fileconnection, , fileconnection
MicroEdition-Configuration: CLDC-1.0
MicroEdition-Profile: MIDP-1.0
MIDlet-JAR-SIZE: 100
```

Socket

A socket is a connection to a port on a remote computer that is used to exchange information using HTTP commands. HTTP commands enable your application to send an HTTP request for a stream of data to a remote computer. In return, the remote computer responds to your application by sending an HTTP response. Let's say your application wants to receive a stream of data from a particular file stored on a remote server. First your application opens a socket connecting to a port on the server. Next, the application sends a GET command followed by the file name as part of an HTTP request. Your application then reads the stream containing the remote server's HTTP response.

You'll learn more about HTTP commands, HTTP requests, and HTTP responses later in this chapter. For now let's focus on opening a socket for two-way transmission with a remote server. A socket is created by calling the Connector open() method and passing it a string containing the socket schema. The socket schema consists of the socket identifier followed by the URL of the remote server. The URL must contain the port number of the remote server that is used to connect the remote server to the client.

The following code segment illustrates a socket schema. In this example, a connection is made to port 80 of www.myserver.com, which is the URL of the remote server.

```
socket://www.myserver.com:80
```

The println() method of the PrintStream is used to send strings containing HTTP commands to the remote server over the socket connection. The following code segment is a typical HTTP request. GET is the HTTP command used to request a file. /my.html is the name of the file being requested. HTTP/0.9 is the version of the protocol being used for transmission, and \r\n are the carriage return and new line characters.

```
GET /my.html HTTP/0.9\r\n
```

The application then uses the read() method of the InputStream to retrieve the HTTP response sent by the remote server along the socket connection. Logic within the application responds appropriately to the HTTP response message.

Listing 13-5 illustrates how to create a socket connection and use it to communicate with a remote computer. Listing 13-6 contains the JAD file for Listing 13-5. The program issues a GET request for the my.html file and then displays the HTTP response in the console. In a real-world program you would include logic to respond to the HTTP response rather than simply displaying the response on the screen.

The MIDlet begins by creating a form that contains two command buttons, one to start the application and the other to exit the application. Each command button is then associated with the form within the constructor. Likewise, a CommandListener is also associated with the form to process these commands. The form is then displayed on the screen by calling the setCurrent() method within the startApp() method. The startApp(), as you'll remember from other chapters, is the method that is automatically called when the MIDlet is loaded into the device.

The commandAction() method is called whenever the user selects a command button. The application terminates if the Exit button is selected. The application sends the HTTP request and processes the HTTP response received from the server.

The open() method is called to create a socket connection with the remote server. The URI for the server is www.myserver.com, and the port used by the socket is port 80. Once the connection is opened, the MIDlet creates a PrintStream that is used to write to the socket by calling the println() method. The string passed to the println() method must contain a properly structured HTTP command statement, which you learn about later in this chapter. The println() method does not validate the HTTP command statement passed to it. The println() method simply treats the HTTP command statement as any string as it passes it through to the socket connection.

In this example, the GET command is issued specifying the requested file and HTTP version used for transmission, as described previously in this section. The flush() method is then called to assure that all pending strings waiting to be sent over the socket connection are actually sent.

Writing to and Reading from a Socket Connection

Here are the steps required to write to and read from a socket connection:

1. Declare references.
2. Obtain a reference to the instance of the Display class.
3. Create an instance of a Command class to exit the MIDlet.
4. Create an instance of a Command class to start the MIDlet.
5. Create an instance of the Form class.
6. Associate the instance of the Command class to the instance of the Form class.
7. Associate a CommandListener with the instance of the Form class.
8. Display the instance of the Form class on the screen.
9. If the Start command is selected, create and open a StreamConnection.
10. Create and open a PrintStream.
11. Print an HTTP request to the PrintStream.
12. Flush the PrintStream.
13. Create an input stream.
14. Read bytes from the input stream and display them on the console.
15. Close the input stream.
16. Close the output stream.
17. Trap errors thrown during this process.
18. If the Exit command is selected, terminate the MIDlet.
19. Trap exceptions thrown within the commandAction() method.
20. If the MIDletStateChangeException is thrown, indicate that conditions are now safe to terminate the MIDlet by assigning a true value to the exit flag variable.
21. Terminate the MIDlet when the Exit command is entered the second time.

Next an InputStream is created and used to receive the server's response from the socket connection. The read() method is called within the conditional statement in the while loop to reach a character from the socket connection. As long as the value returned by the read() method isn't a –1, the return value is converted to a char and then printed on the console.

The InputStream, PrintStream, and socket connection are closed when the read() method returns a –1 indicating that no more characters are to be read from the socket. In a real-world application you include logic within the MIDlet to reply to the remote server's response until communication between both the client and server is no longer necessary.

Listing 13-5
Writing to and reading from a socket connection

```
import javax.microedition.midlet.*;
import javax.microedition.lcdui.*;
import java.io.*;
import javax.microedition.io.*;
public class socketconnection extends MIDlet implements CommandListener {
  private Command exit, start;
  private Display display;
  private Form form;
  public socketconnection ()
  {
    display = Display.getDisplay(this);
    exit = new Command("Exit", Command.EXIT, 1);
    start = new Command("Start", Command.EXIT, 1);
    form = new Form("Read Write Socket");
    form.addCommand(exit);
    form.addCommand(start);
    form.setCommandListener(this);
  }
  public void startApp() throws MIDletStateChangeException
  {
    display.setCurrent(form);
  }
  public void pauseApp()
  {
  }
  public void destroyApp(boolean unconditional)
  {
  }
  public void commandAction(Command command, Displayable displayable)
  {
    if (command == exit)
    {
```

```
        destroyApp(false);
        notifyDestroyed();
      }
    else if (command == start)
    {
      try
      {
        StreamConnection connection = (StreamConnection)
Connector.open("socket://www.myserver.com:80");
        PrintStream output =
          new PrintStream(connection.openOutputStream() );
        output.println( "GET /my.html HTTP/0.9\n\n" );
        output.flush();
        InputStream in = connection.openInputStream();
        int ch;
        while( ( ch = in.read() ) != -1 )
        {
          System.out.print( (char) ch );
        }
        in.close();
        output.close();
        connection.close();
      }
      catch( ConnectionNotFoundException error )
      {
        Alert alert = new Alert(
          "Error", "Cannot access socket.", null, null);
        alert.setTimeout(Alert.FOREVER);
        alert.setType(AlertType.ERROR);
        display.setCurrent(alert);
      }
      catch( IOException error )
      {
        Alert alert = new Alert("Error", error.toString(), null, null);
        alert.setTimeout(Alert.FOREVER);
        alert.setType(AlertType.ERROR);
        display.setCurrent(alert);
      }
    }
  }
}
```

Listing 13-6
The JAD
file for
Listing 13-5

```
MIDlet-Name: socketconnection
MIDlet-Version: 1.0
MIDlet-Vendor: MyCompany
MIDlet-Jar-URL: socketconnection.jar
MIDlet-1: socketconnection, , socketconnection
MicroEdition-Configuration: CLDC-1.0
MicroEdition-Profile: MIDP-1.0
MIDlet-JAR-SIZE: 100
```

Communication Management Using HTTP Commands

HTTP is used by two computers to communicate with each other over a socket connection. HTTP is considered a request/response protocol, meaning that a client is the requestor of information contained on a server and the server responds to the client's request. An HTTP request, called a *request entity*, consists of three components. These are the request method, request header, and request body. The request method describes the way in which information is to be sent to the client by the server. The client specifies the request method as part of the request, as illustrated in the previous section of this chapter. There are three request methods (see Table 13-3). These are GET, POST, and HEAD.

A word of caution: the term *method* used in relationship to an HTTP request is an HTTP method and not a J2ME method.

There are basically two ways in which data is sent—by including the data as part of the URL as a query string, which is called the GET method, or by sending data in a stream aside from the URL, called the POST method. The GET method requires a URL and data separated by a question mark, which is also known as URL encoding. Data is grouped into one or more fields, each of which has a value associated with the field. A value is associated with a field by using an assignment operator (=), and each field-value pair is separated by an ampersand (&).

Request	Description
GET	Send requested data as part of the URL
POST	Send requested data in a separate stream
HEAD	Send only meta-information about the specified resource

Table 13-3.   *Types of HTTP Request Methods*

Data sent in response to a request is assigned to an environment variable within the requestor's operating environment. The requestor then retrieves the data by reading the environment variable.

The following code segment illustrates the form of the data being returned using the GET request method. This example is a response to a request from the client located at www.myclient.com/inventory for the inventory status of product 123 and product 456. The first field is prod123 and has a value of 100 units; the second field is prod456 and has a value of 150 units. Spaces are not permitted in field names and in values. However, you can insert a plus sign (+) in place of a space if a space is required to fulfill the request.

```
http://www.myclient.com/inventory?prod123=100&prod456=150
```

The POST method requires data to be sent in a separate stream, which provides two advantages over the GET method. Data sent using the GET method is visible whenever the URL is visible. You've probably noticed data attached to the end of the URL whenever you select the Submit button after filling out a form in a browser. The POST method causes the data not to be visible as part of the URL.

The other advantage of using the POST method is to be able to send an unlimited amount of data in response to a request. The size of data sent using the GET method is limited by the maximum size of data that can be held by the environment variable. Data exceeding the size of the environment variable will probably be lost after reaching the requestor.

A word of caution: the POST method is not a secure method to transmit data. It is simply less accessible than the GET method because data is sent on a different stream.

The HEAD method requests metadata about the resource. Remember that metadata is information about data, such as the last time inventory data was updated. A MIDlet that wants to retrieve the latest inventory status of a product may do so only if the inventory recently changed. Therefore, the MIDlet uses the HEAD method and follows up with a GET or POST method if the inventory has changed. Metadata is returned using the same technique as the GET request method.

HttpConnection

HttpConnection is used to send an HTTP request method. Implementing the following code segment within your MIDlet creates an HttpConnection. In this example, a connection is made to the inventory.dat resource located on the server associated with the URI www.myserver.com:

```
HttpConnection connection = (HttpConnection)
        Connector.open("http://www.myserver.com/inventory.dat");
```

Once an HttpConnection is opened, you can use HttpConnection client request methods to interact with the remote server. There are two ways to interact with the remote server—by setting or retrieving the request method, or by setting or retrieving the HTTP header information.

The request method is set by calling the setRequestMethod(), which requires a string containing GET, POST, or HEAD as a parameter. The getRequestMethod() is called to retrieve a string that contains the current request method.

The setRequestProperty() method is used to write a value to a field in the HTTP header. Two parameters are required by the setRequestProperty() method. The first parameter is a string containing the field name, called a key, which is being set. The other parameter is a string containing the new value of the specified header field.

A request header is information that describes the request using one or a combination of 40 header fields. Many header fields are used only rarely. Here are commonly used header fields:

- Accept
- Cache-Control
- Content-Type
- Expires
- IF-Modified-Since
- User-Agent

Let's say that a client wants to receive a response using the plain text content type and using the GET request method. Here's the code segment that needs to be included in the MIDlet:

```
HttpConnection connection = (HttpConnection)
        Connector.open("http://www.myserver.com/inventory.dat");
connection.setRequestMethod(HttpConnection.GET);
connection.setRequestProperty("Content-Type","//text/plain");
```

The body of an HTTP request contains any information that is sent to the server as part of the request. This information is transferred to the server using either the GET or POST request method, as described in the request method portion of the request.

The request method, request header, and the body of the request are transmitted over the connection to the server, where software running on the server reads each component of the request, processes the request based on the nature of the application, and returns a response with a response entity.

You are unlikely to create a response entity using a MIDlet because MIDlets are typically clients in an HTTP transmission. You'll find more information about how to create a response entity in *J2EE: The Complete Reference* (McGraw-Hill/Osborne, 2001). However, you will need to understand how to translate a server's response into information that is processed by your MIDlet. A response entity consists of three components: the status line, header response, and the body of the response.

The status line is a snapshot of the server's response to the client's request. There are more than 35 response status codes for the HttpConnection. A three-digit number represents a status code. The first digit represents the category of the status code (see Table 13-4), and the remaining digits represent a specific status within a category.

There are two parts to the status line. The first part is the status code and the other, the status message. You retrieve the status code by calling the getResponseCode(). The getResponseCode() returns an int whose value is the status code. The status message is retrieved by calling the getResponseMessage(). The getResponseMessage() method returns a string containing the status message. The following code segment illustrates how to retrieve the response code and response message from within a MIDlet:

```
HttpConnection connection = (HttpConnection)
Connector.open("http://www.myserver.com/inventory.dat");
System.out.println(connection.getResponseCode());
System.out.println(connection.getResponseMessage());
```

The response header contains header fields and related values similar to the request header discussed previously in this section of the chapter. You can retrieve a header field or field value by calling methods of the HttpConnection class. The most commonly used methods to retrieve the value of a header field are two versions of the getHeaderField() method. The first version retrieves the value by referencing the index of the header field, which is passed to the getHeaderField() as an int. Each header field is assigned an index beginning with zero in the order in which the header field was entered into the header. Therefore, getHeaderField(0) retrieves the value of the first header field of the response header.

The second version of the getHeaderField() retrieves the value of a header field by referencing the name of the header field, which is passed as a string to the getHeaderField() method as a parameter.

Status Code Category	Description
100–199	Information
200–299	Success
300–399	Redirection
400–499	Client Error
500–599	Server Error

Table 13-4. *Response Status Code Categories*

You can retrieve the name of a header field by calling the getHeaderFieldInt() method and passing it a string that contains the name of the header field. Likewise, you can retrieve the name of a header field by calling the getHeaderFieldKey() and passing it an int that represents the index of the header field.

Three useful header fields that are typically included in the response header are the date, expiration, and last modified fields. These are fairly self-explanatory: date contains the date when the header was created. Expiration is the date when information contained in the header is no longer valid. And the last modified field is the date when values in the header changed. You can retrieve these dates by calling the getDate() method, getExpiration() method, and getLastModified() method. All three return the date as a long.

Besides predefined response header fields, a response header can also include customized header fields. Customized header fields are application specific, and their values are generated by the server-side process. The value assigned to a customized header field is retrieved by calling the getHeaderField() method, as described previously in this section.

The third component of a response entity is the body, which contains the information that the client requested from the server. HttpConnection does not contain methods for reading the body of a response entity because you read the body as illustrated previously in this chapter in the "Reading Data from an HTTP Connection" section.

Using HttpConnection in a MIDlet

Listing 13-7 illustrates how to create a MIDlet to send an HTTP request and read an HTTP response, including the body of the response, from a server. Listing 13-8 contains the JAD file for Listing 13-7. The MIDlet sets the request method to GET and then retrieves a text file from the server, which is displayed on the console.

Listing 13-7 begins by creating and displaying a form containing Start and Exit command buttons. The form is displayed when the startApp() method is called. The commandAction() method responds to the selection of either the Exit or Start command. When the Start command is selected, the MIDlet creates references for an HttpConnection and InputStream and then calls the open() method of the Connector to open an HTTP connection to www.myserver.com/myinfo.txt.

Once the connection is opened, the MIDlet tells the server that the GET request method is being used for the transmission by calling the setRequestMethod() and passing it the Http.Connection.GET field. Next, the value of the Content-Type HTTP header field is set to //text/plain by passing the appropriate parameters to the setRequestProperty() method.

The last step in sending the HTTP request is to call the setRequestProperty() method again to close the connection. The MIDlet requests that the connection be closed after the request is received, by setting the value of the Connection HTTP header field to close and passing those values to the setRequestProperty() method. The value of the Connection HTTP header field is then set to close, which tells the server to close the connection once the request is received. It is wise to close the connection explicitly because in a real-world application the connection to the server is reused for other requests. Closing the connection when you no longer require it enables the connection to be reused.

The MIDlet then reads the HTTP response sent by the server. The HTTP response consists of several components, which are discussed in the previous section. Components can be read in any order, although the status line should be read first to determine the status of the response.

The MIDlet calls the getResponseCode() method and getResponseMessage() method to retrieve the status line code and status line message from the HTTP response. Both are displayed on the console for illustrative purposes. If the server successfully fulfills the request, the response code has the value of HTTP_OK; otherwise the request isn't fulfilled and the server sends a different response code. The MIDlet uses a conditional expression in the if statement to determine whether the response code is equivalent to HTTP_OK. If so, then the values of the selected HTTP header fields are read and displayed on the console for illustrative purposes.

You don't need to read HTTP header fields unless you require them to process the HTTP response. The "Quick Reference Guide" section at the end of this chapter contains a list of HttpConnection methods that you can use to retrieve connection information from an HTTP response.

First, the header field and header key field are retrieved by passing the field index to the getHeaderField() method and getHeaderFieldKey() method. Next, the date of the header field is retrieved by passing the getHeaderField() method the name of the header field.

The MIDlet then reads the body of the HTTP response. There are two techniques for reading the body. First, you can read the entire contents of the body into an array, which is possible only if the length of the content can be determined by the MIDlet. If the length cannot be determined, the second technique is used to read each byte of the contents of the body.

The MIDlet begins reading the body of the HTTP response by creating a string to hold the contents and opening an input stream to read the contents. The input stream is opened by calling the openInputStream method(). Once the input stream is opened, the getLength() method is called to determine the length of the content of the body of the HTTP response. The getLength() method returns an int that represents either the length of the body or a –1, which means that the length cannot be established.

If the return value of getLength() is not a –1, the MIDlet proceeds to read the entire contents of the body into an array. First, a byte array is created using the value returned by the getLength() method to determine the size of the array. Next, the read() method is called and passed the name of the byte array. The read() method copies the contents of the body into the byte array. The byte array is then assigned to a string.

If the return value of getLength() is –1, the MIDlet cannot determine the size of the content of the body and therefore must read the content a byte at a time. The MIDlet begins this process by creating a ByteArrayOutputStream.

The read() method is called as a component of the conditional expression in the while loop. The read() method returns a byte from the contents of the body of the HTTP response, which is compared to –1. A –1 indicates the end of the stream. The MIDlet calls

Using an HttpConnection to Communicate with a Server

Here are the steps required to use an HttpConnection to communicate with a server:

1. Declare references.
2. Obtain a reference to the instance of the Display class.
3. Create an instance of a Command class to exit the MIDlet.
4. Create an instance of a Command class to start the MIDlet.
5. Create an instance of the Form class.
6. Associate the instance of the Command class to the instance of the Form class.
7. Associate a CommandListener with the instance of the Form class.
8. Display the instance of the Form class on the screen.
9. If the Start command is selected, create an HttpConnection reference and an InputStream reference.
10. Open an HTTP connection.
11. Set the request method and required properties.
12. Set the Connection field to close.
13. Read the response code and response message, and print them to the console.
14. If HttpConnection.HTTP_OK is received, read header fields and the header field key, and display them on the console.
15. Open the input stream and determine the number of bytes to be read from the input stream (length).
16. If the length of the input stream cannot be determined, create a byte array the size of the length of the input stream.
17. Read bytes from the input stream into the byte array.
18. Assign the byte array to a string.
19. If the length of the input stream can be determined, create a ByteArrayOutputStream.
20. Read each byte from the input stream and into the ByteArrayOutputStream.
21. Assign the ByteArrayOutputStream to a string.
22. Close the byte stream.
23. Print the string to the console.

24. Trap errors thrown during this process.

25. If the Exit command is selected, terminate the MIDlet.

26. Trap exceptions thrown within the commandAction() method.

27. If the MIDletStateChangeException is thrown, indicate that conditions are now safe to terminate the MIDlet by assigning a true value to the exit flag variable.

28. Terminate the MIDlet when the Exit command is entered the second time.

the write() method to write the byte from the content to the ByteArrayOutputStream until the end of the stream is read, at which time the ByteArrayOutputStream is assigned to a string and then closed.

The string containing the contents of the body of the HTTP response is then displayed on the console. In a real-world application, a MIDlet is likely to process the content further rather than display the contents on the console. The nature of this processing is application dependent. Both the input stream and the HttpConnection are closed within the final try {} block as long as each was opened successfully.

Listing 13-7
Using an HttpConnection to communicate with a server

```
input javax.microedition lcdui.*
import javax.microedition.midlet.*;
import javax.microedition.io.*;
import java.io.*;
public class httpconnection extends MIDlet implements CommandListener {
    private Command exit, start;
    private Display display;
    private Form form;
    public httpconnection ()
    {
        display = Display.getDisplay(this);
        exit = new Command("Exit", Command.EXIT, 1);
        start = new Command("Start", Command.EXIT, 1);
        form = new Form("Http Connection");
        form.addCommand(exit);
        form.addCommand(start);
        form.setCommandListener(this);
    }
    public void startApp()
    {
     display.setCurrent(form);
    }
    public void pauseApp()
    {
    }
```

```
public void destroyApp(boolean unconditional)
{
    destroyApp(false);
    notifyDestroyed();
}
public void commandAction(Command command, Displayable displayable)
{
  if (command == exit)
  {
    destroyApp(false);                      .
    notifyDestroyed();
  }
  else if (command == start)
  {
    HttpConnection connection = null;
    InputStream inputstream = null;
    try
    {
      connection = (HttpConnection) Connector.open("http://www.myserver.com/myinfo.txt");
      //HTTP Request
      connection.setRequestMethod(HttpConnection.GET);
      connection.setRequestProperty("Content-Type","//text plain");
      connection.setRequestProperty("Connection", "close");
      // HTTP Response
      System.out.println("
         Status Line Code: " + connection.getResponseCode());
      System.out.println(
         "Status Line Message: " + connection.getResponseMessage());
      if (connection.getResponseCode() == HttpConnection.HTTP_OK)
      {
        System.out.println(
          connection.getHeaderField(0)+ " " + connection.getHeaderFieldKey(0));
        System.out.println(
         "Header Field Date: " + connection.getHeaderField("date"));
        String str;
        inputstream = connection.openInputStream();
        int length = (int) connection.getLength();    .
        if (length != -1)
        {
          byte incomingData[] = new byte[length];
          inputstream.read(incomingData);
          str = new String(incomingData);
        }
        else
        {
          ByteArrayOutputStream bytestream =
                new ByteArrayOutputStream();
```

J2ME NETWORKING
AND WEB SERVICES

```
              int ch;
              while ((ch = inputstream.read()) != -1)
              {
                 bytestream.write(ch);
              }
              str = new String(bytestream.toByteArray());
              bytestream.close();
            }
          System.out.println(str);
        }
      }
      catch(IOException error)
      {
       System.out.println("Caught IOException: " + error.toString());
      }
      finally
      {
        if (inputstream!= null)
        {
          try
          {
            inputstream.close();
          }
          catch( Exception error)
          {
             /*log error*/
          }
        }
        if (connection != null)
        {
          try
          {
             connection.close();
          }
          catch( Exception error)
          {
             /*log error*/
          }
        }
      }
    }
  }
}
```

Listing 13-8
The JAD
file for
Listing 13-7

```
MIDlet-Name: httpconnection
MIDlet-Version: 1.0
MIDlet-Vendor: MyCompany
```

```
MIDlet-Jar-URL: httpconnection.jar
MIDlet-1: httpconnection, , httpconnection
MicroEdition-Configuration: CLDC-1.0
MicroEdition-Profile: MIDP-1.0
MIDlet-JAR-SIZE: 100
```

Sending Data Along with an HTTP Request

Typically, an HTTP request to a server is accompanied by information needed by the server to process the request. A case in point is when a server must authenticate a client using the client's user ID and password. The client sends the user ID and password along with the HTTP request. Data sent to a server must be in a pair value set, where the first element in the pair value is the field name and the second element is the value associated with the field. The field name and value must be separated by an equal sign.

One of two techniques is used to send data to the server depending on whether the GET or POST request method is used for transmission. The GET request method requires that data be concatenated to the URL of the server. The POST request method requires that each pair value be written to the output stream.

The following code segment illustrates how to send data using the GET request method. The URL includes the name of the program that executes on the server to process the data associated with the request. A Java Servlet called my.LoginServlet processes this request by reading both pair value sets sent to the server. The pair value sets are sent as a query string that is separated from the URL by a question mark. Each pair value set is separated from other pair value sets by an ampersand (&).

```
HttpConnection http = (HttpConnection)
        Connector.open("
        http://www.myserver.com/my.LoginServlet?UserID=jim&password=keogh;
```

The next code segment shows how to send data using the POST request method. In this example, each pair value is assigned to a byte array. The byte array is then written to the output stream by calling the write() method. The flush() method is called after the last pair value set is written.

```
byte data[] = ("userID=jim");
outputstream.write(data);
data = ("&password=Keogh");
outputstream.write(data);
outputstream.flush();
```

Session Management

A key drawback of HTTP communication is the lack of persistence. HTTP is a stateless protocol, and there is no record of an HTTP transaction once a server responds to a client. The lack of state becomes a concern if multiple related HTTP transactions occur during the same session. This is the case in an order entry application. A session is created for one order. A separate HTTP transaction occurs each time an item is placed in the shopping cart and when the order is presented to the customer at the checkout counter. Items in the shopping cart are stored on the server. The checkout process summarizes items in the shopping cart and completes the transaction. Therefore, the server needs a way to associate an HTTP request with a session in order to properly relate data stored on the server, which is called *session tracking*.

It is critical that each HTTP transaction is related to a specific session, especially if the server is processing thousands of orders daily. Although HTTP does not have the built-in capability to conduct HTTP transactions within a session, you can work around this problem by managing the session yourself. Two techniques are used to manage an HTTP session—rewriting the URL and using cookies. Rewriting the URL requires that a session identifier be written to a customized HTTP response header field. The server generates a session identifier when the initial request is received from the client. The URL of the server is modified to include the session identifier and is returned to the client as the value of a custom HTTP header field. The client copies the value of the field, appends new data to the end of the URL, and uses the new URL to open an HTTP connection to the server.

A session begins when a client sends an HTTP request to the server. The URL specified in the request contains the domain name followed by the name of the server-side application that will process the request, which you learned previously in this chapter. The client appends a query string to the end of the full URL if the client uses the GET request method. The server-side application generates a session ID, appends the session ID to the full URL (minus the query string), and writes the revised URL to a custom HTTP response field. The HTTP response is then returned to the client.

Let's assume that the custom HTTP response field is called SessionIDURL. The client reads this field by calling the getHeaderField() method, as shown in the following code segment. The getHeaderField() method returns the string value of the HTTP response field, which you learned about earlier in this chapter.

```
String url = http.getHeaderField("SessionIDURL");
```

The client retains this value while waiting for another item to be entered by the user. The next item entered by the user is appended to the modified URL as a query string and used to open the connection to the server. The following code segment illustrates how this is done. In this example, the pair value Prod=012345 represents the product number of the next item.

```
HttpConnection connection = (HttpConnection)
        Connector.open(url + "?" + "Prod=012345");
```

Downloading an Image

From time to time, you will need to download an image from a server. The processing for downloading an image is very similar to processes discussed previously in the chapter for downloading files. However, the MIDlet needs to perform a few additional steps when downloading an image.

Begin by opening a ContentConnection specifying the full path to the image in the URL, as illustrated in this code segment. This example opens a connection to the my.png image located in the image directory on www.myserver.com.

```
ContentConnection connection = (ContentConnection)
        Connector.open("http://www.myserver.com/image/my.png");
```

Next you'll need to open an input stream and call the read() method to read each byte of the file from the input stream and write the byte to a byte array output stream. The byte array output stream is then passed to the createImage() method, which transforms the byte array output stream into an image. These steps are illustrated in the following code segment:

```
InputStream inputstream = (InputStream)
        Connector.openInputStream(connection);
 try
{
  ByteArrayOutputStream bytearray = new ByteArrayOutputStream();
  int ch;
  while ((ch = inputstream.read()) != -1)
  {
     bytearray.write(ch);
  }
  byte imagearray[] = bytearray.toByteArray();
  // Create the image from the byte array
  Image image = Image.createImage(imagearray, 0, imagearray.length);
}
```

Remember that the modified URL received from the server already has reference to the server-side application that will process the request. The server-side application uses the session ID to associate the newly ordered item with other items ordered during the same session.

Cookies

The other alternative to managing an HTTP session is to use a cookie. A cookie is a pair value in the HTTP response field and an HTTP request field that contains the session ID generated by the server-side application.

The session begins when the server receives the client's request. The server generates the session ID, assigns the session ID to the cookie HTTP response field, and then sends the response to the client. The client retrieves and temporarily retains the session ID and then processes the response from the server. The cookie pair value is then written as an HTTP request field in the next request to the server made by the client. The server-side application retrieves the session ID, and the process is repeated until the client terminates the session.

Transmit as a Background Process

Rarely do any of us want to wait very long to send and receive transmissions. Most of us want instant gratification. Unfortunately, network communications are sometimes slow and unable to meet our expectations. Although you are at the mercy of the network infrastructure for the speed of your transmission, you can improve the perception that users have of your application by making transmissions a background process. Running your application as a background process enables users to run another process while transmission occurs in the background.

You can run an application as a background process by using a thread. Listing 13-9 illustrates how this is done. Listing 13-10 contains the JAD file for Listing 13-9. Listing 13-9 is a skeleton of an application to which you'll need to add code that handles the transmission, which is discussed throughout this chapter. You'll also need to include the other process that runs in the foreground.

Two classes are defined in Listing 13-9. The first is the MIDlet and the other is the Process class containing code for the transmission. The MIDlet class is very similar to other MIDlets discussed in this chapter in that a form is created containing Start and Exit command buttons. The Start button launches the background process and the foreground process. Take a look at the start section of the commandAction() method and you'll notice that an instance of the Process class is created; then the start() method of the instance is called to begin the background process as a thread. You place code that starts the foreground process below the call to the start() method.

Transmitting a Background Process

Here are the steps required to transmit a background process:

1. Declare references.
2. Obtain a reference to the instance of the Display class.
3. Create an instance of a Command class to exit the MIDlet.
4. Create an instance of a Command class to start the MIDlet.
5. Create an instance of the Form class.
6. Associate the instance of the Command class to the instance of the Form class.
7. Associate a CommandListener with the instance of the Form class.
8. Display the instance of the Form class on the screen.
9. Create a processing class that runs a thread and contains a method that defines the background process.
10. If the Start command is selected, create an instance of the processing class.
11. Call the start() method of the processing class.
12. Call the foreground process.
13. If the Exit command is selected, terminate the MIDlet.
14. Trap exceptions thrown within the commandAction() method.
15. If the MIDletStateChangeException is thrown, indicate that conditions are now safe to terminate the MIDlet by assigning a true value to the exit flag variable.
16. Terminate the MIDlet when the Exit command is entered the second time.

The Process class defines the start() method. The start() method creates a thread and then calls the start() method to run the thread. The run() method calls the transmit() method. The transmit() method contains all the code to send or receive a transmission.

Listing 13-9
Transmitting as a background process

```
import javax.microedition.midlet.*;
import javax.microedition.lcdui.*;
import javax.microedition.io.*;
import java.io.*;
public class BackgroundProcessing extends MIDlet
            implements CommandListener
{
  private Display display;
```

```
    private Form form;
    private Command exit;
    private Command start;
    public BackgroundProcessing()
    {
      display = Display.getDisplay(this);
      form = new Form("Background Processing");
      exit = new Command("Exit", Command.EXIT, 1);
      start = new Command("Start", Command.SCREEN, 2);
      form.addCommand(exit);
      form.addCommand(start );
      form.setCommandListener(this);
    }
    public void startApp()
    {
      display.setCurrent(form);
    }
    public void pauseApp()
    {
    }
    public void destroyApp(boolean unconditional)
    {
    }
    public void commandAction(Command command, Displayable displayable)
    {
      if (command == exit)
      {
        destroyApp(false);
        notifyDestroyed();
      }
      else if (command == start)
      {
        Process process = new Process(this);
        process.start();
        //Do foreground processing here
      }
    }
}
class Process implements Runnable
{
  private BackgroundProcessing MIDlet;
  public Process(BackgroundProcessing MIDlet)
```

```
    {
     this.MIDlet = MIDlet;
    }
    public void run()
    {
      try
      {
        transmit ();
      }
      catch (Exception error)
      {
        System.err.println(error.toString());
      }
    }
    public void start()
    {
      Thread thread = new Thread(this);
      try
      {
        thread.start();
      }
      catch (Exception error)
      {
      }
    }
    private void transmit() throws IOException
    {
      //Place code here to receive or send transmission.
    }
}
```

```
MIDlet-Name: BackgroundProcessing
MIDlet-Version: 1.0
MIDlet-Vendor: MyCompany
MIDlet-Jar-URL: BackgroundProcessing.jar
MIDlet-1: BackgroundProcessing, , BackgroundProcessing
MicroEdition-Configuration: CLDC-1.0
MicroEdition-Profile: MIDP-1.0
MIDlet-JAR-SIZE: 100
```

Quick Reference Guide

This quick reference guide provides an overview of classes used by J2ME for the GCF. Full details of these classes and all Java classes and interfaces are available at java.sun.com.

javax.microedition.io.Connector Class

Method	Description
static Connection open (string name)	Open a connection in READ_WRITE mode, where name is the connection identifier.
static Connection open(String name, int mode)	Open a connection, where name is the connection identifier and mode is the read/write mode.
static Connection open(String name, int mode, boolean timeouts)	Open a connection, where name is the connection identifier, mode is the read/write mode, and timeouts is a boolean value indicating whether or not the connection can time out.
static InputStream openInputStream (String name)	Open an input stream.
static OutputStream openOutputStream(String name)	Open an output stream.
static DataInputStream openDataInputStream(String name)	Open a data input stream.
static DataOutputStream(String name)	Open a data output stream.

javax.microedition.io.HttpConnection

Method	Description
void setRequestMethod(String method)	Set the request method to either GET, POST, or HEAD.
void setRequestProperty(String key, String value)	Set the header information, where key is the field name in the HTTP header, and value is the new value assigned to the field.
String getRequestMethod()	Retrieve the request method.
String getRequestProperty(String key)	Retrieve the current value of the HTTP field, where key is a string containing the name of the field.

javax.microedition.io.HttpConnection Class

Method	Description
int getResponseCode()	Retrieve the response status line code.
String getResponseMessage()	Retrieve the response status line message.

javax.microedition.io.HttpConnection Class

Method	Description
String getHeaderField (int n)	Retrieve the value of the header field whose index value is represented as n.
String getHeaderField(String name)	Retrieve the value of the header field whose header field name is contained in name.
long getHeaderFieldDate(String name, long deft)	Retrieve the header field date, where the field name is represented by name and the date is represented by deft.
int getHeaderFieldInt(String name, int def)	Retrieve the index of the field name identified as name.
String getHeaderFieldKey (int n)	Retrieve the name of the field using the field name index represented by n.
long getDate()	Retrieve the header field date.
long getExpiration()	Retrieve the expiration of the header field.
long getLastModified()	Retrieve the date when the header field was modified.

javax.microedition.io.HttpConnection

Method	Description
String getFile()	Retrieve the file name from the URL.
String getHost()	Retrieve the host from the URL.
int getPort()	Retrieve the port from the URL.
String getProtocol()	Retrieve the protocol from the URL.
String getQuery()	Retrieve the query string if the GET request method is used.
String getRef()	Retrieve the reference portion of the URL.
String getURL()	Retrieve the complete URL.

J2ME NETWORKING
AND WEB SERVICES

The
Complete
Reference

Chapter 14

Web Services

W ith IT cost escalating, IT departments are always on the hunt for ways to reduce cost without negatively affecting operations. A key target for cost savings is removing unnecessary redundancy within an organization, such as duplicate routines in software applications. A duplicate routine is stealthy in that no one can see its drain on IT resources.

Web services offer a new approach to designing a cost-effective infrastructure by organizing commonly used routines into services that can be invoked by any application that needs them. Let's say that multiple applications need to perform a credit check on customers. The credit check routine can be a web service called by each application, rather than a routine built into each application. This not only reduces redundancy of code but also eliminates the need to modify multiple routines whenever the credit check routines are modified.

A web services infrastructure consists of a client and a web service. A client is software that requests a web service. A J2ME MIDlet is capable of becoming a web service client and can access any web service that it is authorized to use within a corporate web services infrastructure. You'll learn about web services in this chapter and how to make your MIDlet a web services client. You'll need to pick up a copy of *J2EE: The Complete Reference* (McGraw-Hill/Osborne, 2002) if you want to learn how to create a web service. Web services are built using J2EE technology because J2EE addresses the complex issues that a programmer faces when developing a large-scale distributive system.

Web Services Basics

A common misunderstanding regarding web services is that the "web" component comes from the relationship between web services and the Internet. This isn't true. *Web services* are a web of software building blocks (routines) that are available on a network from which programmers can efficiently create large-scale distributive systems.

Three standards were developed with the introduction of web services: Web Services Description Language (WSDL), Universal Description, Discovery, and Integration (UDDI), and Simple Object Access Protocol (SOAP). Programmers use WSDL to publish their web service, thereby making the web service available to other programmers over the network. They use UDDI to locate web services that have been published and SOAP to invoke a particular web service.

The Tier

Numerous web services are used in a typical large-scale distributive system, and each service is associated with a tier in the multi-tier architecture that is used to share resources over a corporate infrastructure. A *tier* is an abstract concept that defines a group of technologies that provide one or more services to clients. One way to understand a tier structure's organization is to draw a parallel to a typical large corporation (see Figure 14-1).

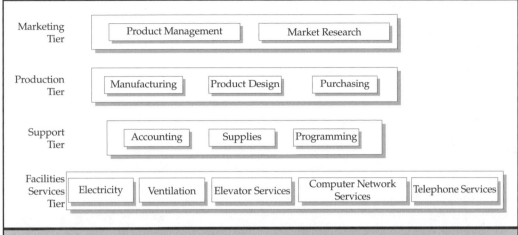

Figure 14-1.   *Resources of a large corporation are typically organized into a tier structure that operates similarly to the tier structure used in distributed systems.*

At the lowest level of a corporation, facilities services consist of resources necessary to maintain the office building. Facilities services encompass a wide variety of resources that typically include electricity, ventilation, elevator services, computer network services, and telephone service. The next tier in the organization contains services such as accounting, supplies, computer programming, and other resources that support the main activity of the company. Above the support tier is the production tier, which has resources necessary to produce the products and services sold by the company. And in our example the highest tier is the marketing tier, consisting of resources used to determine the products and services to sell to customers.

Any resource is considered a client when it sends a request for service to a service provider (also referred to as a service). A service is any resource that receives and fulfills a request from a client. And that resource itself might have to make requests to other resources to fulfill a client's request. Let's say that a product manager working at the marketing tier decides the company could make a profit by selling customers a widget. The product manager requests an accountant to conduct a formal cost analysis of manufacturing a widget. The accountant is on the support tier of the organization. The product manager is the client, and the accountant is the service. However, the accountant requires information from the manufacturing manager to fulfill the product manager's request. The manufacturing manager works on the production tier of the organization. The accountant is the client to the manufacturing manager, who is the service to the accountant.

In multi-tier architecture, each tier contains services that include software objects, database management systems (DBMSs), or connectivity to legacy systems. Information technology departments of corporations employ multi-tier architecture because it is a cost-efficient way to build an application that is flexible, scalable, and responsive to the expectations of clients. The functionality of the application is divided into logical components associated with a tier. Each component is a service that is built and maintained independently of other services. Services are bound together by a communication protocol that enables a service to receive and send information from and to another service.

A client is concerned about sending a request for service and receiving results from a service. A client isn't concerned about how a service provides the results. This means that a programmer can quickly develop a system by creating a client program that formulates a request to services that already exist in the multi-tier architecture. These services already have the functionality built into them to fulfill the request made by the client program.

Services can be modified as changes occur in the functionality without affecting the client program. For example, a client might request the tax owed on a specific order. The request is sent to a service that has the functionality to determine the tax. The business logic for calculating the tax resides within the service. A programmer can modify the business logic in the service to reflect the latest changes in the tax code without having to modify the client program. These changes are hidden from the client program.

Clients, Resources, and Components

Multi-tier architecture is composed of clients, resources, components (web service), and containers (see Figure 14-2). A client is a program that requests service from a component. A resource is anything a component needs to provide a service. A component is part of a tier and consists of a collection of classes or a program that performs a function to provide the service. A container is software that manages a component and provides a component with system services.

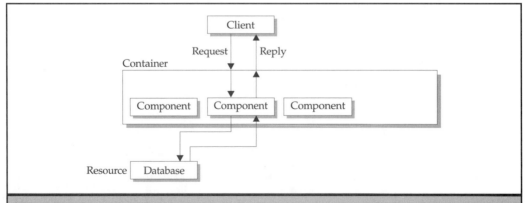

Figure 14-2. *A multi-tier architecture consist of clients, resources, components, and containers that are used by a programmer to create a distributive system.*

The relationship between a container and a component is sometimes referred to as a contract whose terms are governed by an application programming interface (API). An API defines rules that a component must follow and the services a component will receive from the container.

A container handles persistence, resource management, security, threading, and other system-level services for components that are associated with the container. Components are responsible for implementation of business logic. This means programmers can focus on encoding business rules into components without becoming concerned about low-level system services. This is an important concept in multi-tier architecture because modification can be made to low-level security, for example, without requiring any modification to a component. Only the container needs to be modified by the programmer.

The relationship between a component and a container is very similar to the relationship between a program and an operating system. The operating system provides low-level systems services such as I/O to a program. Programs don't need to be modified if a new disk drive is installed in the computer. Instead, the operating system is reconfigured to recognize the new disk drive.

Accessing Services

A client uses a client protocol to access a service associated with a particular tier. A protocol is a standard method of communication that both a client and the tier/ component/resource understands. A number of protocols are used within a multi-tier infrastructure because each tier/component/resource could use different protocols.

One of the most commonly implemented multi-tier architectures is used in web-centric applications where browsers are used to interact with corporate online resources. A browser is a client and requests a service from a web server using HTTP. In a typical enterprise-wide application, a browser requests services from other components within the infrastructure, such as a servlet. A servlet uses a resource protocol to access resources necessary for the servlet to fulfill the request. For example, a servlet will use the JDBC protocol to retrieve data from a DBMS. Pick up a copy of *J2EE: The Complete Reference*, which will introduce you to specific protocols as you learn to build components and use resources.

J2EE Multi-Tier Web Services Architecture

J2EE multi-tier web services architecture is a four-tier architecture (see Figure 14-3). The four tiers are the Client Tier (sometimes referred to as the Presentation Tier or Application Tier), Web Tier, Enterprise JavaBeans Tier (sometimes referred to as the Business Tier), and the Enterprise Information Systems Tier. Each tier focuses on providing a specific type of functionality to an application.

It is important to delineate between physical location and functionality. Two or more tiers can physically reside on the same Java Virtual Machine, although each tier provides a different type of functionality to an application. And since the J2EE multi-tier

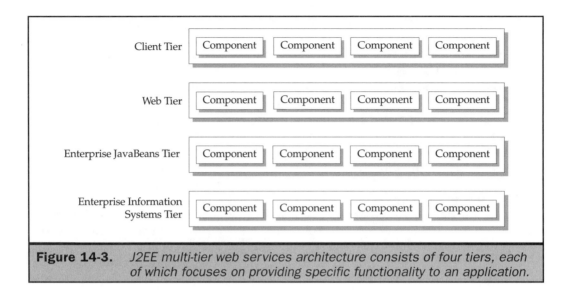

Figure 14-3. *J2EE multi-tier web services architecture consists of four tiers, each of which focuses on providing specific functionality to an application.*

web services architecture is functionality-centric, an application accesses only tiers whose functionality it requires. It is also important to disassociate a J2EE API from a particular tier. That is, some APIs (XML API, for example) and J2EE components can be used on more than one tier, while others (Enterprise JavaBeans API, for example) are associated with a particular tier.

The Client Tier consists of programs that interact with the user. These programs prompt the user for input and then convert the user's response into requests that are forwarded to software on a component that processes the request and returns results to the client program. The component can operate on any tier, although most requests from clients are processed by components on the Web Tier. The client program also translates the server's response into text and screens that are presented to the user.

The Web Tier provides Internet functionality to an application. Components that operate on the Web Tier use HTTP to receive requests from and send responses to clients that could reside on any tier. A client is any component that initiates a request, as explained previously in this chapter.

For example (see Figure 14-4), a client's request for data that is received by a component working on the Web Tier is passed by the component to the Enterprise JavaBeans Tier, where an Enterprise JavaBean working on this tier interacts with a DBMS to fulfill the request. Requests are made to the Enterprise JavaBeans by using the Java Remote Method Invocation (RMI) API. The requested data is then returned by the Enterprise JavaBeans, where the data is then forwarded to the Web Tier, and then relayed to the Client Tier where the data is presented to the user.

The Enterprise JavaBeans (EJB) Tier contains the business logic for applications. One or more Enterprise JavaBeans reside on this tier, each encoded with business rules

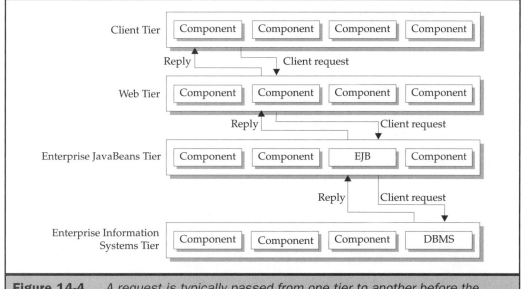

Figure 14-4.   *A request is typically passed from one tier to another before the request is fulfilled.*

that are called upon indirectly by clients. The EJB Tier is the keystone to every application because Enterprise JavaBeans working on this tier enable multiple instances of an application to access business logic and data concurrently so as not to impede performance.

Enterprise JavaBeans are contained on the Enterprise JavaBeans server, which is a distributed object server that works on the EJB Tier. It manages transactions and security, and assures that multi-threading and persistence are properly implemented whenever Enterprise JavaBeans are accessed.

Although Enterprise JavaBeans can access components on any tier, they typically access components and resources such as a DBMS on the Enterprise Information System (EIS) Tier. Access is made using an Access Control List (ACL) that controls communication between tiers. The ACL is a critical design element in the J2EE multi-tier web services architecture because it bridges tiers that are typically located on different virtual local area networks and adds a security level to web applications. Hackers typically focus their attack on the Web Tier to try to directly access the DBMS. ACL prevents direct access to DBMSs and similar resources.

The EIS Tier links an application to resources and legacy systems that are available on the corporate backbone network. This is where an application directly or indirectly interfaces with a variety of technologies, including DBMSs and mainframes that are part of the mission-critical systems keeping the corporation operational. Components that work on the EIS Tier communicate with resources using CORBA or Java connectors referred to as J2EE Connector Extensions.

Client Tier Implementation

The two components on the Client Tier are applet clients and application clients (J2ME MIDlet). An applet client is a component used by a web client that operates within the applet container, which is a Java-enabled browser. An applet uses the browser as a user interface.

An application client is a Java application that operates within the application client container, which is the Java 2 Runtime Environment, Standard Edition (JRE). An application has its own user interface and is capable of accessing all the tiers in the multi-tier architecture, depending on how the ACLs are configured. Typically, an application has access only to the web layer.

A rich client is a third type of client but is not considered a component of the Client Tier because a rich client can be written in a language other than Java. A rich client is similar to an application client in that both contain their own user interface. And as with an application client, a rich client can access any tier in the environment (depending on the ACL configuration), using HTTP, SOAP, ebXML, or an appropriate protocol.

Classification of Clients

Besides being defined as an applet client, application client, or a rich client, clients are also classified by the technology used to access components and resources associated with each tier. There are five classifications: a web client, Enterprise JavaBeans client, Enterprise Information System (EIS) client, web service peers, and a multi-tier client.

A web client consists of software—usually a browser—that accesses resources located on the Web Tier. These resources typically consist of web pages written in HTML or XML. However, a web client can also access other kinds of information located on the Web Tier. Web clients communicate with Web Tier resources using either HTTP or HTTPS (the Hyptertext Transfer Protocol, Secured), which is used to transfer encrypted information.

Enterprise JavaBeans clients are similar to web clients in that they work on the Client Tier and act as an interface between the application and the user. However, an Enterprise JavaBeans client only accesses one or more Enterprise JavaBeans located on the Enterprise JavaBeans Tier rather than resources on the Web Tier. This access is made possible by using the RMI API. RMI handles communication between the Enterprise JavaBeans client and the Enterprise JavaBeans Tier using either the Java Remote Method Protocol (JRMP) or the Internet Inter-ORB Protocol (IIOP).

EIS clients act as the interface between users and resources located on the EIS Tier. These clients use Java connectors, appropriate APIs, or proprietary protocols to utilize resources such as DBMSs and legacy data sources.

A web service peer is a unique type of client because it is also a service that works on the Web Tier. Technically, a web service peer forms a peer-to-peer relationship with other components on the Web Tier rather than a true client/server relationship. However, a web service peer is commonly referred to as a client because it requests service from other components on the Web Tier, although a web service peer can also access other tiers. Typically, a web service peer makes requests over HTTP using either electronic business XML or SOAP.

Multi-tier clients are conceptually similar to a web service peer, except they access components located on tiers other than the tier where the multi-tier client resides. Multi-tier clients typically use the Java Message Service (JMS) to communicate asynchronously with other tiers.

Web Tier Implementation

The Web Tier has several responsibilities in the J2EE multi-tier web services architecture, all of which are provided to the Client Tier using HTTP. These responsibilities are to act as an intermediary between components working on the Web Tier and other tiers and the Client Tier. Intermediary activities include

- Accepting requests from other software that are sent using POST, GET, and PUT operations, which are part of HTTP transmissions
- Transmitting data such as images and dynamic content

Two types of components work on the Web Tier. These are servlets and JavaServer Pages (JSP), although many times they are proxied to the Application or EJB Tier. A servlet is a Java class that resides on the Web Tier and is called by a request from a browser client that operates on the Client Tier. A servlet is associated with a URL that is mapped by the servlet container.

A request for a servlet contains the servlet's URL and is transmitted from the Client Tier to the Web Tier using HTTP. The request generates an instance of the servlet or reuses an existing instance, which receives any input parameters from the Web Tier necessary for the servlet to perform the service. Input parameters are sent as part of the request from the client.

An instance of a servlet fulfills the request by accessing components/resources on the Web Tier or on other tiers as necessary based on the business logic encoded in the servlet. The servlet typically generates an HTML output stream that is returned to the web server. The web server then transmits the data to the client. This output stream is a dynamic web page.

JSP is similar to a servlet in that a JSP is associated with a URL and is callable from a client, but it is different in several ways depending on the container that is used. Some containers translate the JSP into a servlet the first time the client calls the JSP, which is then compiled, and the compiled servlet is loaded into memory. The servlet remains in memory. Subsequent calls by the client to the JSP cause the web server to recall the servlet without translating the JSP and compiling the resulting code. Other containers precompile a JSP into a .java file that looks like a servlet file, which is then compiled into a Java class.

Business logic used by JSP and servlets is contained in one or more Enterprise JavaBeans that are callable from within the JSP and servlet. The code is the same for both JSP and servlet, although the format of the code differs. JSP uses custom tags to access Enterprise JavaBeans, while servlets can access Enterprise JavaBeans directly. You can learn how to create and use servlets in *J2EE: The Complete Reference*.

Enterprise JavaBeans Tier Implementation

J2EE uses distributive object technology to enable Java developers to build portable, scalable, and efficient applications that meet the 24x7 durability expected from an enterprise system. The Enterprise JavaBeans Tier contains the Enterprise JavaBeans server, which is the object server that stores and manages Enterprise JavaBeans.

The EJB Tier is a vital element in the J2EE multi-tier web services architecture because it provides concurrency, scalability, life cycle management, and fault tolerance. This tier automatically handles concurrency issues to assure that multiple clients have simultaneous access to the same object. The EJB Tier is where some vendors include features that enable scalability of an application because the tier is designed to work in a clustered environment. This assumes that vendor components that are used support clustering. If not, a Local Director is typically used for horizontal load balancing.

The Enterprise JavaBeans Tier manages instances of components. This means component containers working on the EJB Tier create and destroy instances of components and also move components in and out of memory.

Fault tolerance is an important consideration in mission-critical applications. The EJB Tier is also where some vendors include features that provide fault-tolerant operation by making it possible to have multiple Enterprise JavaBeans servers available through the tier. This means backup Enterprise JavaBeans servers can be contacted immediately upon the failure of the primary server.

The Enterprise JavaBeans server has an Enterprise JavaBeans container within which is a collection of Enterprise JavaBeans. As discussed in previous sections of this chapter, Enterprise JavaBeans are classes that contain business logic and are callable from a servlet or JSP.

Collectively, the Enterprise JavaBeans server and Enterprise JavaBeans container are responsible for low-level system services required to implement business logic of an Enterprise JavaBean. These system services are

- Resource pooling
- Distributed object protocols
- Thread management
- State management
- Process management
- Object persistence
- Security
- Deploy-time configuration

A key benefit of using the Enterprise JavaBeans server and container technology is that this technology makes proper use of a programmer's expertise. That is, a programmer who specializes in coding business logic isn't concerned about coding system services. Likewise, a programmer whose specialty is system services can focus on developing system services and not be concerned with coding business logic.

Any component, regardless of the tier where it is located, can use Enterprise JavaBeans. This means that an Enterprise JavaBean client can reside outside the client tier. The protocol used to communicate between the Enterprise JavaBeans Tier and other tiers is dependent on the protocol used by the other tier.

Components on the Client Tier and the Web Tier communicate with the Enterprise JavaBeans Tier using the Java RMI API and either IIOP or JRMP. Sometimes software on other tiers, usually the middle tier, uses JMS to communicate with the EJB Tier. This communication isn't exclusively used to send and receive messages between machines. JMS is also used for other communication, such as decoupling tiers using the queue mechanism.

However, the Enterprise JavaBean that is used must be a message-driven bean (MDB). MDBs are commonly used to process messages on a queue that may or may not reside on the local machine. You'll learn more about MDB by reading *J2EE: The Complete Reference*.

Enterprise Information Systems Tier Implementation

The Enterprise Information Systems (EIS) Tier is the J2EE multi-tier web services architecture's connectivity to resources that are not part of J2EE. These include a variety of resources such as legacy systems, DBMSs, and systems provided by third parties that are accessible to components in the J2EE infrastructure. This tier provides flexibility to developers of applications because developers can leverage existing systems and resources currently available to the corporation and do not need to replicate them in J2EE.

Likewise, developers can utilize off-the-shelf software that is commercially available in the marketplace because the EIS Tier provides the connectivity between an application and non-J2EE software. This connectivity is made possible through the use of CORBA and Java connectors or through proprietary protocols.

Java connector technology enables software developers to create a Java connector for legacy systems and for third-party software. The connector defines all the elements that are needed to communicate between the application and the non-J2EE software. This includes rules for connecting to each other and rules for conducting secured transactions. You'll learn more on how these connections are created by reading *J2EE: The Complete Reference*.

XML

The Extensible Markup Language (XML) is used to create other languages that define components of a document, called *elements*. Elements include the title page, table of contents, index, and chapters, each of which conforms to a specific style.

In a relational database, data is described using metadata such as a column name, column data type, and column size. XML is used to create metadata that describes elements in a document, such as a book.

XML is similar in concept to the hypertext markup language (HTML) in that an element is defined using tags and attributes. Tags and attributes are comparable to the metadata of a relational database. XML simplifies data exchange by organizing a document and standardizing data exchange.

An XML Schema contains the definition of the language created using XML that consists of a definition of a customized set of tags. These tags are very similar to HTML tags (tag names and attributes of these tags), except XML is specific to the language created using XML. The XML Schema is referenced whenever the document is accessed.

Elements defined in the XML Schema are used to create an XML document such as a description of a web service. For example, you might define a tag called RetailPrice in the XML Schema. There is a growing trend to standardize XML Schemas such as when describing a web service. You'll enclose the retail price element of your document with the retail price tag as shown here:

```
<RetailPrice>$15.95</RetailPrice>
```

Browsers cannot read an XML document because they read HTML documents that contain HTML tags and not XML tags. XML tags are displayed literally by a browser as if tags are part of text that is displayed on the screen. However, an XML-based document can be converted to an HTML document by server-side software using an XML style sheet—referred to as Extensible Stylesheet Language Transformation (XSLT). An XSLT contains rules used to translate each element of the XML-based document into tags on an HTML page.

An XML parser is a program that transforms an XML document into a structure that allows programmatic access to a document's content. During the transformation process, the XML parser reads the XML document and examines XML syntax, then reports any syntax errors that are encountered. An XML parser is included in Internet Explorer 5 and Netscape 6 browsers.

Two parsers are used to access a document's content: the Document Object Model (DOM) and the Simple API for XML (SAX), which is used by Java, C, and other programming languages to programmatically use the content of an XML document.

Inside WSDL

Organizations that either publish web services or consume web services must be able to communicate with each other using an agreed-upon protocol. Protocols supported by an organization are described using the Web Services Description Language (WSDL). WSDL standardizes XML elements that describe a collection of communication endpoints. A communication *endpoint* is a port that sends and receives messages. Web services providers and web services consumers are endpoints in communication, each of which has one or multiple ports. Each port is associated with a network address. Collectively, ports of a web services provider or web services consumer are called a network service.

WSDL defines a network service using seven XML elements. These are types, message, operation, portType, binding, port, and service. The type element contains data type definitions. The message element contains the data type of the data that is being transmitted. The operation element describes an action supported by the network service. The portType element defines operations supported by the web services provider. The binding element specifies the protocol and data format for a port type. And the service element contains other ports associated with the web services provider. Each WSDL element is discussed in detail later in this chapter.

WSDL has binding extensions for popular protocols and message formats that are positioned on top of the network service definition. These include SOAP 1.1, HTTP GET/POST, and MIME. Other binding extensions can be used with WSDL.

The WSDL Document

The WSDL document should be organized into a set of three documents so that it can be easily maintained and reused as necessary. The first document is the XML Schema, which contains the Data Type Definition (DTD), as shown in Listing 14-1. The next document contains abstract definitions and is shown in Listing 14-2. The third document identifies service bindings and is illustrated in Listing 14-3.

This example illustrates a WSDL document set that is used to provide a product pricing service to a trading partner. The XML Schema in Listing 14-1 identifies the target namespace schemas located at mycompany.com/pricing.

The first element defined in the XML Schema is ProductPriceRequest, which is a complex type that contains the child element called ProductID. ProductID is a string. The other element defined in the XML Schema is called ProductPrice. ProductPrice is also a complex type and has one child element called UnitPrice. UnitPrice is a float.

The next document in the set is the abstract definition called Pricing. The document begins by identifying namespaces. You'll notice that the XML Schema is incorporated into the abstract definition document by using the import element. The import element enables you to divide the WSDL document into a set of three documents and then combine the set into one WSDL document by importing the other documents of the set.

The abstract definition document creates two message elements. The first message element is called GetProductPriceInput, and the body of this message is the ProductPriceRequest element. The other message element is called GetProductPriceOutput, and the body of this message is the ProductPrice element. Both the ProductPriceRequest element and the ProductPrice element are defined in the XML Schema.

Next the abstract definition document creates the portType element called ProductPricePortType that contains one child element, which is called operation. The operation element contains two child elements. These are the input element and the output element. The input element message is the GetProductPriceInput element, and the output element is the GetProductPriceOut element. Both of these elements are defined in the message elements of the abstract definition document.

The last document in the WSDL document set is the service bindings, shown in Listing 14-3. This document begins by identifying namespaces and then imports the XML Schema and the abstract definition documents.

Next the document creates the ProductPriceSoapBinding element that is a ProductPricePortType. ProductPricePortType is defined in the abstract definition document. Within the binding element is the operations element that identifies the location of GetProductPrice, which is used by the trading partner to obtain product pricing. The document also creates a service element that identifies information about the product pricing service offered by the business.

Listing 14-1
XML Schema
(Data Type
Definition)

```
<?xml version="1.0"?>
<schema targetNamespace="http://mycompany.com/pricing/schemas"
        xmlns="http://www.w3.org/2000/10/XMLSchema">
    <element name="ProductPriceRequest">
        <complexType>
            <all>
                <element name="ProductID" type="string"/>
            </all>
        </complexType>
    </element>
    <element name="ProductPrice">
        <complexType>
            <all>
                <element name="UnitPrice" type="float"/>
            </all>
        </complexType>
    </element>
</schema>
```

Listing 14-2
Abstract
definition

```xml
<?xml version="1.0"?>
<definitions name="Pricing"
targetNamespace="http://mycompany.com/pricing/definitions"
           xmlns:tns="http://mycompany.com/pricing/definitions"
           xmlns:xsd1="http://mycompany.com/pricing/schemas"
           xmlns:soap="http://schemas.xmlsoap.org/wsdl/soap/"
           xmlns="http://schemas.xmlsoap.org/wsdl/">
    <import namespace="http://mycompany.com/pricing/schemas"
            location="http://mycompany.com/pricing/pricing.xsd"/>
    <message name="GetProductPriceInput">
        <part name="body" element="xsd1:ProductPriceRequest"/>
    </message>
    <message name="GetProductPriceOutput">
        <part name="body" element="xsd1:ProductPrice"/>
    </message>
    <portType name="ProductPricePortType">
        <operation name="GetProductPrice">
            <input message="tns:GetProductPriceInput"/>
            <output message="tns:GetProductPriceOutput"/>
        </operation>
    </portType>
</definitions>
```

Listing 14-3
Service
bindings

```xml
<?xml version="1.0"?>
<definitions name="pricing"
targetNamespace="http://mycompany.com/pricing/service"
        xmlns:tns="http://mycompany.com/pricing/service"
            xmlns:soap="http://schemas.xmlsoap.org/wsdl/soap/"
            xmlns:defs="http://example.com/stockquote/definitions"
            xmlns="http://schemas.xmlsoap.org/wsdl/">
    <import namespace="http://mycompany.com/pricing/definitions"
            location="http://mycompany.com/pricing/pricing.wsdl"/>
    <binding name="ProductPriceSoapBinding"
             type="defs:ProductPricePortType">
        <soap:binding style="document"
transport="http://schemas.xmlsoap.org/soap/http"/>
        <operation name="GetProductPrice">
            <soap:operation soapAction=
```

```
                    "http://mycompany.com/GetProductPrice"/>
            <input>
                <soap:body use="literal"/>
            </input>
            <output>
                <soap:body use="literal"/>
            </output>
        </operation>
    </binding>
    <service name="ProductPriceService">
        <documentation>Product pricing service</documentation>
        <port name="ProductPricePort" binding="tns:ProductPriceBinding">
            <soap:address location="http://mycompany.com/pricing"/>
        </port>
    </service>
</definitions>
```

Types Element

The types element of the WSDL document contains definitions of data types used within the WSDL document message. WSDL uses XML Schema Definition (XSD) as the canonical type system, so data types are independent of wire format.

WSDL also introduces flexibility when it comes to data type systems through the use of extensibility elements. An extensibility element functions like the XML Schema element in that the extensibility element identifies both the type definition system and the XML container element for the type definition.

Message Element

The message element identifies the body of the WSDL document and is divided into multiple sections, where each section is typed using an extensible message attribute. Two of the commonly used message attributes are element and type. The element attribute identifies the unique name of the message. The type is either simpleType or complexType. You can create your own attributes as necessary. However, your attributes must use a namespace other than the WSDL namespace.

A message is identified by a unique name assigned to the name attribute. The message name must be unique among all messages within the same document. A message can be divided into logical components, where each component is referred to as a message part. Message parts are identified with the part element. Each part element must have a unique name within the message. The name of the part element is identified by the part element's name attribute.

portType Element

The portType element is used to describe abstract operations and messages. This element has a name attribute whose value uniquely identifies the portType element within all the portTypes of the WSDL XML document.

The portType element has a child element called operation, which also has a name attribute used to uniquely identify the operation within the portType element. The portType uses one of four transmission primitives supported by an endpoint.

The first transmission primitive is one way and indicates that the endpoint supports receiving a message. This is identified by using the wsdl:input element, as shown in Listing 14-4. In this example, GetPricing is the name of the wsdl:input operation, and ProductPricing is the message associated with this operation.

Listing 14-4
One-way
transmission
primitive

```
<wsdl:operation name="GetProductPricing">
   <wsdl:input name="GetPricing"? message="InputProductPricing"/>
</wsdl:operation>
```

Next is the request-response transmission primitive that states the endpoint receives and sends a responding message. This is illustrated in Listing 14-5. The operation is called GetProductPricing, and ProductID is the parameterOrder.

The parameterOrder attribute is used with the request-response and solicit-response transmission primitives to capture the function signature of the remote procedure call that made the request. Although this example shows one parameter, there can be other parameters, each separated by a space. Parameters do not need to be used by the operation.

There are three child elements within the operation. These are wsdl:input, wsdl:output, and wsdl:fault. The wsdl:input element called GetPricing indicates that the endpoint receives messages. The InputProductPricing message is associated with the input operation. Next is the wsdl:output operation called SendPricing that indicates the endpoint supports sending a reply message. OutputProductPricing is the message associated with the output operation. The last operation is the wsdl:fault element that sets the default. The default is used if the name attribute is not specified. The wsdl:fault element is called DefaultPricing and is associated with the DefaultProductPricing message.

Listing 14-5
Request-
response
transmission
primitive

```
<wsdl:operation name=" GetProductPricing " parameterOrder="ProductID">
   <wsdl:input name=" GetPricing "? message="InputProductPricing"/>
   <wsdl:output name="SendPricing "? message="OutputProductPricing"/>
   <wsdl:fault name="DefaultPricing" message="DefaultProductPricing"/>*
</wsdl:operation>
```

The third transmission primitive is solicit-response. The solicit-response transmission primitive indicates that the endpoint sends a message and then receives a responding message, and is structured the same as the request-response transmission primitive.

The final transmission primitive is notification, which states that the endpoint sends a message. Listing 14-6 illustrates this structure. In this example, the wsdl:output element called GetPricing is used and is associated with the OutputProductPricing message.

Listing 14-6
Notification transmission primitive

```
<wsdl:operation name=" SendProductPricing ">
    <wsdl:output name="GetPricing"? message="OutputProductPricing"/>
</wsdl:operation>
```

WSDL defines bindings for two of the four transmission primitives, the one-way transmission primitive and the request-response transmission primitive.

Binding Element

The purpose of the binding element is to define details of protocols and message format that are referenced in a portType element. Since a portType can have many operations, there can be multiple binding elements for each portType described in the WSDL XML document.

The binding element requires a name attribute whose value uniquely identifies the binding in the WSDL XML document. The binding element is associated with a portType through the binding element's type attribute.

Within the binding element is the wsdl:operation child element. The wsdl:operation element contains information necessary for binding operations specified in the portType. Listing 14-7 illustrates how operations are specified in the wsdl:operation element of the binding element.

You'll notice that there are three operations. These are input, output, and the default operation. Each operation is identified as an appropriate child element of the operation element. You place the necessary information needed to bind each operation within its operation element.

Listing 14-7
The binding element

```
<wsdl:binding name="ProductPriceSoapBinding" type="ProductPricePortType">
    <wsdl:operation name="GetProductPrice">
        <wsdl:input name="GetProductPriceInput"? > ?
        </wsdl:input>
        <wsdl:output name="GetProductPriceOutput"? > ?
        </wsdl:output>
        <wsdl:fault name="GetProductPriceDefault">
        </wsdl:fault>
    </wsdl:operation>
</wsdl:binding>
```

Port Element

Endpoints are identified by the wsdl:port element in the WSDL XML document. The wsdl:port element is a child element of the wsdl:service element, and each port element contains the URL of a binding. The wsdl:port element requires two attributes: the name attribute and the binding attribute.

The value of the name attribute uniquely identifies the wsdl:port element within the WSDL XML document. The value of the binding attribute identifies the binding associated with the wsdl:port element. Listing 14-8 illustrates the wsdl:port element. This example identifies the location for the ProductPriceBinding at the URL mycompany.com/pricing.

Listing 14-8
The wsdl:port
element

```
< wsdl:port name="ProductPricePort" binding="tns:ProductPriceBinding">
    wsdl:<soap:address location="http://mycompany.com/pricing"/>
</wsdl:port>
```

Service Element

The wsdl:port element is a child element of the wsdl:service element, as discussed in the previous section. The wsdl:service element is used within a WSDL document to group together related wsdl:port elements. The wsdl:service element is the child element of the wsdl:definitions element.

The wsdl:definitions element can have multiple wsdl:service elements, each associated with a group of ports. Therefore, you'll need to use the name attribute to uniquely identify each wsdl:service element contained in the wsdl:definitions element.

A port within a wsdl:service element is restricted from communicating with other ports contained in the same wsdl:service element. Ports within a wsdl:service element that share the same port type and have different binding URLs are semantically similar. A trading partner can choose the appropriate port within the wsdl:service using a port's communication characteristics as criteria for the selection.

Listing 14-9 illustrates the use of the wsdl:service element within a WSDL document. This example defines the wsdl:service called ProductPriceService that contains the wsdl:port ProductPricePort, which was presented in the previous section.

Listing 14-9
The
wsdl:service
element

```
<wsdl:service name="ProductPriceService">
    <wsdl:port name="ProductPricePort" binding="tns:ProductPriceBinding">
        <soap:address location="http://mycompany.com/pricing"/>
    </wsdl:port>
</wsdl:service>
```

J2ME MIDlets and Web Services

A J2ME MIDlet can become a client of a web service but cannot be a web service because a J2ME implementation typically lacks the resources required to be an endpoint. An endpoint is a server-based application that provides a web service. A web service is invoked by calling methods associated with the web service. For example, a web service might have one method that is designed to retrieve the default price of a specified product. Calling this method returns the default price of a product to the client.

A J2ME client uses remote method calls to invoke methods associated with web services. The MIDlet cannot directly call a method of a web service. Instead, the MIDlet must use a proxy, called a *stub interface*, that is used to interact with the web service. A stub that corresponds to the web service must first be created before the MIDlet can invoke the call. Information about the stub is contained within the WSDL description of the web service.

At development time, you must use the wsdl2java tool provided by the implementation. This tool reads the WSDL description of the web service and generates the appropriate Java code that instantiates the stub for the web service. This is the same tool used in JAX-RPC (see *J2EE: The Complete Reference*).

Let's assume that the web service is called ProductInformation. An instance of the stub associated with the ProductInformation web service is created by the following statement. The instance of the stub becomes a proxy for the web service.

```
ProductInformation stub = new ProductInformation();
```

The instance of the stub can be used to set stub properties, such as login information and the address of the web service, and can also be used to invoke methods associated with the web service.

The following example sets a stub's user ID property and then invokes a method that retrieves recent sales data by region. Data returned by the getSalesByRegion() method is assigned to a holder, which is an array. You'll learn more about Holder classes later in this chapter.

```
stub._setProperty(Stub.USER_ID_PROPERTY, "BSmith");
SalesByRegionHolder[] salesByRegion = stub.getSalesByRegion();
```

Both the generated stub and other artifacts generated with the stub, such as Holder classes, must be included in the J2ME client application's deployment bundle. In the previous example, the Stub interface and the SalesByRegionHolder Holder class are artifacts that must be included in the deployment bundle.

The remote method call uses the synchronous request-response mode when invoking a web service, which is conceptually the same mode used in the client/server model.

The client invocation thread is blocked until the remote method call responds with either a return value or an exception. The return value might be void.

All parameters passed to remote method invocation are made by copy and not by reference. The same is true of return values. This also means that the web service cannot expect parameters to be passed by reference or values to be returned by reference. A J2ME client wouldn't be able to utilize any web service that requires passing by reference.

JAX-RPC

J2ME uses a subset of the JAX-RPC 1.9 specification to provide a Java API to SOAP-based web services that is appropriate for the J2ME platform. The JAX-RPC subset is suited for the restricted memory size, processing power, and deployment environment, which has a low bandwidth and high latency.

The JAX-RPC subset run time is identical to the JAX-RPC 1.0 specifications. The implementation supports static stub invocation using the Stub interface, which is commonly referred to as a local stub base. However, there is no support for dynamic proxies or a dynamic invocation interface (DII). Stubs that are generated use the document style and literal use (documents/literal) mode. Although this is restrictive, the document style and literal use mode simplify the implementation.

The implementation supports data types shown in Table 14-1. There is no support for extensible type mapping. Table 14-2 shows the mapping of XML simple data types to Java data types. XML data types are defined in the XML Schema.

Holder Classes

A Holder class is used in the mapping of WSDL operations to Java as a way of preserving the intended WSDL operation signature and parameter. The JAX-RPC subset specification contains Holder classes for simple XML data types and is contained in the javax.xml.rpc.holders package. The name of the Holder class is the concatenation of the name of the Java primitive type and the suffix Holder. The initial letter of the Java type name is capitalized, as in IntegerHolder, and maps to the Java primitive type int. Standard Holder classes specified in the javax.xml.rpc.holders package are shown in Table 14-3.

boolean	byte	short	int
long string	value types	arrays of primitive and value types	QName

Table 14-1.   *Data Types Supported by Web Services Implementation*

XML Data Type	Java Data Type
xsd:string	java.lang.String
xsd:int	int
xsd:long	long
xsd:short	short
xsd:boolean	boolean
xsd:byte	byte
xsd:QName	javax.xml.namespace.QName
xsd:base64Binary	byte[]
xsd:hexBinary	byte[]
xsd:int	java.lang.Integer
xsd:long	java.lang.Long
xsd:short	java.lang.Short
xsd:boolean	java.lang.Boolean
xsd:byte	java.lang.Byte

Table 14-2. *XML Data Type to Java Data Type Mapping*

A Holder class is also constructed for complex XML data types by concatenating the name of the Java class with the prefix Holder, as in SalesByRegionHolder[]. A Holder class has a public field that corresponds to the Java type and a default constructor that initializes the field value to a default value as specified in the Java language specification. The constructor then sets the field value to the passed parameter.

BooleanHolder	BooleanWrapperHolder	ByteArrayHolder	ByteHolder
ByteWrapperHolder	IntHolder	IntegerWrapperHolder	LongHolder
LongWrapperHolder	ObjectHolder	QNameHolder	ShortHolder
ShortWrapperHolder	StringHolder		

Table 14-3. *Standard Holder Classes Specified in the javax.xml.rpc.holders Package*

Remote Method Invocation Concept

An application that operates under a JVM can invoke objects located on a different JVM by using the Java Remote Method Invocation (RMI) system. RMI is used for remote communication between Java applications and components (web services); it connects a client and a server. A client is an application or component that requires the services of an object to fulfill a request. A server creates an object and makes the object available to clients. A client contacts the server to reference and invoke the object by using RMI.

RMI handles transmission of requests and provides the facility to load the object's bytecode, which is referred to as *dynamic code loading*. This means that the behavior of an application can be dynamically extended by the remote JVM.

Remote Interface

Server-side objects that are invoked by remote clients must implement a remote interface and associated method definitions. The remote interface is used by clients to interact with an object using RMI communications. A remote interface extends java.rmi.Remote, and each method must throw a RemoteException.

There are two stubs used in RMI: a local stub, which is the proxy, and a remote stub called a skeleton. A client uses the local stub to interact with a remote object. The skeleton on the web service receives the invocation from the local stub and in turn invokes the web service's method.

SOAP Basics

Simple Object Access Protocol (SOAP) was conceived in 1997 by three industry players: a small software company called Userland Software, Microsoft, and DevelopMentor, which is a Lucent spin-off. Together they set out to develop a communication protocol that would meet three needs: ease of use, flexibility, and the forever-elusive interoperability. Soon after the project began, they focused their attention on XML as the basis for the new communication protocol. XML is straightforward to implement and extensible, providing a structure for flexibility.

XML is the ideal language to use to implement the new communication protocol because of its built-in data types defined in the XML Schema. Data types are used by a communication protocol to define data transmissions. This meant that the team developing SOAP didn't have to reinvent data typing. Instead, they could adopt data types defined in XML. XML defined all but the array data type.

It took the team a year to flesh out the details of the new protocol, and internal squabbles at Microsoft hampered development. Delays frustrated some of the team and resulted in a defection by Dave Winer. Winer created his own communication protocol called XML-Remote Procedure Call (XML-RPC), which gained popularity until the release of SOAP 1.0 in 2000.

SOAP 1.0 used HTTP for transmitting messages sent using SOAP. Although HTTP is a widely used transport protocol, specifying HTTP violated one of the key objectives of SOAP—interoperability. SOAP shouldn't be dependent on one transport protocol. SOAP became fully independent with the introduction of SOAP 1.1. This meant that SOAP messages could use any transport protocol, such as SMTP and FTP, as well as HTTP.

SOAP 1.1 addresses the concerns of the web services industry. However, it wasn't until the end of 2000 before the SOAP team caught the industry's attention, when Microsoft adopted SOAP as the communication protocol used with .NET technology. The SOAP team submitted SOAP 1.1 to the World Wide Web Consortium (W3C), the organization that adopts standards for the World Wide Web community. W3C formed their own committee, which included Sun Microsystems, and set out to develop specifications for a communication protocol based on SOAP 1.1. They adopted a working draft for the new specification called SOAP 1.2.

SOAP Functionality

SOAP is a specification for a messaging system where data is represented as text and defined as a data type. The text that contains this data is called a SOAP message, which is written in XML. Besides transmitting data, SOAP also transmits metadata in the SOAP message header. Anyone familiar with HTML and XML can read and understand a SOAP message and if necessary use XML to modify the SOAP message. Tags are used in XML to define data elements. Unlike HTML, XML enables you to create your own XML tags. This is referred to as *extensibility*, which is critical to implement future developments in SOAP technology.

SOAP is a stateless communication protocol. That is, data and the SOAP message aren't saved during the course of the transmission. For example, SOAP transmits a request to invoke a remote procedure call to the service provider. The service provider responds to the request in a return SOAP message to the calling party. The relationship between the sender and receiver no longer exists once the client receives the response.

SOAP cannot reference objects because all data must be explicitly contained in a SOAP message. This means that a SOAP message cannot contain a reference to data that is external from the message. Let's say that you want to transmit data contained on a remote computer. You cannot include code in the SOAP message that tells SOAP to get this data. Instead, you must invoke a remote procedure by making a remote procedure call within the SOAP message. The remote procedure must then get data from the remote computer. Each SOAP message can contain one remote procedure call.

The SOAP Message and Delivery Structure

There are three parts to a SOAP message. These are the envelope, header, and body. The SOAP envelope is a required XML tag that contains the SOAP header and body. The header is an optional XML tag in the SOAP message that contains metadata. The body of the SOAP message is required and contains the text of the message. The Java API for XML Messaging (JAXM) generates the SOAP message for you based on the JAXM code in your J2EE application, which you'll learn about later in this chapter.

The SOAP envelope is used to contain the SOAP message, similar to an envelope used to post a letter. The header contains additional information and sometimes instructions for use by the SOAP processor to transmit the SOAP message. For example, the body of the SOAP message might have data that is defined in the header as metadata.

Any number of intermediate computers might process a SOAP message between the requestor, who generates the SOAP message, and the receiver, who responds to the request. Intermediate computers are called SOAP nodes that receive and forward a SOAP message until the message reaches the receiver. Some SOAP nodes simply relay the SOAP message to the next SOAP node or directly to the receiver. A SOAP message might need to be processed a particular way based on needs of the SOAP node or the receiver before the SOAP message is relayed to the next SOAP node or receiver. Such processing instructions are generally contained in the SOAP message header, which is read and processed by the SOAP node.

The process performed on the SOAP message by a node before the message is relayed is called a SOAP actor. A SOAP node can have multiple actors, and each actor might involve processing that occurs simultaneously on different machines.

There are three kinds of SOAP message bodies: a request, a response, and a fault. A request message body contains the name of the remote procedure and serialized input parameters, if any, that are passed to the remote procedures when the remote procedure is invoked. The response message body contains the name of the remote procedure and output parameter, if any, that are returned by the remote procedure to the requestor. The fault message body contains fault codes and fault messages, known as the fault string, that describe failure of the message to be successfully distributed. A fault code is an abbreviation indicating the fault. A fault message is text that describes the fault.

The SOAP specification defines four kinds of faults. These are VersionMismatch, MustUnderstand, Client, and Server. The VersionMismatch is sent when an invalid namespace is detected in the envelope. MustUnderstand is generated when the receiving SOAP processor is unable to process the SOAP message header. The Client fault occurs when a client incorrectly formed the SOAP message. The SOAP server sends the Client fault. The Server fault is sent when the SOAP server cannot process the SOAP message, although the SOAP message is not a fault. A SOAP actor can also generate one of the four SOAP faults.

WSDL and SOAP

SOAP facilitates the interaction between applications and web services located on remote computers. WSDL can be used to describe network services used with SOAP by including a binding for SOAP 1.1 protocol endpoints. Two commonly used transmission primitives for SOAP are one-way transmission primitives using SMTP and request-response transmission primitives using HTTP. Listing 14-10 illustrates the one-way transmission primitive, and Listing 14-11 shows the request-response transmission primitive.

SOAP One-Way Transmission Primitive

Similar in design to the one-way transmission primitive described earlier in this chapter for the WSDL document, the SOAP one-way transmission primitive consists of only an input operation. There is no output operation. Listing 14-10 shows how to construct a one-way transmission primitive using SMTP within a SOAP binding. The document is divided into WSDL document components such as message, portType, binding, operation, service, port, and types, all of which are described in the earlier discussion about WSDL.

SOAP elements are placed within the appropriate elements of the WSDL document. The first SOAP element used in the WSDL document is the soap:binding element. The soap:binding element has two attributes—style and transport—that describe the SOAP binding. The value of the style attribute describes the type of binding. There are two types: document and rpc, which is used for a remote procedure call. This example uses the document type. Listing 14-11 uses rpc. The value of the transport attribute is the URI of the SMTP server.

The next two SOAP elements used in the WSDL document appear as child elements of the input element. These are the soap:body element and the soap:header element, each of which describes components of the SOAP message that will be received from a trading partner.

The last SOAP element to appear within this WSDL document is the soap:address element. The soap:address element is a child element of the port element. The soap:address element has one attribute called location. The value of the location attribute is the port binding used to receive requests from potential trading partners.

Listing 14-10
SOAP
one-way
transmission
primitive
using SMTP

```xml
<?xml version="1.0"?>
<definitions name="pricing" targetNamespace=
      "http://mycompany.com/pricing.wsdl"
    xmlns:tns="http://mycompany.com/pricing.wsdl"
    xmlns:xsd1="http://mycompany.com/pricing.xsd"
    xmlns:soap="http://schemas.xmlsoap.org/wsdl/soap/"
    xmlns="http://schemas.xmlsoap.org/wsdl/">
  <message name="ProductPricing">
    <part name="body" element="xsd1:ProductPricing"/>
    <part name="productheader" element="xsd1:ProductHeader"/>
  </message>
  <portType name="ProductPricePortType">
    <operation name="GetProductPricing">
      <input message="tns:GetProductPricingInput"/>
    </operation>
  </portType>
  <binding name="ProductPriceSoapBinding"
      type="tns:ProductPricePortType">
```

```
       <soap:binding style="document"
         transport="http://mycompany.com/smtp"/>
        <operation name="GetProductPricing">
          <input message="tns:GetProductPricing">
            <soap:body parts="body" use="literal"/>
            <soap:header message="tns:GetProductPricing"
               part="productheader" use="literal"/>
          </input>
        </operation>
   </binding>
   <service name="ProductPricingService">
     <port name="ProductPricingPort"
            binding="tns:ProductPricingSoap">
       <soap:address location="mailto:customer@mycompany.com"/>
     </port>
    </service>
   <types>
   <schema targetNamespace="http://mycompany.com/ProductPrice.xsd"
      xmlns="http://www.w3.org/2000/10/XMLSchema">
     <element name="ProductPrice">
       <complexType>
         <all>
           <element name="ProductID" type="string"/>
         </all>
       </complexType>
     </element>
     <element name="ProductPriceHeader" type="uriReference"/>
    </schema>
   </types>
 </definitions>
```

SOAP Request-Response Transmission Primitive

The SOAP request-response transmission primitive is used whenever a web service is designed to receive requests from potential trading partners and is designed to respond to such a request. It is very similar in concept to the WSDL request-response transmission primitive. Listing 14-11 illustrates the SOAP request-response transmission primitive. This example begins by specifying namespaces used in the document. And as with the SOAP one-way transmission primitive, the structure of the document is similar to the WSDL document that uses the request-response transmission primitive.

Within the WSDL elements are SOAP elements, the first of which is the soap:binding element. The soap:binding element, as discussed in the previous section, is a child element within the binding element. In this example, the soap:binding element uses rpc as the value of the style attribute. This means binding is designed for a remote procedure call. The value of the transport attribute identifies HTTP as the protocol used for transmission.

The next SOAP element, soap:operation, appears within the operation element. The soap:operation element requires one attribute, which is the soapAction attribute. The soapAction attribute contains the URI of the operation. In this example GetProductPrice is the operation.

Within the input element is the soap:body element. The soap:body requires three attributes. These are use, namespace, and encodingStyle. The value of the use attribute specifies whether the soap:body is encoded or not. The namespace attribute identifies the namespacing used in the SOAP body. And the encodingStyle attribute specifies the URI of the encoding style if the soap:body is encoded. Likewise, another soap:body element is included in the WSDL document. This one is within the output element and describes the SOAP body of the output.

The last SOAP element in the example is soap:address and is contained within the port element. The soap:address identifies the URI used for the binding.

Listing 14-11
The request-response transmission primitive

```
<?xml version="1.0"?>
<definitions name="pricing"
        targetNamespace="http://mycompany.com/pricing.wsdl"
    xmlns:tns="http://mycompany.com/pricing.wsdl"
    xmlns:xsd="http://www.w3.org/2000/10/XMLSchema"
    xmlns:xsd1="http://mycompany.com/pricing.xsd"
    xmlns:soap="http://schemas.xmlsoap.org/wsdl/soap/"
    xmlns="http://schemas.xmlsoap.org/wsdl/">
    <message name="ProductPricingInput">
        <part name="ProductID" element="xsd:string"/>
    </message>
    <message name="ProductPricingOutput">
        <part name="price" type="xsd:float"/>
    </message>
    <portType name="ProductPricePortType">
        <operation name="GetProductPricing">
            <input message="tns:GetProductPricingInput"/>
            <output message="tns:GetProductPricingOutput"/>
        </operation>
    </portType>
    <binding name="ProductPriceSoapBinding"
            type="tns:ProductPricePortType">
        <soap:binding style="rpc"
                transport="http://schemas.xmlsoap.org/soap/http"/>
    <operation name="GetProductPrice">
        <soap:operation soapAction="http://mycompany/GetProductPrice"/>
```

```
        <input>
          <soap:body use="encoded"
                  namespace="http://mycompany.com/pricing"
              encodingStyle=
                  "http://schemas.xmlsoap.org/soap/encoding/"/>
        </input>
        <output>
          <soap:body use="encoded"
                  namespace="http://mycompany.com/pricing"
              encodingStyle=
                  "http://schemas.xmlsoap.org/soap/encoding/"/>
        </output>
      </operation>
    </binding>
    <service name="ProductPricingService">
      <documentation>My first service</documentation>
      <port name="ProductPricePort" binding="tns:ProductPriceBinding"
        <soap:address location="http://mycompany.com/pricing"/>
      </port>
    </service>
</definitions>
```

SOAP Binding Element

The soap:binding element indicates that the WSDL document is bound to the SOAP 1.1 protocol. Recall that the SOAP protocol defines a SOAP message as having an envelope, header, and body. There are two attributes required by the soap:binding element: the style attribute, which has a value of either document or rpc (as described previously in this chapter), and the transport attribute. The transport attribute contains the URI of the SOAP transport used for the binding. SOAP transports include HTTP, SMTP, and FTP.

Both of these attributes are necessary whenever you need to use a SOAP binding to a WSDL document. However, the value of the style attribute defaults to document if it is excluded from the soap:binding.

SOAP Operation Element

The soap:operation element supplies information about the operation and contains two attributes—style and soapAction. The style attribute states whether the message contains a document or parameters and return values. The value of the style attribute is document if the message contains a document; otherwise, it is rpc. As discussed previously, rpc implies a remote procedure call, which uses parameters and return values. The default value of the style attribute is document.

The style attribute is important to the SOAP binding because the value determines the structure of the message body and the programming model that will be used to access the message. The soapAction attribute is used to identify the contents of the SOAPAction header. The content of the SOAPAction header is specific to an operation. The value of the soapAction attribute is the URI of the SOAPAction header content.

SOAP Body Element

The soap:body element defines the organization of message parts within the body element and provides information on how message parts are assembled. Message parts fall into two categories—abstract type definitions and concrete schema definitions. An abstract type definition defines types that are serialized based on rules of an encoding style. The encoding style is identified by a URI. An encoding style sets rules that enable the message to be formatted in various ways, which requires the message recipient to interpret all the variations in the message format. Alternatively, the concrete schema definition avoids the use of various message formats. Therefore the message recipient needs to be able to interpret one message format as specified in the schema definition.

The soap:body element contains four attributes. These are parts, user, encodingStyle, and namespace. The parts attribute specifies the SOAP message parts contained in the body of the message. It defaults to all parts of a SOAP message if the parts attribute is omitted. The use attribute specifies whether parts of the message use an abstract type definition or concrete schema definition. The value encoded indicates that an abstract type definition is being used and the value literal implies use of a concrete schema definition.

The encodingStyle attribute contains the URI of the abstract type definitions and is required only if the use attribute is assigned the encoded value. The encodingStyle attribute value can contain multiple URIs, each representing a different abstract type definition supported by the message. Each URI assigned to the encodingStyle attribute must be separated by a space.

The namespace attribute identifies the URI of the namespace used by the encodingStyle and is applied to content that isn't defined by the abstract type definition.

SOAP Fault Element

The soap:fault element defines SOAP fault details and follows the style of the soap:body element. The soap:fault has four attributes. These are name, use, encodingStyle, and namespace. The value of the name attribute associates the soap:fault element with the wsdl:fault element that is used for the same operation. The other attributes have the same functionality as they do within the soap:body element.

SOAP Header Element

The SOAP header element actually consists of two elements. These are the soap:header and the soap:headerfault. Both elements define the header for the SOAP envelope header element. The soap:headerfault is the default definition for the header element.

Both the soap:header element and the soap:headerfault element contain five attributes. These are message, part, use, encodingStyle, and namespace. The value of the message attribute identifies the SOAP message whose header is being defined. The value of the part attribute identifies the message part that defines the header type. The other attributes function the same as they do in the soap:body element.

SOAP Address Element

The soap:address element is used to identify the address to be used for binding the SOAP message. The soap:address element contains one attribute called location. The location attribute is assigned the URI of the port used for binding.

WSDL and HTTP Binding

A web browser is typically used to interact with a web site, although there are other programmatic ways of achieving the same interaction. WSDL contains specifications for binding to a web site by using Get and Post, which are components of the HTTP 1.1 protocol. Let's see how this works in Listing 14-12. This example defines two messages. The first message has three parts, where the first and third parts are of xsd:string types, and the second part is xsd:int type. The second message has one part that is of a xsd:binary type.

The portType called FirstPort defines two operations. The first operation is input and receives the FirstMessage, and the second operation is output that is the SecondMessage. This means that the web service receives a three-part message consisting of a xsd:string, xsd:int, and xsd:string. When this message is received, the web service replies with a message that contains an xsd:binary type. As you'll see later in this example, the output operation returns a JPEG file containing an image.

The service element assigns an http:address to each port and associates ports with related bindings. These bindings are defined in subsequent binding elements. You'll notice that both the FirstBinding and SecondBinding use GET and output mime:context. However, input to the FirstBinding is http:urlReplace, and input to the SecondBinding is http:urlEncoded. The ThirdBinding uses POST and input and output mime:content.

The http:address element requires one attribute, which is location. The value of the location attribute is the base address.

The http:operation element contains a location attribute. The value of the location attribute is the URI that is specific for the operation and is combined with the URI of the http:address to become the URI used for the HTTP request.

The http:urlEncoded element signifies that the standard URI-encoding rules are used to encode parts of the message. The URI-encoding rules use a name=value pair, where each pair is separated with an ampersand (&), such as fname="Bob"&lname="Smith" (see Chapter 8).

The http:urlReplacement element specifies that a replacement algorithm is used to encode parts of the message. The replacement algorithm contains steps used to search for a set of patterns in the http:operation element URI. This search occurs prior to the http:operation and http:address values being joined. When a match occurs, the related part of the message replaces the part matching the pattern.

```
<definitions>
  <message name="FirstMessage">
    <part name="FirstPart" type="xsd:string"/>
    <part name="SecondPart" type="xsd:int"/>
    <part name="ThirdPart" type="xsd:string"/>
  </message>
  <message name="SecondMessage">
    <part name="FirstPart" type="xsd:binary"/>
  </message>
  <portType name="FirstPort">
    <operation name="FirstOperation">
      <input message="tns:FirstMessage"/>
      <output message="tns:SecondMessage"/>
    </operation>
  </portType>
  <service name="FirstService">
    <port name="FirstPort" binding="tns:FirstBinding">
      <http:address location="http://mycompany.com/"/>
    </port>
    <port name="SecondPort" binding="tns:SecondBinding">
      <http:address location="http://mycompany.com/"/>
    </port>
    <port name="ThirdPort" binding="tns:ThirdBinding">
      <http:address location="http://mycompany.com/"/>
    </port>
  </service>
  <binding name="FirstBinding" type="FirstPart">
    <http:binding verb="GET"/>
    <operation name="FirstOperation">
      http:operation location=
             "FirstOperation/A(part1)B(part2)/(part3)"/>
        <input>
          <http:urlReplacement/>
        </input>
        <output>
          <mime:content type="image/jpeg"/>
        </output>
    </operation>
  </binding>
  <binding name="SecondBinding" type="FirstPart">
```

```
    <http:binding verb="GET"/>
     <operation name="FirstOperation">
       <http:operation location="FirstOperation"/>
       <input>
         <http:urlEncoded/>
       </input>
       <output>
         <mime:content type="image/jpeg"/>
       </output>
     </operation>
  </binding>
  <binding name="ThirdBinding" type="FirstPart">
    <http:binding verb="POST"/>
      <operation name="FirstOperation">
        <http:operation location="FirstOperation"/>
        <input>
          <mime:content type="application/x-www-form-urlencoded"/>
        </input>
        <output>
          <mime:content type="image/jpeg"/>
        </output>
      </operation>
    </binding>
</definitions>
```

Quick Reference Guide

This quick reference guide provides an overview of classes used by J2ME for web services. Full details of these classes and all Java classes and interfaces are available at java.sun.com.

javax.xml.rpc public interface Stub

Field	Description
static java.lang.String ENDPOINT_ADDRESS_PROPERTY	Address of target service endpoint.
static java.lang.String PASSWORD_PROPERTY	Password for authentication static.
java.lang.String SESSION_MAINTAIN_PROPERTY	This boolean property is used by a service client to indicate whether or not it wants to participate in a session with a service endpoint.
static java.lang.String USERNAME_PROPERTY	User name for authentication.

javax.xml.rpc public interface Stub

Method	Description
java.lang.Object _getProperty(java.lang.String name)	Return the value of a specific configuration property.
Iterator _getPropertyNames()	Return an Iterator view of the names of the properties that can be configured on this stub instance.
void _setProperty(java.lang.String name, java.lang.Object value)	Set the name and value of a configuration property for this Stub instance.

public class NamespaceConstants extends java.lang.Object

Field	Description
static java.lang.String NSPREFIX_SCHEMA_XSD	Namespace prefix for XML schema XSD static.
java.lang.String NSPREFIX_SCHEMA_XSI	Namespace prefix for XML Schema XSI.
static java.lang.String NSPREFIX_SOAP_ENCODING	Namespace prefix for SOAP encoding.
static java.lang.String NSPREFIX_SOAP_ENVELOPE	Namespace prefix for SOAP envelope.
static java.lang.String NSURI_SCHEMA_XSD	Namespace URI for XML Schema XSD.
static java.lang.String NSURI_SCHEMA_XSI	Namespace URI for XML Schema XSI static.
java.lang.String NSURI_SOAP_ENCODING	Namespace URI for SOAP 1.1 encoding.
static java.lang.String NSURI_SOAP_ENVELOPE	Namespace URI for SOAP 1.1 envelope.
static java.lang.String NSURI_SOAP_NEXT_ACTOR	Namespace URI for SOAP 1.1 next actor role.

Method	Description
NamespaceConstants ( )	Constructor.

public class JAXRPCException extends java.lang.RuntimeException

JAXRPCException()	Construct a new exception with null as its detail message.
JAXRPCException(java.lang.String message)	Construct a new exception with the specified detail message.
JAXRPCException(java.lang.String message, java.lang.Throwable cause)	Construct a new exception with the specified detail message and cause.
JAXRPCException(java.lang.Throwable cause)	Construct a new JAXRPCException with the specified cause and a detail message of the cause. This contains the class and detail message of cause.
java.lang.Throwable getLinkedCause()	Retrieve the linked cause of the exception.

The Complete Reference

Appendix

Quick Reference Guide

This quick reference guide provides a brief overview of classes used by J2ME for the Display class, Command class, and Item class. Full details of these classes and all Java classes and interfaces are available at java.sun.com.

▦ **javax.microedition.lcdui.DisplayClass**

Method	Description
static Display getDisplay(MIDlet midlet)	Retrieve an instance of the Display class.
Displayable getCurrent()	Retrieve the current instance of Displayable class.
void setCurrent(Alert alert, Displayable displayable)	Display the specified instance of the alert dialog box and then the specified instance of the Displayable class.
void setCurrent (Displayable displayable)	Display the specified instance of the Displayable class.
boolean isColor()	Determine whether the device supports color.
int numColors()	Retrieve the number of colors or shades of gray that are available on the device.
void callSerial(Runnable runnable)	Call an instance of the Runnable class after repainting.

▦ **javax.microedition.lcdui.DisplayableClass**

Method	Description
void addCommand(Command command)	Associate a command to an instance of the Displayable class.
void removecommand(Command command)	Disassociate a command from an instance of the Displayable class.
void setCommandListener(Command Listener commandlistener)	Associate a CommandListener to an instance of the Displayable class.
boolean isShown()	Determine whether an instance of the Displayable class is shown on the screen.

javax.microedition.lcdui.CommandClass

Method	Description
Command(String label, int commandType, int priority)	Create an instance of the Command class that displays the specified label and is of the specified commandType and has the specified priority.
int getCommandType()	Retrieve the commandType of a command.
String getLabel()	Retrieve the label of a command.
int getPriority()	Retrieve the priority of a command.

javax.microedition.lcdui.CommandListener-Interface

Method	Description
void commandAction (Command command, Displayable displayable)	Process an instance of the Command class.

javax.microedition.lcdui.ItemClass

Method	Description
String getLabel()	Retrieve the label associated with an instance of the Item class.
void setLabel(String label)	Assign a label to an instance of the Item class.

javax.microedition.lcdui.ItemStateListener-Interface

Method	Description
void itemStateChanged (Item item)	Process changes to an instance of the Item class.

javax.microedition.midlet.MIDletClass

Method	Description
abstract void destroyApp (boolean unconditional)	MIDlet is going to shut down.
abstract void pauseApp()	MIDlet is going to pause.
abstract void startApp()	MIDlet is in the active state.
final void notifyDestroyed()	Requesting to shut down the MIDlet.
final void notifyPaused()	Requesting to pause the MIDlet.
final void resumeRequest()	Requesting to activate the MIDlet.
final String getAppProperty(String key)	Retrieve attributes from a JAD or JAR file.

javax.microedition.midlet.MIDletStatechange-ExceptionClass

Method	Description
MIDletStateChangeException()	Create a new MIDletStateChangeException object without a test.
MIDletStatechangeException (String string)	Create a new MIDletStateChangeException object with a message.

javax.microedition.lcdui.Screen Class

Method	Description
String getTitle()	Retrieve the screen's title.
void setTitle(String string)	Set the screen's title.
Ticker getTicker()	Retrieve the screen's Ticker.
void setTicker(Ticker ticker)	Set the screen's Ticker.

javax.microedition.lcdui.Alert Class

Method	Description
Alert(String title)	Create an instance of the Alert class.
Alert(String title, String message, Image image, AlertType, alertType)	Create an instance of the Alert class with an Image and AlertType.
Image getImage()	Retrieve an instance of the Alert class image.
void setImage(Image image)	Associate an image with an instance of the Alert class.
String getString()	Get an instance of the Alert class message.
void setString(String str)	Set an instance of the Alert class message.
int getDefaultTimeout()	Retrieve an instance of the Alert class default time.
int getTimeout()	Retrieve actual time an instance of the Alert class will be displayed.
void setTimeout(int time)	Set the display time of an instance of the Alert class.
AlertType getType()	Retrieve the AlertType of an instance of the Alert class.
void setType(AlertType type)	Set the AlertType of an instance of the Alert class.

javax.microedition.lcdui.Form Class

Method	Description
Form (String title)	Create an instance of the Form class with a title.
Form (String title, Item[] items)	Create an instance of the Form class and append the specified list of array items onto the instance.
int append(Image image)	Append an instance of the Image class to an instance of the Form class.
int append(Item item)	Append an instance of the Item class or subclass to an instance of the Form class.

Method	Description
int append(String string)	Append an instance of the String class to an instance of the Form class.
void delete(int index)	Remove an instance of the Item class or subclass specified by the index from an instance of the Form class.
void insert (int index, Item item)	Insert an instance of the Item class or subclass before the instance of the Item class whose position is specified by the index.
Item get(int index)	Retrieve an instance of the Item class or subclass whose position is specified by the index.
void set(int index, Item item)	Replace an existing instance of the Item class or subclass whose position is specified by the index with the instance of the Item class or subclass reference in the second parameter.
void setItemStateListener(Item-Statelistener itemStateListener)	Associate an ItemStateListener with an instance of the Item class or subclass.
int size()	Retrieve the number of instances of the Item class or subclass in an instance of the Form class.
String getLabel()	Retrieve the label associated with an instance of an Item class.
void setLabel(String label)	Associate a label with an instance of an Item class.

javax.microedition.lcdui.ChoiceGroup Class

Method	Description
ChoiceGroup (String label, int choiceType)	Create an instance of an empty ChoiceGroup class, where label is the title of the instance and choiceType is the type of instance.
ChoiceGroup(String label, int choiceType, String[] string, Image image)	Create an instance of the ChoiceGroup class, where label is the title of the instance and choiceType is the type of instance, and use the image with the instance. Also populate the instance with options contained in the string.

Method	Description
int append (String string, Image image)	Place an option at the end of other options in an instance of the Choice Group class, and associate the image with the option.
void delete (int index)	Remove the option identified by the index number from an instance of the ChoiceGroup class, and associate the image with the option.
void insert (int index, String string, Image image)	Insert an option into an instance of the ChoiceGroup class before the option identified by the index number.
void set (int index, String string, Image image)	Replace an option identified by the index number with the option specified in the string and image.
String getString (int index)	Retrieve the string associated with the option identified by the index number.
Image getImage(int index)	Retrieve the image associated with the option identified by the index number.
int getSelectedIndex()	Retrieve the index associated with an option.
void setSelectedIndex(int index, boolean selected)	Select the option identified by the index and whether the option is selected (true) or unselected (false).
int getSelectedFlags (boolean[] array)	Retrieve the selection status of options and store them in an array.
void setSelectedFlag (boolean[] array)	Set the selection status of options stored in an array.
boolean isSelected (int index)	Determine whether the user selected the option identified by the index number.
int size()	Determine the number of options there are in an instance of the ChoiceGroup.

javax.microedition.lcdui.DateField Class

Method	Description
DateField (String label, int mode)	Create an instance of the DateField class that contains the specified label and uses the specified mode.

Method	Description
DateField (String label, int mode, TimeZone timeZone)	Create an instance of the DateField class that contains the specified label and uses the specified mode and time zone.
Date getDate()	Retrieve the date/time from an instance of the DateField class.
void setDate (Date date)	Set the date for an instance of the DateField class.
int getInputMode()	Retrieve the input mode of an instance of the DateField class.
void setInputMode(int mode)	Replace the existing date field mode with a different mode.

javax.microedition.lcdui.Gauge Class

Method	Description
Gauge(String label, boolean interactive, int maxValue, int initialValue)	Create an instance of the Gauge class, where label is the caption for the instance, interactive is a boolean value indicating whether the instance is interactive, maxValue is the maximum value displayed in the gauge, and the initialValue is the beginning value displayed in the gauge.
int getValue()	Retrieve the current value of the gauge.
void setValue (int value)	Set a new value for the gauge.
int getMaxValue()	Retrieve the maximum value of the gauge.
void setMaxValue(int maxValue)	Set the maximum value of the gauge.
boolean isInteractive()	Determine whether the gauge is interactive.

javax.microedition.lcdui.StringItem Class

Method	Description
StringItem (String label, String text)	Create an instance of a StringItem class, where the label is text describing the StringItem class, and text is the text displayed on the screen.

Method	Description
String getText()	Retrieve the text portion of an instance of a StringItem class.
void setText (String text)	Replace the text portion of an instance of a StringItem class.
String getLabel()	Retrieve the label portion of an instance of a StringItem class.
void setLabel (String text)	Replace the label portion of an instance of a StringItem class.

javax.microedition.lcdui.TextField Class

Method	Description
TextField (String label, String text, int maxSize, int constraint)	Create an instance of a TextField class.
void delete (int offset, int length)	Remove characters from a TextField class at a specified offset.
void insert (String src, int position)	Insert String at a specified offset in a TextField class at a specified offset.
void insert (char[] data, int offset, int length, int position)	Insert characters from an array into a TextField class at a specified offset.
void setChars (char[] data, int offset, int length)	Replace characters of a TextField class with characters from an array.
void setString(String text)	Replace characters of a TextField class with characters in a string.
int getChars (char[] data)	Copy contents of a TextField class into an array.
String getString()	Copy contents of the TextField class into a string.
int getConstraints()	Retrieve the constraint of a TextField class.
void setConstraints (int constraint)	Set the constraint of a TextField class.
int getMaxSize()	Retrieve the maximum number of characters of a TextField class.

Method	Description
int setMaxSize (int maxsize)	Set the maximum number of characters of a TextField class.
int getCaretPosition()	Retrieve the cursor position within a TextField class.
int size()	Retrieve the number of characters in a TextField class.

javax.microedition.lcdui.Image Class

Method	Description
static Image create Image (String name)	Create an immutable image, where name is the name of a resource.
static Image createImage (Image source)	Create an immutable image, where source is reference to an existing Image.
static Image createImage(byte[] imageData, int imageOffset, int imageLength)	Create an immutable image, where byte is an array of data representing the image, imageOffset is the starting position of the image, and imageLength is the length of the image.
static Image createImage(int width, int height)	Create a mutable image that has a specified width and height.
Graphics getGraphics()	Retrieve reference to an instance of the Graphics class.
int getHeight()	Retrieve the image height.
int getwidth()	Retrieve the image width.
boolean isMutable()	Determine whether an image is a mutable image.

javax.microedition.lcdui.ImageItem Class

Method	Description
ImageItem(String label, Image im, int layout, String altText)	Create an instance of the ImageItem class, where label is text describing the image, im is reference to the image, layout is the layout directive, and altText is displayed if the image cannot be shown on the device.

Method	Description
Image getImage()	Retrieve an image associated with an ImageItem class.
voaid setImage (image im)	Associate an image with an ImageItem class.
int getLayout()	Retrieve the layout directive of an ImageItem instance.
void setLayout (int layout)	Replace the layout directive of an ImageItem instance.
String getAltText()	Retrieve the alternate text of an ImageItem instance.
void setAltText(String text)	Replace the alternate text of an ImageItem instance.

javax.microedition.lcdui.List Class

Method	Description
List (String title, int listType)	Create an instance of the List class without assigning elements to the list. The title is the title of the list, and the listType is the type of list being created.
List (String title, int listType, String[] stringElements, Image[] imageElements)	Create an instance of the List class and assign elements to the list. The title is the title of the list; the listType is the type of list being created; stringElements is an array of strings containing text for the list; and imageElements is an array of images associated with each list element.
int append (String stringPart, Image imagePart)	Append an element to the end of the list, where stringPart is the text of the element, and imagePart is the image associated with the element.
void delete(int indexNum)	Remove an element from a list, where the element being removed is identified by the indexNum.
void insert (int indexNum, String stringPart, Image imagePart)	Insert an element into the list at a specific position within the list, where indexNum is the position within the list where the element will be located; stringPart is the text of the element; and imagePart is the image associated with the element.

Method	Description
void set(int indexNum, String stringPart, Image imagePart)	Replace an element in the list at a specific position within the list, where indexNum is the position within the list where the element will be located; stringPart is the text of the element; and imagePart is the image associated with the element.
String getString (int indexNum)	Retrieve the text of an element from a specific position in the list, where indexNum identifies the position of the element.
Image getImage(int indexNum)	Retrieve the image of an element from a specific position in the list, where indexNum identifies the position of the element.
int getSelectedIndex()	Retrieve index of a selected element of a list.
void setSelectedIndex(int indexNum, boolean selected)	Set the default selected flag of an element within the list, where indexNum is the index number of the element, and selected is either true or false.
int getSelectedFlag (boolean[] selectedArray_return)	Retrieve the selection status and store them in the selectedArray.
void setSelectedFlags(boolean[] selectedArray)	Set the selection status based on values stored in the selectedArray.
boolean isSelected(int indexNum)	Determine whether the element identified by indexNum is selected.
int size()	Number of elements in list.

javax.microedition.lcdui.TextBox Class

Method	Description
TextBox(String title, String text, int maxSize, int constraint)	Create a new instance of the TextBox class, where title is the title of the text box; text is the text used to populate the text box; maxSize is the requested maximum number of characters that can be entered into the text box; and constraint identifies character restrictions.
void delete(int offset, int length)	Remove characters from a text box. Characters to be removed begin with the character specified by offset character position until the specified length is reached.

Method	Description
void insert(String src, int position)	Insert characters from a string into the text box, where src is the string, and position is the position within the text box to insert the characters.
void insert(char[] data, in offset, int length, int position)	Insert characters from an array into the text box, where data is the array; offset is the starting position within the array; length is the number of characters to insert; and position is the place within the text box to insert the characters.
void setChars(char[] data, int offset, int length)	Replace contents of the text box with characters in an array, where data is the array; offset is the starting position within the array; and length is the number of characters to insert.
int getChars(char[] data)	Retrieve the contents of a text box into an array, where data is the array that receives the contents of the text box.
String getString()	Retrieve the contents of a text box into a string.
int getConstraints()	Retrieve the constraints of the text box.
void setConstraints(int constraints)	Replace the constraints of a text box, where constraints contains the new constraints.
int getMaxSize()	Retrieve the maximum number of characters that can be stored in a text box.
int setMaxSize(int maxSize)	Set the maximum number of characters that can be stored in a text box, where maxSize is the requested maximum number of characters.
int getCaretPosition()	Retrieve the current cursor position within the text box.
int size()	Retrieve the current number of characters in a text box.

javax.microedition.lcdui.Ticker Class

Method	Description
Ticker(String str)	Create a new Ticker, where str is the text that appears in the ticker.

Method	Description
String getString()	Retrieve the text displayed by the Ticker.
void setString(String str)	Set the text displayed by the Ticker, where str is the text.

javax.microedition.lcdui.Canvas Class

Method	Description
int getWidth()	Return the width of the canvas in pixels.
int getHeight()	Return the height of the canvas in pixels.

Paint	Description
abstract void paint(Graphic g)	Draw an image on the canvas using the instance of the Graphics class passed as a parameter.
final void repaint()	Repaint the full canvas.
final void repaint(int x, int y, int width, int height)	Repaint the specified region of the canvas.
final void servicePaints()	A pending paint request must be processed before other outstanding requests.
boolean isDoubleBuffered()	Determine whether the device supports double buffering.

Notify	Description
void showNotify()	Called before the application manager displays the canvas.
void hideNotify()	Called after the application manager removes the canvas from the screen.

Key and Game Action	Description
void keyPressed(int keycode)	Called whenever a key is pressed and used to process the key code of that key.
void keyReleased(int keycode)	Called whenever a key is released and used to process the key code of that key.
void keyRepeated(int keycode)	Called whenever a key is held down and used to process the key code of that key (not supported by all devices).

Method	Description
boolean hasRepeatEvents()	Determine whether the device supports repeated keys.
String getKeyName(int keycode)	Return the text associated with the key.
int getKeyCode(int gameActionConstant)	Return the key code value for the game action constant.
int getGameAction(int keycode)	Return the game action for a key code value.
String getKeyname(int keycode)	Return the name of the key for a key code. The name returned is not the name of the game action, but is the name of the actual key.

Pointer Event	Description
boolean hasPointerEvents()	Determine whether the device supports a pointer device.
boolean hasPointerMotion Events()	Determine whether the device detects the press, drag, and release motion of a pointer device.
void pointerDragged(int x, int y)	Called in response to a pointer drag event.
void pointerPressed(int x, int y)	Called in response to a pointer press event.
void pointerReleased(int x, int y)	Called in response to a pointer release event.

javax.microedition.lcdui.Graphics Class

Method	Description
void setColor(int RGB)	Change the current color to the integer represented by RGB. Red, green, and blue color values are consolidated into one integer value and passed to the setColor() method.
void setColor(int red, int green, int blue)	Change the current color to integers represented by red, green, and blue color values.
int getColor()	Retrieve the integer value that represents the current color.
int getBlueComponent()	Retrieve the blue color value.
int getGreenComponent()	Retrieve the green color value.
int getRedComponent()	Retrieve the red color value.

Method	Description
void setGrayScale(int value)	Change the value of the current gray scale.
int getGrayScale()	Retrieve the value of the current gray scale.
Stroke Style	**Description**
int getStrokeStyle()	Retrieve the stroke style of a graphic context.
void setStrokeStyle(int style)	Set the stroke style of a graphic context, where style is either SOLID or DOTTED.
Line	**Description**
void drawLine(int x1, int y1, int x2, int y2)	Draw a line beginning at coordinate x1, y1 and ending at coordinate x2, y2.
Arc	**Description**
void drawArc(int x1, int y1, int x2, int y2, startAngle, endAngle)	Draw an outline arc within the rectangle defined as the first four parameters beginning with the startAngle and terminating with the endAngle.
void fillArc(int x1, int y1, int x2, int y2, startAngle, endAngle)	Draw a filled arc within the rectangle defined as the first four parameters beginning with the startAngle and terminating with the endAngle.
Rectangle	**Description**
void drawRect(int x1, int y1, int x2, int y2)	Draw a rectangle, where x1, y1 represents the coordinate of the upper-left corner of the rectangle, and x2, y2 represents the width and height of the rectangle.
void drawroundRect(int x1, int y1, int x2, int y2, int arcW, int arcH)	Draw a rounded rectangle, where x1, y1 represents the coordinate of the upper-left corner of the rectangle, and x2, y2 represents the width and height of the rectangle. arcW is the angle for the width of the arc, and arcH is the angle for the height of the arc.
void fillRect(int x1, int y1, int x2, int y2)	Draw a filled rectangle, where x1, y1 represents the coordinate of the upper-left corner of the rectangle, and x2, y2 represents the width and height of the rectangle.

Method	Description
void fillRoundedRect (int x1, int y1, int x2, int y2, int arcW, int arcH)	Draw a rounded filled rectangle, where x1, y1 represents the coordinate of the upper-left corner of the rectangle, and x2, y2 represents the width and height of the rectangle. arcW is the angle for the width of the arc, and arcH is the angle for the height of the arc.

Text	Description
void drawChar(char character, int x, int y, int anchor)	Draw a character at the x, y coordinate on the canvas using the specified anchor point.
void drawChars(char[] data, int offset, int len, int x, int y, int anchor)	Draw a subset of a character array the length specified by len and beginning with the character indicated by the offset. Draw the subset at the x, y coordinate on the canvas using the specified anchor point.
void drawString (String str, int x, int y, int anchor)	Draw a string at the x, y coordinate on the canvas using the specified anchor point.
void drawSubstring(String str, int offset, int len, int x, int y, int anchor)	Draw a substring the length specified by len and beginning with the character indicated by the offset. Draw the substring at the x, y coordinate on the canvas using the specified anchor point.
Font getFont()	Return the font of the graphic context.
void setFont(Font font)	Set the font of the graphic context, where font is the new font.

Image	Description
void drawImage(Image img, int x, int y, int anchor)	Draw the image specified in img, where the upper-left corner of the image is positioned at coordinate x, y using anchor point referenced by anchor.

Translate	Description
void translate (int x, int y)	Translate the specified by x, y coordinate.
int getTranslateX()	Retrieve the translated x coordinate.
int getTranslateY()	Retrieve the translated y coordinate.

Method	Description
Clip Region	**Description**
void setClip (int x1, int y1, int x2, int y2)	Set the coordinates for the clipping region, where x1, y1 represents the coordinate of the upper-left corner of the region, and x2, y2 represents the coordinate of the lower-right corner of the clipping region.
void clipRect(int x1, int y1, int x2, int y2)	Create a rectangle defined by x1, y1 and x2, y2 coordinates that establish a new clipping region by intersecting the existing clipping region. The coordinate x1, y1 represents the upper-left corner of the region, and x2, y2 represents the coordinate of the lower-right corner of the new clipping region.
int getClipX()	Retrieve the x1 coordinate of the upper-left corner of the clipping region.
int getClipY()	Retrieve the y1 coordinate of the upper-left corner of the clipping region.
int getClipHeight()	Retrieve the x2 coordinate of the lower-right corner of the clipping region.
int getclipWidth()	Retrieve the y2 coordinate of the lower-right corner of the clipping region.

javax.microedition.lcdui.Font Class

Method	Description
static Font getFont(int face, int style, int size)	Create an instance of the Font class that has the specified font face, font style, and font size.
static Font getDefaultfont()	Create an instance of the Font class that uses the default font face, font style, and font size.
Face, Style, Size	**Description**
int getFace()	Retrieve the font face.
int getStyle()	Retrieve the combination of font styles.
int getSize()	Retrieve the font size.

Method	Description
boolean isPlain()	Determine whether the font uses the plain style.
boolean isBold()	Determine whether the font uses the bold style.
boolean isItalic()	Determine whether the font uses the italic style.
boolean isUnderlined()	Determine whether the font uses the underlined style.

Height/Width	Description
int getHeight()	Return the font height.
int getBaselinePosition()	Return the ascent of the text.
int charWidth(char ch)	Return the advance of a character.
int charsWidth(char[] ch, int offset, int length)	Return the advance of a series of characters in a character array that begins with character represented by the offset and has a length represented by the integer length.
int substringWidth(String str, int offset, int length)	Return the advance of a substring that begins with character represented by the offset and has a length represented by the integer length.

javax.microedition.rms.RecordStore Class

Method	Description
static RecordStore openRecordStore(String recordStoreName)	Open the record store specified in recordStoreName.
static RecordStore openRecordStore(String recordStoreName, boolean createIfNecessary)	Open the record store specified in recordStoreName. If createIfNecessary is true, create a new record store if the recordStoreName doesn't exist. If createIfNecessary is false, don't create a new record store.
void closeRecordStore()	Close the currently opened record store.
static void deleteRecordStore (String recordStoreName)	Remove the record store specified in recordStoreName.
static String[] listRecordStores()	Return an array of strings containing the names of record stores in the MIDlet suite.

Method	Description
int addRecord(byte[] data, int offset, int numBytes)	Insert a record into a record store, where data is the record, offset is the index within the data of the first byte of the data, and the numBytes is the total number of bytes of the data.
void setRecord (int recordID, byte[] newData, int offset, int numBytes)	Replace data in the specified record, where recordID is the record ID, newData is the data that will overwrite the existing data in the record, the offset is the index of the first byte in the byte array, and numBytes is the total number of bytes to be written to the record store.
void deleteRecord(int recordID)	Remove a record specified by recordID from the record store.
byte[] getRecord(int recordID)	Retrieve a record specified by recordID from the record store.
int getRecord(int recordID, byte[] buffer, int offset)	Retrieve a record specified by recordID from the record store, where buffer is the destination, and offset is the byte within the record where copying begins.
int getRecordSize(int recordID)	Retrieve the size of the record specified in recordID. Size is returned as bytes.
int getNextRecordID()	Retrieve the next record ID.
int getNumRecords()	Retrieve the number of records that are in a record store.
long getLastModified()	Retrieve the date of the last modification made to the record store.
int getVersion()	Retrieve the version number of the record store.
String getName()	Retrieve the name of the record store.
int getSize()	Retrieve the size of the record.
int getSizeAvailable()	Retrieve the space available within a record store to store records.
RecordEnumeration enumerateRecords (Recordfilter filter, RecordComparator comparator, boolean keepUpdate)	Create an enumeration of records, where filter specifies the argument for placing records within the enumeration, comparator specifies the argument for comparing records, and keepUpdate is a boolean value that determines whether the enumeration should be updated when changes occur to the underlying record store.

Method	Description
void addRecordListener (RecordListener listener)	Associate a RecordListener to the record store.
void removeRecordListener (recordListener listener)	Remove the RecordListener that is associated with a record store.

javax.microedition.rms.RecordEnumeration Interface

Method	Description
int numRecords()	Return the number of records in the RecordEnumeration.
byte[] nextRecord()	Return the next record in the RecordEnumeration.
int nextRecordId()	Return the next record ID in the RecordEnumeration.
byte[] previousRecord()	Return the previous record in the RecordEnumeration.
int previousRecordId()	Return the previous record ID in the RecordEnumeration.
boolean hasNextElement()	Determine whether the enumeration has more records going forward.
boolean hasPreviousElement()	Determine whether there is a previous record in the RecordEnumeration.
void keepUpdated(boolean keepUpdated)	Set the automatic update feature of the RecordEnumeration, where keepUpdated is a boolean value indicating whether or not the feature is activated.
boolean isKeptUpdated()	Determine whether the RecordEnumeration is automatically updated.
void rebuild()	Rebuild the index of the RecordEnumeration.
void reset()	Return to the beginning of the RecordEnumeration.
void destroy()	Release resources reserved for the RecordEnumeration.

javax.microedition.rms.RecordComparator Interface

Method	Description
int compare(byte[], rec1, byte[] rec2)	Compare two records represented as byte array rec1 and byte array rec2 to determine the sort sequence of a RecordEnumeration.

javax.microedition.rms.RecordFilter interface

Method	Description
boolean matches(byte[] candidate)	Search a record for a specific value.

javax.microedition.rms.RecordListener Interface

Method	Description
void recordAdded(RecordStore recordStore, int recordId)	This method is called whenever a record is added to the record store, where recordStore is the record store, and recordID is the record that was added.
void recordChanged(RecordStore recordStore, int recordId)	This method is called whenever a record is changed in the record store, where recordStore is the record store, and recordID is the record that was changed.
void recordDeleted(RecordStore recordStore, int recordId)	This method is called whenever a record is deleted from the record store, where recordStore is the record store, and recordID is the record that was deleted.

Record Management System Exceptions

Exception	Description
public InvalidRecordIDException()	An invalid record number was used.
public InvalidRecordIDException (String message)	An invalid record number was used, where message contains the text of the exception.
public RecordStoreException()	General exception with the record store.
public RecordStoreException (String message)	General exception with the record store, where message contains the text of the exception.
public RecordStoreFullException()	Record store is full.
public RecordStoreFullException (String message)	Record store is full, where message contains the text of the exception.
public RecordStoreNotFound Exception()	Record store does not exist.
public RecordStoreNotFound Exception(String message)	Record store does not exist, where message contains the text of the exception.
public RecordStoreNotOpen Exception()	Record store is not open.
public RecordStoreNotOpen Exception(String message)	Record store is not open, where message contains the text of the exception.

java.sql Package Public Interface CallableStatement

Method	Description
public void registerOutParameter (int parameterIndex, int sqlType) throws SQLException	Register the OUT parameter.
public void registerOutParameter (int parameterIndex, int sqlType, int scale) throws SQLException	Register the OUT parameter.

Method	Description
public boolean wasNull() throws SQLException	Determine an OUT parameter value is null.

set by name

Method	Description
public void setURL(String parameterName,URL val) throws SQLException	Set a parameter to a java.net.URL object.
public void setNull(String parameterName, int sqlType) throws SQLException	Set a parameter to a null value.
public void setBoolean(String parameterName,boolean x) throws SQLException	Set a parameter to a Java boolean value.
public void setByte(String parameterName, byte x) throws SQLException	Set a parameter to a Java byte value.
public void setShort(String parameterName, short x) throws SQLException	Set a parameter to a Java short value.
public void setInt(String parameterName, int x) throws SQLException	Set a parameter to a Java int value.
public void setLong(String parameterName, long x) throws SQLException	Set a parameter to a Java long value.
public void setFloat(String parameterName, float x) throws SQLException	Set a parameter to a Java float value.
public void setDouble(String parameterName, double x) throws SQLException	Set a parameter to a Java double value.
public void setBigDecimal(String parameterName,BigDecimal x) throws SQLException	Set a parameter to a java.math.BigDecimal value.

Method	Description
public void setString(String parameterName,String x) throws SQLException	Set a parameter to a Java String value.
public void setBytes(String parameterName, byte[] x) throws SQLException	Set a parameter to a Java array of bytes.
public void setDate(String parameterName,Date x) throws SQLException	Set a parameter to a java.sql.Date value.
public void setTime(String parameterName, Time x) throws SQLException	Set a parameter to a java.sql.Time value.
public void setTimestamp(String parameterName,Timestamp x) throws SQLException	Set a parameter to a java.sql.Timestamp value.
public void setBinaryStream(String parameterName, InputStream x, int length) throws SQLException	Set the designated parameter to the given input stream, which will have the specified number of bytes.
public void setObject(String parameterName, Object x,int targetSqlType,int scale)throws SQLException	Set a parameter with the given object.
public void setObject(String parameterName, Object x, int targetSqlType) throws SQLException	Set a parameter with the given object.
public void setObject(String parameterName, Object x)throws SQLException	Set a parameter with the given object.
public void setDate(String parameterName, Date x,Calendar cal) throws SQLException	Set a parameter to a java.sql.Date value.
public void setTime(String parameterName, Time x, Calendar cal)throws SQLException	Set a parameter to a java.sql.Time value.

Method	Description
public void setTimestamp(String parameterName, Timestamp x, Calendar cal) throws SQLException	Set a parameter to a java.sql.Timestamp value.
public void setNull(String parameterName, int sqlType, String typeName)throws SQLException	Set a parameter to a null value.

get by index

Method	Description
public String getString(int parameterIndex) throws SQLException	Determine the value of the designated JDBC CHAR, VARCHAR, or LONGVARCHAR parameter.
public boolean getBoolean(int parameterIndex) throws SQLException	Determine the value of the designated JDBC BIT parameter.
public byte getByte(int parameterIndex) throws SQLException	Determine the value of the designated JDBC TINYINT parameter.
public short getShort(int parameterIndex) throws SQLException	Determine the value of the designated JDBC SMALLINT parameter.
public int getInt(int parameter Index) throws SQLException	Determine the value of the designated JDBC INTEGER parameter.
public long getLong(int parameterIndex) throws SQLException	Determine the value of the designated JDBC BIGINT parameter.
public float getFloat(int parameterIndex) throws SQLException	Determine the value of the designated JDBC FLOAT parameter.
public double getDouble(int parameterIndex) throws SQLException	Determine the value of the designated JDBC DOUBLE parameter.
public BigDecimal getBigDecimal (int parameterIndex,int scale) throws SQLException	Determine the value of the designated JDBC NUMERIC parameter.

Method	Description
public byte[] getBytes(int parameterIndex) throws SQLException	Determine the value of the designated JDBC BINARY or VARBINARY parameter.
public Date getDate(int parameterIndex)throws SQLException	Determine the value of the designated JDBC DATE parameter.
public Time getTime(int parameterIndex) throws SQLException	Determine the value of the designated JDBC TIME parameter.
public Timestamp getTimestamp (int parameterIndex) throws SQLException	Determine the value of the designated JDBC TIMESTAMP parameter.
public Object getObject(int parameterIndex)throws SQLException	Determine the value of the designated parameter.
public BigDecimal getBigDecimal (int parameterIndex) throws SQLException	Determine the value of the designated JDBC NUMERIC parameter.
public Object getObject(int i, Map map) throws SQLException	Return an object representing the value of OUT parameter.
public Ref getRef(int i) throws SQLException	Determine the value of the designated JDBC REF parameter.
public Blob getBlob(int i) throws SQLException	Determine the value of the designated JDBC BLOB parameter.
public Clob getClob(int i) throws SQLException	Determine the value of the designated JDBC CLOB parameter.
public Array getArray(int i) throws SQLException	Determine the value of the designated JDBC ARRAY parameter.
public Date getDate(int parameterIndex, Calendar cal) throws SQLException	Determine the value of the designated JDBC DATE parameter.
public Time getTime(int parameterIndex, Calendar cal) throws SQLException	Determine the value of the designated JDBC TIME parameter.

Method	Description
public Timestamp getTimestamp (int parameterIndex, Calendar cal) throws SQLException	Determine the value of the designated JDBC TIMESTAMP parameter.
public void registerOutParameter(int paramIndex, int sqlType,String typeName)throws SQLException	Register the designated output parameter.
public void registerOutParameter (String parameterName, int sqlType) throws SQLException	Register the OUT parameter named parameterName.
public void registerOutParameter(String parameterName, int sqlType, int scale)throws SQLException	Determine the parameter named parameterName.
public void registerOutParameter (String parameterName, int sqlType, String typeName)throws SQLException	Determine the designated output parameter.
public URL getURL(int parameterIndex)throws SQLException	Determine the value of the designated JDBC DATALINK parameter.

get by name

Method	Description
public String getString(String parameterName) throws SQLException	Determine the value of a JDBC CHAR, VARCHAR, or LONGVARCHAR parameter.
public boolean getBoolean(String parameterName) throws SQLException	Determine the value of a JDBC BIT parameter.
public byte getByte(String parameterName) throws SQLException	Determine the value of a JDBC TINYINT parameter.
public short getShort(String parameterName) throws SQLException	Determine the value of a JDBC SMALLINT parameter.

Method	Description
public int getInt(String parameterName) throws SQLException	Determine the value of a JDBC INTEGER parameter.
public long getLong(String parameterName) throws SQLException	Determine the value of a JDBC BIGINT parameter.
public float getFloat(String parameterName) throws SQLException	Determine the value of a JDBC FLOAT parameter.
public double getDouble(String parameterName) throws SQLException	Determine the value of a JDBC DOUBLE parameter.
public byte[] getBytes(String parameterName) throws SQLException	Determine the value of a JDBC BINARY or VARBINARY parameter.
public Date getDate(String parameterName) throws SQLException	Determine the value of a JDBC DATE parameter.
public Time getTime(String parameterName) throws SQLException	Determine the value of a JDBC TIME parameter.
public Timestamp getTimestamp(String parameterName) throws SQLException	Determine the value of a JDBC TIMESTAMP parameter.
public Object getObject(String parameterName) throws SQLException	Determine the value of a parameter as an Object.
public BigDecimal getBigDecimal(String parameterName)throws SQLException	Determine the value of a JDBC NUMERIC parameter.
public Object getObject(String parameterName, Map map) throws SQLException	Return an object representing the value of OUT parameter.

Method	Description
public Ref getRef(String parameterName) throws SQLException	Determine the value of a JDBC REF parameter.
public Blob getBlob(String parameterName) throws SQLException	Determine the value of a JDBC BLOB parameter.
public Clob getClob(String parameterName)throws SQLException	Determine the value of a JDBC CLOB parameter.
public Array getArray(String parameterName)throws SQLException	Determine the value of a JDBC ARRAY.
public Date getDate(String parameterName, Calendar cal)throws SQLException	Determine the value of a JDBC DATE parameter.
public Time getTime(String parameterName, Calendar cal)throws SQLException	Determine the value of a JDBC TIME parameter.
public Timestamp getTimestamp(String parameterName, Calendar cal)throws SQLException	Determine the value of a JDBC TIMESTAMP parameter.
public URL getURL(String parameterName) throws SQLException	Determine a URL.

java.sql Package Public Interface Connection Interface

Method	Description
public void close()throws SQLException	Close a Connection.
public boolean isClosed()throws SQLException	Determine whether a Connection object is closed.

Method	Description
public DatabaseMetaData getMetaData()throws SQLException	Retrieve a DatabaseMetaData.
public void setReadOnly(boolean readOnly)throws SQLException	Place a connection in read-only.
public boolean isReadOnly() throws SQLException	Determine whether a Connection object is in read-only.
public String getCatalog()throws SQLException	Determine a Connection's catalog name.

Warnings

Method	Description
public SQLWarning getWarnings()throws SQLException	Retrieve the first warning reported.
public void clearWarnings() throws SQLException	Clear all warnings reported.

Holdability

Method	Description
public void setHoldability(int holdability)throws SQLException	Change the holdability of ResultSet objects.
public int getHoldability() throws SQLException	Determine the holdability of a ResultSet.

Transactions

Method	Description
public Savepoint setSavepoint() throws SQLException	Create an unnamed savepoint.
public Savepoint setSavepoint(String name) throws SQLException	Create a named savepoint.
public void rollback(Savepoint savepoint) throws SQLException	Reverse all changes made after a savepoint was set.
public void releaseSavepoint (Savepoint savepoint)throws SQLException	Remove a Savepoint object.

Method	Description
public void commit()throws SQLException	Make all changes permanent.
public void rollback()throws SQLException	Reverse changes made to a transaction and release any database locks.
public void setAutoCommit(boolean autoCommit)throws SQLException	Set the autocommit mode.
public boolean getAutoCommit()throws SQLException	Determine whether the autocommit mode is set.

CallableStatement

Method	Description
public CallableStatement prepareCall(String sql, int resultSetType, int resultSetConcurrency, int resultSetHoldability)throws SQLException	Create a CallableStatement object that generates a ResultSet.
public CallableStatement prepareCall(String sql,int resultSetType,int resultSetConcurrency)throws SQLException	Create a CallableStatement object that generates a ResultSet.
public CallableStatement prepareCall(String sql)throws SQLException	Create a CallableStatement object.

Statement

Method	Description
public Statement createStatement(int resultSetType,int resultSetConcurrency,int resultSetHoldability) throws SQLException	Create a Statement object that will generate ResultSet.

Method	Description
public Statement createStatement(int resultSetType,int resultSetConcurrency) throws SQLException	Create a Statement object that generates ResultSet.
public Statement createStatement()throws SQLException	Create a Statement object.

PrepareStatement

Method	Description
public PreparedStatement prepareStatement(String sql)throws SQLException	Create a PreparedStatement object.
public PreparedStatement prepareStatement(String sql, int resultSetType,int resultSetConcurrency,int resultSetHoldability)throws SQLException	Create a PreparedStatement object that will generate ResultSet.
public PreparedStatement prepareStatement(String sql, int[] columnIndexes)throws SQLException	Create a PreparedStatement object that returns autogenerated keys.
public PreparedStatement prepareStatement(String sql, int resultSetType,int resultSetConcurrency)throws SQLException	Create a PreparedStatement object that generates ResultSet.
public PreparedStatement prepareStatement(String sql,String[] columnNames) throws SQLException	Create a PreparedStatement object that returns autogenerated keys.

java.sql Package Public Interface DatabaseMetaData

Method	Description
public Connection getConnection() throws SQLException	Retrieve the connection that produced metadata.
public boolean supportsSavepoints() throws SQLException	Determine whether a database supports savepoints.
public boolean supportsNamedParameters() throws SQLException	Determine whether a database supports named parameters to callable statements.
public boolean supports MultipleOpenResults() throws SQLException	Determine whether it is possible to have multiple ResultSet objects returned from a CallableStatement simultaneously.
public int getMaxUserName Length() throws SQLException	Determine the maximum number of characters in a user name.
public boolean supports Transactions() throws SQLException	Determine whether a database supports transactions.
public int getJDBCMajorVersion() throws SQLException	Determine the major JDBC version number of a driver.
public int getJDBCMinorVersion() throws SQLException	Determine the minor JDBC version number of a driver.

Database

Method	Description
public String getURL() throws SQLException	Retrieve the URL for a DBMS.
public String getDatabaseProductName() throws SQLException	Determine the name of a DBMS.
public String getDatabaseProductVersion() throws SQLException	Determine the version number of a DBMS.

Method	Description
public ResultSet getSchemas() throws SQLException	Determine the schema names.
public ResultSet getCatalogs() throws SQLException	Determine the catalog names.
public ResultSet getTypeInfo() throws SQLException	Retrieve a description of standard SQL types supported by a database.
public int getDatabaseMajorVersion() throws SQLException	Determine the major version number of a database.
public int getDatabaseMinorVersion() throws SQLException	Determine the minor version number of a database.

Columns and Rows

Method	Description
public int getMaxColumnNameLength() throws SQLException	Determine the maximum number of characters allowed in a column name.
public int getMaxColumnsInGroupBy() throws SQLException	Determine the maximum number of columns allowed in a GROUP BY clause.
public int getMaxColumnsInIndex() throws SQLException	Determine the maximum number of columns allowed in an index.
public int getMaxColumnsInOrderBy() throws SQLException	Determine the maximum number of columns allowed in an ORDER BY clause.
public int getMaxColumnsInSelect() throws SQLException	Determine the maximum number of columns allowed in a SELECT list.
public int getMaxColumnsInTable() throws SQLException	Determine the maximum number of columns allowed in a table.
public int getMaxConnections() throws SQLException	Determine the maximum number of concurrent connections that are possible to a database.
public int getMaxIndexLength() throws SQLException	Determine the maximum number of bytes allowed for an index.
public int getMaxRowSize() throws SQLException	Determine the maximum number of bytes allowed in a row.

APPENDIX

Method	Description
public ResultSet getColumns(String catalog, String schemaPattern, String tableNamePattern, String columnNamePattern) throws SQLException	Retrieve a description of table columns.
public ResultSet getColumnPrivileges(String catalog,String schema,String table,String columnNamePattern) throws SQLException	Determine access rights for columns.

Statement

Method	Description
public int getMaxStatementLength() throws SQLException	Determine the maximum number of characters permitted in an SQL statement.
public int getMaxStatements() throws SQLException	Determine the maximum number of active statements that can be open at the same time.
public boolean supportsBatchUpdates() throws SQLException	Determine whether a database supports batch updates.

Table

Method	Description
public int getMaxTableNameLength() throws SQLException	Determine the maximum number of characters in a table name.
public int getMaxTablesInSelect() throws SQLException	Determine the maximum number of tables allowed in a SELECT statement.
public ResultSet getTables(String catalog, String schemaPattern, String tableNamePattern, String[] types) throws SQLException	Determine tables available in a catalog.
public ResultSet getTablePrivileges(String catalog,String schemaPattern,String tableNamePattern)throws SQLException	Determine access rights for each table.

Method	Description

Keys

Method	Description
public ResultSet getPrimaryKeys(String catalog,String schema,String table)throws SQLException	Retrieve a description of a table's primary key.
public ResultSet getIndexInfo(String catalog, String schema,String table,boolean unique, boolean approximate)throws SQLException	Retrieve a description of table's indices and statistics.
public boolean supportsGetGeneratedKeys() throws SQLException	Determine whether autogenerated keys can be retrieved.

Procedure

Method	Description
public ResultSet getProcedureColumns(String catalog,String schemaPattern,String procedureNamePattern,String columnNamePattern)throws SQLException	Determine a catalog's stored procedure parameter and result columns.
public ResultSet getProcedures(String catalog,String schemaPattern,String procedureNamePattern)throws SQLException	Determine the stored procedures available in a catalog.

Holdability

Method	Description
public boolean supportsResultSetHoldability(int holdability) throws SQLException	Determine whether a database supports holdability.

Method	Description
public int getResultSetHoldability() throws SQLException	Determine the default holdability of a ResultSet.

java.sql Package Public Class DriverManager

Method	Description
public static Connection getConnection(String url, Properties info)throws SQLException	Open a connection to a database.
public static Connection getConnection(String url, String user, String password)throws SQLException	Open a connection to a database.
public static Connection getConnection(String url) throws SQLException	Open a connection to a database.

Timeout

Method	Description
public static void setLoginTimeout(int seconds)	Set the maximum time in seconds before the login to the database times out.
public static int getLoginTimeout()	Determine the maximum time in seconds before the login to the database times out.

java.sql Package Public Interface PreparedStatement

Method	Description
public ResultSetMetaData getMetaData() throws SQLException	Retrieve a ResultSetMetaData object.
public ParameterMetaData getParameterMetaData() throws SQLException	Determine the metadata for a PreparedStatement's parameters.

Method	Description
public void addBatch() throws SQLException	Add a parameter to PreparedStatement batch of commands.

Execute

Method	Description
public ResultSet executeQuery() throws SQLException	Execute a query in a PreparedStatement and return a ResultSet.
public int executeUpdate() throws SQLException	Execute the SQL statement that contains an INSERT, UPDATE, or DELETE statement in a PreparedStatement.
public boolean execute() throws SQLException	Execute an SQL statement in a PreparedStatement.

Parameters

Method	Description
public void setNull(int parameterIndex,int sqlType)throws SQLException	Set the parameter to a null value.
public void setString(int parameterIndex, String x) throws SQLException	Set the String value.
public void setDate(int parameterIndex, Date x) throws SQLException	Set the java.sql.Date value.
public void setTime(int parameterIndex, Time x) throws SQLException	Set the java.sql.Time value.
public void setTimestamp(int parameterIndex, Timestamp x) throws SQLException	Set the java.sql.Timestamp value.
public void clearParameters() throws SQLException	Clear the current parameter values.
public void setNull(int paramIndex, int sqlType, String typeName)throws SQLException	Set a parameter to a null value.

java.sql Package Public Interface ResultSet

Method	Description
public void close() throws SQLException	Close a ResultSet.

Method	Description
public ResultSetMetaData getMetaData() throws SQLException	Retrieve metadata.
public Statement getStatement()throws SQLException	Retrieve the Statement object.

Warnings

Method	Description
public SQLWarning getWarnings() throws SQLException	Retrieve the first warning reported on a ResultSet.
public void clearWarnings() throws SQLException	Clear all warnings reported on a ResultSet.

Virtual Cursor Movement

Method	Description
public boolean next() throws SQLException	Move the virtual cursor down one row.
public boolean isFirst()throws SQLException	Determine whether the virtual cursor is on the first row.
public boolean isLast()throws SQLException	Determine whether the virtual cursor is on the last row.
public boolean first()throws SQLException	Move the virtual cursor to the first row.
public boolean last()throws SQLException	Move the virtual cursor to the last row.
public int getRow()throws SQLException	Determine the current row number.
public boolean absolute(int row)throws SQLException	Move the virtual cursor to the row specified by the row parameter.
public boolean relative(int rows)throws SQLException	Move the virtual cursor a relative number of rows.
public boolean previous()throws SQLException	Move the virtual cursor to the previous row.

Fetch Size

Method	Description
public void setFetchSize(int rows)throws SQLException	Give the database driver a hint as to how many rows should be fetched when more rows are needed for this ResultSet.

Method	Description
public int getFetchSize()throws SQLException	Determine the fetch size for this ResultSet.

Rows

Method	Description
public boolean rowUpdated()throws SQLException	Determine whether a row has been updated.
public boolean rowInserted()throws SQLException	Determine whether a row has had an insertion.
public boolean rowDeleted()throws SQLException	Determine whether a row is deleted.
public void updateNull(int columnIndex)throws SQLException	Insert a null into a column.
public void insertRow()throws SQLException	Insert a row into a ResultSet and into the database.
public void updateRow()throws SQLException	Update the underlying database with the row of this ResultSet.
public void deleteRow()throws SQLException	Delete a row from a ResultSet and from the database.
public void refreshRow()throws SQLException	Refresh the current row with the current value in the database.
public void cancelRowUpdates()throws SQLException	Cancel updates.

java.sql Package Public Interface ResultSetMetaData

Method	Description
public int getColumnCount()throws SQLException	Retrieve the number of columns in a ResultSet object.
public boolean isCaseSensitive(int column) throws SQLException	Determine whether a column is case sensitive.

Method	Description
public boolean isSearchable(int column) throws SQLException	Determine whether a column can be used in a where clause.
public boolean isCurrency(int column) throws SQLException	Determine whether a column is a cash value.
public int isNullable(int column)throws SQLException	Determine whether a null value can be placed in the column.
public boolean isSigned(int column)throws SQLException	Determine whether values are signed numbers.

Columns

Method	Description
public int getColumnDisplaySize(int column)throws SQLException	Retrieve the column's maximum width in characters.
public String getColumnLabel(int column)throws SQLException	Retrieve the column's label.
public String getColumnName(int column) throws SQLException	Retrieve the column's name.
public int getPrecision(int column) throws SQLException	Retrieve the column's precision.
public int getColumnType(int column)throws SQLException	Retrieve the data type of the column.
public String getColumnTypeName(int column)throws SQLException	Retrieve the name of the column data type.
public boolean isReadOnly(int column) throws SQLException	Indicate whether a column is read-only.
public boolean isWritable(int column)throws SQLException	Indicate whether a column is writable.

java.sql Package Public Interface Savepoint

Method	Description
public int getSavepointId()throws SQLException	Retrieve a savepoint ID.

Method	Description
public String getSavepointName()throws SQLException	Retrieve a savepoint name.

java.sql Package Public Interface Statement

Method	Description
public void close() throws SQLException	Release a Statement object.
public ResultSet getResultSet() throws SQLException	Retrieve the current ResultSet object.
public int getUpdateCount()throws SQLException	Determine the number of rows that were updated.
public Connection getConnection() throws SQLException	Retrieve a Connection object.
public ResultSet getGeneratedKeys() throws SQLException	Retrieve autogenerated keys.

Timeout

Method	Description
public int getQueryTimeout()throws SQLException	Determine the maximum number of seconds for a Statement object to execute.
public void setQueryTimeout(int seconds) throws SQLException	Set the maximum number of seconds for a Statement object to execute.

Rows

Method	Description
public int getMaxRows() throws SQLException	Retrieve the maximum number of rows for a ResultSet object.
public void setMaxRows(int max) throws SQLException	Set the maximum number of rows for a ResultSet object.
public void setFetchSize(int rows)throws SQLException	Give database a hint for how many rows to retrieve when more rows are needed for the ResultSet.
public int getFetchSize()throws SQLException	Determine the number of rows for the fetch size.

APPENDIX

Method	Description
Warnings	
Method	Description
public SQLWarning getWarnings() throws SQLException	Retrieve the first warning on a Statement object.
public void clearWarnings() throws SQLException	Clear all the warnings reported on a Statement object.
Execute	
Method	Description
public boolean execute(String sql) throws SQLException	Execute an SQL statement.
public ResultSet executeQuery(String sql)throws SQLException	Execute an SQL statement and return a ResultSet object.
public int executeUpdate(String sql) throws SQLException	Execute an SQL statement that contains INSERT, UPDATE, or DELETE statements or DDL statements.
Batch	
Method	Description
public void addBatch(String sql)throws SQLException	Add an SQL statement to a batch.
public void clearBatch() throws SQLException	Empty a batch of SQL statements.
public int[] executeBatch()throws SQLException	Execute a batch of SQL statements.

javaxsql Package Public Interface DataSource

Method	Description
public Connection getConnection() throws SQLException	Open a connection to a data source.
public Connection getConnection(String username, String password) throws SQLException	Open a connection to a data source.

javaxsql Package Public Interface RowSet

Method	Description
public void setUrl(String url) throws SQLException	Set the URL of a RowSet.
public boolean isReadOnly()	Determine whether a RowSet object is read-only.
public void setReadOnly(boolean value) throws SQLException	Set a RowSet object to read-only.
public int getMaxFieldSize() throws SQLException	Determine the maximum number of bytes that can be placed in a column.
public int getMaxRows() throws SQLException	Determine the maximum number of rows that can be in a RowSet.

DataSource

Method	Description
public String getDataSourceName()	Determine the logical name of the data source for a RowSet.
public void setDataSourceName(String name) throws SQLException	Set the data source name for a RowSet.

User Name and Password

Method	Description
public String getUsername()	Determine the user name used to create a database connection for a RowSet.
public void setUsername(String name) throws SQLException	Set the user name for a RowSet.
public String getPassword()	Determine the password used to create a database connection.
public void setPassword(String password) throws SQLException	Set the database password for a RowSet.

Timeout

Method	Description
public int getQueryTimeout() throws SQLException	Determine the maximum time the driver will wait for a statement to execute.
public void setQueryTimeout(int seconds) throws SQLException	Set the maximum time the driver will wait for a statement to execute.

javax.sql Public Class RowSetEvent Extends java.util.EventObject

Method	Description
public RowSetEvent(RowSet source)	Create an instance of a RowSetEvent that is associated with the RowSet specified by the source parameter.

javax.sql Public Interface RowSetInternal

Method	Description
public Object[] getParams() throws SQLException	Return an array of Objects containing parameter values for a RowSet.
public Connection getConnection() throws SQLException	Return the Connection object associated with a RowSet. A null is returned if there is no Connection object associated with a RowSet.
public void setMetaData(RowSetMetaData md) throws SQLException	Set the metadata for a RowSet, where md is the RowSetMetaData.
public ResultSet getOriginal() throws SQLException	Return a ResutSet containing the original value of the RowSet.
public ResultSet getOriginalRow() throws SQLException	Return a ResutSet containing the original value of the current row of the RowSet. An exception is thrown if there is no current row.

javax.sql Public Interface RowSetListener Extends java.util.EventListener

Method	Description
public void rowSetChanged(RowSetEvent event)	Send a RowSetListener notification that the entire content of a RowSet has changed. RowSetEvent is the object that contains the RowSet associated with the change.

Method	Description
public void rowChanged(RowSetEvent event)	Send a RowSetListener notification that the one row of a RowSet has changed. RowSetEvent is the object that contains the RowSet associated with the change.
public void cursorMoved(RowSetEvent event)	Send a RowSetListener notification that the cursor of a RowSet has moved. RowSetEvent is the object that contains the RowSet associated with the cursor.

javax.sql Public Interface RowSetMetaData Extends ResultSetMetaData

Method	Description
public void setColumnCount(int columnCount) throws SQLException	Determine the number of columns in a RowSet, where columnCount specifies the number of columns.
public void setAutoIncrement(int columnIndex, boolean property) throws SQLException	Determine whether the specified column is numbered automatically, where columnIndex is the index of the column, and property is a boolean value indicating whether or not the column is automatically numbered. The property value is false by default.
public void setCaseSensitive(int columnIndex, boolean property) throws SQLException	Determine whether the specified column is case sensitive, where columnIndex is the index of the column, and property is a boolean value indicating whether or not the column is case sensitive. The property value is false by default.
public void setSearchable(int columnIndex,boolean property) throws SQLException	Determine whether the specified column can be used in a where clause, where columnIndex is the index of the column, and property is a boolean value indicating whether or not the column can be used in a where clause. The property value is false by default.
public void setCurrency(int columnIndex, boolean property) throws SQLException	Determine whether the specified column is a cash value, where columnIndex is the index of the column, and property is a boolean value indicating whether or not the column is a cash value. The property value is false by default.

Method	Description
public void setNullable(int columnIndex, int property) throws SQLException	Determine whether the specified column can be set to null, where columnIndex is the index of the column, and property is an int indicating whether or not the column can be set to null. The property value is one of the following constants: ResultSetMetaData.columnNoNulls, ResultSetMetaData.columnNullable, or ResultSetMetaData.columnNullableUnknown
public void setSigned(int columnIndex, boolean property) throws SQLException	Determine whether the specified column is a signed number, where columnIndex is the index of the column, and property is a boolean value indicating whether or not the column is a signed number. The property value is false by default.
public void setColumnDisplaySize(int columnIndex, int size) throws SQLException	Determine the maximum width in chars when displaying the column, where columnIndex is the index of the column, and property is an int indicating the maximum number of characters that will be displayed.
public void setColumnLabel(int columnIndex, String label) throws SQLException	Determine the suggested label for the column, where columnIndex is the index of the column, and label is the String containing the text of the suggested label.
public void setColumnName(int columnIndex, String columnName) throws SQLException	Determine the name for the column, where columnIndex is the index of the column, and columnName is the String containing the text of the column name.
public void setSchemaName(int columnIndex, String schemaName) throws SQLException	Determine the name of the table's schema that contains the column, where columnIndex is the index of the column, and schemaName is the String containing the text of the schema name.
public void setPrecision(int columnIndex, int precision) throws SQLException	Determine the number of decimal digits, where columnIndex is the index of the column, and precision is an int indicating the maximum number of decimal digits contained in the column.
public void setScale(int columnIndex, int scale) throws SQLException	Determine the number of digits to the right of the decimal point, where columnIndex is the index of the column, and scale is an int indicating the number of digits to the right of the decimal point in the value within the column.

Method	Description
public void setTableName(int columnIndex, String tableName) throws SQLException	Determine the name of the table that contains the column, where columnIndex is the index of the column, and tableName is a String containing the text of the table name.
public void setCatalogName(int columnIndex, String catalogName) throws SQLException	Determine the name of the table catalog that contains the column, where columnIndex is the index of the column, and catalogName is a String containing the text of the catalog.
public void setColumnType(int columnIndex, int SQLType) throws SQLException	Determine SQL type of the column, where columnIndex is the index of the column, and SQLType is an int containing the SQL type.
public void setColumnTypeName(int columnIndex, String typeName) throws SQLException	Determine the name of the column type in the data source of the column, where columnIndex is the index of the column, and typeName is the String containing the text of the column type.

javax.sql Public Interface RowSetReader

Method	Description
public void readData(RowSetInternal caller) throws SQLException	Read the content of a RowSet, where the caller is the RowSetInternal that is implemented by a RowSet object and is registered with the RowSetReader.

javax.sql Public Interface RowSetWriter

Method	Description
public boolean writeData(RowSetInternal caller) throws SQLException	Write changes to the RowSet associated with the RowSetWriter to the data source, where caller is the RowSetInternal associated with the RowSetWriter. A true is returned if the data was successfully written to the data source, otherwise a false is returned.

Public Interface Contact Extends PIMItem

Field	Description
static int ADDR	Specify an address for a Contact.
static int ADDR_COUNTRY	Index into the string array for an address field representing the country of an address.
static int ADDR_EXTRA	Index into the string array for an address field representing any extra info of an address.
static int ADDR_LOCALITY	Index into the string array for an address field representing the locality (for example, a city) of an address.
static int ADDR_POBOX	Index into the string array for an address field representing the post office box of an address.
static int ADDR_POSTALCODE	Index into the string array for an address field representing the postal code (for example, a zip code) of an address.
static int ADDR_REGION	Index into the string array for an address field representing the region (for example, a province, state, or territory) of an address.
static int ADDR_STREET	Index into the string array for an address field, where the data at this index represents the street information of a particular address.
static int ADDRSIZE	The size of an address string array.
static int ATTR_ASST	Attribute classifying data as related to an ASSISTANT.
static int ATTR_AUTO	Attribute classifying a data as related to AUTO.
static int ATTR_FAX	Attribute classifying a data as related to FAX.
static int ATTR_HOME	Attribute classifying a data as related to HOME.
static int ATTR_MOBILE	Attribute classifying a data as related to MOBILE.
static int ATTR_OTHER	Attribute classifying a data as "OTHER."
static int ATTR_PAGER	Attribute classifying a data as related to PAGER.
static int ATTR_PREFERRED	Attribute classifying a data with preferred status for retrieval or display purposes (platform specific).
static int ATTR_SMS	Attribute classifying a data as related to SMS.

Field	Description
static int ATTR_WORK	Attribute classifying a data as related to WORK.
static int BIRTHDAY	Field for birthday.
static int CLASS	Field specifying access class for a contact.
static int CLASS_CONFIDENTIAL	Constant indicating contact's class is confidential.
static int CLASS_PRIVATE	Constant indicating contact's class is private.
static int CLASS_PUBLIC	Constant indicating contact's class is public.
static int EMAIL	Field for email address.
static int FORMATTED_ADDR	Field for a formatted version of a contact address.
static int FORMATTED_NAME	Field for a formatted version of a contact name.
static int NAME	Field for a contact name.
static int NAME_FAMILY	Index into the string array for an address field, where the data at this index represents a family name.
static int NAME_GIVEN	Index into the string array for an address field, where the data at this index represents a given name.
static int NAME_OTHER	Index into the string array for an address field, where the data at this index represents other alternate name or names.
static int NAME_PREFIX	Index into the string array for an address field, where the data at this index represents a prefix to a name.
static int NAME_SUFFIX	Index into the string array for an address field, where the data at this index represents a suffix to a name.
static int NAMESIZE	Indicate the size of a name string array.
static int NICKNAME	Field where the data is a nickname.
static int NOTE	Field for supplemental information or a comment associated with a Contact.
static int ORG	Field for the organization name or units associated with a Contact.

APPENDIX

Field	Description
static int PHOTO	Field for a photo of a Contact.
static int PHOTO_URL	Field for a URL for a photo of a Contact.
static int PUBLIC_KEY	Field for the public encryption key for a Contact.
static int PUBLIC_KEY_STRING	Field for the public encryption key for a Contact.
static int REVISION	Field for the last modification date and time of a Contact item.
static int TEL	Field for a voice telephone number.
static int TITLE	Field for the job title for a Contact.
static int UID	Field for a unique ID for a Contact.
static int URL	Field for the uniform resource locator for a Contact.
Method	**Description**
int getPreferredIndex(int field)	Return the index of the value marked with the attribute ATTR_PREFERRED for a field.

Public Interface ContactList Extends PIMItem

Method	Description
Contact createContact()	Create a Contact for this contact list.
Contact importContact(Contact contact)	Import the given Contact into this contact list.
void removeContact(Contact contact)	Remove a Contact from the list.

Public Interface Event Extends PIMItem

Field	Description
static int ALARM	Field for the relative time for an Alarm for this Event.
static int CLASS	Field for the desired access class for this contact.
static int CLASS_CONFIDENTIAL	Indicate this event's class is confidential.

Field	Description
static int CLASS_PRIVATE	Indicate this event's class is private.
static int CLASS_PUBLIC	Indicate this event's class is public.
static int END	Field for the noninclusive date and time a single Event ends.
static int LOCATION	Field for the venue for this Event.
static int NOTE	A String for a complete description of an Event.
static int REVISION	Field for the last modification date and time of an Event item.
static int START	Field for the inclusive date and time a single Event starts.
static int SUMMARY	Field for the summary or subject for this Event.
static int UID	Field for a unique ID for an Event.

Method	Description
RepeatRule getRepeat()	Retrieve a RepeatRule object that specifies how often and when this event occurs.
void setRepeat(RepeatRule value)	Set the RepeatRule that specifies how often and when this event occurs.

Public Interface EventList Extends PIMItem

Field	Description
static int ENDING	Represents a search type for Events based on the event end date/time.
static int OCCURRING	Represents a search type for Events based on the event during a time period.
static int STARTING	Represents a search type for Events based on the event start date/time.

Method	Description
Event createEvent()	Create an Event for this event list.
Event importEvent(Event item)	Import the given Event into this list by making a new Event for the list.

Field	Description
java.util.Enumeration items(int searchType, long startDate, long endDate, boolean initialEventOnly)	Return an enumeration of all the Events where at least one of the Event's occurrences falls in the specified startDate to endDate inclusive.
void removeEvent(Event item)	Remove a specific Event from the list.

Public Class FieldEmptyException Extends java.lang.RuntimeException

Method	Description
FieldEmptyException()	Construct an instance of this class with its stack trace filled.
FieldEmptyException(java.lang .String detailMessage)	Construct an instance of this class with its stack trace and message filled.
FieldEmptyException(java.lang .String detailMessage, int field)	Construct an instance of this class with its stack trace, message, and offending field filled.
int getField()	Access the field that caused the exception to be thrown.

Public Class FieldFullException Extends java.lang.RuntimeException

Method	Description
FieldFullException()	Construct an instance of this class with its stack trace filled.
FieldFullException(java.lang.String detailMessage)	Construct an instance of this class with its stack trace and message filled.
FieldFullException(java.lang.String detailMessage, int field)	Construct an instance of this class with its stack trace, message, and offending field filled.
int getField()	Access the field that caused the exception to be thrown.

Public Class PIMException Extends java.lang.Exception

Field	Description
static int FEATURE_NOT_SUPPORTED	Functionality is not supported in this implementation.
static int GENERAL_ERROR	General PIM exception error.
static int LIST_CLOSED	List is closed and access is attempted.
static int LIST_NOT_ACCESSIBLE	List is no longer accessible by the application, such as if the underlying PIM database is deleted.
static int MAX_CATEGORIES_EXCEEDED	Maximum number of categories is exceeded.
static int UNSUPPORTED_VERSION	Data is in an unsupported PIM version.
static int UPDATE_ERROR	The update could not continue.

Method	Description
PIMException()	Construct an instance of this class with its stack trace filled.
PIMException(java.lang.String detailMessage)	Construct an instance of this class with its stack trace and message filled.
PIMException(java.lang.String detailMessage, int reason)	Construct an instance of this class with its stack trace, message, and reason filled.
int getReason()	Return the reason for the PIM Exception.

Public Interface PIMItem

Field	Description
static int ATTR_NONE	No additional attributes are applicable to a data value for a field.
static int BINARY	Data is binary in a byte array.
static int BOOLEAN	Data is of boolean primitive data type.

Field	Description
static int DATE	Data is a Date in long primitive data type format expressed in the same long value format as java.util.Date, which is milliseconds since the epoch (00:00:00 GMT, January 1, 1970).
static int EXTENDED_ATTRIBUTE_MIN_VALUE	The minimum possible value for an extended attribute constant.
static int EXTENDED_FIELD_MIN_VALUE	The minimum possible value for an extended field constant.
static int INT	Data is of int primitive data type.
static int STRING	Data is a String object.
static int STRING_ARRAY	Data is an array of related fields returned in a string array.

Method	Description
void addBinary(int field, int attributes, byte[] value, int offset, int length)	Add a binary data value to a field.
void addBoolean(int field, int attributes, boolean value)	Add a boolean value to a field.
void addDate(int field, int attributes, long value)	Add a date value to a field.
void addInt(int field, int attributes, int value)	Add an integer value to a field.
void addString(int field, int attributes, java.lang.String value)	Add a String value to a field.
void addStringArray(int field, int attributes, java.lang.String[] value)	Add an array of related string values as a single entity to a field.
void addToCategory(java.lang.String category)	Add a category to this item.
void commit()	Persist the data in the item to its PIM list.
int countValues(int field)	Return the number of values assigned to a field.
int getAttributes(int field, int index)	Return the attributes associated with the data value at the given index for the indicated field.

Field	Description
byte[] getBinary(int field, int index)	Return a binary data value for a field from the item.
boolean getBoolean(int field, int index)	Return a boolean value from a field in the item.
java.lang.String[] getCategories()	Return all categories for the item.
long getDate(int field, int index)	Return a date value from a field in the item.
int[] getFields()	Return all fields in the item that have data stored for them.
int getInt(int field, int index)	Return an integer value from a field in the item.
PIMList getPIMList()	Return the PIMList associated with this item.
java.lang.String getString(int field, int index)	Return a String value from a field in the item.
java.lang.String[] getStringArray(int field, int index)	Return an array of related values from a field in the item.
boolean isModified()	Return a boolean indicating whether any of this item's fields have been modified since the item was retrieved or last committed.
int maxCategories()	Return the maximum number of categories that this item can be assigned to.
void removeFromCategory(java.lang.String category)	Remove a category from this item.
void removeValue(int field, int index)	Remove the value at the given index for the indicated field in an item.
void setBinary(int field, int index, int attributes, byte[] value, int offset, int length)	Set an existing binary data value in a field to a new value.
void setBoolean(int field, int index, int attributes, boolean value)	Set an existing boolean data value in a field to a new value.
void setDate(int field, int index, int attributes, long value)	Set an existing date data value in a field to a new value.
void setInt(int field, int index, int attributes, int value)	Set an existing int data value in a field to a new value.

Field	Description
void setString(int field, int index, int attributes, java.lang.String value)	Set an existing String data value in a field to a new value.
void setStringArray(int field, int index, int attributes, java.lang.String[] value)	Set an existing String array data value in a field to a new value.

Public Interface PIMList

Field	Description
static java.lang.String UNCATEGORIZED	Constant for the itemsByCategory(java.lang.String) method to indicate to search for uncategorized items.

Method	Description
void addCategory(java.lang.String category)	Add a category to the PIM list.
void close()	Close the list, releasing any resources.
void deleteCategory(java.lang.String category)	Delete a category from the PIM list.
java.lang.String getAttributeLabel(int attribute)	Return a String label associated with an attribute.
java.lang.String[] getCategories()	Return the categories defined for the PIM list.
int getFieldDataType(int field)	Return an int representing the data type of the data associated with a field.
java.lang.String getFieldLabel(int field)	Return a String label associated with a field.
java.lang.String getName()	Return the name of the list.
int[] getSupportedArrayElements(int stringArrayField)	Return an integer array containing all of the supported elements of a string array for a field.
int[] getSupportedAttributes(int field)	Return an integer array containing all of the supported attributes for a field.
int[] getSupportedFields()	Return all fields that are supported in this list.
boolean isCategory(java.lang.String category)	Return whether a category is a valid, existing category for this list.

APPENDIX

Field	Description
boolean isSupportedArrayElement(int stringArrayField, int arrayElement)	Return whether or not the element in an array is supported for a field in this PIM list.
boolean isSupportedAttribute(int field, int attribute)	Return whether or not the given attribute is supported in this PIM list for a field.
boolean isSupportedField(int field)	Return whether or not the given field is supported in this PIM list.
java.util.Enumeration items()	Return an Enumeration of all items in the list.
java.util.Enumeration items(PIMItem matchingItem)	Return an Enumeration of all items in the list that contain fields that match all fields specified in the matching item.
java.util.Enumeration items(java.lang.String matchingValue)	Return an Enumeration of all items in the list that contain at least one String field data value that matches the specified string value.
java.util.Enumeration itemsByCategory(java.lang.String category)	Return an enumeration of all items in the PIM list that match the category.
int maxCategories()	Return the maximum number of categories that this list can have.
void renameCategory(java.lang.String currentCategory, java.lang.String newCategory)	Rename a category to a new name.
int supportsMultipleValues(int field)	Determine whether a field supports adding more than one value to the field.

Public Class RepeatRule Extends java.lang.Object

Field	Description
static int APRIL	Constant for the month of April.
static int AUGUST	Constant for the month of August.
static int COUNT	Specify the number of times this event repeats, including the first time, starting from the first time the event starts (derived from Event.START) and continuing to the last date of the repeat (defined by RepeatRule.END).

Field	Description
static int DAILY	Indicate frequency when the Event happens every day.
static int DAY_IN_MONTH	Specify the day of the month an Event occurs; for example, 15.
static int DAY_IN_WEEK	Specify the days of the week an Event occurs.
static int DAY_IN_YEAR	Specify the day of the year an Event occurs; for example, 134.
static int DECEMBER	Constant for the month of December.
static int END	Specify the ending date of the repeating event.
static int FEBRUARY	Constant for the month of February.
static int FIFTH	Constant for the fifth week of the month.
static int FIFTHLAST	Constant for the fifth to last week of the month.
static int FIRST	Constant for the first week of the month.
static int FOURTH	Constant for the fourth week of the month.
static int FOURTHLAST	Constant for the fourth to last week of the month.
static int FREQUENCY	Specify the frequency of the Repeat.
static int FRIDAY	Constant for the day of week Friday.
static int INTERVAL	Specify the number of iterations of the frequency between occurring dates, or how often the frequency repeats.
static int JANUARY	Constant for the month of January.
static int JULY	Constant for the month of July.
static int JUNE	Constant for the month of June.
static int LAST	Constant for the last week of the month.
static int MARCH	Constant for the month of March.
static int MAY	Constant for the month of May.
static int MONDAY	Constant for the day of week Monday.
static int MONTH_IN_YEAR	Specify the month in which an event occurs.
static int MONTHLY	Specify the frequency when the Event happens every month.
static int NOVEMBER	Constant for the month of November.
static int OCTOBER	Constant for the month of October.
static int SATURDAY	Constant for the day of week Saturday.

Field	Description
static int SECOND	Constant for the second week of the month.
static int SECONDLAST	Constant for the second to last week of the month.
static int SEPTEMBER	Constant for the month of September.
static int SUNDAY	Constant for the day of week Sunday.
static int THIRD	Constant for the third week of the month.
static int THIRDLAST	Constant for the third to last week of the month.
static int THURSDAY	Constant for the day of week Thursday.
static int TUESDAY	Constant for the day of week Tuesday.
static int WEDNESDAY	Constant for the day of week Wednesday.
static int WEEK_IN_ MONTH	Specify which week in a month a particular event occurs.
static int WEEKLY	Specify frequency when the Event happens every week.
static int YEARLY	Specify frequency when the Event happens every year.

Method	Description
RepeatRule()	Default constructor.
void addExceptDate(long date)	Add a Date for which the RepeatRule should not occur.
java.util.Enumeration dates(long startDate, long subsetBeginning, long subsetEnding)	Return an Enumeration of dates on which an Event will occur.
long getDate(int field)	Return a Date field.
java.util.Enumeration getExceptDates()	Return the Dates for which the RepeatRule should not occur.
int[] getFields()	Return a list of fields that currently have values assigned to them.
int getInt(int field)	Return an integer field.
void removeExceptDate(long date)	Delete a Date for which the RepeatRule should not occur.
void setDate(int field, long value)	Set a Date field.
void setInt(int field, int value)	Set an integer field.

Public Interface ToDo Extends PIMItem

Field	Description
static int CLASS	Specify the desired access class for this contact.
static int CLASS_CONFIDENTIAL	Constant indicating the to do's class is confidential.
static int CLASS_PRIVATE	Constant indicating the to do's class is private.
static int CLASS_PUBLIC	Constant indicating the to do's class is public.
static int COMPLETED	Field ID indicating a ToDo has been completed.
static int COMPLETION_DATE	Field ID indicating a ToDo has been completed on the date specified by this field.
static int DUE	The date a ToDo is due expressed in the same long value format as java.util.Date, which is milliseconds since the epoch (00:00:00 GMT, January 1, 1970).
static int NOTE	Specify a more complete description than the SUMMARY for this ToDo.
static int PRIORITY	Specify the priority of this ToDo.
static int REVISION	Specify the last modification date and time of a ToDo item.
static int SUMMARY	Specify the summary or subject for this ToDo.
static int UID	Specify a unique ID for a ToDo.

Public Interface ToDoList Extends PIMList

Method	Description
ToDo createToDo()	Create a ToDo entry for this ToDo list.
ToDo importToDo(ToDo item)	Import the ToDo into this list by making a new ToDo for the list and filling its information with as much information as it can from the provided ToDo.

Method	Description
java.util.Enumeration items(int field, long startDate, long endDate)	Return an enumeration of all the ToDos in the list, where the value of the specified date field falls in the range from startDate to endDate inclusive.
void removeToDo(ToDo item)	Delete a specific ToDo from the list.

Public Class UnsupportedFieldException Extends java.lang.RuntimeException

Method	Description
UnsupportedFieldException()	Construct an instance of this class with its stack trace filled.
UnsupportedFieldException(java .lang.String detailMessage)	Construct an instance of this class with its stack trace and message filled.
UnsupportedFieldException(java .lang.String detailMessage, int field)	Construct an instance of this class with its stack trace, message, and offending field filled.

javax.microedition.io.Connector Class

Method	Description
static Connection open (string name)	Open a connection in READ_WRITE mode, where name is the connection identifier.
static Connection open(String name, int mode)	Open a connection, where name is the connection identifier and mode is the read/write mode.
static Connection open(String name, int mode, boolean timeouts)	Open a connection, where name is the connection identifier, mode is the read/write mode, and timeouts is a boolean value indicating whether or not the connection can time out.
static InputStream openInputStream(String name)	Open an input stream.
static OutputStream openOutputStream(String name)	Open an output stream.

Method	Description
static DataInputStream openDataInputStream(String name)	Open a data input stream.
static DataOutputStream(String name)	Open a data output stream.

javax.microedition.io.HttpConnection

Method	Description
void setRequestMethod(String method)	Set the request method to either GET, POST, or HEAD.
void setRequestProperty(String key, String value)	Set the header information, where key is the field name in the HTTP header, and value is the new value assigned to the field.
String getRequestMethod()	Retrieve the request method.
String getRequestProperty(String key)	Retrieve the current value of the HTTP field, where key is a string containing the name of the field.

javax.microedition.io.HttpConnection Class

Method	Description
int getResponseCode()	Retrieve the response status line code.
String getResponseMessage()	Retrieve the response status line message.

javax.microedition.io.HttpConnection Class

Method	Description
String getHeaderField (int n)	Retrieve the value of the header field whose index value is represented as n.

Method	Description
String getHeaderField(String name)	Retrieve the value of the header field whose header field name is contained in name.
long getHeaderFieldDate(String name, long deft)	Retrieve the header field date, where the field name is represented by name and the date is represented by deft.
int getHeaderFieldInt(String name, int def)	Retrieve the index of the field name identified as name.
String getHeaderFieldKey (int n)	Retrieve the name of the field using the field name index represented by n.
long getDate()	Retrieve the header field date.
long getExpiration()	Retrieve the expiration of the header field.
long getLastModified()	Retrieve the date when the header field was modified.

javax.microedition.io.HttpConnection

Method	Description
String getFile()	Retrieve the file name from the URL.
String getHost()	Retrieve the host from the URL.
int getPort()	Retrieve the port from the URL.
String getProtocol()	Retrieve the protocol from the URL.
String getQuery()	Retrieve the query string if the GET request method is used.
String getRef()	Retrieve the reference portion of the URL.
String getURL()	Retrieve the complete URL.

javax.xml.rpc public interface Stub

Field	Description
static java.lang.String ENDPOINT_ADDRESS_PROPERTY	Address of target service endpoint.

Field	Description
static java.lang.String PASSWORD_ PROPERTY	Password for authentication static.
java.lang.String SESSION_ MAINTAIN_PROPERTY	This boolean property is used by a service client to indicate whether or not it wants to participate in a session with a service endpoint.
static java.lang.String USERNAME_PROPERTY	User name for authentication.

Method	Description
java.lang.Object _getProperty(java.lang.String name)	Return the value of a specific configuration property.
Iterator _getPropertyNames()	Return an Iterator view of the names of the properties that can be configured on this stub instance.
void _setProperty(java.lang.String name, java.lang.Object value)	Set the name and value of a configuration property for this Stub instance.

Public Class NamespaceConstants Extends java.lang.Object

Field	Description
static java.lang.String NSPREFIX_SCHEMA_XSD	Namespace prefix for XML schema XSD static.
java.lang.String NSPREFIX_SCHEMA_XSI	Namespace prefix for XML Schema XSI.
static java.lang.String NSPREFIX_SOAP_ENCODING	Namespace prefix for SOAP encoding.
static java.lang.String NSPREFIX_SOAP_ENVELOPE	Namespace prefix for SOAP envelope.
static java.lang.String NSURI_SCHEMA_XSD	Namespace URI for XML Schema XSD.
static java.lang.String NSURI_SCHEMA_XSI	Namespace URI for XML Schema XSI static.

Field	Description
java.lang.String NSURI_SOAP_ENCODING	Namespace URI for SOAP 1.1 encoding.
static java.lang.String NSURI_SOAP_ENVELOPE	Namespace URI for SOAP 1.1 envelope.
static java.lang.String NSURI_SOAP_NEXT_ACTOR	Namespace URI for SOAP 1.1 next actor role.

Method	Description
NamespaceConstants ( )	Constructor.

Public Class JAXRPCException Extends java.lang.RuntimeException

JAXRPCException()	Construct a new exception with null as its detail message.
JAXRPCException(java.lang.String message)	Construct a new exception with the specified detail message.
JAXRPCException(java.lang.String message, java.lang.Throwable cause)	Construct a new exception with the specified detail message and cause.
JAXRPCException(java.lang.Throwable cause)	Construct a new JAXRPCException with the specified cause and a detail message of the cause. This contains the class and detail message of cause.
java.lang.Throwable getLinkedCause()	Retrieve the linked cause of the exception.

APPENDIX

Index

INTERNATIONAL CONTACT INFORMATION

AUSTRALIA
McGraw-Hill Book Company Australia Pty. Ltd.
TEL +61-2-9900-1800
FAX +61-2-9878-8881
http://www.mcgraw-hill.com.au
books-it_sydney@mcgraw-hill.com

CANADA
McGraw-Hill Ryerson Ltd.
TEL +905-430-5000
FAX +905-430-5020
http://www.mcgraw-hill.ca

GREECE, MIDDLE EAST, & AFRICA
(Excluding South Africa)
McGraw-Hill Hellas
TEL +30-210-6560-990
TEL +30-210-6560-993
TEL +30-210-6560-994
FAX +30-210-6545-525

MEXICO (Also serving Latin America)
McGraw-Hill Interamericana Editores S.A. de C.V.
TEL +525-117-1583
FAX +525-117-1589
http://www.mcgraw-hill.com.mx
fernando_castellanos@mcgraw-hill.com

SINGAPORE (Serving Asia)
McGraw-Hill Book Company
TEL +65-863-1580
FAX +65-862-3354
http://www.mcgraw-hill.com.sg
mghasia@mcgraw-hill.com

SOUTH AFRICA
McGraw-Hill South Africa
TEL +27-11-622-7512
FAX +27-11-622-9045
robyn_swanepoel@mcgraw-hill.com

SPAIN
McGraw-Hill/Interamericana de España, S.A.U.
TEL +34-91-180-3000
FAX +34-91-372-8513
http://www.mcgraw-hill.es
professional@mcgraw-hill.es

UNITED KINGDOM, NORTHERN,
EASTERN, & CENTRAL EUROPE
McGraw-Hill Education Europe
TEL +44-1-628-502500
FAX +44-1-628-770224
http://www.mcgraw-hill.co.uk
computing_europe@mcgraw-hill.com

ALL OTHER INQUIRIES Contact:
Osborne/McGraw-Hill
TEL +1-510-549-6600
FAX +1-510-883-7600
http://www.osborne.com
omg_international@mcgraw-hill.com